PROBABILITY AND PROBABILITY DISTRIBUTIONS

Probability

Bayes' theorem

$$P(B_i|A) = \frac{P(B_i) \cdot P(A|B_i)}{P(B_1) \cdot P(A|B_1) + P(B_2) \cdot P(A|B_2) + \cdots + P(B_k) \cdot P(A|B_k)}$$

Conditional probability

$$P(A|B) = \frac{P(A \cap B)}{P(B)}$$

General addition rule

$$P(A \cup B) = P(A) + P(B) - P(A \cap B)$$

General multiplication rule

$$P(A \cap B) = P(B) \cdot P(A|B) \qquad \text{or} \qquad P(A \cap B) = P(A) \cdot P(B|A)$$

Mathematical expectation

$$E = a_1 p_1 + a_2 p_2 + \cdots + a_k p_k$$

Probability Distributions

Binomial distribution

$$f(x) = \binom{n}{x} p^x (1 - p)^{n-x}$$

Mean of probability distribution

$$\mu = \sum x \cdot f(x)$$

Standard deviation of probability distribution

$$\sigma = \sqrt{\sum (x - \mu)^2 \cdot f(x)}$$

Continued inside back cover

NINTH EDITION
REVISED

MODERN
ELEMENTARY
STATISTICS

JOHN E. FREUND
Arizona State University

GARY A. SIMON
New York University

PRENTICE HALL
Upper Saddle River, New Jersey 07458

Library of Congress Cataloging-in-Publication Data

Freund, John E.
    Modern elementary statistics / John E. Freund, Gary A. Simon —
rev. 9th ed.
        p.   cm.
    Includes bibliographical references and index.
    ISBN 0-13-858291-2 (hard)
    1. Statistics.   I. Simon, Gary A.   II. Title.
QA276. 12.F738   1997
519.5—dc20   96-22742
                                                  CIP

Editorial director: TIM BOZIK
Editor-in-chief: JEROME GRANT
Acquisition editor: ANN HEATH
Development editor: MILLICENT TRELOAR
Assistant VP production and manufacturing: DAVID RICCARDI
Executive managing editor: KATHLEEN SCHIAPARELLI
Managing editor: LINDA MIHATOV BEHRENS
Editorial assistants: NANCY BAUER / MINDY INCE
Creative director: PAULA MAYLAHN
Art director: AMY ROSEN
Interior designer: KEVIN KALL
Cover designer: JOSEPH SENGOTTA
Assistant to art director: ROD HERNANDEZ
Art manager: GUS VIBAL
Marketing manager: EVAN GIRARD
Marketing assistant: BILL PAQUIN
Manufacturing manager: TRUDY PISCIOTTI
Manufacturing buyer: ALAN FISCHER

©1997, 1992, 1988, 1984, 1979, 1973, 1967, 1960, 1952
by Prentice-Hall, Inc.
Simon & Schuster / A Viacom Company
Upper Saddle River, NJ 07458

Cover photo: Frank Lloyd Wright's May House in Grand Rapids Michigan (1908)

Printed in the United States of America
10 9 8 7 6 5 4 3 2

ISBN 0-13-858291-2

Prentice-Hall International (UK) Limited, *London*
Prentice-Hall of Australia Pte. Limited, *Sydney*
Prentice-Hall Canada, Inc., *Toronto*
Prentice-Hall Hispanoamericana, S.A., *Mexico*
Prentice-Hall of India Private Limited, *New Delhi*
Prentice-Hall of Japan, Inc., *Tokyo*
Simon & Schuster Asia Pte. Ltd., *Singapore*
Editora Prentice-Hall do Brasil Ltda., *Rio de Janeiro*

CONTENTS

PREFACE

$\mathcal{T}$he principal objective for this, the ninth edition of *Modern Elementary Statistics,* is to introduce beginning students to the fundamental ideas of modern statistics. The organization of the text is unchanged, but there are modifications in content, emphasis, and visual presentation.

This ninth edition contains some 1400 exercises that involve both conceptual and computational challenges. Our purpose here is to make the reader familiar with the mechanics of calculations but also to think about the relevance of techniques introduced.

This edition offers greater opportunity for the student to use the computer in the study of statistics. The computer is spectacularly effective for producing graphic displays such as scatter plots and box-and-whisker plots, and can be used to great advantage to simulate values of random variables in connection with the law of large numbers or the sampling distribution of the mean; to determine tail probabilities for the values of n and p not found in tables and thus ascertain the proximity of the Poisson approximation to the binomial. Moreover, the computer is indispensable for multiple-regression computations that are intricate and not amenable to manual calculation.

We do not state specifically the subjects, sections, or chapters to study, but we do indicate which topics can be omitted without loss of continuity. Such "optional" sections are identified by an icon, $\ominus$, preceding the topic heading. For example, some instructors will not cover the material on grouped data, yet those who must deal with published government data may consider it essential.

NEW TO THIS EDITION

Supplementing the innovations highlighted as follows, this edition is enhanced by an "open" style of presentation, meaning that important equations or statements and lists of data are displayed rather than embedded in the text.

topic selection

The selection of topics for this text has evolved during its eight preceding editions, and the experience and classroom use implied by the wide, implicit acceptance of its presentation. Additionally, for this edition we have included, in Chapter 14, material concerning multiple comparisons. As a logical follow-up to comparative experiments, frequently involving consumer goods, decisions concerning the relative merits of individual products must be made; this section provides guidance for that process.

computer printouts

Illustrated copiously with computer output, this edition uses MINITAB 10 for Windows, for which most of the commands are executed by using menus. As the menu item is selected, this program creates automatically the command code familiar to previous releases of MINITAB. In this edition the command code illustrates the applications. Instructors should have no difficulty in using this text with other software packages.

reduced complexity of exercises

In the early chapters the student will make computations of the form $\Sigma\, x$, $\Sigma\, x^2$, and $\Sigma\, (x - \bar{x})^2$ during the process of learning about the mean and the standard deviation. For the more advanced topics, later in the book, the exercises simply present the student with values of $\bar{x}$ and s, rather than requiring that these be computed from raw data. Thus, students can devote their concentration to the new subject and avoid calculations related to topics studied previously.

icons to classify exercises

Three icons are used for the reader's convenience: The icon ▣ precedes exercises requiring computer software. The more challenging exercises are denoted by the symbol ▦. Finally, the icon ⬦ is used to flag exercises related to the material covered in "optional" sections. Occasionally, more than one icon may apply to a given exercise.

data disk

Exercise data sets are now provided on disk. These exercises pertain to topics requiring extensive data entries.

acknowledgments

Our appreciation goes to our colleagues and students for their helpful suggestions and reviews of the present as well as preceding editions of this text. For this revision, we are grateful to Leslie Ribera of the University of Central Oklahoma, Dee Cyler of Utah Valley State College, Louis Bianco of the University of Massachusetts at Dartmouth, David Lund of the University of Wisconsin at Eau Claire, and Bernard Okun of Brooklyn College for their helpful comments. We also thank Zhenhong Fan for his assistance in preparing the exercise solutions. Finally, our gratitude to our editors at Prentice Hall, Ann Heath and Millicent Treloar, and to Nicholas Romanelli for his help during the production process.

The revisions in the original version of the 9th edition of this book are entirely the work of Gary Simon.

GARY SIMON

CHAPTER 1

INTRODUCTION

he collection, processing, interpretation, and presentation of numerical data all belong to the domain of statistics. These tasks include the calculation of baseball batting averages, collecting data on births and deaths, evaluating the effectiveness of commercial products, and forecasting the weather. Statistical information is presented to us constantly on radio and television. Our enthusiasm for statistical facts is encouraged by national newspapers such as The Wall Street Journal *and* USA Today.

The word "statistics" is used in several ways. It can refer not only to the mere tabulation of numeric information, as in reports of stock market transactions, but also to the body of techniques used in processing or analyzing data.

The word "statistician" is also used in several ways. The term can be applied to those who simply collect information, as well as to those who prepare analyses or interpretations, and it is also applied to scholars who develop the mathematical theory on which statistics is based.

In Sections 1.1 and 1.2 we discuss the recent growth of statistics and its ever-widening range of applications. In Section 1.3 we explain the distinction between the two major branches of statistics, descriptive statistics and statistical inference, and in the optional Section 1.4 we discuss the nature of various kinds of data and in connection with this warn the reader against the indiscriminate mathematical treatment of statistical data. ◪

1.1   THE GROWTH OF MODERN STATISTICS

There are several reasons why the scope of statistics and the need to study statistics have grown enormously in the last fifty or so years. One reason is the increasingly quantitative approach employed in all the sciences, as well as in business and many other activities which directly affect our lives. This includes the use of mathematical techniques in the evaluation of antipollution controls, in inventory planning, in the analysis of traffic patterns, in the study of the effects of various kinds of medications, in the evaluation of teaching techniques, in the analysis of competitive behavior of business managers and governments, in the study of diet and longevity, and so forth. The availability of powerful computers has greatly increased our ability to deal with numerical information. Many types of computers are also inexpensive, so that sophisticated statistical work can be done by small businesses, college students, and even high school students.

The other reason is that the amount of data that is collected, processed, and disseminated to the public for one reason or another has increased almost beyond comprehension, and what part is good statistics and what part is bad statistics is anybody's guess. To act as watchdogs, more and more persons with some knowledge of statistics are needed to take an active part in the collection of the data, in the analysis of the data, and, what is equally important, in all of the preliminary planning. Without the latter, it is frightening to think of all the things that can go wrong in the compilation of statistical data. The results of costly surveys can be useless if questions are ambiguous or asked in the wrong way, if they are asked of the wrong persons, in the wrong place, or at the wrong time. Much of this is just common sense, as is illustrated by the following examples:

Example

To determine public sentiment about the continuation of a certain government program, an interviewer asks: "Do you feel that this wasteful program should be stopped?" Explain why this question will probably not yield the desired information.

solution

The interviewer is begging the question by suggesting, in fact, that the program is wasteful.   ▰ ▰ ▰

Example

To study consumer reaction to a new convenience food, a house-to-house survey is conducted during weekday mornings, with no provisions for return visits in case no one is home. Explain why this approach may well yield misleading information.

solution

This survey will fail to reach those who are most likely to use the product: single persons and married couples with both spouses employed.   ▰ ▰ ▰

Although much of the above-mentioned growth of statistics began prior to the computer revolution, the widespread availability and use of computers have greatly accelerated the process. In particular, computers enable us to handle, analyze, and dissect large masses of data, and they enable us to perform calculations which previously had been too cumbersome even to contemplate. Our objective in this book is your gaining an understanding of the ideas of statistics. Access to a computer is not critical for this objective. Computer uses are occasionally illustrated in this textbook, but nearly all the exercises can be done with nothing more than a four-function calculator.

1.2   THE STUDY OF STATISTICS

The subject of statistics can be presented at various levels of mathematical difficulty, and it may be directed toward applications in various fields of inquiry. Accordingly, many textbooks have been written on business statistics, educational statistics, medical statistics, psychological statistics, . . . , and even on statistics for historians. Although problems arising in these various disciplines will sometimes require special statistical techniques, none of the basic methods discussed in this book is restricted to any particular field of application. In the same way in which $2 + 2 = 4$ regardless of whether we are adding dollar amounts, horses, or trees, the methods we shall present provide **statistical models** which apply regardless of whether the data are IQs, tax payments, reaction times, humidity readings, test scores, and so on. To illustrate this further, consider an exercise from Chapter 13, specifically exercise 13.104

13.104   In a random sample of 200 retired persons, 137 stated that they prefer living in an apartment to living in a one-family home. At the 0.05 level of significance does this refute the claim that 60 percent of all retired persons prefer living in an apartment to living in a one-family home?

The question asked here should be clear, and it should also be clear that the answer would be of interest mainly to social scientists or to persons in the construction industry. However, if we wanted to cater to the special interests of students of biology, engineering, education, or ecology, we might rephrase the exercise as follows:

13.104   In a random sample of 200 citrus trees exposed to a 20° frost, 137 showed some damage to their fruit. At the 0.05 level of significance does this refute the claim that 60 percent of all citrus trees exposed to a 20° frost will show some damage to their fruit?

13.104   In a random sample of 200 transistors made by a given manufacturer, 137 passed an accelerated performance test. At the 0.05 level of significance does this refute the claim that 60 percent of all the transistors made by the manufacturer will pass the test?

13.104   In a random sample of 200 high school seniors in a large city, 137 said that they will go on to college. At the 0.05 level of significance does this refute the claim that 60 percent of all the high school seniors in this city will go on to college?

13.104   In a random sample of 200 cars tested for the emission of pollutants, 137 failed to meet a state's legal standards. At the 0.05 level of significance does this refute the claim that 60 percent of all cars tested in this state will fail to meet its legal emission standards?

Insofar as the work in this book is concerned, the statistical treatment of all these versions of Exercise 13.104 is the same, and with some imagination the reader should be able to rephrase it for virtually any field of specialization. As some authors do, we could present, and so designate, special problems for readers with special interests, but this would defeat our goal of impressing upon the reader the importance of statistics in all of science, business, and everyday life. To attain this goal, we have included in this text exercises covering a wide spectrum of interests.

To avoid the possibility of misleading anyone with our various versions of Exercise 13.104, let us make it clear that we cannot squeeze all statistical problems into the same mold. Although the methods we study in this book are all widely applicable, it is always important to make sure that the statistical model we are using is the right one.

EXERCISES

1.1   Rephrase Exercise 13.104 referred to above, so that it will be of special interest to

(a) a cosmetics salesperson;   (b) a musician;   (c) a traffic engineer.

1.2   Bad statistics may well result from asking questions in the wrong way or of the wrong persons. Explain why the following may lead to useless data:

(a) To determine public sentiment about a certain foreign trade restriction, an interviewer asks voters: "Do you feel that this unfair practice should be stopped?"

(b) To predict a municipal election, a public opinion poll telephones persons selected haphazardly from the city's telephone directory.

1.3 Bad statistics may well result from asking questions in the wrong place or at the wrong time. Explain why the following may lead to useless data:

(a) To predict an election, a poll taker interviews persons coming out of the building which houses the national headquarters of a political party.

(b) To study the spending patterns of families in a certain income group, a survey is conducted during the first three weeks of December.

1.4 Explain why each of the following studies may fail to yield the desired information:

(a) To determine the proportion of improperly sealed cans of coffee, a quality control inspector examines every 50th can coming off a production line.

(b) To determine the average annual income of its graduates 10 years after graduation, a college's alumni office sent questionnaires in 1995 to all members of the class of 1985, and the estimate was based on the questionnaires returned.

(c) To ascertain facts about tooth-brushing habits, a sample of the residents of a community are asked how many times they brush their teeth each day.

1.5 Consider this exercise: In an experiment comparing two skin cleansing products, lotion *A* caused irritation in 14 of 45 subjects, while lotion *B* caused irritation in 8 of 41 subjects. At the 0.05 level of significance, does this information refute the claim that the two lotions are equally irritating?

Rephrase this exercise so that it would be of interest to

(a) an agronomist comparing the benefits of two fertilizers;

(b) a political scientist comparing the opinions of two groups of voters;

(c) an educator comparing the merits of two instructional methods.

1.6 Explain why each of the following studies may fail to yield useful information:

(a) To estimate the value of stolen merchandise, employees of a business are asked, in confidence, about pilferage.

(b) To assess the level of usage of illegal drugs, employees of a business are given appointments for drug tests.

(c) To obtain information about recent purchases of expensive consumer appliances, residents of a certain town are sent questionnaires.

1.3 DESCRIPTIVE STATISTICS AND STATISTICAL INFERENCE

The origin of modern statistics can be traced to two areas of interest which, on the surface, have very little in common: government (political science) and games of chance.

Governments have long used censuses to count persons and property, and the problem of describing, summarizing, and analyzing census data has led to the development of methods which, until recently, constituted about all there was to the subject of statistics. These methods, which at first consisted primarily of presenting data in the form of tables and charts, make up what we now call **descriptive statistics.** This includes anything done to data which is designed to summarize, or describe, without going any further; that is, without attempting to infer anything that goes beyond the data, themselves. For instance, if tests performed on six small cars imported in 1996 showed that they were able to accelerate from 0 to 60 miles per hour (mph) in

$$18.7 \quad 19.2 \quad 16.2 \quad 12.3 \quad 17.5 \quad 13.9$$

seconds, and we report that half of them accelerated from 0 to 60 mph in less than 17.0 seconds, our work belongs to the domain of descriptive statistics. This would also be the case if we claim that these six cars averaged

$$\frac{18.7 + 19.2 + 16.2 + 12.3 + 17.5 + 13.9}{6} = 16.3 \text{ seconds}$$

but not if we conclude that half of *all* cars imported that year could accelerate from 0 to 60 mph in less than 17.0 seconds.

Although descriptive statistics is an important branch of statistics and it continues to be widely used, statistical information usually arises from samples (from observations made on only part of a large set of items), and this means that its analysis requires generalizations which go beyond the data. As a result, the most important feature of the recent growth of statistics has been a shift in emphasis from methods which merely describe to methods which serve to make generalizations, that is, a shift in emphasis from descriptive statistics to the methods of **statistical inference.**

Such methods are required, for instance, to predict the operating life span of a hand-held calculator (on the basis of the performance of several such calculators); to estimate the 2005 assessed value of all privately owned property in Orange County, California (on the basis of business trends, population projections, and so forth); to compare the effectiveness of two reducing diets (on the basis of the weight losses of persons who have been on the diets); to determine the most effective dose of a new medication (on the basis of tests performed with volunteer patients from selected hospitals); or to predict the flow of traffic on a freeway which has not yet been built (on the basis of past traffic counts on alternative routes).

In each of the situations described in the preceding paragraph, there are uncertainties because there is only partial, incomplete, or indirect information; therefore, the methods of statistical inference are needed to judge the merits of our results, to choose a "most promising" prediction, or to select a "most reasonable" (perhaps, a "potentially most profitable") course of action.

In view of the uncertainties, we handle problems like these with statistical methods which find their origin in games of chance. Although the mathematical study of games of chance dates back to the seventeenth century, it was not until the early part of the nineteenth century that the theory developed for "heads or tails," for example, or "red or black" or "even or odd," was applied also to real-life situations where the outcomes were "boy or girl," "life or death," "pass or fail," and so forth. Thus, **probability theory** was applied to many problems in the behavioral, natural, and social sciences, and at present provides an important tool for the analysis of any situation (in science, in business, or in everyday life) which in some way involves an element of uncertainty or chance. In particular, it provides the basis for the methods which we use when we generalize from observed data, namely, when we use the methods of statistical inference.

In recent years it has been suggested that the emphasis has swung too far from descriptive statistics to statistical inference, and that more attention should be paid to the treatment of problems requiring only descriptive techniques. To accommodate these needs, some new descriptive methods have recently been developed under the general heading of **exploratory data analysis.** Two of these methods are presented in Sections 2.1 and 3.5.

1.4 THE NATURE OF STATISTICAL DATA[†] ⇔

Statistical data are the raw material of statistical investigations—they arise whenever measurements are made or observations are recorded. They may be weights of animals, measurements of personality traits, or earthquake intensities, and they may be simple "yes or no" answers or descriptions of persons' marital status as single, married, widowed, or divorced. Since we said on page 2 that statistics deals with numerical data, this requires some explanation, because "yes or no" answers and descriptions of marital status would hardly seem to qualify as being numerical. Observe, however, that we can record "yes or no" answers to a question as 0 and 1 (or as 1 and 2, or perhaps as 29 and 30 if we are referring to the 15th "yes or no" question of a test), and that we can record a person's marital status as 1, 2, 3, or 4, depending on whether the person is single, married, widowed, or divorced. In this artificial, or nominal, way, categorical (qualitative, or descriptive) data can be made into numerical data, and if we thus code the various categories, we refer to the numbers we record as **nominal data.**

Nominal data are numerical in appearance only, because they do not share any of the properties of the numbers we deal with in ordinary arithmetic. For instance, if we record marital status as 1, 2, 3, or 4 as suggested above, we cannot write $3 > 1$ or $2 < 4$, and we cannot write

$$2 - 1 = 4 - 3, \qquad 1 + 3 = 4, \quad \text{or} \quad 4 \div 2 = 2.$$

It is important, therefore, always to check whether mathematical calculations performed in a statistical analysis are really legitimate.

Let us now consider some examples where data share some, but not necessarily all, of the properties of the numbers we deal with in ordinary arithmetic. For instance, in mineralogy the hardness of solids is sometimes determined by observing "what scratches what." If one mineral can scratch another it receives a higher hardness number, and on Mohs' scale the numbers from 1 to 10 are assigned, respectively, to talc, gypsum, calcite, fluorite, apatite, feldspar, quartz, topaz, sapphire, and diamond. With these numbers we can write $6 > 3$, for example, or $7 < 9$, since feldspar is harder than calcite and quartz is softer than sapphire. On the other hand, we cannot write $10 - 9 = 2 - 1$, for example, because the difference in hardness between diamond and sapphire is actually much greater than that between gypsum and talc. Also, it would be meaningless to say that topaz is twice as hard as fluorite simply because their respective hardness numbers on Mohs' scale are 8 and 4.

[†]As is explained in the Preface, all sections marked ⇔ are optional. The material in this section is meant to serve as a warning against the indiscriminate mathematical treatment of statistical data. It is most relevant to students of the behavioral and social sciences, where artificial scales serve to measure, say, neurotic tendencies, happiness, or conformity to social standards.

If we cannot do anything except set up inequalities, as was the case in the preceding example, we refer to the data as **ordinal data.** In connection with ordinal data, $>$ does not necessarily mean "greater than." It may be used to denote "happier than," "preferred to," "more difficult than," "tastier than," and so forth.

If we can also form differences, but not multiply or divide, we refer to the data as **interval data.** To give an example, suppose we are given the following temperature readings in degrees Fahrenheit:

$$63° \quad 68° \quad 91° \quad 107° \quad 126° \quad 131°$$

Here we can write $107° > 68°$ or $91° < 131°$, which simply means that $107°$ is warmer than $68°$ and that $91°$ is colder than $131°$. Also, we can write

$$68° - 63° = 131° - 126°$$

since equal temperature differences are equal in the sense that the same amount of heat is required to raise the temperature of an object from $63°$ to $68°$ as from $126°$ to $131°$. On the other hand, it would not mean much if we say that $126°$ is twice as hot as $63°$, even though $126 \div 63 = 2$. To show why, we have only to change to the Celsius scale, where the first temperature becomes

$$\frac{5}{9}(126 - 32) = 52.2°,$$

the second temperature becomes

$$\frac{5}{9}(63 - 32) = 17.2°$$

and the first figure is now more than three times the second. This difficulty arises because the Fahrenheit and Celsius scales both have artificial origins (zeros); in other words, the number 0 of neither scale is indicative of the absence of whatever quantity we are trying to measure.

If we can also form quotients, we refer to the data as **ratio data,** and such data are not difficult to find. They include all the usual measurements (or determinations) of length, height, money amounts, weight, volume, area, pressure, elapsed time (though not calendar time), sound intensity, density, brightness, velocity, and so on.

The distinction we have made here between nominal, ordinal, interval, and ratio data is important, for as we shall see, the nature of a set of data may suggest the use of particular statistical techniques. To emphasize the point that what we can and cannot do arithmetically with a given set of data depends on the nature of the data, consider the following scores which four students obtained in the three parts of a comprehensive history test:

	American History	European History	Ancient History
Linda	89	51	40
Tom	61	56	54
Henry	40	70	55
Rose	13	77	72

The totals for the four students are 180, 171, 165, and 162, so that Linda scored highest, followed by Tom, Henry, and Rose.

Suppose now that somebody proposes that we compare the overall performance of the four students by ranking their scores from high to low for each part of the test, and then average their ranks. What we get is shown in the following table:

	American History	European History	Ancient History	Average Rank
Linda	1	4	4	3
Tom	2	3	3	$2\frac{2}{3}$
Henry	3	2	2	$2\frac{1}{3}$
Rose	4	1	1	2

Here Linda's average rank was calculated as

$$\frac{1 + 4 + 4}{3} = \frac{9}{3} = 3,$$

Tom's as

$$\frac{2 + 3 + 3}{3} = \frac{8}{3} = 2\frac{2}{3},$$

and so forth.

Now, if we look at the average ranks, we find that Rose came out best, followed by Henry, Tom, and Linda, so that the order has been reversed from what it was before. How can this be? Well, strange things can happen when we average ranks. For instance, when it comes to their ranks, Linda's outscoring Tom by 28 points in American history counts just as much as Tom's outscoring her by 5 points in European history, and Tom's outscoring Henry by 21 points in American history counts just as much as Henry's outscoring him by a single point in ancient history. We conclude that, perhaps, we should not have averaged the ranks, but it might also be pointed out that, perhaps, we should not even have totaled the original scores. The variation of the American history scores, which go from 13 to 89, is much greater than that of the other two kinds of scores, and this strongly affects the total scores and suggests a possible shortcoming of the procedure. We shall not go into this here, as it has been our goal merely to alert the reader against the indiscriminate use of statistical techniques.

◢ EXERCISES†

1.7   In five biology tests a student received grades of 46, 61, 74, 79, and 88. Which of the following conclusions can be obtained from these figures by purely descriptive methods and which require generalizations? Explain your answers.

(a) Only two of the grades exceeded 75.

(b) The student's grades increased from each test to the next.

†Exercises marked ⬦ pertain to material from optional sections.

(c) The student must have studied harder for each successive test.

(d) The difference between the highest and lowest grades is 42.

1.8 Mary and Jean are in real estate sales. In the first three months of 1996 Mary sold 3, 6, and 2 one-family homes and Jean sold 4, 0, and 5 one-family homes. Which of the following conclusions can be obtained from these figures by purely descriptive methods and which require generalizations? Explain your answers.

(a) During the three months Mary sold more one-family homes than Jean.

(b) Mary is a better real estate salesperson than Jean.

(c) Mary sold at least two one-family homes during each of the three months.

(d) Jean probably took her annual vacation during the second month.

1.9 On three consecutive days, a traffic officer issued 9, 14, and 10 speeding tickets, and 5, 10, and 12 tickets for passing through red lights. Which of the following conclusions can be obtained from these data by purely descriptive methods and which require generalizations? Explain your answers.

(a) Altogether on these three days, the officer issued more speeding tickets than tickets for passing red lights.

(b) On two of the three days, the officer issued more speeding tickets than tickets for passing red lights.

(c) The officer issued the smallest number of tickets on the first day because he was new on the job.

(d) The officer will seldom write more than 15 speeding tickets on any one day.

1.10 The three lemons which a person bought at a supermarket weighed 7, 8, and 12 ounces. Which of the following conclusions can be obtained from these data by purely descriptive methods and which require generalizations? Explain your answers.

(a) The average weight of the three lemons is 9 ounces.

(b) The average weight of lemons sold at that supermarket is 9 ounces.

⇧ 1.11 State whether we get nominal data or ordinal data if

(a) mechanics have to say whether changing the spark plugs on a new model car is very difficult, difficult, easy, or very easy;

(b) the religion of persons attempting suicide is coded 1, 2, 3, 4, or 5, representing Protestant, Catholic, Jewish, other, and none;

(c) consumers must say whether they prefer brand A to brand B, like them equally, or prefer brand B to brand A;

(d) consumers must say whether they prefer brand A to brand B, like them equally, prefer brand B to brand A, or have no opinion.

⇧ 1.12 Are the following nominal, ordinal, interval, or ratio data? Explain your answers.

(a) Social Security numbers.

(b) The number of passengers on buses from Los Angeles to San Diego.

(c) Vocational interest scores consisting of the total number of "yes" answers given to a set of questions, if it can be assumed that each "yes" answer represents the same increment of vocational interest.

(d) Military ranks.

⇧ 1.13 IQ scores are sometimes looked upon as interval data. What assumption would this entail about the differences in intelligence of three persons with IQs of 95, 105, and 135? Is this assumption reasonable?

⇧ 1.14 On page 8 we indicated that data pertaining to calendar time (for instance, the years in which Army beat Navy in football) are not ratio data. Explain why. What kind of time measurements do constitute ratio data?

1.5 CHECKLIST OF KEY TERMS[†] *(with page references to their definitions)*

Descriptive statistics, 5   Probability theory, 6
Exploratory data analysis, 7   ⇔ Ratio data, 8
⇔ Interval data, 8   Statistical inference, 6
⇔ Nominal data, 7   Statistical model, 3
⇔ Ordinal data, 8

1.6 REVIEW EXERCISES[††]

1.15   The paid attendance at a small college's home football games was

$$12{,}305 \quad 10{,}984 \quad 6{,}850 \quad 11{,}733 \quad 10{,}641$$

Which of the following conclusions can be obtained from these figures by purely descriptive methods and which require generalizations? Explain your answers.

(a) The attendance at the third home game was so low because it rained.

(b) Among the five games, the paid attendance was highest at the first game.

(c) The paid attendance exceeded 11,000 at two of the five games.

(d) The paid attendance increased from the third home game to the fourth home game because the college's football team had been winning.

⇔ 1.16   Are the following nominal, ordinal, interval, or ratio data? Explain your answers.

(a) Elevations above sea level.

(b) Responses to the question whether (in the downtown area of a large city) living conditions are

"getting much worse," "getting a little worse,"

"staying the same," "getting a little better," or "getting much better."

(c) Ages of secondhand cars.

(d) Responses on drivers' licenses with regard to eye color.

1.17   Explain why each of the following data may well fail to yield the desired information:

(a) To predict a municipal election, a public opinion poll questions persons walking in front of the municipal government office.

(b) To determine public sentiment about certain import restrictions, an interviewer asks voters: "Do you feel that American consumers should be denied the use of these products?"

1.18   If students calculate their grade-point indexes (that is, average their grades) by counting

$$A, \ B, \ C, \ D, \ \text{and} \ F \ \text{as} \ 4, \ 3, \ 2, \ 1, \ \text{and} \ 0$$

what does this assume about the nature of the grades?

1.19   Explain why each of the following data may well fail to yield the desired information:

(a) To see how the public feels about imports from India, selected persons are asked whether they like Indian art.

(b) To ascertain facts about their bathing habits, a sample of the citizens of a European country are asked how many times on the average they bathe per week.

[†]Terms marked ⇔ pertain to material from optional sections.

[††]Review exercises marked ⇔ pertain to material from optional sections.

1.20   Using the same model car, five drivers averaged

$$23.4, \quad 22.5, \quad 24.0, \quad 23.4, \quad \text{and} \quad 22.7$$

miles per gallon. Which of the following conclusions can be obtained by purely descriptive methods and which require generalizations? Explain your answers.

(a) More often than any of the other figures, the drivers averaged 23.4 miles per gallon.

(b) More often than any of the other figures, drivers of this kind of car will average 23.4 miles per gallon.

(c) None of the averages differs from 23.5 by more than 1.0 mile.

(d) If the whole experiment is repeated, none of the drivers will average less than 22.5 or more than 24.5 miles per hour.

1.21   In two major golf tournaments one professional finished second and ninth, while another finished sixth and fifth. Comment on the argument that since $2 + 9 = 6 + 5$, the overall performance of the two golfers in these two tournaments was equally good.

1.22   Rephrase the exercise referred to on page 4 so that it would be of special interest to

(a) a lawyer;   (b) a travel agent;   (c) an author.

1.23   Five members of a secretarial pool have weekly commuting expenses of

$$\$13 \quad \$25 \quad \$22 \quad \$45 \quad \$15$$

Which of the following conclusions are descriptive and which are generalizations? Explain your answers.

(a) The average expenses are $24.

(b) Only one person has expenses in excess of $30.

(c) The person who spends $13 lives closest to the office.

(d) If bus fares increase, the average expense will also increase.

1.24   A baseball fan claims that a player with a batting average of .350 is 40% better than a player with a batting average of .250. Comment on this assertion.

1.7   REFERENCES

Brief and informal discussions of what statistics is and what statisticians do may be found in pamphlets titled *Careers in Statistics* and *Statistics as a Career: Women at Work,* which are published by the American Statistical Association. They may be obtained by writing to this organization at 1429 Duke Street, Alexandria, VA 22314-3402. Among the few books on the history of statistics, there is on the elementary level

WALKER, H. M., *Studies in the History of Statistical Method.* Baltimore: The Williams & Wilkins Company, 1929.

and on the more advanced level

KENDALL, M.G., and PLACKETT, R. L., eds. *Studies in the History of Statistics and Probability,* Vol. II. New York: Macmillan Publishing Co., Inc., 1977.

PEARSON, E. S., and KENDALL, M. G., eds. *Studies in the History of Statistics and Probability,* New York: Hafner Press, 1970.

STIGLER, S.M., *The History of Statistics.* Cambridge, Mass.: Harvard University Press, 1986.

A more detailed discussion of the nature of statistical data and the general problem of **scaling** (namely, the problem of constructing scales of measurement or assigning scale scores) may be found in

AGRESTI, A., *Analysis of Ordinal Categorical Data.* New York: John Wiley & Sons, Inc., 1984.

HILDEBRAND, D. K., LAING, J. D., and ROSENTHAL, H., *Analysis of Ordinal Data.* Beverly Hills, Calif.: Sage Publications, Inc., 1977.

REYNOLDS, H. T., *Analysis of Nominal Data.* Beverly Hills, Calif.: Sage Publications, Inc., 1977.

SIEGEL, S., *Nonparametric Statistics for the Behavioral Sciences.* New York: McGraw-Hill Book Company, 1956.

The following are some titles from the ever-growing list of books on statistics which are written for the layperson.

BROOK, R. J., ARNOLD, G. C., HASSARD, T. H., and PRINGLE, R. M., eds., *The Fascination of Statistics.* New York: Marcel Dekker, Inc., 1986.

CAMPBELL, S. K., *Flaws and Fallacies in Statistical Thinking.* Englewood Cliffs, N.J.: Prentice-Hall, Inc., 1974.

HOLLANDER, M., and PROSCHAN, F., *The Statistical Exorcist: Dispelling Statistics Anxiety.* New York: Marcel Dekker, Inc., 1984.

HOOKE, R., *How to Tell the Liars from the Statisticians.* New York: Marcell Dekker, Inc., 1983.

JOFFE, A., and SPIRER, H. F., *Misused Statistics: Straight Talk for Twisted Numbers.* New York: Marcel Dekker, Inc., 1987.

KIMBLE, G. A., *How to Use (and Misuse) Statistics.* Englewood Cliffs, N.J.: Prentice-Hall, Inc., 1978.

LARSEN, R. J., and STROUP, D. F., *Statistics in the Real World.* New York: Macmillan Publishing Co., Inc., 1976.

PAULOS, J. A., *Innumeracy: Mathematical Illiteracy and Its Consequences.* New York: Hill and Wang, 1988.

RUNYON, R. P., *Winning with Statistics.* Reading, Mass.: Addison-Wesley Publishing Company, Inc., 1977.

TANUR, J. M., ed., *Statistics: A Guide to the Unknown.* San Francisco: Holden-Day, Inc., 1972.

WANG, C., *Sense and Nonsense of Statistical Inference.* New York: Marcel Dekker, Inc., 1993.

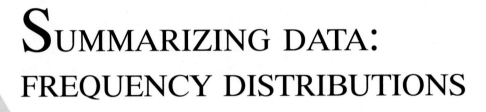

Summarizing Data: Frequency Distributions

*I*n recent years the collection of statistical data has grown at such a rate that it would be impossible to keep up with even a small part of the things which directly affect our lives unless this information is disseminated in predigested, or summarized, form. The whole matter of putting large masses of data into usable form has always been important, but it has multiplied greatly in the last few decades. This has been due partly to the development of computers which now make it possible to accomplish in seconds what was previously left undone because it would have taken months or years, and partly to the deluge of data generated by the increasingly quantitative approach of the sciences, especially the behavioral and social sciences, where nearly every aspect of human life is measured in one way or another.

The most common method of summarizing data is to present them in condensed form in tables or charts, and at one time this took up the better part of an elementary course in statistics. However, there is so much else to learn in statistics that very little time is now devoted to this kind of work. This is unfortunate, because one does not have to look far in newspapers, magazines, and even professional journals to find unintentionally or intentionally misleading statistical charts.

Section 2.1 deals with the task of sorting numeric values and presents a new technique, the stem-and-leaf display. Section 2.2 deals with frequency distributions, the standard method for grouping data. Section 2.3 shows some graphical methods. ◪

2.1   DISPLAYING NUMERIC VALUES

Organizing and presenting numeric information is one of the first tasks in understanding a problem. As a typical situation, consider the values below, which represent the travel time to work of 100 employees in a large downtown office building. The times are given in minutes, and each value represents an employee's average time over five consecutive workdays. The mere gathering together of this information is no small task, but it is clear that more must be done to make the numbers comprehensible.

44.0	35.4	28.4	37.0	46.0	35.4	19.4	20.4	56.4	43.2
36.2	38.4	49.2	31.8	86.4	12.6	27.4	14.0	39.4	39.4
15.8	28.8	38.0	44.0	38.4	74.0	23.0	11.4	39.8	30.2
29.2	40.6	49.6	30.4	12.2	123.8	42.0	47.0	32.4	39.2
35.2	56.4	31.0	45.0	90.2	100.0	39.0	37.0	49.4	28.2
12.6	27.0	47.8	52.6	41.0	40.0	28.0	23.6	37.6	37.8
30.0	45.8	18.0	41.0	22.6	24.2	89.6	90.4	43.0	29.8
56.2	24.8	12.6	53.6	125.4	16.2	39.0	40.8	33.6	39.4
45.6	37.4	18.0	50.6	103.4	52.4	20.2	64.6	22.2	60.0
42.2	42.0	16.2	108.2	44.0	42.6	39.4	37.6	41.4	40.4

What can be done to make this mass of information more usable? Some people find it interesting to locate the extreme values.

For this list, the smallest value is 11.4 minutes, and the largest is 125.4 minutes. It is occasionally useful to sort the data values into increasing or decreasing order. The list below gives these sorted values, and it is now possible to learn more about these travel times. For instance, we see now that there are many values near 40 minutes.

11.4	12.2	12.6	12.6	12.6	14.0	15.8	16.2	16.2	18.0
18.0	19.4	20.2	20.4	22.2	22.6	23.0	23.6	24.2	24.8
27.0	27.4	28.0	28.2	28.4	28.8	29.2	29.8	30.0	30.2
30.4	31.0	31.8	32.4	33.6	35.2	35.4	35.4	36.2	37.0
37.0	37.4	37.6	37.6	37.8	38.0	38.4	38.4	39.0	39.0
39.2	39.4	39.4	39.4	39.4	39.8	40.0	40.4	40.6	40.8
41.0	41.0	41.4	42.0	42.0	42.2	42.6	43.0	43.2	44.0
44.0	44.0	45.0	45.6	45.8	46.0	47.0	47.8	49.2	49.4
49.6	50.6	52.4	52.6	53.6	56.2	56.4	56.4	60.0	64.6
74.0	86.4	89.6	90.2	90.4	100.0	103.4	108.2	123.8	125.4

Sorting a large set of numbers into increasing or decreasing order is a surprisingly difficult task.

This list of numbers, even in sorted form, is still a ponderous piece of information. It will be helpful to have other ways of dealing with these values. A recently developed technique, the **stem-and-leaf display,** will give a good overall impression of the data.

To illustrate this technique, consider the following scores on a test of physical coordination given to 20 students who had consumed an amount of alcohol equal to 0.1% of their weight:

69 84 52 93 61 74 79 65 88 63
57 64 67 72 74 55 82 61 68 77

Now break each number into its tens and units digits, tallying together values which share the tens digit. That is, we will think of the number 69 as 6 | 9. The tens digits will then be aligned vertically with the units digits displayed to the side. For the set of 20 physical coordination scores, the picture is this:

```
5 | 2 7 5
6 | 9 1 5 3 4 7 1 8
7 | 4 9 2 4 7
8 | 4 8 2
9 | 3
```

The first row of the display, namely 5 | 2 7 5, tells us that the list contains values 52, 57, and 55. The second row tells us that the list contains eight values in the 60s.

This table is referred to as a stem-and-leaf display, since each row represents a **stem** position and each digit to the right of the vertical line can be thought of as a **leaf.** To make this stem-and-leaf display, begin with the stems only, as

```
5 |
6 |
7 |
8 |
9 |
```

This step need not be perfect; after all, it's easy to stick on additional stem positions at the top or bottom. Then mark the leaves by going through the individual data items sequentially. After the first three values (69, 84, 52) the stem-and-leaf display will look like this:

```
5 | 2
6 | 9
7 |
8 | 4
9 |
```

After just one pass through the data, the complete stem-and-leaf display is done.

The stem-and-leaf display conveys the same information as the original list, but is much more compact, and highlights the important aspects of the data. For instance, in this case the display reveals immediately that most of the values are in the 60s.

The stem-and-leaf display accomplishes most of the task of sorting the values. Most people like to complete the sorting by ordering the leaves as well. In this example, it gives the following:

```
5 | 2 5 7
6 | 1 1 3 4 5 7 8 9
7 | 2 4 4 7 9
8 | 2 4 8
9 | 3
```

Not every set of values can be placed into a stem-and-leaf display this easily. The treatment of more complicated situations is a matter of taste. Let's consider the 100 travel times noted before. These numbers were given to *tenths* of minutes. In making the stem-and-leaf display, we recommend ignoring the tenths rather than rounding the values to the nearest minute. This introduces a half-minute bias to the display, but produces with less effort nearly the same result as proper rounding.[†] We will use the tens digit to label the stem, and this produces the display below:

```
 1 | 1 2 2 2 4 5 6 6 8 8 9
 2 | 0 0 2 2 3 3 4 4 7 7 8 8 8 8 9 9
 3 | 0 0 0 1 1 2 3 5 5 5 6 7 7 7 7 7 8 8 8 9 9 9 9 9 9 9 9
 4 | 0 0 0 0 1 1 1 2 2 2 2 3 3 4 4 4 5 5 5 6 7 7 9 9 9
 5 | 0 2 2 3 6 6 6
 6 | 0 4
 7 | 4
 8 | 6 9
 9 | 0 0
10 | 0 3 8
11 |
12 | 3 5
13 |
```

Note: 7 | 4 means   74 minutes
         12 | 3 means 123 minutes

[†]Dropping off digits has a number of advantages over the process of careful rounding, and it is the procedure recommended by John Tukey, the inventor of the stem-and-leaf display. His book appears in the References at the end of this chapter.

This stem-and-leaf display requires just looking through the original list once and its picture conveys the message of the original list in a very clean pictorial form. It is helpful to attach a note as above to help people read the display. This is certainly helpful when the stem labels are not the tens digits.

There are various ways in which stem-and-leaf displays can be modified to meet particular needs. If we want to construct a stem-and-leaf display with more stems than there would be otherwise, we can divide each stem position in two. Use the first stem position to hold leaves 0, 1, 2, 3, and 4, and use the second stem position to hold leaves 5, 6, 7, 8, and 9. For the second set of data on page 16, we would thus get the **double-stem display:**

```
5 | 2
5 | 5  7
6 | 1  1  3  4
6 | 5  7  8  9
7 | 2  4  4
7 | 7  9
8 | 2  4
8 | 8
9 | 3
```

In this display, we doubled the number of stem positions by cutting in half the interval covered by each tens digit.

We will use the displays for some further descriptions (see Section 3.4). In Figure 2.1 we used a computer to construct the double-stem display shown above. Computer-generated stem-and-leaf displays tally cumulative counts from the high and low ends. The first three rows of Figure 2.1 contain seven values, while the final four rows contain six values. The count for the row containing the middle value is given in parentheses; this is the notation (4) in Figure 2.1.

FIGURE 2.1

Computer printout for the construction of a double-stem display (MINITAB 10 for Windows).

```
MTB  > SET  C1
DATA > 69   84   52   93   61   74   79   65   88   63
DATA > 57   64   67   72   74   55   82   61   68   77
MTB  > STEM  C1

Character  Stem-and-Leaf  Display

Stem-and-leaf of C1          N = 20
Leaf  Unit = 1.0

    1        5  2
    3        5  57
    7        6  1134
   (4)       6  5789
    9        7  244
    6        7  79
    4        8  24
    2        8  8
    1        9  3
```

We shall not treat stem-and-leaf displays in any great detail, as it has been our objective mainly to present one of the relatively new techniques which come under the general heading of **exploratory data analysis.** These techniques are used primarily to explore data without, or before, using the more traditional methods of statistical analysis.

◢ EXERCISES

2.1 The following are the heights in centimeters of 16 high school students:

> 172 182 177 174 166 158 170 178
> 163 161 191 167 171 201 166 172

Construct a stem-and-leaf display with the stem labels 15, 16, 17, 18, 19, and 20.

2.2 The following are the weights in pounds of 20 applicants for jobs with a city's fire department:

> 225 182 194 210 205 172 181 198 164 176
> 180 193 178 193 208 186 183 170 186 188

Construct a stem-and-leaf display with the stem labels 16, 17, 18, 19, 20, 21, and 22.

2.3 The following are the weekly earnings in dollars of 15 salespersons:

> 425 440 610 518 324 482 624 390
> 468 457 509 561 482 480 520

Construct a stem-and-leaf display with the stem labels 3, 4, 5, and 6; the tens digits should be used as the leaves.

2.4 List the data values which are given in the stem-and-leaf display below.

$$
\begin{array}{c|cccccc}
4 & 0 & 2 & 3 \\
5 & 1 & 1 & 8 & 9 \\
6 & 2 & 3 & 3 & 7 & 7 & 9 \\
7 & 0
\end{array}
$$

2.5 Construct a double-stem display for the data of Exercise 2.2.

2.6 The following are the ages of 32 heads of household in a retirement community:

> 68 81 62 61 76 65 69 73 66 68 71 74 70 68 73 64
> 82 79 63 69 68 66 73 74 77 80 73 66 67 81 77 66

Construct a double-stem display (see page 18) for these values.

2.7 The following number of products were completed on a particular day by 20 employees of a handcrafts factory:

> 61 58 59 72 47 55 40 73 66 60
> 71 69 63 58 51 42 67 80 62 53

Construct a stem-and-leaf display with the stem labels 4, 5, 6, 7, and 8.

2.8 The margin of victory (meaning winning score minus losing score) for 43 high school basketball games in a particular league are

> 10   5   7 13   9 12 14   7 15   6
> 1   8 12   7 26   3 19   2 11 14
> 8 10   4   9 12 16   7   5   1   9
> 14   8 14 16   8   7   9 10 10 22
> 6   1 19

Construct a double-stem display for these data.

2.2 FREQUENCY DISTRIBUTIONS

When we deal with large sets of data, a good overall picture and all the information we need can often be conveyed by grouping the data into a number of classes, intervals, or categories. For instance, a survey of local weekly newspaper subscription bases in 1994 may be summarized as follows:

Number of Subscribers	Number of Newspapers
Less than 1,000	244
1,000– 3,499	157
3,500– 9,999	96
10,000–19,999	37
20,000–49,999	24
50,000 or more	6
Total	564

This table is called a **frequency distribution** (or simply a **distribution)**—it shows how the local weekly newspapers are distributed among the six classes. When data are thus grouped according to size, we refer to such a table as a **numerical** (or **quantitative**) **distribution.**

In the newspaper subscriber example, each class covered a wide range of values, but there are also numerical distributions where each class covers only a single value. The following example is based on a study in which 200 persons were asked how many times they had visited a local zoo during the last 12 months:

Number of Visits to Local Zoo	Number of Persons
0	90
1	72
2	26
3	8
4	3
5	0
6	1
Total	200

If data are grouped into nonnumerical categories, such a table is called a **categorical** (or **qualitative**) **distribution.** This kind of distribution is illustrated by the following table pertaining to 2,439 complaints about comfort-related characteristics of an airline's planes:

Nature of Complaint	Number of Complaints
Inadequate leg room	719
Uncomfortable seats	914
Narrow aisles	146
Insufficient carry-on facilities	218
Insufficient restrooms	58
Miscellaneous other complaints	384
Total	2,439

We could convert a distribution like this into a numerical distribution by **coding** the data, say, by assigning the six alternatives the numbers 1, 2, 3, 4, 5, and 6, but this would give us nominal data, which are numerical only in a trivial sense.

Frequency distributions present data in a relatively compact form, give a good overall picture, and contain adequate information for many purposes, but there are usually some things which cannot be determined without referring to the original data. For instance, from the first table of this section we can find neither the size of the smallest of the 564 newspapers, nor the average number of subscribers for the ten largest newspapers. Similarly, from the third table we cannot tell how many of the complaints about uncomfortable seats were over the width of the seats, or how many of the complaints about insufficient carry-on facilities were over space for suit carriers. Nevertheless, frequency distributions present **raw** (unprocessed) **data** in a more readily usable form, and the price we have to pay for this—the loss of some information—is usually worthwhile.

The construction of a frequency distribution consists essentially of three steps:

1. Choosing the **classes** (intervals or categories)
2. Sorting or tallying the data into these classes
3. Counting the number of items in each class

Since the second and third steps are purely mechanical, we concentrate here on the first, namely, that of choosing a suitable classification.

For numerical distributions, this consists of deciding how many classes we are going to use and from where to where each class should go. Both of these choices are essentially arbitrary, but the following rules are usually observed:

We seldom use fewer than six or more than 15 classes; the exact number we use in a given situation depends largely on how many measurements or observations there are.

Clearly, we would lose more than we gain if we group five observations into 12 classes with most of them empty, and we would probably discard too much information if we group a thousand measurements into three classes.

We always make sure that each item (measurement or observation) goes into one and only one class.

To this end we must make sure that the smallest and largest values fall within the classification, that none of the values can fall into a gap between successive classes, and that the classes do not overlap, namely, that successive classes have no values in common.

Whenever possible, we make the classes cover equal ranges of values.

Also, if we can, we make these ranges multiples of numbers that are easy to work with, such as 5, 10, or 100, since this will tend to facilitate the construction and the use of a distribution.

In connection with these rules, the newspaper subscriber distribution on page 20 satisfies the first two, but violates the third. Actually, the third rule is violated in several ways, since the classes

1,000–3,499,   3,500–9,999,   10,000–19,999,   20,000–49,999

all cover different ranges of values, the first class has no specified lower limit, and the last class has no specified upper limit. Presumably, the statisticians responsible for this table had good reasons for choosing the classes as they did.

Classes of the "less than," "or less," "more than," or "or more" variety are referred to as **open classes,** and they are used to reduce the number of classes that are needed when some of the values are much smaller than or much greater than the rest. Generally, open classes should be avoided, however, because they make it impossible to calculate certain values of interest, such as averages or totals (see Exercise 3.58 on page 71).

Insofar as the second rule is concerned, we have to watch whether the data are given to the nearest dollar or to the nearest cent, whether they are given to the nearest inch or to the nearest tenth of an inch, whether they are given to the nearest ounce or to the nearest hundredth of an ounce, and so on. For instance, if we want to group the weights of certain animals, we might use the first of the following classifications when the weights are given to the nearest kilogram, the second when the weights are given to the nearest tenth of a kilogram, and the third when the weights are given to the nearest hundredth of a kilogram:

Weight (kilograms)	Weight (kilograms)	Weight (kilograms)
10–14	10.0–14.9	10.00–14.99
15–19	15.0–19.9	15.00–19.99
20–24	20.0–24.9	20.00–24.99
25–29	25.0–29.9	25.00–29.99
30–34	30.0–34.9	30.00–34.99
etc.	etc.	etc.

To illustrate a frequency distribution, discussed in this section, we now proceed through the actual steps of grouping a set of data into a frequency distribution.

Example

Construct a distribution of the following amounts of sulfur oxides (in tons) emitted by an industrial plant in 80 days:

15.8	26.4	17.3	11.2	23.9	24.8	18.7	13.9	9.0	13.2
22.7	9.8	6.2	14.7	17.5	26.1	12.8	28.6	17.6	23.7
26.8	22.7	18.0	20.5	11.0	20.9	15.5	19.4	16.7	10.7
19.1	15.2	22.9	26.6	20.4	21.4	19.2	21.6	16.9	19.0
18.5	23.0	24.6	20.1	16.2	18.0	7.7	13.5	23.5	14.5
14.4	29.6	19.4	17.0	20.8	24.3	22.5	24.6	18.4	18.1
8.3	21.9	12.3	22.3	13.3	11.8	19.3	20.0	25.7	31.8
25.9	10.5	15.9	27.5	18.1	17.9	9.4	24.1	20.1	28.5

solution

Since the smallest value is 6.2 and the largest value is 31.8, we might choose the six classes

5.0–9.9, 10.0–14.9, ..., and 30.0–34.9,

the seven classes

5.0–8.9, 9.0–12.9, ..., and 29.0–32.9,

the nine classes

5.0–7.9, 8.0–10.9, ..., and 29.0–31.9,

or numerous other classifications. Note that in each of the classifications cited, the classes accommodate all the data, they do not overlap, and they are all of the same size.

Essentially, the choice among these classifications is arbitrary, but supposing that for some legal reason (say, government regulations) it is necessary to keep all values greater than 16.9 but less than 21.0 in one class, we choose the second one. Then, tallying the 80 measurements into the seven classes, we obtain the following table:

Tons of Sulfur Oxides	Tally	Frequency
5.0– 8.9	///	3
9.0–12.9	### ###	10
13.0–16.9	### ### ////	14
17.0–20.9	### ### ### ### ###	25
21.0–24.9	### ### ### //	17
25.0–28.9	### ////	9
29.0–32.9	//	2
	Total	80

The tally is usually omitted in a final presentation of such a table.

The numbers shown in the right-hand column of the table above, which show how many items fall into each class, are called the **class frequencies.** The smallest and largest values that can go into any given class are called its **class limits,** and for the distribution of the emission data they are

5.0 and 8.9, 9.0 and 12.9, 13.0 and 16.9, ..., and 29.0 and 32.9

More specifically,

5.0, 9.0, 13.0, ..., and 29.0

are called the **lower class limits,** and

$$8.9, \quad 12.9, \quad 16.9, \quad \ldots, \quad \text{and} \quad 32.9$$

are called the **upper class limits.**

The amounts which we grouped in our example were all given to the nearest tenth of a ton, so that 5.0 actually includes everything from 4.95 to 5.05, 8.9 includes everything from 8.85 to 8.95, and the class 5.0–8.9 includes everything from 4.95 to 8.95. Similarly, the second class includes everything from 8.95 to 12.95, . . ., and the seventh class includes everything from 28.95 to 32.95. It is customary to refer to

$$4.95, \quad 8.95, \quad 12.95, \quad \ldots, \quad 32.95$$

as the **class boundaries** or the **real class limits.** Although 8.95 is the upper boundary of the first class and also the lower boundary of the second class, . . . , and 28.95 is the upper boundary of the sixth class and also the lower boundary of the seventh class, there is no cause for alarm. The class boundaries are, by their very nature, impossible values which cannot occur among the data being grouped. For instance, in the newspaper subscriber example on page 20, the class boundaries are the impossible values

$$999.5, \quad 3,499.5, \quad 9,999.5, \quad 19,999.5, \quad 49,999.5$$

They are impossible values because a newspaper cannot very well have half a subscriber.

To avoid gaps in the continuous number scale, some statistics texts and some widely used computer programs (Minitab, for example) include in each class its lower boundary. They would include 4.95, but not 8.95, in the first class of the distribution of the sulfur oxides emission data. Similarly, they would include 8.95, but not 12.95, in the second class, and so forth. All this is totally immaterial, of course, so long as the class boundaries are impossible values which cannot occur among the data being grouped. Especially for this reason, the use of impossible class boundaries can be very helpful.

Numerical distributions also have what we call **class marks** and **class intervals.** Class marks are simply the midpoints of the classes, and they are found by adding the lower and upper limits of a class (or its lower and upper boundaries) and dividing by 2. A class interval is merely the length of a class, or the range of values it can contain, and it is given by the difference between its boundaries. If the classes of a distribution are all equal in length, their common class interval, which we call the **class interval of the distribution,** is also given by the difference between any two successive class marks.

Example

Find the class marks and the class interval of the distribution of the sulfur oxides emission data.

solution

The class marks are

$$\frac{5.0 + 8.9}{2} = 6.95, \quad \frac{9.0 + 12.9}{2} = 10.95, \quad \frac{13.0 + 16.9}{2} = 14.95, \quad \frac{17.0 + 20.9}{2} = 18.95,$$

$$\frac{21.0 + 24.9}{2} = 22.95, \quad \frac{25.0 + 28.9}{2} = 26.95, \quad \frac{29.0 + 32.9}{2} = 30.95$$

Therefore, since the class intervals are

$$8.95 - 4.95 = 4, \quad 12.95 - 8.95 = 4, \quad \ldots, \quad \text{and } 32.95 - 28.95 = 4,$$

and they are all equal, the class interval of the distribution is 4. Note that if we had taken the differences between the class limits instead of the differences between the class boundaries, we would have obtained 3.9 instead of 4, and 3.9 is not the class interval. ◪ ◪ ◪

There are two ways in which frequency distributions can be modified to suit particular needs. One way is to convert a distribution into a **percentage distribution** by dividing each class frequency by the total number of items grouped, and then multiplying by 100%.

Example

Convert the distribution of the sulfur oxides emission data into a percentage distribution.

solution

The first class contains

$$\frac{3}{80} \cdot 100\% = 3.75\% \text{ of the data,}$$

the second class contains

$$\frac{10}{80} \cdot 100\% = 12.50\% \text{ of the data,} \quad \ldots,$$

and the seventh class contains

$$\frac{2}{80} \cdot 100\% = 2.50\% \text{ of the data}$$

These results are shown in the following table:

Tons of Sulfur Oxides	Percentage
5.0– 8.9	3.75
9.0–12.9	12.50
13.0–16.9	17.50
17.0–20.9	31.25
21.0–24.9	21.25
25.0–28.9	11.25
29.0–32.9	2.50
Total	100.00

Percentage distributions are often used when we want to compare two or more distributions; for instance, if we want to compare oxides emission of the plant considered in our example with that of a plant at a different location. ◪ ◪ ◪

The other way of modifying a frequency distribution is to convert it into a "less than," "or less," "more than," "or more" **cumulative distribution.** To construct a cumulative distribution, we simply add the class frequencies, starting either at the top or at the bottom of the distribution.

Example

Convert the distribution on page 23 into a "less than" cumulative distribution.

solution

Since

none of the values is less than 5.0,
3 of the values are less than 9.0,

$3 + 10 = 13$ of the values are less than 13.0,

$3 + 10 + 14 = 27$ of the values are less than 17.0, and so on,

we obtain the results shown in the following table:

Tons of Sulfur Oxides	Cumulative Frequency
Less than 5.0	0
Less than 9.0	3
Less than 13.0	13
Less than 17.0	27
Less than 21.0	52
Less than 25.0	69
Less than 29.0	78
Less than 33.0	80

Note that instead of

"less than 5.0," "less than 9.0," "less than 13.0," ...,

we could have written

"4.9 or less," "8.9 or less," "12.9 or less," ...,

or

"less than 4.95," "less than 8.95," "less than 12.95," ....

In the same way we can also convert a percentage distribution into a **cumulative percentage distribution.** We simply add the percentages instead of the frequencies, starting either at the top or at the bottom of the distribution.

So far we have discussed only the construction of numerical distributions, but the general problem of constructing categorical (or qualitative) distributions is about the same. Here again we must decide how many categories (classes) to use and what kind of items each category is to contain, making sure that all the items are accommodated and that there are no ambiguities. Since the categories must often be chosen before any data are actually collected, it is usually prudent to include a category labeled "others" or "miscellaneous."

For categorical distributions, we do not have to worry about such mathematical details as class limits, class boundaries, and class marks. On the other hand, there is often a serious problem with ambiguities and we must be very careful and explicit in defining what each category is to contain. For instance, if we had to classify items sold at a supermarket into "meats," "frozen foods," "baked goods," and so forth, it would be difficult to decide, for example, where to put frozen beef pies. Similarly, if we had to classify occupations, it would be difficult to decide where to put a farm manager, if our table contained (without qualification) the two categories "farmers" and "managers." For this reason, it is advisable, where possible, to use standard categories developed by the Bureau of the Census and other government agencies. References to lists of such categories may be found in the book by P. M. Hauser and W. R. Leonard listed among the references on page 42.

◪ EXERCISES

2.9 The weights of the members of a university football team vary from 168 to 266 pounds. Indicate the limits of 11 classes into which these weights might be grouped.

2.10 The three-month rates of return for a group of 250 mutual funds vary from −10.5% to +26.8%. Indicate the limits you would use if you would like to group these values into at least eight classes but no more than 12 classes.

2.11 Measurements of the boiling point of a flavoring extract, measured to the nearest tenth of a Celsius degree, vary from 148.2° to 160.6°. Indicate the limits of seven classes into which these measurements might be grouped.

2.12 The weekly earnings of the piecework employees of a furniture factory vary from $227.82 to $396.05. Indicate the limits of seven classes with an interval of $25 into which these values might be grouped.

2.13 The numbers of empty seats on bus runs from Philadelphia to Baltimore are grouped into a table with classes

0–4, 5–9, 10–14, 15–19, 20–24, and 25 or more

Will it be possible to determine exactly from this table the number of bus runs on which there were

(a) at least 10 empty seats;   (b) more than 10 empty seats;

(c) more than 14 empty seats;   (d) at least 14 empty seats;

(e) exactly 9 empty seats?

2.14 A suburban postmaster groups the values of stamp purchases into a frequency distribution with the classes

$0.00–4.99, $5.00–9.99, $10.00–14.99, $15.00–19.99,

$20.00–24.99, $25.00–29.99, and $30.00 and over

Is it possible to determine from this distribution the proportion of purchases valued at

(a) less than $10.00;   (b) $10.00 or less;   (c) more than $25.00;   (d) $25.00 or more?

2.15   The following is the distribution of the weights of 125 mineral specimens collected on a field trip:

Weight (grams)	Number of specimens
0.0– 19.9	16
20.0– 39.9	38
40.0– 59.9	35
60.0– 79.9	20
80.0– 99.9	11
100.0–119.9	4
120.0–139.9	1
Total	125

If possible, find how many of the specimens weigh

(a) at most 59.9 grams;   (b) more than 59.9 grams;   (c) more than 80.0 grams;

(d) 80.0 grams or less;   (e) exactly 70.0 grams;

(f) anywhere from 60.0 grams to 100.0 grams.

2.16   The numbers of nurses on duty each day at a hospital are grouped into a distribution having the classes

15–29,   30–44,   45–59,   60–74,   75–89

Find

(a) the class limits;   (b) the class boundaries;   (c) the class marks;

(d) the class interval of the distribution.

2.17   The declared values of packages mailed from Great Britain to the United States are grouped into a distribution with classes

$0.00–49.99, $50.00–99.99, $100.00–149.99, $150.00–199.99,

$200.00–249.99, $250.00–299.99,   and $300.00 and over

Find

(a) the class limits;   (b) the class boundaries;   (c) the class marks;

(d) the class interval of the distribution.

2.18   The class marks of a distribution of the daily number of burglaries reported by a police precinct are 4, 13, 22, 31, and 40. If the class intervals are all equal, find

(a) the class boundaries;   (b) the class limits.

2.19   The class marks of a distribution of the daily number of VCRs (videocassette recorders) repaired by a manufacturer's regional service center are 6, 19, 32, and 45. If the class intervals are all equal, find

(a) the class boundaries;   (b) the class limits.

2.20   To group data on the number of rainy days reported by a weather station for the month of August during the last 60 years, a meteorologist uses the classes

0–5,   6–11,   12–16,   18–24,   24–30

Explain where difficulties might arise.

2.21   To group sales receipts ranging from $10.00 to $60.00, a clerk uses the following classifications:

$10.00–19.99, $20.00–35.99, $35.00–49.90, $50.00–59.99

Explain where difficulties might arise.

2.22   The following are the grades which 40 students obtained in a psychology test:

75 89 66 52 90 68 83 94 77 60
38 47 87 65 97 49 65 72 73 81
63 77 91 88 74 37 85 76 74 63
69 72 31 87 76 58 63 70 72 65

Group these grades into a distribution having the classes

20–29, 30–39, 40–49, 50–59, 60–69, 70–79, 80–89, 90–99

2.23   Convert the distribution obtained in Exercise 2.22 into a percentage distribution.

2.24   Convert the distribution obtained in Exercise 2.22 into a "less than" cumulative distribution, beginning with "less than 20."

2.25   The following are the body weights (in grams) of 50 rats used in a study of vitamin deficiencies:

136 92 115 118 121 137 132 120 104 125
119 115 101 129 87 108 110 133 135 126
127 103 110 126 118 82 104 137 120 95
146 126 119 119 105 132 126 118 100 113
106 125 117 102 146 129 124 113 95 148

Group these weights into a distribution having the classes

80–89, 90–99, 100–109, ..., 140–149

2.26   Convert the distribution obtained in Exercise 2.25 into a percentage distribution.

2.27   Convert the distribution obtained in Exercise 2.25 into an "or more" cumulative distribution, beginning with "80 or more."

2.28   The following are the numbers of customers a restaurant served for lunch on 120 weekdays:

50 64 55 51 60 41 71 53 63 64 46 59 66 45 61
57 65 62 58 65 55 61 50 55 53 57 58 66 53 56
64 46 59 49 64 60 58 64 42 47 59 62 56 63 61
68 57 51 61 51 60 59 67 52 52 58 64 43 60 62
48 62 56 63 55 73 60 69 53 66 54 52 56 59 65
60 61 59 63 56 62 56 62 57 57 52 63 48 58 64
59 43 67 52 58 47 63 53 54 67 57 61 76 78 60
66 63 58 60 55 61 59 74 62 49 63 65 55 61 54

Group these figures into a distribution having the classes

40–44, 45–49, 50–54, 55–59, 60–64, 65–69, 70–74, 75–79

2.29   Convert the distribution obtained in Exercise 2.28 into a

(a) percentage distribution;

(b) "less than" cumulative percentage distribution.

2.30   The following are the miles per gallon obtained with 40 tanks of gas:

24.5 23.6 24.1 25.0 22.9 24.7 23.8 25.2 23.7 24.4
24.7 23.9 25.1 24.6 23.3 24.3 24.6 23.9 24.1 24.4
24.5 25.7 23.6 24.0 23.9 24.2 24.7 24.9 25.0 24.8
24.5 23.4 24.9 24.8 24.7 24.1 22.8 23.1 25.3 24.6

Group these figures into a distribution having the classes

22.5–22.9, 23.0–23.4, 23.5–23.9, 24.0–24.4, 24.5–24.9, 25.0–25.4, 25.5–25.9

2.31   Convert the distribution obtained in Exercise 2.30 into a
(a) "more than" cumulative distribution;
(b) "more than" cumulative percentage distribution.

2.32   On a certain freeway there were the following numbers of traffic accidents during 50 afternoon rush hours.

```
1 0 3 2 3 5 3 0 2 7
0 4 3 1 3 1 5 3 4 4
2 1 3 1 2 2 1 0 2 0
0 1 1 2 4 5 3 4 3 4
3 3 5 2 1 6 1 2 4 6
```

Construct a distribution showing on how many afternoons there were

0, 1, 2, 3, 4, 5, 6, or 7

accidents.

2.33   An audit of 60 sales invoices reveals the following number of mistakes in quoting prices.

```
0 0 2 1 4 1 0 1 3 2 2 0
1 1 1 4 0 3 1 5 1 1 0 2
0 0 1 1 4 3 0 1 0 2 1 4
3 1 0 0 5 1 2 0 3 0 2 1
1 3 1 4 3 0 2 0 1 1 0 1
```

Construct a distribution showing how many of the invoices contained

0, 1, 2, 3, 4, or 5

mistakes.

2.34   Convert the distribution obtained in Exercise 2.33 into a cumulative "less than" distribution.

2.35   A survey taken at a New York hotel indicated that 40 guests arrived by the following means of transportation:

car	car	bus	plane	train	bus	bus	plane
car	plane	plane	bus	plane	car	car	train
train	car	car	car	car	plane	plane	car
bus	car	bus	car	plane	car	plane	plane
car	car	car	bus	train	car	bus	car

Construct a categorical distribution showing the frequencies corresponding to the different means of transportation.

2.36   In a categorical distribution, women's dresses are classified according to whether they are made of wool, cotton, silk, or synthetic fibers. Explain where difficulties might arise.

2.37   In a categorical distribution, customer complaints at a furniture store are classified, according to whether they involve defective merchandise, merchandise of incorrect color or size, failure to adhere to delivery schedule, or damage during delivery. In what ways might there be difficulties with this approach?

2.3   GRAPHICAL PRESENTATIONS

When frequency distributions are constructed primarily to condense large sets of data and display them in an easy-to-digest form, it is usually best to present such distributions graphically. A picture speaks louder than a thousand words, and this was true even before the current availability of computer graphics.

For frequency distributions, the most common form of graphical presentation is the **histogram,** like the one shown in Figure 2.2. Histograms are constructed by representing the measurements or observations that are grouped (in Figure 2.2 the sulfur oxides emission data) on a horizontal scale and the class frequencies on a vertical scale, and drawing rectangles whose bases equal the class intervals and whose heights are the corresponding class frequencies.

The markings on the horizontal scale of a histogram can be the class marks as in Figure 2.2, the class limits, the class boundaries, or arbitrary key values. Observe that the rectangles of a histogram go from one class boundary to the next. Histograms cannot be drawn for distributions with open classes, and special care is required when the class intervals are not all equal (see Exercise 2.45 on page 38).

The data which led to Figure 2.2 were easy to group because there were only 80 values in the sample. For really large sets of data, it may be convenient to construct histograms directly from raw data by using a suitable computer package. In fact, Figure 2.2 was constructed by computer, using the code which appears in Figure 2.3.[†] The computer code sets the class marks at

$$6.95, \quad 10.95, \quad \dots, \quad \text{and} \quad 30.95$$

so that the histogram will be comparable to the table on page 23.

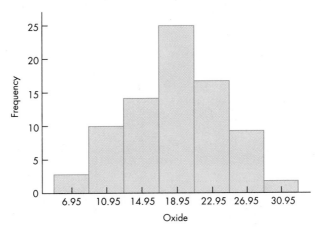

[†]In the printout of Figure 2.3 and in others appearing in this text, words and numbers appear which relate to the technical aspects of operating the particular computer program employed. If a computer is available, the reader should refer to the appropriate manuals for operating instructions and for a list of problems which can be solved with existing programs. Trained users can create additional programs as needed.

FIGURE 2.3

Computer code to create the histogram of Figure 2.2 (MINITAB 10 for Windows).

```
MTB  ># Opening worksheet from file: A:\DATA\OXIDE.DAT
MTB  ># File was last modified on 1/10/96
MTB  >Set C2
DATA>   1( 6.95 : 30.95 / 4)1
DATA>   End.
MTB  >Histogram C1;
SUBC>   MidPoint C2;

SUBC>   Bar;
SUBC>     Type 3;
SUBC>     Color 0.
```

Similar to histograms are **bar charts,** as shown in Figure 2.4. The heights of the rectangles, or bars, represent the class frequencies as in a histogram, but there is no pretense of having a continuous horizontal scale.

Another, less widely used form of graphical presentation is the **frequency polygon,** as shown in Figure 2.5. Here the class frequencies are plotted at the class marks and the successive points are connected by straight lines. Note that we added classes with zero frequencies at both ends of the distribution to tie down the graph to the horizontal scale. If we apply a similar technique to a cumulative distribution, we obtain what is called an **ogive.** However, in an ogive the cumulative frequencies are plotted at the class boundaries instead of the class marks—it stands to reason that the cumulative frequency corresponding to, say, "less than 13.0" should be plotted at the class boundary 12.95, since "less

FIGURE 2.4

Bar chart of the distribution of the sulfur oxides emission data.

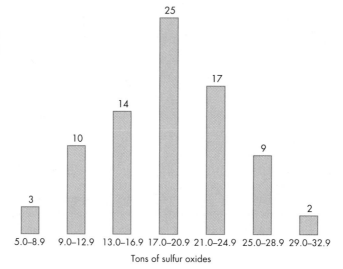

Tons of sulfur oxides

FIGURE 2.5

FIGURE 2.5

Frequency polygon of the distribution of the sulfur oxides emission data.

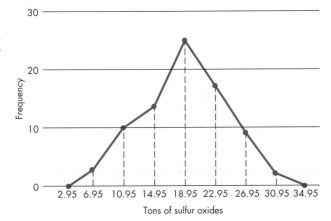

than 13.0" actually includes everything up to 12.95. Figure 2.6 shows an ogive of the "less than" cumulative distribution obtained on page 26 for the sulfur oxides emission data.

Although the visual appeal of histograms, bar charts, frequency polygons, and ogives is a marked improvement over that of mere tables, there are various ways in which distributions can be presented even more dramatically and often more effectively. An example of pictorial presentations of data taken over time (often seen in newspapers, magazines, and reports of various sorts) is the **pictogram** shown in Figure 2.7.

Categorical (or qualitative) distributions are often presented graphically as **pie charts,** like the one shown in Figure 2.8, where a circle is divided into sectors—pie-shaped pieces—which are proportional in size to the corresponding frequencies or percentages. To construct a pie chart, we first convert the distribution into a percentage distribution. Then since a complete circle corresponds to 360 degrees, we obtain the central angles of the various sectors by multiplying the percentages by 360.

Many computers are preprogrammed so that, once the data have been entered, a simple command will produce a pie chart or variations thereof. Some

FIGURE 2.6

Ogive of the cumulative distribution of the sulfur oxides emission data.

FIGURE 2.7

Pictogram of the population of the United States.

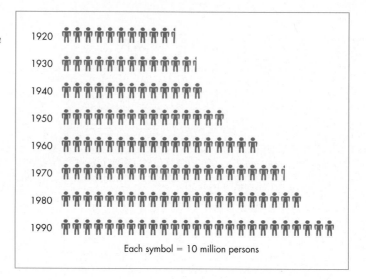

Each symbol = 10 million persons

computer-generated pie charts use color, some are three dimensional, some cut out sectors (like a pieces of pie) for emphasis, and some shade or tint the different sectors.

Research on reading graphical displays indicates that untrained users have trouble interpreting pie graphs. Comparing information from two adjacent pie charts is particularly difficult. The comparison of bar heights in histograms is not difficult. We recommend that pie charts be used rarely and with great care.

Numerical information can be summarized with **maps,** a process that is facilitated by graphical computer programs. When information is shown on a map, each number is associated with and displayed with a particular geographic region. Maps generally do not provide statistical summaries.

FIGURE 2.8

Electric energy production data.

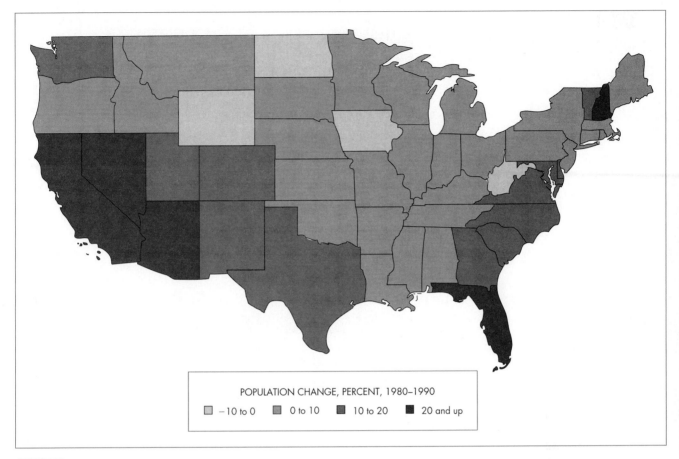

FIGURE 2.9

Percentages of U.S. population changes from 1980–1990.

The success of a numerical map is difficult to assess. Figure 2.9 shows, by state, percentage changes in population in the United States (excluding Alaska and Hawaii). This map can be regarded as successful, since most persons in the United States are familiar with its geography and can obtain desired facts from the map. Figure 2.10 shows the population densities of the counties of Arkansas. Most Americans (including even those who live in Arkansas) would have difficulty with using this map. The identities of the counties are not known to most people. Moreover, there is no apparent regularity in the shading, and therefore the map does not provide any geographical insight.

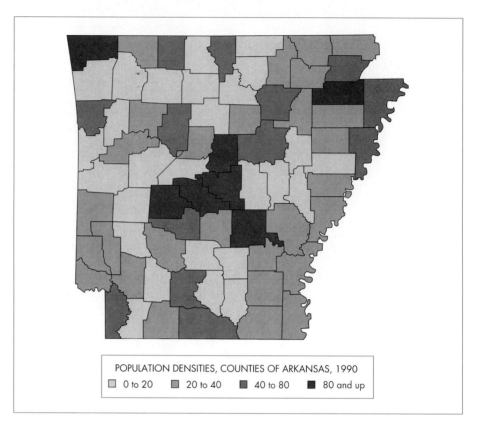

FIGURE 2.10

Population densities for the counties of Arkansas in 1990.

POPULATION DENSITIES, COUNTIES OF ARKANSAS, 1990

☐ 0 to 20   ▨ 20 to 40   ▨ 40 to 80   ■ 80 and up

◢ EXERCISES

2.38   The following is the distribution of the monthly bills for 200 charge accounts at a department store:

Amount (dollars)	Frequency
0.00– 19.99	22
20.00– 39.99	47
40.00– 59.99	66
60.00– 79.99	35
80.00– 99.99	21
100.00–119.99	9
Total	200

(a) Draw a histogram of this distribution.

(b) Draw a bar chart of this distribution.

2.39   Convert the distribution of Exercise 2.38 into a cumulative "less than" distribution and draw an ogive.

2.40   The following is the distribution of the weights of the 150 freshmen women entering a certain college:

Weight (pounds)	Frequency
90– 99	6
100–109	25
110–119	46
120–129	37
130–139	22
140–149	7
150–159	3
160–169	3
170–179	0
180–189	1
Total	150

(a) Draw a histogram of this distribution.

(b) Draw a frequency polygon of this distribution.

2.41 Convert the distribution of Exercise 2.40 into a cumulative "less than" distribution and draw an ogive.

2.42 The weight distribution for 90 players trying out for a college football team is:

Weight (pounds)	Frequency
160–169	2
170–179	6
180–189	12
190–199	13
200–209	18
210–219	17
220–229	7
230–239	8
240–249	4
250–259	1
260–269	2
Total	90

Draw a histogram of this distribution.

2.43 Convert the distribution of Exercise 2.42 into a cumulative "less than" distribution and draw an ogive.

2.44 The following table shows how workers in Denver, Colorado, get to work:

Means of Transportation	Percentage
Ride alone	82
Car pool	13
Ride bus	2
Varies or work at home	3
Total	100

Construct a pie chart of this percentage distribution.

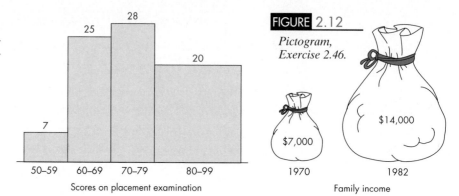

FIGURE 2.11

Distribution of scores on foreign-language placement examination.

Scores on placement examination

FIGURE 2.12

Pictogram, Exercise 2.46.

$7,000   1970 $14,000   1982

Family income

2.45   Figure 2.11 shows the distribution of the scores of 80 entering college freshmen on a foreign-language placement examination. Explain why it might easily give a misleading impression and indicate how it might be improved.

2.46   The pictogram of Figure 2.12 is intended to illustrate that in a certain region average family income has doubled from $7,000 in 1970 to $14,000 in 1982. Explain why this pictogram conveys a misleading impression and indicate how it might be modified.

2.47   Construct a pie chart of the following distribution, which shows the numbers of motor vehicle registrations at a state office:

Type of Vehicle	Number
Passenger car	248
Minivan	62
Two-axle truck	42
Multiaxle truck	12
Motorcycle	55
Motorboat	9
Total	428

2.48   Here, again, are the grades (from Exercise 2.22) which 40 students obtained in a psychology test:

75 89 66 52 90 68 83 94 77 60
38 47 87 65 97 49 65 72 73 81
63 77 91 88 74 37 85 76 74 63
69 72 31 87 76 58 63 70 72 65

Use a computer package to construct a histogram with the classes

20–29, 30–39, 40–49, 50–59, 60–69, 70–79, 80–89, 90–99

Also construct a histogram with the classes

20–39, 40–59, 60–79, 80–99

Which histogram do you prefer?

2.49   Use a computer package to construct a histogram with the classes

40–44, 45–49, 50–54, 55–59, 60–64, 65–69, 70–74, 75–79

for the number of lunch customers given in Exercise 2.28.

2.50   Use a computer package to construct a histogram with the classes

22.5–22.9,   23.0–23.4,   23.5–23.9,   24.0–24.4,   24.5–24.9,   25.0–25.4,   25.5–25.9

for the miles-per-gallon data of Exercise 2.30 on pages 29–30.

2.4   CHECKLIST OF KEY TERMS   (*with page references to their definitions*)

Bar chart, 32
Categorical distribution, 20
Class, 21
Class boundary, 24
Class frequency, 23
Class interval, 24
Class limit, 23
Class mark, 24
Coding, 21
Cumulative distribution, 26
Cumulative percentage distribution, 26
Distribution, 20
Double-stem display, 18
Exploratory data analysis, 19
Frequency distribution, 20
Frequency polygon, 32

Histogram, 31
Lower class limit, 23
Map, 34
Numerical distribution, 20
Ogive, 32
Open class, 22
Percentage distribution, 25
Pictogram, 33
Pie chart, 33
Qualitative distribution, 20
Quantitative distribution, 20
Raw data, 21
Real class limits, 24
Stem-and-leaf display, 16
Upper class limit, 24

2.5   REVIEW EXERCISES

2.51   The class marks of a distribution of the daily number of calls received by a small cab company are

18,   25,   32,   39,   46,   and   53

If the class intervals are all equal, what are the class limits?

2.52   A distribution has class marks of

40,   47,   54,   61,   68

If the class intervals are all equal, what are the class limits?

2.53   The following are the numbers of deer observed in 72 sections of land in a wildlife count:

```
18   8   9  22  12  16  20  33  15  21  18  13
13  19   0   2  14  17  11  18  16  13  12   6
 8  12  13  21   8  11  19   1  14   4  19  16
 2  16  11  18  10  28  15  24   8  20   6   7
21   0  16  12  20  17  13  20  10  16   5  10
15  10  16  14  29  17   4  18  21  10  16   9
```

Group these data into a distribution having the classes

0–4,   5–9,   10–14,   15–19,   20–24,   25–29,   30–34

2.54   Draw a histogram of the distribution obtained in Exercise 2.53.

2.55   Convert the distribution of Exercise 2.53 into an "or less" cumulative distribution and draw an ogive.

2.56   The ages of a company's employees are to be grouped into the following classes:

under 19   20–24,   25–29,   30–34,   34–39,   and over   39

Explain where difficulties may arise.

2.57   The number of persons attending an art exhibit daily are grouped into a distribution with the classes

0–39,   40–79,   80–119,   120–159

Is it possible to determine from this distribution on how many days

(a) at least 79 persons attended the exhibit;

(b) more than 79 persons attended the exhibit;

(c) 40 or more persons attended the exhibit;

(d) at most 120 persons attended the exhibit?

2.58   The following is the distribution of the number of meals which 60 real estate salespersons charged as business expenses in a given week:
Find:

Number of Meals	Frequency
0–1	16
2–3	25
4–5	13
6–7	4
8–9	2
Total	60

(a) the class marks;

(b) the class boundaries;

(c) the class interval of the distribution.

2.59   Convert the distribution of Exercise 2.58 into an "or more" cumulative percentage distribution and draw a bar chart.

2.60   A college freshman class has 1,517 students. Their application forms contain an entry for preferred areas of study. There are 347 who indicate engineering, 122 who indicate science, 288 who indicate humanities, and 550 who indicate social science. The remaining 210 students either leave this area blank or write "undecided." Present this information in the form of a

(a) bar chart;   (b) pie chart.

2.61   In 1986, the annual salaries paid to teachers in a certain school district varied from $18,400 to $32,600. Indicate the limits of six classes, each with an interval of $2,500, into which these salaries might be grouped.

2.62   Among histograms, bar charts, and pie charts, which ones can be used to represent

(a) nominal data;   (b) ordinal data;   (c) interval data?

2.63   Measurements of the lengths of fish to the nearest tenth of an inch are grouped into a table whose classes have the boundaries

5.95,   7.95,   9.95,   11.95,   13.95,   15.95

What are the lower and upper limits of each class?

2.64   Asked whether they ever attend meetings of their town council, 50 residents of a community reply as follows:

never	occasionally	rarely	rarely	never
rarely	occasionally	frequently	never	rarely
rarely	rarely	occasionally	rarely	occasionally
never	never	rarely	frequently	never
never	rarely	occasionally	occasionally	rarely
rarely	never	never	rarely	rarely
frequently	occasionally	occasionally	never	rarely
never	rarely	rarely	occasionally	rarely
never	never	rarely	occasionally	never
rarely	rarely	occasionally	rarely	never

Construct a categorical distribution and draw a pie chart.

2.65   List the data that correspond to the following stems of stem-and-leaf displays:

(a) 125 | 3 0 4 8 7 6 5
(b) 34 | 67 05 19 48
(c)   1 | 1 0
      1 | 8 6 7 7
      2 | 2 4 0 1 1 3
      2 | 9 6 7 7
      3 | 3 1 2
      3 | 8 5
      4 | 2

2.66   The following are the numbers of false alarms (tripped accidentally or by equipment malfunction) which a security monitoring service received in 30 days:

```
3  6  2  4  5  8  2  5  6  3  4  7  4  6  5
5  5  4  3  7  4  4  6  3  9  5  7  4  4  6
```

Construct a frequency distribution.

2.67   Construct a histogram of the distribution obtained in Exercise 2.66.

2.68   The following are the systolic blood pressures of 20 hospital patients:

```
165  135  151  153  155  182  152  158  146  149
124  162  173  204  159  130  177  162  141  156
```

Construct a stem-and-leaf display with one-digit leaves.

2.69   In a survey, persons are asked if they

(1) finished high school;

(2) finished college;

(3) have an advanced degree.

Explain where difficulties might arise.

2.6   REFERENCES

Detailed information about statistical charts may be found in

CLEVELAND, W. S., *The Elements of Graphing Data.* Monterey, Calif.: Wadsworth Advanced Books and Software, 1985.

SCHMID, C. F., *Statistical Graphics: Design Principles and Practices.* New York: John Wiley & Sons, Inc., 1983.

TUFTE, E. R., *The Visual Display of Quantitative Information.* Cheshire, Conn.: Graphics Press, 1985.

and some interesting information about the history of the graphical presentation of statistical data is given in an article by E. Royston in

PEARSON, E. S., and KENDALL, M. G., eds., *Studies in the History of Statistics and Probability.* New York: Hafner Press, 1970.

Discussions of what not to do in the presentation of statistical data may be found in

CAMPBELL, S. K., *Flaws and Fallacies in Statistical Thinking.* Englewood Cliffs, N.J.: Prentice-Hall, Inc., 1974.

HUFF, D., *How to Lie with Statistics.* New York: W.W. Norton & Company, Inc., 1954.

REICHMAN, W. J., *Use and Abuse of Statistics.* New York: Penguin Books, 1971.

Useful references to lists of standard categories are given in

HAUSER, P. M., and LEONARD, W. R., *Government Statistics for Business Use,* 2nd ed. New York: John Wiley & Sons, Inc., 1956.

For further information about exploratory data analysis and stem-and-leaf displays in particular, see

HARTWIG, F., and DEARING, B. E., *Exploratory Data Analysis.* Beverly Hills, Calif.: Sage Publications, Inc., 1979.

HOAGLIN, D. C., MOSTELLER, F., and TUKEY, J. W., *Understanding Robust and Exploratory Data Analysis.* New York: John Wiley & Sons, Inc., 1983.

KOOPMANS, L. H., *An Introduction to Contemporary Statistics.* North Scituate, Mass.: Duxbury Press, 1981.

TUKEY, J. W., *Exploratory Data Analysis.* Reading, Mass.: Addison-Wesley Publishing Company, Inc., 1977.

VELLEMAN, P. F., and HOAGLIN, D. C., *Applications, Basics, and Computing for Exploratory Data Analysis.* North Scituate, Mass.: Duxbury Press, 1980.

CHAPTER 3

SUMMARIZING DATA: MEASURES OF LOCATION

When we describe a set of data, we try to say neither too little nor too much. Statistical descriptions can be brief or elaborate, depending on the purposes they are to serve. Sometimes we present data in raw form and let them speak for themselves. On other occasions we present data as frequency distributions or as graphs. Most of the time, however, we must describe data by one or two carefully chosen numbers.

It is often necessary to summarize data by means of a single number which, in its way, is descriptive of the entire set. Exactly what sort of number we choose depends on the particular characteristic we want to describe. In one study we may be interested in the value which is exceeded by only 25 percent of the data; in another, in the value which exceeds the lowest 10 percent of the data; and in still another, in a value which somehow describes the center or middle of the data. The statistical measures which describe such characteristics are called measures of location; *among them, the ones which describe the center or middle of the data are called* measures of central location.*

In Sections 3.2, 3.3, 3.4, and 3.6 we present four of the most widely used measures of central location; some measures of location other than central location and the description of grouped data are discussed in Sections 3.5 and 3.7, which are optional. ◰

3.1   POPULATIONS AND SAMPLES

Before we study particular statistical descriptions, notice the following distinction:

If a set of data consists of all conceivably possible (or hypothetically possible) observations of a given phenomenon, we call it a **population;** if a set of data consists of only a part of these observations, we call it a **sample.**

Here we added the phrase "hypothetically possible" to take care of such clearly hypothetical situations as where we look at the outcomes (heads or tails) of 12 flips of a coin as a sample from the potentially unlimited number of flips of the coin, where we look at the weights of ten 30-day-old lambs as a sample of the weights of all (past, present, and future) 30-day-old lambs raised at a certain farm, or where we look at four determinations of the uranium content of an ore as a sample of the many determinations that could conceivably be made. In fact, we often look at the results of an experiment as a sample of what we might get if the experiment were repeated over and over again.

Originally, statistics dealt with the description of human populations, census counts and the like (see page 5), but as it grew in scope, the term "population" took on the much wider connotation given to it above. Whether or not it sounds strange to refer to the heights of all the trees in a forest or the speeds of all the cars passing a checkpoint as populations is beside the point—in statistics, "population" is a technical term with a meaning of its own.

Although we are free to call any group of items a population, what we do in practice depends on the context in which the items are to be viewed. Suppose, for instance, that we are offered a lot of 400 ceramic tiles, which we may or may not buy depending on their strength. If we measure the breaking strength of 20 of these tiles in order to estimate the average breaking strength of all the tiles, these 20 measurements are a sample from the population which consists of the breaking strengths of the 400 tiles. In another context, however, if we consider entering into a long-term contract calling for the delivery of tens of thousands of such tiles, we would look upon the breaking strengths of the original 400 tiles only as a sample. Similarly, the complete figures for a recent year, giving the elapsed times between the filing and disposition of divorce suits in San Diego County, can be looked upon as either a population or a sample. If we are interested only in San Diego County and that particular year, we would look upon the data as a population; on the other hand, if we want to generalize about the time that is required for the disposition of divorce suits in the entire United States, in some other county, or in some other year, we would look upon the data as a sample.

As we have used it here, the word "sample" has very much the same meaning as it has in everyday language. A newspaper considers the attitudes of 150 readers toward a proposed school bond to be a sample of the attitudes of all its readers toward the bond. A consumer considers a box of Mrs. See's candy a sample of the firm's product. Later, we shall use the word "sample" only when referring to data which can reasonably serve as the basis for valid generalizations about the populations from which they came; in this more technical sense, many sets of data which are popularly called samples are not samples at all.

In this chapter and in Chapter 4 we describe things statistically without making any generalizations. For future reference, though, it is important even here to distinguish between populations and samples. Thus, we shall use different symbols depending on whether we are describing populations or samples.

3.2 THE MEAN

The most popular measure of central location is what the layman calls an "average" and what the statistician calls an **arithmetic mean,** or simply a **mean.**[†]

> The mean of n numbers is their sum divided by n.

It is alright to use the word "average" and on occasion we also use it, but there are other kinds of averages in statistics and we cannot afford to speak loosely when there is any danger of ambiguity.

[†]The term "arithmetic mean" is used mainly to distinguish the mean from the **geometric mean** and the **harmonic mean,** two other kinds of averages used only in very special situations (see Exercises 3.19 and 3.21).

Example

For the 12 months of 1990, a police department reported

$$4 \quad 3 \quad 5 \quad 5 \quad 10 \quad 8 \quad 9 \quad 6 \quad 3 \quad 4 \quad 8 \quad 7$$

armed robberies. Find the mean, namely, the average number of armed robberies per month.

solution

The total for the 12 months is

$$4 + 3 + 5 + 5 + 10 + 8 + 9 + 6 + 3 + 4 + 8 + 7 = 72$$

and therefore

$$\text{mean} = \frac{72}{12} = 6$$

Example

A supermarket manager, who wants to study the traffic in her store, finds that

$$295 \quad 1{,}002 \quad 941 \quad 768 \quad 1{,}283$$

persons entered the store during the past five days. Find the mean number of persons who entered the supermarket during these five days.

solution

Altogether the number of persons who entered the supermarket during the past five days is

$$295 + 1{,}002 + 941 + 768 + 1{,}283 = 4{,}289$$

Since

$$\frac{4{,}289}{5} = 857.8$$

this is the mean (or average) number of persons who entered the store per day.

Since we shall have occasion to calculate the means of many different sets of sample data, it is convenient to have a simple formula which is always applicable. This requires that we represent the figures to be averaged by some general symbol such as *x, y,* or *z;* the number of values in a sample, the **sample size,** is usually denoted by the letter *n.* Choosing the letter *x,* we can refer to the *n* values in a sample as

$x_1, x_2, \ldots,$ and x_n (read "*x* sub-one," "*x* sub-two," ..., and "*x* sub-*n*")

and write

$$\text{sample mean} = \frac{x_1 + x_2 + x_3 + \cdots + x_n}{n}$$

This formula will take care of any set of sample data, but it can be made more compact by assigning the sample mean the symbol $\bar{x}$ (read "x bar") and using the **summation (Σ) notation.** The symbol Σ is capital *sigma,* the Greek letter for S. In this notation we let Σx stand for

"the sum of the x's"   (that is, $\Sigma x = x_1 + x_2 + \cdots + x_n$)

and we can write

Sample Mean	$$\bar{x} = \frac{\Sigma x}{n}$$

If we refer to the measurements as y's or z's, we write their mean as $\bar{y}$ or $\bar{z}$. In the formula for $\bar{x}$, the term Σx does not state explicitly which values of x are added; let it be understood, however, that Σx always refers to the sum of all the x's under consideration in a given situation. In the technical note of Section 3.8 the use of the sigma notation is discussed in more detail.

The number of values in a population, the **population size,** is usually denoted by N. The mean of a population of N items is defined in the same way. It is the sum of the N items,

$$x_1 + x_2 + x_3 + \cdots + x_N, \quad \text{or} \quad \Sigma x, \text{ divided by N.}$$

Assigning the population mean the symbol μ (*mu,* the Greek letter for lower-case m), we write

Population Mean	$$\mu = \frac{\Sigma x}{N}$$

with the reminder that Σx is now the sum of all N values of x which constitute the population.[†]

Also, to distinguish between descriptions of populations and descriptions of samples, we not only use different symbols such as μ and $\bar{x}$, but we refer to a description of a population as a **parameter** and a description of a sample as a **statistic.** Parameters are usually denoted by Greek letters.

To illustrate the terminology and notation introduced in this section, suppose that we are interested in the mean lifetime of a production lot of $N = 40{,}000$ light bulbs. Obviously, we cannot test all of the light bulbs for there would be none left to use or sell, so we take a sample, calculate $\bar{x}$, and use this quantity to estimate μ. If $n = 5$ and the light bulbs in the sample last

967, 949, 940, 952, and 922 hours

[†]In cases in which the population size is unlimited, as discussed in Section 3.1, the population mean cannot be defined in this manner. The mean of an infinite population is discussed in the references in Section 3.11.

we have

$$\bar{x} = \frac{967 + 949 + 940 + 952 + 922}{5} = 946 \text{ hours}$$

If these lifetimes constitute a sample in the technical sense (that is, a set of data from which valid generalizations can be made), we can estimate the mean lifetime μ of all the 40,000 light bulbs as 946 hours.

For non-negative data, the mean not only describes the middle of a set of data, but it also puts some limitation on their size. If we multiply by n on both sides of the equation

$$\bar{x} = \frac{\Sigma x}{n} \quad \text{it follows that} \quad \Sigma x = n \cdot \bar{x}$$

and, hence, no single x-value can exceed $n \cdot \bar{x}$.

Example

If the mean annual salary paid to the three top executives of a firm is $156,000, can one of them receive an annual salary of $500,000?

solution

Since $n = 3$ and $\bar{x} = \$156,000$, we get

$$\Sigma x = 3 \cdot 156,000 = \$468,000$$

and it is impossible for any of the executives to receive more than that.   ▰ ▰ ▰

Example

If nine high school juniors averaged 41 on the verbal part of the PSAT/NMSQT test, at most how many of them can have scored 65 or more?

solution

Since $n = 9$ and $\bar{x} = 41$, we get

$$\Sigma x = 9 \cdot 41 = 369$$

and since 65 goes into 369 five times ($369 = 5 \cdot 65 + 44$), it follows that at most five of the nine high school juniors can have scored 65 or more.   ▰ ▰ ▰

The popularity of the mean as a measure of the "middle" or "center" of a set of data is not accidental. Any time we use a single number to describe some aspect of a set of data, there are certain requirements, or desirable features, that should be kept in mind. Aside from the fact that the mean is a simple and familiar measure, the following are some of its noteworthy properties:

It can be calculated for any set of numerical data, so it always exists.

A set of numerical data has one and only one mean, so it is always unique.

It lends itself to further statistical treatment; as we shall see, for example, the means of several sets of data can always be combined into the overall mean of all the data.

It is relatively reliable in the sense that means of many samples drawn from the same population usually do not fluctuate, or vary, as widely as other statistical measures used to estimate the mean of a population.

The last of these properties is of fundamental importance in statistical inference, and we shall study it in some detail in Chapter 10.

There is another property of the mean which, on the surface, seems desirable:

It takes into account every item of a set of data.

However, sometimes samples contain very small or very large values which are so far removed from the main body of the data that the appropriateness of including them in a sample is questionable. Such values may be due to chance, or they may be due to gross errors in recording the data, gross errors in calculations, malfunctioning of equipment, or other identifiable sources of contamination. In any case, when such values are averaged in with the other values, they can affect the mean to such an extent that it is debatable whether it really provides a useful description of the "middle" of the data.

Example

With reference to the illustration dealing with the light bulbs on page 47, suppose that the second value is recorded incorrectly as 499 instead of 949. Find the error this would cause in calculating the mean lifetime of the five light bulbs.

solution

The mean of 967, 499, 940, 952, and 922 is

$$\bar{x} = \frac{967 + 499 + 940 + 952 + 922}{5} = 856$$

and this differs from 946, the mean obtained on page 48, by

$$946 - 856 = 90 \text{ hours}$$

Example

The ages of six students who went on a geology field trip are

$$18 \quad 19 \quad 20 \quad 17 \quad 19 \quad 18$$

and the age of the instructor who went with them is 50. Find the mean age of these seven persons.

solution

The mean is

$$\bar{x} = \frac{18 + 19 + 20 + 17 + 19 + 18 + 50}{7} = 23$$

but any statement to the effect that the mean age of the group is 23 could easily be misinterpreted. We might well infer incorrectly that the persons who went on the field trip are all in their early 20s.

To avoid the possibility of being misled by a mean affected by a very small value or a very large value, we sometimes find it preferable to describe the middle or center of a set of data with a statistical measure other than the mean; perhaps, with the **median,** which we discuss in Section 3.4.

3.3   THE WEIGHTED MEAN

When we calculate an average, we may be making a serious mistake if we overlook the fact that the quantities are not all of equal importance with reference to the phenomenon being described. Consider, for example, the following information on the percentage of housing units that were owner occupied in selected neighborhoods of three California cities:

	Percent Owner Occupied
Los Angeles	40.3
Sacramento	56.4
San Jose	62.1

The mean of these three percentages is

$$\frac{40.3 + 56.4 + 62.1}{3} = 52.9$$

but we cannot very well say that this is the average owner occupancy rate for the three cities. The three figures do not carry equal weight because there are great differences in the size of the three cities.

To give quantities being averaged their proper degree of importance, it is necessary to assign them (relative importance) **weights,** and then calculate a **weighted mean.** In general, the weighted mean $\bar{x}_w$ of a set of numbers x_1, x_2, $x_3, \ldots$, and x_n, whose relative importance is expressed numerically by a corresponding set of numbers w_1, w_2, $w_3, \ldots$, and w_n, is given by

Weighted Mean

$$\bar{x}_w = \frac{w_1 x_1 + w_2 x_2 + \cdots + w_n x_n}{w_1 + w_2 + \cdots + w_n} = \frac{\Sigma\, w \cdot x}{\Sigma\, w}$$

Here $\Sigma\, w \cdot x$ is the sum of the products obtained by multiplying each x by the corresponding weight, and $\Sigma\, w$ is simply the sum of the weights. Note that when the weights are all equal, the formula for the weighted mean reduces to that for the ordinary (arithmetic) mean.

Example

Given that, in the selected neighborhoods, there were 1,135 thousand housing units in Los Angeles, 113 thousand in Sacramento, and 210 thousand in San Jose, use these figures and the percentages in the text above to determine the average owner occupancy rate (percentage) for the three cities.

solution

Substituting

$$x_1 = 40.3, \quad x_2 = 56.4, \quad x_3 = 62.1, \quad w_1 = 1{,}135, \quad w_2 = 113, \quad w_3 = 210$$

into the formula for $\bar{x}_w$, we get

$$\bar{x}_w = \frac{(1{,}135)(40.3) + (113)(56.4) + (210)(62.1)}{1{,}135 + 113 + 210} = \frac{65{,}154.7}{1{,}458} \approx 44.7^{\dagger}$$

Note that the value we obtained for $\bar{x}_w$ is much smaller than that of $\bar{x}$, 44.7 compared to 52.9, and this is due entirely to the large size of Los Angeles and its low owner-occupancy rate. ◪ ◪ ◪

A special application of the formula for the weighted mean arises when we must find the overall mean, or **grand mean,** of k sets of data having the means

$$\bar{x}_1, \bar{x}_2, \bar{x}_3, \ldots, \text{ and } \bar{x}_k, \quad \text{and consisting} \quad \text{of } n_1, n_2, n_3, \ldots, \text{ and } n_k$$

measurements or observations. The result is given by

Grand Mean of Combined Data	$\bar{\bar{x}} = \dfrac{n_1\bar{x}_1 + n_2\bar{x}_2 + \cdots + n_k\bar{x}_k}{n_1 + n_2 + \cdots + n_k} = \dfrac{\Sigma\, n \cdot \bar{x}}{\Sigma\, n}$

where the weights are the sizes of the respective sets of data, the numerator is the total of all the measurements or observations, and the denominator is the total number of items in the combined data.

Example

In a biology class there are 20 freshmen, 18 sophomores, and 12 juniors. If the freshmen averaged 68 in an examination, the sophomores averaged 75, and the juniors averaged 86, find the mean grade for the entire class.

solution

Substituting

$$n_1 = 20, \quad n_2 = 18, \quad n_3 = 12, \quad \bar{x}_1 = 68, \quad \bar{x}_2 = 75, \quad \text{and} \quad \bar{x}_3 = 86$$

into the formula for the grand mean of combined data, we get

$$\bar{\bar{x}} = \frac{20 \cdot 68 + 18 \cdot 75 + 12 \cdot 86}{20 + 18 + 12} = \frac{3{,}742}{50} \approx 74.84$$ ◪ ◪ ◪

◪ EXERCISES

3.1 Suppose that we are given complete information about the travel expenses which the administrators of a business's computer support staff charged to their expense accounts during

†In this book we use the symbol $\approx$ to mean "approximately equal to." We use this symbol only for the step where numerical rounding occurs.

1990. Give one illustration each of a situation where these data would be looked upon as

(a) a population;   (b) a sample.

3.2   The final election returns from a county show that the three candidates for a certain office received 14,276, 10,210, and 2,873 votes. Indicate an office that these candidates might be running for so that these figures would constitute

(a) a population;   (b) a sample.

3.3   Suppose that we have the complete information on the number of purchase returns at each of 23 department stores. Give one illustration each of a situation where these data would be looked upon as

(a) a population;   (b) a sample.

3.4   Suppose that we have just obtained the results of a questionnaire given to 848 students of a particular college. Indicate a situation in which these data would be looked upon as

(a) a population;   (b) a sample.

3.5   The following are the ages of thirty persons empaneled for jury duty by a court:

42 45 51 39 32 61 27 62 53 51 48 40 34 37 28
58 55 43 29 39 40 22 58 28 31 31 52 44 38 36

Find their mean age.

3.6   The following are the numbers of stray dogs captured or turned in to a town animal shelter on twenty working days:

4 6 8 4 2 6 4 3 4 9
5 8 5 3 5 7 6 3 8 6

Find the mean.

3.7   At a roadblock, twelve drivers cited for speeding were going

8 11 14 6 8 10 20 11 13 18 9 15

miles per hour over the speed limit.

(a) On the average, by how many miles per hour were these drivers exceeding the speed limit?

(b) If a driver exceeding the speed limit by less than 15 miles per hour was fined $60 and the others were fined $88, find the mean of the fines which these drivers had to pay.

3.8   During a one-hour period an ice cream store had 20 customers, and the purchase amounts in dollars were the following:

1.25 2.50 1.25 5.50 3.25 3.75 2.75 6.25 4.00 2.50
1.25 1.25 3.75 6.00 4.50 3.25 1.25 4.50 2.50 1.25

(a) Find the mean purchase amount.

(b) If each purchase under $5 gets a 50-cent off coupon and each purchase of $5 or over gets a one-dollar off coupon, find the mean value of the 20 coupons.

3.9   At their first inaugurations, the first ten presidents of the United States were

57 61 57 57 58 57 61 54 68 51

years old. Find the mean age of those presidents at their first inauguration.

3.10   As part of a laboratory assignment in nutrition, fifteen students determined the number of calories in a serving of lasagna. They obtained the values

329 335 347 318 322 330 351 362 315 342 346 353 316 327 333

    (a) Find the mean.

    (b) Subtract 300 from each value and then find the mean of the numbers thus obtained. Add 300 to the result. Does this suggest a simplification for the calculation of a mean?

3.11   A bridge is designed to carry a maximum load of 150,000 pounds. Is this bridge overloaded if it is carrying 18 vehicles having a mean weight of 4,630 pounds?

3.12   An elevator in an office building is designed to carry a maximum load of 2,000 pounds. Is it overloaded if it is carrying nine women whose mean weight is 123 pounds and five men whose mean weight is 174 pounds?

3.13   A clerk lost one of 10 sales slips for purchases made in the closing hour. The mean value of all 10 slips was $7.20, and the remaining nine slips had the values

$$\$4.80 \quad \$7.10 \quad \$7.90 \quad \$9.55 \quad \$4.45 \quad \$5.72 \quad \$7.54 \quad \$8.34 \quad \$9.70$$

What is the value of the slip that was lost?

3.14   For three rounds of golf, Peter scores 88, 79, and 82. What fourth-round score would he need reduce his mean score to 81 for all four rounds?

3.15   Careful measurements show that the actual amounts of coffee in six four-ounce jars of instant coffee are

$$4.02 \quad 3.98 \quad 4.01 \quad 4.05 \quad 3.97 \quad 4.03$$

ounces.

    (a) Find the mean coffee content of these six jars.

    (b) What would be the error in calculating the mean coffee content of the six jars if the fourth value is recorded incorrectly as 4.50 instead of 4.05?

3.16   The mean weight of the 45 members of a football team is 215 pounds. If none of the players weighs less than 170 pounds, at most how many of them can weigh 250 pounds or more?

⊞ 3.17   The argument of the examples on page 48 can be generalized. For any set of non-negative data with the mean $\bar{x}$, the fraction of the data that are greater than or equal to any positive value k cannot exceed $\bar{x}/k$. Use this result, called **Markov's theorem,** in solving the following:

    (a) If the mean adult weight of a certain breed of dog is 35 pounds, at most what fraction can have a weight exceeding 40 pounds?

    (b) If the citrus trees in a certain orchard have a mean diameter of 16.0 cm, at most what fraction of the trees can have a diameter of 24 cm or more?

3.18   Records show that in Phoenix, Arizona, the normal daily maximum temperature for each month is

$$65 \quad 69 \quad 74 \quad 84 \quad 93 \quad 102 \quad 105 \quad 102 \quad 98 \quad 88 \quad 74 \quad \text{and} \quad 66$$

degrees Fahrenheit. Verify that the mean of these figures is 85, and comment on the claim that the average daily maximum temperature in Phoenix is a very comfortable 85 degrees.

⊞ 3.19   The **geometric mean** of n positive numbers is the nth root of their product. For example, the geometric mean of 3 and 12 is

$$\sqrt{(3)(12)} = \sqrt{36} = 6$$

The geometric mean of 2, 3, and 36 is

$$\sqrt[3]{(2)(3)(36)} = \sqrt[3]{216} = 6$$

The geometric mean is used mainly in averaging ratios, rates of change, and economic indices.

(a) Find the geometric mean of 0.8 and 3.2.

(b) Find the geometric mean of 1, 2, 8, and 16.

(c) During a flu epidemic, 12 cases were reported on the first day, 18 on the second day, and 48 on the third day. From the first day to the second day, the number of cases was multiplied by $\frac{18}{12}$, and from the second day to the third day the number of cases was multiplied by $\frac{48}{18}$. Find the geometric mean of these two growth rates and (assuming that the growth pattern continues) predict the numbers of cases that will be reported on the fourth and fifth days.

3.20   An investment grew at the rate of 7.79% for the first year, 4.27% for the second year, and 9.00% for the third year. Find the overall mean rate of growth for the three years. *Hint:* Consider the growth rate method used for part (c) of Exercise 3.19.

⊞ 3.21   The **harmonic mean** of n numbers $x_1, x_2, \ldots,$ and x_n is defined as n divided by the sum of the reciprocals of the n numbers. The calculation required is

$$\frac{n}{\Sigma \, 1/x}$$

The harmonic mean is used in dealing with musical frequencies and in some other special situations. For instance, if a commuter drives 10 miles on a freeway at 60 miles per hour and then the next 10 miles off the freeway at 30 miles per hour, his average speed is *not* 45 miles an hour. He will have driven a total of 20 miles in 30 minutes, so that his correct average speed is 40 miles per hour.

(a) Verify that the harmonic mean of 60 and 30 is 40, so that it is the appropriate "average" for this example.

(b) If an investor buys $18,000 worth of a company's stock at $45 a share and then buys $18,000 worth at $36 a share, find the average price that the investor has paid per share. Verify that this price is the harmonic mean of $45 and $36.

(c) If a bakery buys $36 worth of an ingredient at 60 cents per pound, $36 worth at 72 cents per pound, and $36 worth at 90 cents per pound, what is the average cost per pound?

3.22   An instructor counts the final examination in a course three times as much as each of the three one-hour examinations. What is the average grade of a student who received grades of 72, 86, and 80 in the three one-hour examinations and 90 in the final examination?

3.23   The average salaries of elementary school teachers in three cities are

$$\$38,300, \quad \$44,500, \quad \text{and} \quad \$41,000$$

Given that there are 720, 660, and 520 elementary school teachers in these cities, find their average salary.

3.24   A sample survey conducted by a public health organization yielded the following data on the average number of times that persons in various age groups visit a dentist:

Age Group	Number of Persons in the Sample	Mean Number of Visits
Under 6	55	0.6
6–24	112	1.9
25–64	145	1.8
65 and over	88	1.5
Total	400	

What is the mean for all persons in the sample?

3.25   A sample survey of students in a junior high school yields the following data on the mean daily time (in hours) spent in doing homework:

Grade	Number of Students in the Sample	Mean Homework Hours
7	80	0.9
8	70	0.7
9	65	1.0
Total	215	

Find the mean for all 215 students in the sample.

3.26   In a recent season, an amateur baseball team's five best hitters had batting averages of

.381 .367 .321 .312 .293

If these players had, respectively,

223 180 274 125 and 191

at bats, find their combined batting average.

3.4   THE MEDIAN

To avoid the possibility of being misled by very small or very large values, we sometimes describe the "middle" or "center" of a set of data with statistical measures other than the mean. One of these, the **median** of n values, requires that we arrange the data according to size, and it is defined as

the value of the middle item if n is odd, and the mean of the two middle items if n is even.

In either case, when no two values are alike, the median is exceeded by as many values as it exceeds. When some of the values are alike, this may not be the case.

Example

In a recent month, a state's Game and Fish Department reported

53 31 67 53 and 36

hunting or fishing violations for five different regions. Find the median number of violations for these months.

solution

The median is not 67, the third (or middle) item, because the figures must first be arranged according to size (lowest to highest). Thus, we get

31 36 53 53 67

and it can be seen that the median is 53.

Note in this example that there are two 53's among the data and that we do not refer to either of them as *the* median—the median is a number and not necessarily a particular measurement or observation.

Example

In some areas, persons cited for certain minor traffic violations can attend a class on defensive driving instead of paying a fine. If 12 such classes were attended by

40   32   37   30   24   40   38   35   40   28   32   37

persons, find the median attendance.

solution

Arranging these figures according to size, we get

24   28   30   32   32   35   37   37   38   40   40   40

and we find that the median is

$$\frac{35 + 37}{2} = 36$$

namely, the mean of the two values nearest the middle.

Some of the values were alike in the preceding example, but this did not affect the median, which exceeds six of the values and is exceeded by the other six. The situation is quite different, though, in the example that follows:

Example

On the third hole of a golf course, nine golfers scored

4   3   4   5   4   3   3   4   3

Find the median.

solution

Arranging these figures from lowest to highest, we get

3   3   3   3   4   4   4   4   5

and it can be seen that the median, the fifth value, is 4.

This time the median exceeds four of the values but is exceeded by only one, and it would be misleading to think of it as the "middle" of the scores—it is not exceeded by as many values as it exceeds.

The symbol that we use for the median of n sample values $x_1, x_2, x_3, \ldots,$ and x_n is $\tilde{x}$ (and, hence, $\tilde{y}$ or $\tilde{z}$ if we refer to the values of y's or z's). The symbol $\tilde{x}$ is usually read as "*x* tilde." If a set of data constitutes a population, we denote its median by $\tilde{\mu}$.

Thus, we have a symbol for the median, but no formula; there is only a formula for the **median position.** Referring again to data arranged according to size, usually ranked from low to high, we can write

Median Position	*The median is the value of the* $\left(\dfrac{n+1}{2}\right)$ *th item.*

When n is odd, $\frac{n+1}{2}$ is an integer and it gives the position of the median; when n is even, $\frac{n+1}{2}$ is halfway between two integers and the median is the mean of the values of the corresponding items.

Example
_____

Find the median position for (a) $n = 15$ and (b) $n = 45$.

solution
_____

With the data arranged according to size (and counting from either end)

(a) $\frac{n+1}{2} = \frac{15+1}{2} = 8$, so the median is the value of the 8th item;

(b) $\frac{n+1}{2} = \frac{45+1}{2} = 23$, so the median is the value of the 23rd item.

Example
_____

Find the median position for (a) $n = 20$ and (b) $n = 48$.

solution
_____

With the data arranged according to size (and counting from either end)

(a) $\frac{n+1}{2} = \frac{20+1}{2} = 10.5$, so the median is the mean of the values of the 10th and 11th items;

(b) $\frac{n+1}{2} = \frac{48+1}{2} = 24.5$, so the median is the mean of the values of the 24th and 25th items.

It is important to remember that

$$\frac{n+1}{2}$$

is a formula for the median position, and not a formula for the median itself. The determination of a median can sometimes be simplified, particularly for larger sets of data, by utilizing the grouping provided by a stem-and-leaf display.

Example
_____

The following are the numbers of passengers on 50 runs of a ferryboat:

```
61  52   65  84  35  57  58  95  82  64
50  53  103  40  62  77  78  66  60  41
58  92   51  65  71  75  89  37  54  67
59  79   80  73  49  71  97  62  68  53
43  80   75  70  45  91  50  64  56  86
```

Construct a stem-and-leaf display with one-digit leaves and use it to find the median.

solution

First conducting the stem-and-leaf display, we get

3	5 7
4	0 1 3 5 9
5	0 0 1 2 3 3 4 6 7 8 8 9
6	0 1 2 2 4 4 5 5 6 7 8
7	0 1 1 3 5 5 7 8 9
8	0 0 2 4 6 9
9	1 2 5 7
10	3

Since the median position is

$$\frac{50 + 1}{2} = 25.5$$

and 19 of the values fall on the first three stems, we must find the mean of the 6th and 7th values on the fourth stem. These values are 64 and 65, so that the median is

$$\frac{64 + 65}{2} = 64.5$$

Besides the median and the mean there are many other measures of central location (see, for example, the **midrange** described in Exercise 3.41 and the **midquartile** defined on page 61). Each describes the "middle" or "center" of a set of data in its own way and it should not come as a surprise that their values may not be the same. For instance, for the example where the seven students read 16, 10, 14, 13, 20, 11, and 17 of the books that were assigned, the median is 14 and the mean is

$$\frac{16 + 10 + 14 + 13 + 20 + 11 + 17}{7} = \frac{101}{7} \approx 14.4$$

The median is average in the sense that it splits the data into two parts so that, unless there are duplicates, as many values are below the median as there are above it. The mean, on the other hand, is average in the sense that if each value in a set of data is replaced by some number k while the total remains unchanged, this number k will have to be the mean. This follows directly from the relationship

$$n \cdot \bar{x} = \Sigma\, x$$

The median shares some, but not all, of the properties of the mean which we list on pages 48–49. Like the mean, the median always exists and it is unique for any set of data. Also like the mean, the median is simple enough to find once the data have been arranged according to size, but ordering a large set of data manually can be a fairly tedious task.

Unlike the mean, the medians of several sets of data cannot generally be combined into an overall median of all the data, and in problems of statistical inference the median is usually less reliable than the mean. This is meant to say that the medians of many samples drawn from the same population will usually vary more widely than the corresponding sample means (see Exercises 3.38 on page 64 and 10.55 on page 310). On the other hand, in some situations the median may be preferable to the mean because it is not so easily affected by extreme (very small or very large) values. For instance, on page 48 we show that the mean of 967, 949, 940, 952, and 922 (the lifetimes of five light bulbs) is 946, and on page 49 we show that if 949 is misread as 499, the mean becomes 856. Thus, the error of this mistake is

$$946 - 856 = 90$$

Had we used the median instead of the mean, we would have obtained 949 and 940, and the error would have been only

$$949 - 940 = 9$$

Finally, the median can be used to define the middle of a number of objects, properties, or qualities which can be ranked, namely, when we deal with ordinal data. For instance, we might rank a number of tasks according to their difficulty and then describe the middle (or median) one as being of "average" difficulty; also, we might rank samples of chocolate fudge according to their consistency and then describe the middle (or median) one as having "average" consistency. Since numbers were not used, the mean cannot be calculated for these situations.

3.5   OTHER FRACTILES

The median is but one of many **fractiles** that divide data into two or more parts, as nearly equal as they can be made. Among them we also find **quartiles, deciles, and percentiles,** which are intended to divide data into four, 10, and 100 parts. Until recently, fractiles were determined mainly for distributions of large sets of data, and in this connection we shall study them in Section 3.7.

In this section we concern ourselves mainly with a problem that has arisen in **exploratory data analysis**—in the preliminary analysis of relatively small sets of data. It is the problem of dividing such data into four nearly equal parts, where we say "nearly equal" because there is no way in which we can divide a set of data into four equal parts for, say, $n = 27$ or $n = 33$. Statistical measures designed for this purpose have traditionally been referred to as the three **quartiles,** Q_1, Q_2, and Q_3. There is no argument about Q_2, which is simply the median. On the other hand, there is ample room for arbitrariness in the definition of the **lower quartile** Q_1 and the **upper quartile** Q_3.

The following are some of the desirable properties we would like the quartiles Q_1 and Q_3 to have:

1. Q_1 is exceeded by three times as many values as it exceeds, and it is the other way around for Q_3.

2. There are as many values less than Q_1 as there are between Q_1 and Q_2, between Q_2 and Q_3, and greater than Q_3.

3. Half the data fall between Q_1 and Q_3.

It is assumed here that no two values are alike; otherwise, the wording would have to be changed as indicated on page 61.

To illustrate, consider the following high temperature readings in 12 European cities on a June day:

90 75 86 77 85 72 78 79 94 82 74 93

Arranging these figures in sequence from lowest to highest reading,

72 74 75 77 78 79 82 85 86 90 93 94

The dashed lines in the upper part of Figure 3.1 divide the data into four equal parts. If we let the midpoints between 75 and 77, 79 and 82, and 86 and 90 be the three quartiles, we have

$$Q_1 = \frac{75 + 77}{2} = 76, \quad Q_2 = \frac{79 + 82}{2} = 80.5, \quad \text{and} \quad Q_3 = \frac{86 + 90}{2} = 88$$

Of course, $Q_2 = 80.5$ is also the median and it can be verified readily that all three of the desirable properties listed above for the quartiles are satisfied.

Everything worked nicely in this example because 12, the sample size, happened to be a multiple of 4. What can we do, though, when this is not the case? Suppose, for instance, that the city where the high temperature was 77 failed to report, so that we are left with the following 11 numbers arranged according to size:

72 74 75 78 79 82 85 86 90 93 94

The median, or Q_2, is now 82, but what can we do about the other two dividing lines? If it is felt that the second of the three properties listed on page 59 is most relevant, the dividing lines can be drawn as in the lower part of Figure 3.1, so that

$$Q_1 = 75, \quad Q_2 = 82, \quad \text{and} \quad Q_3 = 90.$$

There are two values less than Q_1, two values between Q_1 and Q_2, two values between Q_2 and Q_3, and two values greater than Q_3, but Q_1 is exceeded by four times as many values as it exceeds and only five of the eleven values fall between Q_1 and Q_3.

The procedures for finding the quartiles are as follows—assuming that no two values are alike:

The lower quartile is the median of all values less than the median of the whole set of data.

The upper quartile is the median of all values greater than the median of the whole set of data.

FIGURE 3.1

Quartiles.

Example

The following are the scores of nine students on a history test:

$$86 \quad 82 \quad 73 \quad 94 \quad 88 \quad 66 \quad 79 \quad 90 \quad 74$$

Find the median and the two quartiles.

solution

For $n = 9$, the median position is

$$\frac{9 + 1}{2} = 5$$

The lower quartile is the median of the four values below the median, and the upper quartile is the median of the four values above the median. Arranging the data according to size, we have

$$66 \quad 73 \quad 74 \quad 79 \quad 82 \quad 86 \quad 88 \quad 90 \quad 94$$

Thus the median is 82,

the lower quartile is $\dfrac{73 + 74}{2} = 73.5$,

and the upper quartile is $\dfrac{88 + 90}{2} = 89$. ◪ ◪ ◪

If some of the values are alike, we modify the definition of quartiles by replacing "less than the median" by "to the left of the median position" and "greater than the median" by "to the right of the median position." For instance, the nine golfers in the example on page 56 scored

$$3 \quad 3 \quad 3 \quad 3 \quad 4 \quad 4 \quad 4 \quad 4 \quad 5$$

on the third hole. The lower quartile, the mean of the second and third values, is 3. The median, the fifth value, is 4. The upper quartile, the mean of the second and third values from the right, is 4.

Another definition for the quartiles is provided in the exercises.

Quartiles are not intended to be descriptive of the "middle" or "center" of a set of data, and we have given them here mainly because, like the median, they are fractiles and they are determined in more or less the same way. The **midquartile,** $\frac{Q_1 + Q_3}{2}$, has been used on occasion as a measure of central location.

The information provided by the median, the two quartiles, and the smallest and largest values is sometimes presented in the form of a **box-and-whisker plot,** often just called a **box plot.** Such a plot is shown in Figure 3.2 for the data on the history test scores above. In practice, this figure is sometimes embellished with other features of the data, but the simple form shown here is adequate for most purposes.

FIGURE 3.2

Box-and-whisker plot for data on history test scores.

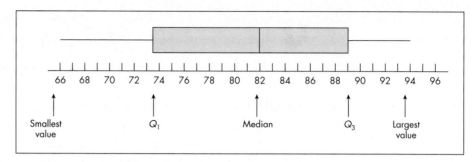

3.6   THE MODE

Another measure that is sometimes used to describe the "middle" or "center" of a set of data is the **mode,** defined simply as the value that occurs with the highest frequency and more than once. Its two main advantages are that it re- quires no calculation, only counting, and it can be determined even for qualita- tive, or nominal, data.

Example

The 20 meetings of a square dance club were attended by

$$26 \quad 25 \quad 28 \quad 23 \quad 25 \quad 24 \quad 24 \quad 21 \quad 23 \quad 26$$
$$28 \quad 26 \quad 24 \quad 32 \quad 25 \quad 27 \quad 24 \quad 23 \quad 24 \quad 22$$

of its members. Find the mode.

solution

Among the 20 numbers, 21, 22, 27, and 32 each occurs once; 28 occurs twice; 23, 25, and 26 each occurs three times; and 24 occurs five times. Thus, 24 is the **modal** attendance.   ▰ ▰ ▰

   Also, if more visitors to California want to see Disneyland than any other tourist attraction, we say that Disneyland is their **modal** choice.
   Aside from the fact that the mode is seldom of any use in statistical inference, it also has the disadvantage that it may not exist (which is the case when no two values are alike) or that it may not be unique.

Example

A sample of the records of a motor vehicle bureau shows that 18 drivers in a cer- tain age group received

$$3 \quad 2 \quad 0 \quad 0 \quad 2 \quad 3 \quad 3 \quad 1 \quad 0 \quad 1 \quad 0 \quad 3 \quad 4 \quad 0 \quad 3 \quad 2 \quad 3 \quad 0$$

traffic tickets during the last three years. Find the mode.

solution

As can be seen, the number 4 occurs once, the number 1 occurs twice, the num- ber 2 occurs three times, and the numbers 0 and 3 each occurs six times. So, there are the two modes, 0 and 3.   ▰ ▰ ▰

An additional difficulty with the mode is that it behaves erratically when data values are rounded (see Exercise 3.57 on pages 66–67).

There are many other measures of central location besides the ones we have mentioned, and at least one more, the **midrange,** is given in Exercise 3.41. What particular average should be used in a given situation can depend on many things (see Section 7.3, for example) and the choice may be difficult to make. Since the selection of statistical descriptions often contains an element of arbitrariness, there are persons who believe that the magic of statistics can be used to prove almost anything. Indeed, a famous nineteenth-century British statesman said that there are three kinds of lies: *lies, damned lies, and statistics.* Exercises 3.40 and 3.41 on pages 64–65 describe a situation where this criticism is well justified.

◢ EXERCISES

3.27   Find the median position for
(a) $n = 25$;   (b) $n = 32$.

3.28   Find the median position for
(a) $n = 37$;   (b) $n = 64$.

3.29   On 15 days, a restaurant serves breakfast to

40 52 55 38 40 48 56 56 60 37 58 63 46 50 61

customers. Find the median.

3.30   In 1991, 12 used-car salespersons sold, respectively,

58 70 85 42 64 46 66 89 44 93 58 79

used cars. Find the median.

3.31   Twenty power failures last

18 125 44 96   31 26 80 49 125 63
45   33 89 12 103 75 40 80   61 28

minutes. Find the median.

3.32   Find the median number of traffic tickets for the 18 drivers cited in the example on page 62.

3.33   On the 20 pages of a report, a typist made the following number of mistakes:

0 0 1 2 0 3 1 0 0 0
0 1 0 0 4 1 0 0 2 1

(a) Find the mean.
(b) Find the median.
(c) How many of the 20 values are above the mean?
How many are below the mean?
(d) How many of the 20 values are above the median?
How many are below the median?

3.34   A public school that operates on a 35-week school year schedule reports the following number of absences due to measles:

0	0	2	0	0	1	0	0	2	1
1	1	4	8	15	39	42	12	6	4
2	1	0	0	0	1	0	0	0	0
0	0	1	0	0					

Calculate the mean and median of these values, and then indicate which of the two measures gives a better indication of the "average" number of measles absences.

3.35   The following values are the times (in minutes) of 25 National Basketball Association (NBA) games:

138	142	113	126	135	142	159	157	140
157	121	128	142	164	155	139	143	158
140	118	142	146	123	130	137		

(a) Find the median directly by arranging the data according to size.

(b) Find the median by first constructing a stem-and-leaf display.

3.36   Use the stem-and-leaf display on page 17 to find the median of the scores which the 20 students received on the physical coordination test.

3.37   In one month, 15 salespersons reach

107 90 80 92 86 109 102 92 353 78 74 102 106 95 91

percent of their sales quotas. Calculate the mean and the median of these percentages, and indicate which of the two measures gives a better indication of these salespersons' "average" performance.

3.38   To verify the claim that the mean is generally more reliable than the median (namely, that the mean is subject to smaller chance fluctuations), a student conducts an experiment consisting of 12 tosses of three dice. The following are his results:

2, 4, and 6,   5, 3, and 5,   4, 5, and 3,   5, 2, and 3,   6, 1, and 5,   3, 2, and 1,
3, 1, and 4,   5, 5, and 2,   3, 3, and 4,   1, 6, and 2,   3, 3, and 3,   4, 5, and 3.

(a) Calculate the 12 medians and the 12 means.

(b) Group the medians and the means obtained in part (a) into separate distributions having the classes

1.5–2.5,   2.5–3.5,   3.5–4.5,   4.5–5.5

(Note that there will be no ambiguities since the medians of three whole numbers and the means of three whole numbers cannot equal 2.5, 3.5, or 4.5.)

(c) Draw histograms of the two distributions obtained in part (b) and explain how they illustrate the claim that the mean is generally more reliable than the median.

3.39   Repeat Exercise 3.38 with your own data by repeatedly rolling three dice (or one die three times) and constructing corresponding distributions of the medians and means.

3.40   A consumer testing service obtains the following mileage per gallon during five test runs performed with each of three compact cars:

Car A: 27.9   30.4   30.6   31.4   31.7
Car B: 31.2   28.7   31.3   28.7   31.3
Car C: 28.6   29.1   28.5   32.1   29.7

(a) If the manufacturer of car *A* wants to advertise that their car performed best in this test, which of the "averages" discussed in this book could they use to substantiate their claim?

(b) If the manufacturer of car *B* wants to advertise that their car performed best in this test, which of the "averages" discussed in this book could they use to substantiate their claim?

3.41 Suppose that the manufacturer of car C of Exercise 3.40 hires an unscrupulous statistician and instructs him to find some kind of "average" which will show that their car performed best in the test. Show that the **midrange** (the mean of the smallest and largest values) will serve their purpose.

3.42 The library records of a large university show that 22 senior philosophy majors checked out the following number of books during the academic year:

$$62 \quad 73 \quad 40 \quad 72 \quad 79 \quad 88 \quad 35 \quad 51 \quad 48 \quad 42 \quad 75$$
$$65 \quad 69 \quad 82 \quad 50 \quad 66 \quad 103 \quad 68 \quad 54 \quad 38 \quad 52 \quad 72$$

(a) Find the median.

(b) Find the quartiles Q_1 and Q_3.

3.43 Automotive engineers testing a new brake system found that 21 drivers traveling 30 mph stopped within the following number of feet:

$$69 \quad 58 \quad 70 \quad 80 \quad 46 \quad 61 \quad 65 \quad 74 \quad 75 \quad 55 \quad 67$$
$$56 \quad 70 \quad 72 \quad 61 \quad 66 \quad 58 \quad 68 \quad 70 \quad 68 \quad 58$$

(a) Find the median.

(b) Find the quartiles Q_1 and Q_3.

3.44 Find the two quartiles for the lengths of the NBA games cited in Exercise 3.35.

3.45 If *n* sample values are arranged according to size, find the positions of the median and the two quartiles:

(a) when $n = 40$; (b) when $n = 41$;

(c) when $n = 42$; (d) when $n = 43$.

3.46 An alternative method for finding quartiles would replace Q_1 with the median of all values less than *or equal to* the median of the whole set of data. This method would also replace Q_3 with the median of all values greater than *or equal to* the median of the whole set of data. These replacements are called **hinges.** Find the positions of the hinges in a sample of *n* values arranged according to the following sizes:

(a) when $n = 40$; (b) when $n = 41$;

(c) when $n = 42$; (d) when $n = 43$.

The use of hinges as an alternative to using quartiles was once popular in exploratory data analysis, but that popularity has diminished.

3.47 Find the quartiles for the power failure data of Exercise 3.31.

3.48 In this problem we explain a procedure for finding general **fractiles** or **percentiles.** Let *p* be a fraction between 0 and 1. Find the fractile corresponding to *p* as follows:

Compute *pn*. If this is not an integer, use the next highest integer for the *p*th fractile position; if it is an integer, use the mean of the values in positions *pn* and $pn + 1$ as the *p*th fractile.

For example, if you wanted fractile $p = 0.6$ in a list with $n = 103$, you would find $pn = 61.8$ and use the value in position 62. If you wanted fractile $p = 0.6$ in a list with $n = 110$, you would find $pn = 66$ and use the mean of the values in positions 66 and 67. Fractiles are often expressed as percentiles; for example, the 0.6 fractile is called the 60th percentile. Find the 60th percentile for the lengths of the NBA games cited in Exercise 3.35.

3.49 Find the 30th percentile for the stopping distances in Exercise 3.43.

3.50   Some statisticians and some computer packages use **interpolation** to determine the position of quartiles and other fractiles. This technique begins by finding the position for the fractile corresponding to p as $p(n + 1)$. For instance, to find the position of the lower quartile of 30 values we substitute $p = 0.25$ and $n = 30$ to get

$$0.25(30 + 1) = 7.75$$

This means that we must go three-fourths of the way between the seventh and eight values. If these values happen to be 146 and 148, the lower quartile is

$$146 + \frac{3}{4}(148 - 146) = 147.5$$

A college had

$$8 \quad 3 \quad 20 \quad 5 \quad 2 \quad 8 \quad 14 \quad 2 \quad 6 \quad 10 \quad 7 \quad 15$$

applicants for 12 different teaching positions. Find the hinges and also find the quartiles, using the technique of Exercise 3.48. Then use the interpolation method to obtain the quartiles.

3.51   Use the results of Exercises 3.31 and 3.47 to construct a box-and-whisker plot for the lengths of the power failures.

3.52   Use the results of Exercises 3.35 and 3.44 to construct a box-and-whisker plot for the lengths of the NBA games.

3.53   The following are the number of days in advance that 17 persons purchased tickets for a sporting event:

$$7 \quad 3 \quad 4 \quad 12 \quad 18 \quad 3 \quad 8 \quad 14 \quad 6 \quad 16 \quad 7 \quad 6 \quad 11 \quad 7 \quad 9 \quad 5 \quad 2$$

Find the mode.

3.54   On 50 days, these were the number of students absent from an algebra class:

```
1 3 0 0 1 0 4 1 1 0 1 2 6 0 1
0 0 1 0 0 0 0 1 3 3 2 5 0 1 1
1 0 3 0 0 0 4 1 1 2 1 2 0 1 0
1 0 0 3 2
```

Find the mode.

3.55   Find the mode (if it exists) of each of the following sets of blood pressure readings:
(a) 144, 145, 146, 146, 148, 146, 146, 145, 147, 145, 144;
(b) 146, 149, 146, 141, 146, 149, 147, 147, 149, 149, 145;
(c) 167, 151, 175, 144, 152, 148, 156, 169, 143, 177, 161.

3.56   Thirty persons were asked for their favorite color. These are their responses:

red	blue	blue	green	yellow	blue	brown	red	red	red
green	white	blue	red	yellow	blue	blue	red	green	yellow
blue	blue	orange	green	blue	blue	green	red	purple	blue

What is their modal choice?

3.57   The figures below are a local bakery's daily flour utilization, in pounds, for 20 consecutive weekdays:

$$440 \quad 677 \quad 481 \quad 690 \quad 707 \quad 514 \quad 671 \quad 488 \quad 483 \quad 554$$
$$611 \quad 638 \quad 572 \quad 514 \quad 623 \quad 664 \quad 631 \quad 570 \quad 484 \quad 612$$

(a) Find the mean, median, and mode for this set of values.

(b) Round the 20 values to the nearest ten pounds. Then again give the mean, median, and mode.

(c) Round the 20 values to the nearest hundred pounds. Then again give the mean, median, and mode.

(d) State a conclusion about the effect of rounding on the mean, median, and mode.

3.7 THE DESCRIPTION OF GROUPED DATA ⇔

In the past, considerable attention was paid to the description of grouped data because it was generally advantageous to group data before calculating various statistical descriptions. This is no longer the case, since the necessary calculations can now be made in a matter of seconds by using computers or even hand-held calculators. Nevertheless, we devote this section and Section 4.4 to the description of grouped data, since some data (published government figures, for example) are available only in the form of frequency distributions.

As we have already seen, the grouping of data entails some loss of information. Each item loses its identity, so to speak; we only know how many items there are in each class, so we must be satisfied with approximations. To determine the mean, we can usually get a good approximation by **assigning to each item falling into a class the value of the corresponding class mark.** For instance, to calculate the mean of the grouped sulfur oxides emission data on page 23, we treat the three values in the first class as if they were all 6.95, the 10 values in the second class as if they were all 10.95, . . ., and the two values falling into the seventh class as if they were all 30.95. This procedure is usually quite satisfactory, since the errors that are thus introduced into the calculations will tend to average out.

To find a general formula for the mean of a distribution with k classes, let us denote the successive class marks by $x_1, x_2, \ldots$, and x_k, and the corresponding class frequencies by $f_1, f_2, \ldots$, and f_k. Then, the sum of all the measurements is approximated by

$$x_1 \cdot f_1 + x_2 \cdot f_2 + \cdots + x_k \cdot f_k = \Sigma\, x \cdot f,$$

and the mean of the distribution is given by

Mean of Grouped Data

$$\bar{x} = \frac{\Sigma\, x \cdot f}{n}$$

Here n is the size of the sample, $f_1 + f_2 + \cdots + f_k$, and to write a corresponding formula for the mean of a population, we substitute μ for $\bar{x}$ and N for n.

Example

Calculate the mean of the distribution of the sulfur oxides emission data on page 23.

solution

To get $\Sigma\, x \cdot f$, we perform the calculations shown in the following table, where the first column contains the class marks, the second column is copied from the original distribution, and the third column contains the products $x \cdot f$:

Class mark x	Frequency f	x · f
6.95	3	20.85
10.95	10	109.50
14.95	14	209.30
18.95	25	473.75
22.95	17	390.15
26.95	9	242.55
30.95	2	61.90
Total	80	1,508.00

Then, substitution into the formula yields

$$\bar{x} = \frac{1,508.00}{80} = 18.85$$

To check on the **grouping error**, namely, the error introduced by replacing each value in a class by the class mark, let us refer to the computer printout of Figure 3.3, which shows that the mean of the original ungrouped data is 18.896. Thus, the error is only

$$18.85 - 18.896 = -0.046,$$

which is very small.

FIGURE 3.3

Computer printout for the mean of the sulfur oxides emission data.
(Minitab 10 for Windows).

```
MTB > set cl
DATA > 15.8  26.4  17.3  11.2  23.9  24.8  18.7  13.9   9.0  13.2
DATA > 22.7   9.8   6.2  14.7  17.5  26.1  12.8  28.6  17.6  23.7
DATA > 26.8  22.7  18.0  20.5  11.0  20.9  15.5  19.4  16.7  10.7
DATA > 19.1  15.2  22.9  26.6  20.4  21.4  19.2  21.6  16.9  19.0
DATA > 18.5  23.0  24.6  20.1  16.2  18.0   7.7  13.5  23.5  14.5
DATA > 14.4  29.6  19.4  17.0  20.8  24.3  22.5  24.6  18.4  18.1
DATA >  8.3  21.9  12.3  22.3  13.3  11.8  19.3  20.0  25.7  31.8
DATA > 25.9  10.5  15.9  27.5  18.1  17.9   9.4  24.1  20.1  28.5
DATA > end
MTB > mean cl

Column Mean

    Mean of Cl      =       18.896

MTB > stan cl

Column Standard Deviation
    Standard deviation of Cl     =      5.6565
```

Once a set of data has been grouped, we can still determine most other statistical measures besides the mean, but we may have to make special assumptions or modify the definitions. For instance, we define the median of a distribution in the following way:

The median of a distribution is such that half the total area of the rectangles of the histogram of the distribution lies to its left and the other half lies to its right.

This definition, illustrated by Figure 3.4, assumes that the values in the class containing the median of the ungrouped data are distributed evenly—that is, spread out evenly—throughout that class.

FIGURE 3.4

Median of the distribution of the sulfur oxides emission data.

To find the dividing line between the two halves of a histogram (each of which represents $\frac{n}{2}$ of the items grouped), we must count $\frac{n}{2}$ of the items starting at either end of the distribution. How this is done is illustrated by the following example:

Example

Find the median of the distribution of the sulfur oxides emission data.

solution

Since

$$\frac{n}{2} = \frac{80}{2} = 40$$

we must count 40 of the items starting at either end. Starting at the bottom of the distribution (that is, beginning with the smallest values), we find that

$$3 + 10 + 14 = 27$$

of the values fall into the first three classes, and that

$$3 + 10 + 14 + 25 = 52$$

of the values fall into the first four classes. Therefore, we must count $40 - 27 = 13$ more values beyond the 27 which fall into the first three classes. On the assumption that the 25 values in the fourth class are spread evenly throughout that class, we can do this by adding $\frac{13}{25}$ of the class interval of 4 to 16.95, the lower boundary of the fourth class. This gives us

$$\tilde{x} = 16.95 + \frac{13}{25} \cdot 4 = 19.03$$

for the median of the distribution.   ◪ ◪ ◪

In general, if L is the lower boundary of the class into which the median must fall, f is its frequency, c is its class interval, and j is the number of items we still lack when we reach L, then the median of the distribution is given by

Median of Grouped Data	
	$$\tilde{x} = L + \frac{j}{f} \cdot c$$

If we prefer, we can find the median of a distribution by starting to count at the other end (beginning with the largest values) and subtracting an appropriate fraction of the class interval from the upper boundary of the class into which the median must fall.

Example

Use this alternative approach to find the median of the distribution of the sulfur oxides emission data.

solution

Since $2 + 9 + 17 = 28$ of the values fall above 20.95, we need $40 - 28 = 12$ of the 25 values which fall into the next class to reach the median, and we write

$$\tilde{x} = 20.95 - \frac{12}{25} \cdot 4 = 19.03$$

The result is, of course, the same.   ◪ ◪ ◪

Note that the median of a distribution can be found regardless of whether the class intervals are all equal; in fact, it can usually be found even when either or both of the classes at the top and at the bottom of a distribution are open (see Exercise 3.58).

The method by which we found the median of a distribution can also be used to determine other fractiles. For instance, the three quartiles (which are intended to divide a set of data into four more-or-less equal parts) are defined for grouped data so that 25 percent of the total area of the rectangles of the histogram lies to the left of Q_1, 25 percent lies between Q_1 and Q_2, 25 percent lies between Q_2 and Q_3, and 25 percent lies to the right of Q_3. Similarly, the nine deciles (which are intended to divide a set of data into 10 more or less equal parts) are defined for grouped data so that 10 percent of the total area of the rectangles of the histogram lies to the left of D_1, 10 percent lies between D_1 and D_2, ..., and 10 percent lies to the right of D_9. And finally, the 99 percentiles (which are intended to divide a set of data into 100 more-or-less equal parts) are defined for grouped data so that 1 percent of the total area of the rectangles of the histogram lies to the left of P_1, 1 percent lies between P_1 and P_2, ..., and 1 percent lies to the right of P_{99}. Note that Q_2, D_5, and P_{50} are all equal to the median, and that P_{25} equals Q_1 and P_{75} equals Q_3. See also Exercise 3.48 on page 65.

Example

Find Q_1 and Q_3 for the distribution of the sulfur oxides emission data.

solution

To find Q_1 we must count $\frac{80}{4} = 20$ of the items starting at the bottom of the distribution. Since there are $3 + 10 = 13$ values in the first two classes, we must count $20 - 13 = 7$ of the 14 values in the third class to reach Q_1, and we get

$$Q_1 = 12.95 + \frac{7}{14} \cdot 4 = 14.95$$

To find Q_3 we must count 20 of the items starting at the other end of the distribution. Since $2 + 9 = 11$ of the values fall into the two classes at the top of the distribution, we must count $20 - 11 = 9$ of the 17 values in the next class to reach Q_3, and we get

$$Q_3 = 24.95 - \frac{9}{17} \cdot 4 \approx 22.83$$

Example

Find D_8 and P_2 for the distribution of the sulfur oxide emission data.

solution

Counting $80(0.20) = 16$ of the items starting with the largest values, we get

$$D_8 = 24.95 - \frac{5}{17} \cdot 4 \approx 23.77$$

and counting $80(0.02) = 1.6$ of the items starting with the smallest values, we get

$$P_2 = 4.95 + \frac{1.6}{3} \cdot 4 \approx 7.08$$

Note that when we determine a fractile of a distribution, the number of items we have to count and the quantity j in the formula on page 70 need not be a whole number.

◪ EXERCISES

3.58 For each of the following distributions determine whether it is possible to find the mean and/or the median:

(a)

Grade	Freq.
40–49	5
50–59	18
60–69	27
70–79	15
80–89	6
Total	71

(b)

IQ	Freq.
< 90	3
90–99	14
100–109	22
110–119	19
> 119	7
Total	65

(c)

Weight	Freq.
100 or less	41
101–110	13
111–120	8
121–130	3
131–140	1
Total	66

3.59   Find the mean of the following distribution of the grades that 500 students obtain in a geography test:

Grade	Number of Students
10–24	44
25–39	70
40–54	92
55–69	147
70–84	115
85–99	32
Total	500

3.60   With reference to the distribution of Exercise 3.59, find

(a) the median;   (b) the quartiles Q_1 and Q_3.

3.61   At the end of each working day, at a large retail store, the total of the prices entered into its cash registers is compared with money actually in the registers. The excess money differences, meaning money in drawers minus cash register totals, for 120 business days, are noted in the distribution below:

Excess Money		Frequency
−$150.00 to −$100.01		3
−$100.00 to −$50.01		12
−$50.00 to −$0.01		31
$0.00 to $49.99		66
$50.00 to $99.99		6
$100.00 to $149.99		2
Total		120

(a) Find the median of these values.

(b) Find the percentiles P_{20} and P_{80}.

3.62   With reference to the distribution of Exercise 3.59, find

(a) the deciles D_1 and D_9;

(b) The percentiles P_5 and P_{95}.

3.63   Find the mean of the following distribution of the percentages of the students belonging to a certain ethnic group in a sample of 50 elementary schools:

Percentage	Number of Schools
0–4	18
5–9	15
10–14	9
15–19	7
20–24	1
Total	50

3.64   With reference to the distribution of Exercise 3.63, find

(a) the median;   (b) the quartiles Q_1 and Q_3.

3.65 With reference to the distribution of Exercise 3.63, find
(a) the deciles D_3 and D_7; (b) the percentiles P_5 and P_{98}.

3.66 Find the mean of the following distribution of the ages of the members of a labor union:

Age (years)	Frequency
15–19	18
20–24	42
25–29	78
30–34	115
35–39	178
40–44	107
45–49	88
50–54	52
55–59	30
60–64	11
Total	719

3.67 With reference to the distribution of Exercise 3.66, find
(a) the median;
(b) the quintiles, meaning $P_{20}, P_{40}, P_{60}, P_{80}$.

3.68 With reference to the distribution of Exercise 3.66, find the two fractiles that divide the distribution into three equal parts.

3.69 Find the mean of the distribution obtained in Exercise 2.25 on page 29 for the weights of the 50 rats. Also, use a computer package or a calculator to find the mean of the original (ungrouped) data, and thus determine the size of the grouping error.

3.70 Find the mean of the distribution obtained in Exercise 2.30 on page 29 for the mileages obtained with 40 tanksful of gas. Also, use a computer package or a calculator to find the mean of the original (ungrouped) data, and thus determine the size of the grouping error.

3.71 Suppose that data values have been grouped into a distribution with class interval c. It is guaranteed that the grouping error in computing the mean cannot exceed c. For each of Exercises 3.69 and 3.70, compare the grouping error to the class interval.

3.8 TECHNICAL NOTE (Summations)

In the notation introduced on page 47, Σx does not tell us which, or how many, values of x we must add. This omission is taken care of by the more explicit notation

$$\sum_{i=1}^{n} x_i = x_1 + x_2 + \cdots + x_n$$

where it is made clear that we are adding the x's whose subscripts i are $1, 2, \ldots$, and n. We are not using the more explicit notation in this book so as to simplify the overall appearance of the formulas, assuming that it is clear in each case which x's we are referring to and how many there are.

Using the Σ notation, we shall also have occasion to write such expressions as

$$\Sigma x^2, \quad \Sigma xy, \quad \Sigma x^2 f \quad \ldots$$

which (more explicitly) represent the sums

$$\sum_{i=1}^{n} x_i^2 = x_1^2 + x_2^2 + x_3^2 + \cdots + x_n^2$$

$$\sum_{j=1}^{n} x_j y_j = x_1 y_1 + x_2 y_2 + \cdots + x_n y_n$$

$$\sum_{i=1}^{n} x_i^2 f_i = x_1^2 f_1 + x_2^2 f_2 + \cdots + x_n^2 f_n$$

Working with two subscripts, we shall also have the occasion to evaluate **double summations** such as

$$\sum_{j=1}^{3} \sum_{i=1}^{4} x_{ij} = \sum_{j=1}^{3} (x_{1j} + x_{2j} + x_{3j} + x_{4j})$$

$$= x_{11} + x_{21} + x_{31} + x_{41} + x_{12} + x_{22} + x_{32} + x_{42}$$

$$+ x_{13} + x_{23} + x_{33} + x_{43}$$

To verify some of the formulas involving summations that are stated but not proved in the text, the reader needs the following rules:

Rules for Summations	Rule A: $\sum_{i=1}^{n} (x_i \pm y_i) = \sum_{i=1}^{n} x_i \pm \sum_{i=1}^{n} y_i$
	Rule B: $\sum_{i=1}^{n} k \cdot x_i = k \cdot \sum_{i=1}^{n} x_i$
	Rule C: $\sum_{i=1}^{n} k = k \cdot n$

The first of these rules states that the summation of the sum (or difference) of two terms equals the sum (or difference) of the individual summations, and it can be extended to the sum or difference of more than two terms. The second rule states that we can factor a constant out of a summation, and the third rule states that the summation of a constant is simply n times that constant. All of these rules can be proved by actually writing out in full what each of the summations represents.

◢ EXERCISES

3.72   Write each of the following in full; that is, without summation signs:

(a) $\sum_{i=1}^{6} x_i$;   (b) $\sum_{i=1}^{5} y_i$;   (c) $\sum_{i=1}^{3} x_i y_i$;

(d) $\sum_{j=1}^{8} x_j f_j$;   (e) $\sum_{i=3}^{7} x_i^2$;   (f) $\sum_{j=1}^{4} (x_j + y_j)$.

3.73   Write each of the following without summation signs and simplify if possible:

(a) $\sum_{i=1}^{5} (x_i + 1)$;   (b) $\sum_{j=1}^{4} (3y_j)$;   (c) $\sum_{i=1}^{4} x_i + \sum_{j=1}^{4} (2x_j)$.

3.74 Write each of the following as summations:

(a) $z_1 + z_2 + z_3 + z_4$;

(b) $x_6 + x_7 + x_8 + x_9 + x_{10} + x_{11}$;

(c) $x_1 f_1 + x_2 f_2 + x_3 f_3 + x_4 f_4 + x_5 f_5 + x_6 f_6$;

(d) $y_1^2 + y_2^2 + y_3^2 + y_4^2 + y_5^2$;

(e) $3x_1 + 3x_2 + 3x_3 + 3x_4 + 3x_5 + 3x_6$;

(f) $(x_1 - y_1) + (x_2 - y_2) + (x_3 - y_3) + (x_4 - y_4)$;

(g) $(w_1 - 5) + (w_2 - 5) + (w_3 - 5)$;

(h) $a_1 b_1 c_1 + a_2 b_2 c_2 + a_3 b_3 c_3 + a_4 b_4 c_4$.

3.75 Given $x_1 = 1$, $x_2 = 3$, $x_3 = 5$, $x_4 = 7$, $x_5 = 9$, $f_1 = 1$, $f_2 = 5$, $f_3 = 3$, $f_4 = 3$, and $f_5 = 2$, find

(a) $\sum_{i=1}^{5} x_i$; (b) $\sum_{i=1}^{5} f_i$; (c) $\sum_{i=1}^{5} x_i \cdot f_i$; (d) $\sum_{i=1}^{5} x_i^2 \cdot f_i$;

3.76 Given $x_1 = -2$, $x_2 = 3$, $x_3 = 1$, and $x_4 = 4$, find

(a) $\sum_{i=1}^{4} x_i$; (b) $\sum_{i=1}^{4} x_i^2$

3.77 Given $x_{11} = 3$, $x_{12} = 1$, $x_{13} = -2$, $x_{14} = 2$, $x_{21} = 1$, $x_{22} = 4$, $x_{23} = -2$, $x_{24} = 5$, $x_{31} = 3$, $x_{32} = -1$, $x_{33} = 2$, and $x_{34} = 3$, find

(a) $\sum_{i=1}^{3} x_{ij}$ separately for $j = 1, 2, 3$, and 4;

(b) $\sum_{j=1}^{4} x_{ij}$ separately for $i = 1, 2$, and 3.

3.78 With reference to Exercise 3.77, evaluate the double summation

$$\sum_{i=1}^{3} \sum_{j=1}^{4} x_{ij}$$

using

(a) the results of part (a) of that exercise;

(b) the results of part (b) of that exercise.

3.79 Show that

$$\sum_{i=1}^{n} (x - \bar{x}) = 0$$

for any set of x's whose mean is $\bar{x}$.

3.80 Is it true in general that

$$\left(\sum_{i=1}^{n} x_i \right)^2 = \sum_{i=1}^{n} x_i^2 ?$$

(*Hint:* Check whether the equation holds for $n = 2$.)

3.81 For any positive (or zero) values a_1 through a_n it is always the case that

$$\left(\sum_{i=1}^{n} a_i^2 \right) \le \left(\sum_{i=1}^{n} a_i \right)^2$$

(a) Verify this assertion with $n = 4$,

$$a_1 = 5, \quad a_2 = 3, \quad a_3 = 2, \quad a_4 = 1$$

(b) Verify this assertion with $n = 5$,

$$a_1 = 1, \quad a_2 = 2, \quad a_3 = 0, \quad a_4 = 1, \quad a_5 = 6$$

(c) Devise an example showing that an assertion may be false if negative numbers are permitted. (*Hint:* Consider $n = 2$ and $a_2 = -a_1$.)

(d) Prove this result by starting from

$$\sum_{i=1}^{n} \left(a_i - \frac{\sum_{j=1}^{n} a_j}{n} \right)^2 \geq 0$$

3.82   The notation $|a|$ denotes the **absolute value** of a number, meaning the number with the sign converted to positive. For example,

$$|3| = 3, \quad |-8| = 8, \quad |-13.2| = 13.2, \quad |0| = 0$$

and so on. For any values b_1 through b_n it is always true that

$$\left(\sum_{i=1}^{n} b_i^2 \right) \leq \left(\sum_{i=1}^{n} |b_i| \right)^2$$

(a) Verify this assertion with $n = 4$,

$$b_1 = 5, \quad b_2 = -3, \quad b_3 = 2, \quad b_4 = -1$$

(b) Verify this assertion with $n = 5$,

$$b_1 = 1, \quad b_2 = -2, \quad b_3 = 0, \quad b_4 = 1, \quad b_5 = -6$$

3.83   For any two sets of values, x_1 through x_n and y_1 through y_n, it is always true that

$$\left(\sum_{i=1}^{n} |x_i| \, |y_i| \right) \leq \left(\sum_{i=1}^{n} |x_i| \right) \left(\sum_{i=1}^{n} |y_i| \right)$$

(a) Verify this assertion with $n = 3$,

$$x_1 = 2, \quad x_2 = -3, \quad x_3 = 5, \quad y_1 = 100, \quad y_2 = 200, \quad y_3 = 300$$

(b) Verify this assertion with $n = 4$,

$$x_1 = 0, \quad x_2 = 2, \quad x_3 = 0, \quad x_4 = 4, \quad y_1 = 0, \quad y_2 = 20, \quad y_3 = 0, \quad y_4 = 50.$$

3.9   CHECKLIST OF KEY TERMS[†] *(with page references to their definitions)*

Absolute value, 76

Arithmetic mean, 45

Box-and-whisker plot, 61

Box plot, 61

⇔ Decile, 59

Double summation, 74

⇔ Exploratory data analysis, 59

⇔ Fractile, 59

Geometric mean, 53

Grand mean, 51

[†]Terms introduced in exercises are shown in *italics.*

⇔ Grouping error, 68
Harmonic mean, 54
⇔ Hinge, 65
⇔ *Interpolation,* 66
⇔ Lower quartile, 59
Markov's theorem, 53
Mean, 45
Measures of central location, 44
Measures of location, 44
Median, 55
Median position, 56
⇔ Midquartile, 61
Midrange, 65

Mode, 62
Parameter, 47
⇔ Percentile, 59
Population, 44
Population size, 47
⇔ Quartile, 59
Sample, 44
Sample size, 46
Statistic, 47
Summation notation, 47
⇔ Upper quartile, 59
Weighted mean, 50
Weights, 50

3.10 ◼ REVIEW EXERCISES

3.84   The following are the estimated television audience ratings for 16 professional football games:

$$1.46 \quad 1.32 \quad 1.58 \quad 1.88 \quad 1.32 \quad 1.39 \quad 1.72 \quad 1.66$$
$$1.82 \quad 1.21 \quad 1.36 \quad 1.76 \quad 1.86 \quad 1.63 \quad 1.55 \quad 1.57$$

Find the median and the mode for these values.

3.85   Find the quartiles for the audience ratings of Exercise 3.84.

3.86   In a benefit sale, a service organization sells 120 books at a mean price of $2.10, 80 cakes at a mean price of $2.75, and 50 craft items at a mean price of $4.55. Find the total sales amount, and provide the mean price per item sold.

3.87   The following is the distribution of the number of rainy days in Seattle in 60 months:

Number of Days	Frequency
5– 7	5
8–10	9
11–13	12
14–16	18
17–19	13
20–22	3
Total	60

Calculate the mean.

3.88   With reference to Exercise 3.87, find

(a) the median of the distribution;

⇔ (b) the quartiles of the distribution.

3.89   With reference to Exercise 3.87, find the 60th percentile of the distribution.

3.90   A producer of television commercials knows exactly how much money was spent on the production of each of 10 one-minute commercials. Give one example each of a problem in which these data would be looked upon as

(a) a population;   (b) a sample.

3.91   Find the median position for

(a) $n = 31$;   (b) $n = 80$.

3.92   The 1990 earnings, in thousands of dollars, for 10 women working in industrial sales are

28.2   30.5   25.8   20.4   23.2   32.5   33.0   26.4   28.8   27.3

(a) Find the median of these earnings.

(b) Find the mean of these earnings.

3.93   For the data of Exercise 3.92, find the quartiles of the women's 1990 earnings.

3.94   A student scores 78 on her first test, 83 on the second test, and 88 on the final. The instructor considers the second test to be twice as important as the first test and the final to be three times as important as the second test. What is the student's weighted mean score for the three tests?

3.95   During the three weeks before Christmas, 12 persons shopped, on the average, in 5.75 clothing stores. Is it possible that at least seven of them shopped in 10 or more stores?

3.96   Twenty registered voters are asked whether they consider themselves Democrats, Republicans, or Independents. Use the following results to determine their modal choice:

Democrat	Democrat	Democrat	Democrat	Independent
Independent	Independent	Independent	Republican	Democrat
Independent	Independent	Independent	Republican	Independent
Republican	Democrat	Democrat	Independent	Republican

3.97   Given a sample of 23 observations, find the positions of the median and the two quartiles.

3.98   Given a sample of 24 observations, find the positions of the median and the two quartiles.

3.99   The following values are the percentage of sulfur retention in 42 watershed areas of the northeastern United States, reported in 1989:

18.3	41.9	32.4	33.2	25.9	60.6	19.0	54.7	48.8	43.0
57.4	44.2	56.2	59.6	43.5	17.8	37.6	66.2	49.7	39.0
53.7	39.8	21.8	43.2	24.3	42.0	19.3	42.1	53.9	28.2
47.8	34.3	33.0	33.2	42.2	31.7	38.0	45.3	41.7	45.7
37.0	51.0								

Construct a stem-and-leaf display and use it to find the median of these data.

3.100   The following are the number of passengers on 46 sightseeing buses in Boston, Massachusetts:

Number of Persons	Frequency
15 or fewer	5
16–20	8
21–25	11
26–30	13
31–35	6
36–40	3
Total	46

If possible, find the mean and the median.

3.101   With reference to the distribution of the preceding exercise, find, if possible,

(a) the lower quartile;   (b) the upper quartile;

(c) the 40th percentile;   (d) the 80th percentile.

3.102 Given

$$x_1 = 3, \quad x_2 = 5, \quad x_3 = -2, \quad x_4 = 1, \quad x_5 = 3, \quad x_6 = -4, \quad x_7 = 2, \quad x_8 = 4$$

find

(a) $\sum_{i=1}^{6} x_i$; (b) $\sum_{i=3}^{8} x_i$.

3.103 If the mean salary of all male employees of company *A* exceeds that of all male employees of company *B*, and the mean salary of all female employees of company *A* exceeds that of all female employees of company *B*, does it follow that the mean salary of all employees of company *A* exceeds that of all employees of company *B*? Explain your answer.

3.104 Baseball batting averages are obtained by dividing the number of hits that a player gets by his number of at-bats, expressing the result as a three-figure decimal. For example, a player with 30 hits and 100 at-bats has a batting average of .300. Here are some values from the 1990 baseball season:

Player	League	Hits	At-bats
George Brett	American	179	544
Willie McGee	American	31	113
Willie McGee	National	168	501
Eddie Murray	National	184	558

George Brett had the highest batting average in the American League, and Willie McGee had the highest batting average in the National League. McGee, however, played in both leagues. Show that Eddie Murray had the highest overall batting average, even though he was not best in his league.

3.11 REFERENCES

Informal discussions of the ethics involved in choosing among averages and other questions of ethics in statistics in general are given in

HOOKE, R., *How to Tell the Liars from the Statisticians.* New York: Marcel Dekker, Inc., 1983.

HUFF, D., *How to Lie with Statistics.* New York: W.W. Norton & Company, Inc., 1954.

For further information about the use and interpretation of hinges, see the books on exploratory data analysis referred to on page 42.

Simplification of calculations in grouped data by use of "coding" is explained in Appendix C of

HAMBURG, M., *Basic Statistics: A Modern Approach.* New York: Harcourt Brace Jovanovich, Inc., 1974.

A discussion of the mean of an infinite population is found on page 187 of

NETER, J., WASSERMAN, W., and WHITMORE, G., *Applied Statistics,* 2nd ed. Boston: Allyn and Bacon, Inc., 1982.

CHAPTER 4

SUMMARIZING DATA: MEASURES OF VARIATION

*F*or *most sets of data the values are not all alike. The extent to which they vary is a serious concern of statistics. Consider the following examples:*

In a hospital where each patient's pulse rate is taken three times a day, that of patient A is 72, 76, and 74, and that of patient B is 72, 91, and 59. The mean pulse rate of the two patients is the same, 74, but observe the difference in variability. Whereas patient A's pulse rate is stable, that of patient B fluctuates widely.

A supermarket stocks certain 1-pound bags of mixed nuts, which on the average contain 12 almonds per bag. If all the bags contain anywhere from 10 to 14 almonds, the product is consistent and satisfactory, but the situation is quite different if some of the bags have no almonds but others have 20 or more.

Consider a basketball player who scores 22, 26, and 24 points in his first three games. A teammate scores 41, 13, and 18 in those games. Both players have the same average, 24, but the first player is much more consistent.

Measuring variability is of special importance in statistical inference. Suppose, for instance, that we have a coin which is slightly bent and we wonder whether there is still a fifty–fifty chance for a heads. What if we toss the coin 100 times and get 28 heads and 72 tails? Does the shortage of heads—only 28 where we might have expected 50—imply that the coin is not "fair"? To answer such questions we must have some idea about the magnitude of the fluctuations, or variations, that are brought about by chance when coins are tossed 100 times.

We need to assess the extent to which data disperse; the measures that will provide this information are called **measures of variation.** *In Sections 4.1 through 4.3 we present the most widely used measures of variation and some of their special applications. Measuring the variation of grouped data and some statistical descriptions other than measures of location and variation are explained in Sections 4.4 and 4.5, which are optional.* ◼

4.1   THE RANGE

To introduce a simple way of measuring variability, refer to the first of the three examples above, where the pulse rate of patient *A* varied from 72 to 76 while that of patient *B* varied from 59 to 91. These extreme (smallest and largest) values are indicative of the variability of the two sets of data, and just about the same information is conveyed if we take the differences between the respective extremes. So, let us make the following definition:

The **range** of a set of data is the largest value minus the smallest.

For patient *A* of the example above we get a range of 76 − 72 = 4, and for patient *B* a range of 91 − 59 = 32. Also, for the sulfur oxides emission data on page 23 the smallest value is 6.2, the largest value is 31.8, and the range is 31.8 − 6.2 = 25.6; and for the lifetimes of the five light bulbs on page 47 the smallest value is 922, the largest value is 967, and the range is 967 − 922 = 45.

The range is not difficult to calculate and to understand, and there is a natural curiosity about the minimum and maximum values. Nonetheless, it is not generally a useful measure of variation—the main shortcoming being that there is no indication concerning the dispersion of the values which fall between the two extremes. Each of the following sets of data

$$
\begin{array}{llllllllll}
\text{Set 1:} & 5 & 20 & 20 & 20 & 20 & 20 & 20 & 20 \\
\text{Set 2:} & 5 & 5 & 5 & 5 & 20 & 20 & 20 & 20 \\
\text{Set 3:} & 5 & 7 & 9 & 12 & 15 & 17 & 19 & 20
\end{array}
$$

has a range of 20 − 5 = 15, but the dispersion is entirely different in each case. Thus, the range is used mainly as a "quick and easy" indication of variability, for instance, in industrial quality control to keep a close check on raw materials or products by observing, and charting, the range of small samples taken at regular intervals of time.

Whereas the range covers all the values in a sample, a similar measure of variation covers (more or less) the middle 50 percent. It is the **interquartile range** $Q_3 − Q_1$ where Q_1 and Q_3 can be defined in various ways for ungrouped or grouped data as in Sections 3.5 and 3.7. For instance, for the nine history test scores on page 61 we might use

$$Q_3 − Q_1 = 89 − 73.5 = 15.5$$

and for the distribution of the sulfur oxides emission data we might use the values of Q_1 and Q_3 on page 71 and write

$$22.83 − 14.95 = 7.88$$

Some statisticians also use the **semi-interquartile range,** $\frac{1}{2}(Q_3 − Q_1)$, sometimes called the **quartile deviation.**

4.2   THE VARIANCE AND THE STANDARD DEVIATION

To define the **standard deviation,** by far the most generally useful measure of variation, let us observe that the dispersion of a set of data is small if the values are closely bunched about their mean, and that it is large if the values are scattered widely about their mean. It would seem reasonable, therefore, to measure the variation of a set of data in terms of the amounts by which the values deviate from their mean. If a set of numbers

$$x_1, \quad x_2, \quad x_3, \quad \ldots, \quad \text{and} \quad x_n$$

constituting a sample, has the mean $\bar{x}$, the differences

$$x_1 − \bar{x}, \quad x_2 − \bar{x}, \quad x_3 − \bar{x}, \quad \ldots, \quad \text{and} \quad x_n − \bar{x}$$

are called the **deviations from the mean,** which suggests that we might use their average (namely, their mean) as a measure of the variation of the sample. Unfortunately, this will not do. Unless the x's are all equal, some of the deviations will be positive, some will be negative, and as the reader was asked to show in Exercise 3.79 on page 75, the sum of the deviations from the mean, $\Sigma(x - \bar{x})$, and hence also their mean, is always zero.

Since we are really interested in the magnitude of the deviations, and not in whether they are positive or negative, we might simply ignore the signs and define a measure of variation in terms of the absolute values of the deviations from the mean. Indeed, if we add the deviations from the mean as if they were all positive or zero and divide by n, we obtain the statistical measure which is called the **mean deviation.** This measure has intuitive appeal, but because of the absolute values it leads to serious theoretical difficulties in problems of inference, and it is rarely used.

An alternative approach is to work with the squares of the deviations from the mean, as this will also eliminate the effect of the signs. Squares of real numbers cannot be negative; in fact, squares of the deviations from a mean are all positive unless a value happens to coincide with the mean. Then, if we average the squared deviations from the mean and take the square root of the result (to compensate for the fact that the deviations were squared), we have

$$\sqrt{\frac{\Sigma (x - \bar{x})^2}{n}}$$

which is how, traditionally, the standard deviation used to be defined. Expressing literally what we have done here mathematically, it is also called the **root-mean-square deviation.**

It is customary to modify this formula by dividing the sum of the squared deviations from the mean by $n - 1$ instead of n. Following this practice, which will be explained below, let us define the **sample standard deviation,** denoted by s, as

Sample Standard Deviation

$$s = \sqrt{\frac{\Sigma (x - \bar{x})^2}{n - 1}}$$

and its square, the **sample variance,** as

Sample Variance

$$s^2 = \frac{\Sigma (x - \bar{x})^2}{n - 1}$$

These formulas for the standard deviation and the variance apply to samples, but if we substitute μ for $\bar{x}$ and N for n, we obtain analogous formulas for the standard deviation and the variance of a population. It is common practice to denote the **population standard deviation** by σ (*sigma,* the Greek letter for lowercase s) when dividing by N. Thus we write

Population Standard Deviation

$$\sigma = \sqrt{\frac{\Sigma (x - \mu)^2}{N}}$$

Its square is the **population variance**

Population Variance	$$\sigma^2 = \frac{\Sigma (x - \mu)^2}{N}$$

Ordinarily, the purpose of calculating a sample statistic (such as the mean, the standard deviation, or the variance) is to estimate the corresponding population parameter. If we actually took many samples from a population which has the mean μ calculated the sample means $\bar{x}$, and then averaged all these estimates of μ, we should find that their average is very close to μ. However, if we calculated the variance of each sample by means of the formula

$$\frac{\Sigma (x - \bar{x})^2}{n}$$

and then averaged all these supposed estimates of σ^2, we would probably find that their average is less than σ^2. Theoretically, it can be shown that we can compensate for this by dividing by $n - 1$ instead of n in the formula for s^2. Estimators which have the desirable property that their values will on the average equal the quantity they are supposed to estimate are said to be **unbiased;** otherwise, they are said to be **biased.** So, we say that $\bar{x}$ is an unbiased estimator of the population mean μ, and that s^2 is an unbiased estimator of the population variance σ^2. It does not follow from this that s is also an unbiased estimator of σ, but when n is large the bias is small and can usually be ignored.

In calculating the sample standard deviation using the formula by which it is defined, we must

1. Find $\bar{x}$.
2. Determine the n deviations from the mean $x - \bar{x}$.
3. Square these deviations.
4. Add all the squared deviations.
5. Divide by $n - 1$.
6. Take the square root of the result obtained in step 5.

In actual practice, this formula is rarely used, but we shall illustrate it here to emphasize what is really measured by σ and s.

Example

On six consecutive Sundays, a tow-truck operator received

$$9 \quad 7 \quad 11 \quad 10 \quad 13 \quad 7$$

service calls. Calculate s.

solution

First calculating the mean, we obtain

$$\bar{x} = \frac{9 + 7 + 11 + 10 + 13 + 7}{6} = \frac{57}{6} = 9.5$$

and the work required to find $\Sigma \, (x - \bar{x})^2$ may be arranged as in the following table:

x	$x - \bar{x}$	$(x - \bar{x})^2$
9	−0.5	0.25
7	−2.5	6.25
11	1.5	2.25
10	0.5	0.25
13	3.5	12.25
7	−2.5	6.25
Total	0.0	27.50

Then, dividing by $6 - 1 = 5$ and taking the square root, we have

$$s = \sqrt{\frac{27.50}{5}} = \sqrt{5.5} \approx 2.3^{\dagger}$$

Note in the table above that the total for the middle column is zero; since that must always be the case, it provides a check on the calculations. ◪ ◪ ◪

It was easy to calculate s in this example because the data were whole numbers and the mean was exact to one decimal. Otherwise, the calculations required by the formula defining s can be quite tedious, and, unless we can get s directly with a statistical calculator or a computer, it helps to use the computing formula

Sample Standard Deviation

$$s = \sqrt{\frac{S_{xx}}{n - 1}} \qquad where \; S_{xx} = \Sigma \, x^2 - \frac{(\Sigma \, x)^2}{n}$$

Example

Use this computing formula for s to rework the preceding example.

solution

First we calculate $\Sigma \, x$ and $\Sigma \, x^2$, getting

x	x^2
9	81
7	49
11	121
10	100
13	169
7	49
57	569

[†]See the footnote on page 51 regarding the use of the symbol $\approx$.

Then, substituting $\Sigma x = 57$ and $\Sigma x^2 = 569$, together with $n = 6$, we find that

$$S_{xx} = 569 - \frac{(57)^2}{6} = 27.50$$

This gives us

$$s = \sqrt{\frac{27.50}{6 - 1}} = \sqrt{5.5} \approx 2.3,$$

agreeing with the result we obtained before.　　　　◪ ◪ ◪

The computing formula for s can also be used to find σ; the denominator $n - 1$ must be replaced by N.

4.3　APPLICATIONS OF THE STANDARD DEVIATION

In subsequent chapters, sample standard deviations are used mainly to estimate population standard deviations in problems of inference. To give you more of a feeling for what a standard deviation really measures, we devote this section to some applications.

In the argument which led to the definition of the standard deviation, we observed that the dispersion of a set of data is small if the values are bunched closely about their mean, and that it is large if the values are scattered widely about their mean. Correspondingly, we can now say that if the standard deviation of a set of data is small, the values are concentrated near the mean, and if the standard deviation is large, the values are scattered widely about the mean. This idea is expressed more formally by the following theorem, called **Chebyshev's theorem** after the Russian mathematician P. L. Chebyshev (1821–1894):

Chebyshev's Theorem	*For any set of data (population or sample) and any constant k greater than 1, the proportion of the data that must lie within k standard deviations on either side of the mean is at least* $$1 - \frac{1}{k^2}$$

Thus, we can be sure that at least

$$1 - \frac{1}{2^2} = \frac{3}{4}, \quad \text{or 75 percent}$$

of the values in any set of data must lie within two standard deviations on either side of the mean; at least

$$1 - \frac{1}{3^2} = \frac{8}{9}, \quad \text{or 88.9 percent}$$

must lie within three standard deviations on either side of the mean; and at least

$$1 - \frac{1}{5^2} = \frac{24}{25} \quad \text{or 96 percent}$$

must lie within five standard deviations on either side of the mean. Here we arbitrarily let $k = 2, 3,$ and 5.

Example

If all the 1-pound cans of coffee filled by a food processor have a mean weight of 16.00 ounces with a standard deviation of 0.02 ounce, at least what percentage of the cans must contain between 15.80 and 16.20 ounces of coffee?

solution

Since k standard deviations, or $k(0.02)$, equals

$$16.20 - 16.00 = 16.00 - 15.80 = 0.20$$

we have

$$k(0.02) = 0.20 \quad \text{and} \quad k = \frac{0.20}{0.02} = 10$$

According to Chebyshev's theorem, it follows that at least

$$1 - \frac{1}{10^2} = 0.99 \quad \text{or 99 percent}$$

of the cans must contain between 15.80 and 16.20 ounces of coffee.   ◢ ◢ ◢

Chebyshev's theorem applies to any kind of data, but it tells us only "at least what percentage" must lie between certain limits. For nearly all sets of data, the actual percentage of data lying between the limits is much greater than that specified by Chebyshev's theorem.

For distributions having the general shape of the cross section of a bell (see Figure 4.1), we can make the following much stronger statement:

(1) about 68% of the values will lie within one standard deviation of the mean, that is, between $\bar{x} - s$ and $\bar{x} + s$;

Bell-shaped distribution.

(2) about 95% of the values will lie within two standard deviations of the mean, that is, between $\bar{x} - 2s$ and $\bar{x} + 2s$;

(3) about 99.7% of the values will lie between three standard deviations of the mean, that is, between $\bar{x} - 3s$ and $\bar{x} + 3s$.

This result is sometimes referred to as the **empirical rule,** presumably because such percentages are observed in practice. Actually, it is a theoretical result based on the normal distribution, which we shall study in Chapter 9 (in particular, see Exercise 9.14 on page 263).

Example

Use the values of $\bar{x}$ and s given in the computer printout of Figure 3.3 on page 68 to determine what percentage of the sulfur oxides emission data on page 23 actually falls within one standard deviation of the mean, within two standard deviations of the mean, and within three standard deviations of the mean.

solution

Since $\bar{x} = 18.896$ and $s = 5.6565$, we shall first have to determine what percentage of the data falls between

$$18.896 - 5.6565 = 13.2395 \quad \text{and} \quad 18.896 + 5.6565 = 24.5525.$$

Counting 14 values below 13.2395 and 14 values above 24.5525, we find that $80 - 28 = 52$ values, and hence

$$\frac{52}{80} \cdot 100\% = 65 \text{ percent}$$

of the data, falls between the two limits. Similarly, we find that

$$\frac{78}{80} \cdot 100\% = 97.5 \text{ percent}$$

of the data falls within two standard deviations of the mean, and that

$$\frac{80}{80} \cdot 100 = 100 \text{ percent}$$

of the data fall within three standard deviations of the mean.

The results which we have obtained here are not exactly 68, 95, and 99.7 percent but it would seem reasonable to say that they are "about 68 percent," "about 95 percent," and "about 99.7 percent." Also, Figure 2.2 on page 31 shows that the distribution of the data has the shape of a somewhat lopsided bell, so we cannot really expect perfect results.

On page 81 we gave examples in which knowledge about the variability of the data was of importance. This is also the case when we want to compare numbers belonging to different sets of data. To illustrate, suppose that the final examination in a French course consists of two parts, vocabulary and grammar, and that a certain student scored 66 points in the vocabulary part and 80 points in the grammar part. At first glance it would seem that the student did much better in grammar than in vocabulary, but suppose that all the students in the class averaged 51 points in the vocabulary part with a standard deviation of 12, and 72 points in the grammar part with a standard deviation of 16. Thus, we can argue that the student's score in the vocabulary part is

$$\frac{66 - 51}{12} = 1.25$$

standard deviations above the average for the class, while her score in the grammar part is only

$$\frac{80 - 72}{16} = 0.50$$

standard deviation above the average for the class. Whereas the original scores cannot be meaningfully compared, these new scores, expressed in terms of standard deviations, can. Clearly, the given student rates much higher on her command of French vocabulary than on her knowledge of French grammar, compared to the rest of the class.

What we have done here consisted of converting the grades into **standard units** or **z-scores**. In general, if x is a measurement belonging to a set of data having the mean $\bar{x}$ (or μ) and the standard deviation s (or σ), then its value in standard units, denoted by z, is

Converting to Standard Units	$$z = \frac{x - \bar{x}}{s} \quad \text{or} \quad z = \frac{x - \mu}{\sigma}$$

depending on whether the data constitute a sample or a population. In these units, z tells us how many standard deviations a value lies above or below the mean of the set of data to which it belongs. Standard units will be used frequently in later chapters.

Example

Two-year-old models of a certain kind of car have been selling on the average for $7,860 with a standard deviation of $820, while three-year-old models of the same kind of car have been selling on the average for $6,400 with a standard deviation of $960. Leaving all other considerations aside, is a two-year-old model priced at $6,960 a better buy than a three-year-old model priced at $5,400?

solution

Converting both prices into standard units, we get

$$\frac{6,960 - 7,860}{820} \approx -1.10$$

for the two-year-old car, and

$$\frac{5,400 - 6,400}{960} \approx -1.04$$

for the three-year-old car. Even though the two-year-old model is priced $900 below average and the three-year-old model is priced $1,000 below average, the two-year-old model is priced relatively lower for cars of the same kind and, hence, it is a greater bargain. ◪ ◪ ◪

One disadvantage of the standard deviation as a measure of variation is that it depends on the units of measurement. For instance, the weights of certain objects may have a standard deviation of 0.1 ounce or 2,835 milligrams, which is the same, but neither value really tells us whether it reflects a great deal of variation or very little variation. If we are weighing the eggs of small birds, either figure would reflect a great deal of variation, but this would not be the case if we are weighing 100-pound bags of potatoes. What we need in a situation like this is a **measure of relative variation,** such as the **coefficient of variation**

Coefficient of Variation	$V = \dfrac{s}{\bar{x}} \cdot 100\%$ *or* $V = \dfrac{\sigma}{\mu} \cdot 100\%$

which expresses the standard deviation as a percentage of what is being measured, at least on the average.

Example

Several measurements of the diameter of a ball bearing made with one micrometer had a mean of 2.49 mm and a standard deviation of 0.012 mm, and several measurements of the unstretched length of a spring made with another micrometer had a mean of 0.75 in. with a standard deviation of 0.002 in. Which of the two micrometers is relatively more precise?

solution

Calculating the two coefficients of variation, we get

$$\frac{0.012}{2.49} \cdot 100\% \approx 0.48\% \quad \text{and} \quad \frac{0.002}{0.75} \cdot 100\% \approx 0.27\%$$

Thus, the measurements of the length of the spring are relatively less variable, which means that the second micrometer is more precise. Both coefficients of variation are less than 1 percent, so that both micrometers qualify as highly precise. ◪ ◪ ◪

◪ EXERCISES

4.1 The following are the response times in seconds of a smoke alarm after the release of smoke from a fixed source:

$$12 \quad 9 \quad 11 \quad 7 \quad 9 \quad 14 \quad 6 \quad 10$$

Find the range.

4.2 The numbers that follow are the yields (in trays per acre) for sun-dried raisins over a 10-year period in California.

$$715 \quad 825 \quad 640 \quad 900 \quad 790$$
$$965 \quad 895 \quad 700 \quad 915 \quad 945$$

Find the range.

4.3   The following are the closing prices for two stocks on five consecutive Fridays:

$$\text{Stock A: } 15\tfrac{7}{8} \quad 15\tfrac{1}{2} \quad 16\tfrac{3}{8} \quad 16\tfrac{5}{8} \quad 15\tfrac{3}{4}$$
$$\text{Stock B: } 22\tfrac{1}{8} \quad 22 \quad 21\tfrac{7}{8} \quad 22\tfrac{1}{8} \quad 22\tfrac{1}{4}$$

Find the range for each stock.

4.4   Twenty-five employees of a motel chain, given a course in first aid, obtained these scores on a test administered after the course:

$$17 \quad 19 \quad 14 \quad 20 \quad 17 \quad 17 \quad 12 \quad 15 \quad 15 \quad 16 \quad 16 \quad 19 \quad 18$$
$$15 \quad 16 \quad 16 \quad 17 \quad 18 \quad 17 \quad 13 \quad 17 \quad 16 \quad 14 \quad 18 \quad 17$$

Find the range.

4.5   Find the quartiles for the data of Exercise 4.4, and then find the interquartile range. Is it surprising that the interquartile range is less than half the range?

4.6   In Exercise 3.43 on page 65, we noted the stopping distances for 21 drivers traveling at 30 miles per hour. These values were

$$69 \quad 58 \quad 70 \quad 80 \quad 46 \quad 61 \quad 65 \quad 74 \quad 75 \quad 55 \quad 67$$
$$56 \quad 70 \quad 72 \quad 61 \quad 66 \quad 58 \quad 68 \quad 70 \quad 68 \quad 58$$

Find the range of these values.

4.7   Find the interquartile range for the stopping distances in Exercise 4.6.

4.8   In the ferryboat example on page 57, the number of passengers in 50 runs were tabulated in the following stem-and-leaf display:

3	57		3 | 5 means 35
4	01359		
5	001233467889		
6	01224455678		
7	011355789		
8	002469		
9	1257		
10	3		

Find the range.

4.9   In the ferryboat example of Exercise 4.8, find the quartiles and the semi-interquartile range.

4.10   In five attempts, it took a person

$$12 \quad 18 \quad 14 \quad 11 \quad 15$$

minutes to change the oil in a particular make of automobile. Calculate the standard deviation of this sample using

(a) the formula which defines s;   (b) the computing formula for s.

4.11   Four purchases of jelly beans in bags labeled "one pound" contained

$$16.2 \quad 15.9 \quad 15.8 \quad 16.1$$

ounces. Calculate s using

(a) the formula which defines s;   (b) the computing formula for s.

4.12   The numbers of misdirected luggage cases reported for six consecutive weeks at a small airport were

$$13 \quad 8 \quad 15 \quad 11 \quad 3 \quad 10$$

Find the variance of these figures using

(a) the formula by which s^2 is defined;   (b) the computing formula for s^2.

4.13   On four days it took a person

$$37 \quad 32 \quad 35 \quad 41$$

minutes to drive to work.

(a) Use the computing formula which defines s to compute the standard deviation of these data.

(b) Subtract 30 from each and then use the computing formula for s to calculate the standard deviation. What general rule does this suggest for simplifying the calculation of s?

4.14   The following values are the daily sales, Monday through Friday, of newspapers at a newsstand outside an office building:

$$231 \quad 228 \quad 244 \quad 240 \quad 236$$

Find the standard deviation s.

4.15   Each of the following lists contains an even number of items. Further, each list contains just two different values. Find the standard deviation for each list. Can you relate this standard deviation to the difference between the values? For this exercise, the formula which defines s will be somewhat easier to use.

(a)   16   16   20   20

(b) 100   100   100   200   200   200

(c)   60   60   60   60   80   80   80   80

4.16   Each of the following lists contains just one value that is different from all the others. Find the standard deviation for each list. Can you relate this standard deviation to the difference between the values?

(a) 6   6   6   10

(b) 6   10   10   10

(c) 20   20   20   24

(d) 20   20   20   20   24

(e) 20   20   20   20   20   24

4.17   It is asserted that for samples of size $n = 4$, the range should be roughly twice as large as the standard deviation. Check this claim with reference to the following data, representing the numbers of emergency surgeries that were performed at a hospital on four days:

$$3 \quad 6 \quad 2 \quad 6$$

4.18   It has been claimed that for samples of size $n = 10$, the range should be roughly three times as large as the standard deviation. Check this claim with reference to the following data, representing the emission scores of 10 automobiles:

$$18 \quad 21 \quad 16 \quad 24 \quad 28 \quad 20 \quad 22 \quad 29 \quad 19 \quad 25$$

4.19   If we add the same constant c to each item in a set of data, the mean and the median of the new set equal the mean and the median of the original set plus the constant c, while the range and the standard deviation remain unchanged.

(a) Verify that for a sample consisting of the values

$$-3 \quad 4 \quad 1 \quad 5 \quad 3 \quad 4 \quad 0$$

the mean is 2, the median is 3, the range is 8, and the standard deviation is $\sqrt{8}$, and that after we add 3 to each value the mean becomes 5, the median becomes 6, but the range is still 8 and the standard deviation is still $\sqrt{8}$.

(b) Find the standard deviation of the data in Exercise 4.4 after subtracting 10 from each value.

4.20   If we multiply each item in a set of data by the same positive constant b, the mean, median, range, and standard deviation of the new set equal the mean, median, range, and standard deviation of the original set multiplied by b.

(a) With reference to the seven sample values of part (a) of Exercise 4.19, show that if each value is multiplied by 2 the mean becomes 4, the median becomes 6, the range becomes 16, and the standard deviation becomes

$$\sqrt{32} = 2\sqrt{8}$$

(b) During four pit stops, the front-tire man changed a racing car's right front tire in

$$10.8 \quad 12.0 \quad 10.5 \quad 10.7$$

seconds. Calculate the standard deviation by first multiplying each figure by 10, subtracting 110, determining s for the resulting figures, and then dividing by 10.

4.21   According to Chebyshev's theorem, what can we assert about the proportion of any set of data that must lie within k standard deviations of the mean when

(a) $k = 6$;   (b) $k = 12$?

4.22   According to Chebyshev's theorem, what can we assert about the percentage of any set of data that must lie within k standard deviations of the mean when

(a) $k = 4$;   (b) $k = 9$?

4.23   The weights of a certain brand of imported Puerto Rican mangoes have a mean weight of 360 grams and a standard deviation of 40 grams. What does Chebyshev's theorem tell us about the percentage of mangoes with weights between 340 and 380 grams?

4.24   The orders received by a mail-order company have a mean dollar amount of $34 and a standard deviation of $40. What does Chebyshev's theorem tell us about the percentage of orders below $114?

4.25   According to Chebyshev's theorem, what can we assert about the percentage of any set of data that must lie within k standard deviations on either side of the mean when

(a) $k = 5$;   (b) $k = 8$;   (c) $k = 10$;   (d) $k = 20$?

4.26   An airline's records show that its flights between two cities arrive on the average 5.4 minutes late with a standard deviation of 1.4 minutes. At least what percentage of its flights between the two cities arrive anywhere between

(a) 2.6 minutes late and 8.2 minutes late;

(b) 1.6 minutes early and 12.4 minutes late?

4.27   A study of the nutritional value of a certain kind of bread shows that on the average one slice contains 0.260 milligram of thiamine (vitamin B_1) with a standard deviation of 0.005 milligram. According to Chebyshev's theorem, between what values must the thiamine content be of

(a) at least $\frac{35}{36}$ of all slices of this bread;

(b) at least $\frac{80}{81}$ of all slices of this bread?

4.28   With reference to Exercise 4.27, at least what percentage of the slices of the given kind of bread must have a thiamine content between 0.245 and 0.275 milligram? What can we say about this percentage if it can be assumed that the distribution of the thiamine contents of the slices of bread is bell-shaped?

4.29   The data below are the numbers of customers a restaurant served for lunch on 120 weekdays. These were given in Exercise 2.28 on page 29.

50	64	55	51	60	41	71	53	63	64	46	59	66	45	61
57	65	62	58	65	55	61	50	55	53	57	58	66	53	56
64	46	59	49	64	60	58	64	42	47	59	62	56	63	61
68	57	51	61	51	60	59	67	52	52	58	64	43	60	62
48	62	56	63	55	73	60	69	53	66	54	52	56	59	65
60	61	59	63	56	62	56	62	57	57	52	63	48	58	64
59	43	67	52	58	47	63	53	54	67	57	61	76	78	60
66	63	58	60	55	61	59	74	62	49	63	65	55	61	54

(a) Use a computer package to determine $\bar{x}$ and s for these data.

(b) Use the results of part (a) to find the percentages of the data values that lie within one, two, and three standard deviations of the mean. Compare these with the percentages expected according to the rule on pages 87–88. (Exercise 2.28 indicates that the distribution of these values is reasonably bell-shaped.)

4.30   In a Southeastern city, supermarkets charge on the average $3.67 per pound for sirloin steak (with a standard deviation of $0.40), $1.12 per pound for chicken drumsticks (with a standard deviation of $0.11), and $8.18 per pound for leg of veal (with a standard deviation of $0.92). If a supermarket in this city charges $3.59 per pound for sirloin steak, $1.09 per pound for chicken drumsticks, and $7.69 per pound for leg of veal, which of the three items is, relatively speaking, the best bargain?

4.31   Two men are on a weight-reducing diet. The first belongs to an age/body type group for which the mean weight is 145 pounds with a standard deviation of 15 pounds. The second belongs to an age/body type group for which the mean weight is 165 pounds with a standard deviation of 20 pounds. If their respective weights are 178 and 204 pounds, who is more definitely overweight for his age/body type group?

4.32   A laboratory technician studied recent measurements made with two different instruments. The first measured the diameter of a ball bearing and obtained a mean of 4.96 mm with a standard deviation of 0.022 mm. The second measured the diameter of a metal rod and obtained a mean of 6.48 mm with a standard deviation of 0.032 mm. Which of the two instruments was relatively more precise?

4.33   One patient's blood pressure was measured daily for several weeks. These measurements had mean 188 with standard deviation 14.2. A second patient was also measured daily, obtaining an average of 136 with standard deviation 8.6. Which patient's blood pressure is relatively more variable?

4.34   On sixteen days a restaurant had the following numbers of orders for chicken and steak:

Chicken	46	55	43	48	54	65	36	40	51	53	64	32	41	46	53	47
Steak	39	41	25	30	46	36	37	23	30	33	50	44	41	28	35	37

Calculate the two coefficients of variation to determine for which item the number of orders is relatively more variable.

4.35   An alternative measure of relative variation is the **coefficient of quartile variation,** defined as

$$\frac{Q_3 - Q_1}{Q_3 + Q_1} \cdot 100\%$$

where Q_1 and Q_3 are the lower and upper quartiles. Find the coefficient of quartile variation for the stopping distances of Exercise 4.6 on page 91.

4.36 Compute the coefficient of quartile variation for the data given in Exercise 4.4 and used in Exercise 4.5 on page 91.

4.4   THE DESCRIPTION OF GROUPED DATA �

To determine the standard deviation of a distribution, we make the same approximation as on page 67—**to each value falling into a class we assign the value of the corresponding class mark.** Again letting $x_1, x_2, ...,$ and x_k denote the class marks, and $f_1, f_2, ...,$ and f_k the corresponding class frequencies, then the sum of all the measurements or observations is represented by

$$x_1 f_1 + x_2 f_2 + x_3 f_3 + \cdots + x_k f_k = \Sigma\, x \cdot f$$

and the sum of their squares is represented by

$$x_1^2 f_1 + x_2^2 f_2 + x_3^2 f_3 + \cdots + x_k^2 f_k = \Sigma\, x^2 \cdot f$$

The formula for $\bar{x}$ and the computing formula for s can be written as

$$\bar{x} = \frac{\Sigma\, x \cdot f}{n} \quad \text{and} \quad S_{xx} = \Sigma\, x^2 \cdot f - \frac{(\Sigma\, x \cdot f)^2}{n}$$

Then

$$s = \sqrt{\frac{S_{xx}}{n-1}}$$

To get the corresponding formulas for $\bar{x}$ and S_{xx} for a population, we replace n by N; then in the formula for s, we replace $n-1$ by N.

Example

Find the mean and the standard deviation of the following distribution, giving the amounts of time that 80 college students devoted to leisure activities during a typical school week:

Hours	Frequency
10–14	8
15–19	28
20–24	27
25–29	12
30–34	4
35–39	1
Total	80

solution

To obtain $\Sigma\, x \cdot f$ and $\Sigma\, x^2 \cdot f$, we perform the calculations shown in the following table:

Class Mark x	Frequency			
	x^2	f	$x \cdot f$	$x^2 \cdot f$
12	144	8	96	1,152
17	289	28	476	8,092
22	484	27	594	13,068
27	729	12	324	8,748
32	1,024	4	128	4,096
37	1,369	1	37	1,369
	Total	80	1,655	36,525

Then, substitution into the formulas yields

$$\bar{x} = \frac{1,655}{80} = 20.6875 \approx 20.69$$

and

$$S_{xx} = 36,525 - \frac{(1,655)^2}{80} \approx 2287.19 \quad \text{and then} \quad s = \sqrt{\frac{2287.19}{79}} \approx 5.38$$

4.5   SOME FURTHER DESCRIPTIONS �

So far we have discussed only statistical descriptions that come under the general heading of measures of location or measures of variation. Actually, there is no limit to the number of ways in which statistical data can be described, and statisticians continually develop new methods of describing characteristics of numerical data that are of interest in particular problems. In this section we consider briefly the problem of describing the overall shape of a distribution.

Although frequency distributions can assume almost any shape or form, most of the distributions we meet in practice can be described fairly well by a few standard types. Foremost in importance is the symmetrical **bell-shaped distribution** shown in Figure 4.2; it is symmetrical about the dashed vertical line. The other two distributions of Figure 4.2 can still, by a stretch of the imagination, be called bell-shaped, but they are not symmetrical. Distributions like these, having a "tail" on one side or the other, are said to be **skewed;** if the tail is on the left we say it is **negatively skewed,** and if the tail is on the right we say that it is

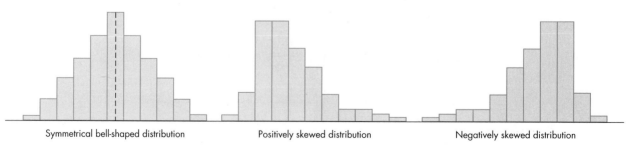

Symmetrical bell-shaped distribution   Positively skewed distribution   Negatively skewed distribution

FIGURE 4.2 _____ *Bell-shaped distribution and skewed distributions.*

positively skewed. Distributions of incomes or wages are often positively skewed because of the presence of some relatively high values that are not offset by correspondingly low values.

The concepts of symmetry and skewness apply to any kind of data, not only distributions. Of course, for a large set of data we may just group the data and draw and study a histogram, but if that is not enough, we can use any one of several statistical **measures of skewness.** A relatively easy one is based on the fact that when there is perfect symmetry as in the distribution at the left of Figure 4.2, the mean and the median will coincide. When there is positive skewness and some of the high values are not offset by correspondingly low values, the mean will be greater than the median (see Figure 4.3); and when there is negative

FIGURE 4.3

Mean and median of a positively skewed distribution.

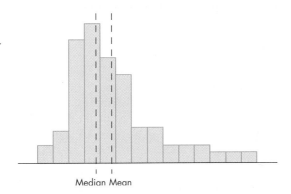

Median Mean

skewness and some of the low values are not offset by correspondingly high values, the mean will be smaller than the median. This relationship between the mean and the median can be used to define a relatively simple measure of skewness. It is called the **Pearsonian coefficient of skewness,** and it is given by

Pearsonian Coefficient of Skewness	$SK = \dfrac{3(mean - median)}{standard\ deviation}$

For a perfectly symmetrical distribution the value of SK is 0, and in general its values must fall between −3 and 3. (Division by the standard deviation makes SK independent of the scale of measurement.)

Example

Use the results obtained on pages 67–68 and 70, along with $s = 5.55$, to find the Pearsonian coefficient of skewness for the distribution of the sulfur oxides emission data.

solution

Substituting $\bar{x} = 18.85$, $\tilde{x} = 19.03$, and $s = 5.55$ into the formula, we get

$$SK = \frac{3(18.85 - 19.03)}{5.55} \approx -0.01$$

Since this value is so close to zero, we can say that the distribution is nearly symmetrical. This is also apparent from the histogram of Figure 2.2 on page 31. ◪ ◪ ◪

Besides the distributions we have discussed in this section, two others sometimes met in practice are the **reverse J-shaped** and **U-shaped** distributions shown in Figure 4.4. As can be seen from this figure, the names of these distributions literally describe their shape. Examples of such distributions may be found in Exercises 4.47 on page 99 and Exercise 4.50 on page 100.

FIGURE 4.4

Reverse J-shaped and U-shaped distributions.

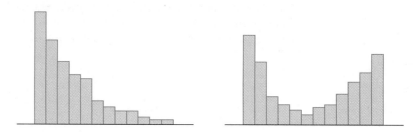

Note that the U-shaped distribution has two peaks, so that it is often described as **bimodal;** distributions with one peak are called **unimodal.**

Box plots, introduced in Section 3.5, can also be useful in describing distributions.

◪   EXERCISES

4.37   In a factory or office, the time during working hours in which a machine is not operating as a result of breakage or failure is called a **downtime.** The following distribution shows a sample of the length of the downtimes of a certain machine:

Downtime (minutes)	Frequency
0– 9	2
10–19	15
20–29	17
30–39	13
40–49	3
Total	50

Find (a) the mean and the median;   (b) the standard deviation.

4.38   Find $\bar{x}$ and s for the following distribution of the weekly earnings of 125 wage earners.

Weekly earnings (*dollars*)	Frequency
120.00–129.99	9
130.00–139.99	20
140.00–149.99	36
150.00–159.99	30
160.00–169.99	15
170.00–179.99	11
180.00–189.99	4
Total	125

Observe that the class marks are

$$\$124.995 \quad \$134.995 \quad \$144.995$$

and so on. The computations will be somewhat easier if you raise these by $0.005 to

$$\$125 \quad \$135 \quad \$145$$

and so on. This action will have the effect of raising each value in the list, on average, by one-half cent.

4.39   Calculate the Pearsonian coefficient of skewness for the distribution of the preceding exercise and discuss the symmetry or skewness of the data.

4.40   Exercise 3.59 lists this distribution of grades on a geography exam:

Grade	Number of students
10–24	44
25–39	70
40–54	92
55–69	147
70–84	115
85–99	32
Total	500

Calculate s for this grade distribution.

4.41   Discuss the symmetry or skewness of the data of Exercise 4.40, using the Pearsonian coefficient of skewness. The results of Exercises 3.59 and 3.60 on page 72 may be helpful.

4.42   In a sample of 30 three-minute intervals, a fast-food restaurant served

$$\begin{array}{cccccccccccccccc} 4 & 5 & 5 & 8 & 7 & 3 & 5 & 6 & 9 & 5 & 6 & 5 & 4 & 7 & 3 \\ 5 & 10 & 6 & 4 & 5 & 6 & 9 & 4 & 5 & 3 & 8 & 6 & 7 & 4 & 5 \end{array}$$

customers. Calculate the Pearsonian coefficient of skewness and discuss the symmetry or skewness of these data.

4.43   Construct a boxplot for the data of the preceding exercise and discuss the symmetry or skewness of the data.

4.44   Draw a boxplot for the data of Exercise 3.42 on page 65 and discuss their symmetry or skewness.

4.45   Draw a boxplot for the data of Exercise 4.6 on page 91, and discuss the symmetry or skewness of the stopping distances. The results of Exercise 3.43 on page 65 may be helpful.

4.46   Draw a boxplot for the NBA data of Exercise 3.35 on page 64 and discuss their symmetry or skewness.

4.47   The following are the numbers of 6's obtained in 50 rolls of four dice:

$$\begin{array}{cccccccccccccccc} 0 & 0 & 1 & 0 & 0 & 0 & 2 & 0 & 0 & 1 & 0 & 0 & 0 & 0 & 1 \\ 1 & 0 & 1 & 2 & 0 & 0 & 1 & 0 & 0 & 1 & 1 & 0 & 1 & 0 \\ 0 & 1 & 2 & 1 & 0 & 0 & 3 & 1 & 1 & 0 & 0 & 0 & 0 & 1 & 2 \\ 1 & 0 & 0 & 1 & 1 \end{array}$$

Construct a frequency distribution and a histogram, and discuss the overall shape of the data.

4.48   Draw a boxplot for the data of Exercise 4.47. What features of the boxplot suggest that the data have a somewhat unusual shape?

4.49   The following values are the number of loaves of unsold bread at Carl's bakery at closing time:

```
0  0  4  2  0  1  0  2  0  4
1  0  0  3  2  0  1  0  0  0
2  0  0  1  0  0  3  2  1  7
0  1  0  0  2  0  0  3  2  1
```

Construct a boxplot for these values and discuss the overall shape of the data.

4.50   If a coin is flipped five times in a row, the result may be represented by a sequence of H's and T's, where H stands for heads and T for tails. Having obtained such a sequence of H's and T's, we can then check after each successive flip whether the number of heads exceeds the number of tails. For instance, for the sequence

HHTTH,

heads is ahead after the first flip, after the second flip, after the third flip, not after the fourth flip, but again after the fifth flip; altogether, it is ahead four times. Actually repeating this experiment sixty times, we got

TTHHH,   THHTT,   ...,   and   TTTHT

and found that heads was ahead

```
1  1  5  0  0  5  0  1  2  0  1  0  5  1  0
0  5  0  0  0  0  1  0  0  5  0  2  0  1  0
5  5  0  5  4  3  5  0  5  0  1  5  0  1  5
3  1  5  5  1  2  4  2  3  0  5  5  0  0  0
```

times. Construct a frequency distribution and a histogram, and discuss the overall shape of the data.

4.51   Draw a boxplot for the data of the preceding exercise. What feature of the boxplot suggests that the data have a very unusual shape?

4.6   CHECKLIST OF KEY TERMS[†]   *(with page references to their definitions)*

⬦ Bell-shaped distribution, 96
Biased estimator, 84
⬦ Bimodal, 98
Chebyshev's theorem, 86
⬦ *Coefficient of quartile variation*, 94
Coefficient of variation, 90
Deviation from mean, 82
Empirical rule, 88
Interquartile range, 82
Mean deviation, 83
Measures of relative variation, 90
⬦ Measures of skewness, 97
Measures of variation, 81
⬦ Negatively skewed distribution, 96

⬦ Pearsonian coefficient of skewness, 97
Population standard deviation, 83
Population variance, 84
⬦ Positively skewed distribution, 97
Quartile deviation, 82
Range, 81
⬦ Reverse J-shaped distribution, 98
Root-mean-square deviation, 83
Sample standard deviation, 83
Sample variance, 83
Semi-interquartile range, 82
⬦ Skewed distribution, 96
Standard deviation, 82
Standard units, 89

[†]Terms introduced in exercises are shown in *italics*.

4.7 REVIEW EXERCISES

4.52 Find the standard deviation for a set of data for which

$$n = 15, \quad \Sigma\, x = 202, \quad \text{and} \quad \Sigma\, x^2 = 3{,}452$$

4.53 The purchase amounts for the customers at a particular supermarket on a Saturday morning between 8 a.m. and noon had a mean of $56.42 and a standard deviation of $12.40. At least what proportion of the amounts must lie between $37.82 and $75.02?

⇔ 4.54 The following is the distribution of the sizes of a sample of 60 orders receiving by a mail-order seed business:

Size of order	Number of orders
$ 0.00–$ 19.99	6
$ 20.00–$ 39.99	16
$ 40.00–$ 59.99	12
$ 60.00–$ 79.99	11
$ 80.00–$ 99.99	8
$100.00–$119.99	7
Total	60

Calculate

(a) the quartiles Q_1 and Q_3;

(b) the interquartile range;

(c) the coefficient of quartile variation.

⇔ 4.55 The following are the number of false alarms which a fire department recorded during 17 consecutive weeks:

8 3 12 5 6 12 6 3 4 11 8 7 5 6 8 8 4.

Construct a boxplot and discuss the symmetry or skewness of these data.

4.56 A survey of 218 families in Massachusetts indicated that the standard deviation of the number of empty deposit bottles that they had on hand was 14.6. If the coefficient of variation was 74%, what is the mean of the sample data?

4.57 Calculate σ^2 for the population which consists of the integers 1, 2, 3, 4, and 5. Does your calculation support the claim that for a population consisting of the first k positive integers the variance is $\dfrac{k^2 - 1}{12}$?

4.58 A quality control inspector examined 15 crates of ceramic tiles, each containing 144 tiles. The numbers of cracked tiles in these boxes were

2 5 3 4 2 0 1 5 7 3 0 2 2 4 3

Calculate s for these data.

4.59 The market weight of a certain variety of watermelon has a mean of 28 pounds and a coefficient of variation of 22%. What is the z-score for a watermelon that weighs 35 pounds?

⊞ 4.60   A list of numbers has

$$\Sigma x = 40 \quad \text{and} \quad \Sigma x^2 = 156$$

How many values are in the list if its standard deviation is 2.0?

⇔ 4.61   The distribution of the number of mistakes made by 200 students taking German in a multiple-choice quiz on vocabulary is as follows:

Number of mistakes	Number of students
6–10	12
11–15	73
16–20	52
21–25	39
26–30	24
Total	200

Find

(a) the mean;   (b) the standard deviation.

⇔ 4.62   Calculate the Pearsonian coefficient of skewness for the distribution of Exercise 4.61 and discuss the symmetry or skewness of the data.

4.63   For a certain variety of light bulb, a bulb that lasts 1,020 hours has a standard score of $z = 2$. Given that the lifetimes of these bulbs have a coefficient of variation of 14%, find the mean and standard deviation of the lifetimes.

4.64   According to Chebyshev's theorem, what can we assert about the percentage of any set of data that must lie within k standard deviations on either side of the mean when

(a) $k = 6$;   (b) $k = 8$;   (c) $k = 15$?

4.65   The following are the number of accidents that occurred in July of 1990 in a certain town at 18 intersections without left-turn arrows:

$$\begin{array}{ccccccccc} 8 & 29 & 31 & 14 & 35 & 28 & 12 & 18 & 22 \\ 13 & 6 & 32 & 2 & 10 & 26 & 22 & 32 & 25 \end{array}$$

Find

(a) the median;   (b) Q_1 and Q_3.

4.66   Use the results of Exercise 4.65 to draw a boxplot for the accident data.

4.67   For a large group of students the mean score on a historical events quiz is 160 points, with a standard deviation of 22 points. At least what percentage of the scores must lie between

(a) 127 and 193 points;   (b) 116 and 204 points;   (c) 105 and 215 points?

4.68   If a set of measurements has the mean $\bar{x} = 48$ and the standard deviation $s = 12$, convert each of the following into standard units:

(a) 54;   (b) 72;   (c) 78.

4.69   Find the variance of the sample data of Exercise 4.65.

4.70   Explain why it is impossible to have

$$n = 10, \quad \Sigma x = 40, \quad \Sigma x^2 = 140$$

for a given set of data.

4.71   If Chebyshev's theorem indicates that at least 75% of a set of data must lie between 245 and 285, what is the coefficient of variation?

4.8   REFERENCES

A proof that division by $n - 1$ makes the sample variance an unbiased estimator of the population variance may be found in most textbooks on mathematical statistics; for instance, in

FREUND, J. E., *Mathematical Statistics,* 5th ed. Englewood Cliffs, N.J.: Prentice-Hall, Inc., 1992.

An unbiased estimator of the population standard deviation σ is given on pages 62–63 of

JOHNSON, N. L., and KOTZ, S., *Distributions in Statistics: Continuous Univariate Distributions.* Boston: Houghton Mifflin, 1970.

For further information about the use and interpretation of boxplots, see the books on exploratory data analysis listed on page 42. Some information about the effect of grouping on the calculation of various statistical descriptions may be found in some of the older textbooks on statistics; for instance, in

MILLS, F. C., *Introduction to Statistics.* New York: Holt, Rinehart and Winston, 1956.

POSSIBILITIES AND PROBABILITIES

*T*he central problem of statistics is dealing with chance and uncertainty. Chance events have always been regarded as mysterious. The Book of Job pondered long ago the role of divine intent in chance occurrences, and it was many centuries later that the power of mathematics was used to explain randomness. The scientific advances of the centuries following the Renaissance, emphasizing careful observation and experimentation, brought forth **probability theory** to study the laws of nature and the problems of everyday life.

In this chapter we shall see how uncertainties can actually be measured, how they can be assigned numbers, and how these numbers are to be interpreted. In subsequent chapters we shall see how these numbers, called **probabilities,** can be used to live with uncertainties, enabling us to make decisions which are likely to be fruitful.

In Sections 5.1 through 5.3 we present mathematical preliminaries dealing with the question of "what is possible" in given situations. After all, we can hardly predict the outcome of a football game unless we know what teams are playing, and we cannot very well predict what will happen in an election unless we know what candidates are running for office. Then, in Section 5.4 we shall learn how to judge also "what is probable;" that is, we shall learn about several ways in which probabilities are defined, or interpreted, and their values are determined.

5.1   COUNTING

In the study of "what is possible," there are essentially two kinds of problems. There is the problem of listing everything that can happen in a given situation, and then there is the problem of determining how many different things can happen (without actually constructing a complete list). The second kind of problem is especially important, because there are many situations in which we do not need a complete list and, hence, can save ourselves a great deal of work. Although the first kind of problem may seem straightforward and easy, the following example illustrates that this is not always the case:

Example

A governmental agency is committed to the purchase of three vehicles from a local automobile dealer. Each of these vehicles will be either a jeep, a pickup truck, a minivan, or some other vehicle. List the different ways in which the purchases can be made.

solution

There are many possibilities. All three vehicles may be jeeps; two may be jeeps while the other is a minivan; two may be pickup trucks while the other is a minivan; and so forth. If we continue in this manner, it is likely that we will omit some of the possibilities.

FIGURE 5.1

Tree diagram for choice
of vehicle example.

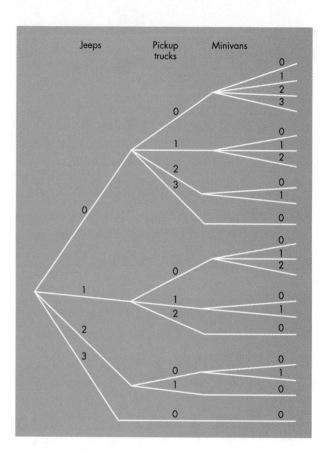

The problem can be handled systematically by drawing a **tree diagram** such as
Figure 5.1. This shows that there are four possibilities (four branches) corresponding to 0, 1, 2, or 3 of the vehicles being jeeps. For pickup trucks there are
four branches coming from the top branch (0 jeeps), three branches coming from
the next branch (1 jeep), two branches coming from the following branch (2 jeeps),
and just one branch coming from the bottom branch. For the number of minivans,
the reasoning is similar. You can see that twenty branches end at the right side of
Figure 5.1. In other words, there are altogether twenty possibilities.   ◩ ◩ ◩

Example
_____

In a medical study, patients are classified according to whether they have blood
type A, B, AB, or O, and also according to whether their blood pressure is low,
normal, or high. In how many different ways can a patient thus be classified?

solution
_____

As is apparent from the tree diagram of Figure 5.2, the answer is 12. Starting at
the top, the first path along the "branches" corresponds to a patient having blood
type A and low blood pressure, the second path corresponds to a patient having
blood type A and normal blood pressure, ..., and the twelfth path corresponds to
a patient having blood type O and high blood pressure.   ◩ ◩ ◩

FIGURE 5.2

Tree diagram for classification of patients.

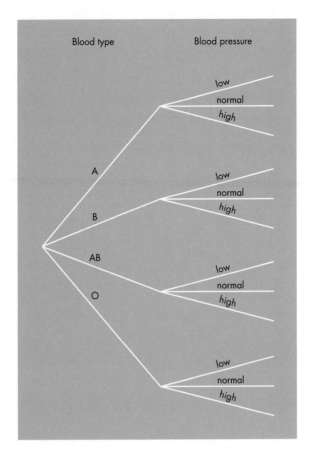

The answer we got in this example is $4 \cdot 3 = 12$, namely, the product of the number of blood types and the number of blood pressure levels. Generalizing from this example, let us state the following rule:

Multiplication of Choices	*If a choice consists of two steps, of which the first can be made in m ways and for each of these the second can be made in n ways, then the whole choice can be made in m · n ways.*

To prove this we have only to draw a tree diagram like that of Figure 5.2. First there are *m* branches corresponding to the *m* possibilities in the first step, and then there are *n* branches emanating from each of these branches corresponding to the *n* possibilities in the second step. This leads to $m \cdot n$ paths along the branches of the tree diagram, and hence to $m \cdot n$ possibilities.

Example

If a travel agency offers special weekend trips to 12 different cities, by air, rail, or bus, in how many different ways can such a trip be arranged?

solution

Since $m = 12$ and $n = 3$, there are $12 \cdot 3 = 36$ ways in which such a trip can be arranged. ◪ ◪ ◪

Example

If an ice-cream shop offers one-scoop mini-sundaes with a choice of 20 ice-cream flavors along with a choice of eight toppings, in how many different ways can a customer order a mini-sundae?

solution

Since $m = 20$ and $n = 8$, there are

$$20 \cdot 8 = 160$$

ways in which a customer can order a mini-sundae. ◪ ◪ ◪

By using appropriate tree diagrams, we can easily generalize the above rule so that it will apply to choices involving more than two steps. For k steps, where k is a positive integer, we get the following rule:

Multiplication of Choices	*If a choice consists of k steps, of which the first can be made in n_1 ways, for each of these the second can be made in n_2 ways, ..., and for each of these the kth can be made in n_k ways, then the whole choice can be made in $n_1 \cdot n_1 \cdot \cdots \cdot n_k$ ways.*

We simply keep multiplying the numbers of ways in which the different steps can be made.

Example

A luncheonette offers a special meal consisting of a sandwich (using one of eight different meats and one of four different types of bread), one of four different types of soup, and one of three different beverages. In how many ways can a person choose one of these special meals?

solution

Since $n_1 = 8$, $n_2 = 4$, $n_3 = 4$, and $n_4 = 3$, there are

$$8 \cdot 4 \cdot 4 \cdot 3 = 384$$

ways in which the special meal may be chosen. ◪ ◪ ◪

Example

A test consists of 15 multiple-choice questions, with each question having four possible answers. In how many different ways can a student check off one answer to each question?

solution

Since $n_1 = n_2 = n_3 = \cdots = n_{15} = 4$, there are altogether

$$4 \cdot 4 \cdot 4 \cdot 4 \cdot 4 \cdot 4 \cdot 4 \cdot 4 \cdot 4 \cdot 4 \cdot 4 \cdot 4 \cdot 4 \cdot 4 \cdot 4 = 1{,}073{,}741{,}824$$

different ways in which a student can check off one answer to each question. Note that in only one of the 1,073,741,824 possibilities all the answers are correct and in

$$3 \cdot 3 \cdot 3 \cdot 3 \cdot 3 \cdot 3 \cdot 3 \cdot 3 \cdot 3 \cdot 3 \cdot 3 \cdot 3 \cdot 3 \cdot 3 \cdot 3 = 14{,}348{,}907$$

of them all the answers are wrong.   ▮ ▮ ▮

5.2   PERMUTATIONS

The rule for the multiplication of choices and its generalization are often used when several choices are made from one and the same set and we are concerned with the order in which they are made.

Example

If 20 paintings are entered in an art show, in how many different ways can the judges award a first prize and a second prize?

solution

Since the first prize can be awarded in $m = 20$ ways and the second prize must be awarded to one of the other $n = 19$ paintings, there are altogether

$$20 \cdot 19 = 380$$

ways in which the judges can make the two awards.   ▮ ▮ ▮

Example

In how many different ways can the 52 members of a labor union choose a president, a vice-president, a secretary, and a treasurer?

solution

Since $n_1 = 52$, $n_2 = 51$, $n_3 = 50$, and $n_4 = 49$ (regardless of which officer is chosen first, second, third, and fourth), there are altogether

$$52 \cdot 51 \cdot 50 \cdot 49 = 6{,}497{,}400$$

different possibilities.   ▮ ▮ ▮

In general, if r objects are selected from a set of n distinct objects, any particular arrangement (order) of these objects is called a **permutation.** For instance, 4 1 2 3 is a permutation of the first four positive integers; Maine, Vermont, and Connecticut is a permutation (a particular ordered arrangement) of three of the six New England states; and

| Red Sox | Tigers | Indians | Orioles |
| Blue Jays | Red Sox | Yankees | Tigers |

are two different permutations (ordered arrangements) of four of the 14 baseball teams of the American League.

Example

Determine the number of different permutations of two of the five vowels *a, e, i, o,* and *u,* and list them all.

solution

Since $m = 5$ and $n = 4$, there are $5 \cdot 4 = 20$ different permutations, and they are

$$ae \quad ai \quad ao \quad au \quad ei \quad eo \quad eu \quad io \quad iu \quad ou$$
$$ea \quad ia \quad oa \quad ua \quad ie \quad oe \quad ue \quad oi \quad ui \quad uo$$

A formula for the total number of permutations of *r* objects selected from a set of *n* distinct objects, such as the 14 baseball teams, would be useful. Observe that the first selection is made from the whole set of *n* objects, the second selection is made from the $n - 1$ objects which remain after the first selection has been made, the third selection is made from the $n - 2$ objects which remain after the first two selections have been made, ..., and the *r*th and final selection is made from the

$$n - (r - 1) = n - r + 1$$

objects that remain after the first $r - 1$ selections have been made. Therefore, direct application of the generalized rule for the multiplication of choices yields the result that the total number of permutations of *r* objects selected from a set of *n* distinct objects, which we shall denote by $_nP_r$, is

$$n(n - 1)(n - 2) \cdot \cdots \cdot (n - r + 1)$$

Since products of consecutive integers arise in many problems relating to permutations and other kinds of special arrangements or selections, it is convenient to introduce here the **factorial notation.** In this notation, the product of all positive integers less than or equal to the positive integer *n* is called "*n* factorial" and denoted by *n*!. Thus,

$$1! = 1$$
$$2! = 2 \cdot 1 = 2$$
$$3! = 3 \cdot 2 \cdot 1 = 6$$
$$4! = 4 \cdot 3 \cdot 2 \cdot 1 = 24$$
$$5! = 5 \cdot 4 \cdot 3 \cdot 2 \cdot 1 = 120$$
$$6! = 6 \cdot 5 \cdot 4 \cdot 3 \cdot 2 \cdot 1 = 720$$

$$\cdots \cdots \cdots \cdots \cdots \cdots$$

and in general

$$n! = n(n - 1)(n - 2) \cdot \cdots \cdot 3 \cdot 2 \cdot 1$$

Also, to make various formulas more generally applicable, we let $0! = 1$ by definition.

The factorials grow so quickly that some have claimed that the exclamation point indicates surprise. The value of 10! exceeds three million, and 70! exceeds the memory limit of most hand-held calculators.

To express the formula for $_nP_r$ in terms of factorials, we note, for example, that

$$12 \cdot 11 \cdot 10! = 12!, 9 \cdot 8 \cdot 7 \cdot 6! = 9! \quad \text{and} \quad 37 \cdot 36 \cdot 35 \cdot 34 \cdot 33! = 37!$$

Similarly,

$$_nP_r \cdot (n-r)! = n(n-1)(n-2) \cdot \cdots \cdot (n-r+1) \cdot (n-r)! = n!$$

so that

$$_nP_r = \frac{n!}{(n-r)!}$$

To summarize:

Permutations of n Objects Taken r at a Time	*The number of permutations of r objects selected from a set of n distinct objects is* $$_nP_r = n(n-1)(n-2) \cdot \cdots \cdot (n-r+1)$$ *or, in factorial notation,* $$_nP_r = \frac{n!}{(n-r)!}$$

where either formula can be used for $r = 1, 2, ..., $ or n. (The second formula, but not the first, could be used also for $r = 0$, for which we would get the trivial result that there is

$$_nP_0 = \frac{n!}{(n-0)!} = 1$$

way of selecting none of n objects.) The first formula is generally easier to use because it requires fewer steps, but many students find the one in factorial notation easier to remember.

Example

Find the number of permutations of four objects selected from a set of 12 distinct objects (say, the number of ways in which four of 12 basketball teams can be ranked first, second, third, and fourth by a panel of coaches).

solution

For $n = 12$ and $r = 4$, the first formula yields

$$_{12}P_4 = 12 \cdot 11 \cdot 10 \cdot 9 = 11,880$$

and the second formula yields

$$_{12}P_4 = \frac{12!}{(12-4)!} = \frac{12!}{8!} = \frac{12 \cdot 11 \cdot 10 \cdot 9 \cdot 8!}{8!} = 11,880$$

Essentially, the work is the same, but the second formula requires a few extra steps. ◪ ◪ ◪

To find the formula for the number of permutations of n distinct objects taken all together, we substitute $r = n$ into either formula for $_nP_r$ and get

Permutations of n Objects Taken n at a Time	$_nP_n = n!$

Example

In how many ways can 10 instructors be assigned to 10 sections of a course in economics?

solution

Substituting $n = 10$, we have

$$_{10}P_{10} = 10! = 3,628,800$$

Throughout this discussion it has been assumed that the n objects are all distinct. When this is not the case, the formula for $_nP_n$ can be easily modified, but we shall not go into that in this book. (The modification of $_nP_r$ with $r < n$ is complicated.) Exercises 5.26 and 5.27 deal with nondistinct objects in the case $r = n$.   ◪ ◪ ◪

5.3   COMBINATIONS

There are many problems in which we want to know the number of ways in which r objects can be selected from a set of n objects, but we do not care about the order in which the selection is made. For instance, we may want to know in how many ways a committee of four can be selected from among the 45 members of a college fraternity, or the number of ways in which the IRS can choose five of 36 tax returns for a special audit. To derive a formula which applies to problems like these, let us first examine the following 24 permutations of three of the first four letters of the alphabet:

abc	acb	bac	bca	cab	cba
abd	adb	bad	bda	dab	dba
acd	adc	cad	cda	dac	dca
bcd	bdc	cbd	cdb	dbc	dcb

If we do not care about the order in which the three letters are chosen from among the four letters a, b, c, and d, there are only four ways in which the selection can be made: *abc, abd, acd,* and *bcd.* Note that these are the groups of letters shown in the first column of the table, and that each row contains the $_3P_3 = 3! = 6$ permutations of the three letters in the first column.

In general, there are $_rP_r = r!$ permutations of r distinct objects, so that the $_nP_r$ permutations of r objects selected from among n distinct objects contain each group of r objects $r!$ times. (In our example, the $_4P_3 = 4 \cdot 3 \cdot 2 = 24$ permutations of three letters selected from among the first four letters of the alphabet contain each group of three letters $_3P_3 = 3! = 6$ times.) Therefore, to get a formula for the number of ways in which r objects can be selected from a set of n distinct objects *without regard to their order,* we divide $_nP_r$ by $r!$. Referring to such a selection as a **combination** of n objects taken r at a time, we denote the number of combinations of n objects taken r at a time by

$$_nC_r \quad \text{or} \quad \binom{n}{r}$$

and write

Combinations of n Objects Taken r at a Time	The number of ways in which r objects can be selected from a set of n distinct objects is $$\binom{n}{r} = \frac{n(n-1)(n-2)\cdot\cdots\cdot(n-r+1)}{r!}$$ or, in factorial notation, $$\binom{n}{r} = \frac{n!}{r!(n-r)!}$$

Like the two formulas for $_nP_r$, either formula can be used for $r = 1, 2, ...,$ or n, but only the second one for $r = 0$. Again, the first formula is generally easier to use because it requires fewer steps, but many students find the one in factorial notation easier to remember.

For $n = 0$ to $n = 20$, the values of $\binom{n}{r}$ may be read from Table X, where these quantities are referred to as **binomial coefficients.** The reason for this is explained in Exercise 5.41 on page 119.

Example

In how many ways can a person choose three books from a list of eight best-sellers?

solution

As it is assumed here that the order in which the three books are selected does not matter, we substitute $n = 8$ and $r = 3$ into the first formula and get

$$\binom{8}{3} = \frac{8 \cdot 7 \cdot 6}{3!} = 8 \cdot 7 = 56$$

Similarly, substitution into the second formula yields

$$\binom{8}{3} = \frac{8!}{3!5!} = \frac{8 \cdot 7 \cdot 6 \cdot 5!}{3!5!} = \frac{8 \cdot 7 \cdot 6}{3 \cdot 2 \cdot 1} = 56$$

Essentially, the work is the same, but the first formula requires fewer steps.

It is possible to list all the possible selections. If we agree to identify the eight books by the letters a through h, then the $\binom{8}{3} = 56$ possible selections are these:

abc	abd	abe	abf	abg	abh	acd
ace	acf	acg	ach	ade	adf	adg
adh	aef	aeg	aeh	afg	afh	agh
bcd	bce	bcf	bcg	bch	bde	bdf
bdg	bdh	bef	beg	beh	bfg	bfh
bgh	cde	cdf	cdg	cdh	cef	ceg
ceh	cfg	cfh	cgh	def	deg	deh
dfg	dfh	dgh	efg	efh	egh	fgh

Once the books have been identified with letters, it is possible to list the selections methodically in alphabetical order.   ◪ ◪ ◪

Example

In how many different ways can a committee of five be selected from the 62 members of the clerical staff at a large legal firm?

solution

Since the order in which the committee members are selected does not matter, we substitute $n = 62$ and $r = 5$ into the first formula to get

$$\binom{62}{5} = \frac{62 \cdot 61 \cdot 60 \cdot 59 \cdot 58}{5!} = 6,471,002$$

Note that the result of the first example, but not that of the second, can be verified in Table X.

Example

In how many different ways can the director of a research laboratory choose two chemists from among seven applicants and three physicists from among nine applicants?

solution

The two chemists can be selected in $\binom{7}{2}$ ways, the three physicists can be selected in $\binom{9}{3}$ ways, so that, by the multiplication of choices, all five of them can be selected in

$$\binom{7}{2} \cdot \binom{9}{3} = 21 \cdot 84 = 1,764$$

ways. The values of the two binomial coefficients were obtained from Table X.

Using $r = n$ in either formula for $\binom{n}{r}$ yields

$$\binom{n}{n} = 1$$

In other words, there is one and only one way in which we can select all n of the elements which constitute a set.

When we take 7 objects from a set of 10 distinct objects, then $10 - 7 = 3$ of the objects are left. Thus, there are as many ways of leaving (or selecting) 3 objects from a set of 10 distinct objects as there are ways of selecting 7 objects, and we can write

$$\binom{10}{7} = \binom{10}{3}$$

In general, when r objects are selected from a set of n distinct objects, $n - r$ of the objects are left, and consequently, there are as many ways of leaving (or selecting) $n - r$ objects from a set of n distinct objects as there are ways of selecting r objects. Symbolically, we write

Rule for Binomial Coefficients	$$\binom{n}{r} = \binom{n}{n-r} \qquad \text{for } r = 0, 1, 2, ..., n$$

Sometimes this rule serves to simplify calculations and sometimes it is needed in connection with the use of Table X.

Example

Determine the value of $\binom{75}{72}$.

solution

To avoid having to write down the product

$$75 \cdot 74 \cdot 73 \cdot \;\cdots\; \cdot 4$$

and to cancel

$$72 \cdot 71 \cdot 70 \cdot \;\cdots\; \cdot 4$$

we write directly

$$\binom{75}{72} = \binom{75}{3} = \frac{75 \cdot 74 \cdot 73}{3!} = 67,525$$

Example

Find the value of $\binom{18}{13}$.

solution

$\binom{18}{13}$ cannot be looked up directly in Table X, but by making use of the fact that

$$\binom{18}{13} = \binom{18}{18-13} = \binom{18}{5}$$

we look up $\binom{18}{5}$ and obtain 8,568.

If we substitute $r = 0$ into the second of the two formulas for $\binom{n}{r}$, or if we write

$$\binom{n}{0} = \binom{n}{n-0} = \binom{n}{n} \qquad \text{we get} \qquad \binom{n}{0} = 1$$

Evidently, there are as many ways of selecting none of the objects in a set as there are ways of choosing the n objects which are left.

◢ EXERCISES

5.1   In the World Series of baseball the winner is the first team to win four games. Suppose that the American League champions lead the National League champions by three games to one. Construct a tree diagram showing the number of ways that these teams may continue to the completion of the series.

5.2   A person with $3 in his pocket bets $1, even money, on the flip of a coin. He continues to bet $1 as long as he has any money. Draw a tree diagram to show the various things that can happen in the first four flips of the coin. In how many of the cases will he be

(a) exactly $4 ahead;   (b) exactly $2 ahead;

(c) exactly even;   (d) exactly $2 behind;

(e) exactly $3 behind?

5.3   A student can study 0, 1, or 2 hours for a statistics test on any given night. Draw tree diagrams to find the number of ways in which the student can study

(a) a total of exactly five hours on three consecutive nights;

(b) a total of at least five hours on three consecutive nights.

5.4   A food specialty store receives two cherry cheesecakes each morning. Cheesecakes not sold by closing time are discarded. Construct a tree diagram to show the number of ways in which the store can sell a total of five cherry cheesecakes on four consecutive days.

5.5   The store of Exercise 5.4 also receives three cream cakes each morning, and cream cakes which are not sold by closing time must be discarded. Construct a tree diagram to show the number of ways in which the store can sell a total of five cream cakes on three consecutive days.

5.6   In a union election, Mr. Brown, Ms. Green, and Ms. Jones are running for president. Mr. Adams, Ms. Roberts, and Mr. Smith are running for vice-president. Construct a tree diagram showing the nine possible outcomes, and use it to determine the number of ways in which the two unions officials will not be of the same sex.

5.7   In a political science survey, voters are classified into six income categories and five education categories. In how many different ways can a voter be classified?

5.8   A chain of convenience stores has four warehouses and operates 35 retail outlets. In how many different ways can this chain ship a carton of cola syrup from one of the warehouses to one of the retail outlets?

5.9   A purchasing agent places his orders by phone, by fax, by mail, or by express carrier. He requests that the order be confirmed by phone or by fax. In how many different ways can one of his orders be placed and confirmed?

5.10   There are six routes between Connie's home and her place of work.

(a) In how many different ways can she go to and from work?

(b) In how many different ways can she go to and from work if she does not want to use the same route both ways?

(c) If two of her six routes have been made into one-way streets (in opposite directions), in how many ways can she go to and from work, assuming that she is willing to use the same route both ways?

(d) If two of her six routes have been made into one-way streets (in opposite directions), in how many ways can she go to and from work, assuming that she does not want to use the same route both ways?

5.11   In an optics kit there are six concave lenses, four convex lenses, two prisms, and two mirrors. In how many different ways can one choose a concave lens, a convex lens, a prism, and a mirror from this kit?

5.12   A psychologist is preparing three-letter nonsense words for use in a memory test. He chooses the first letter from the consonants *k, m, w,* and *z.* He chooses the middle letter from the vowels *a, i,* and *u.* He chooses the final letter from the consonants *b, d, f, k, m,* and *t.*

(a) How many different three-letter nonsense words can he construct?

(b) How many of these nonsense words will begin with the letter *z*?

(c) How many of these nonsense words will end with either *k* or *m*?

(d) How many of these nonsense words will begin and end with the same letter?

5.13 In Dr. Freud's waiting room there are eight recent issues of *Newsweek*, six issues of *The New Yorker*, and five issues of the *Reader's Digest*. In how many different ways can a patient, while waiting to see the doctor, glance at one of each of the magazines if the order does not matter?

5.14 A true–false test consists of 10 questions. In how many ways can a student mark one answer to each question?

5.15 A pizzeria offers 10 toppings for its pizzas. The customer can order any combination of these toppings, including all of them or none of them. How many different types of pizza are possible? (*Hint*: For each topping, the diner must decide whether to select it.)

5.16 Determine whether each of the following is true or false:

(a) $18! = 18 \cdot 17 \cdot 16!$; (b) $4! \cdot 5! = 20!$ (c) $6! = 30 \cdot 4!$; (d) $15! = \dfrac{16!}{16}$.

5.17 Determine whether each of the following is true or false:

(a) $\dfrac{1}{2!} + \dfrac{1}{3!} = \dfrac{5}{6!}$; (b) $5! + 2! = 7!$; (c) $\dfrac{6!}{2! \cdot 4!} + \dfrac{6!}{3! \cdot 3!} = \dfrac{7!}{3! \cdot 4!}$; (d) $\dfrac{1}{3!} + \dfrac{1}{3!} = \dfrac{1}{3}$.

5.18 For his vacation, Carl would like to visit three of 10 historical sights in Philadelphia. If the order of the visits matters, in how many different ways can the trip be planned?

5.19 Waldo plans to spend seven nights in Cleveland and has obtained a list of the city's eight best Italian restaurants and nine best Chinese restaurants. In how many ways can Waldo eat seven evening meals at these restaurants, assuming that he wishes to try a different restaurant each night and also that he wishes to alternate between Italian and Chinese food?

5.20 In how many ways can four new corporate clients be assigned to eleven service representatives, assuming that each service representative can be assigned at most one of the corporate clients?

5.21 An amusement park has 28 rides. Of these, 10 are popular, meaning that the wait in line exceeds 30 minutes. In how many different ways can a visitor try six of these rides, assuming that he wishes to try two of the popular rides and four of the others, and assuming that order matters and that he does not wish to try any ride more than once?

5.22 If there are nine horses in a race, in how many different ways can they finish first, second, and third?

5.23 In how many different ways can eight books be placed on a shelf?

5.24 In how many different ways can the manager of a baseball team arrange the batting order of nine players in the starting lineup? In how many different ways can this be done if he insists that the pitcher should bat ninth?

5.25 Four married couples have purchased eight seats in a row for a football game. In how many different ways can they be seated if

(a) each couple is to sit together;

(b) all the men are to sit together and all the women are to sit together;

(c) all the men are to sit together;

(d) the men and women are to sit in alternate seats;

(e) no man is to sit next to another man?

5.26 If among n objects r are alike, and the others are all distinct, the number of permutations of these n objects taken all together is $\frac{n!}{r!}$.

(a) How many permutations are there of the letters in the word "silly"?

(b) How many permutations are there of the letters in the word "bubble"?

(c) In how many ways can a radio director select six consecutive commercials, using one commercial for product A, one commercial for product B, one commercial for product C, and three identical commercials for product D?

(d) Present an argument to justify the formula given in this exercise.

5.27 If among n objects r_1 are identical, another r_2 are identical, and the remaining (if any) are all distinct, the number of permutations of these n objects taken all together is

$$\frac{n!}{r_1! \cdot r_2!}$$

(a) How many permutations are there of the letters in the word "better"?

(b) How many permutations are there of the letters in the word "hubbub"?

(c) In how many ways can the radio director of the previous problem select six consecutive commercials, using three identical commercials for product E and three identical commercials for product F?

(d) Generalize the formula so that it applies to the permutations of n objects taken all together if there are r_1 identical, another r_2 identical, another r_3 identical, and so on.

(e) How many permutations are there of the letters in "Mississippi"?

5.28 There is no simple formula for the number of permutations of n nonidentical objects when fewer than n are selected.

(a) List all possible permutations of three letters taken from the letters of the word "fever." Note that "e" may appear 0, 1, or 2 times among the selected letters.

(b) List all possible permutations of four letters taken from the letters of the word "bubble."

5.29 The number of ways in which n distinct objects can be arranged in a circle is $(n-1)!$.

(a) Present an argument to justify this formula.

(b) In how many ways can six persons be seated at a round table, if we care only who sits on whose left or right side?

(c) In how many ways can eight persons form a circle for a folk dance?

(d) Four men and four women are forming a circle for a folk dance. In how many ways can this be done if we require that the men and women alternate positions?

5.30 The number of ways in which n distinct keys can be placed on a key ring is $(n-1)!/2$.

(a) Show that there is only one way in which three keys can be placed on a ring.

(b) In how many ways can four keys be placed on a ring?

(c) In how many ways can six keys be placed on a ring?

5.31 The gift shop of a tourist resort has 15 different scenic postcards. In how many ways can one select four of these as souvenirs?

5.32 A pizza shop offers 10 different toppings for its pizza. In how many ways can a customer select three toppings for his pizza?

5.33 A bookstore has a sale in which a customer gets a special price for buying four of the current 10 best-sellers. In how many ways can a customer make such a selection?

5.34 A true–false test contains 12 questions. Calculate the numbers of ways in which a student can mark each question either true or false and get

(a) eight right and four wrong;   (b) ten right and two wrong.

5.35   A high-school student doing a report on ancient Greece has found 15 books on this subject in the school library. The library rules permit him to check out only five books at a time. Find the number of ways in which the student can select five books, and verify your answer in Table X.

5.36   A carton of 12 eggs contains one egg that is spoiled. In how many ways can a person choose three of these eggs and

(a) get the one egg that is spoiled;

(b) not get the one egg that is spoiled?

5.37   A 10-pack of batteries has two defective batteries. In how many ways can one select three of these batteries and get

(a) neither of the defective batteries;

(b) one of the defective batteries;

(c) both of the defective batteries?

5.38   Among the eight nominees for two vacancies on a school board are four men and four women. In how many ways can these vacancies be filled

(a) with any two of the eight nominees;

(b) with any two of the female nominees;

(c) with any two of the male nominees;

(d) with one of the male nominees and one of the female nominees?

5.39   A men's clothing store carries eight kinds of sweaters, six kinds of slacks, and 10 kinds of shirts. In how many ways can two of each kind be chosen for a special sale?

用 5.40   Counting the number of outcomes in games of chance has been popular for many centuries. Not only was gambling involved, but the outcomes were also taken as indications of divine intent. It was just about 1,000 years ago that a bishop in what is now Belgium determined that there are 56 different ways in which three dice can fall, provided one is interested only in the overall result and not in the outcomes of the individual dice. He assigned a virtue to each of these possibilities and each sinner had to concentrate for some time on the virtue which corresponded to his cast of the dice.

(a) Find the number of ways in which three dice can all come up with the same number of points.

(b) Find the number of ways in which two of the three dice can come up with the same number of points while the third die comes up with a different number of points.

(c) Find the number of ways in which all three of the dice can come up with a different number of points.

(d) Use parts (a), (b), and (c) to verify the bishop's calculation that there are altogether 56 possibilities.

5.41   The quantity $\binom{n}{r}$ is called a **binomial coefficient** because it is the coefficient of $a^{n-r} b^r$ in the binomial expansion of $(a + b)^n$.

(a) Verify this fact for $n = 1$.

(b) Verify this fact for $n = 2$ by expanding $(a + b)^2$.

(c) Verify this fact for $n = 3$ by expanding $(a + b)^3$.

(d) Verify this fact for $n = 4$ by expanding $(a + b)^4$.

(e) Compare your findings to the corresponding entries of Table X.

5.42   Use Table X to determine the values of the following binomial coefficients:

(a) $\binom{18}{6}$;   (b) $\binom{14}{6}$;   (c) $\binom{18}{15}$;   (d) $\binom{16}{11}$.

5.43   Verify that

(a) $\binom{12}{8} = 3 \cdot \binom{11}{8}$; (b) $10 \cdot \binom{14}{4} = 14 \cdot \binom{13}{4}$; (c) $\dfrac{\binom{10}{4}}{\binom{9}{3}} = \dfrac{5}{2}$.

⊞ 5.44   A table of binomial coefficients is easy to construct by following the pattern below.

$$
\begin{array}{ccccccccccc}
 & & & & & 1 & & & & & \\
 & & & & 1 & & 1 & & & & \\
 & & & 1 & & 2 & & 1 & & & \\
 & & 1 & & 3 & & 3 & & 1 & & \\
 & 1 & & 4 & & 6 & & 4 & & 1 & \\
1 & & 5 & & 10 & & 10 & & 5 & & 1 \\
\end{array}
$$

. . . .

Called **Pascal's triangle,** in this arrangement each row begins with a 1, ends with a 1, and each entry is the sum of the nearest two values from the row above. Construct the next three rows of Pascal's triangle, and verify from Table X that they are, respectively, the binomial coefficients corresponding to

$$n = 6, \quad n = 7, \quad \text{and} \quad n = 8.$$

⊞ 5.45   In Pascal's triangle, denote the row

1 2 1   as row 2

row

1 3 3 1   as row 3

row

1 4 6 4 1   as row 4

and so on. The row beginning 1 n . . . will be row n. Within row n, label the $n + 1$ positions as 0, 1, 2, . . . , n. Observe that $\binom{n}{r}$ appears in position r of row n.

(a) What is row 7?   (b) Give the value of $\binom{7}{3}$.

(c) The triangle is constructed by the relationship

$$\binom{n}{r} = \binom{n-1}{r-1} + \binom{n-1}{r}$$

Verify this relationship by expressing the binomial coefficients in factorial form.

⊞ 5.46   Pascal's triangle has several useful patterns.

(a) Show that row 2, meaning the row 1 2 1, has total 4, and then show that rows 3, 4, 5, and 6 have totals 8, 16, 32, and 64.

(b) Without doing the arithmetic, what do you think should be the total for row 11?

⊞ 5.47   Susan is one of seven office workers in a small business. Three of these workers will be selected to serve on a committee.

(a) In how many different ways can three of these persons be chosen to be on the committee?

(b) In how many different ways can three of these persons be chosen so that Susan is *not* on the committee?

(c) In how many different ways can three of the persons be chosen so that Susan is one of the chosen persons?

(d) Verify that your solutions to parts (b) and (c) add up to the solution to part (a). This is an example of the result given by Exercise 5.45.

5.4   PROBABILITY

Thus far in this chapter we have studied only what is possible in a given situation. In some instances we listed all the possibilities and in others we merely determined how many different possibilities there are. Now we shall go one step further and judge also what is probable and what is improbable.

The most common way of measuring the uncertainties connected with events (say, the outcome of a presidential election, the side effects of a new medication, the durability of an exterior paint, or the total number of points we may roll with a pair of dice) is to assign them **probabilities** or to specify the **odds** at which it would be fair to bet that the events will occur. In this section we shall learn how probabilities are interpreted and how their numerical values are determined; odds will be discussed in Section 6.3.

Historically, the oldest way of measuring uncertainties is the **classical probability concept.** It was developed originally in connection with games of chance, and it lends itself most readily to bridging the gap between possibilities and probabilities. The classical probability concept applies only when all possible outcomes are equally likely, in which case we say that

Classical Probability Concept	*If there are n equally likely possibilities, of which one must occur and s are regarded as favorable, or as a "success," then the probability of a "success" is $\frac{s}{n}$.*

In the application of this rule, the terms "favorable" and "success" are used rather loosely—what is favorable to one player is unfavorable to his opponent, and what is a success from one point of view is a failure from another. Thus, the terms "favorable" and "success" can be applied to any particular kind of outcome, even if "favorable" means that a television set does not work, or "success" means that someone catches the flu. This usage dates back to the days when probabilities were quoted only in connection with games of chance.

Example

What is the probability of drawing an ace from a well-shuffled deck of 52 playing cards?

solution

By "well-shuffled" we mean that each card has the same chance of being drawn, so that the classical probability concept can be applied. Since there are $s = 4$ aces among the $n = 52$ cards, we find that the probability of drawing an ace is

$$\frac{s}{n} = \frac{4}{52} = \frac{1}{13}$$

Example
_____

What is the probability of rolling a 3 or a 4 with a balanced die?

solution
_____

By "balanced" we mean that each face of the die has the same chance, so that the classical probability concept can be applied. Since $n = 6$ and $s = 2$, we find that the probability of rolling a 3 or a 4 is

$$\frac{s}{n} = \frac{2}{6} = \frac{1}{3}$$

▟ ▟ ▟

Example
_____

If H stands for heads and T for tails, the four possible outcomes for two flips of a coin are

HH HT TH TT

If it can be assumed that these four possibilities are equally likely, what are the probabilities of getting zero, one, or two heads?

solution
_____

Since $n = 4$ and

$$s = 1 \text{ for zero heads,} \quad s = 2 \text{ for one head,} \quad \text{and} \quad s = 1 \text{ for two heads}$$

the probability of getting zero heads is $\frac{1}{4}$, the probability of getting one head is

$$\frac{2}{4} = \frac{1}{2},$$

and the probability of getting two heads is $\frac{1}{4}$.

▟ ▟ ▟

Although equally likely possibilities are found mostly in games of chance, the classical probability concept applies also in a great variety of situations where gambling devices are used to make **random selections**—say, when offices are assigned to research assistants by lot, when laboratory animals are chosen for an experiment so that each one has the same chance of being selected (perhaps, by the method which is described in Section 10.1), when each family in a township has the same chance of being included in a survey, or when machine parts are chosen for inspection so that each part produced has the same chance of being selected.

Example
_____

If three of 20 tires are defective and four of them are randomly chosen for inspection, what is the probability that one of the defective tires will be included?

solution
_____

There are

$$n = \binom{20}{4} = 4{,}845$$

ways of choosing four of the 20 tires, which may be regarded as equally likely by virtue of the random selection. The number of favorable outcomes is the number of ways in which one of the three defective tires and three of the 17 nondefective tires can be selected, namely,

$$s = \binom{3}{1}\binom{17}{3} = 3 \cdot 680 = 2{,}040$$

It follows that the probability of getting one defective tire and three nondefective tires is

$$\frac{s}{n} = \frac{2{,}040}{4{,}845} = \frac{8}{19} \approx 0.42^{\dagger}$$

The values of the various binomial coefficients were read directly from Table X.

▰ ▰ ▰

A major shortcoming of the classical probability concept is its limited applicability, for there are many situations in which the various possibilities cannot all be regarded as equally likely. This would be the case, for instance, if we are concerned with the question of whether it will rain on a certain day; when we wonder whether a person will get a raise; when we want to predict the outcome of an election or the score of a baseball game; or when we want to judge whether a stock market index will go up or down.

Among the various probability concepts, most widely held is the **frequency interpretation,** according to which probabilities are interpreted as follows:

Frequency Interpretation of Probability	*The probability of an event (happening or outcome) is the proportion of the time that events of the same kind will occur in the long run.*

If we say that the probability is 0.78 that a jet from San Francisco to Phoenix will arrive on time, we mean that such flights arrive on time 78 percent of the time. Also, if the Weather Service predicts that there is a 40 percent chance for rain (that the probability is 0.40 that it will rain), they mean that under the same weather conditions it will rain 40 percent of the time. More generally, we say that an event has a probability of, say 0.90, in the same sense in which we might say that our car will start in cold weather 90 percent of the time. We cannot guarantee what will happen on any particular occasion—the car may start and then it may not—but if we kept records over a long period of time, we should find that the proportion of "successes" is very close to 0.90.

In accordance with the frequency interpretation of probability, we estimate the probability of an event by observing what fraction of the time similar events have occurred in the past.

---

†See the footnote on page 51 regarding the use of the symbol ≈.

Example

If an airline's records show that (over a period of time) 468 of 600 of its jets from San Francisco to Phoenix arrived on time, what is the probability that any one of the airline's jets from San Francisco to Phoenix will arrive on time?

solution

Since in the past $\frac{468}{600} = 0.78$ of the flights arrived on time, we use this figure as an estimate of the desired probability.   ◢ ◢ ◢

Example

If records show that 504 of 813 automatic dishwashers sold by a large retailer required repairs within the warranty year, what is the probability that an automatic dishwasher sold by the retailer will not require repairs within the warranty year?

solution

Since $813 - 504 = 309$ of the dishwashers did not require repairs, we estimate the probability as

$$\frac{309}{813} \approx 0.38.$$ ◢ ◢ ◢

When probabilities are estimated in this way, it is only reasonable to ask whether the estimates are any good. In Chapter 13 we shall answer this question in some detail, but for now let us refer to an important theorem called the **Law of Large Numbers.** Informally, this theorem may be stated as follows:

Law of Large Numbers	*If a situation, trial, or experiment is repeated again and again, the proportion of successes will tend to approach the probability that any one outcome will be a success.*

This theorem is known informally as the "law of averages." It is a statement about the long-run proportion of successes, and it has little to say about any single trial.

An easy illustration of the Law of Large Numbers can be obtained through a **computer simulation** of the repeated flipping of a balanced coin. This is shown in Figure 5.3, where the 1's and 0's denote heads and tails.

Reading across successive rows, we find that among the first five simulated flips there are 3 heads, among the first 10 there are 6 heads, among the first 15 there are 8 heads, among the first 20 there are 12 heads, among the first 25 there are 14 heads, ..., and among all 100 there are 51 heads. The corresponding proportions, plotted in Figure 5.4 are

$$\frac{3}{5} = 0.60, \quad \frac{6}{10} = 0.60, \quad \frac{8}{15} \approx 0.53, \quad \frac{12}{20} = 0.60, \quad \frac{14}{25} = 0.56, \quad \ldots, \quad \frac{51}{100} = 0.51$$

Observe that the proportion of heads fluctuates but comes closer and closer to 0.50, the probability of heads for each flip of the coin.

FIGURE 5.3

Computer simulation of 100 flips of a balanced coin (MINITAB 10 for Windows).

```
MTB > Random 100 cl;
SUBC>     Bernoulli .5.
MTB > write cl
```

Data Display (WRITE)

```
0  0  1  1  1  1  1  0  0  1
1  0  0  1  0  1  1  1  0  1
0  0  1  0  1  1  0  1  0  0
1  1  0  1  0  0  1  1  1  0
1  0  1  0  0  0  0  1  0  0
1  1  0  0  0  0  0  1  0  0
1  1  0  0  1  1  1  0  1  1
1  0  1  1  0  1  1  0  0  0
0  0  0  1  0  0  1  0  1  1
1  0  1  1  1  1  0  1  0  1
```

```
MTB > Tally cl;
SUBC>     Counts.
```

Summary Statistics for Discrete Variables

```
      Cl     Count
       0       49
       1       51
```

FIGURE 5.4

Graph illustrating Law of Large Numbers.

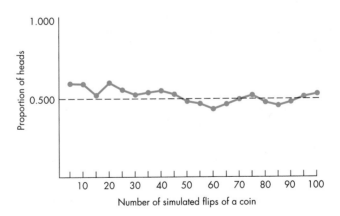

In the frequency interpretation, the probability of an event is defined in terms of what happens to similar events in the long run, so let us examine briefly whether it is at all meaningful to talk about the probability of an event which can occur only once. For instance, can we assign a probability to the event that Ms. Bertha Jones will be able to leave the hospital within four days after having an appendectomy, or to the event that a certain major-party candidate will win an upcoming gubernatorial election? If we put ourselves in the position of Ms. Jones' doctor, we might check medical records, discover that patients left the hospital within four days after an appendectomy in, say 78 percent of hundreds of cases, and apply this figure to Ms. Jones. This may not be of much comfort to Ms. Jones, but it does provide a meaning for a probability statement about her leaving the hospital within four days—the probability is 0.78.

This illustrates that when we make a probability statement about a specific (nonrepeatable) event, the frequency interpretation of probability leaves us no choice but to refer to a set of similar events. As can well be imagined, however, this can easily lead to complications, since the choice of similar events is generally neither obvious nor straightforward. With reference to Ms. Jones' appendectomy, we might consider as similar only cases in which the patients were of the same sex, only cases in which the patients were also of the same age as Ms. Jones, or only cases in which the patients were also of the same height and weight as Ms. Jones. Ultimately, the choice of similar events is a matter of personal judgment, and it is by no means contradictory that we can arrive at different probability estimates, all valid, concerning the same event.

With regard to the question whether a certain major-party candidate will win an upcoming gubernatorial election, suppose that we ask the persons who have conducted a poll how sure they are that the candidate will win. If they say they are "95 percent sure" (that is, if they assign a probability of 0.95 to the candidate's winning the election), this is not meant to imply that he would win 95 percent of the time if he ran for office a great number of times. Rather, it means that the pollsters' prediction is based on a method which works 95 percent of the time. It is in this way that we must interpret many of the probabilities attached to statistical results.

Finally, let us mention a third probability concept which is currently enjoying favor. According to this point of view, probabilities are interpreted as **personal** or **subjective** evaluations. They reflect one's belief with regard to the uncertainties that are involved, and they apply especially when there is little or no direct evidence, so that there really is no choice but to consider collateral (indirect) information, educated guesses, and perhaps intuition and other subjective factors. Subjective probabilities are sometimes determined by putting the issues in question on a money basis, as will be explained in Sections 6.3 and 7.1

◢ EXERCISES

5.48   When one card is drawn from a well-shuffled deck of 52 standard playing cards, what are the probabilities of getting
(a) the queen of hearts;
(b) a face card (meaning jack, queen, or king) of any suit;
(c) a red card;
(d) any one of a 2, 3, or 4;
(e) a diamond?

5.49   Two cards are dealt from a well-shuffled deck. What are the probabilities of getting
(a) two aces;   (b) two face cards;
(c) two black cards; (d) two diamonds?

5.50   If three cards are dealt from a well-shuffled deck, find the probabilities of getting

(a) three face cards;   (b) three jacks;

(c) two aces and one king;   (d) three hearts.

5.51   If we roll a balanced die, what are the probabilities of getting

(a) a 6; (b) an even number?

5.52   If we roll a pair of balanced dice, what are the probabilities of getting

(a) a 5; (b) a 7;

(c) an 11; (d) either a 7 or an 11?

5.53   If H stands for heads and T for tails, the sixteen possible outcomes for four flips of a coin are

HHHH	HTHH	THHH	TTHH
HHHT	HTHT	THHT	TTHT
HHTH	HTTH	THTH	TTTH
HHTT	HTTT	THTT	TTTT

If these 16 outcomes are equally likely, what are the probabilities of getting 0, 1, 2, 3, or 4 heads?

5.54   A bowl contains 15 red beads, 30 white beads, 20 blue beads, and 7 black beads. If one of the beads is drawn at random, what are the probabilities that it will be

(a) red; (b) white or blue;

(c) black; (d) neither white nor black?

5.55   A bowl contains 25 red marbles, 18 yellow marbles, and 11 blue marbles. If one of the marbles is selected at random, find the probabilities that it will be

(a) red; (b) yellow or blue

(c) blue; (d) neither red nor blue.

5.56   The balls used in selecting numbers for BINGO carry the numbers 1, 2, 3, ..., 75. If one of the balls is selected at random, what are the probabilities that it will be

(a) an even number;

(b) a number which is 15 or below;

(c) a number which is 60 or above?

5.57   If a game has *n* equally likely outcomes, what is the probability of each individual outcome?

5.58   Among the 15 applicants for three positions at a newspaper, 10 are college graduates. If the selections are random, what are the probabilities that the positions will be filled with

(a) three applicants with college degrees;

(b) two applicants with college degrees and one without;

(c) three applicants without college degrees?

5.59   A carton of 24 light bulbs includes two that are defective. If two of the bulbs are chosen at random, what are the probabilities that

(a) neither bulb will be defective;

(b) one of the bulbs will be defective;

(c) both bulbs will be defective?

5.60   A hoard of medieval coins discovered in Spain includes 24 struck in Seville and 16 struck in Toledo. If a person chooses four of these coins at random, what is the probability that he or she will get two coins from each city?

5.61   The seven cities in the United States with the most murders in 1990 were New York, Los Angeles, Chicago, Detroit, Houston, Philadelphia, and Washington. If a television news program randomly selects two of these cities as a subject for a special report, what is the probability that the selection

(a) will include Chicago;

(b) will consist of Detroit and Houston?

5.62   On a tray there are six pieces of chocolate cake and five pieces of walnut cake. If a waiter randomly picks two pieces of cake from the tray and gives them to diners who ordered chocolate cake, what is the probability that he is making a mistake?

5.63   If 226 of 300 randomly selected newspaper subscribers indicated that they read the comics section daily, estimate the probability that any one subscriber selected randomly would read the comics section daily.

5.64   If 103 of 150 randomly selected riders of a bus line felt that the buses were too dirty, estimate the probability that any one rider selected randomly would feel that the buses were too dirty.

5.65   Among the 842 armed robberies that occurred in a certain city during the last five years, 143 were never solved. Assuming that conditions have not changed, estimate the probability that an armed robbery in this city will not be solved.

5.66   With reference to Exercise 5.65, give an example of a change in conditions which would make the estimate of the probability unreasonable.

5.67   In a sample of 325 cars using a state-run emissions testing station, it was found that 62 of the cars had one or more defective exterior lights. Estimate the probability that a car using the emissions testing station will have one or more defective exterior lights.

5.68   A survey of 1,290 persons randomly selected from the visitors to a national park found that 726 did not walk farther than one-half mile from their parking space. Estimate the probability that any randomly chosen visitor would not walk farther than one-half mile from his or her parking space.

5.69   You can get a feeling for the Law of Large Numbers by flipping coins. Flip a coin 100 times, and plot the accumulated proportion of heads after each five flips, as in Figure 5.4 on page 125. By how much do these proportions differ from 0.50 after the first 50 flips?

5.70   Record the last digit on the license plates of 300 cars. After each 10 cars plot the accumulated proportions of 5's, as in Figure 5.4 on page 125. By how much do these proportions differ from 0.10 after the first 200 cars?

5.71   Record the first 200 numbers encountered in a newspaper, beginning with page 1 and proceeding in any convenient systematic fashion. Include also numbers appearing in advertisements. For each of these numbers note the leftmost digit and record the proportions of 1's, 2's, 3's, ..., and 9's. Note that 0 cannot be a leftmost digit. In the decimal number 0.0056, the leftmost digit is the 5. The results will be quite surprising, but the Law of Large Numbers tells you that you must be estimating correctly.

5.5   CHECKLIST OF KEY TERMS† *(with page references to their definitions)*

Binomial coefficients, 113

Classical probability concept, 121

Combinations, 112

Computer simulation, 124

Factorial notation, 110

Frequency interpretation of probability, 123

Law of Large Numbers, 124

Multiplication of choices, 107

Odds, 121

▥ *Pascal's triangle,* 120

Permutations, 109

Personal probability, 126

Probability, 121

Random selection, 122

Subjective probability, 126

Tree diagram, 106

†Terms introduced in exercises are shown in *italics.*

REVIEW EXERCISES

5.72   Certain government employees are classified into six categories according to age and four categories according to marital status. In how many ways can one of these employees be classified?

5.73   In the meat department of a supermarket there are 10 rib steaks and 12 sirloin steaks. If the first customer buys one of the steaks and the second customer buys one of each kind, how many choices does the second customer have if

(a) the first customer buys a rib steak;

(b) the first customer buys a sirloin steak?

5.74   Determine whether each of the following is true or false:

(a) $\dfrac{1}{3!} + \dfrac{1}{4!} = \dfrac{5}{4!}$;   (b) $4! + 5! = 6 \cdot 4!$;

(c) $\dfrac{16!}{13!} = 16 \cdot 15 \cdot 14 \cdot 13$;   (d) $2! + 2! + 1! + 0! = 3!$.

5.75   A market research organization surveyed 625 people and found that 102 of them would like more baseball games shown on network television. Estimate the probability that any one person would express this opinion.

5.76   The five finalists in a college art competition are identified as

BG   CW   RM   JE   MK

Draw a tree diagram showing the different ways in which the judges can choose the winner and the first runner-up.

5.77   What is the probability of rolling a total of five with a pair of balanced dice?

5.78   In how many different ways can you arrange eight books on a shelf

(a) if all eight books are different;

(b) if the books include three identical copies of one title, two identical copies of another title, and three one-of-a-kind titles?

5.79   A questionnaire on personality consists of ten questions, having four different answers. In how many different ways can you choose one answer for each question?

5.80   In how many ways can three newspaper reporters, *A*, *B*, and *C*, divide up 12 assignments so that *A* will cover three, *B* will cover five, and *C* will cover four?

5.81   A business employs three persons named Jones: Harry Jones, Norma Jones, and Richard Jones. Draw a tree diagram to show the different ways in which the payroll department can distribute their paychecks so that each of them receives a check made out to a Jones. In how many of the possibilities will

(a) none of them get the right check;

(b) only one of them get the right check;

(c) only two of them get the right check;

(d) all three of them get the right check?

5.82   In how many ways can a person buy a pound each of three of the 16 kinds of cheese carried by a gourmet food shop?

5.83   A women's clothing shop has three mannequins for the left, center, and right positions in its small display window. The store manager has eight different fall outfits, and she wants to select three of these for display. In how many different ways can she design the store window

(a) if the mannequins are identical;

(b) if the mannequins are distinguishable but cannot be moved;

(c) if the mannequins are distinguishable and can be moved among the three positions in the window?

5.84   Suppose that Christine flips a coin 100 times and gets 32 heads, which is far short of the number of heads she might expect. Then she flips the coin another 100 times and gets 44 heads, which is again short of the number of heads she might expect. Can she accuse the Law of Large Numbers of "letting her down"? Explain.

⊞ 5.85   How many different gin rummy hands, consisting of 10 cards, can be dealt from an ordinary deck of 52 playing cards?

⊞ 5.86   How many different bridge hands, consisting of 13 cards, can be dealt from an ordinary deck of 52 playing cards?

5.87   If H stands for heads and T for tails, the 32 possible outcomes for five flips of a coin are

HHHHH	HTHHH	THHHH	TTHHH
HHHHT	HTHHT	THHHT	TTHHT
HHHTH	HTHTH	THHTH	TTHTH
HHHTT	HTHTT	THHTT	TTHTT
HHTHH	HTTHH	THTHH	TTTHH
HHTHT	HTTHT	THTHT	TTTHT
HHTTH	HTTTH	THTTH	TTTTH
HHTTT	HTTTT	THTTT	TTTTT

If these 32 outcomes are equally likely, what are the probabilities of getting 0, 1, 2, 3, 4, or 5 heads?

5.88   If one letter is chosen at random from the word "anemone," what is the probability that it will be a consonant?

5.89   Among 800 married women interviewed, 648 said that they prefer to be called "Mrs." rather than "Ms." Estimate the probability that a married woman prefers to be called "Mrs." rather than "Ms."

5.90   A restaurant has on its menu eight fish dishes, four potato dishes, and three green vegetables. In how many ways can a diner choose

   (a)   one of the fish dishes and one of the potato dishes;

   (b)   one of the fish dishes, one of the potato dishes, and one of the green vegetables?

5.91   A carton of 16 hair dryers contains one with serious damage, two which have minor blemishes, and the others in perfect condition. If three of the dryers are randomly selected from the carton, find the probability that

   (a)   all three will be in perfect condition;

   (b)   two will be in perfect condition and one will have a minor blemish;

   (c)   two will be in perfect condition and one will have serious damage;

   (d)   two will have minor blemishes and one will have serious damage.

5.92   If 756 of 1,200 letters mailed by a government agency were delivered within 48 hours, estimate the probability that any one letter mailed by the agency will be delivered within 48 hours.

5.93   In Daddy Dee's ice cream parlor, you have a choice of 24 flavors with or without chocolate syrup, whipped cream, chopped nuts, crushed pineapple, or marshmallow syrup. In how many different ways can you order your ice cream?

5.94   On his weight-reducing diet Freddy is allowed to have, at most, eight eggs in five days, with no more than two eggs for any single day. Construct a tree diagram to determine the number of ways in which Freddy can consume exactly eight eggs in five days.

5.95 A food editor and three friends are trying out a new restaurant. If the menu lists 19 different entrees, in how many ways can these diners each order a different entree?

5.7 REFERENCES

Informal introductions to probability, written primarily for the layperson, may be found in

GARVIN, A. D., *Probability in Your Life.* Portland, Maine: J. Weston Walch Publisher, 1978.

HUFF, D., and GEIS, I., *How to Take a Chance.* New York: W.W. Norton & Company, Inc., 1959.

KOTZ, S., and STROUP, D. E., *Educated Guessing: How to Cope in an Uncertain World.* New York: Marcel Dekker, Inc., 1983.

LEVINSON, H. C., *Chance, Luck, and Statistics.* New York: Dover Publications, Inc., 1963.

MOSTELLER, F., KRUSKAL, W. H., LINK, R. F., PIETERS, R. S., and RISING, G. R., *Statistics by Example: Weighing Chances.* Reading, Mass.: Addison-Wesley Publishing Company, Inc., 1973.

WEAVER, W., *Lady Luck: The Theory of Probability.* New York: Dover Publications, Inc., 1982.

For fascinating reading on the history of probability, see

DAVID, F. N., *Games, Gods and Gambling.* New York: Hafner Press, 1962.

and the first three chapters of

STIGLER, S. M., *The History of Statistics.* Cambridge, Mass.: Harvard University Press, 1986.

Some rules
of probability

*I*n the study of probability there are three fundamental kinds of questions:

1. *What do we mean when we say that the probability of an event is, say, 0.50, 0.78, or 0.44?*

2. *How are the numbers we call probabilities determined, or measured, in practice?*

3. *What are the mathematical rules that probabilities must obey?*

For the most part, we have already studied the first two kinds of questions in Chapter 5. In the classical probability concept we are concerned with equally likely possibilities, count the ones that are favorable, and use the formula s/n. In the frequency interpretation we are concerned with proportions of "successes" in the long run and base our estimates on what has happened in the past. When it comes to subjective probabilities, we are concerned with a measure of a person's belief. In Section 6.3, and also in Section 7.1, we shall see how such subjective probabilities can actually be determined.

*In this chapter, after some preliminaries in Section 6.1, we concentrate on the rules that probabilities must obey, namely, on the **theory of probability**. This includes the basic postulates, the relationship between probabilities and odds, the addition rules, the definition of conditional probability, the multiplication rules, and finally, Bayes' theorem.* ■

6.1 SAMPLE SPACES AND EVENTS

In statistics, the word *experiment* is used in a very broad and unconventional sense. "Experiment" refers to any process of observation or measurement. Thus, an **experiment** may consist of counting how many times a student has been absent; or the simple process of noting whether a light is on or off; or whether a person is single or married; or it may consist of the very complicated process of obtaining and evaluating data to predict trends in the economy, to find the source of social unrest, or study the cause of a disease. The results that one obtains from an experiment, whether they are instrument readings, counts, "yes or no" answers, or values obtained through extensive calculations, are called the **outcomes** of the experiment.

For each experiment, the set of all possible outcomes is called the **sample space,** usually denoted by the letter S. For instance, if a zoologist must choose three of 24 guinea pigs for an experiment, the sample space consists of the $\binom{24}{3} = 2{,}024$ ways that the selection can be made. If a college dean must assign two of 84 faculty members as advisors to a political science club, the sample space consists of the $\binom{84}{2} = 3{,}486$ ways in which this can be done. Also, if we are concerned with the number of days it rains in Chicago during the month of January, the sample space is the set

$$S = \{0, 1, 2, 3, 4, \ldots, 30, 31\}$$

When we study the outcomes of an experiment, we usually identify the various possibilities with numbers, points, or some other kind of symbol, so that we can treat all questions about them mathematically, without having to go through long verbal descriptions of what has taken place, is taking place, or will take place. For instance, if there are eight candidates for a scholarship and we let *a*, *b*, *c*, *d*, *e*, *f*, *g*, and *h* denote that it is awarded to Ms. Adam, Mr. Bean, Miss Clark, and so on, then the sample space for this experiment is the set

$$S = \{a,\ b,\ c,\ d,\ e,\ f,\ g,\ h\}$$

The use of points rather than letters or numbers is advantageous because it is easier to visualize the various possibilities, and perhaps discover special features that several of the outcomes may have in common.

Example

A used-car dealer has two 1992 Dodge Caravans on his lot and we are interested in how many each of two salespersons will sell in a given week.

(a) Using two coordinates, so that (0, 1), for example, represents the outcome that the first salesperson will sell neither of the Caravans and the second salesperson will sell one, (1, 1) represents the outcome that each of the two salespersons will sell one of the Caravans, and (2, 0) represents the outcome that the first salesperson will sell them both, list all possible outcomes of this experiment.

(b) Draw a figure showing the corresponding points of the sample space.

solution

(a) The six possible outcomes are

$$(0, 0) \quad (1, 0) \quad (0, 1) \quad (2, 0) \quad (1, 1) \text{ and } (0, 2)$$

(b) The corresponding points are shown in Figure 6.1, from which it is apparent, for instance, that they sell equally many 1992 Caravans in two of the six possibilities, and that they sell both vans in three of the six possibilities.   ◤ ◤ ◤

FIGURE 6.1

Sample space for two-salespersons example.

Number of vans sold by first salesperson

Usually, we classify sample spaces according to the number of elements, or points, which they contain. The ones that we have mentioned thus far in this section contained 2,024, 3,486, 32, 8, and 6 elements, and we refer to them all as **finite.** In this chapter we consider only sample spaces that are finite, but in later chapters we also consider sample spaces that are **infinite.** An infinite sample space arises, for example, when we throw a dart at a target and there is a continuum of points that we may hit.

In statistics, any subset of a sample space is called an **event.** By **subset** we mean any part of a set, including the set as a whole. An **empty set,** denoted by $\emptyset$, has no elements at all.

For instance, for the example dealing with the number of days that it rains in Chicago during the month of January,

$$F = \{18, 19, 20, 21, 22, 23, 24\}$$

is the event that there will be from 18 to 24 rainy days, and

$$G = \{20, 21, 22, ..., 30, 31\}$$

is the event that there will be at least 20 rainy days. As is the custom, we denoted these events by capital letters.

Example

With reference to Figure 6.1, express in words what events are represented by
  (a) $C = \{(0, 0), (1, 1)\}$;
  (b) $D = \{(1, 0), (1, 1)\}$;
  (c) $E = \{(0, 2)\}$.

solution

(a) C is the event that the two salespersons will sell equally many of the 1992 Dodge Caravans.
(b) D is the event that the first salesperson will sell one and only one of the two vans.
(c) E is the event that the second salesperson will sell both vans. ◪ ◪ ◪

In this example, the events C and E have no elements in common. Such events are called **mutually exclusive,** meaning that they cannot occur at the same time. If the two salespersons sell equally many of these vans (event C), then it is impossible for the second salesperson to sell them both (event E). Observe also that events C and D are not mutually exclusive since they both contain the outcome $(1, 1)$, in which each of the salespersons sells one of the vans.

In many probability problems we are interested in events that can be expressed in terms of two or more events by forming **unions, intersections,** and **complements.** In general, the union of two events A and B, denoted by $A \cup B$, is the event that consists of all the elements (outcomes) contained in A, in B, or in both. The intersection of two events A and B, denoted by $A \cap B$, is the event that consists of all the elements contained in both A and B. And the complement of A, denoted by A', is the event that consists of all the elements of the sample space that are not contained in A. We usually read $\cup$ as "or," $\cap$ as "and," and A' as "not A." One sometimes encounters the symbols A_c or $\overline{A}$ for "not A." We will use A'.

Example

With reference to the example dealing with the number of days that it rains in Chicago in January and the events F and G defined on page 135, list the outcomes comprising each of the following events, and express the events in words:
(a) $F \cup G$; (b) $F \cap G$; (c) G'; (d) $F' \cap G'$.

solution

(a) Since $F \cup G$ contains all the elements that are in F, in G, or in both, we find that

$$F \cup G = \{18, 19, 20, ..., 30, 31\}$$

and this is the event that there will be at least 18 rainy days.
(b) Since $F \cap G$ contains all the elements that are in both F and G, we find that

$$F \cap G = \{20, 21, 22, 23, 24\}$$

and this is the event that there will be from 20 to 24 rainy days.
(c) Since G' contains all the elements of the sample space that are not in G, we find that

$$G' = \{0, 1, 2, ..., 18, 19\}$$

and this is the event that there will be at most 19 rainy days.
(d) Since $F' \cap G'$ contains all the elements of the sample space that are neither in F nor in G, we find that

$$F' \cap G' = \{0, 1, 2, ..., 16, 17\}$$

and this is the event that there will be at most 17 rainy days.   ◢ ◢ ◢

Sample spaces and events, particularly relationships among events, are often illustrated by **Venn diagrams** such as those of Figures 6.2 and 6.3. In each case, the sample space is represented by a rectangle, and events by circles or parts of circles within the rectangle. The tinted regions of the four Venn diagrams of Figure 6.2 represent event X, the complement of event X, the union of events X and Y, and the intersection of events X and Y.

X

X'

$X \cup Y$

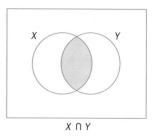

$X \cap Y$

FIGURE 6.2   *Venn diagram*

Example

If X is the event that Mr. Green is a naturalized citizen and Y is the event that his wife is a naturalized citizen, what events are represented by the tinted regions of the four Venn diagrams of Figure 6.2?

solution

The tinted region of the first diagram represents the event that Mr. Green is a naturalized citizen; the tinted region of the second diagram represents the event that Mr. Green is not a naturalized citizen; the tinted region of the third diagram represents the event that Mr. Green, his wife, or both are naturalized citizens; and the tinted region of the fourth diagram represents the event that Mr. Green and his wife are both naturalized citizens. ◪ ◪ ◪

When we deal with three events, we draw circles as in Figure 6.3. In this diagram, the circles divide the sample space into eight regions, numbered 1 through 8, and it is easy to determine whether the corresponding events are in X or in X', in Y or in Y', and in Z or Z'.

Example

If X is the event that hamburgers will be served at the company picnic, Y is the event that beer will be served, and Z is the event that watermelon will be served, express in words the events which are represented by the following regions of the Venn diagram of Figure 6.3:
  (a) region 3;
  (b) regions 1 and 2 together;
  (c) regions 4, 6, 7, and 8 together.

solution

  (a) Since this region is part of Y and part of Z, but not part of X, it represents the event that beer and watermelon will be served at the picnic, but hamburgers will not be served.
  (b) Since this region is part of both X and Y, it represents the event that hamburgers and beer will be served.
  (c) Since these are the entire region outside Y, the event is that beer will not be served. ◪ ◪ ◪

FIGURE 6.3

Venn diagram.

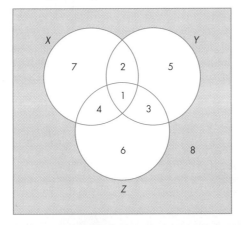

◢ EXERCISES

6.1   With reference to the example on page 134, suppose that a, b, c, d, e, f, g, and h denote the events that Ms. Adam, Mr. Bean, Miss Clark, Mrs. Daly, Mr. Earl, Ms. Fuentes, Ms. Gardner, and Mr. Hall is awarded the scholarship, and that

$$U = \{b, e, h\} \quad \text{and} \quad V = \{a, c, e, f, g\}$$

List the outcomes that comprise each of the following events and also express the events in words:

(a) U';   (b) $U \cup V$;   (c) $U \cap V$.

6.2   With reference to Exercise 6.1, are the two events U and V mutually exclusive?

6.3   In an experiment, individuals are asked to pick a number from 1 to 10, so that for each individual the sample space is the set

$$S = \{1, 2, 3, ..., 10\}$$

If $R = \{1, 2, 3, 4, 5\}$ and $S = \{4, 5, 6, 7\}$, express in terms of R and S the event that a person will

(a) pick a number greater than 5;

(b) pick a 4 or a 5;

(c) pick a number greater than 7;

(d) pick a number less than 6.

6.4   For an experiment related to a certain popular game involving the selection of a number from 1 to 75, the sample space is

$$S = \{1, 2, 3, ..., 75\}$$

Consider the events

$$B = \{1, 2, ..., 15\}$$

$$I = \{16, 17, ..., 30\}$$

$$N = \{31, 32, ..., 45\}$$

$$G = \{46, 47, ..., 60\}$$

$$O = \{61, 62, ..., 75\}$$

In terms of these events, express the event that the selected number will be

(a) greater than 30;   (b) at most 45;

(c) less than 16;   (d) less than 80.

(e) Which of the 10 pairs of the events B, I, N, G, O are mutually exclusive?

6.5   To construct sample spaces for experiments where we deal with categorical data, we often code the various alternatives by assigning them numbers. For instance, if individuals are asked whether their favorite color is red, yellow, blue, green, brown, white, purple, or some other color, we might assign these alternatives the codes 1, 2, 3, 4, 5, 6, 7, and 8. If

$$A = \{3, 4\}, \quad B = \{1, 2, 3, 4, 5, 6, 7\}, \quad \text{and} \quad C = \{6, 7, 8\}$$

list the outcomes that comprise each of the following events and also express the events in words:

(a) B';   (b) $A \cap C$;   (c) $B \cap C'$;   (d) $A \cup B'$.

6.6   With reference to Exercise 6.5, which of the pairs of events, A and B, A and C, and B and C, are mutually exclusive?

6.7   With reference to the two automobile salespeople and Figure 6.1, describe each of the following events in words:

      (a) $N = \{(1, 0), (1, 1)\}$;   (b) $O = \{(0, 1), (0, 2)\}$;

      (c) $P = \{(0, 0), (1, 1)\}$;   (d) $Q = \{(1, 0), (2, 0)\}$.

6.8   With reference to Exercise 6.7, which of the six pairs of events, N and O, N and P, N and Q, O and P, O and Q, and P and Q, are mutually exclusive?

6.9   With reference to the two automobile salespeople and Figure 6.1, list the points of the sample space that comprise the following events:

      (a) Between them, the two salespeople will sell both vans.

      (b) The first salesperson will sell more vans than the second salesperson.

      (c) The first salesperson will sell at least as many vans as the second salesperson.

6.10   A movie critic has two days in which to view some of the pictures that have recently been released. She wants to see at least three of the movies but not more than three on either day.

      (a) Using two coordinates so that (3, 1), for example, represents the event that she will see three of the movies on the first day and one on the second day, draw a diagram similar to that of Figure 6.1 showing the 10 points of the corresponding sample space.

      (b) If T is the event that altogether she will see three of the movies, U is the event that she will see more of the movies on the second day than on the first, V is the event that she will see three of the movies on the first day, and W is the event that she will see equally many movies on both days, list the outcomes comprising each of these events.

6.11   With reference to Exercise 6.10, which of the six pairs of events, T and U, T and V, T and W, U and V, U and W, and V and W, are mutually exclusive?

6.12   With reference to Exercise 6.10, list the outcomes that comprise each of the following events and express the events in words:

      (a) V';   (b) $T \cap U$;   (c) $V' \cap W$.

6.13   A small marina has three fishing boats which are sometimes in dry dock for repairs.

      (a) Using two coordinates, so that (2, 1), for example, represents the event that two of the fishing boats are in dry dock and one is rented out for the day, and (0, 2) represents the event that none of the boats is in dry dock and two are rented out for the day, draw a diagram similar to that of Figure 6.1 showing the 10 points of the corresponding sample space.

      (b) If K is the event that at least two of the boats are rented out for the day, L is the event that more boats are in dry dock than are rented out for the day, and M is the event that all the boats that are not in dry dock are rented out for the day, list the outcomes that comprise each of these events.

      (c) Which of the three pairs of events, K and L, K and M, and L and M, are mutually exclusive?

6.14   With reference to Exercise 6.13, list the outcomes that comprise each of the following events and express the events in words:

      (a) K';   (b) $L \cap M$.

Applicant	Native Born?	College Graduate?	Marital Status
A	No	Yes	Single
B	No	No	Married
C	Yes	Yes	Married
D	Yes	No	Single
E	Yes	Yes	Married
F	Yes	No	Married

6.15   There are six applicants for an executive job, and the table above gives some facts about their backgrounds:
One of these applicants is to get the job, and the event that the job is given to a native-born person, for example, is denoted {C, D, E, F}. State in a similar manner the event that the job is awarded to

(a) a single person;

(b) a native-born college graduate;

(c) a married person who is foreign born;

(d) a college graduate.

6.16   Which of the following pairs of events are mutually exclusive? Explain your answers.

(a) A driver getting a ticket for speeding and a ticket for going through a red light.

(b) Being foreign-born and being President of the United States.

(c) A baseball player getting a walk and hitting a home run in the same at bat.

(d) A baseball player getting a walk and hitting a home run in the same game.

(e) Having rain and sunshine on July 4, 1990.

6.17   In Figure 6.4, L is the event that a driver has liability insurance and C is the event that he has collision insurance. Explain in words what events are represented by regions 1, 2, 3, and 4.

6.18   With reference to Exercise 6.17, what events are represented by

(a) regions 1 and 2 together;

(b) regions 2 and 4 together;

(c) regions 1, 2, and 3 together?

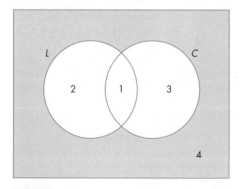

FIGURE 6.4   *Venn diagram for Exercise 6.17.*

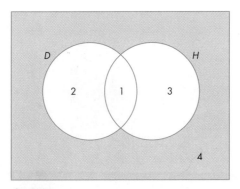

FIGURE 6.5 _____ *Venn diagram for Exercise 6.19.*

6.19   In Figure 6.5, *D* is the event that a flight leaves Denver on time and *H* is the event that it arrives in Houston on time. Explain in words what events are represented by regions 1, 2, 3, and 4.

6.20   With reference to Exercise 6.19 what events are represented by

(a) regions 1 and 3 together;

(b) regions 3 and 4 together;

(c) regions 2, 3, and 4 together?

6.21   Venn diagrams are also useful in determining the numbers of outcomes associated with various events. One of the 240 members of a tennis club is to be named Player of the Year. If 145 of the members are women, 85 use a two-handed backhand, and 50 are women who use a two-handed backhand, how many of the outcomes correspond to the choice of a man who does not use a two-handed backhand?

6.22   One of the 200 business majors at a college is to be chosen for the student senate. If 77 of these students are enrolled in a course in accounting, 64 are enrolled in a course in business law, and 92 are not enrolled in either course, how many of the outcomes correspond to the choice of a business major who is enrolled in both courses?

6.23   With reference to the example of page 137 and Figure 6.3, what regions or combinations of regions represent the events that

(a) hamburgers will not be served;

(b) hamburgers will be served, but watermelon will not;

(c) beer and watermelon will both be served;

(d) neither beer nor watermelon will be served?

6.24   In Figure 6.6, *E, T,* and *N* are the events that a car brought to a garage needs an engine overhaul, transmission repairs, or new tires. Express in words what events are represented by

(a) region 1;

(b) region 3;

(c) region 7;

(d) regions 1 and 4 together;

(e) regions 2 and 5 together;

(f) regions 3, 5, 6, and 8 together.

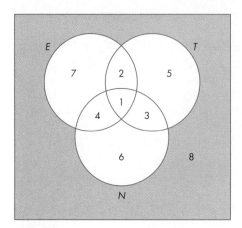

FIGURE 6.6   *Venn diagram for Exercise 6.24.*

6.25   With reference to Exercise 6.24 and the Venn diagram of Figure 6.6, list the regions or combinations of regions which represent the events that a car brought to the garage needs

(a) transmission repairs, but neither an engine overhaul nor new tires;

(b) an engine overhaul and transmission repairs;

(c) transmission repairs or new tires, but not an engine overhaul;

(d) new tires.

6.26   As we pointed out in Exercise 6.21, Venn diagrams are also useful in determining the numbers of outcomes associated with various circumstances. Among 60 houses advertised for sale there are 8 with swimming pools, three or more bedrooms, and wall-to-wall carpeting; 5 with swimming pools, three or more bedrooms, but no wall-to-wall carpeting; 3 with swimming pools, wall-to-wall carpeting, but fewer than three bedrooms; 8 with swimming pools but neither wall-to-wall carpeting nor three or more bedrooms; 24 with three or more bedrooms, but neither a swimming pool nor wall-to-wall carpeting; 2 with three or more bedrooms, wall-to-wall carpeting, but no swimming pool; 3 with wall-to-wall carpeting, but neither a swimming pool nor three or more bedrooms; and 7 without any of these features. If one of these houses is to be chosen for a television commercial, how many outcomes correspond to the choice of

(a) a house with a swimming pool;

(b) a house with wall-to-wall carpeting?

6.27   Venn diagrams are often used to verify relationships among sets, subsets, or events, without requiring formal proofs based on the algebra of sets. We simply check whether the expressions that are supposed to be equal are represented by the same region of a Venn diagram. Use Venn diagrams to show that

(a) $A \cup (A \cap B) = A$;

(b) $(A \cap B) \cup (A \cap B') = A$;

(c) $(A \cap B)' = A' \cup B'$ and also $(A \cup B)' = A' \cap B'$;

(d) $A \cup B = (A \cap B) \cup (A \cap B') \cup (A' \cap B)$;

(e) $A \cap (B \cup C) = (A \cap B) \cup (A \cap C)$.

6.2 THE POSTULATES OF PROBABILITY

Probabilities always pertain to the occurrence of events, and now that we have learned how to deal mathematically with events, let us turn to the rules that probabilities must obey. To formulate these rules, we continue the practice of denoting events by capital letters and write the probability of event A as $P(A)$, the probability of event B as $P(B)$, and so on. As before, we denote the set of all possible outcomes, the sample space, by the letter S.

Most basic among all the rules of probability are the three **postulates,** which, as we shall state them here, apply when the sample space S is finite. Beginning with the first two, we write

First Two Postulates of Probability

> *1. Probabilities are positive real numbers or zero; symbolically,*
>
> $$P(A) \geq 0 \quad \text{for any event } A.$$
>
> *2. Every sample space has probability 1; symbolically,*
>
> $$P(S) = 1 \quad \text{for any sample space } S.$$

To justify these two postulates, as well as the third one which follows, let us show that they are in agreement with the classical probability concept as well as the frequency interpretation. In section 6.3 we shall see to what extent the postulates are compatible also with subjective probabilities.

The first two postulates are in agreement with the classical probability concept because the fraction $\frac{s}{n}$ is always positive or zero, and for the entire sample space (which includes all n outcomes) the probability is

$$\frac{s}{n} = \frac{n}{n} = 1$$

When it comes to the frequency interpretation, the proportion of the time that an event will occur cannot be a negative number, and one of the outcomes in the sample space must occur 100 percent of the time, that is, with probability 1.

Although a probability of 1 is thus identified with certainty, in actual practice we also assign a probability of 1 to events that are "practically certain" to occur. For instance, we would assign a probability of 1 to the event that at least one person will vote in the next presidential election, even though it is not logically certain. Similarly, we would assign a probability of 1 to the event that not every student entering college in the fall of 1997 will apply for admission to Princeton University.

The third postulate of probability is especially important, but it is not quite as obvious as the other two.

Third Postulate of Probability

> *3. If two events are mutually exclusive, the probability that one or the other will occur equals the sum of their probabilities. Symbolically,*
>
> $$P(A \cup B) = P(A) + P(B)$$
>
> *for any two mutually exclusive events A and B.*

For instance, if the probability that weather conditions will improve during a certain week is 0.62 and the probability that they will remain unchanged is 0.23, then the probability that they will either improve or remain unchanged is

$$0.62 + 0.23 = 0.85$$

Similarly, if the probabilities that a student will get an A or a B in a course are 0.13 and 0.29, then the probability that he or she will get either an A or a B is

$$0.13 + 0.29 = 0.42$$

To show that the third postulate is also compatible with the classical probability concept, let s_1 and s_2 denote the number of equally likely possibilities that comprise events A and B. Since A and B are mutually exclusive, no two of these possibilities are alike and all $s_1 + s_2$ of them comprise event $A \cup B$. Thus,

$$P(A) = \frac{s_1}{n}, \qquad P(B) = \frac{s_2}{n}, \qquad P(A \cup B) = \frac{s_1 + s_2}{n}$$

and

$$P(A) + P(B) = P(A \cup B)$$

Insofar as the frequency interpretation is concerned, if one event occurs, say, 36 percent of the time, another event occurs 41 percent of the time, and they cannot both occur at the same time (that is, they are mutually exclusive), then one or the other will occur $36 + 41 = 77$ percent of the time. This is in agreement with the third postulate.

By using the three postulates of probability, we can derive many further rules according to which probabilities must "behave"—some of them are easy to prove and some are not, but they all have important applications. Among the immediate consequences of the three postulates we find that probabilities can never be greater than 1, that an event which cannot occur has probability 0, and that the probabilities that an event will occur and that it will not occur always add up to 1. Symbolically,

Other Rules of Probability	
	$P(A) \leq 1$ for any event A
	$P(\varnothing) = 0$
	$P(A) + P(A') = 1$ for any event A

The first of these results simply expresses the fact that there cannot be more favorable outcomes than there are outcomes, or that an event cannot occur more than 100 percent of the time. The second result expresses the fact that when an event cannot occur there are $s = 0$ favorable outcomes, or that such an event occurs zero percent of the time. In actual practice, we also assign 0 probability to events which are so unlikely that we are "practically certain" they will not occur. For instance, in flipping a coin we will assign 0 probability to the event that the coin lands on its edge.

The third result can also be derived from the postulates of probability, and it can easily be seen that it is compatible with the classical probability concept and the frequency interpretation. In the classical concept, if there are s "successes" there are $n - s$ "failures," the corresponding probabilities are

$$\frac{s}{n} \quad \text{and} \quad \frac{n - s}{n},$$

and their sum is

$$\frac{s}{n} + \frac{n - s}{n} = \frac{n}{n} = 1$$

In accordance with the frequency interpretation, we can say that if some given investments are successful 22 percent of the time, then they are not successful 78 percent of the time, the corresponding probabilities are 0.22 and 0.78, and their sum is 1.

The examples that follow show how the postulates and the rules we gave above are put to use in actual practice.

Example

If A is the event that a student will stay home to study and B is the event that she will instead go to a movie, $P(A) = 0.64$, and $P(B) = 0.21$, find
(a) $P(A')$;   (b) $P(A \cup B)$;   (c) $P(A \cap B)$.

solution

(a) Using the final rule, we find that the probability of A', the event that the student will not stay home to study, is

$$1 - P(A) = 1 - 0.64 = 0.36$$

(b) Since A and B are mutually exclusive, we can use the third postulate and write

$$P(A \cup B) = P(A) + P(B) = 0.64 + 0.21 = 0.85$$

for the probability that the student will either stay home to study or go to a movie.

(c) Since A and B are mutually exclusive, they cannot possibly both occur and, hence,

$$P(A \cap B) = P(\varnothing) = 0$$

In problems like this, it often helps to draw a Venn diagram, fill in the probabilities associated with the various regions, and then read the answers directly off the diagram.

Example

If C is the event that at 9:30 A.M. a certain doctor is in his office and D is the event that he is in the hospital,

$$P(C) = 0.48 \quad \text{and} \quad P(D) = 0.27$$

find $P(C' \cap D')$, which is the probability that he is neither in his office nor in the hospital.

FIGURE 6.7

Venn diagram.

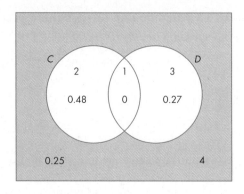

solution

Drawing the Venn diagram as in Figure 6.7, we first put a 0 probability into region 1 because the events C and D are mutually exclusive. It follows that the 0.48 probability of event C must go into region 2, the 0.27 probability of event D must go into region 3, and since the probability for the entire sample space must total 1, we put

$$1 - (0.48 + 0.27) = 0.25$$

into region 4. Since the event $C' \cap D'$ is represented by the region outside both circles, namely, region 4, we find that the answer is

$$P(C' \cap D') = 0.25$$

◢ ◢ ◢

6.3   PROBABILITIES AND ODDS

If an event is twice as likely to occur than not to occur, we say that the **odds** are 2 to 1 that it will occur; if an event is three times as likely to occur than not to occur, we say that the odds are 3 to 1; if an event is ten times as likely to occur than not to occur, we say that the odds are 10 to 1; and so on. In general,

> The odds that an event will occur are given by the ratio of the probability that it will occur to the probability that it will not occur.

Symbolically, if the probability of an event is p, the odds for its occurrence are a to b, where a and b are positive values such that

$$\frac{a}{b} = \frac{p}{1 - p}$$

It is customary to express odds in terms of positive integers having no common factors.

Example

What are the odds for the occurrence of an event if its probability is
(a) $\frac{5}{9}$;
(b) 0.85?

solution

(a) By definition, the odds are

$$\frac{5}{9} \text{ to } 1 - \frac{5}{9} = \frac{4}{9}, \quad \text{or} \quad 5 \text{ to } 4$$

(b) By definition, the odds are

0.85 to $1 - 0.85 = 0.15$,   85 to 15,   or better, 17 to 3   ◪ ◪ ◪

If an event is more likely not to occur than to occur, it is customary to quote the odds that it will not occur rather than the odds that it will occur.

Example

What are the odds, if the probability of an event is 0.20?

solution

The odds for the occurrence of the event are

0.20 to $1 - 0.20 = 0.80$,   or   1 to 4

but it is customary to say instead that the odds against the occurrence of the event are 4 to 1.   ◪ ◪ ◪

In betting, the term "odds" is also used to denote the ratio of the wager of one party to that of another. For instance, if a gambler says that he will give 3 to 1 odds on the occurrence of an event, he means that he is willing to bet $3 against $1 (or perhaps $30 against $10 or $1,500 against $500) that the event will occur. If such **betting odds** actually equal the odds that the event will occur, we say that the betting odds are **fair.** If a gambler really believes that a bet is fair, then he is, at least in principle, willing to bet on either side. The gambler in this situation would also be willing to bet $1 against $3 (or $10 against $30 or $500 against $1,500) that the event will not occur.

Example

Records show that $\frac{1}{12}$ of the trucks weighed at a certain check point in Nevada carry too heavy a load. If someone offers to bet $40 against $4 that the next truck weighed at this check point will not carry too heavy a load, are these betting odds fair?

solution

Since the probability is $1 - \frac{1}{12} = \frac{11}{12}$ that the truck will not carry too heavy a load, the odds are 11 to 1, and the bet would be fair if the person offered to bet $44 against $4 that the next truck weighed at the check point will not carry too heavy a load. Thus, the $40 against $4 bet is not fair; it favors the person offering the bet.   ◪ ◪ ◪

In most betting situations outside of casinos, the actual odds that an event will occur are unknown and opinions will be different. Suppose, for example, that a football game between the Wildcats and the Magpies is about to take place. Suppose also that Al believes that the odds that the Wildcats will win are 2 to 3. It happens that Bob believes that the odds that the Wildcats will win are 1 to 1.

Observe that Al is willing to bet $20 on the Wildcats to win $30. He is also willing to bet $30 on the Magpies to win $20.

Since Bob believes that the game is even, he is willing to bet $25 on either team to win $25.

If Al and Bob actually discuss the game with each other, they will probably make a bet somewhere around $27 to $23. In this example, Al will bet $27 on the Magpies and Bob will bet $23 on the Wildcats. Each believes that he has a good bet. (The actual dollar amounts depend on negotiating skill. It could well be that the amounts bet will be $29 to $21.)

This discussion of odds and betting odds provides the groundwork for a way of measuring **subjective probabilities.** If a businessman "feels" that the odds for the success of a new clothing store are 3 to 2, this means that he is willing to bet (or considers it fair to bet) $300 against $200, or perhaps $3,000 against $2,000, that the new store will be a success. In this way he is expressing his belief regarding the uncertainties connected with the success of the store, and to convert it into a probability we take the equation

$$\frac{a}{b} = \frac{p}{1 - p}$$

and solve it for p. Leaving details to the reader in Exercise 6.60, let us merely state the result that

Relating Probabilities to Odds	*If the odds are a to b that an event will occur, the probability of its occurrence is* $$p = \frac{a}{a + b}$$

Example

Convert the businessman's 3 to 2 odds for the success of the new clothing store into a probability.

solution

Substituting $a = 3$ and $b = 2$ into the formula for p, we get

$$p = \frac{3}{3 + 2} = \frac{3}{5}$$

Example

If an applicant for a managerial position feels that the odds are 7 to 4 that she will get the job, what probability is she thus assigning to her getting the job?

solution

Substituting $a = 7$ and $b = 4$ into the formula for p, we have

$$p = \frac{7}{7 + 4} = \frac{7}{11}$$

or approximately 0.64.

Let us now see whether subjective probabilities, determined in this way, behave in accordance with the postulates of probability on page 143. Insofar as the first postulate is concerned, this is easy to see. Since a and b are positive quantities,

$$\frac{a}{a+b}$$

is certainly greater than or equal to zero. For the second postulate, observe that the surer we are that an event will occur, the "better" odds we should be willing to give—say 100 to 1, 1,000 to 1, or perhaps even 1 million to 1. The corresponding probabilities are

$$\frac{100}{100+1} \approx 0.99, \quad \frac{1,000}{1,000+1} \approx 0.999, \quad \text{and} \quad \frac{1,000,000}{1,000,000+1} \approx 0.999999$$

and it can be seen that the surer we are that an event will occur, the closer its probability will be to 1.

This leaves only the third postulate,

$$P(A \cup B) = P(A) + P(B)$$

for any two mutually exclusive events A and B, and this rule is not necessarily satisfied when it comes to subjective probabilities. Indeed, proponents of the subjectivist point of view impose it as a **consistency criterion,** and this provides a means of "policing" a person's subjective probabilities.

Example

An economist feels that the odds are 2 to 1 that the price of beef will go up during the next month, 1 to 5 that it will remain unchanged, and 8 to 3 that it will go up or remain unchanged. Are the corresponding probabilities consistent?

solution

The corresponding probabilities that the price of beef will go up during the next month, that it will remain unchanged, and that it will go up or remain unchanged are, respectively,

$$\frac{2}{2+1} = \frac{2}{3}, \quad \frac{1}{1+5} = \frac{1}{6}, \quad \text{and} \quad \frac{8}{8+3} = \frac{8}{11}$$

and since

$$\frac{2}{3} + \frac{1}{6} = \frac{5}{6} \quad \text{and not} \quad \frac{8}{11},$$

the probabilities are not consistent. Hence, the economist's judgment must be questioned. ◪ ◪ ◪

EXERCISES

6.28   In a study of the future needs of a community, C is the event that there will be enough capital for expansion and T is the event that there will be adequate transportation. State in words what probabilities are expressed by

(a) $P(C')$;   (b) $P(T')$;   (c) $P(C \cup T)$;   (d) $P(C \cap T)$.

6.29   With reference to Exercise 6.28, express symbolically the probabilities that there will be

(a) adequate transportation but not enough capital for expansion;

(b) neither enough capital for expansion nor adequate transportation.

6.30   In a student evaluation of faculty, V is the event that a professor is well versed in his field, D is the event that he gives difficult tests, and R is the event that he is a rough grader. State in words what probabilities are expressed by

(a) $P(D')$;   (b) $P(D \cup R)$;   (c) $P(V' \cap D)$;   (d) $P(V \cap R')$.

6.31   With reference to Exercise 6.30, express symbolically the probabilities that a professor

(a) is not a rough grader;

(b) does not give difficult tests but is a rough grader;

(c) is not well versed in his field and/or does not give difficult tests.

6.32   Which of the postulates of probability are violated by the following statements?

(a) Since there is no cloud in the sky, the probability that it will rain later on in the day is -0.90.

(b) The probability that a mineral specimen will contain copper is 0.28 and the probability that it will not contain copper is 0.55.

(c) The probability that a lawyer will win his case is 0.30, and the probability that he will lose it is five times as large.

(d) The probabilities that a person will spend an evening at the movies or at home watching television are 0.27 and 0.35, and the probability that it will be one or the other is 0.52.

Explain your answers.

6.33   Which of the rules on page 144 are violated by the following statements?

(a) The probability that a chemistry experiment will succeed is 0.44 and the probability that it will fail is 0.53.

(b) According to the doctor, the probability that a certain patient has the flu is 1.12.

(c) The probability that two mutually exclusive events will both occur is always equal to 1.

(d) At a certain time of the year, the probability of seeing a whale off the San Diego coast is only 0.18, but the probability of seeing a seal is six times as large.

Explain your answers.

6.34   Express symbolically what general rule is violated by each of the following assertions:

(a) The probability that a person will buy a cake at a certain bakery is 0.48, and the probability that the person will buy a cake or a pie is 0.35.

(b) The probability that a student will get a passing grade in English is 0.77, and the probability that he or she will get a passing grade in English as well as psychology is 0.85.

6.35   Indicate which rules of probability are violated by the following statements:

(a) The probability that a particular house will be sold next week is 0.14, whereas the probability that it will not be sold is 0.92.

(b) The probability that a customer in a stationery store will purchase at least one item is 0.60, while the probability that a customer will purchase two or more items is 0.70.

(c) The event that an automobile salesman will sell at most one car today is mutually exclusive from the event that the salesman will sell at least one car today.

(d) The probability that in flipping a five-cent coin the coin will land on edge is so small that we can assign it the probability -0.01.

6.36   On Friday and Saturday, John will go to the theater and the opera. The probability that he will enjoy the theater is 0.38, the probability that he will enjoy them both is 0.23, and the probability that he will enjoy the theater but not the opera is 0.17. Use part (b) of Exercise 6.27 on page 142 to show that these probabilities cannot all be correct.

6.37 Since $A \cup A' = S$ in accordance with the definition of A', we can write

$$P(A \cup A') = P(S)$$

Then, making use of the fact that A and A' are mutually exclusive, we get

$$P(A) + P(A') = P(S) \qquad \text{step 1}$$
$$P(A) + P(A') = 1 \qquad \text{step 2}$$

which proves the third of the three rules on page 144. State which of the postulates of probability justify steps 1 and 2.

6.38 Since $S \cup \varnothing = S$ for any sample space S, we can write

$$P(S \cup \varnothing) = P(S)$$

Then, making use of the fact that S and $\varnothing$ are mutually exclusive (by default), we get

$$P(S) + P(\varnothing) = P(S) \qquad \text{step 1}$$
$$1 + P(\varnothing) = 1 \qquad \text{step 2}$$

and $P(\varnothing) = 0$, which proves the second of the three rules on page 144. State which of the postulates of probability justify steps 1 and 2.

6.39 Using the result of Exercise 6.37 we can write

$$P(A) = 1 - P(A')$$

and hence $P(A) \le 1$, which proves the first of the three rules on page 144. State which of the postulates of probability justifies the last step.

6.40 Given $P(M) = 0.30$ and $P(N) = 0.22$, where M and N are mutually exclusive, find

(a) $P(M')$; (b) $P(N')$; (c) $P(M \cup N)$;
(d) $P(M' \cap N')$; (e) $P(M' \cup N')$; (f) $P(M' \cap N)$.

6.41 If $P(Q) = 0.32$, $P(R) = 0.25$, and $P(Q' \cap R') = 0.42$, determine whether or not Q and R are mutually exclusive.

6.42 Provide examples in which events A and B are mutally exclusive and also

(a) A' and B' are not mutually exclusive;

(b) A' and B' are also mutually exclusive.

(*Hint:* Use Venn diagrams.)

6.43 A data processing firm evaluates its data-entry personnel in terms of the numbers of errors made in performing 1,000 keystrokes. For one of its data-entry persons, the probability of making at most five errors (per 1,000 keystrokes) is 0.62, and the probability of making six to 10 errors (per 1,000 keystrokes) is 0.28. Find the probability that in the next 1,000 keystrokes she will make

(a) at least six mistakes;

(b) at least 11 mistakes;

(c) at most 10 mistakes.

6.44 A large industrial building contains over 2,400 panes of window glass. The probability that, in any one-month period, 1 to 10 panes of glass must be replaced is 0.65, the probability that 11 to 20 panes of glass must be replaced is 0.32, and the probability that 21 or more panes of glass must be replaced is 0.02. Find the probability that next month the following must be replaced:

(a) zero panes of glass;

(b) at least 11 panes of glass;

(c) at most 20 panes of glass;

(d) at most 10 panes of glass.

6.45   The probabilities that a missile will explode during liftoff or have its guidance system fail in flight are 0.002 and 0.005. Use the postulates and/or the rules on page 144 to find the probabilities that the missile will

(a) not explode during liftoff;

(b) explode during liftoff or have its guidance system fail in flight;

(c) not explode during liftoff nor have its guidance system fail in flight.

6.46   The probability that a university student selected at random will have one or more failing grades on his or her transcript is 0.22, and the probability of having two or more failing grades is 0.18. What is the probability that a randomly selected student will have

(a) no failing grades?

(b) exactly one failing grade?

6.47   Convert each of the following probabilities to odds:

(a) The probability that the last digit of a car's license plate is a 2, 3, 4, 5, 6, or 7 is $\frac{6}{10}$.

(b) The probability of getting at least two heads in four flips of a balanced coin is $\frac{11}{16}$.

(c) The probability of rolling "7 or 11" with a pair of balanced dice is $\frac{2}{9}$.

6.48   If the probability is 0.65 that next year's inflation rate will exceed this year's, what are the corresponding odds?

6.49   If the probability is $\frac{4}{13}$ that a shipment of laboratory supplies will arrive on time, what are the odds that it will not arrive on time?

6.50   If the odds that a college football team will win its next game are better than 5 to 4, what can be said about the probability of winning its next game?

6.51   Convert each of the following odds to probabilities:

(a) If three eggs are randomly chosen from a carton of twelve eggs of which three are cracked, the odds are 34 to 21 that at least one of them will be cracked.

(b) If a person has eight $1 bills, five $5 bills, and one $20, and randomly selects three of them, the odds are 11 to 2 that they will not all be $1 bills.

(c) If we arbitrarily arrange the letters in the word "nest," the odds are 5 to 1 that we will not get a meaningful word in the English language.

6.52   A government economist claims that the odds are 3 to 1 that interest rates will go down and 5 to 1 that they will go up. Can these odds be right? Explain your answer.

6.53   A football fan is offered a bet of $12 against her $4 that her team will lose an upcoming game. What does it tell us about the subjective probability she assigns to her team winning the game, if

(a) she considers this bet to be fair;

(b) she is unwilling to bet?

6.54   A television producer is willing to bet $1,500 against $1,000, but not $2,000 against $1,000, that a new game show will be a success. What does this tell us about the probability that the producer assigns to the show's success?

6.55   Asked about his political future, a party official replies that the odds are 2 to 1 that he will not run for the House of Representatives and 4 to 1 that he will not run for the Senate. Furthermore, he feels that the odds are 7 to 5 that he will run for one or the other. Are the corresponding probabilities consistent?

6.56   A high school principal feels that the odds are 7 to 5 against her getting a $1,000 raise and 11 to 1 against her getting a $2,000 raise. Furthermore, she feels that it is an even-money bet that she will get one of these raises or the other. Discuss the consistency of the corresponding subjective probabilities.

6.57   There are two Porsches in a race, and a reporter feels that the odds against their winning are, respectively, 4 to 1 and 5 to 1. To be consistent, what odds should he assign to the event that neither car will win?

6.58   The odds against the Muskrats winning the division title of a local softball league are 2 to 1, and the odds against the Otters winning are 8 to 1. What is the probability that neither of these teams will win the division title?

6.59   Some events are so unlikely that we choose to assign them probabilities of zero. Would you assign probability zero to the event that

      (a)   a coin flip will result in the coin's landing on its edge;

      (b)   10 successive flips of a coin will all be heads;

      (c)   a monkey sitting at a typewriter and striking randomly at the keys will correctly type Lincoln's Gettysburg Address;

      (d)   three U.S. commercial airline crashes will occur on the same day?

田 6.60   Verify algebraically that the equation

$$\frac{a}{b} = \frac{p}{1-p},$$

     solved for p, yields

$$p = \frac{a}{a+b}$$

6.61   A gambler believes that the true odds favoring team Y in a coming game are 5 to 3. Which of the following bets would be attractive to him?

      (a)   Bet $5 on team Y to win $5.

      (b)   Bet $6 on team Y to win $4.

      (c)   Bet $4 against team Y to win $6.

      (d)   Bet $40 against team Y to win $60.

6.62   Alan and Ben are debating the coming football game between the Rockets and the Pythons. Alan believes that the odds are 14 to 11 in favor of the Rockets. Ben believes that the odds are 3 to 2 in favor of the Rockets. Will the two men be able to agree on a wager? If so, what will it be?

6.4   ADDITION RULES

The third postulate of probability applies only to two mutually exclusive events, but it can easily be generalized so that it applies to more than two mutually exclusive events. We say that k events are mutually exclusive if no two of them have any elements in common. Repeatedly using the third postulate, we can show that

Generalization of Postulate 3	*If k events are mutually exclusive, the probability that one of them will occur equals the sum of their individual probabilities; symbolically,* $$P(A_1 \cup A_2 \cup \cdots \cup A_k) = P(A_1) + P(A_2) + \cdots + P(A_k)$$ *for any mutually exclusive events A_1, A_2, ..., and A_k.*

Here again, we read $\cup$ as "or."

Example

A person is looking for a new car. The probabilities that she will buy a Chrysler, a Ford, or a Toyota are

$$0.17, \quad 0.22, \quad \text{and} \quad 0.08$$

respectively. Assuming that she will buy just one car, what is the probability that she will buy one of these three?

solution

Since the three possibilities are mutually exclusive, direct substitution into the formula yields

$$0.17 + 0.22 + 0.08 = 0.47$$

Example

The probabilities that a consumer testing service will rate a new washing machine as very poor, poor, fair, good, very good, or excellent are

$$0.06, \quad 0.13, \quad 0.17, \quad 0.32, \quad 0.22, \quad \text{and} \quad 0.10$$

What are the probabilities that it will rate the new washing machine
   (a) very poor, poor, fair, or good;
   (b) good, very good, or excellent?

solution

Since the six possibilities are mutually exclusive, direct substitution into the formula yields
   (a) $0.06 + 0.13 + 0.17 + 0.32 = 0.68$;
   (b) $0.32 + 0.22 + 0.10 = 0.64$.

The job of assigning probabilities to all possible events connected with a given situation can be very tedious. Indeed, it can be shown that if a sample space has 10 elements (points or outcomes) we can form more than 1,000 different events, and if a sample space has 20 elements we can form more than 1 million.[†] Fortunately, it is seldom necessary to assign probabilities to all possible events (that is, to all possible subsets of a sample space). The following rule, which is a direct application of the generalization of the third postulate above, makes it easy to determine the probability of any event on the basis of the probabilities assigned to the individual elements of a sample space:

[†]In general, if a sample space has n elements, we can form 2^n different events. Each element is either included or excluded for a given event, so by the multiplication of choices there are

$$2 \cdot 2 \cdot 2 \cdot \cdots \cdot 2 = 2^n$$

possibilities. Note that

$$2^{10} = 1,024 \text{ and } 2^{20} = 1,048,576$$

Calculating the Probability of an Event	*The probability of any event A is given by the sum of the probabilities of the individual outcomes comprising A.*

In the special case where the outcomes are all equiprobable, this rule leads to the formula

$$P(A) = \frac{s}{n}$$

which we used earlier in connection with the classical probability concept. Here, n is the total number of outcomes in the sample space and s is the number of "successes," namely, the number of outcomes in event A.

Example

Referring again to the example on page 134, which dealt with the two salespersons trying to sell two 1992 Dodge Caravans, suppose that the six points of the sample space have the probabilities shown in Figure 6.8. Find the probabilities that

(a) the first salesperson will not sell either of the two vans;
(b) both vans will be sold;
(c) the second salesperson will sell at least one of the two vans.

solution

(a) Adding the probabilities associated with the points $(0, 0)$, $(0, 1)$, and $(0, 2)$, we get

$$0.06 + 0.17 + 0.22 = 0.45$$

(b) Adding the probabilities associated with the points $(2, 0)$, $(1, 1)$, and $(0, 2)$, we get

$$0.22 + 0.16 + 0.22 = 0.60$$

FIGURE 6.8

Sample space for two-salespersons example with probabilities assigned to the outcomes.

(c) Adding the probabilities associated with the points (0, 1), (1, 1), and (0, 2), we get

$$0.17 + 0.16 + 0.22 = 0.55$$

■ ■ ■

FIGURE 6.9

Sample space with 44 outcomes.

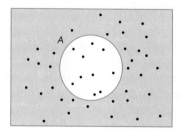

Example

Assuming that the 44 points (outcomes) of the sample space of Figure 6.9 are all equiprobable, find $P(A)$.

solution

Since there are $s = 10$ outcomes in A and the $n = 44$ outcomes of the sample space are all equiprobable, it follows that

$$P(A) = \frac{10}{44} = \frac{5}{22} \quad \text{or approximately } 0.23$$

■ ■ ■

Since the third postulate and its generalization apply only to mutually exclusive events, they cannot be used, for example, to find the probability that at least one of the two friends will pass a language examination, the probability that a birdwatcher will spot a roadrunner, a cactus wren, or a Gila woodpecker, or the probability that a customer will buy a shirt, a sweater, a belt, or a tie at a department store. Both friends can pass the examination, a birdwatcher can spot more than one of these birds, and the customer of the department store can buy any number of these items.

To find a formula for $P(A \cup B)$ that holds regardless of whether A and B are mutually exclusive, let us consider the Venn diagram of Figure 6.10. It concerns

FIGURE 6.10

Venn diagram.

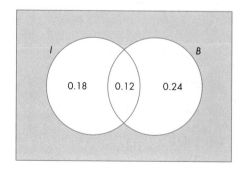

the job applications of a recent business school graduate, and the letters I and B denote her getting a job offer from an investment broker or a bank. It follows from the figures in the Venn diagram that

$$P(I) = 0.18 + 0.12 = 0.30$$

$$P(B) = 0.12 + 0.24 = 0.36$$

and

$$P(I \cup B) = 0.18 + 0.12 + 0.24 = 0.54$$

where we could add the respective probabilities because they pertain to mutually exclusive events (nonoverlapping regions of the Venn diagram).

Had we erroneously used the third postulate to calculate $P(I \cup B)$, we would have obtained $P(I) + P(B) = 0.30 + 0.36 = 0.66$, which exceeds the correct value by 0.12. This error results from adding $P(I \cap B) = 0.12$ in twice, once in $P(I) = 0.30$ and once in $P(B) = 0.36$, and we could correct for this by subtracting 0.12 from 0.66. Thus, we could write

$$P(I \cup B) = P(I) + P(B) - P(I \cap B)$$

$$= 0.30 + 0.36 - 0.12 = 0.54$$

and this agrees, as it should, with the result obtained before.

Since the argument used in this example holds for any two events A and B, we can now state the following **general addition rule**, which applies regardless of whether A and B are mutually exclusive events:

General Addition Rule	$P(A \cup B) = P(A) + P(B) - P(A \cap B)$

When A and B are mutually exclusive, $P(A \cap B) = 0$ and the formula above reduces to that of the third postulate of probability. In this connection, the third postulate is also referred to as the **special addition rule**. To add to this terminology, the generalization of the third postulate on page 153 is sometimes referred to as the **generalized** (special) **addition rule**.

Example

If one card is drawn from an ordinary deck of 52 playing cards, what is the probability that it will be either a club or a face card (king, queen, or jack)?

solution

If C denotes drawing a club and F denotes drawing a face card, then

$$P(C) = \frac{13}{52}, \quad P(F) = \frac{12}{52}, \quad \text{and} \quad P(C \cap F) = \frac{3}{52}$$

so that

$$P(C \cup F) = \frac{13}{52} + \frac{12}{52} - \frac{3}{52} = \frac{22}{52}$$

Example

If the probabilities are, respectively, 0.92, 0.33, and 0.29 that a person vacationing in Washington, D.C., will visit the Capitol building, the Smithsonian Institution, or both, what is the probability that a person vacationing there will visit at least one of these buildings?

solution

Substituting into the formula, we obtain

$$0.92 + 0.33 - 0.29 = 0.96$$

Note that if we had incorrectly used the special addition rule (for mutually exclusive events), we would have obtained the impossible answer $0.92 + 0.33 = 1.25$. ◪ ◪ ◪

The general addition rule can be generalized further so that it will apply to more than two events, but we do not go into that in this book.

◪ EXERCISES

6.63   The Warwick police department needs new tires for its patrol cars. The probabilities that it will buy Uniroyal, Goodyear, Michelin, General, or Goodrich tires are

$$0.16 \quad 0.29 \quad 0.20 \quad 0.12 \quad 0.23$$

Find the probabilities that it will buy
(a) Goodyear or Goodrich tires;
(b) Uniroyal, Michelin, General, or Goodrich tires;
(c) Uniroyal, Michelin, or General tires.

6.64   The probabilities that a student will get an A, a B, or a C in a linguistics course are 0.22, 0.42, and 0.25. What is the probability that a student will get a grade lower than C?

6.65   The Warwick police department maintains a telephone line to register complaints about the behavior of its officers. The table below gives the probabilities for the number of complaints in one month:

Number of complaints	At most 4	5	6	7	8	9	10	11 or more
Probability	0.02	0.12	0.21	0.29	0.24	0.08	0.03	0.01

What are the probabilities that, in any month, the department will receive
(a) at most 7 complaints;
(b) at least 5 complaints;
(c) anywhere from 6 to 9 complaints;
(d) more than 8 complaints?

6.66   With reference to Figure 6.9 on page 156, suppose that each of the 10 outcomes in A is three times as likely as each of the 34 outcomes in A'. Find $P(A)$.

6.67   Figure 6.11 indicates the number of guests invited to a dinner party and the number that attend. If each of the 45 points of the sample space has the probability $\frac{1}{45}$, find the probabilities that
(a) at most four persons will attend;
(b) at least six persons will attend;
(c) all those invited will attend;
(d) exactly two invited persons will not attend.

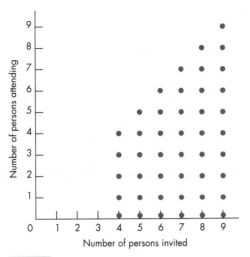

FIGURE 6.11   *Sample space for Exercise 6.67.*

6.68   With reference to Exercise 6.10 on page 139, suppose that each of the 10 points of the sample space has the probability 0.10. Find the probabilities of events *T, U, V,* and *W.*

6.69   With reference to Figure 6.3 on page 137, suppose that probabilities are assigned to the regions as follows:

Region	Probability
1	0.15
2	0.13
3	0.10
4	0.17
5	0.15
6	0.12
7	0.10
8	0.08

Find the probabilities that
(a) hamburgers will be served;
(b) beer will be served;
(c) neither hamburgers nor watermelon will be served;
(d) beer and/or hamburgers will be served.

6.70   If H stands for heads and T for tails, the 32 possible outcomes for five flips of a coin are

HHHHH	HTHHH	THHHH	TTHHH
HHHHT	HTHHT	THHHT	TTHHT
HHHTH	HTHTH	THHTH	TTHTH
HHHTT	HTHTT	THHTT	TTHTT
HHTHH	HTTHH	THTHH	TTTHH
HHTHT	HTTHT	THTHT	TTTHT
HHTTH	HTTTH	THTTH	TTTTH
HHTTT	HTTTT	THTTT	TTTTT

If these 32 outcomes are equally likely, what is the probability of getting more heads than tails?

6.71   The probabilities that a person convicted of reckless driving will be fined, have his license revoked, or both are 0.88, 0.62, and 0.55. What is the probability that a person convicted of reckless driving will be fined and/or have his license revoked?

6.72   A geology professor has two graduate assistants helping with her research. The probability that the older of the two will be absent on any given day is 0.08, the probability that the younger of the two will be absent on any given day is 0.06, and the probability that they will both be absent on any given day is 0.02. Find the probability that either or both of the graduate assistants will be absent on any given day.

6.73   The probability that a person stopping at a service station, will ask to have his oil checked is 0.28, the probability that he will ask to have his tire pressures checked is 0.11, and the probability that he will ask to have both checked is 0.04. What are the probabilities that a person stopping at this service station, will ask to have

(a) his oil, his tire pressures, or both checked?

(b) neither his oil nor his tire pressures checked?

6.74   Among the 64 doctors on the staff of a hospital, 58 carry malpractice insurance, 33 are surgeons, and 31 of the surgeons carry malpractice insurance. If one of these doctors is chosen by lot to represent the hospital staff at an AMA convention, so that each doctor has the probability $\frac{1}{64}$ of being selected, what is the probability that he or she will not be a surgeon nor carry malpractice insurance?

6.75   The probabilities that in any one year a teenage girl will attend a professional football game, a professional tennis match, or both are 0.37, 0.13, and 0.10. Draw a Venn diagram, fill in the probabilities associated with the various regions, and thus determine the probabilities that in any one year a teenage girl will attend

(a) a professional football game but no professional tennis match;

(b) a professional football game and/or a professional tennis match;

(c) neither a professional football game nor a professional tennis match.

6.76   Lois feels that the odds are 3 to 2 against her getting a promotion an even bet that she will get a raise, and 4 to 1 against getting both. What are the odds that Lois will get a promotion and/or a raise?

6.77   Explain why there must be a mistake in each of the following statements:

(a) The probabilities that the University of Georgia football team will win the first game of the season, the second game of the season, or the first two games of the season are 0.84, 0.71, and 0.53.

(b) At a certain medical clinic, the probabilities that a patient with a fever will get a shot, some medicine but no shot, or no medicine and no shot are 0.48, 0.36, and 0.12.

6.78   It can be shown that for any three events *A, B,* and *C,* the probability that at least one of them will occur is given by

$$P(A \cup B \cup C) = P(A) + P(B) + P(C)$$

$$- P(A \cap B) - P(A \cap C) - P(B \cap C) + P(A \cap B \cap C)$$

Use this formula for the following problems:

(a) The probability that a person visiting his dentist will have

his teeth cleaned is 0.47;

a cavity filled is 0.29;

a tooth extracted is 0.09;

his teeth cleaned and a cavity filled is 0.13;

his teeth cleaned and a tooth extracted is 0.03;

a cavity filled and a tooth extracted is 0.02;

his teeth cleaned, a cavity filled, and a tooth extracted is 0.01.

Find the probability that the person will have at least one of these things done.

(b) For a visitor to Disneyland, the probability that he or she will go on

the Jungle Cruise is 0.74;

the Monorail is 0.70;

the Matterhorn ride is 0.62;

the Jungle Cruise and the Monorail is 0.52;

the Jungle Cruise and the Matterhorn ride is 0.46;

the Monorail and the Matterhorn ride is 0.44;

the Jungle Cruise, the Monorail, and the Matterhorn ride is 0.34.

What is the probability that a person visiting Disneyland will go on at least one of these three rides?

6.5   CONDITIONAL PROBABILITY

If we ask for the probability of an event without specifying the sample space, we can easily get different answers and they may all be correct. For instance, if we ask for the probability that a lawyer will make more than $200,000 a year within 10 years after passing the bar, we may get one answer that applies to all persons practicing law in the United States, another one that applies to corporation lawyers, another one that applies to lawyers employed by the federal government, another one that applies to lawyers who specialize in divorce cases, and so on. Since the choice of the sample space is by no means always self-evident, it helps to use the symbol

$$P(A|S)$$

to denote the **conditional probability** of event A relative to the sample space S, or as we often call it "the probability of A given S." The symbol $P(A\,|\,S)$ makes it explicit that we are referring to a particular sample space S, and it is generally preferable to the abbreviated notation $P(A)$ unless the tacit choice of S is clearly understood. It is also preferable when we have to refer to different sample spaces in the same problem.

To elaborate on the idea of a conditional probability, suppose that a consumer research organization has studied the service under warranty provided by the 200 tire dealers in a large city, and that their findings are summarized in the following table:

	Good service under warranty	Poor service under warranty	Total
Name-brand tire dealers	64	16	80
Off-brand tire dealers	42	78	120
Total	106	94	200

If one of these tire dealers is randomly selected (that is, each dealer has the probability $\frac{1}{200}$ of being selected), we find that the probabilities of choosing a name-brand dealer, a dealer who provides good service under warranty, or a name-brand dealer who provides good service under warranty are

$$P(N) = \frac{80}{200} = 0.40$$

$$P(G) = \frac{106}{200} = 0.53$$

and

$$P(N \cap G) = \frac{64}{200} = 0.32$$

All these probabilities were calculated by means of the formula $\frac{s}{n}$ for equally likely possibilities.

Since the second of these possibilities is particularly disconcerting—there is almost a fifty–fifty chance of choosing a dealer who does not provide good service under warranty—let us see what will happen if we limit the choice to name-brand dealers. This reduces the sample space to the 80 choices corresponding to the first row of the table, and we find that the probability of choosing a name-brand dealer who will provide good service under warranty is

$$P(G|N) = \frac{64}{80} = 0.80$$

This is quite an improvement over $P(G) = 0.53$, as might have been expected. Note that the conditional probability which we have obtained here,

$$P(G|N) = 0.80,$$

can also be written as

$$P(G|N) = \frac{\frac{64}{200}}{\frac{80}{200}} = \frac{P(N \cap G)}{P(N)}$$

namely, as the ratio of the probability of choosing a name-brand dealer who provides good service under warranty to the probability of choosing a name-brand dealer.

Generalizing from this example, let us now make the following definition of conditional probability, which applies to any two events A and B belonging to a given sample space S:

Conditional Probability	*If $P(B)$ is not equal to zero, then the conditional probability of A relative to B, namely, the probability of A given B, is* $$P(A|B) = \frac{P(A \cap B)}{P(B)}$$

When $P(B)$ is equal to zero, the conditional probability of A relative to B is undefined.

Example

With reference to the tire dealers of the example above, what is the probability that a dealer will provide good service under warranty given that he is not a name-brand dealer?

solution

As can be seen from the table,

$$P(G \cap N') = \frac{42}{200} = 0.21 \quad \text{and} \quad P(N') = \frac{120}{200} = 0.60$$

so that substitution into the formula yields

$$P(G|N') = \frac{P(G \cap N')}{P(N')} = \frac{0.21}{0.60} = 0.35$$

Of course, by writing $\frac{42}{120} = 0.35$, we could have obtained this result directly from the second row of the table on page 161.   ◩ ◩ ◩

Although we introduced the formula for $P(A|B)$ by means of an example in which the possibilities were all equally likely, this is not a requirement for its use.

Example

At a certain elementary school, the probability that a student who is randomly selected will come from a two-parent home is 0.75, and the probability that he or she will come from a two-parent home and be a low achiever (get mostly D's and F's) is 0.18. What is the probability that such a randomly selected student will be a low achiever given that he or she comes from a two-parent home?

solution

Letting L denote a low achiever and T a student from a two-parent home, we have

$$P(T) = 0.75 \quad \text{and} \quad P(L \cap T) = 0.18$$

and we get

$$P(L|T) = \frac{P(L \cap T)}{P(T)} = \frac{0.18}{0.75} = 0.24 \qquad ◩ ◩ ◩$$

To introduce another concept that is important in the study of probability, let us consider the following example.

Example

If H stands for heads and T for tails, the four equally likely outcomes for two flips of a balanced coin are HH, HT, TH, and TT. If A and B denote the respective events of getting heads on the first and second flips of the coin, find
   (a) $P(A)$ and $P(B)$;   (b) $P(B \cap A)$;   (c) $P(B|A)$.

solution

Using the formula $\frac{s}{n}$ for equally likely outcomes, we get

(a) $P(A) = \frac{2}{4} = 0.50$ and $P(B) = \frac{2}{4} = 0.50$;

(b) $P(B \cap A) = \frac{1}{4} = 0.25$;

and, hence

(c) $P(B|A) = \dfrac{P(B \cap A)}{P(A)} = \dfrac{0.25}{0.50} = 0.50.$ ◪ ◪ ◪

What is special, and interesting, about this result is that $P(B|A) = P(B) = 0.50$, so that the probability of event B is the same regardless of whether event A has occurred. Actually, this should not come as a surprise, since the coin has no memory and what happens in the second flip is in no way affected by what happened in the first.

If $P(B)$ is not equal to zero and if $P(A|B) = P(A)$, we say that event A is **independent** of event B; that is,

Event A is independent of event B if the probability of A is not affected by the occurrence or nonoccurrence of B.

Since it can be shown that event B is independent of event A whenever event A is independent of event B, it is customary to say simply that **A and B are independent** whenever one is independent of the other (see Exercise 6.102 on page 171). If two events A and B are not independent, we say that they are **dependent.**

This notion of independence is satisfied by events of probability zero, even though certain conditional probabilities are not defined. Some people use the special multiplication rule on page 166 as the definition of independence.

Example

The probabilities that a student will get passing grades in mathematics, in English, or in both are

$$P(M) = 0.70, \quad P(E) = 0.80, \quad \text{and} \quad P(M \cap E) = 0.56$$

Check whether events M and E are independent.

solution

Substituting into the formula for a conditional probability, we get

$$P(M|E) = \frac{P(M \cap E)}{P(E)} = \frac{0.56}{0.80} = 0.70$$

Since $P(M|E) = 0.70 = P(M)$, we find that events M and E are independent.

◪ ◪ ◪

Example

The probabilities that it will rain or snow in a given city on Christmas Day, on New Year's Day, or on both days are

$$P(C) = 0.60, \quad P(N) = 0.60, \quad \text{and} \quad P(C \cap N) = 0.42$$

Check whether events N and C are independent.

solution

Substituting into the formula for a conditional probability, we get

$$P(N|C) = \frac{P(C \cap N)}{P(C)} = \frac{0.42}{0.60} = 0.70$$

Since $P(N|C) = 0.70$ does not equal $P(N) = 0.60$, we find that events N and C are dependent. ▰ ▰ ▰

In the next section we shall see that there is another way of working the two preceding examples.

Note that we did not use Venn diagrams in discussing independence. Independence is not easily displayed graphically.

6.6   MULTIPLICATION RULES

In Section 6.5 we used the formula

$$P(A|B) = \frac{P(A \cap B)}{P(B)}$$

only to calculate conditional probabilities, but if we multiply on both sides of the equation by $P(B)$, we get the following formula, called the **general multiplication rule**, which enables us to calculate the probability that two events will both occur:

General Multiplication Rule	$P(A \cap B) = P(B) \cdot P(A|B)$

In words, this formula states that the probability that two events will both occur is the product of the probability that one of the events will occur and the conditional probability that the other event will occur given that the first event has occurred (occurs, or will occur). As it does not matter which event is referred to as A and which is referred to as B, the formula above can also be written as

General Multiplication Rule	$P(A \cap B) = P(A) \cdot P(B|A)$

Example

A jury consists of nine persons who are native-born and three persons who are foreign-born. If two of the jurors are randomly picked for an interview, what is the probability that they will both be foreign-born?

solution

Let A be the event that the first juror is foreign-born and B the event that the second juror is foreign-born. If we assume equal probabilities for each choice (which is, in fact, what we mean by the selection being random), the probability that the first juror picked will be foreign-born is

$$P(A) = \frac{3}{12}$$

Then, if the first juror picked is foreign-born, the probability that the second juror will also be foreign-born is

$$P(B|A) = \frac{2}{11}$$

Hence, the probability of getting two jurors who are both foreign-born is

$$P(A \cap B) = P(A) \cdot P(B|A) = \frac{3}{12} \cdot \frac{2}{11} = \frac{1}{22}$$

When A and B are independent, we can substitute

$$P(A) \qquad \text{for} \qquad P(A|B)$$

in the first of the two formulas for $P(A \cap B)$, or

$$P(B) \qquad \text{for} \qquad P(B|A)$$

in the second, and we obtain

Special Multiplication Rule (independent events)	*If A and B are independent events, then* $$P(A \cap B) = P(A) \cdot P(B)$$

In words, the probability that two independent events will both occur is simply the product of their respective probabilities. This rule is sometimes used as the definition of independence; in any case, it may be used to check whether two given events are independent.

Example

What is the probability of getting two heads in two flips of a balanced coin?

solution

Since the probability of heads is $\frac{1}{2}$ for each flip of the coin, the answer is

$$\frac{1}{2} \cdot \frac{1}{2} = \frac{1}{4}$$

Example

If

$$P(C) = 0.65, \quad P(D) = 0.40, \quad \text{and} \quad P(C \cap D) = 0.26$$

are the events C and D independent?

solution

Since

$$P(C) \cdot P(D) = (0.65)(0.40) = 0.26 = P(C \cap D)$$

the two events are independent.

Example

With reference to the first example on page 164, use the special multiplication rule to verify that events M and E are independent.

solution

Since

$$P(M) \cdot P(E) = (0.70)(0.80) = 0.56 = P(M \cap E),$$

the special multiplication rule is satisfied and the two events are independent.

Example

With reference to the second example on page 164, use the special multiplication rule to verify that events N and C are dependent.

solution

Since

$$P(C) \cdot P(N) = (0.60)(0.60) = 0.36$$

does not equal $P(C \cap N) = 0.42$, the special multiplication rules is not satisfied and the two events are not independent; that is, they are dependent.

Example

What is the probability of getting two aces in a row when two cards are drawn from an ordinary deck of 52 playing cards, if
(a) the first card is replaced before the second card is drawn;
(b) the first card is not replaced before the second card is drawn?

solution

(a) Since there are four aces among the 52 cards, we get

$$\frac{4}{52} \cdot \frac{4}{52} = \frac{1}{169}$$

(b) Since there are only three aces among the 51 cards that remain after one ace has been removed from the deck, we get

$$\frac{4}{52} \cdot \frac{3}{51} = \frac{1}{221}$$

The distinction between the two parts of this example is important in statistics. What we did in part (a) is called **sampling with replacement**, and what we did in part (b) is called **sampling without replacement**.

The special multiplication rule can easily be generalized so that it applies to the occurrence of three or more independent events—again, we multiply together all the individual probabilities.

Example

What is the probability of getting three heads in three flips of a balanced coin?

solution

Since the flips of the coin are independent, we obtain $\frac{1}{2} \cdot \frac{1}{2} \cdot \frac{1}{2} = \frac{1}{8}$.   ▰ ▰ ▰

Example

If the probability is 0.70 that any person interviewed at a shopping mall will be against rezoning a certain piece of property for industrial development, what is the probability that among four persons interviewed at the mall the first three will be against the rezoning but the fourth one will not be against it?

solution

Assuming independence, we multiply the respective probabilities and get

$$(0.70)(0.70)(0.70)(0.30) = 0.1029 \approx 0.10^\dagger$$ ▰ ▰ ▰

When three or more events are not independent, the multiplication rule becomes more complicated—we form the product of the probability that one of the events will occur, the probability that a second event will occur given that the first event has occurred, the probability that a third event will occur given that the first two events have occurred, and so on.

Example

With reference to the example on page 165, what is the probability that if three of the 12 jurors are randomly picked for an interview, they will all be foreign born?

solution

Since the probabilities are $\frac{3}{12}$, $\frac{2}{11}$, and $\frac{1}{10}$ that the first juror picked will be foreign born, that the second juror picked will be foreign born given that the first juror picked is foreign born, and that the third juror picked will be foreign born given that the first two jurors picked are foreign born, the probability is

$$\frac{3}{12} \cdot \frac{2}{11} \cdot \frac{1}{10} = \frac{1}{220}$$ ▰ ▰ ▰

▰ EXERCISES

6.79   If W is the event that a worker is well trained and Q is the event that he or she meets the production quota, express symbolically the probabilities that

(a) a worker who is well trained will meet the production quota;

(b) a worker who meets the production quota is not well trained;

(c) a worker who is not well trained will not meet the production quota.

†See the footnote on page 51 regarding the use of $\approx$.

6.80 A guidance department tests students in various ways. If I is the event that a student scores high in intelligence, A is the event that a student rates high on a social adjustment scale, and N is the event that a student displays neurotic tendencies, express symbolically the probabilities that

(a) a student who scores high in intelligence will display neurotic tendencies;

(b) a student who does not rate high on the social adjustment scale will not score high in intelligence;

(c) a student who displays neurotic tendencies will neither score high in intelligence nor rate high on the social adjustment scale.

6.81 With reference to Exercise 6.79 state in words what probabilities are expressed by

(a) $P(W|Q)$; (b) $P(Q'|W)$; (c) $P(W'|Q')$.

6.82 With reference to Exercise 6.80, state in words what probabilities are expressed by

(a) $P(I|A)$; (b) $P(A'|N')$; (c) $P(N'|I \cap A)$.

6.83 If E is the event that an applicant for a home mortgage is employed, G is the event that she has a good credit rating, and A is the event that the application is approved, express symbolically the probabilities that

(a) an applicant who has a good credit rating will be employed;

(b) an applicant whose application is not approved will not have a good credit rating;

(c) an applicant who is employed and has a good credit rating will have the application approved.

6.84 If F is the event that an applicant to a college has applied for financial aid, H is the event that he or she has a high academic ranking, and C is the event that he or she resides in California, express symbolically the probabilities that

(a) an applicant who is a resident of California will apply for financial aid;

(b) an applicant who does not have high academic ranking will not apply for financial aid;

(c) an applicant who does not apply for financial aid and who has high academic ranking will reside in California;

(d) an applicant who does not reside in California will not apply for financial aid.

6.85 With reference to Exercise 6.83, state in words what probabilities are expressed by

(a) $P(A|E)$; (b) $P(A'|E')$; (c) $P(E' \cup G'|A)$.

6.86 With reference to Exercise 6.84, state in words what probabilities are expressed by

(a) $P(C|H)$; (b) $P(F|H)$; (c) $P(F \cap H|C)$; (d) $P(F'|H \cap C)$.

6.87 There are 80 applicants seeking to obtain a fast–food franchise. Some of these persons are college graduates and some are not. Some have prior experience in the food service industry and some do not. The exact breakdown is

	College graduates	*Not college graduates*
Prior food service experience	24	36
No prior food service experience	12	8

If the order in which the applicants are processed is random, G is the event that the first applicant processed is a college graduate, and E is the event that the first applicant processed has prior food service experience, determine each of the following probabilities directly from the entries and the row and column totals of the table:

(a) $P(G)$;   (b) $P(E')$;   (c) $P(E \cap G)$;   (d) $P(E' \cap G')$;

(e) $P(E|G)$;   (f) $P(G'|E')$;   (g) $P(E'|G')$;   (h) $P(E \cup G)$.

6.88 Among the 400 inmates of a prison, some are first offenders, some are hardened criminals, some serve terms of less than five years, and some serve longer terms, with the exact breakdown being

	Terms of less than five years	Longer terms
First offenders	120	40
Hardened criminals	80	160

If one of the inmates is to be selected at random to be interviewed about prison conditions, H is the event that he is a hardened criminal, and L is the event that he is serving a longer term, determine each of the following probabilities directly from the entries and the row and column totals of the table:

(a) $P(H)$;   (b) $P(L)$;   (c) $P(L \cap H)$;

(d) $P(H' \cap L)$;   (e) $P(L|H)$;   (f) $P(H'|L)$.

6.89 Use the results of Exercise 6.87 to verify that

(a) $P(E|G) = \dfrac{P(E \cap G)}{P(G)}$;   (b) $P(G'|E') = \dfrac{P(E' \cap G')}{P(E')}$.

6.90 Use the results of Exercise 6.88 to verify that

(a) $P(L|H) = \dfrac{P(L \cap H)}{P(H)}$;   (b) $P(H'|L) = \dfrac{P(H' \cap L)}{P(L)}$.

6.91 The probabilities are 0.45, 0.36, and 0.18 that a person traveling in the northeastern United States will visit Boston, Providence, or both. Find the probabilities that

(a) such a traveler who is visiting Boston will also visit Providence;

(b) such a traveler who is visiting Providence will also visit Boston.

6.92 A survey of women in executive positions showed that the probability is 0.60 that such a woman will enjoy making financial decisions, and 0.42 that such a woman will enjoy making financial decisions and be willing to assume substantial risks. What is the probability that a woman in an executive position who enjoys making financial decisions will be willing to assume substantial risks?

6.93 The probability that a bus from Cleveland to Chicago will leave on time is 0.80, and the probability that it will leave on time and also arrive on time is 0.72.

(a) What is the conditional probability that if such a bus leaves on time it will also arrive on time?

(b) If the probability is 0.75 that such a bus will arrive on time, what is the conditional probability that if such a bus does not leave on time it will nevertheless arrive on time?

6.94 Given $P(A) = 0.50$, $P(B) = 0.30$,   and $P(A \cap B) = 0.15$ verify that

(a) $P(A|B) = P(A)$;   (b) $P(A|B') = P(A)$;

(c) $P(B|A) = P(B)$;   (d) $P(B|A') = P(B)$.

6.95 The probability that a certain person will go out for breakfast is 0.40, and the probability that if she goes out for breakfast she will spend more than $5.00 is 0.75. What is the probability that she will go out for breakfast and spend more than $5.00?

6.96 The probability that a student attending a certain Ohio college will purchase a portable computer is 0.65. The probability that if he purchases a portable computer his grades will go up is 0.80. What is the probability that a student at this college will purchase a personal computer and have his grades go up?

6.97 If two cards are drawn from an ordinary deck of 52 playing cards, what are the probabilities that they will both be diamonds if the drawing is

(a) with replacement; (b) without replacement?

6.98 Among 80 pieces of luggage loaded on a plane in San Francisco, 60 are destined for Seattle and 20 for Vancouver. If two of the pieces of luggage are unloaded in Portland by mistake, and if the "selection" is random, what are the probabilities that

(a) both should have gone to Seattle;

(b) both should have gone to Vancouver;

(c) one should have gone to Seattle and one to Vancouver?

6.99 In a fifth-grade class of 18 boys and 12 girls, one pupil is chosen each week by lot to act as an assistant to the teacher. What is the probability that a girl will be chosen two weeks in a row if

(a) the same pupil cannot serve two weeks in a row;

(b) the restriction of part (a) is removed?

6.100 If A and B are independent events and $P(A) = 0.20$ and $P(B) = 0.45$, find

(a) $P(A \cap B)$; (b) $P(A|B)$; (c) $P(B|A)$; (d) $P(A' \cap B)$;

(e) $P(A \cap B')$; (f) $P(B'|A')$; (g) $P(A' \cap B')$; (h) $P(A \cup B)$.

6.101 If $P(A) = 0$ and $P(B) > 0$, show that A is independent of B, in the sense that $P(A|B) = P(A)$.

6.102 If $P(A) > 0$ and $P(B) > 0$, and if A is independent of B, show that B is independent of A.

6.103 If $P(A) = 0.80$, $P(C) = 0.95$, and $P(A \cap C) = 0.76$ are events A and C independent?

6.104 If $P(K) = 0.15$, $P(L) = 0.82$, and $P(K \cap L) = 0.12$ are events K and L independent?

6.105 If the odds are 5 to 3 that event M will not occur, 2 to 1 that event N will occur, and 4 to 1 that they will not both occur, are the two events M and N independent?

6.106 The odds are 3 to 2 that event Q will occur, 5 to 4 that event R will occur, and 37 to 8 that at least one of them will occur. Are events Q and R independent?

6.107 What is the probability of getting eight heads in a row with a balanced coin?

6.108 What is the probability of getting no 3's in four rolls of a balanced die?

田 6.109 Some special cards are prepared for an unusual game. There are four varieties: cards with red letter X, cards with green letter X, cards with red letter Y, and cards with green letter Y. Decks A and B contain different numbers of these cards.

	D e c k A			*D e c k B*	
	Red	*Green*		*Red*	*Green*
X	5	14	X	5	2
Y	5	16	Y	20	13

(a) If you use deck A, show that

$$P(X|\text{red, deck } A) > P(X|\text{green, deck } A)$$

(b) If you use deck B, show that

$$P(X|\text{red, deck } B) > P(X|\text{green, deck } B)$$

(c) Suppose that the two decks are combined to make a single deck of 80 cards. How many cards of each of the four varieties are in that deck?

(d) Suppose that a single card is to be selected randomly from that deck. Is it true that

$$P(X|\text{red, combined deck}) > P(X|\text{green, combined deck})?$$

(*Note:* Conditional probabilities behave in peculiar ways. This problem is an example of **Simpson's paradox.**)

6.110   Abel and Baker are quarterbacks on the Middletown football team. The coach uses both players during each game. In the first game of the season, Abel got to throw 20 passes, and 11 of them were complete. Also in the first game, Baker threw five passes, completing three of them.

In the second game, Abel threw five passes, completing only one. Baker threw 16 passes, completing six.

(a) Show that Baker's proportion of pass completions was better than Abel's proportion of pass completions in the first game.

(b) Show that Baker's proportion of pass completions was better than Abel's proportion of pass completions in the second game.

(c) The Middletown newspaper combined the data from the two games, to get the "season-to-date" data. According to the combined information, which quarterback has the higher proportion of pass completions?

6.111   If five of a company's 10 delivery trucks do not meet emission standards and three of them are chosen for inspection, what is the probability that none of the trucks chosen will meet emission standards?

6.112   If a person randomly picks four of the 15 gold coins a dealer has in stock, and six of the coins are counterfeits, what is the probability that the coins picked will all be counterfeits?

6.113   In a certain city, the probability that it will rain on a November day is 0.60, the probability that a rainy November day will be followed by another rainy day is 0.80, and the probability that a sunny November day will be followed by a rainy day is 0.30. What is the probability that it will rain, rain, not rain, and rain in this city on four consecutive November days?

6.114   A department store that bills its charge-account customers once a month has found that if a customer pays promptly one month, the probability is 0.90 that he will also pay promptly the next month; however, if a customer does not pay promptly one month, the probability that he will pay promptly the next month is only 0.40.

(a) What is the probability that a customer who pays promptly one month will also pay promptly the next three months?

(b) What is the probability that a customer who does not pay promptly one month will also not pay promptly the next two months and then make a prompt payment the month after that?

6.7   BAYES' THEOREM ⇔

Although the symbols $P(A|B)$ and $P(B|A)$ may look alike, there is a great difference between the probabilities which they represent. For instance, on page 162 we calculated the probability $P(G|N)$ that a name-brand tire dealer will provide good service under warranty, but what do we mean when we write $P(N|G)$? This is the probability that a tire dealer who provides good service under warranty is a name-brand dealer. To give another example, suppose that B represents the event that a person committed a burglary and G represents the event that he or she is found guilty of the crime. Then $P(G|B)$ is the probability that the person who committed the burglary will be found guilty of the crime, and $P(B|G)$ is the probability that the person who is found guilty of the burglary actually committed it. Thus, in both of these examples we turned things around—cause, so to speak, became effect and effect became cause.

Since there are many problems in statistics that involve such pairs of conditional probabilities, let us find a formula that expresses $P(B|A)$ in terms of $P(A|B)$ for any two events A and B. To this end we equate the expressions for $P(A \cap B)$ in the two forms of the general multiplication rule on page 165 and we get

$$P(A) \cdot P(B|A) = P(B) \cdot P(A|B) \quad \text{and, hence,} \quad P(B|A) = \frac{P(B) \cdot P(A|B)}{P(A)}$$

after we divide by $P(A)$.

Example

In a state where cars have to be tested for the emission of pollutants, 25 percent of all cars emit excessive amounts of pollutants. When tested, 99 percent of all cars that emit excessive amounts of pollutants will fail, but 17 percent of the cars that do not emit excessive amounts of pollutants will also fail. What is the probability that a car that fails the test actually emits excessive amounts of pollutants?

solution

Letting A denote the event that a car fails the test and B the event that it emits excessive amounts of pollutants, we can translate the given percentages into probabilities and write

$$P(B) = 0.25, \quad P(A|B) = 0.99, \quad \text{and} \quad P(A|B') = 0.17$$

Before we can calculate $P(B|A)$ by means of the formula given above on this page, we will first have to determine $P(A)$, and to this end let us look at the tree diagram of Figure 6.12. Here A is reached either along the branch which passes through B or along the branch which passes through B', and the probabilities of this happening are

$$(0.25)(0.99) = 0.2475 \quad \text{and} \quad (0.75)(0.17) = 0.1275$$

Since the alternatives represented by the two branches are mutually exclusive, we find that $P(A) = 0.2475 + 0.1275 = 0.3750$, and substitution into the formula for $P(B|A)$ yields

FIGURE 6.12

Tree diagram for emission-testing example.

$$P(B|A) = \frac{P(B) \cdot P(A|B)}{P(A)} = \frac{(0.25)(0.99)}{0.3750} = 0.66$$

This is the probability that a car which fails the test actually emits excessive amounts of pollutants.   ◪ ◪ ◪

FIGURE 6.13

Tree diagram for Bayes' theorem.

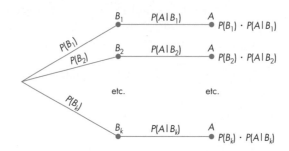

With reference to the tree diagram of Figure 6.12, we can say that $P(B|A)$ is the probability that event A was reached via the upper branch of the tree, and we showed that its value is given by the ratio of the probability associated with that branch of the tree to the sum of the probabilities associated with both branches. This argument can be generalized to the case where there are more than two possible "causes," namely, more than two branches leading to an event A. With reference to Figure 6.13, we can say that $P(B_i|A)$ is the probability that event A was reached via the ith branch of the tree (for $i = 1, 2, ..., $ or k), and it can be shown that its value is given by the ratio of the probability associated with the ith branch to the sum of the probabilities associated with all the branches leading to A. Formally, we write

Bayes' Theorem	*If B_1, B_2, ..., and B_k are mutually exclusive events of which one must occur, then* $$P(B_i|A) = \frac{P(B_i) \cdot P(A|B_i)}{P(B_1) \cdot P(A|B_1) + P(B_2) \cdot P(A|B_2) + \cdots + P(B_k) \cdot P(A|B_k)}$$ *for $i = 1, 2, ..., $ or k.*

Note that the expression in the denominator actually equals $P(A)$. This formula for calculating $P(A)$ when A is reached via one of several intermediate steps, is called the **rule of elimination** or the **rule of total probability.**

Example

In a cannery, assembly lines I, II, and III account for 50, 30, and 20 percent of the total output. If 0.4 percent of the cans from assembly line I are improperly sealed, and the corresponding percentages for assembly lines II and III are 0.6 and 1.2 percent, what is the probability that
   (a) a can produced by this cannery will be improperly sealed;
   (b) an improperly sealed can (discovered at the final inspection of outgoing products) will have come from assembly line I?

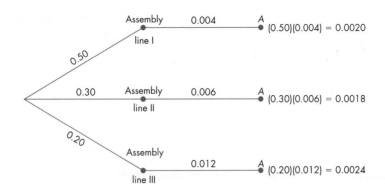

FIGURE 6.14

Tree diagram for cannery example.

solution

(a) Letting A denote the event that a can is improperly sealed, and B_1, B_2, and B_3 denote the events that a can comes from assembly lines I, II, or III we can translate the given percentages into probabilities and write

$$P(B_1) = 0.50, \qquad P(B_2) = 0.30, \qquad P(B_3) = 0.20$$

$$P(A|B_1) = 0.004, \quad P(A|B_2) = 0.006, \quad P(A|B_3) = 0.012$$

Thus, the probabilities associated with the three branches of the tree diagram of Figure 6.14 are

$$(0.50)(0.004) = 0.0020, \qquad (0.30)(0.006) = 0.0018$$

and

$$(0.20)(0.012) = 0.0024$$

and the rule of elimination yields

$$P(A) = 0.0020 + 0.0018 + 0.0024 = 0.0062$$

(b) Substituting this result together with the probability associated with the first branch of the tree diagram into the formula for Bayes' theorem, we get

$$P(B_1|A) = \frac{0.0020}{0.0062} \approx 0.32$$

Problems like these may be solved by creating a fictitious production run. Suppose that we imagine a run of, say, 10,000 cans. Of these cans, 5,000 will come from line I, 3,000 will come from line II, and 2,000 will come from line III. Of the 5,000 cans from line I, there will be

$$0.004 \cdot 5,000 = 20$$

cans with improper seals. Similar logic applied to the other two lines lets us fill in the following chart:

Production Line	Number of Cans	Number with Improper Seals
I	5,000	20
II	3,000	18
III	2,000	24
Total	10,000	62

This fictitious run produces, on average, 62 improperly sealed cans. Of these, 20 came from line I, so the conditional probability $P(B_1|A)$ is $\frac{20}{62} \approx 0.32$, exactly as before. The method does not allow for chance variation in the numbers of cans produced, so it is a bit unrealistic. It does, however, lead easily to the solution.

As can be seen from the two examples of this section, Bayes' formula is a relatively simple mathematical rule. There can be no question about its validity, but criticism has frequently been raised about its applicability. This is because it involves a "backward" or "inverse" sort of reasoning, namely, reasoning from effect to cause. For instance, in the example on page 173 we wondered whether a car's failing the test was brought about, or caused, by its emitting excessive amounts of pollutants. Similarly, in the example immediately above we wondered whether an improperly sealed can was produced, or caused, by assembly line I. It is precisely this aspect of Bayes' theorem that makes it play an important role in statistical inference, where our reasoning goes from sample data that are observed to the populations from which they came. Brief discussions of such inferences, appropriately called **Bayesian inferences,** may be found in Sections 11.3 and 13.2.

EXERCISES

6.115 The probability that a one-car accident is caused by faulty brakes is 0.04, the probability that a one-car accident is correctly attributed to faulty brakes is 0.82, and the probability that a one-car accident is incorrectly attributed to faulty brakes is 0.03. What is the probability that

(a) a one-car accident will be attributed to faulty brakes;

(b) a one-car accident attributed to faulty brakes was actually due to faulty brakes?

6.116 In a T-maze, a rat is given food if it turns left and an electric shock if it turns right. On the first trial there is a fifty–fifty chance that a rat will turn either way; then, if it receives food on the first trial, the probability that it will turn left on the second trial is 0.68, and if it receives a shock on the first trial, the probability that it will turn left on the second trial is 0.84. What is the probability that

(a) a rat will turn left on the second trial;

(b) a rat that turns left on the second trial will have also turned left on the first trial?

6.117 At an electronics plant, it is known from past experience that the probability is 0.86 that a new worker who has attended the company's training program will meet his production quota, and that the corresponding probability is 0.35 for a new worker who has not attended the company's training program. If 80 percent of all new workers attend the training program, what is the probability that

(a) a new worker will not meet his production quota;

(b) a new worker who does not meet his production quota will not have attended the company's training program?

6.118 Two firms, V and W, consider bidding on a road-building job which may or may not be awarded, depending on the amounts of the bids. Firm V submits a bid and the probability is $\frac{3}{4}$ that it will get the job provided that firm W does not bid. The odds are 3 to 1 that W will bid, and if it does, the probability that V will get the job is only $\frac{1}{3}$.

(a) What is the probability that V will get the job?

(b) If V gets the job, what is the probability that W did not bid?

6.119 In a certain community, 8 percent of all adults over age 50 have diabetes. If a doctor in this community correctly diagnoses 95 percent of all persons with diabetes as having the disease and incorrectly diagnoses 2 percent of all persons without diabetes as having the disease, what is the probability that an adult over 50 diagnosed by this doctor as having diabetes actually has the disease?

6.120 Regarding the example on page 173, the state agency doing the testing has acquired new equipment. With this new equipment, 99 percent of all cars emitting excessive amounts of pollutants will fail and three percent of all cars not emitting excessive amounts of pollution will fail. If it is still the case that 25 percent of all cars emit excessive amounts of pollutants, find the probability that a car which fails the test actually emits excessive amounts of pollutants.

6.121 A blood disease is found in 2 percent of the persons in a certain population. A new blood test will correctly identify 96 percent of the persons with the disease and 94 percent of the persons without the disease

(a) What is the probability that a person who is called positive by the blood test actually has the disease?

(b) What is the probability that a person who is called negative by the blood test actually does not have the disease?

6.122 At the public affairs office of a large department store, the probability that a consumer complaint will concern faulty merchandise is 0.65, the probability that it will concern late delivery is 0.30, and the probability that it will concern billing errors is 0.05. Complaints about faulty merchandise can be resolved to the consumer's satisfaction with probability 0.70, complaints about late delivery can be resolved with probability 0.10, and complaints about billing errors can be resolved with probability 0.90.

(a) Find the probability that a complaint can be resolved to the consumer's satisfaction.

(b) If a complaint was resolved successfully, find the probability that it concerned a billing error.

6.123 A computer software firm maintains a telephone hotline service for its customers. The firm finds that 48 percent of the calls involve questions about the application of the software, 38 percent involve issues of incompatibility with the hardware, and 14 percent involve the inability to install the software on the user's machine. These three categories of problems can be resolved with probabilities 0.90, 0.15, and 0.80, respectively.

(a) Find the probability that a call to the hotline involves a problem that can be resolved.

(b) If a call involves a problem that cannot be resolved, find the probability that this problem concerned incompatibility with the hardware.

6.124 A retailer of automobile parts has four employees, K, L, M, and N, who make mistakes in filling orders one time in 100, four times in 100, six times in 100, and two times in 100. Of all the orders filled, K, L, M, and N fill 20, 30, 10, and 40 percent. What is the probability that

(a) a mistake will be made in an order;

(b) if a mistake is made in an order, the order was filled by K;

(c) if a mistake is made in an order, the order was filled by N?

6.125 An explosion in a liquefied natural gas tank undergoing repair could have occurred as the result of static electricity, malfunctioning electrical equipment, an open flame in contact with the liner, or purposeful action (industrial sabotage). Interviews with engineers who were analyzing the risks led to estimates that such an explosion would occur with probability 0.25 as a result of static electricity, 0.20 as a result of malfunctioning electric equipment, 0.40 as a result of an open flame, and 0.75 as a result of purposeful action. These interviews also yielded subjective estimates of the probabilities of the four causes of 0.30, 0.40, 0.15, and 0.15, respectively. Based on all this information, what is the most likely cause of the explosion? (From I. Miller, and J. E. Freund, *Probability and Statistics for Engineers,* 3rd ed., Prentice Hall, Upper Saddle River, N.J., 1985.)

6.126   To get answers to sensitive questions, we sometimes use a method called the **randomized response technique.** Suppose, for instance, that we want to determine what percentage of the students at a large university smoke marijuana. We construct 20 flash cards, write "I smoke marijuana at least once a week" on 12 of the cards, where 12 is an arbitrary choice, and "I do not smoke marijuana at least once a week" on the others. Then, we let each student (in the sample interviewed) select one of the cards at random, and respond "yes" or "no" without divulging the question.

   (a) Establish a relationship between $P(Y)$, the probability that a student will give a "yes" response, and $P(M)$, the probability that a student randomly selected at that university smokes marijuana at least once a week.

   (b) If 106 of 250 students answered "yes" under these conditions, use the result of part (a) and $\frac{106}{250}$ as an estimate of $P(Y)$ to estimate $P(M)$.

6.127   The following story illustrates what can happen when we use "common sense," or intuition, in connection with probabilities:

   Among three indistinguishable boxes one contains two pennies, one contains a penny and a dime, and one contains two dimes. We randomly choose one of the three boxes, and randomly pick one of the two coins in that box without looking at the other. If the coin we pick is a penny, what is the probability that the other coin in the box is also a penny? Without giving the matter too much thought, we might argue that there is a fifty–fifty chance that the other coin is also a penny. After all, the coin we picked must have come from the box with the penny and the dime or from the box with the two pennies. In the first case the other coin is a dime, in the second case the other coin is a penny, and it would seem reasonable to say that these two possibilities are equally likely.

   Use Bayes' theorem to show that the probability is actually $\frac{2}{3}$ that the other coin is also a penny.

6.8   CHECKLIST OF KEY TERMS[†] (*with page references to their definitions*)

[†]Terms introduced in exercises are shown in *italics.*

6.9   REVIEW EXERCISES

6.128   Convert each of the following probabilities to odds:

(a) The probability of rolling eight or less with a pair of balanced dice is $\frac{26}{36}$.

(b) If a researcher randomly selected 8 of 80 households to be included in a study, the probability is $\frac{1}{10}$ that any particular household will be included.

(c) The probability of getting at least three heads in six flips of a balanced coin is $\frac{42}{64}$.

6.129   A small real estate office has five part-time salespersons. Using two coordinates, so that (3, 1), for example, represents the event that three of the salespersons are at work and one of them is busy with a customer, and (2, 0) represents the event that two of the salespersons are at work but neither of them is busy with a customer, draw a diagram similar to that of Figure 6.1, showing the 21 points of the corresponding sample space.

6.130   With reference to Exercise 6.129, assume that each of the 21 points of the sample space has the probability $\frac{1}{21}$, find the probabilities that

(a) there are no salespersons at work;

(b) there is at least one salesperson at work, and all the salespersons that are at work are busy with customers;

(c) at least three salespersons are at work;

(d) at least three salespersons are busy with customers;

(e) none of the salespersons are busy with customers;

(f) there is at least one salesperson who is at work but not busy with customers.

⬦ 6.131   A hotel gets cars for its guests from three rental agencies, 20 percent from agency X, 40 percent from agency Y, and 40 percent from agency Z. If 14 percent of the cars from X, 4 percent from Y, and 8 percent from Z need tune-ups, what is the probability that

(a) a car needing a tune-up will be delivered to one of the guests;

(b) if a car needing a tune-up is delivered to one of the guests, it came from agency Z?

6.132   If R and D are the events that a person will have regular coffee or decaffeinated coffee after dinner at a certain restaurant, $P(R) = 0.63$ and $P(D) = 0.28$, find the probabilities that after dinner at this restaurant a person will

(a) not have decaffeinated coffee;

(b) have regular or decaffeinated coffee;

(c) have neither kind of coffee.

6.133   If the probability is 0.26 that any one woman will name yellow or orange as her favorite color, what is the probability that four women, selected at random, will all name yellow or orange as their favorite color?

6.134   If Q is the event that a person is qualified for a job and G is the event that he or she will get the job, express in words what probabilities are represented by

(a) $P(G|Q)$;   (b) $P(G'|Q')$;   (c) $P(Q|G)$;   (d) $P(Q|G')$.

6.135   If $P(M) = 0.55$, $P(N) = 0.18$, and $P(M \cap N) = 0.099$, are the events M and N independent or dependent?

6.136   Discuss the following assertion: Since probabilities are measures of uncertainty, the probability we assign to a future event will always increase when we get more information.

6.137   Convert each of the following odds to probabilities:

(a) The odds are 19 to 5 that a given horse will not win the Kentucky Derby.

(b) If five cards are drawn with replacement from an ordinary deck of 52 playing cards, the odds are 13 to 3 that at most three of them will be red.

(c) If two persons are chosen at random from a group of 10 men and 12 women, the odds are 40 to 37 that one man and one woman will be selected.

6.138   Suppose that the numbers 1, 2, 3, 4, 5, and 6 are used to denote that a committee of parents and teachers decides that a certain education program is terrible, poor, fair, good, very good, or excellent. If

$$L = \{2, 3, 4, 5\} \quad \text{and} \quad R = \{4, 5, 6\}$$

list the elements of the sample space comprising each of the following events, and express the events in words:

(a) L';   (b) $L \cup R$;   (c) $L \cap R$;   (d) $L \cap R'$.

6.139   If someone feels that 17 to 8 are fair odds that a paint job will be finished on time, what subjective probability does he assign to this event?

6.140   The probabilities are 0.15, 0.26, and 0.08 that a family driving through a western city will spend the night at one of its hotels, at one of its motels, or at its campground. What is the probability that a family driving through this city will spend the night at one of these kinds of facilities?

6.141   The probabilities that a newspaper will receive 0, 1, 2, ..., 7, or at least 8 letters to the editor about an unpopular decision of the school board are

$$0.01, \quad 0.02, \quad 0.05, \quad 0.14, \quad 0.16, \quad 0.20, \quad 0.18, \quad 0.15, \quad 0.09$$

What are the probabilities that the newspaper will receive

(a) at most 4 letters to the editor about the school board decision;

(b) at least 6;

(c) from 3 to 5?

6.142   Mr. Smith is willing to bet Mrs. Smith $24 to her $8, but not $24 to her $6, that they will be late for the opera. What does this tell us about the probability which he assigns to their being late for the opera?

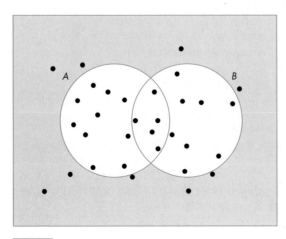

FIGURE 6.15   *Sample space for Exercise 6.144.*

6.143   Joe and Walter both enjoy sports betting, and the two are currently discussing the next Rams–49ers football game. Joe feels that the odds should be 7 to 4 in favor of the 49ers, while Walter feels that the odds should be 5 to 2 in favor of the 49ers. Describe a bet that would be agreeable to both men.

6.144   If each point of the sample space of Figure 6.15 represents an outcome having the probability $\frac{1}{32}$, find

(a) $P(A)$;   (b) $P(B')$;   (c) $P(A \cap B')$;   (d) $P(A \cup B)$;

(e) $P(A' \cap B')$;   (f) $P(A|B)$;   (g) $P(B|A')$;   (h) $P(B|A \cup B)$;

6.145   A plant nursery has discovered an old batch of seeds for a plant species that it has not grown in many years. The nursery manager would like to grow at least one plant from these seeds, in order to prepare a fresh batch of new seeds. If the germination probability for each seed is 0.025, find the smallest number of seeds that should be planted in order that the probability of getting at least one plant will be 0.90 or more.

6.146   As part of a promotional scheme in Arizona and New Mexico, a company distributing frozen foods will award a grand prize of $100,000 to some person sending in his or her name on an entry blank, with the option of including a label from one of the company's products. A breakdown of the 225,000 entries received is shown in the following table:

	With label	*Without label*
Arizona	120,000	42,000
New Mexico	30,000	33,000

If the winner of the grand prize is chosen by lot, A represents the event that it will be won by an entry from Arizona, and L represents the event that it will be won by an entry which included a label, find each of the following probabilities:

(a) $P(A)$;   (b) $P(L)$;   (c) $P(A|L)$;

(d) $P(L|A)$;   (e) $P(A'|L')$;   (f) $P(L|A')$.

6.147   Suppose that in Exercise 6.146 the drawing is rigged so that by including a label each entry's probability of winning the grand prize is doubled. Recalculate the probabilities of parts (a) through (f).

6.148   A box contains 100 beads, some red and some white. One bead will be drawn at random, and you are asked to call beforehand whether it is going to be red or white. What odds would constitute a fair bet on this game if

(a) you have no idea how many of the beads are red and how many are white;

(b) you are told that 50 of the beads are red and 50 are white?

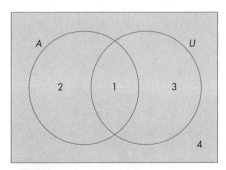

FIGURE 6.16   *Venn diagram for Exercise 6.150.*

6.149   A library received 40 new books, including 12 historical novels. If four of these books are selected at random, what is the probability that not one of them is a historical novel?

6.150   If A is the event that a university's football team is rated among the top 20 by AP and U is the event that it is rated among the top 20 by UPI, what events are represented by the four regions of the Venn diagram of Figure 6.16?

6.151   A movie producer feels that the odds are 8 to 1 that his new movie will not be rated G, 15 to 3 that it will not be rated PG, and 13 to 5 that it will not get either of these two ratings. Are the corresponding probabilities consistent?

6.152   The probability that George will get an M.A. degree is 0.40, and the probability that with an M.A. degree he will get a well-paying job is 0.85. What is the probability that he will get an M.A. degree and a well-paying job?

6.153   Lie detectors have been used during wartime to uncover security risks. As is well known, lie detectors are not infallible. Let us suppose that the probability is 0.10 that the lie detector will fail to detect a person who is a security risk and that the probability is 0.08 that the lie detector will incorrectly label a person who is not a security risk. If 2 percent of the persons who are given the test are actually security risks, what is the probability that

(a) a person labeled a security risk by a lie detector test is in fact a security risk;

(b) a person who is cleared by a lie detector test is in fact not a security risk?

6.154   Explain why there must be a mistake in each of the following statements:

(a) The probability that a new safety feature in cars will be able to prevent injuries is −0.02.

(b) The probability that a student will get a B in a course is 0.11, but she is 10 times as likely to get a C.

(c) The probability that a teachers' conference will be well attended is 0.59, and the probability that it will not be well attended is 0.31.

6.155   If a student answers the 12 questions on a true–false test by flipping a balanced coin, what is the probability that he will answer all questions

(a) correctly; (b) incorrectly?

6.156   Provide an example in which $P(A|B)$ is positive while $P(B|A') = 0$.

6.157   In Figure 6.17, B is the event that a person traveling in Europe will visit Belgium, P is the event that he or she will visit Portugal, and E is the event that he or she will visit

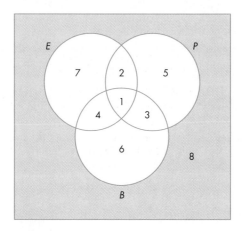

FIGURE 6.17   *Venn diagram for Exercise 6.157.*

England. Explain in words what events are represented by the following regions or combinations of regions of the Venn diagram:

(a) region 5;   (b) regions 1 and 4 together;

(c) regions 3 and 6 together;   (d) regions 3, 5, and 6 together;

(e) regions 5 and 8 together.

6.158 The odds for event A are 1 to 4 and for event B are 1 to 5. If A and B are independent, what are the odds for $A \cup B$?

6.159 The four checkout clerks of a supermarket are supposed to ask for two identifications when they cash a check. George, who cashes 30 percent of all the checks, fails to do so 1 time in 50; Tracy, who also cashes 30 percent of all the checks, fails to do so 1 time in 40; Charles, who cashes 20 percent of all the checks, fails to do so 1 time in 10; and Susan, who also cashes 20 percent of all the checks, fails to do so 1 time in 20.

(a) What is the probability that a check will be cashed at this supermarket without two identifications?

(b) If a check is found to have been cashed without two identifications, what is the probability that it was cashed by Tracy or Charles?

6.160 Among a company's replacement parts for a given assembly, 20 percent are defective and the rest are good, 60 percent were bought from external sources and the rest were made by the company itself, and of those bought from external sources 80 percent are good and the rest are defective. What are the probabilities that a replacement part selected randomly from this stock is

(a) bought from an external source and good;

(b) bought from an external source and defective;

(c) company made and defective;

(d) company made given that it is defective?

6.161 Surgical operations can be classified as to level of risk. The data below give the numbers of operations and the numbers of deaths at each of two hospitals:

	HOSPITAL A		HOSPITAL B	
Risk	Operations	Deaths	Operations	Deaths
Low	120	2	40	0
Medium	100	6	90	4
High	60	20	160	36

(a) Show that the death rate is higher in hospital A for low-risk operations, for medium-risk operations, and for higher-risk operations.

(b) Show that the overall death rate is higher in hospital B.

(c) Explain the apparent inconsistency between the answers to parts (a) and (b).

6.162 A horse breeder has entered one of his horses in a race in Florida and a race in Kentucky. If the odds are 3 to 1 that it will not win in Florida and 7 to 1 that it will not win in Kentucky, what are the odds that it will not win either race? Assume independence.

6.10 REFERENCES

More detailed, though still elementary treatments of probability may be found in

BARR, D. R., and ZEHNA, P. W., *Probability: Modeling Uncertainty.* Reading, Mass.: Addison-Wesley Publishing Company, Inc., 1983.

DRAPER, N. R., and LAWRENCE, W. E., *Probability: An Introductory Course.* Chicago: Markham Publishing Co., 1970.

FREUND, J. E., *Introduction to Probability.* New York: Dover Publications, Inc., 1993.

GOLDBERG, S., *Probability—An Introduction.* Englewood Cliffs, N.J.: Prentice Hall, 1960.

HODGES, J. L., and LEHMANN, E. L., *Elements of Finite Probability,* 2nd ed. San Francisco: Holden-Day, Inc., 1970.

MOSTELLER, F., ROURKE, R. E. K., and THOMAS, G. B., *Probability with Statistical Applications,* 2nd ed. Reading, Mass.: Addison-Wesley Publishing Company, Inc., 1970.

SCHEAFFER, R. L. and MENDENHALL, W., *Introduction to Probability: Theory and Applications.* North Scituate, Mass.: Duxbury Press, 1975.

and interesting data on probabilities and odds in

NEFT, D. S., COHEN, R. M., and DEUTCH, J. A., *The World Book of Odds.* New York: Grosset & Dunlap, Inc., 1978.

The following is an introduction to the mathematics of gambling and various games of chance:

PACKEL, E. W., *The Mathematics of Games and Gambling.* Washington, D.C.: Mathematics Association of America, 1981.

The following is a collection of entertaining, and sometimes difficult, problems in probability:

MOSTELLER, F., *Fifty Challenging Problems in Probability with Solutions.* Reading, Mass.: Addison-Wesley Publishing Company, Inc., 1965.

EXPECTATIONS AND DECISIONS

*hen decisions are made in the face of uncertainty, they are rarely based on probabilities alone; in most cases we must also know something about the potential consequences (profits, losses, penalties, or rewards). If we must decide whether to buy a new car, knowing that our old car will soon require repairs is not enough—to make an intelligent decision we must know, among other things, the cost of the repairs and the trade-in value of the old car. Also, suppose that a building contractor has to decide whether to bid on a construction job that promises a profit of $120,000 with probability 0.20, or a loss of $27,000 (perhaps due to a strike) with probability 0.80. The probability that the contractor will make a profit is not very high but, on the other hand, the amount he stands to gain is much greater than the amount he stands to lose. Both of these examples demonstrate the need for a method of combining probabilities and consequences, and that is why we introduce the concept of a **mathematical expectation** in Section 7.1.*

Chapters 11 through 17 deal with many different problems of inference. We estimate unknown quantities, test hypotheses (assumptions or claims), and make predictions, and for such problems it is essential that, directly or indirectly, we pay attention to the consequences of what we do. After all, if there is nothing at stake, no penalties or rewards, and nobody cares, why not estimate the average weight of gray squirrels as 315.2 pounds, why not accept the claim that by adding water to gasoline we can get 150 miles per gallon with the old family car, and why not predict that by the year 2500 the average person will live to be 200 years old? Why not—if there is nothing at stake, no penalties or rewards, and no one cares? In Section 7.2 we give some examples showing how mathematical expectations based on penalties, rewards, and other kinds of payoffs can be used in making decisions, and in Section 7.3 we show how such factors may have to be considered so as to choose appropriate statistical techniques.

7.1 MATHEMATICAL EXPECTATION

If a mortality table tells us that in the United States a 50-year-old woman can expect to live 31 more years, this does not mean that anyone really expects a 50-year-old woman to live until her 81st birthday and then die the next day. Similarly, if we read that in the United States a person can expect to eat 104.4 pounds of beef and drink 39.6 gallons of soft drinks per year, or that a child in the age group from 6 to 16 can expect to visit a dentist 2.2 times a year, it must be apparent that the word "expect" is not being used in its usual sense. A child cannot go to the dentist 2.2 times, and it would be surprising, indeed, if we found somebody who actually ate 104.4 pounds of beef and drank 39.6 gallons of soft drinks in any given year. Insofar as 50-year-old women are concerned, some will live another 12 years, some will live another 20 years, some will live another 33 years, . . ., and the life expectancy of "31 more years" will have to be interpreted as an average or, as we call it here, a **mathematical expectation.**

Originally, the concept of a mathematical expectation arose in connection with games of chance, and in its simplest form it is the product of the amount that a player stands to win and the probability that he or she will win.

Example

What is our mathematical expectation when we will win $10 if and only if a balanced coin comes up heads?

solution

If we assume that the coin is balanced and randomly tossed, namely, that the probability of heads is $\frac{1}{2}$, our mathematical expectation is $10 \cdot \frac{1}{2} = \$5$.

Example

What is our mathematical expectation if we buy one of 2,000 raffle tickets for a television set worth $640?

solution

Since the probability of winning the television set is

$$\frac{1}{2,000} = 0.0005$$

our mathematical expectation is

$$640(0.0005) = \$0.32$$

Thus, from an economic standpoint, it would be foolish to spend more than 32 cents for the ticket. We might be willing to pay more if we derive pleasure from placing the bet or if the proceeds of the raffle go to a worthy cause.

Each of these two examples has a single prize, but two possible payoffs—$0 or $10 in the first example and $0 or the television set worth $640 in the other. Indeed, in the second example we can argue that one of the tickets will pay $640 (in merchandise), each of the other 1,999 tickets will pay $0, so that, altogether, the 2,000 tickets will pay $640 (in merchandise) or on the average $0.32 per ticket. This is the mathematical expectation.

To generalize this concept consider the following change in the raffle of the preceding example.

Example

What is our mathematical expectation if we buy one of 2,000 raffle tickets for a first prize of a television set worth $640, a second prize of a tape recorder worth $120, and a third prize of a radio worth $40?

solution

Now we can argue that one of the tickets will pay $640 (in merchandise), another will pay $120 (in merchandise), a third will pay $40 (in merchandise), and each of the other 1,997 tickets will pay $0. Altogether, the 2,000 tickets will thus pay

$$640 + 120 + 40 = \$800 \text{ (in merchandise),} \quad \text{or on the average } \frac{800}{2,000} = \$0.40$$

per ticket. Again, this is the mathematical expectation.   ◪ ◪ ◪

Looking at the preceding example in a different way, we can argue that if the raffle were repeated many times, we would lose

$$\frac{1,997}{2,000} \cdot 100\% = 99.85\%$$

of the time (or with probability 0.9985) and win each of the prizes

$$\frac{1}{2,000} \cdot 100\% = 0.05\%$$

of the time (or with probability 0.0005). On the average we would thus win

$$0(0.9985) + 640(0.0005) + 120(0.0005) + 40(0.0005) = \$0.40$$

which is the sum of the products obtained by multiplying each payoff by the corresponding proportion or probability. Generalizing from this example leads to the following definition:

Mathematical Expectation	*If the probabilities of obtaining the amounts a_1, a_2, ..., or a_k are p_1, p_2, ..., and p_k, where $p_1 + p_2 + \cdots + p_k = 1$, then the mathematical expectation is* $$E = a_1p_1 + a_2p_2 + \cdots + a_kp_k$$

Each amount is multiplied by the corresponding probability, and the mathematical expectation, E, is given by the sum of all these products. In the Σ notation,

$$E = \Sigma \, a \cdot p$$

Insofar as the a's are concerned, it is important to keep in mind that they are positive when they represent profits, winning, or gains (namely, amounts that we receive), and that they are negative when they represent losses, penalties, or deficits (namely, amounts that we have to pay).

Example

What is our mathematical expectation if we win $10 when a die comes up 1 or 6, and lose $5 when it comes up 2, 3, 4, or 5?

solution

The amounts are $a_1 = 10$ and $a_2 = -5$, and the probabilities are

$$p_1 = \frac{2}{6} = \frac{1}{3} \quad \text{and} \quad p_2 = \frac{4}{6} = \frac{2}{3}$$

(if we can assume that the die is balanced and randomly tossed). Thus, the mathematical expectation is

$$E = 10 \cdot \frac{1}{3} + (-5) \cdot \frac{2}{3} = 0$$ ◪ ◪ ◪

Example

The probabilities are 0.22, 0.36, 0.28, and 0.14 that an investor will be able to sell a piece of property at a profit of $2,500, at a profit of $1,500, at a profit of $500, or at a loss of $500. What is the investor's expected profit?

solution

Substituting

$$a_1 = 2,500, \quad a_2 = 1,500, \quad a_3 = 500, \quad a_4 = -500,$$

$$p_1 = 0.22, \quad p_2 = 0.36, \quad p_3 = 0.28, \quad \text{and} \quad p_4 = 0.14$$

into the formula for E, we get

$$E = 2,500(0.22) + 1,500(0.36) + 500(0.28) - 500(0.14) = \$1,160 \quad \blacksquare \ \blacksquare \ \blacksquare$$

The first of these two examples illustrates what we mean by an **equitable** or **fair game.** It is a game that does not favor either player; namely, a game in which each player's mathematical expectation is zero.

Although we referred to the quantities $a_1, a_2, \ldots,$ and a_k as "amounts," they need not be amounts of money. On page 186 we said that a child in the 6 to 16 age group can expect to visit a dentist 2.2 times a year. This value is a mathematical expectation, the sum of the products obtained by multiplying 0, 1, 2, 3, 4, ..., by the corresponding probabilities that a child in that age group will visit a dentist that many times a year.

Example

If the probabilities are

0.06   0.21   0.24   0.18   0.14   0.10   0.04   0.02   0.01

that an airline office at a certain airport will receive 0, 1, 2, 3, 4, 5, 6, 7, or 8 complaints per day about its luggage handling, how many such complaints can it expect per day?

solution

Substituting into the formula for a mathematical expectation, we get

$$E = 0(0.06) + 1(0.21) + 2(0.24) + 3(0.18) + 4(0.14)$$

$$+ 5(0.10) + 6(0.04) + 7(0.02) + 8(0.01)$$

$$= 2.75 \quad \blacksquare \ \blacksquare \ \blacksquare$$

In all of the examples of this section we were given the values of a and p (or the values of the a's and p's) and calculated E. Now let us consider an example where we are given values of a and E to arrive at some result about p, and also an example where we are given values of p and E to arrive at some result about a.

Example

To defend a client in a liability suit resulting from a car accident, a lawyer must decide whether to charge a straight fee of $6,000 or a contingent fee which she will receive only if her client wins. How does the lawyer feel about her client's chances if

(a) she prefers a straight fee of $6,000 rather than a contingent fee of $20,000;
(b) she prefers a contingent fee of $48,000 rather than a straight fee of $6,000?

solution

(a) If she feels that the probability is p that her client will win, the lawyer associates a mathematical expectation of $20{,}000p$ with the contingent fee of $20,000. Since she feels that the straight fee of $6,000 is preferable to this expectation, we can express her belief as

$$6{,}000 > 20{,}000p \quad \text{so that} \quad p < \frac{6{,}000}{20{,}000} = 0.30$$

(b) If the mathematical expectation associated with the contingency fee is $48{,}000p$, and if the lawyer feels that this is preferable to the straight fee of $6,000$, we can write

$$48{,}000p > 6{,}000 \quad \text{and therefore} \quad p > \frac{6{,}000}{48{,}000} = 0.125 \quad \blacksquare\,\blacksquare\,\blacksquare$$

Combining the results of parts (a) and (b) of the preceding example, we have shown here that $0.125 < p < 0.30$, where p is the lawyer's personal probability about her client's success. To narrow it further, we might vary the contingent fees as in Exercises 7.15 and 7.16 on page 192.

Example

A friend says that he would "give his right arm" for our two tickets to an NBA play-off game. To put this on a cash basis, we propose that he pay us $120 (the actual price of the two tickets), but he will get the tickets only if he draws a jack, queen, king, or ace from an ordinary deck of 52 playing cards; otherwise, we keep the tickets and his $120. What are the two tickets worth to our friend if he feels that this arrangement is fair?

solution

Since there are four jacks, four queens, four kings, and four aces, the probability that our friend will get the tickets is $\frac{16}{52}$. Hence, the probability that he will not get the tickets is

$$1 - \frac{16}{52} = \frac{36}{52}$$

and the mathematical expectation associated with the gamble is

$$E = a \cdot \frac{16}{52} + 0 \cdot \frac{36}{52} = a \cdot \frac{16}{52}$$

where a is the value he places on these tickets. Putting this mathematical expectation equal to $120, which he considers a fair price to pay for taking the risk, we get

$$a \cdot \frac{16}{52} = 120 \quad \text{and} \quad a = \frac{52 \cdot 120}{16} = \$390$$

This is what the two tickets are worth to our friend.   ▰ ▰ ▰

▰ EXERCISES

7.1   If a service club sells 600 raffle tickets for a cash prize of $120, what is the mathematical expectation of a person who buys one of the tickets?

7.2   At a church lottery 1,000 tickets are sold for a drawing for two prizes. One of the prizes is worth $400, and the other $250. What is the mathematical expectation of someone who buys one of the tickets?

7.3   At a bazaar held to raise money for a charity, it costs $1.00 to try one's luck at drawing an ace from an ordinary deck of 52 playing cards. What is the bazaar's organizers' expected profit per customer, if the organizers pay $10 if and only if a customer draws an ace?

7.4   If someone gives us $15 if we draw a spade from an ordinary deck of 52 playing cards, how much should we pay him if we draw a heart, diamond, or club, so as to make the game fair?

7.5   A celebrity bowling tournament pays $10,000 to the winner. What are the two finalists' mathematical expectations if

(a) they are evenly matched;

(b) their probabilities of winning are 0.65 and 0.35;

(c) their probabilities of winning are 0.85 and 0.15?

7.6   The winner of a tennis tournament gets $40,000 and the runner-up gets $15,000. What are the two finalists' mathematical expectations if

(a) they are evenly matched;

(b) their probabilities of winning are 0.60 and 0.40;

(c) their probabilities of winning are 0.70 and 0.30?

7.7   Box 1 contains 20 slips of paper, of which 19 are marked $0 and the other is marked $5; box 2 contains 50 slips of paper of which 49 are marked $0 and the other is marked $14. If a person gets whatever is on the slip he or she draws, would it be smarter to draw a slip of paper from box 1 or from box 2?

7.8   As part of a promotional scheme, the manufacturer of a new breakfast food offers a prize of $50,000 to someone willing to try the new product (distributed without charge) and send in his or her name on the label. The winner is to be drawn at random from all the entries received.

(a) What is each entrant's mathematical expectation if 200,000 persons send in their names?

(b) Was sending in the label worth the cost of postage?

7.9   If the two league champions are evenly matched, the probabilities that a "best of seven" basketball play-off will take 4, 5, 6, or 7 games are

$$\frac{1}{8}, \quad \frac{1}{4}, \quad \frac{5}{16}, \quad \text{and} \quad \frac{5}{16}$$

Under these conditions, how many games can we expect such a play-off to last?

7.10   A student's parents promise her a gift of $100 if she gets an A in statistics, $50 if she gets a B, and no reward otherwise. What is her mathematical expectation if the probabilities of her getting an A or B are 0.32 and 0.40?

7.11   The wage negotiator of a labor union feels that the odds are 3 to 1 that the members of the union will get a $1.00 raise in their hourly wage, 17 to 3 that they will not get a $1.40

raise in their hourly wage, and 9 to 1 that they will not get a $2.00 raise in their hourly wage. What is the corresponding expected raise in the hourly wage?

7.12   A fabrics dealer has an opportunity to buy a shipment of Turkish wool for $26,000. The probability that he will be able to sell this wool for $22,000 is 0.35, and the probability that he will be able to sell it for $32,000 is 0.65. What is the dealer's expected gross profit?

7.13   A police chief knows that the probabilities of 0, 1, 2, 3, or 4 burglaries on any given day are

$$0.12 \quad 0.25 \quad 0.39 \quad 0.18 \quad \text{and} \quad 0.06$$

How many burglaries can the police chief expect per day? It is assumed here that the probability of more than 4 burglaries is negligible.

7.14   The probabilities that a person who enters Merton's Department Store will make 0, 1, 2, 3, 4, or 5 purchases are

$$0.24 \quad 0.31 \quad 0.22 \quad 0.15 \quad 0.06 \quad \text{and} \quad 0.02$$

How many purchases can a person entering this store be expected to make?

7.15   With reference to the example on pages 189–190, how does the lawyer feel about her client's chances if

(a) she prefers the straight fee of $6,000 to a contingent fee of $24,000;

(b) she prefers a contingent fee of $40,000 to a straight fee of $6,000?

7.16   With reference to the example on pages 189–190, how does the lawyer feel about her client's chances if she cannot decide whether to accept a straight fee of $6,000 or a contingent fee of $30,000?

7.17   A baseball pitcher has to choose between a straight salary of $2,000,000 and a salary of $1,800,000 with a bonus of $350,000 if he wins 20 or more games. How does the pitcher feel about his chances of winning twenty games if he decides to take the straight salary of $2,000,000?

7.18   Mr. Williams is negotiating with his teenage son, Tommy, regarding payment for mowing the lawn during the summer months. Mr. Williams offers his son a choice: $100 for the season or $10 for each time he mows the lawn, as determined by the height of the grass. What does Tommy believe about the anticipated number of mowings if he prefers the second choice?

7.19   Mr. Smith feels that it is a toss-up as to whether to accept a cash prize of $26 or to gamble on two flips of a coin, where he is to receive an electric drill if the coin comes up heads both times, while otherwise he is to receive $5. What cash value does he attach to owning the drill?

7.20   Jones would like to beat Brown in an upcoming golf tournament, but his chances are nil unless he takes $400 worth of lessons, which (according to the pro at his club) will give him a fifty–fifty chance. If Jones can expect to break even if he takes the lessons, and bets Brown $1,000 against x dollars that he will win, find x.

7.2   DECISION MAKING ⊖

In the face of uncertainty, mathematical expectations can often be used to great advantage in making decisions. In general, if we must choose between two or more alternatives, it is considered rational to select the one with the "most promising" mathematical expectation: the one that maximizes expected profits, minimizes expected costs, maximizes expected tax advantages, minimizes expected losses, and so on.

Example

A furniture manufacturer must decide whether to expand his plant capacity now or wait at least another year. His advisors tell him that if he expands now and economic conditions remain good, there will be a profit of $328,000 during the next fiscal year; if he expands now and there is a recession, there will be a loss (negative profit) of $80,000; if he waits at least another year and economic conditions remain good, there will be a profit of $160,000; and if he waits at least another year and there is a recession, there will be a small profit of $16,000. If the furniture manufacturer feels that the probabilities for economic conditions remaining good or there being a recession are $\frac{1}{3}$ and $\frac{2}{3}$, will expanding his plant capacity now maximize his expected profit?

solution

In problems like this it often helps to present the given information in a table such as the following:

	Expand now	*Delay expansion*
Economic conditions remain good	$328,000	$160,000
There is a recession	−$80,000	$16,000

As can be seen from this table, it will be advantageous to expand the plant capacity right away only if economic conditions remain good, and the furniture manufacturer's decision will, therefore, have to depend on the chances that this will be the case. Using the manufacturer's probabilities of $\frac{1}{3}$ and $\frac{2}{3}$ for economic conditions remaining good or there being a recession, we find that the expected profit is

$$328,000 \cdot \frac{1}{3} + (-80,000) \cdot \frac{2}{3} = \$56,000$$

if he expands his plant capacity right away, and

$$160,000 \cdot \frac{1}{3} + (16,000) \cdot \frac{2}{3} = \$64,000$$

if the expansion is delayed. Since the second of these figures exceeds the first, it follows that delaying the expansion maximizes the furniture manufacturer's expected profit. ◪ ◪ ◪

The way in which we have studied this problem is called a **Bayesian analysis.** In this kind of analysis, probabilities are assigned to the alternatives about which uncertainties exist (the **states of nature,** which in our example were economic conditions remaining good and a recession); then we choose whichever alternative promises the greatest expected profit or the smallest expected loss.

This approach to decision making has great intuitive appeal, but it is not without complications. If mathematical expectations are to be used for making decisions, it is essential that our appraisals of all relevant probabilities and payoffs be very close to correct. An additional difficulty is that two persons dealing with the same problem may have different opinions about the probabilities or the payoffs and come to different conclusions.

Example

Suppose that an expert forecaster feels that the probabilities for economic conditions remaining good or there being a recession are 0.40 and 0.60. Based on these probabilities, what should the furniture manufacturer do so as to maximize his expected profit?

solution

Now the expected profit is

$$328,000(0.40) + (-80,000)(0.60) = \$83,200$$

if the furniture manufacturer expands his plant capacity right away, and

$$160,000(0.40) + 16,000(0.60) = \$73,600$$

if the expansion is delayed. Since the first of these two figures exceeds the second, the furniture manufacturer will maximize his expected profit if he expands his plant capacity right away. Note that by changing the probabilities from $\frac{1}{3}$ and $\frac{2}{3}$ to 0.40 and 0.60, the decision has been reversed.   ▨ ▨ ▨

Example

Now suppose that the furniture manufacturer is told by his accountant that the \$328,000 figure is incorrect and that it should be \$352,000. If the furniture manufacturer uses his own appraisal of the probabilities for economic conditions remaining good or there being a recession, will this change in the payoffs affect his decision?

solution

With this change, the expected profit is

$$352,000 \cdot \frac{1}{3} + (-80,000) \cdot \frac{2}{3} = \$64,000$$

if the manufacturer expands his plant capacity right away, and

$$160,000 \cdot \frac{1}{3} + 16,000 \cdot \frac{2}{3} = \$64,000$$

if the expansion is delayed. Since the two figures are the same, it does not matter now whether the furniture manufacturer expands his plant capacity right away or delays the expansion. Again, a minor change in the figures has affected the result.   ▨ ▨ ▨

7.3   STATISTICAL DECISION PROBLEMS ⇧

Modern statistics, with its emphasis on inference, may be looked upon as the art, or science, of decision making under uncertainty. This approach to statistics, called **decision theory,** dates back only to the middle of this century and the publication of John von Neumann and Oscar Morgenstern's *Theory of Games and Economic Behavior* in 1944 and Abraham Wald's *Statistical Decision Functions* in 1950. Since the study of decision theory is quite complicated mathematically, we limit our discussion here to an example in which the method of Section 7.2 is applied to a problem that is of a statistical nature.

Example

A government agency creates five groups to study gender discrimination in business. The groups contain 1, 2, 5, 1, and 6 women, and are assigned randomly to various cities. The mayor of one city hires a consultant to predict how many women will be in the group sent to his city. The consultant will be paid a flat fee of $100, plus a bonus of $200 if his prediction is correct. What prediction maximizes the amount of money the consultant can obtain?

solution

If the consultant's prediction is 1, which is the mode of the five numbers, he will make $100 with probability $\frac{3}{5}$ and $300 with probability $\frac{2}{5}$. So he can expect to make

$$100 \cdot \frac{3}{5} + 300 \cdot \frac{2}{5} = \$180$$

and we can readily verify that this is the best he can do. If his prediction is 2, 5, or 6, he can expect to make

$$100 \cdot \frac{4}{5} + 300 \cdot \frac{1}{5} = \$140$$

and for any other prediction his expectation is only $100.   ◪ ◪ ◪

This example illustrates the (perhaps obvious) fact that if one has to pick an exact value "on the nose" and there is no reward for being close, the best prediction is the mode. To illustrate further how the consequences of one's decisions may dictate the choice of a statistical method of decision or prediction, let us consider the following variation of our example.

Example

Suppose that the consultant is paid $300 minus an amount of money equal in dollars to 40 times the magnitude of his error. What prediction will maximize the amount of money that he can expect to get?

solution

Now it is the median that yields the best predictions. If the consultant's prediction is 2, which is the median of the five numbers, the magnitude of the error will be 1, 0, 3, or 4, depending on whether 1, 2, 5, or 6 of the members of the team sent to the city will be women. Consequently, he will get $260, $300, $180, or $140 with probabilities $\frac{2}{5}, \frac{1}{5}, \frac{1}{5}$, and $\frac{1}{5}$, and he can expect to make

$$260 \cdot \frac{2}{5} + 300 \cdot \frac{1}{5} + 180 \cdot \frac{1}{5} + 140 \cdot \frac{1}{5} = \$228$$

It can be shown that the consultant's expectation is less than $228 for any value other than 2, but let us verify it here merely for 3, which is the mean of the five numbers. In that case the magnitude of the error will be 2, 1, 2, or 3, depending on whether 1, 2, 5, or 6 of the members of the team sent to the city will be women, the consultant will get $220, $260, $220, or $180 with probabilities $\frac{2}{5}, \frac{1}{5}, \frac{1}{5}$, and $\frac{1}{5}$, and he can expect to make

$$220 \cdot \frac{2}{5} + 260 \cdot \frac{1}{5} + 220 \cdot \frac{1}{5} + 180 \cdot \frac{1}{5} = \$220 \qquad \blacksquare \ \blacksquare \ \blacksquare$$

The mean comes into its own right when the penalty, the amount subtracted, increases more rapidly with the size of the error: namely, when it is proportional to its square.

Example

Suppose that the consultant is paid $300 minus an amount of money equal in dollars to 20 times the square of the error. What prediction will maximize the amount of money that he can expect to get?

solution

If the consultant's prediction is 3, which is the mean of the five numbers, the squares of the errors will be 4, 1, 4, or 9 depending on whether 1, 2, 5, or 6 of the members of the team sent to the city will be women. Correspondingly, the consultant will get $220, $280, $220, or $120 with probabilities $\frac{2}{5}, \frac{1}{5}, \frac{1}{5}$, and $\frac{1}{5}$, and he can expect to make

$$220 \cdot \frac{2}{5} + 280 \cdot \frac{1}{5} + 220 \cdot \frac{1}{5} + 120 \cdot \frac{1}{5} = \$212$$

As can be verified, the consultant's expectation is less than $212 for any other prediction (see Exercise 7.35 on page 199). $\qquad \blacksquare \ \blacksquare \ \blacksquare$

This third case is of special importance in statistics, as it ties in closely with the method of least squares. We study this method in Chapter 15, where it is used in fitting curves to observed data, but besides this it has other important applications in the theory of statistics. The idea of working with the squares of the errors is justified on the grounds that in actual practice the seriousness of an error often increases rapidly with the size of the error, more rapidly than the magnitude of the error itself.

The greatest difficulty in applying the methods of this chapter to realistic problems in statistics is that we seldom know the exact values of all the risks that are involved; that is, we seldom know the exact values of the "payoffs" corresponding to the various eventualities. For instance, if the Food and Drug Administration must decide whether or not to release a new drug for general use, how can it put a cash value on the damage that might be done by not waiting for a more thorough analysis of possible side effects or on the lives that might be lost by not making the drug available to the public right away? Similarly, if a faculty committee must decide which of several applicants should be admitted to a medical school or, perhaps, receive a scholarship, how can they possibly foresee all the consequences that might be involved?

The fact that we seldom have adequate information about relevant probabilities also provides obstacles to finding suitable decision criteria; without them, is it reasonable to base decisions, say, on pessimism or optimism as in Exercises 7.30 and 7.31 on page 198? Questions like these are difficult to answer, but their analysis serves the important purpose of revealing the logic that underlies statistical thinking.

◢ EXERCISES

7.21   A grab-bag contains 5 packages worth $1 apiece, 5 packages worth $3 apiece, and 10 packages worth $5 apiece. Is it rational to pay $4 for the privilege of selecting one of these packages at random?

7.22   A contractor must choose between two jobs. The first promises a profit of $120,000 with a probability of $\frac{3}{4}$ or a loss of $30,000 (due to strikes and other delays) with a probability of $\frac{1}{4}$; the second job promises a profit of $180,000 with a probability of $\frac{1}{2}$ or a loss of $45,000 with a probability of $\frac{1}{2}$. Which job should the contractor choose so as to maximize his expected profit?

7.23   A landscape architect must decide whether to bid on the landscaping of a public building. What should she do if she figures that the job promises a profit of $10,800 with probability of 0.40 or a loss of $7,000 (due to a lack of rain or perhaps an early frost) with probability 0.60, and it is not worth her time unless the expected profit is at least $1,000?

7.24   A truck driver has to deliver a load of building materials to one of two construction sites, a barn that is 18 miles from the lumberyard or a shopping center that is 22 miles from the lumberyard. He has misplaced the order indicating where the loads should go. Also, he must return to the lumberyard after the delivery. The barn and shopping center are 8 miles apart. To complicate matters, the telephone at the lumberyard is not working. If the driver feels that the probability is $\frac{1}{6}$ that the load should go to the barn and $\frac{5}{6}$ that the load should go to the shopping center, where should he go first so as to minimize the distance that he will have to drive?

7.25   With reference to Exercise 7.24, where should the driver go first so as to minimize the expected driving distance if instead of $\frac{1}{6}$ and $\frac{5}{6}$ the probabilities are

(a) $\frac{1}{3}$ for the barn and $\frac{2}{3}$ for the shopping center;

(b) $\frac{1}{4}$ for the barn and $\frac{3}{4}$ for the shopping center?

7.26   The management of a mining company must decide whether to continue an operation at a certain location. If they continue and are successful, they will make a profit of $4,500,000; if they continue and are not successful, they will lose $2,700,000; if they do not continue but would have been successful if they had continued, they will lose $1,800,000 (for competitive reasons); and if they do not continue and would not have been successful if they had continued, they will make a profit of $450,000 (because funds allocated to the operation remain unspent). What decision would maximize the company's expected profit if it is felt that there is a fifty–fifty chance for success?

7.27   With reference to Exercise 7.26, show that it does not matter what they decide to do if it is felt that the probabilities for and against success are $\frac{1}{3}$ and $\frac{2}{3}$.

7.28   A small delicatessen has shelf space for four highly perishable cream pies which are destroyed at the end of the day if they are not sold. The cream pies cost $2 each and sell for $6 each, so that the profit is $4 for each cream pie sold. How many cream pies should the retailer stock so as to maximize his expected profit if he knows that the probabilities of a demand for 0, 1, 2, 3, or 4 cream pies are, respectively,

0.10   0.30   0.35   0.15   and   0.10 ?

⇦ 7.29   With reference to the furniture manufacturer on page 193, suppose that the $80,000 loss is in error and should be a $120,000 loss. What decision would maximize his expected profit if the probabilities are 0.40 and 0.60 that the economic conditions will remain good or that there will be a recession?

⊞ 7.30   In the absence of any information about relevant probabilities, a pessimist may well try to minimize the maximum loss or maximize the minimum profit. This person would be using the **minimax** or **maximin criterion.**

(a)   With reference to the furniture manufacturer on page 193, suppose that he has no idea about the probabilities that economic conditions will remain good or that there will be a recession. What decision would minimize his maximum loss?

(b)   With regard to Exercise 7.28, suppose that the delicatessen owner has no idea about the probabilities for the demand for the cream pies. How many cream pies should he stock if he wishes to minimize the maximum loss to which he could be exposed? Discuss the reasonableness of using the minimax criterion in a problem of this kind.

⊞ 7.31   In the absence of any information about relevant probabilities, an optimist may well try to minimize the minimum loss or maximize the maximum profit. This person would be using the **minimin** or **maximax criterion.**

(a)   With reference to the furniture manufacturer on page 193, suppose that he has no idea about the probabilities that economic conditions will remain good or that there will be a recession. What decision would maximize his maximum profit?

(b)   With regard to Exercise 7.28, suppose that the delicatessen owner has no idea about the probabilities for the demand for the cream pies. How many cream pies should he stock if he wishes to maximize his maximum profit?

⊞ 7.32   With reference to Exercise 7.26, suppose that the management of the mining company has no idea about the chances for success. What decision will

(a)   maximize their minimum profit;

(b)   maximize their maximum profit?

⊞ 7.33   With reference to the furniture manufacturer on page 193, suppose that before he must decide whether or not to expand the capacity of his plant, he has the option of paying an infallible consultant $25,000 to find out for sure whether economic conditions will remain good or whether there will be a recession. This raises the question whether it is worthwhile for him to spend the $25,000. To answer this question, let us use his $\frac{1}{3}$ and $\frac{2}{3}$ probabilities that economic conditions will remain good or that there will be a recession. If he knew for sure what was going to happen, the right decision would yield a profit of $328,000 or a profit of $16,000. Since the corresponding probabilities are $\frac{1}{3}$ and $\frac{2}{3}$, we find that (with the help of the infallible expert) the furniture manufacturer's expected profit is

$$328,000 \cdot \frac{1}{3} + 16,000 \cdot \frac{2}{3} = \$120,000$$

This is called the **expected profit with perfect information.** On page 193 we showed that without the help of the infallible expert, the expected profit was either $56,000 or $64,000, so that there is an improvement of at least

$$\$120,000 - \$64,000 = \$56,000$$

and this makes the $25,000 fee well worthwhile. It is customary to refer to the amount by which perfect information improves one's expectation, $56,000 in our example, as the **expected value of perfect information.**

(a)   With reference to Exercise 7.24, find the expected distance with perfect information and the expected value (in miles) of perfect information.

(b)   With reference to Exercise 7.26, find the expected profit with perfect information and the expected value of perfect information. Would it be worthwhile to spend $500,000 beforehand to find out for sure whether the operation will be a success?

⊞ 7.34   There are situations where the various criteria we have discussed are all outweighed by special considerations. For instance, with reference to the furniture manufacturer on page 193, what may well be his decision if he knows that

(a) he will be bankrupt unless he makes a profit of at least $200,000 during the next fiscal year;

(b) he will be bankrupt unless he shows a profit, no matter how small, during the next fiscal year?

⊞ 7.35   With reference to the example on page 195, where the consultant is paid $300 minus an amount of money equal to 20 times the square of the error, what can the consultant expect to make if

(a) his prediction is 1;   (b) his prediction is 2?

In general, it can be shown that for any set of numbers, $x_1, x_2, \ldots,$ and x_n, the quantity

$$\sum_{i=1}^{n}(x_i - k)^2$$

is smallest when $k = \bar{x}$. In this case, the amount subtracted from $300 is smallest when the prediction is $\bar{x} = 3$.

7.36   The ages of the seven entries in an essay contest are

$$17 \quad 17 \quad 17 \quad 18 \quad 20 \quad 21 \quad 23$$

and their chances of winning are equal. We want to predict the age of the winner. What prediction maximizes the expected reward if

(a) there is a reward for being right, but none for being close;

(b) there is a penalty proportional to the size of the error;

(c) there is a penalty proportional to the square of the error?

7.37   Some of the used cars on Harry's parking lot are priced at $1,200, some at $1,500, some at $2,000, and some at $2,800. If we want to predict the price of the car that will be sold first, what prediction minimizes the maximum size of the error? What is the name of this statistic, which is given in an exercise in Chapter 3?

7.38   There are sometimes occasions in which we select an option that has an inferior mathematical expectation. Suppose that you have a choice between two investments for $10,000. One option is a bank certificate of deposit (CD) which will certainly return to you the amount $10,800 after one year. The second option consists of shares in a silver-prospecting company; in one year these shares will be worth nothing with probability 0.80 and will be worth $60,000 with probability 0.20. Which investment do you prefer? Why?

⊞ 7.39   The situation of Exercise 7.28 is sometimes described as the **newsboy problem.** Suppose that a newspaper seller buys papers at the beginning of the day for 15 cents each and sells them for 40 cents each. If he buys more papers than he can sell, the leftovers must be discarded as a complete loss. Suppose that the probability is 0.01 that he will have a demand for one paper, 0.01 that he will have a demand for two papers, 0.01 that he will have a demand for three papers, . . ., 0.01 that he will have a demand for 100 papers. How many papers should he purchase at the beginning of the day so as to maximize his expected profit?

7.4   CHECKLIST OF KEY TERMS[†]   (*with page references to their definitions*)

†Terms introduced in exercises are shown in *italics*.

7.5   REVIEW EXERCISES

7.40   The probabilities that a person shopping at "The Bookstore," will buy 0, 1, 2, 3, or 4 books are

$$0.22 \quad 0.54 \quad 0.17 \quad 0.06 \quad \text{and } 0.01$$

How many books can a person shopping at this bookstore be expected to buy?

⬦ 7.41   A playwright feels that she stands to make $250,000 if her new play is a success, but nothing if it is a flop. How does she feel about the chances that the play will be a success if prior to its opening she sells the play outright for $150,000?

7.42   The mortgage manager for a bank figures that if an applicant for a $150,000 home mortgage is a good risk and the bank accepts him, the bank's profits will be $8,000. If the applicant is a bad risk and the bank accepts him, the bank will lose $20,000. If the manager turns down the applicant, there will be no profit or loss either way. What should the manager do if

(a) he wishes to maximize expected profit and feels that the probability is 0.10 that the applicant is a bad risk;

(b) he wishes to maximize expected profit and feels that the probability is 0.30 that the applicant is a bad risk;

(c) he wishes to minimize the maximum loss and has no idea about the probability that the applicant is a bad risk?

7.43   Ms. McCall contemplates buying a raffle ticket from a charity organization. The raffle has 1,200 tickets, and there are two prizes. One prize is $500 in cash and the other prize is a week's stay at a hotel in San Diego. What value does Ms. McCall place on the hotel stay if she is willing to spend $2 for a ticket?

7.44   If the probabilities are

$$0.09 \quad 0.25 \quad 0.29 \quad 0.18 \quad 0.14 \quad 0.03 \quad \text{and} \quad 0.02$$

that a child in the age group from 6 to 16 will visit a dentist 0, 1, 2, 3, 4, 5, or 6 times a year, how many times can a child in this age group expect to visit a dentist in any given year?

7.45   Mrs. Black feels that it is about a toss-up whether to accept $20 cash or to gamble on drawing a bead from an urn containing 15 white beads and 45 red beads, where she is to receive $2 if she draws a white bead or a bottle of fancy perfume if she draws a red bead. What value, or utility, does she attach to the bottle of perfume?

⬦ 7.46   The five kinds of cars considered by a police department average

$$31, \quad 30, \quad 30, \quad 33, \quad 30$$

miles per gallon, and their chances of being chosen are all equal. We wish to predict the average miles per gallon of the kind of car they will choose. What prediction maximizes the expected reward if

(a) there is a $200 reward for being right, but no reward for being close;

(b) there is a reward of $200, minus $10 times the square of the error?

7.47   An athlete is willing to give odds of 2 to 1, but not odds of 3 to 1, that he will be able to beat his roommate at arm wrestling. What does this tell us about the probability he assigns to his being able to win?

7.48   A person gets $40 if he or she gets three heads in three random flips of a balanced coin; otherwise, there is no reward. How much should the person pay to play this game so as to make it fair?

7.49   The manufacturer of a new battery additive has to decide whether to sell his product for $1.00 a can or for $1.25 with a "double-your-money-back-if-not-satisfied guarantee." How does he feel about the chances that a person will actually ask for double his or her money back if

(a) he decides to sell the product for $1.00;

(b) he decides to sell the product for $1.25 with the guarantee;

(c) he cannot make up his mind?

7.50   Ms. Cooper is planning to attend a convention in San Diego and must send in her room reservations immediately. The convention is so large that the activities are held partly in hotel A and partly in hotel B, and Ms. Cooper does not know whether the particular session she wants to attend will be held in hotel A or hotel B. She is planning to stay only one day, which would cost her $80.00 at hotel A and $72.80 at hotel B, but it will cost her an extra $12.00 for cab fare if she stays at the wrong hotel. Where should she make her reservation if she feels that the probability is 0.75 that the session she wants to attend will be held at hotel A and she wants to minimize her expected cost?

7.51   With reference to Exercise 7.50, would it be worthwhile to spend $2.40 on a long-distance call to find out where the session will be held?

7.52   With reference to Exercise 7.50, where should Ms. Cooper make her reservation if she feels that the probability is 0.80 that the session she wants to attend will be held at hotel A?

7.53   With reference to Exercise 7.50, where should Ms. Cooper make her reservation if she is a confirmed optimist but has no idea about the probability that the session she wants to attend will be held at hotel A?

7.54   An insurance company agrees to pay the promoter of a drag race $8,000 in case the event has to be canceled because of rain. If the company's actuary feels that a fair net premium for this risk is $1,280, what probability does she assign to the possibility that the race will have to be canceled because of rain?

7.55   With reference to Exercise 7.46, suppose that there is a penalty of 100 times the size of the error. What prediction will minimize the maximum penalty?

7.56   Two friends are betting on repeated flips of a balanced coin. One has $5 at the start and the other has $3, and after each flip the loser pays the winner $1. If p is the probability that the one who starts with $5 will win his friend's $3 before he loses his own $5, explain why

$$3p - 5(1 - p)$$

should equal 0, and then solve the equation

$$3p - 5(1 - p) = 0$$

for p. Generalize this result to the case where two players start with a dollars and b dollars, respectively.

7.6   REFERENCES

More detailed treatments of the subject matter of this chapter may be found in

BROSS, I. D. J., *Design for Decision.* New York: Macmillan Publishing Co., Inc., 1953.

JEFFREY, R. C., *The Logic of Decision.* New York: McGraw-Hill Book Company, 1965.

and in many textbooks on business statistics; for instance, in Chapter 7 of

FREUND, J. E., WILLIAMS, F. J., and PERLES, B. M., *Elementary Business Statistics: The Modern Approach,* 6th ed. Upper Saddle River, N.J.: Prentice Hall, 1993.

Decision theory, including the newsboy problem, is discussed in Chapter 14 of

EPPEN, G. D., GOULD, F. J., and SCHMIDT, C. P., *Introductory Management Science,* 4th ed. Upper Saddle River, N.J.: Prentice Hall, 1993.

"The Dowry Problem" and "A Tie Is Like Kissing Your Sister" are two amusing examples of decision making given in

HOLLANDER, M., and PROSCHAN, F., *The Statistical Exorcist: Dispelling Statistics Anxiety.* New York: Marcel Dekker, Inc., 1984.

PROBABILITY DISTRIBUTIONS

*F*or most statistics problems we are interested in one aspect, or at most in a few aspects, of the outcomes of experiments. For instance, a student taking a true–false test may be interested only in the number of questions he answers correctly and not which ones; a geologist may be interested only in the age of a rock sample and not in its hardness; and a sociologist may be interested only in the socioeconomic status of a person interviewed in a survey and not in her age or weight. Also, an agronomist may be interested in determining not only the yield per acre of a new variety of corn but also the temperature at which it will germinate; and an automotive engineer may be interested in the brightness and the durability of the headlights proposed for a new model car and also in their projected cost.

In these five examples, the student, the geologist, the sociologist, the agronomist, and the automotive engineer are all interested in numbers that are associated with the outcomes of situations involving an element of chance or, more specifically, in values of **random variables.** Since random variables are neither random nor variables, why do they go by this name? This is hard to say, but a mathematics professor with a good sense of humor likened them to alligator pears, or avocados, which are neither alligators nor pears.

In the study of random variables we are usually interested in the probabilities with which they take on the various values within their range, namely, in their **probability distributions.** The general introduction of random variables and probability distributions in Sections 8.1 and 8.2 is followed by a discussion of some of the most important probability distributions in Sections 8.3 through 8.6. Then in Sections 8.7 and 8.8 we discuss some ways of describing the most relevant features of probability distributions. Section 8.9 contains optional material on the simulation of values of random variables.

8.1　RANDOM VARIABLES

To be more explicit about the concept of a random variable, let us consider Figure 8.1, which shows the sample space for a situation in which an Allstate agent and a State Farm agent are trying to sell three insurance policies—home, automobile, and life—to a family that has just moved. The point (2, 1), for example, labels the outcome in which the Allstate agent sells two of the policies and the State Farm agent sells one. In Figure 8.1 we place another number (in green) next to each point—

　0 to the point (0, 0);
　1 to the points (1, 0) and (0, 1);
　2 to the points (2, 0), (1, 1), and (0, 2); and
　3 to the points (3, 0), (2, 1), (1, 2), and (0, 3)

In this way we have associated with each point of the sample space the number of policies that, between them, the two agents sell to the family.

Since associating numbers with the points of a sample space is just a way of defining a function over the points of the sample space, random variables are re-

FIGURE 8.1

Sample space with values of random variable.

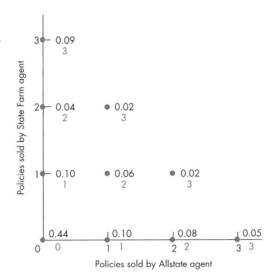

ally functions and not variables. Conceptually, though, most beginners find it easier to think of random variables simply as quantities that can take on different values depending on chance. For instance, the number of speeding tickets issued each day on the freeway between Indio and Blythe in California is a random variable, and so are the annual production of coffee in Brazil, the number of persons visiting Disneyland each week, the wind velocity at Kennedy airport, the size of the audience at a baseball game, and the number of mistakes a person makes when typing a report.

It is customary to classify random variables according to the number of values which they can assume, and in this chapter we consider only random variables that are **discrete,** namely, random variables that can take on a finite number of values or a countable infinity (as many values as there are whole numbers). For nearly all discrete random variables, the possible values form a subset of the integers. For instance, the number of policies which, between them, the two insurance agents sell to the given family is a discrete random variable that can take on a finite number of values, the four values 0, 1, 2, and 3. In contrast, the number of the roll on which a die comes up 6 for the first time is a discrete random variable that can take on the countable infinity of values 1, 2, 3, 4, ... It is possible, although highly unlikely, that it will take 1,000 rolls of the die, 1 million rolls, or even more, until we finally get a 6. There are also **continuous random variables,** which arise when we deal with quantities measured on a continuous scale, say, time, weight, or distance. These will be taken up in Chapter 9.

8.2 PROBABILITY DISTRIBUTIONS

The points of the sample space illustrated in Figure 8.1 are also labeled with their probabilities (in black). For instance, the value 0.06 on the point (1, 1) means that the probability is 0.06 that each agent will sell one policy. We find from this figure that the random variable "the number of policies which, between them, they sell to the given family" takes on

the value 0 with probability 0.44;
the value 1 with probability 0.10 + 0.10 = 0.20;
the value 2 with probability 0.08 + 0.06 + 0.04 = 0.18; and
the value 3 with probability 0.05 + 0.02 + 0.02 + 0.09 = 0.18.

All this is summarized in the following table:

Number of policies sold	Probability
0	0.44
1	0.20
2	0.18
3	0.18

This table, and the two that follow, serve to illustrate what we mean by a **probability distribution**. As this table shows, a **probability distribution is a correspondence that assigns probabilities to the values of a random variable.** Another example of such a correspondence is given by the following table, which pertains to the number of points we roll with a balanced die:

Number of points we roll with a die	Probability
1	$\frac{1}{6}$
2	$\frac{1}{6}$
3	$\frac{1}{6}$
4	$\frac{1}{6}$
5	$\frac{1}{6}$
6	$\frac{1}{6}$

Finally, for four flips of a balanced coin there are the 16 equally likely possibilities

```
HHHH   HHHT   HHTH   HTHH
THHH   HHTT   HTHT   HTTH
THHT   THTH   TTHH   HTTT
THTT   TTHT   TTTH   TTTT
```

where H stands for heads and T for tails. Counting the number of heads in each case and using the formula $\frac{s}{n}$ for equiprobable outcomes, we get the following probability distribution for the total number of heads:

Number of heads	Probability
0	$\frac{1}{16}$
1	$\frac{4}{16}$
2	$\frac{6}{16}$
3	$\frac{4}{16}$
4	$\frac{1}{16}$

When possible, we try to express probability distributions by means of for-mulas that enable us to calculate the probabilities associated with the various values of a random variable. For instance, for the number of points we roll with a balanced die we can write

$$f(x) = \frac{1}{6} \quad \text{for } x = 1, 2, 3, 4, 5, \text{ and } 6$$

where $f(1)$ denotes the probability of rolling a 1, $f(2)$ denotes the probability of rolling a 2, and so on, in the usual functional notation. Here we wrote the prob-ability that the random variable will take on the value x as $f(x)$, but we could just as well write it as

$$g(x), \quad h(x), \quad m(x), \quad \text{and so on.}$$

Example

Verify that for the number of heads obtained in four flips of a balanced coin the probability distribution is given by

$$f(x) = \frac{\binom{4}{x}}{16} \quad \text{for } x = 0, 1, 2, 3, \text{ and } 4$$

solution

By direct calculation, or by using Table X at the end of the book, we find that

$$\binom{4}{0} = 1, \quad \binom{4}{1} = 4, \quad \binom{4}{2} = 6, \quad \binom{4}{3} = 4, \quad \text{and} \quad \binom{4}{4} = 1.$$

Thus, the probabilities for $x = 0, 1, 2, 3,$ and 4 are

$$\frac{1}{16}, \quad \frac{4}{16}, \quad \frac{6}{16}, \quad \frac{4}{16}, \quad \text{and} \quad \frac{1}{16},$$

which agrees with the results obtained above ▰ ▰ ▰

Since the values of probability distributions are probabilities, and since ran-dom variables have to take on one of their values, we have these two rules that apply to any probability distribution.

The values of a probability distribution must be numbers on the interval from 0 to 1.

The sum of all the values of a probability distribution must be equal to 1.

These rules enable us to determine whether or not a function (given by an equation or by a table) can serve as the probability distribution of some random variable.

Example

Check whether the correspondence given by

$$f(x) = \frac{x + 3}{15} \quad \text{for } x = 1, 2, \text{ and } 3$$

can serve as the probability distribution of some random variable.

solution

Substituting $x = 1, 2$, and 3 into $\dfrac{x + 3}{15}$, we get

$$f(1) = \frac{4}{15}, \quad f(2) = \frac{5}{15}, \quad \text{and} \quad f(3) = \frac{6}{15}.$$

Since none of these values is negative or greater than 1, and since their sum is

$$\frac{4}{15} + \frac{5}{15} + \frac{6}{15} = 1$$

the given function can serve as the probability distribution of some random variable.

◤ ◤ ◤

8.3   THE BINOMIAL DISTRIBUTION

There are many applied problems in which we are interested in the probability that an event will occur x times out of n. For instance, we may be interested in the probability of getting 45 responses to 400 questionnaires sent out as part of a sociological study, the probability that 5 of 12 mice will survive for a given length of time after the injection of a cancer-inducing substance, the probability that 45 of 300 drivers stopped at a road block will be wearing their seat belts, or the probability that 66 of 200 television viewers (interviewed by a rating service) will recall what products were advertised on a given program. To borrow from the language of games of chance, we could say that in each of these examples we are interested in the probability of getting "x successes in n trials," or in other words, "x successes and $n - x$ failures in n attempts."

In the problems we shall study in this section, we always make the following assumptions:

1. There is a fixed number of trials.
2. The probability of a success is the same for each trial.
3. The trials are all independent.

Thus, the theory we develop does not apply, for example, if we are interested in the number of dresses that a woman may try on before she buys one (where the number of trials is not fixed), if we check every hour whether traffic is congested at a certain intersection (where the probability of "success" is not constant), or if we are interested in the number of times that a person voted for the Republican candidate in the last five presidential elections (where the trials are not independent).

We will be able to obtain a formula to solve problems that meet the conditions listed in the preceding paragraph. If p and $1 - p$ are the probabilities of success and failure for any given trial, then the probability of getting x successes and $n - x$ failures *in some specific order* is $p^x(1 - p)^{n-x}$. In this product, there is one factor of p for each success and one factor of $1 - p$ for each failure. The x and $n - x$ factors are multiplied together by virtue of the generalization of the special multiplication rule for more than two independent events, as on page 168.

Since this probability applies to any point of the sample space which represents x successes and $n - x$ failures (in some specific order), we have only to count how many points of this kind there are, and then multiply

$$p^x(1 - p)^{n-x}$$

by this number. Clearly, the number of ways in which we can choose the x trials on which the successes are to occur is $\binom{n}{x}$, and we have thus arrived at the following result:

Binomial Distribution	The probability of getting x successes in n independent trials is $$f(x) = \binom{n}{x} p^x (1 - p)^{n-x} \qquad \text{for } x = 0, 1, 2, \ldots, \text{ or } n$$ where p is the constant probability of a success for each trial.

It is customary to say here that the number of successes in n trials is a random variable having the **binomial probability distribution,** or simply the **binomial distribution.** The binomial distribution is called by this name because for

$$x = 0, \quad 1, \quad 2, \quad \ldots, \quad \text{and } n$$

the values of the probabilities are the successive terms of the binomial expansion of

$$[(1 - p) + p]^n.$$

Example

Verify that the formula on page 207 (for the probability of getting x heads in four flips of a balanced coin) is, in fact, the one for the binomial distribution with $n = 4$ and $p = \frac{1}{2}$.

solution

Substituting $n = 4$ and $p = \frac{1}{2}$ into the formula for the binomial distribution, we obtain

$$f(x) = \binom{4}{x}\left(\frac{1}{2}\right)^x\left(1 - \frac{1}{2}\right)^{4-x} = \binom{4}{x}\left(\frac{1}{2}\right)^4 = \frac{\binom{4}{x}}{16}$$

for $x = 0, 1, 2, 3,$ and 4. This is exactly the formula given on page 207. ◪ ◪ ◪

Example

If the probability is 0.70 that any one registered voter (randomly selected from official rolls) will vote in a given election, what is the probability that two of five registered voters will vote in the election?

solution

Substituting

$$x = 2, \quad n = 5, \quad p = 0.70, \quad \text{and} \quad \binom{5}{2} = 10$$

into the formula for the binomial distribution, we have

$$f(2) = \binom{5}{2}(0.70)^2(1 - 0.70)^{5-2} = 10(0.70)^2(0.30)^3 \approx 0.132^\dagger \qquad ◪ ◪ ◪$$

The following is an example where we calculate all the probabilities of a binomial distribution.

Example

The probability is 0.30 that a person shopping at a certain supermarket will take advantage of its special promotion of ice cream. Find the probabilities that among six persons shopping at this market there will be 0, 1, 2, 3, 4, 5, or 6 who will take advantage of the promotion. Also, draw a histogram of this probability distribution.

solution

Assuming that the selection is random, we substitute $n = 6$, $p = 0.30$, and, respectively, $x = 0, 1, 2, 3, 4, 5,$ and 6 into the formula for the binomial distribution, and we have

$$f(0) = \binom{6}{0}(0.30)^0(0.70)^6 \approx 0.118$$

$$f(1) = \binom{6}{1}(0.30)^1(0.70)^5 \approx 0.303$$

$$f(2) = \binom{6}{2}(0.30)^2(0.70)^4 \approx 0.324$$

$$f(3) = \binom{6}{3}(0.30)^3(0.70)^3 \approx 0.185$$

$$f(4) = \binom{6}{4}(0.30)^4(0.70)^2 \approx 0.060$$

$$f(5) = \binom{6}{5}(0.30)^5(0.70)^1 \approx 0.010$$

$$f(6) = \binom{6}{6}(0.30)^6(0.70)^0 \approx 0.001$$

A histogram of this distribution is shown in Figure 8.2.   ◪ ◪ ◪

If you do not care much for ice cream and are not interested in personal buying habits, let us stress the importance of the binomial distribution as a statistical model. The results of the preceding example apply also if

$\dagger$See the footnote on page 51 regarding use of the symbol $\approx$.

FIGURE 8.2

Histogram of binomial distribution with n = 6 and p = 0.30.

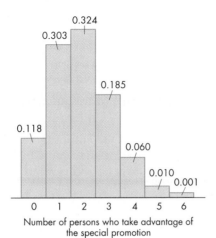

Number of persons who take advantage of the special promotion

- the probability is 0.30 that the battery of a watch will last two years of normal usage, and we want to know the probabilities that, among six of these batteries, 0, 1, 2, 3, 4, 5, or 6 will last two years of normal usage;
- the probability is 0.30 that an embezzler will be caught and brought to trial, and we want to know the probabilities that, among six embezzlers, 0, 1, 2, 3, 4, 5, or 6 will be caught and brought to trial;
- the probability is 0.30 that the head of a household has no life insurance, and we want to know the probabilities that, among six heads of household, 0, 1, 2, 3, 4, 5, or 6 will have no life insurance;
- the probability is 0.30 that a person having serious heart disease will survive another five years, and we want to know the probabilities that, among six persons having serious heart disease, 0, 1, 2, 3, 4, 5, or 6 will live another five years.

The argument we have presented here is precisely like the one we used in Section 1.2, where we tried to impress upon the reader the generality of statistical techniques.

In actual practice, binomial probabilities are rarely found by direct substitution into the formula. Sometimes we use approximations such as those discussed later in this chapter and in Chapter 9, and sometimes we use special tables such as Table V at the end of this book. Computer software is now the most common source for binomial probabilities. At the end of this chapter are listed some references for detailed binomial tables in book form (although falling into disuse).

Table V is limited to the binomial probabilities for

$$n = 2 \text{ to } n = 20$$

and

$$p = 0.05, \ 0.1, \ 0.2, \ 0.3, \ 0.4, \ 0.5, \ 0.6, \ 0.7, \ 0.8, \ 0.9, \ 0.95$$

The probabilities are all rounded to three decimals. Where values are omitted in Table V, they are all 0.0005 or less and have been rounded to 0.000.

Example

Suppose that the probability is 0.60 that a car stolen in a certain southern city will be recovered. Use Table V to find the probabilities that
  (a) at most three of 10 cars stolen in this city will be recovered;
  (b) at least seven of 10 cars stolen in this city will be recovered.

solution

  (a) For $n = 10$ and $p = 0.60$, the entries in Table V corresponding to $x = 0, 1, 2$, and 3 are 0.000, 0.002, 0.011, and 0.042. Thus, the probability that at most three of 10 cars will be recovered is

$$0.000 + 0.002 + 0.011 + 0.042 = 0.055$$

  (b) For $n = 10$ and $p = 0.60$, the entries in Table V corresponding to $x = 7, 8, 9$, and 10 are 0.215, 0.121, 0.040, and 0.006. Thus, the probability that at least seven of 10 cars will be recovered is

$$0.215 + 0.121 + 0.040 + 0.006 = 0.382$$

Example

If the probability is 0.05 that there will be a serious accident at a certain intersection on a weekday, what is the probability that there will be a serious accident at that intersection on at least three of 20 weekdays?

solution

For $n = 20$ and $p = 0.05$, the entries in Table V corresponding to $x = 3, 4$, and 5 are 0.060, 0.013, 0.002 and those corresponding to $x = 6, 7, 8, \ldots$, and 20 are all 0.000. Thus, the probability that there will be a serious accident at the intersection on at least three of 20 weekdays is

$$0.060 + 0.013 + 0.002 = 0.075$$

In the first of the two examples immediately above, we could not have used Table V if the probability that a stolen car will be recovered in the given city had been 0.63 instead of 0.60. In general, if n is greater than 20 or p takes on a value other than

$$0.05, \quad 0.1, \quad 0.2, \quad \ldots, \quad 0.9, \quad \text{or} \quad 0.95$$

we will have to use one of the more detailed tables referred to on page 250, use a computer printout as in the example that follows, or, as a last resort, refer to the formula for the binomial distribution.

Example

Rework the example dealing with the stolen cars, using 0.63 instead of 0.60 as the probability that a car stolen in the given city will be recovered.

solution

  (a) Using the computer printout of Figure 8.3, we find that the probabilities corresponding to $x = 0, 1, 2$, and 3 are

$$0.0000, \quad 0.0008, \quad 0.0063, \quad 0.0285$$

FIGURE 8.3

Computer printout for the binomial distribution with n = 10 and p = 0.63 (MINITAB 10 for Windows).

```
MTB  > Set c1
DATA >    1( 0 : 10 / 1 )1
DATA >    End.
MTB  > PDF c1;
SUBC >    Binomial 10 0.63


Probability Density Function

Binomial with n = 10 and p = 0.630000

             x           P( X = x)
          0.00            0.0000
          1.00            0.0008
          2.00            0.0063
          3.00            0.0285
          4.00            0.0849
          5.00            0.1734
          6.00            0.2461
          7.00            0.2394
          8.00            0.1529
          9.00            0.0578
         10.00            0.0098


MTB  > CDF c1;
SUBC >    Binomial 10 0.63


Cumulative Distribution Function

Binomial with n = 10 and p = 0.630000

             x           P( X ≤ x)
          0.00            0.0000
          1.00            0.0009
          2.00            0.0071
          3.00            0.0356
          4.00            0.1205
          5.00            0.2939
          6.00            0.5400
          7.00            0.7794
          8.00            0.9323
          9.00            0.9902
         10.00            1.0000
```

Thus, the probability that at most three of 10 cars will be recovered is

$$0.0000 + 0.0008 + 0.0063 + 0.0285 = 0.0356$$

Note that this answer is actually shown in the lower part of the printout under the $P(X \le x)$ caption in the row for $x = 3$.

(b) Also using the printout of Figure 8.3, we find that the probabilities corresponding to $x = 7, 8, 9,$ and 10 are

$$0.2394, \quad 0.1529, \quad 0.0578, \quad 0.0098$$

Thus, the probability that at least seven of 10 cars will be recovered is

$$0.2394 + 0.1529 + 0.0578 + 0.0098 = 0.4599$$

Since the probability of "at least 7" is 1 minus the probability of "6 or fewer," we can get this answer as

$$1 - 0.5400 = 0.4600$$

where 0.4600 is the entry under $P(X \leq x)$ for the row $x = 6$. The difference between the two results, 0.4599 and 0.4600, is due to rounding.   ▟ ▟ ▟

When we observe a value of a random variable having the binomial distribution—for instance, when we observe the number of heads in 25 flips of a coin, the number of seeds (in a package of 24 seeds) that germinate, the number of students (among 200 interviewed) who are opposed to a change in student activity fees, or the number of automobile accidents (among 20 investigated) that are due to drunk driving—we say that we are **sampling a binomial population.** This terminology is widely used in statistics.

▟ EXERCISES

8.1   In each case determine whether the given values can serve as the values of a probability distribution of some random variable that can take on only the values 1, 2, and 3, and explain your answers:
(a) $f(1) = 0.42$, $f(2) = 0.31$, and $f(3) = 0.37$;
(b) $f(1) = 0.08$, $f(2) = 0.12$, and $f(3) = 1.03$;
(c) $f(1) = \frac{10}{33}$, $f(2) = \frac{1}{3}$, and $f(3) = \frac{12}{33}$.

8.2   In each case determine whether the given values can serve as the values of a probability distribution of some random variable that can take on only the values 1, 2, 3, and 4, and explain your answers:
(a) $f(1) = 0.25$, $f(2) = 0.75$, $f(3) = 0.25$, and $f(4) = -0.25$;
(b) $f(1) = 0.15$, $f(2) = 0.27$, $f(3) = 0.29$, and $f(4) = 0.29$;
(c) $f(1) = \frac{1}{19}$, $f(2) = \frac{10}{19}$, $f(3) = \frac{2}{19}$, and $f(4) = \frac{5}{19}$.

8.3   For each of the following, determine whether it can serve as the probability distribution of some random variable:
(a) $f(x) = \frac{1}{10}$ for $x = 1, 2, 3, \ldots, 10$;
(b) $f(x) = \frac{1}{8}$ for $x = 0, 1, 2, \ldots, 8$;
(c) $f(x) = \frac{x+1}{20}$ for $x = 1, 2, 3, 4, 5$;
(d) $f(x) = \frac{2x+1}{15}$ for $x = 0, 1, 2, 3$.

8.4   For each of the following, determine whether it can serve as the probability distribution of some random variable:
(a) $f(x) = \frac{x-2}{5}$ for $x = 1, 2, 3, 4, 5$;
(b) $f(x) = \frac{12}{25x}$ for $x = 1, 2, 3, 4$;
(c) $f(x) = \frac{3+x}{3-x}$ for $x = 0, 1, 2, 3, 4$;

(d) $f(x) = \dfrac{x^2 - 1}{50}$ for $x = 1, 2, 3, 4, 5$.

8.5   In a given city, medical expenses are given as the reason for 60 percent of all personal bankruptcies. What is the probability that medical expenses will be given as the reason for four of the next six personal bankruptcies filed in that city?

8.6   If the probability is 0.15 that a set of tennis between two professional players will go into a tie breaker, what is the probability that two of three sets between these players will go into tie breakers?

8.7   Incompatibility is given as the legal reason for 55 percent of all divorce cases filed in a given county. Find the probability that incompatibility will be given as the reason in four of the next six divorce cases filed in that county.

8.8   A multiple-choice test consists of 10 questions with four answers to each question, of which only one is correct. A student answers each question by flipping a dime and a quarter and checking the first answer if he gets heads on both coins, the second answer if he gets heads on the dime and tails on the quarter, the third answer if he gets tails on the dime and heads on the quarter, and the fourth answer if he gets tails on both coins. Find the probabilities that he will get

(a) exactly three correct answers;

(b) no correct answers;

(c) at most four correct answers.

8.9   If the probability is 0.20 that a person traveling on a certain airplane route will request a vegetarian dinner, what is the probability that three of 10 people traveling on this route will request a vegetarian dinner?

8.10 The probability is 0.30 that a person who purchases a particular type of life insurance policy will allow that policy to lapse within five years. Of eight persons purchasing this policy, what is the probability that three of them will allow the policy to lapse within five years?

8.11 If 40 percent of the mice used in an experiment will become very aggressive within 1 minute after having been administered an experimental drug, find the probability that exactly four of 10 mice which have been administered the drug become very aggressive within 1 minute, using

(a) the formula for the binomial distribution;

(b) Table V.

8.12 If it is true that 80 percent of all industrial accidents can be prevented by paying strict attention to safety regulations, find the probability that four of seven industrial accidents can thus be prevented, using

(a) the formula for the binomial distribution;

(b) Table V.

8.13 A civil service examination is prepared so that 80 percent of all persons with a high-school diploma can pass it. Use Table V to find the probabilities that among 14 persons with a high-school diploma

(a) at most 10 will pass;

(b) at least 9 will pass;

(c) exactly 12 will pass;

(d) from 8 through 12 will pass.

8.14 A study shows that 50 percent of the families in a certain large metropolitan area have at least two cars. Use Table V to find the probabilities that among 16 families randomly selected in this metropolitan area

(a) exactly nine have at least two cars;

(b) at most six have at least two cars;

(c) anywhere from eight to 12 have at least two cars.

8.15   An agricultural cooperative claims that 95 percent of the watermelons shipped out are ripe and ready to eat. Find the probabilities that among 18 watermelons that are shipped out

(a) all 18 are ripe and ready to eat;

(b) at least 16 are ripe and ready to eat;

(c) at most 14 are ripe and ready to eat.

8.16   It is known that 20 percent of all persons given a certain medication get very drowsy within 2 minutes. Find the probabilities that among 14 persons given the medication

(a) at most two will get very drowsy within 2 minutes;

(b) at least five will get very drowsy within 2 minutes;

(c) two, three, or four will get very drowsy within 2 minutes.

8.17   A food distributor claims that 80 percent of her 6-ounce cans of mixed nuts contain at least three pecans. To check on this, a consumer testing service decides to examine eight of these 6-ounce cans of mixed nuts from a very large production lot and reject the claim if fewer than six of them contain at least three pecans. Find the probabilities that the testing service will commit the error of

(a) rejecting the claim even though it is true;

(b) not rejecting the claim when in reality only 60 percent of the cans of mixed nuts contain at least three pecans;

(c) not rejecting the claim when in reality only 40 percent of the cans of mixed nuts contain at least three pecans.

8.18   A quality control engineer wants to check whether, in accordance with specifications, 95 percent of the products shipped are in perfect condition. To this end, he randomly selects 10 items from each large lot ready to be shipped and passes the lot only if all 10 are in perfect condition. If all 10 are not in perfect condition, he holds the lot for a complete inspection. Use Table V to find the probabilities that he will commit the error of

(a) holding a lot for further inspection even though 95 percent of the items are in perfect condition;

(b) letting a lot pass through even though only 90 percent of the items are in perfect condition;

(c) letting a lot pass through even though only 80 percent of the items are in perfect condition;

(d) letting a lot pass through even though only 70 percent of the items are in perfect condition.

8.19   A study shows that 40 percent of all patients coming to a certain hospital emergency room will have nonemergency conditions. Find the probabilities that among nine patients coming to the emergency room, 0, 1, 2, . . . , 8, or 9 will have nonemergency conditions.

8.20   The records of a computer retail store indicate that 70 percent of all purchasers of new computers will request an internal modem. Find the probabilities that, among 10 purchasers of new computers, 0, 1, 2, . . . , 9, or 10 will request an internal modem.

8.21   With reference to Exercise 8.16, suppose that 24 percent of all persons given the medication get very drowsy within 2 minutes. Use a suitable table or a computer printout of the binomial distribution with $n = 14$ and $p = 0.24$ to rework the three parts of that exercise.

8.22   Seventy-two percent of all persons who enter a particular stationery store are repeat customers. Use a suitable table or a computer listing of the binomial distribution with $n = 26$ and $p = 0.72$ to find the probabilities that, among the next 26 persons to enter the store,

(a) at least 20 are repeat customers;

(b) at most 21 are repeat customers;

(c) exactly 19 are repeat customers;

(d) from 15 to 21 are repeat customers.

⊞ 8.23   If we have to determine all the values of a binomial distribution, it is sometimes helpful to calculate $f(0)$ using the formula for the binomial distribution, and then calculate the other values, one after the other, using the formula

$$\frac{f(x + 1)}{f(x)} = \frac{n - x}{x + 1} \cdot \frac{p}{1 - p}$$

(a) Verify this formula by substituting for $f(x)$ and $f(x + 1)$ the corresponding expressions given by the formula for the binomial distribution.

(b) Use this method to find all the values of the binomial distribution with $n = 6$ and $p = \frac{1}{4}$, writing them as common fractions with the denominator 4,096.

⊞ 8.24   Use Exercise 8.23 to determine whether it can ever happen that

$$\frac{f(x + 1)}{f(x)} = 1$$

⊞ 8.25   In some situations where otherwise the binomial distribution applies, we are interested in the probability that the first success will occur on a given trial. For this to happen on the xth trial, it must be preceded by $x - 1$ failures for which the probability is $(1 - p)^{x-1}$, and it follows that the probability that the first success will occur on the xth trial is

Geometric Distribution	$f(x) = p(1 - p)^{x-1} \qquad for\ x = 1, 2, 3, 4, \ldots$

This distribution is called the **geometric distribution** (because its successive values constitute a geometric progression) and it should be observed that there is a countable infinity of possibilities.[†] Using the formula, we find, for example, that for repeated rolls of a balanced die the probability that the first 6 will occur on the fifth roll is

$$\frac{1}{6}\left(\frac{5}{6}\right)^{5-1} = \frac{625}{7,776} \approx 0.080$$

(a) When taping a television commercial, the probability that a certain actor will get his lines straight on any one take is 0.40. What is the probability that this actor will get his lines straight for the first time on the fourth take?

(b) Suppose the probability is 0.25 that any given person will believe a rumor about the private life of a certain politician. What is the probability that the fifth person to hear the rumor will be the first one to believe it?

(c) The probability is 0.70 that a child exposed to a certain contagious disease will catch it. What is the probability that the third child exposed to the disease will be the first one to catch it?

⊞ 8.26   For the geometric distribution of Exercise 8.25 in which

$$f(x) = p(1 - p)^{x-1}$$

find the probability that the first success will come *after* the mth trial.

⊞ 8.27   A florist needs 12 exotic potted ferns for a floral exhibition to take place in six months. He knows that the probability is 0.70 that a fern planted now will be suitable for the exhibition in six months. His concern is the minimum number of ferns he should plant if he wants the probability of having 12 suitable ferns in six months to be at least 0.90.

[†]As formulated in Chapter 6, the postulates of probability apply only when the sample space is finite. When the sample space is countably infinite, as is the case here, the third postulate must be modified accordingly. This is explained on page 223.

(a) Will 15 be enough? Find the probability that, if he plants 15 ferns, he will have at least 12 suitable.

(b) Will 20 be enough? Find the probability that if he plants 20 ferns, he will have at least 12 suitable.

(c) Will 30 be enough? Find the probability that if he plants 30 ferns, he will have at least 12 suitable.

(d) Find the smallest number of ferns for which the probability of 12 or more suitable is 0.90 (or more).

8.28   It is known in a certain seaside town that 43 percent of lobsters caught during spawning season will have edible roe. A restaurant owner would like to have 20 lobsters with roe in order to prepare a special banquet. What is the minimum number of lobsters that she should order if she wants the probability of having at least 20 with roe to be 95 percent or more?

8.4   THE HYPERGEOMETRIC DISTRIBUTION

In Chapter 6 we spoke of sampling with and without replacement to illustrate the multiplication rules for independent and dependent events. The binomial distribution applies when we sample with replacement and the trials are all independent, but not when we sample without replacement. To introduce a probability distribution that applies when we sample without replacement, let us consider the following example: A factory ships audio tape players in lots of 24, and when they arrive at their destination, an inspector randomly selects three from each lot. If they are all in good working condition, the entire lot is accepted; otherwise, the entire lot is inspected. Since a lot can be accepted without further inspection even though quite a few of the tape players are defective, there is a considerable risk. So let us find the probability that a lot will be accepted without further inspection even though, say, six of the 24 tape players are defective. This means that we must find the probability of three successes (three nondefective tape players) in three trials (among the three tape players inspected), and we might be tempted to argue that since 18 of the 24 tape players are not defective, the probability of a success is $\frac{18}{24} = \frac{3}{4}$, and hence the desired probability is

$$f(3) = \binom{3}{3}\left(\frac{3}{4}\right)^3\left(1 - \frac{3}{4}\right)^{3-3} \approx 0.42$$

This result, obtained with the formula for the binomial distribution, would be correct if sampling is with replacement, but that is not what we do in realistic problems of sampling inspection. To get the correct answer for our problem when sampling is without replacement, we might argue as follows: There are altogether

$$\binom{24}{3} = 2{,}024$$

ways of choosing three of the tape players, and they are all equiprobable by virtue of the assumption that the selection is random. Among these, there are

$$\binom{18}{3} = 816$$

ways of selecting three of the nondefective tape players, and it follows by the special formula $\frac{s}{n}$ for equiprobable outcomes that the desired probability is

$$\frac{816}{2,024} \approx 0.40.$$

To generalize the method we used here, suppose that n objects are to be chosen from a set of a objects of one kind (successes) and b objects of another kind (failures), the selection is without replacement, and we are interested in the probability of getting x successes and $n - x$ failures. Arguing as before, we find that the n objects can be chosen from the entire set of $a + b$ objects in $\binom{a + b}{n}$ ways, and that x of the a successes and $n - x$ of the b failures can be chosen in

$$\binom{a}{x} \cdot \binom{b}{n - x}$$

ways. It follows that for sampling without replacement the probability of "x successes in n trials" is

Hypergeometric Distribution	$$f(x) = \frac{\binom{a}{x} \cdot \binom{b}{n - x}}{\binom{a + b}{n}} \qquad \text{for } x = 0, 1, 2, \ldots, \text{or } n$$

where x cannot exceed a and $n - x$ cannot exceed b. This is the formula for the **hypergeometric distribution.**

The following are two examples where we sample without replacement and, hence, can use the formula for the hypergeometric distribution.

Example

A mailroom clerk is supposed to send six of 15 packages to Europe by airmail, but he gets them all mixed up and randomly puts airmail postage on six of the packages. What is the probability that only three of the packages which are supposed to go by airmail will go by airmail?

solution

Substituting $a = 6$, $b = 9$, $n = 6$, and $x = 3$ into the formula for the hypergeometric distribution, we get

$$f(3) = \frac{\binom{6}{3} \cdot \binom{9}{6 - 3}}{\binom{15}{6}} = \frac{20 \cdot 84}{5,005} \approx 0.336$$

Example

Among a department store's 16 delivery trucks, five emit excessive amounts of pollutants. If eight of the trucks are randomly picked for inspection, what is the probability that this sample will include at least three of the trucks which emit excessive amounts of pollutants?

The probability we must find is $f(3) + f(4) + f(5)$, where each term in this sum is a value of the hypergeometric distribution with $a = 5$, $b = 11$, and $n = 8$. Substituting these quantities together with $x = 3, 4,$ and 5 into the formula for the hypergeometric distribution, we get

$$f(3) = \frac{\binom{5}{3} \cdot \binom{11}{5}}{\binom{16}{8}} = \frac{10 \cdot 462}{12{,}870} \approx 0.359$$

$$f(4) = \frac{\binom{5}{4} \cdot \binom{11}{4}}{\binom{16}{8}} = \frac{5 \cdot 330}{12{,}870} \approx 0.128$$

$$f(5) = \frac{\binom{5}{5} \cdot \binom{11}{3}}{\binom{16}{8}} = \frac{1 \cdot 165}{12{,}870} \approx 0.013$$

and the probability that the sample will include at least three of the trucks which emit excessive amounts of pollutants is

$$0.359 + 0.128 + 0.013 = 0.500$$

In the beginning of this section we gave an example where we erroneously used the binomial distribution instead of the hypergeometric distribution. The error was quite small, however—we got 0.42 instead of 0.40—and in actual practice the binomial distribution is often used to approximate the hypergeometric distribution. It is generally agreed that this approximation is satisfactory if n does not exceed 5 percent of $a + b$, namely, if

$$n \leq (0.05)(a + b)$$

The main advantages of the approximation are that the binomial distribution has been tabulated much more extensively than the hypergeometric distribution, and that, between the two formulas, the one for the binomial distribution is easier to use.

In a federal prison, 120 of the 300 inmates are serving time for drug-related offenses. If eight of them are to be chosen at random to appear before a legislative committee, what is the probability that three of the eight will be serving time for drug-related offenses?

Since $n = 8$, $a + b = 300$, and 8 is less than $0.05(300) = 15$, we can use the binomial approximation. From Table V we find that for

$$n = 8, \qquad p = \frac{120}{300} = 0.40, \quad \text{and} \quad x = 3$$

the probability asked for is 0.279. Fairly extensive calculations will show that the error of this approximation is 0.003. ◪ ◪ ◪

Also, the binomial calculations are generally less complicated. Observe that the binomial distribution is described by two parameters (n and p) while the hypergeometric distribution requires three (a, b, and n.)

◢ EXERCISES

8.29   Among the 16 used cars on Harry's lot, five have four-wheel drive. If three cars are randomly chosen for a newspaper ad, what is the probability that all three will have four-wheel drive?

8.30   Among the 20 solar collectors on display at a trade show, 12 are flat-plate collectors and the others are concentrating collectors. If a person visiting the show randomly selects six of the solar collectors to check out, what is the probability that three of them will be flat-plate collectors?

8.31   Among 15 male applicants for a postal service job, nine have working wives. If three of the male applicants are randomly chosen for further consideration, find the probabilities that

(a) none have working wives;

(b) only one has a working wife;

(c) two have working wives;

(d) all three have working wives.

8.32   A customs inspector decides to inspect three of 16 shipments that arrive from Madrid by plane. If the selection is random and five of the shipments contain contraband, find the probabilities that the customs inspector will catch

(a) none of the shipments with contraband;

(b) one of the shipments with contraband;

(c) two of the shipments with contraband;

(d) three of the shipments with contraband.

8.33   To pass a quality control inspection, two batteries are chosen from each lot of 12 car batteries, and the lot is passed only if neither battery has any defects; otherwise, each of the batteries in the lot is checked. If the selection of the batteries is random, find the probabilities that a lot will

(a) pass the inspection when one of the 12 batteries is defective;

(b) fail the inspection when three of the batteries are defective;

(c) fail the inspection when six of the batteries are defective.

8.34   Packages of 16 computer boards are subjected to an inspection in which two of the boards are selected at random and tested thoroughly. The package of 16 passes the inspection only if both tested boards are acceptable. Find the probability that the package of 16 computer boards

(a) will pass the inspection when one of the boards is defective;

(b) will pass the inspection when two of the boards are defective;

(c) will pass the inspection when three of the boards are defective;

(d) will pass the inspection when four of the boards are defective.

8.35   Check in each case whether the condition for the binomial approximation to the hypergeometric distribution is satisfied:

(a) $a = 140$, $b = 60$,   and $n = 12$;

(b) $a = 220$, $b = 280$, and $n = 20$;

(c) $a = 250$, $b = 390$, and $n = 30$;

(d) $a = 220$, $b = 220$, and $n = 25$.

8.36   A shipment of 200 burglar alarms contains 10 that are defective. Five of the burglar alarms are randomly selected to be shipped to a customer.

(a) Use the hypergeometric distribution to find the probability that the customer will receive exactly one defective burglar alarm.

(b) Use the binomial approximation to the hypergeometric distribution to find the probability that the customer will receive exactly one defective burglar alarm.

(c) Find the error of the approximation.

8.37   Among the 180 employees of a company, 144 are union members; the others are not. Five of these are to be chosen by lot to serve on the pension fund advisory committee.

(a) Use the hypergeometric distribution to find the probability that three of the five chosen for the committee will be union members.

(b) Use the binomial approximation to the hypergeometric distribution to find the probability that three of the five chosen for the committee will be union members.

(c) Find the error of the approximation.

田 8.38   In certain sampling inspection schemes, the sampling continues until a defective item is found. We will assume that the lot contains a defective and b nondefective items. We are interested in the trial number at which the first defective item is encountered. For this to happen on the xth trial, it must be preceded by $x - 1$ nondefectives. Accordingly, the probability that the first defective item is encountered on the xth trial is

Negative Hypergeometric Distribution	$$f(x) = \dfrac{\dbinom{b}{x-1}}{\dbinom{a+b}{x-1}} \cdot \dfrac{a}{a+b-(x-1)} \qquad \text{for } x = 1, 2, 3, \ldots, b, b+1$$

This distribution is called the **negative hypergeometric distribution.** Using this formula for a lot with $a = 10$ defectives and $b = 30$ nondefectives, we find that the probability that the first defective will be encountered on the fourth trial is

$$\frac{\dbinom{30}{3}}{\dbinom{40}{3}} \cdot \frac{10}{37} = \frac{30 \cdot 29 \cdot 28 \cdot 10}{40 \cdot 39 \cdot 38 \cdot 37} \approx 0.111$$

(a) Find the probability that in a lot with 20 defectives and 180 nondefectives, the first defective will be encountered at the fifth trial.

(b) Find the probability that in a lot with 8 defectives and 42 nondefectives, the first defective will be encountered at the first trial.

(c) Simplify the negative hypergeometric formula when $x = 1$.

田 8.39   A box contains 200 baseball cards, of which 25 are special commemorative cards. The cards cannot be identified other than by purchasing them and opening the wrapper. Moreover, their locations within the box of 200 are random. Suppose that you purchase cards one at a time. Using the result of Exercise 8.38, find the probability that you will purchase exactly 10 cards before obtaining exactly one commemorative card.

8.40 The negative hypergeometric distribution can also be used for defectives beyond the first.
(a) Give the formula for the probability that the *k*th defective will be encountered at the *x*th trial in selecting from a lot with *a* defectives and *b* nondefectives.
(b) Show that if $k = 1$, your result for part (a) agrees with Exercise 8.38.
(c) What are the minimum and maximum possible values for *x* in part (a)?

8.41 An ice bucket contains cans of soft drinks for a picnic. Suppose that the bucket contains 40 cans, of which 12 are diet colas, and that you select cans randomly until you obtain exactly four diet colas. Use the results of Exercise 8.40 to find the probability that you will obtain the fourth diet cola on the 12th selection.

8.5 THE POISSON DISTRIBUTION

When *n* is large and *p* is small, binomial probabilities are often approximated by means of the formula

Poisson Approximation to Binomial Distribution

$$f(x) = \frac{(np)^x \cdot e^{-np}}{x!} \qquad for \ x = 0, 1, 2, 3, \ldots$$

which is a special form of the **Poisson distribution,** named after the French mathematician and physicist S. D. Poisson (1781–1840); the more general form is given on page 227. In this formula, the irrational number

$$e = 2.71828 \ldots$$

is the base of the system of natural logarithms, and the necessary values of e^{-np} may be obtained from Table XI at the end of the book. Note also that as in Exercise 8.25 on page 217, we are faced here with a random variable that can take on a countable infinity of values (namely, as many values as there are whole numbers). Correspondingly, the third postulate of probability must be modified so that for any sequence of mutually exclusive events $A_1, A_2, A_3, \ldots$, the probability that one of them will occur is

$$P(A_1 \cup A_2 \cup A_3 \cup \cdots) = P(A_1) + P(A_2) + P(A_3) + \cdots$$

It is difficult to give precise conditions under which the Poisson approximation to the binomial distribution may be used; that is, explain precisely what we mean here by "when *n* is large and *p* is small." Although other books may give less stringent rules of thumb, we shall play it relatively safe and use the Poisson approximation to the binomial distribution only when

$$n \geq 100 \quad and \quad np < 10$$

To get some idea about the closeness of the Poisson approximation to the binomial distribution, consider the computer printouts of Figure 8.4, which show, next to each other, the binomial distribution with

$$n = 150 \quad and \quad p = 0.05$$

and the Poisson distribution with

$$np = 150(0.05) = 7.5$$

```
MTB > Set cl                            
DATA>    1( 0 : 20 / 1 )1               
DATA>    End.                           
MTB > PDF cl;                           MTB > PDF cl;
SUBC>    Binomial 150 0.05.             SUBC >   Poisson 7.5.

Probability Density Function           Probability Density Function

Binomial with n = 150 and p = 0.050    Poisson with mu = 7.50000

          x       P( X = x)                     x       P( X = x)
       0.00        0.0005                     0.00        0.0006
       1.00        0.0036                     1.00        0.0041
       2.00        0.0141                     2.00        0.0156
       3.00        0.0366                     3.00        0.0389
       4.00        0.0708                     4.00        0.0729
       5.00        0.1088                     5.00        0.1094
       6.00        0.1384                     6.00        0.1367
       7.00        0.1499                     7.00        0.1465
       8.00        0.1410                     8.00        0.1373
       9.00        0.1171                     9.00        0.1144
      10.00        0.0869                    10.00        0.0858
      11.00        0.0582                    11.00        0.0585
      12.00        0.0355                    12.00        0.0366
      13.00        0.0198                    13.00        0.0211
      14.00        0.0102                    14.00        0.0113
      15.00        0.0049                    15.00        0.0057
      16.00        0.0022                    16.00        0.0026
      17.00        0.0009                    17.00        0.0012
      18.00        0.0003                    18.00        0.0005
      19.00        0.0001                    19.00        0.0002
      20.00        0.0000                    20.00        0.0001
```

FIGURE 8.4   *Computer printout of the binomial distribution with n = 150 and p = 0.05 and the Poisson distribution with np = 7.5. The computer output has been rearranged to make it easier to compare the second and fourth columns* (MINITAB 10 for Windows).

Comparing the probabilities in the columns headed $P(X = x)$, we find that the greatest difference, corresponding to $x = 8$, is

$$0.1410 - 0.1373 = 0.0037$$

Example

It is known that 2 percent of the books bound at a certain bindery have defective bindings. Use the Poisson approximation to the binomial distribution to find the probability that 5 of 400 books bound by this bindery will have defective bindings.

solution

Substituting $x = 5$ and $np = 400(0.02) = 8$ into the formula for the Poisson distribution and getting

$$e^{-8} = 0.000335$$

from Table XI, we find that

$$f(5) = \frac{8^5 \cdot e^{-8}}{5!} = \frac{(32,768)(0.000335)}{120} \approx 0.0915$$

Example

Records show that the probability is 0.00006 that a car tire will go flat while being driven through a certain tunnel. Use the Poisson approximation to the binomial distribution to find the probability that at least 2 of 10,000 cars passing through that tunnel will get flat tires.

solution

Rather than add the probabilities for $x = 2, 3, 4, \ldots$, we shall subtract from 1 the sum of the probabilities for $x = 0$ and $x = 1$. Then, substituting

$$np = 10,000(0.00006) = 0.6, \ e^{-0.6} = 0.5488$$

from Table XI, and, respectively, $x = 0$ and $x = 1$ into the formula for the Poisson distribution, we get

$$f(0) = \frac{(0.6)^0(0.5488)}{0!} = 0.5488$$

$$f(1) = \frac{(0.6)^1(0.5488)}{1!} \approx 0.3293$$

Our answer is then

$$1 - (0.5488 + 0.3293) = 0.1219$$

In actual practice, Poisson probabilities are seldom obtained by either direct substitution into the formula or by the use of statistical tables. These tasks are made much easier by utilizing computer software. For instance, had we used the computer printout of Figure 8.5 in the preceding example, we would have obtained the solution directly as

$$1 - 0.8781 = 0.1219,$$

where 0.8781 is the value under the heading $P(X \le x)$ corresponding to $x = 1$.

Since in some cases the hypergeometric distribution may be approximated by a binomial distribution, and the binomial distribution may in some cases be approximated by a Poisson distribution, there will exist situations in which the hypergeometric distribution may be approximated by a Poisson distribution. Consider the following example.

FIGURE 8.5

*Computer printout of the
Poisson distribution
with np = 0.60
(MINITAB 10 for Windows).*

```
MTB > Set c1
DATA>    1( 0 : 6 / 1)1
DATA>    End.
MTB > PDF c1;
SUBC>   Poisson 0.6.

Probability Density Function

Poisson with mu = 0.600000

          x          P( X = x)
        0.00           0.5488
        1.00           0.3293
        2.00           0.0988
        3.00           0.0198
        4.00           0.0030
        5.00           0.0004
        6.00           0.0000

MTB > CDF c1;
SUBC>   Poisson 0.6.

Cumulative Distribution Function

Poisson with mu = 0.600000

          x          P( X <= x)
        0.00           0.5488
        1.00           0.8781
        2.00           0.9769
        3.00           0.9966
        4.00           0.9996
        5.00           1.0000
        6.00           1.0000
```

Example

An auditor has been asked to investigate a collection of 4,000 sales invoices, of which 28 contain errors. A sample of 150 invoices is selected. What is the probability that this set of 150 invoices will contain exactly 2 with errors?

solution

This is a hypergeometric problem with

$$a = 28, \quad b = 3{,}972, \quad n = 150, \quad \text{and} \quad x = 2$$

Since $150 \le 0.05(4{,}000) = 200$, it is reasonable to use the binomial approximation. This binomial distribution has

$$n = 150, \quad p = \frac{a}{a+b} = \frac{28}{4{,}000} = 0.007, \quad \text{and} \quad x = 2$$

Since $n \ge 100$ and $n \cdot p = 150 \cdot 0.007 = 1.05 < 10$, it would also be reasonable to use the Poisson approximation with $np = 1.05$. This yields

$$f(2) = \frac{1.05^2 \cdot e^{-1.05}}{2!} = \frac{(1.1025) \cdot 0.349938}{2} \approx 0.1929$$

The value of $e^{-1.05}$ was obtained from a calculator.   ◪ ◪ ◪

Since auditors deal frequently with situations with large values of n and even larger values of $a + b$, they find the Poisson distribution to be quite useful. Observe that, aside from x, the hypergeometric distribution involves three parameters, (a, b, and n), whereas, the binomial distribution involves two, (n and p), and the Poisson distribution involves only one, (np).

The Poisson distribution has many important applications that have no direct connection with the binomial distribution. In that case np is replaced by the parameter λ (Greek lowercase *lambda*) and we calculate the probability of getting x successes by means of the formula

Poisson Distribution

$$f(x) = \frac{\lambda^x \cdot e^{-\lambda}}{x!} \qquad for\ x = 0, 1, 2, 3, \ldots$$

where λ is interpreted as the expected, or average, number of successes (see discussion on page 233).

This formula applies to many situations where we can expect a fixed number of "successes" per unit time (or for some other kind of unit), say, when a bank can expect to receive six bad checks per day, when 1.6 accidents can be expected per day at a busy intersection, when eight small pieces of meat can be expected in a frozen meat pie, when 5.6 imperfections can be expected per roll of cloth, when 0.03 complaint per passenger can be expected by an airline, and so on.

Example

If a bank receives on the average $\lambda = 6$ bad checks per day, what is the probability that it will receive four bad checks on any given day?

solution

Substituting $\lambda = 6$ and $x = 4$ into the formula, we have

$$f(4) = \frac{6^4 \cdot e^{-6}}{4!} = \frac{(1,296)(0.002479)}{24} \approx 0.1339$$

where the value of e^{-6} was obtained from Table XI.   ◪ ◪ ◪

Example

If $\lambda = 5.6$ imperfections can be expected per roll of a certain kind of cloth, what is the probability that a roll will have three imperfections?

solution

Substituting $\lambda = 5.6$ and $x = 3$ into the formula, we obtain

$$f(3) = \frac{(5.6)^3 \cdot e^{-5.6}}{3!} = \frac{(175.616)(0.003698)}{6} \approx 0.1082$$

where the value of $e^{-5.6}$ was obtained from Table XI.   ◪ ◪ ◪

8.6 THE MULTINOMIAL DISTRIBUTION ◈

An important generalization of the binomial distribution arises when there are more than two possible outcomes for each trial, the probabilities of the various outcomes remain the same for each trial, and the trials are all independent. This is the case, for example, when we repeatedly roll a die, where each trial has six possible outcomes; when students are asked whether they like a certain new recording, dislike it, or don't care; or when a U.S. Department of Agriculture inspector grades beef as prime, choice, good, commercial, or utility.

If there are k possible outcomes for each trial and their probabilities are

$$p_1, \quad p_2, \quad \ldots, \quad \text{and} \quad p_k$$

it can be shown that the probability of x_1 outcomes of the first kind, x_2 outcomes of the second kind, ..., and x_k outcomes of the kth kind in n trials is given by

Multinomial Distribution

$$\frac{n!}{x_1!x_2! \cdot \ldots \cdot x_k!} p_1^{x_1} \cdot p_2^{x_2} \cdot \ldots \cdot p_k^{x_k}$$

This distribution is called the **multinomial distribution.**

Example

In a very large city, network TV has 40 percent of the viewing audience on Friday nights, a local channel has 20 percent, cable TV has 30 percent, and 10 percent are viewing videocassettes. What is the probability that among seven television viewers randomly selected in that city on a Friday night, two will be viewing network TV, one will be watching the local channel, three will be watching cable TV, and one will be watching a videocassette?

solution

Substituting $n = 7$,

$$x_1 = 2, \quad x_2 = 1, \quad x_3 = 3, \quad x_4 = 1,$$
$$p_1 = 0.40, \quad p_2 = 0.20, \quad p_3 = 0.30, \quad \text{and} \quad p_4 = 0.10$$

into the formula, we get

$$\frac{7!}{2! \cdot 1! \cdot 3! \cdot 1!} (0.40)^2(0.20)^1(0.30)^3(0.10)^1 \approx 0.036$$

◪ ◪ ◪

Strictly speaking, the multinomial distribution does not apply when we sample without replacement, but in the example above this does not matter since the sample is very small and the city is very large (see Exercise 8.60).

◪ EXERCISES

8.42   Check in each case whether the values of n and p satisfy the rules of thumb that we gave on page 223 for using the Poisson approximation to the binomial distribution:
(a) $n = 200$ and $p = \frac{1}{25}$;

(b) $n = 400$ and $p = \frac{1}{32}$;

(c) $n = 80$ and $p = \frac{1}{10}$.

8.43 Check in each case whether the values of n and p satisfy the rules of thumb given on page 223 for using the Poisson approximation to the binomial distribution:

(a) $n = 500$ and $p = 0.001$;

(b) $n = 100$ and $p = 0.12$;

(c) $n = 60$ and $p = 0.002$.

8.44 It is known from experience that 2 percent of the calls received by a switchboard are wrong numbers. Use the Poisson approximation to the binomial distribution to determine the probability that three of 200 calls received by the switchboard will be wrong numbers.

8.45 If 0.6 percent of the fuses delivered to an arsenal are defective, use the Poisson approximation to the binomial distribution to determine the probability that in a random sample of 500 fuses, four will be defective.

8.46 Records show that the probability is 0.0012 that a person will get food poisoning spending a day at a certain state fair. Use the Poisson approximation to the binomial distribution to find the probability that among 1,000 persons attending the fair, at most two will get food poisoning.

8.47 In a certain city, 3.2 percent of all licensed drivers will be involved in at least one car accident in any given year. Use the Poisson approximation to the binomial distribution to determine the probability that, among 200 drivers chosen at random in this city,

(a) exactly six will be involved in at least one accident in any given year;

(b) at most eight will be involved in at least one accident in any given year;

(c) five or more will be involved in at least one accident in any given year.

8.48 The number of monthly breakdowns of a computer is a random variable having the Poisson distribution with $\lambda = 1.8$. Find the probabilities that this computer will function for a month

(a) without a breakdown; (b) with only one breakdown.

8.49 The number of lost-and-found requests received each day by a railroad ticket office is a random variable having the Poisson distribution with $\lambda = 4.2$. Find the probability that on any given day, the number of such requests will be

(a) exactly five; (b) at most seven.

8.50 The number of emergency calls that an ambulance service gets per day is a random variable having the Poisson distribution with $\lambda = 5.5$. What is the probability that on any given day it will receive only four emergency calls?

8.51 The number of inquiries a person gets in response to a newspaper ad listing a piano for sale is a random variable having the Poisson distribution with $\lambda = 4.4$. What are the probabilities that in response to such an ad a person will receive

(a) only two inquiries;

(b) only three inquiries;

(c) at most three inquiries?

8.52 The number of loan applications that a bank gets per day is a random variable having the Poisson distribution with $\lambda = 7.5$. Use the computer printout of Figure 8.4 on page 224 to find the probabilities that on any one day the bank will get

(a) exactly six loan applications;

(b) at most four loan applications;

(c) at least eight loan applications;

(d) anywhere from five to 10 loan applications.

8.53 With reference to the example on page 225 and the computer printout of Figure 8.5 on page 226, find the probabilities that among 10,000 cars passing through the tunnel

(a) two will have a flat tire;

(b) four or more will have a flat tire.

8.54 For an auto being driven to a state inspection station, the probabilities are

0.20 that it will fail the emissions test while passing the brake test,
0.10 that it will pass the emissions test while failing the brake test,
0.10 that it will fail both the emissions test and the brake test,
0.60 that it will pass both the emissions test and the brake test.

Find the probability that, among 12 autos inspected,

three will fail only the emissions test,

two will fail only the brake test,

one will fail both tests,

six will pass both tests.

8.55 As we have seen, the probabilities of getting 0, 1, 2, or 3 heads when flipping three balanced coins are $\frac{1}{8}, \frac{3}{8}, \frac{3}{8}$, and $\frac{1}{8}$. What are the probabilities of getting

(a) three tails once, one head and two tails twice, two heads and one tail once, and three heads once in five flips of three balanced coins;

(b) three tails once, one head and two tails three times, and two heads and one tail twice in six flips of three balanced coins?

8.56 The probabilities are 0.60, 0.20, 0.10, and 0.10 that a state income tax form will be filled out correctly, that it will contain only errors favoring the taxpayer, that it will contain only errors favoring the government, and that it will contain both kinds of errors. What is the probability that among 10 such tax forms (randomly selected for audit) seven will be filled out correctly, one will contain only errors favoring the taxpayer, one will contain only errors favoring the government, and one will contain both kinds of errors?

8.57 According to the Mendelian theory of heredity, if plants with round yellow seeds are crossbred with plants with wrinkled green seeds, the probabilities of getting a plant that produces round yellow seeds, wrinkled yellow seeds, round green seeds, or wrinkled green seeds are, respectively, $\frac{9}{16}, \frac{3}{16}, \frac{3}{16}$, and $\frac{1}{16}$. What is the probability that among nine plants thus obtained there will be four that produce round yellow seeds, two that produce wrinkled yellow seeds, three that produce round green seeds, and none that produce wrinkled green seeds?

8.58 Suppose that *n* objects are to be chosen without replacement from a group consisting of a_1 of type 1, a_2 of type 2, . . . , a_k of type *k*. The probability of obtaining in the sample

$$x_1 \text{ of type 1}, \quad x_2 \text{ of type 2}, \quad \ldots, \quad x_k \text{ of type } k$$

is given by

Multivariate Hypergeometric Distribution

$$f(x_1, x_2, \ldots, x_k) = \frac{\binom{a_1}{x_1}\binom{a_2}{x_2}\cdots\binom{a_k}{x_k}}{\binom{a_1 + a_2 + \cdots + a_k}{n}}$$

This distribution is called the **multivariate hypergeometric distribution.** In using this formula, it is assumed that there are exactly *k* different types of objects, and it is also assumed that

$$x_1 + x_2 + \cdots + x_k = n$$

Use this formula to determine the probability that

(a) among five cards drawn without replacement from a standard deck of 52, there will be one spade, two hearts, one diamond, and one club;

(b) among 10 balls drawn without replacement from a jar containing 20 red, 10 green, and 12 yellow balls, there will be six red, one green, and three yellow balls;

(c) among five cards drawn without replacement from a standard deck of 52, there will be two aces, one king, one queen, and one jack.

8.59   Each bridge player receives 13 cards dealt from a well-shuffled deck. Find the probability that a particular player's 13 cards will consist of

(a) four spades, three hearts, three diamonds, and three clubs;

(b) four of one of the suits and three of each of the other three suits.

8.60   If the drawings in Exercise 8.59 were done with replacement, the multinomial distribution would be utilized. The multinomial may be a reasonable approximation to the multivariate hypergeometric when n, the number of objects to be chosen, is small relative to

$$a = a_1 + a_2 + \cdots + a_k.$$

The approximation can be regarded as adequate when $n \leq 0.05a$, and it may still give reasonably good answers even when $n > 0.05a$. Recalculate parts (a), (b), and (c) of Exercise 8.59 assuming sampling with replacement, and compare the solutions.

8.7   THE MEAN OF A PROBABILITY DISTRIBUTION

When we showed on page 189 that an airline office at a certain airport can expect 2.75 complaints per day about its luggage handling, we arrived at this result by using the formula for a mathematical expectation, namely, by adding the products obtained by multiplying 0, 1, 2, 3, . . . , by the corresponding probabilities that it will receive 0, 1, 2, 3, . . . , complaints about its luggage handling on any given day. Here the number of complaints is a random variable and 2.75 is its **expected value.**

If we apply the same argument to the first example of Section 8.2, we find that, between them, the two insurance agents can expect to sell

$$0(0.44) + 1(0.20) + 2(0.18) + 3(0.18) = 1.10$$

insurance policies to the given family. In this case, the number of policies is a random variable and 1.10 is its expected value.

As we explained in Chapter 7, mathematical expectations must be interpreted as averages, or means, and it is customary to refer to the expected value of a random variable as its **mean,** or as the **mean of its probability distribution.** In general, if a random variable takes on the values $x_1, x_2, x_3, \ldots,$ or x_k, with the probabilities

$$f(x_1), \quad f(x_2), \quad f(x_3), \quad \ldots, \quad \text{and} \quad f(x_k),$$

its expected value is

$$x_1 \cdot f(x_1) + x_2 \cdot f(x_2) + x_3 \cdot f(x_3) + \cdots + x_k \cdot f(x_k)$$

and in the $\sum$ notation we write

Mean of a Probability Distribution	$\mu = \sum x \cdot f(x)$

Like the mean of a population, it is denoted by the Greek lowercase μ (*mu*). The notation is the same, for as we pointed out in connection with the binomial distribution, when we observe a value of a random variable, we refer to its distribution as the population we are sampling. For instance, the histogram of Figure 8.2 on page 211 may be looked upon as the population we are sampling when we observe a value of a random variable having the binomial distribution with $n = 6$ and $p = 0.30$.

Example

Find the mean of the second probability distribution of Section 8.2, which pertains to the number of points we roll with a balanced die.

solution

Since the probabilities of rolling a 1, 2, 3, 4, 5, or 6 are all equal to $\frac{1}{6}$, we get

$$1 \cdot \tfrac{1}{6} + 2 \cdot \tfrac{1}{6} + 3 \cdot \tfrac{1}{6} + 4 \cdot \tfrac{1}{6} + 5 \cdot \tfrac{1}{6} + 6 \cdot \tfrac{1}{6} = 3\tfrac{1}{2}$$

Example

With reference to the example on page 210, find the mean number of persons, among six shopping at the market, who will take advantage of the special promotion.

solution

Substituting $x = 0, 1, 2, 3, 4, 5,$ and 6, and the probabilities on page 210 into the formula for μ we get

$$\mu = 0(0.118) + 1(0.303) + 2(0.324) + 3(0.185) + 4(0.060) + 5(0.010) + 6(0.001)$$
$$= 1.802$$

When a random variable can take on many different values, the calculation of μ may become very laborious. For instance, if we want to know how many persons can be expected to contribute to a charity, when 2,000 are solicited for funds and the probability is 0.40 that any one of them will make a contribution, we might consider calculating the 2,001 probabilities corresponding to 0, 1, 2, 3, . . . , 1,999 or 2,000 of them making a contribution. Not seriously, though, and we might argue instead that in the long run 40 percent of the persons will make a contribution, 40 percent of 2,000 is 800, and hence we can expect that 800 of the 2,000 persons will make a contribution. Similarly, if a balanced coin is flipped 1,000 times, we might argue that in the long run heads will come up 50 percent of the time, and hence that we can expect

$$1{,}000(0.50) = 500 \quad \text{heads.}$$

These two results are correct; both problems deal with random variables having binomial distributions, and it can be shown that in general

Mean of a Binomial Distribution	$\mu = n \cdot p$

In words, the mean of a binomial distribution is simply the product of the number of trials and the probability of success on an individual trial.

Example

With reference to the example on page 210, use this formula to find the mean number of persons, among six shopping at the market, who will take advantage of the special promotion.

solution

Since we are dealing with a binomial distribution with $n = 6$ and $p = 0.30$, we get

$$\mu = 6(0.30) = 1.80$$

The small difference of 0.002 between the values obtained here and on page 232 is due to rounding the probabilities to three decimals.   ▰ ▰ ▰

It is important to remember that the formula $\mu = n \cdot p$ applies only to binomial distributions. There are other formulas for other distributions; for instance, for the hypergeometric distribution the formula for the mean is

Mean of a Hypergeometric Distribution	$\mu = \dfrac{n \cdot a}{a + b}$

Example

Among 12 school buses, five have worn brakes. If six of the school buses are randomly picked for inspection, how many of them can be expected to have worn brakes?

solution

Since we are sampling without replacement, we have here a hypergeometric distribution with $a = 5$, $b = 7$, and $n = 6$. Substituting these values into the formula above, we get

$$\mu = \frac{6 \cdot 5}{5 + 7} = 2.5$$

This should not come as a surprise—half of the school buses are selected and half of the ones with worn brakes are expected to be included in the sample.   ▰ ▰ ▰

Also, the mean of the Poisson distribution with the parameter λ is $\mu = \lambda$, and this agrees with what we suggested earlier, namely, that λ is to be interpreted as an average. Derivations of all these special formulas may be found in textbooks on mathematical statistics.

8.8   THE STANDARD DEVIATION OF A PROBABILITY DISTRIBUTION

In Chapter 4 we saw that the most widely used measures of variation are variance and its square root, the standard deviation, which both measure variability by averaging the squared deviations from the mean. For probability distributions we measure variability in almost the same way, but instead of averaging the squared deviations from the mean, we find their expected value. In general, if a random variable takes on the values $x_1, x_2, x_3, \ldots,$ or x_k, with the probabilities

$$f(x_1), \quad f(x_2), \quad f(x_3), \quad \ldots, \quad f(x_k)$$

and the mean of this probability distribution is μ, the deviations from the mean are

$$x_1 - \mu, \quad x_2 - \mu, \quad x_3 - \mu, \quad \ldots, \quad x_k - \mu,$$

and the expected value of their squares is

$$(x_1 - \mu)^2 \cdot f(x_1) + (x_2 - \mu)^2 \cdot f(x_2) + \cdots + (x_k - \mu)^2 \cdot f(x_k)$$

Thus in the Σ notation we write

Variance of a Probability Distribution	$\sigma^2 = \Sigma(x - \mu)^2 \cdot f(x)$

which we refer to as the **variance of the random variable** or the **variance of its probability distribution.** As in Section 8.7, and for the same reason, we denote this description of a probability distribution with the same symbol as the corresponding description of a population.

The square root of the variance defines the **standard deviation of a probability distribution** and we write

Standard Deviation of a Probability Distribution	$\sigma = \sqrt{\Sigma (x - \mu)^2 \cdot f(x)}$

Example

With reference to the example on page 210, find the standard deviation of the number of persons, among six shopping at the market, who will take advantage of the special promotion.

solution

As we have seen, $\mu = 6(0.30) = 1.80$, so that we can arrange the calculations as follows:

Number of persons	Probability	Deviation from mean	Squared deviation from mean	$(x - \mu)^2 f(x)$
0	0.118	−1.8	3.24	0.38232
1	0.303	−0.8	0.64	0.19392
2	0.324	0.2	0.04	0.01296
3	0.185	1.2	1.44	0.26640
4	0.060	2.2	4.84	0.29040
5	0.010	3.2	10.24	0.10240
6	0.001	4.2	17.64	0.01764
				$\sigma^2 = 1.26604$

The values in the right-hand column were obtained by multiplying the squared deviations from the mean by their probabilities, and the total of this column is the variance of the distribution. Thus, the standard deviation is

$$\sigma = \sqrt{1.26604} \approx 1.13$$

The calculations were easy in this example because the deviations from the mean were small numbers given to one decimal. If the deviations from the mean are large numbers, or if they are given to several decimals, it is usually worthwhile to simplify the calculations by using the following computing formula, which does not require that we work with the deviations from the mean:

Variance of a Probability Distribution

$$\sigma^2 = \sum x^2 \cdot f(x) - \mu^2$$

Example

On page 189 we showed that if the probabilities are

0.06, 0.21, 0.24, 0.18, 0.14, 0.10, 0.04, 0.02, 0.01

that an airline office at a certain airport will receive 0, 1, 2, 3, 4, 5, 6, 7, or 8 complaints per day about its luggage handling. The mean of this probability distribution is $\mu = 2.75$. Find its standard deviation.

solution

First calculating

$$\sum x^2 \cdot f(x) = 0^2(0.06) + 1^2(0.21) + 2^2(0.24) + 3^2(0.18)$$
$$+ 4^2(0.14) + 5^2(0.10) + 6^2(0.04) + 7^2(0.02) + 8^2(0.01) \approx 10.59$$

we get

$$\sigma^2 = 10.59 - (2.75)^2 \approx 3.03$$

and, hence,

$$\sigma = \sqrt{3.03} \approx 1.74$$

The calculations would have been much more tedious in this case if we had not used the computing formula.

As in the case of the mean, the calculation of the variance or the standard deviation can generally be simplified when we deal with special kinds of probability distributions. For instance, for the binomial distribution we have the formula

Standard Deviation of a Binomial Distribution

$$\sigma = \sqrt{np(1 - p)}$$

Example

Use this formula to verify the result obtained just above for the example dealing with the number of persons, among six shopping at the market, who will take advantage of the special promotion.

solution

Since we are dealing with a binomial distribution with $n = 6$ and $p = 0.30$, the formula yields

$$\sigma = \sqrt{6(0.30)(0.70)} \approx 1.12$$

The difference, due to rounding, is only $1.13 - 1.12 = 0.01$. ◪ ◪ ◪

There also exist formulas for the standard deviations of other special probability distributions (see, for example, Exercises 8.72 and 8.77).

In Chapter 4 we mentioned Chebyshev's theorem because it gave us some idea how the standard deviation "controls" the spread or variation of a set of data. If we replace "the proportion of the data that must lie within k standard deviations on either side of the mean" by "the probability that a random variable will take on a value within k standard deviations on either side of the mean," the theorem applies also to random variables. From page 86, this probability is at least

$$1 - \frac{1}{k^2}$$

Example

The number of customers that a restaurant serves on a Friday night is a random variable with $\mu = 160$ and $\sigma = 7.5$. According to Chebyshev's theorem, what is the probability that it will serve between 145 and 175 customers on a Friday night?

solution

Since 175 is

$$\frac{175 - 160}{7.5} = 2$$

standard deviations above the mean and 145 is

$$\frac{160 - 145}{7.5} = 2$$

standard deviations below the mean, $k = 2$, the probability is at least

$$1 - \frac{1}{2^2} = 0.75.$$ ◪ ◪ ◪

Example

What does Chebyshev's theorem with $k = 5$ tell us about the number of heads, and hence the proportion of heads, we will get in 400 flips of a balanced coin?

solution

Since we are dealing with a random variable having the binomial distribution with $n = 400$ and $p = 0.50$,

$$\mu = 400(0.50) = 200 \quad \text{and} \quad \sigma = \sqrt{400(0.50)(0.50)} = 10$$

Thus, the probability is at least $1 - \frac{1}{5^2} = 0.96$ that we will get between

$$200 - 5 \cdot 10 = 150 \quad \text{and} \quad 200 + 5 \cdot 10 = 250 \text{ heads},$$

or that the proportion of heads will be between

$$\frac{150}{400} = 0.375 \quad \text{and} \quad \frac{250}{400} = 0.625$$ ◢ ◢ ◢

To continue with this example, the reader is asked to show in Exercise 8.81 on page 240 that for 10,000 flips of a balanced coin the probability is at least 0.96 that the proportion of heads will be between 0.475 and 0.525, and that for 1,000,000 flips of a balanced coin the probability is at least 0.96 that the proportion of heads will be between 0.4975 and 0.5025. All this provides support for the Law of Large Numbers, introduced in Section 5.4 in connection with the frequency interpretation of probability.

◢ EXERCISES

8.61   Suppose that the probabilities are 0.2, 0.4, 0.3, and 0.1 that the number of wills filed on any day at Polk County Courthouse will be 0, 1, 2, or 3.
   (a) Use the formula that defines μ to find the mean of this probability distribution.
   (b) Use the formula that defines σ^2 to find the variance of this probability distribution.
   (c) Use the computing formula for σ^2 to rework part (b).

8.62   The following table gives the probabilities that a probation officer will receive 0, 1, 2, 3, 4, or 5 reports of probation violations on any given day:

Number of violations	0	1	2	3	4	5
Probability	0.15	0.25	0.36	0.18	0.04	0.02

   (a) Use the formula that defines μ to find the mean of this probability distribution.
   (b) Use the formula that defines σ to find the standard deviation of this probability distribution.
   (c) Use the computing formula for σ to rework part (b).

8.63   The probabilities that a building inspector will observe 0 through 5 infractions of the building code in a home built in a large subdivision are

Number of infractions	0	1	2	3	4	5
Probability	0.48	0.25	0.14	0.08	0.04	0.01

   Find the mean and standard deviation of this distribution.

8.64   As mentioned at the beginning of Section 8.2, the probabilities of getting 0, 1, 2, 3, or 4 heads in four flips of a balanced coin are

$$\frac{1}{16}, \quad \frac{4}{16}, \quad \frac{6}{16}, \quad \frac{4}{16}, \quad \frac{1}{16}$$

For this random variable, find

(a) the mean, using the formula that defines μ;

(b) the mean, using the special formula for the mean of the binomial distribution;

(c) the variance, using the formula that defines σ^2;

(d) the variance, using the computing formula for σ^2;

(e) the variance, using the special formula for the standard deviation of the binomial distribution.

8.65   A study shows that 60 percent of all first-class letters between two cities are delivered within 48 hours. Find the mean and the variance of the number of first-class letters between the two cities, among eight randomly selected, which will be delivered within 48 hours, using

(a) Table V, the formula that defines μ, and the computing formula for σ^2;

(b) the special formulas for the mean and the standard deviation of a binomial distribution.

8.66   If 80 percent of certain videocassette recorders will function successfully through the 90-day warranty period, find the mean and standard deviation of the number of these videocasette recorders, among 10 randomly selected, which will function successfully through the 90-day warranty period, using

(a) Table V, the formula that defines μ, and the computing formula for σ^2;

(b) the special formulas for the mean and standard deviation of the binomial distribution.

8.67   A study shows that 80 percent of all patients coming to a certain medical building have to wait at least 30 minutes to see their doctor. Use the special formulas for the mean and the standard deviation of a binomial distribution to find μ and σ for the number of patients, among 20 coming to this medical building, who have to wait at least 30 minutes to see their doctor.

8.68   If 64 percent of all patients with a certain type of cancer will survive five years from the date of diagnosis, use the special formulas for the mean and standard deviation of a binomial distribution to find μ and σ for the number of patients, out of 80 newly diagnosed, who will survive for five years.

8.69   Find the mean and the standard deviation of the binomial random variable that is

(a) the number of heads obtained in 460 flips of a balanced coin;

(b) the number of 4's obtained in 1,200 rolls of a balanced die;

(c) the number of persons, among 200 invited, who will come to a reception honoring the author of a new book, when the probability is 0.36 that any one of them will attend;

(d) the number of videotapes, out of 450 rentals, returned late to a video store, when the probability is 0.08 that any one videotape will be returned late;

(e) the number of elementary school students, among 650 interviewed, who do not like the food served in the school's cafeteria, when the probability is 0.68 that any one of them does not like the food.

8.70   Exercise 8.31 on page 221 considers, among three selected male applicants, the number who have working wives.

(a) Using the probabilities found in that exercise, find the mean of this distribution.

(b) Use the special formula for the mean of a hypergeometric distribution to verify the result of part (a).

8.71   Exercise 8.32 on page 221 considers, among three selected airplane shipments, the number containing contraband.

(a) Using the probabilities found in that exercise, find the mean of this distribution.

(b) Use the special formula for the mean of a hypergeometric distribution to verify the result of part (a).

8.72   Among 10 faculty members considered for promotion, seven are Ph.D.'s and three are not.

(a) If four of them are chosen at random, find the probabilities that 0, 1, 2, 3, or all 4 are Ph.D.'s.

(b) Use the special formula for the mean of a hypergeometric distribution to find the mean of the distribution of part (a).

(c) There is a special formula for the variance of a hypergeometric distribution with parameters a, b, and n:

$$\sigma^2 = n \cdot \frac{ab}{(a+b)^2} \cdot \frac{a+b-n}{a+b-1}$$

Use this formula to find the variance of the distribution of part (a).

8.73 Use the special formula for the variance of the hypergeometric distribution given in part (c) of Exercise 8.72 to find the standard deviation of

(a) the distribution of the number of applicants with working wives in Exercise 8.70, in which $a = 9$, $b = 6$, and $n = 3$;

(b) the distribution of the number of shipments with contraband in Exercise 8.71, in which $a = 5$, $b = 11$, and $n = 3$.

⊞ 8.74 If sampling is done with replacement from a group consisting of a of one type and b of another type, then the binomial probability distribution applies, and the variance of the number of the first type, out of n drawings, is

$$\sigma^2 = n \cdot \frac{ab}{(a+b)^2}$$

Only the factor $\frac{a+b-n}{a+b-1}$ distinguishes the binomial and hypergeometric variances. Compute this factor for the following cases:

(a) $a + b = 20$, $n = 5$;

(b) $a + b = 100$, $n = 4$;

(c) $a + b = 1,000$, $n = 40$;

(d) $a + b = 200$, $n = 60$.

8.75 The probabilities that there will be 0, 1, 2, 3, 4, or 5 fires caused by lightning during a summer storm are, respectively,

0.449   0.360   0.144   0.038   0.008   0.001

Calculate the mean of this Poisson distribution with $\lambda = 0.8$, and use the result to verify the special formula $\mu = \lambda$ mentioned on page 233.

8.76 If the number of gamma rays emitted per second by a certain radioactive substance is a random variable having the Poisson distribution with $\lambda = 2.4$, then the probabilities that it will emit certain numbers of gamma rays in 1 second are given by

Number of gamma rays	Probability
0	0.091
1	0.218
2	0.261
3	0.209
4	0.125
5	0.060
6	0.024
7	0.008
8	0.003
9	0.001

The probability of 10 or more gamma rays is less than 0.001. Calculate the mean and use the result to verify the special formula $\mu = \lambda$ for a random variable having the Poisson distribution with the parameter λ.

用 8.77   For the standard deviation of a Poisson distribution there is the special formula $\sigma = \sqrt{\lambda}$. Calculate the standard deviation of the probability distribution of Exercise 8.75 and use the result to verify this special formula.

8.78   If a student answers the 144 questions of a true–false test by flipping a balanced coin—heads is "true" and tails is "false"—what does Chebyshev's theorem with $k = 4$ tell us about the number of correct answers he will get?

8.79   For the probability distribution of Exercise 8.76 in which the mean is 2.4 and the standard deviation is $\sqrt{2.4} \approx 1.549$, what does Chebyshev's theorem with $k = 2$ tell us about the number of gamma rays emitted in 1 second?

8.80   The annual number of rainy days in a certain city is a random variable with $\mu = 126$ and $\sigma = 9$.

(a)   What does Chebyshev's theorem with $k = 12$ tell us about the number of days it will rain in the given city in any one year?

(b)   According to Chebyshev's theorem, with what probability can we assert that it will rain in the given city between 96 and 156 days in any one year?

8.81   Use Chebyshev's theorem to show that the probability is at least 0.96 that

(a)   for 10,000 flips of a balanced coin the proportion of heads will be between 0.475 and 0.525;

(b)   for 1,000,000 flips of a balanced coin the proportion of heads will be between 0.4975 and 0.5025.

8.9   TECHNICAL NOTE (Simulation) ⇔

During the last few decades, **simulation** techniques have been applied to many problems in business and scientific research, and if the processes being simulated involve an element of chance, we refer to these techniques as **Monte Carlo methods.** Such methods have been used, for example, to study traffic flow on proposed freeways, to conduct war games, to study the spread of epidemics or human behavior during times of natural disaster (say, a flood or an earthquake), and to study the scattering of neutrons or the collisions of photons with electrons. Also, in business research, such methods are used to solve inventory problems, production scheduling, or the effects of advertising campaigns, and to study many other situations involving overall planning and organization. In most cases, this will eliminate the cost of building and operating expensive equipment, and in some instances it can be used when direct experimentation is impossible.

The name Monte Carlo evokes the casino in Monaco, and thus suggests that gambling devices are used for this technique. In fact, applications of Monte Carlo methods invariably use **random numbers** (called **random digits**) generated by computers. The method formerly used published tables of random digits; see the references on page 250.

To illustrate the use of random numbers, let us show how we might play "heads or tails" without actually flipping a coin. Let us suppose that we have programmed a computer to produce random digits from 0 to 9. Letting the even numbers represent heads and the odd numbers tails, the string of computer values

3 9 8 1 5 1 6 3 2 4 . . .

would be interpreted as tail, tail, head, tail, tail, tail, head, tail, head, head, . . .
In the computer printout of Figure 5.3 on page 125 we actually simulated 100
flips of a balanced coin. The commands `Random 100 c1;` and `Bernoulli .5.`
caused the computer to generate 100 values of a random variable having the binomial distribution with $n = 1$ and $p = .50$; here 1 and 0 denote heads and tails.[†]

Repeated flips of any number of coins could be simulated by extending this
technique. For example, to deal with flips of three coins we can ask a computer
to provide random numbers from 000 to 999. This details are shown in Figure
8.6. The request has produced values

$$594 \quad 839 \quad 363 \quad 522 \quad 737 \quad 276 \quad 495 \quad 840 \quad 792 \quad 546 \quad . . . .$$

Then by counting the number of even digits in each case, we interpret these as

$$1 \quad 1 \quad 1 \quad 2 \quad 0 \quad 2 \quad 1 \quad 3 \quad 1 \quad 2 \quad . . . \text{ heads.}$$

To save ourselves the job of having to count the even digits, we might use instead the following scheme, where we made use of the fact that for three balanced coins the probabilities of 0, 1, 2, or 3 heads are

$$\frac{1}{8} \quad \frac{3}{8} \quad \frac{3}{8} \text{ and } \frac{1}{8} \quad \text{or, in decimal notation, } 0.125 \quad 0.375 \quad 0.375 \text{ and } 0.125.$$

Number of heads x	Probability of x heads	Probability of x or fewer heads	Random numbers
0	0.125	0.125	000–124
1	0.375	0.500	125–499
2	0.375	0.875	500–874
3	0.125	1.000	875–999

```
MTB  > Random 25 C1;
SUBC >   Integer Ø 999.

MTB  > write C1

Data Display (WRITE)

594      839      363      522      737      276
495      84Ø      792      546      537      3Ø4
968        6      174       12      725      979
916      184      921      559      583      753
168
```

[†]The semicolon at the end of the first command and the period at the end of the second
command are critical parts of MINITAB syntax if these commands are actually typed. In
MINITAB 10 for Windows, the commands will be generated in proper syntax by click-
ing on menu items.

Here we used three-digit random numbers because the probabilities are given to three decimals, and we allocated 125 of the 1,000 random numbers from 000 to 999 to 0 heads, 375 to 1 head, 375 to 2 heads, and 125 to 3 heads. The column of cumulative probabilities was added to facilitate the assignment of the random numbers. Observe that in each case the last random number is one less than the number formed by the three decimal digits of the corresponding cumulative probability.

   The method explained here regarding a game of chance can be used to simulate observations of any discrete random variable with a given probability distribution.

Example

Use this scheme to simulate 10 flips of three balanced coins. Assume that the three-digit computer random numbers are

$$974 \quad 611 \quad 345 \quad 664 \quad 041 \quad 203 \quad 531 \quad 421 \quad 031 \quad 925$$

solution

The value 974 occurs in the range 875–999, which corresponds to $x = 3$ in the preceding table. Thus, the first flip of three coins produces three heads. The value 611 occurs in the range 500–874, corresponding to $x = 2$, or two heads. We thus interpret this string of random numbers as producing

$$3 \quad 2 \quad 1 \quad 2 \quad 0 \quad 1 \quad 2 \quad 1 \quad 0 \quad 3 \text{ heads} \qquad \blacksquare \blacksquare \blacksquare$$

   We could have worked this example by using the computer software that generated Figure 5.3. Figure 8.7 provides an illustration.

Example

The probabilities that 0, 1, 2, 3, . . ., or 13 cars will arrive at the tollbooth of a certain bridge in any 1 minute during the early afternoon are

$$0.008 \quad 0.037 \quad 0.089 \quad 0.146 \quad 0.179 \quad 0.175 \quad 0.143$$
$$0.100 \quad 0.062 \quad 0.034 \quad 0.016 \quad 0.007 \quad 0.003 \quad 0.001$$

(a) Distribute the three-digit random numbers from 000 to 999 among the 14 values of this random variable, so that they can be used to simulate the arrival of cars at the tollbooth.
(b) Suppose that a computer program has produced the three-digit numbers

$$
\begin{array}{ccccc}
836 & 712 & 524 & 762 & 325 \\
081 & 960 & 594 & 473 & 370 \\
305 & 178 & 523 & 184 & 368 \\
864 & 676 & 975 & 553 & 618 \\
\end{array}
$$

FIGURE 8.7

Computer generation of 10 random flips of three coins (MINITAB 10 for Windows).

```
MTB > Random 1Ø C1;
SUBC >   Binomial 3 Ø.5.

MTB > write C1

Data Display (WRITE)

1  3  1  2  Ø  3  3  1  1  1
```

Use this to simulate the arrivals of cars at the tollbooth during twenty 1-minute intervals in early afternoon.

(a) Calculating the cumulative probabilities and following the suggestion on page 241, we arrive at the following scheme:

Number of cars	Probability	Cumulative probability	Random numbers
0	0.008	0.008	000–007
1	0.037	0.045	008–044
2	0.089	0.134	045–133
3	0.146	0.280	134–279
4	0.179	0.459	280–458
5	0.175	0.634	459–633
6	0.143	0.777	634–776
7	0.100	0.877	777–876
8	0.062	0.939	877–938
9	0.034	0.973	939–972
10	0.016	0.989	973–988
11	0.007	0.996	989–995
12	0.003	0.999	996–998
13	0.001	1.000	999

(b) The value 836 is found in the interval 777–876, corresponding to 7 cars. In this fashion, we are able to produce the simulated list as

7 6 5 6 4 2 9 5 5 4 4 3 5 3 4 7 6 10 5 5

The simulation of the preceding example was fairly easy and straightforward, but clever use of computer software can make it even easier. Making use of the fact that the distribution we gave is that of a random variable having the Poisson distribution with $\lambda = 4.9$, we get the printout of Figure 8.8, which tells us that

5 9 4 2 6 5 5 5 4 7
3 4 2 7 5 5 5 6 5 9

cars arrived at the tollbooth during 20 simulated 1-minute intervals.

It is important to remember that simulations are not necessarily exact replacements for real experiments. Simulations are designed to exhibit the mathematical aspects of real situations, but they sometimes do a poor job of captur-

FIGURE 8.8

Computer simulation of 20 values of a random variable having the Poisson distribution with $\lambda = 4.9$.

```
MTB  > Random 20 C1;
SUBC >   Poisson 4.9.
MTB  > write C1

Data Display (WRITE)

5  9  4  2  6  5  5  5  4  7
3  4  2  7  5  5  5  6  5  9
```

ing behavioral peculiarities. The simulations of coin flips and traffic at a toll booth illustrated in this section are quite reliable. A simulation of an inventory management scheme, however, cannot deal with the possibility that persons managing an inventory scheme might invent new procedures as they go along or might fail to follow established rules.

EXERCISES

8.82   Letting the digits 1, 2, 3, 4, 5, and 6 represent the corresponding faces of a die, use a computer to simulate 120 rolls of a balanced die. (In MINITAB this can be done with the commands Random 120 C1; and Integer 1 6. If you use computer-generated random digits, simply ignore 0, 7, 8, and 9.) Also determine the accumulated proportion of 6's after each tenth roll, and draw a diagram like that of Figure 5.4. Does it seem to support the Law of Large Numbers?

8.83   As we have seen, the probabilities of getting 0, 1, or 2 heads in two flips of a balanced coin (or when flipping a pair of balanced coins) are 0.25, 0.50, and 0.25.

  (a) Distribute the two-digit random numbers from 00 to 99 among the three possibilities so that the corresponding random numbers can be used to simulate repeated flips of a pair of balanced coins.

  (b) Simulate 200 flips of a pair of balanced coins and determine the accumulated proportion of the time that both coins came up heads after each tenth pair of flips. Also draw a diagram like that of Figure 5.4 and check whether the simulation supports the Law of Large Numbers.

8.84   The probabilities that a real estate broker will sell 0, 1, 2, 3, 4, 5, or 6 houses in a week are

$$0.14 \quad 0.27 \quad 0.27 \quad 0.18 \quad 0.09 \quad 0.04 \quad 0.01$$

  (a) Distribute the two-digit random numbers from 00 through 99 among these seven possibilities so that the corresponding random numbers can be used to simulate the number of houses the real estate broker sells in a week.

  (b) Use the results of part (a) to simulate the real estate broker's weekly sales during 25 consecutive weeks.

8.85   With reference to Exercise 8.84, how big is the difference between the mean of the simulated numbers of sales and $\mu = 1.97$, the mean of the given probability distribution?

8.86   Suppose that the probabilities are

$$0.41 \quad 0.37 \quad 0.16 \quad 0.05 \quad 0.01$$

that there will be 0, 1, 2, 3, or 4 UFO sightings in a certain region on any one day.

  (a) Distribute the two-digit random numbers from 00 through 99 among the five values of this random variable so that the corresponding random numbers can be used to simulate the sighting of UFOs in the given region.

  (b) Use the result of part (a) to simulate the sighting of UFOs in the given region on 30 days.

8.87   Suppose that the probabilities are

$$0.2466 \quad 0.3452 \quad 0.2417 \quad 0.1128 \quad 0.0395 \quad 0.0111 \quad 0.0026 \quad 0.0005$$

that there will be 0, 1, 2, 3, 4, 5, 6, or 7 polluting spills in the Great Lakes on any one day.

  (a) Distribute the four-digit random numbers from 0000 through 9999 among the eight values of this random variable so that the corresponding random numbers can be used to simulate the occurrence of polluting spills in the Great Lakes.

(b) Use the results of part (a) to simulate the number of polluting spills in the Great Lakes on 40 consecutive days.

8.88 The owner of a bakery knows that the probabilities are

$$0.05 \quad 0.15 \quad 0.25 \quad 0.25 \quad 0.20 \quad 0.10$$

that the demands for a highly perishable cheese cake will be 0, 1, 2, 3, 4, or 5.

(a) Distribute the two-digit random numbers from 00 through 99 among these six possibilities so that the corresponding random numbers can be used to simulate the daily demand.

(b) Use the results of part (a) to simulate the demand for the cheese cake on 30 consecutive business days.

(c) If the baker makes a profit of $2.00 on each cake that he sells, but loses $1.00 on each cake that goes to waste (namely, each cake that cannot be sold on the day it is baked), find the baker's profit or loss for each of the 30 days of part (b) assuming that each day he bakes three of these cakes. Also find the baker's average profit for the 30 days.

(d) Repeat part (c), assuming that each day he bakes four rather than three of the cakes. Do not repeat part (b) in doing this. Which of the two appears to be more profitable?

8.89 Depending on the availability of parts, a company can manufacture 3, 4, 5, or 6 units of a certain item per week with corresponding probabilities of 0.10, 0.40, 0.30, and 0.20. The probabilities that there will be a weekly demand for 0, 1, 2, 3, ..., or 8 units are

$$0.05 \quad 0.10 \quad 0.30 \quad 0.30 \quad 0.10 \quad 0.05 \quad 0.05 \quad 0.04 \quad 0.01$$

If a unit is sold during the week that it is made, it will yield a profit of $100; this profit is reduced by $20 each week that a unit has to be stored. Use random numbers to simulate the operations of this company for 50 consecutive weeks and estimate its expected weekly profit.

8.10 CHECKLIST OF KEY TERMS[†] *(with page references to their definitions)*

8.11 REVIEW EXERCISES

8.90 If 12 percent of all medical students want to specialize in surgery, what are the probabilities that in a random sample of three medical students

(a) none wants to specialize in surgery;

(b) only one wants to specialize in surgery?

[†]Terms introduced in exercises are shown in *italics*.

8.91   A panel of 300 persons chosen for jury duty included only 30 persons under 25 years of age. For a particular narcotics case, the actual jury of 12 selected from this panel did not contain anyone under the age of 25. The youthful defendant's attorney complained that this jury of 12 is not representative. He argued that the probability of having one of the 12 jurors under 25 years of age should be *many times* the probability of having none of them under 25 years of age.

(a) Find the ratio of these two probabilities, using the hypergeometric distribution.

(b) Find the ratio of these two probabilities, using the binomial distribution as an approximation.

8.92   Referring to the computer printout of Figure 8.5 on page 226, find the probability that a random variable having the Poisson distribution with $\lambda = 0.6$ will take on a value greater than 2 by

(a) adding the probabilities corresponding to 3, 4, 5, 6;

(b) working with the cumulative probabilities.

8.93   In each case determine whether the given values can be looked upon as the values of a probability distribution of a random variable that can take on the values 1, 2, 3, 4, and 5, and explain your answers.

(a) $f(1) = 0.18$ (b) $f(1) = 0.10$ (c) $f(1) = 0.15$

    $f(2) = 0.20$ $f(2) = 0.10$ $f(2) = 0.20$

    $f(3) = 0.22$ $f(3) = 0.80$ $f(3) = 0.25$

    $f(4) = 0.20$ $f(4) = -0.10$ $f(4) = 0.30$

    $f(5) = 0.18$ $f(5) = 0.10$ $f(5) = 0.35$

8.94   The values given below are the probabilities that 0 through 5 of a doctor's patients will come down with the flu during the first week of January:

Number of patients	0	1	2	3	4	5
Probability	0.08	0.18	0.34	0.28	0.10	0.02

(a) Find the mean of this probability distribution.

(b) Use the computing formula to find the standard deviation of this probability distribution.

8.95   The probability that a burglar will get caught on any given job is 0.20. Use the formula for the geometric distribution on page 217 to find the probability that he will get caught for the first time on his fifth job.

8.96   Among 30 workers on a picket line, 17 are men and 13 are women. If a television news reporter randomly picks four of them to be shown on camera, what are the probabilities that those shown will be

(a) two men and two women;

(b) one man and three women;

(c) no men and four women?

8.97   Suppose that the probabilities are 0.46, 0.27, 0.15, 0.08, and 0.04 that it will take an accountant 1, 2, 3, 4, or 5 hours to complete a certain income tax form. Distribute the two-digit random numbers from 00 to 99 among the five values of this random variable so that they can be used to simulate the amount of time it takes the accountant to complete such forms.

8.98 A certain supermarket carries four grades of ground beef, and the probabilities that a shopper will buy the poorest, third best, second best, or best grade are, respectively, 0.10, 0.20, 0.40, and 0.30. Find the probability that among 12 (randomly chosen) shoppers buying ground beef at this supermarket, one will choose the poorest kind, two will choose the third best kind, six will buy the second best kind, and three will buy the best kind.

8.99 Check in each case whether the condition for the binomial approximation to the hypergeometric distribution is satisfied:

(a) $a = 80$, $b = 120$, and $n = 8$;

(b) $a = 75$, $b = 75$, and $n = 10$;

(c) $a = 136$, $b = 164$, and $n = 24$.

8.100 Give the mean and standard deviation for each of the following binomial distributions:

(a) $n = 9$ and $p = 0.5$;

(b) $n = 16$ and $p = 0.36$;

(c) $n = 21$ and $p = 0.7$;

(d) $n = 91$ and $p = 0.65$.

8.101 Use the computer printout of Figure 8.9 on page 248 to find that probabilities that a random variable having the binomial distribution with $n = 18$ and $p = 0.27$ will take on

(a) the value 4;

(b) a value less than 7;

(c) a value anywhere from 3 to 8.

8.102 It is known that 4 percent of all rats carry a certain disease.

(a) If we examine 200 rats, constituting a random sample, will we satisfy the condition in the text for using the Poisson approximation to the binomial distribution of the number carrying the disease?

(b) Calculate the probability that exactly 6 of the 200 rats will carry the disease.

8.103 During the month of August, the daily number of persons visiting a certain tourist attraction is a random variable with $\mu = 1,200$ and $\sigma = 80$.

(a) What does Chebyshev's theorem with $k = 7$ tell us about the number of persons who will visit the tourist attraction on an August day?

(b) According to Chebyshev's theorem, with what probability can we assert that between 1,000 and 1,400 persons will visit the tourist attraction on an August day?

8.104 The size of an animal population is sometimes estimated by the **capture–recapture method.** In this method, n_1 of the animals are captured, marked, and released. Later, n_2 of the animals are captured, x of them are found to be marked, and all this information is used to estimate N, the size of the population. If $n_1 = 3$ rare owls are captured, marked, and released and later $n_2 = 4$ such owls are captured and $x = 1$ of them is found to be marked, for what value of N is the probability of getting $x = 1$ a maximum? (Hint: Try $N = 9, 10, 11, 12, 13,$ and 14.)

8.105 A restaurant manager wants to review the calculations on the diner checks presented to his customers. During the preceding week, 1,428 of these checks were written, and 35 of these have errors in prices or in addition. The manager selects 50 of these at random to review, and we would like to calculate the probability of finding exactly 2 with errors.

(a) Write the expression which gives the exact probability, using the hypergeometric distribution. Do not complete the calculation.

(b) Use the binomial distribution as an approximation to obtain the probability of finding exactly 2 errors.

(c) Use the Poisson distribution as an approximation to obtain the probability of finding exactly 2 errors.

FIGURE 8.9

*Computer printout the
binomial distribution
with n = 18 and p = 0.27.*

```
MTB  > Set c1
DATA >    1( 0 : 12 / 1 )1
DATA >    End.
MTB  > PDF c1;
SUBC >    Binomial 18 0.27.

Probability Density Function

Binomial with n = 18 and p = 0.270000

             x        P( X = x)
           0.00         0.0035
           1.00         0.0231
           2.00         0.0725
           3.00         0.1431
           4.00         0.1985
           5.00         0.2055
           6.00         0.1647
           7.00         0.1044
           8.00         0.0531
           9.00         0.0218
          10.00         0.0073
          11.00         0.0020
          12.00         0.0004

MTB  > CDF c1;
SUBC >    Binomial 18 0.27.

Cumulative Distribution Function

Binomial with n = 18 and p = 0.270000

             x        P( X  ≤ x)
           0.00         0.0035
           1.00         0.0265
           2.00         0.0991
           3.00         0.2422
           4.00         0.4406
           5.00         0.6462
           6.00         0.8109
           7.00         0.9153
           8.00         0.9684
           9.00         0.9903
          10.00         0.9975
          11.00         0.9995
          12.00         0.9999
```

8.106   Among 600 plants exposed to excessive radiation, 90 show abnormal growth. If a scientist collects the seed of three of the plants chosen at random, find the probability that he will
get the seed from one plant with abnormal growth and two plants with normal growth by
using

(a) the hypergeometric distribution;

(b) the binomial distribution as an approximation.

8.107 The probabilities that 0, 1, 2, 3, 4, 5, or 6 fires will break out in a national forest on a July morning are

$$0.120, \quad 0.207, \quad 0.358, \quad 0.162, \quad 0.096, \quad 0.043, \quad 0.014$$

Find the mean and the variance of this probability distribution.

8.108 If 12 of 18 medieval gold coins are genuine, 4 are gold-plated counterfeits, and 2 are pure brass counterfeits, and if three of these coins are randomly selected to be sold at auction, what are the probabilities that

(a) all three coins will be genuine;

(b) two of the coins will be genuine;

(c) one coin will be genuine;

(d) one coin will be genuine, one will be a gold-plated counterfeit, and one will be a pure brass counterfeit?

8.109 The probabilities are 0.70, 0.20, and 0.10 that an automobile using a certain road will have tires that can be classified as adequate, worn, and dangerous, respectively. Ten cars are stopped in a random safety check. Find the probabilities that

(a) at least 8 of the 10 will have adequate tires,

(b) at most 2 of the 10 will have dangerous tires;

(c) 6 will have adequate tires, 3 will have worn tires, and 1 will have dangerous tires.

8.110 Determine whether the following can be probability distributions (defined in each case only for the given values of x) and explain your answers:

(a) $f(x) = \frac{x}{10}$ for $x = 0, 1, 2, 3, 4$;

(b) $f(x) = \frac{x-1}{2}$ for $x = 0, 1, 2, 3$;

(c) $f(x) = \frac{1}{5}\binom{2}{x}$ for $x = 0, 1,$ and 2.

8.111 A study shows that 95 percent of the families in a certain suburban area have a color television set. Use Table V to find the probabilities that among 16 families randomly selected in this area

(a) 14 will have a color television set;

(b) at least 14 will have a color television set;

(c) at most 14 will have a color television set.

8.112 The number of blossoms on a rare plant is a random variable having the Poisson distribution with $\lambda = 2.4$. What are the probabilities that such a plant will have

(a) no blossoms;

(b) at most two blossoms?

8.113 Using the special formula for the mean of the hypergeometric distribution and also the special formula given in Exercise 8.74 on page 239, give the mean and standard deviation for each of the following hypergeometric distributions:

(a) $a = 20,$ $b = 20,$ $n = 5$;

(b) $a = 2,$ $b = 198,$ $n = 15$;

(c) $a = 200,$ $b = 19,800,$ $n = 15$;

(d) $a = 28,$ $b = 12,$ $n = 30$.

8.114 According to Chebyshev's theorem, with what probability can we assert that in 40,000 flips of a balanced coin the proportion of heads will be between 0.45 and 0.55?

8.12 REFERENCES

A great deal of information about various probability distributions may be found in

HASTINGS, N. A. J., and PEACOCK, J. B., *Statistical Distributions.* London: Butterworth & Company (Publishers) Ltd., 1975.

More detailed tables of binomial probabilities may be found in

ROMIG, H. G., *50–100 Binomial Tables.* New York: John Wiley & Sons, Inc., 1953.

Tables of the Binomial Probability Distribution, National Bureau of Standards Applied Mathematics Series No. 6. Washington, D.C.: U.S. Government Printing Office, 1950.

and a detailed table of Poisson probabilities is given in

MOLINA, E. C., *Poisson's Exponential Binomial Limit.* Princeton, N.J.: D. Van Nostrand Company, Inc., 1947.

The wide availability of computer programs for binomial and Poisson probabilities makes it unlikely that the above-named tables will be extended or updated.

Among the many published tables of random numbers, one of the most widely used is

RAND CORPORATION, *A Million Random Digits with 100,000 Normal Deviates.* New York: Macmillan Publishing Co., Inc., third printing, 1966.

There also exist calculators that are preprogrammed to generate random numbers and it is fairly easy to program a computer so that a person can generate his or her own random numbers. The following is one of many articles on this subject.

KIMBERLING, C., "Generate Your Own Random Numbers," *Mathematics Teacher,* February 1984.

A book discussing the use of random numbers in programming is

HENNEFELD, J., *Using Microsoft and IBM BASIC.* Boston: PWS Publishers, 1987.

For more information about simulation and Monte Carlo methods, see

RUBINSTEIN, R. Y., *Simulation and the Monte Carlo Method.* New York: John Wiley & Sons, Inc., 1981.

TRAVERS, K. J., "Using Monte Carlo Methods to Teach Probability and Statistics," in *Teaching Statistics and Probability,* 1981 Yearbook of the National Council of Teachers of Mathematics. Reston, Va.: NCTM, 1981.

CHAPTER 9

THE NORMAL DISTRIBUTION

*C*ontinuous *sample spaces and* **continuous random variables** *occur when we deal with quantities that are measured on a continuous scale—for instance, when we measure the speed of a car, the amount of alcohol in a person's blood, the net weight of a package of frozen food, or the amount of tar in a cigarette. Continuums exist for such situations, but we normally round measurements to the nearest whole unit or to a few decimal places. In actual practice, we are interested in probabilities associated with intervals or regions of a sample space, and not with probabilities associated with individual points. For instance, we may need to know the probability that, at a given time, a car is moving between 50 and 55 miles per hour, or that a package of frozen peas weighs more than 5.95 ounces. We will not ask the probability that the car is moving exactly at $16\pi \approx 50.2685482\ldots$ miles per hour, nor that the package of frozen peas weighs exactly $\sqrt{36.2} \approx 6.0166\ldots$ ounces.*

In this chapter we learn how to determine, and work with, probabilities relating to continuous random variables. Histograms will be superseded by continuous curves, as in Figure 9.1; we can visualize such curves as being approached by histograms with narrower and narrower classes.

After a general introduction to **continuous distributions** *in Section 9.1, we devote the remainder of the chapter to the* **normal distribution** *which is basic to most of the techniques of practical modern statistics. Various applications are discussed in Sections 9.4 and 9.5, and the optional material in Sections 9.3 and 9.6 cover a test to decide whether observed data follow the general pattern of the normal distribution and the simulation of normally distributed random variables.* ◪

9.1   CONTINUOUS DISTRIBUTIONS

In the histograms we have seen thus far, the frequencies, percentages, proportions, or probabilities were represented by the heights of the rectangles, or by their areas. In the continuous case, we also represent probabilities by areas—not

FIGURE 9.1

Continuous distribution curve.

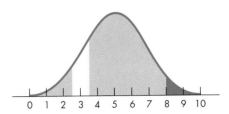

FIGURE 9.2

Histogram of probability distribution and graph of continuous distribution.

by areas of rectangles—but by areas under continuous curves. Figure 9.2 shows a histogram of the probability distribution of a discrete random variable that assumes only the values 0, 1, 2, . . ., and 10. The probability that it will take on the value 3, for example, is given by the area of the white rectangle, and the probability that it will take on a value greater than or equal to 8 is given by the sum of the areas of the three tinted rectangles on the right-hand side. The right-hand diagram of Figure 9.2 refers to a continuous random variable that can take on any value on the interval from 0 to 10. The probability that it will take on a value on the interval from 2.5 to 3.5, for example, is given by the area of the white region under the curve, and the probability that it will take on a value greater than or equal to 8 is given by the area of the tinted region under the curve on the right-hand side.

   Continuous curves such as the one shown on the right in Figure 9.2 are the graphs of functions called **probability densities,** or informally, **continuous distributions.** The term "probability density" comes from physics, where the terms "weight" and "density" are used in just about the same way in which we use the terms "probability" and "probability density" in statistics. As is illustrated by Figure 9.3, probability densities are characterized by the fact that

   The area under the curve between any two values *a* and *b* gives the probability that a random variable having this continuous distribution will take on a value on the interval from *a* to *b*.

   It follows that the values of a continuous distribution must be non-negative, and that the total area under the curve, representing the certainty that a random variable must take on one of its values, is always equal to 1. In contrast with the two rules on page 207, there is no requirement that the values of a continuous distribution be less than or equal to 1.

FIGURE 9.3

Continuous distribution.

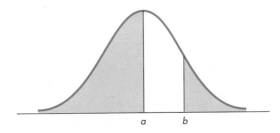

Example

Verify that $f(x) = \frac{x}{8}$ can serve as the probability density of a continuous random variable that can take on any value on the interval from 0 to 4.

solution

The first condition is satisfied since $\frac{x}{8}$ is 0 for $x = 0$, and positive for any other value of x on the interval from 0 to 4. Insofar as the second condition is concerned, it can be seen from Figure 9.4 that the total area under the curve is that of a triangle, and that the base and the height of the triangle are, respectively, 4 and $\frac{4}{8} = \frac{1}{2}$. The usual formula for the area of a triangle yields $\frac{1}{2} \cdot 4 \cdot \frac{1}{2} = 1$. ▱ ▱ ▱

Example

With reference to the preceding example, find the probabilities that a random variable having the given probability density will take on a value
(a) less than 2;
(b) less than or equal to 2.

solution

(a) The probability is indicated by the area of the smaller triangle of Figure 9.4, which is bounded on the right by the dashed vertical line at $x = 2$. Its base is 2, its height is $\frac{2}{8} = \frac{1}{4}$, so its area is $\frac{1}{2} \cdot 2 \cdot \frac{1}{4} = \frac{1}{4}$.
(b) The probability is the same as that of part (a), namely, $\frac{1}{4}$.   ▱ ▱ ▱

This example illustrates the important fact that, in the continuous case, the probability is zero that a random variable will take on any particular value. In our example, the probability is zero that the random variable will take on the value 2, and by 2 we mean *exactly* 2, and we do not include nearby values such as 1.9999998 or 2.0000001.

A consequence of measuring (rather than counting) is that we must assign probability zero to any particular outcome. We assert the probability must be zero that an individual will have a weight of *exactly* 145.27 pounds or that a horse will run a race in *exactly* 58.442 seconds. Observe, however, that even though every particular outcome has probability zero, the process will still produce a value (whether or not we can measure it with extra-fine precision); thus,

FIGURE 9.4

Continuous distribution

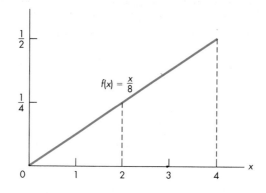

events of probability zero not only can occur but must occur when we deal with measured random quantities.

Statistical descriptions of continuous distributions are as important as descriptions of probability distributions or distributions of observed data, but most of them, including the mean and the standard deviation, cannot be defined without using calculus. Informally, though, we can always picture continuous distributions as being approximated by histograms of probability distributions (see Figure 9.1), whose mean and standard deviation we can calculate. Then, if we choose histograms with narrower and narrower classes, the means and the standard deviations of the corresponding probability distributions will approach the mean and the standard deviation of the continuous distribution. Actually, the mean and the standard deviation of a continuous distribution measure the same properties as the mean and the standard deviation of a probability distribution—the expected value of a random variable having the given distribution, and the expected value of its squared deviations from the mean. More intuitively, the mean μ of a continuous distribution is a measure of its center, or middle, and the standard deviation σ of a continuous distribution is a measure of its dispersion, or spread.

9.2   THE NORMAL DISTRIBUTION

Among many different continuous distributions used in statistics, the most important is the **normal distribution,** whose study dates back to eighteenth-century investigations concerning the nature of errors of measurement. It was observed that discrepancies among repeated measurement of the same physical quantity displayed a surprising degree of regularity. The distribution of the discrepancies could be closely approximated by a certain continuous curve, referred to as the "normal curve of errors" and attributed to the laws of chance. The mathematical equation for this type of curve is

$$f(x) = \frac{1}{\sigma\sqrt{2\pi}}\, e^{-\frac{1}{2}\left(\frac{x-\mu}{\sigma}\right)^2}$$

for $-\infty < x < \infty$, where e is the irrational number 2.71828 . . ., which we met on page 223 in connection with the Poisson distribution. We have given this equation only to point out some of the key features of normal distributions; it is not used in any of our calculations.

The graph of a normal distribution is a bell-shaped curve that extends indefinitely in both directions. Although this may not be apparent from a small drawing like that of Figure 9.5, the curve comes closer and closer to the horizontal

Normal distribution curve.

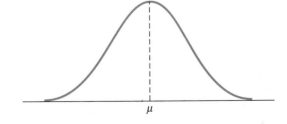

μ

axis without ever reaching it, no matter how far we go in either direction away from the mean. Fortunately, it is seldom necessary to extend the tails of a normal distribution very far because the area under the curve more than four or five standard deviations away from the mean is negligible for most practical purposes (see Exercise 9.14 on page 263.)

An important feature of normal distributions, apparent from the equation above, is that they depend only on the two quantities μ and σ, which are, indeed, the mean and the standard deviation. In other words, there is one and only one normal distribution with a given mean μ and a given standard deviation σ. The fact that we will get different curves depending on the values of μ and σ is illustrated by Figure 9.6. At the top there are two normal curves with unequal means but equal standard deviations; the curve to the right has the higher mean. In the middle are two normal curves with equal means but unequal standard deviations; the lower and flatter curve has the higher standard deviation. At the bottom are two normal curves with unequal means and unequal standard deviations.

In all our work with normal distributions, we shall be concerned only with areas under their curves—so-called **normal-curve areas**—and such areas are found in practice from tables such as Table I at the end of the book. As it is physically impossible, but also unnecessary, to construct separate tables of normal-curve areas for all conceivable pairs of values of μ and σ, we tabulate these areas only for the normal distribution with $\mu = 0$ and $\sigma = 1$, called the **standard normal distribution.** Then, we obtain areas under any normal curve by per-

Three pairs of normal distributions.

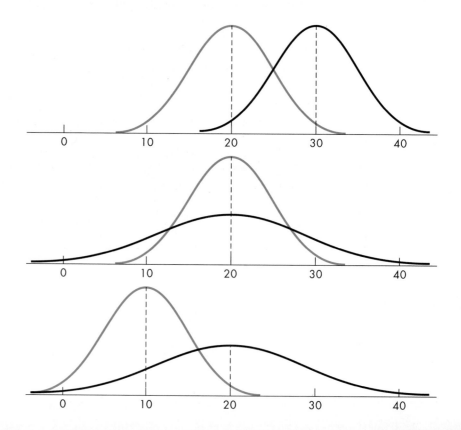

FIGURE 9.7

*Change of scale to
standard units.*

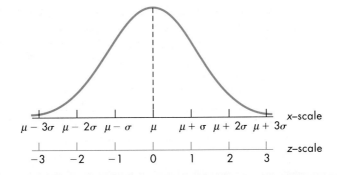

forming the change of scale (see Figure 9.7) which converts the units of measurement from the original scale, or x-scale, into **standard units, standard scores,
or z-scores,** by means of the formula

Standard Units

$$z = \frac{x - \mu}{\sigma}$$

In this new scale, the z-scale, a value of z simply tells us how many standard deviations the corresponding value of x lies above or below the mean of its distribution.

The entries in Table I are the areas under the standard normal curve between
the mean

$$z = 0 \quad \text{and} \quad z = 0.00, 0.01, 0.02, \quad \ldots, \quad 3.08, \quad \text{and} \quad 3.09$$

and also

$$z = 4.00, \quad z = 5.00, \quad \text{and} \quad z = 6.00$$

In other words, the entries in Table I are normal-curve areas like that of the
white region of Figure 9.8.

Table I has no entries corresponding to negative values of z, for these are not
needed by virtue of the symmetry of any normal curve about its mean. This follows from the equation on page 255, which remains unchanged when we substitute $-(x - \mu)$ for $x - \mu$. Specifically,

$$f(\mu - a) = f(\mu + a)$$

meaning that we get the same value for $f(x)$ when we go the distance a to the
left or right of μ.

FIGURE 9.8

*Tabulated normal-curve
areas.*

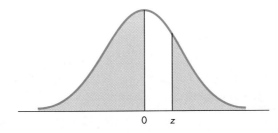

Example

Find the standard-normal-curve area between $z = -1.20$ and $z = 0$.

solution

As can be seen from Figure 9.9, the area under the curve between $z = -1.20$ and $z = 0$ equals the area under the curve between $z = 0$ and $z = 1.20$. So we look up the entry corresponding to $z = 1.20$ in Table I and we get 0.3849.   ◢ ◢ ◢

FIGURE 9.9

Symmetry of normal distribution.

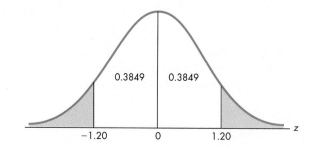

Questions concerning areas under normal distributions arise in various ways, and the ability to find any desired area quickly can be a big help. Although the table gives only areas between $z = 0$ and selected positive values of z, we often have to find areas to the left or to the right of given positive or negative values of z, or areas between two given values of z. This is easy, provided that we remember exactly what areas are represented by the entries in Table I, and also that the standard normal distribution is symmetrical about $z = 0$, so that the area under the curve to the left of $z = 0$ and that to the right of $z = 0$ are both equal to 0.5000.

Example

Find the standard-normal-curve area

(a) to the left of $z = 0.94$;   (b) to the right of $z = -0.65$;
(c) to the right of $z = 1.76$;   (d) to the left of $z = -0.85$;
(e) between $z = 0.87$ and $z = 1.28$;   (f) between $z = -0.34$ and $z = 0.62$.

solution

For each part refer to the corresponding diagram in Figure 9.10.

(a) The area to the left of $z = 0.94$ is 0.5000 plus the entry in Table I corresponding to $z = 0.94$ or

$$0.5000 + 0.3264 = 0.8264$$

(b) The area to the right of $z = -0.65$ is 0.5000 plus the entry in Table I corresponding to $z = 0.65$ or

$$0.5000 + 0.2422 = 0.7422$$

(c) The area to the right of $z = 1.76$ is 0.5000 minus the entry in Table I corresponding to $z = 1.76$ or

$$0.5000 - 0.4608 = 0.0392$$

(a)

(b)

(c)

(d)

(e)

(f)
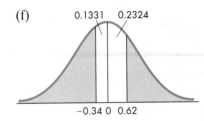

FIGURE 9.10   *Standard-normal-curve areas.*

(d)   The area to the left of $z = -0.85$ is 0.5000 minus the entry in Table I corresponding to $z = 0.85$ or

$$0.5000 - 0.3023 = 0.1977$$

(e)   The area between $z = 0.87$ and $z = 1.28$ is the difference between the entries in Table I corresponding to $z = 0.87$ and $z = 1.28$, or

$$0.3997 - 0.3078 = 0.0919$$

(f)   The area between $z = -0.34$ and $z = 0.62$ is the sum of the entries in Table I corresponding to $z = 0.34$ and $z = 0.62$, or

$$0.1331 + 0.2324 = 0.3655$$

In both of the preceding examples we dealt directly with the standard normal distribution. Now let us consider an example where μ and σ are not 0 and 1, so that we must first convert to standard units.

Example

If a random variable has the normal distribution with $\mu = 10$ and $\sigma = 5$, what is the probability that it will take on a value on the interval from 12 to 15?

solution

The probability is given by the area of the white region of Figure 9.11. Converting $x = 12$ and $x = 15$ to standard units, we get

$$z = \frac{12 - 10}{5} = 0.40 \quad \text{and} \quad z = \frac{15 - 10}{5} = 1.00$$

and since the corresponding entries in Table I are 0.1554 and 0.3413, we find that the probability asked for in this example is

$$0.3413 - 0.1554 = 0.1859$$

FIGURE 9.11

Normal-curve area.

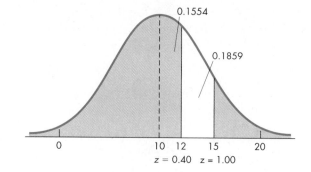

There are also problems in which we are given areas under normal curves and asked to find the corresponding values of z. The results of the example that follows will be used extensively in subsequent chapters.

Example

If z_α denotes the value of z for which the standard-normal-curve area to its right is equal to α (Greek lowercase *alpha*), find
(a) $z_{0.01}$; (b) $z_{0.05}$.

solution

For both parts refer to the diagram of Figure 9.12.
(a) Since $z_{0.01}$ corresponds to an entry of

$$0.5000 - 0.0100 = 0.4900$$

in Table I, we look for the entry closest to 0.4900 and find 0.4901 corresponding to $z = 2.33$; thus, we let

$$z_{0.01} = 2.33.$$

(b) Since $z_{0.05}$ corresponds to an entry of

$$0.5000 - 0.0500 = 0.4500$$

FIGURE 9.12

Determination of z_α.

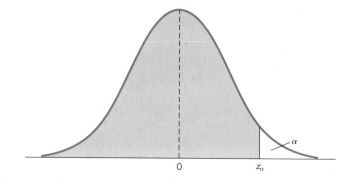

in Table I, we look for the entry closest to 0.4500 and find 0.4495 and 0.4505 corresponding to $z = 1.64$ and $z = 1.65$. Since 0.4500 is precisely halfway between these values, we let

$$z_{0.05} = 1.645.$$ ◢ ◢ ◢

Table I also enables us to verify the remark on pages 87 and 88 that for frequency distributions having the general shape of the cross section of a bell, about 68 percent of the values will lie within one standard deviation of the mean, about 95 percent will lie within two standard deviations of the mean, and about 99.7 percent will lie within three standard deviations of the mean. These percentages apply to frequency distributions having the general shape of a normal distribution, and the reader will be asked to verify them in the first three parts of Exercise 9.14. The other two parts of that exercise show that although the "tails" extend indefinitely in both directions, the standard-normal-curve area to the right of $z = 4$ or $z = 5$, or to the left of $z = -4$ or $z = -5$, is negligible.

Although this chapter is devoted to the normal distribution and its importance cannot be denied, it would be a serious mistake to think that the normal distribution is the only continuous distribution that matters in the study of statistics. In Chapter 11 and in subsequent chapters we shall meet other continuous distributions that play important roles in problems of statistical inference.

◢ EXERCISES

9.1   Explain in each case why the given equation cannot serve as that of the probability density of a continuous random variable that takes on values on the interval from 1 to 4:

(a) $f(x) = \frac{1}{4}$ for $1 \le x \le 4$;

(b) $f(x) = \frac{2}{15}(4x - 7)$ for $1 \le x \le 4$.

9.2   Explain in each case why the given equation cannot serve as that of a probability density of a continuous random variable on the interval from 0 to 10:

(a) $f(x) = \frac{1}{10}(x - 4)$ for $0 \le x \le 10$;

(b) $f(x) = \frac{1}{307}(64 - x^2)$ for $0 \le x \le 10$.

9.3   Figure 9.13 shows the graph of the **uniform distribution** of a random variable that takes on values on the interval from 2 to 10. Find the probabilities that this random variable will take on a value

(a) less than 7;   (b) between 2.4 and 8.8.

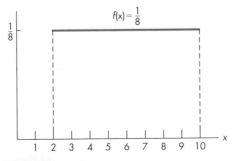

FIGURE 9.13   *Diagram for Exercise 9.3.*

9.4   Suppose that a random variable has the uniform distribution on the interval from 10 to 50 (see Exercise 9.3). Find the probabilities that this random variable will take on a value

(a) from 20 to 50;   (b) less than 20;

(c) greater than 45; (d) between 15 and 45.

9.5   With reference to the example on page 254 and Figure 9.4, what is the probability that the random variable will take on a value greater than 3?

9.6   Figure 9.14 shows the graph of the distribution of a continuous random variable that takes on values on the interval from -1 and 1. Find the probabilities that this random variable will take on a value

(a) between $\frac{1}{2}$ and 1;   (b) between $-\frac{1}{3}$ and $\frac{1}{3}$.

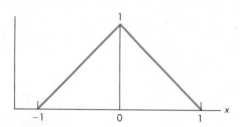

FIGURE 9.14   *Diagram for Exercise 9.6.*

9.7   For each of the cases cited below, involving areas under the standard normal curve, decide whether the first area is bigger, the second area is bigger, or the two areas are equal:

(a) the area to the right of $z = 1.5$ or the area to the right of $z = 2$;

(b) the area to the left of $z = -1.5$ or the area to the left of $z = -2$;

(c) the area to the right of $z = 1$ or the area to the left of $z = -1.5$;

(d) the area to the right of $z = 2$ or the area to the left of $z = -2$;

(e) the area to the right of $z = -2.5$ or the area to the right of $z = -1.5$;

(f) the area to the left of $z = 0$ or the area to the right of $z = -0.1$;

(g) the area to the right of $z = 0$ or the area to the left of $z = 0$;

(h) the area to the right of $z = -1.4$ or the area to the left of $z = -1.4$.

9.8   For each of the cases cited below, involving areas under the standard normal curve, decide whether the first area is bigger, the second area is bigger, or the two areas are equal:

(a) the area between $z = 0$ and $z = 1.3$ or the area between $z = 0$ and $z = 1$;

(b) the area between $z = -0.2$ and $z = 0.2$ or the area between $z = -0.4$ and $z = 0.4$;

(c) the area between $z = -1$ and $z = 1$ or the area between $z = 0$ and $z = 2$;

(d) the area between $z = 0.1$ and $z = 0.2$ or the area between $z = 1.1$ and $z = 1.2$;

(e) the area between $z = -1$ and $z = -0.5$ or the area between $z = 0.5$ and $z = 1$;

(f) the area to the left of $z = -1.5$ or the area to the right of $z = -0.5$;

(g) the area between $z = -1$ and $z = 1.5$ or the area between $z = -1.5$ and $z = 1$;

(h) the area between $z = 1$ and $z = 2$ or the area between $z = 2$ and $z = 4$.

9.9   Find the standard-normal-curve area that lies

(a) between $z = 0$ and $z = 0.87$;

(b) between $z = -1.66$ and $z = 0$;

(c) to the right of $z = 0.48$;

(d) to the right of $z = -0.27$;

(e) to the left of $z = 1.30$;

(f) to the left of $z = -0.79$.

9.10 Find the standard-normal-curve area that lies

(a) between $z = 0.28$ and $z = 1.28$;

(b) between $z = -1.08$ and $z = -0.55$;

(c) between $z = -0.35$ and $z = 0.25$;

(d) between $z = -0.90$ and $z = 1.35$.

9.11 Find the standard-normal-curve area that lies

(a) between $z = -0.70$ and $z = 0.92$;

(b) to the right of $z = 1.15$;

(c) to the left of $z = 0.22$;

(d) between $z = 0.24$ and $z = 1.82$;

(e) to the left of $z = -1.14$;

(f) to the right of $z = -0.76$;

(g) between $z = -1.82$ and $z = -0.79$.

9.12 Find z if the standard-normal-curve area

(a) is the area between 0 and z is 0.1915;

(b) to the left of z is 0.8078;

(c) to the left of z is 0.0132;

(d) between $-z$ and z is 0.8502.

9.13 Find z if the standard-normal-curve area

(a) between 0 and z is 0.4306;

(b) to the right of z is 0.7704;

(c) to the right of z is 0.1314;

(d) between $-z$ and z is 0.9700.

9.14 Find the standard-normal-curve area that lies between $-z$ and z if

(a) $z = 1$ or $z = -1$; (b) $z = 2$ or $z = -2$;

(c) $z = 3$ or $z = -3$; (d) $z = 4$ or $z = -4$;

(e) $z = 5$ or $z = -5$.

9.15 Find z if the area between z and $-z$ is

(a) 0.4038; (b) 0.8812;

(c) 0.3400; (d) 0.9576.

9.16 Verify that

(a) $z_{0.025} = 1.96$; (b) $z_{0.005} = 2.575$.

9.17 For each of the cases cited below, involving random variables with normal distributions, decide whether the first probability is bigger, the second probability is bigger, or the two probabilities are equal:

(a) for a random variable with a normal distribution with $\mu = 100$ and $\sigma = 20$, the probability of a value greater than 140 or the probability of a value greater than 130;

(b) for a random variable with a normal distribution with $\mu = 80$ and $\sigma = 20$, the probability of a value greater than 100 or the probability of a value less than 70;

(c) for a random variable with a normal distribution with $\mu = 60$ and $\sigma = 12$, the probability of a value between 48 and 72 or the probability of a value between 60 and 84;

(d) for a random variable with a normal distribution with $\mu = 200$ and $\sigma = 40$, the probability of a value greater than 250 or the probability of a value less than 140.

9.18   For each of the cases cited below, involving random variables with normal distributions, decide whether the first probability is bigger, the second probability is bigger, or the two probabilities are equal:

(a) the probability that a random variable having the normal distribution with $\mu = 50$ and $\sigma = 10$ takes a value less than 60 or the probability that a random variable having the normal distribution with $\mu = 500$ and $\sigma = 100$ takes a value less than 600;

(b) the probability that a random variable having the normal distribution with $\mu = 40$ and $\sigma = 5$ takes a value greater than 40 or the probability that a random variable having the normal distribution with $\mu = 50$ and $\sigma = 5$ takes a value greater than 40;

(c) the probability that a random variable having the normal distribution with $\mu = 50$ and $\sigma = 10$ takes a value less than 60 or the probability that a random variable having the normal distribution with $\mu = 50$ and $\sigma = 20$ takes a value less than 60;

(d) the probability that a random variable having the normal distribution with $\mu = 100$ and $\sigma = 5$ takes a value greater than 110 or the probability that a random variable having the normal distribution with $\mu = 108$ and $\sigma = 5$ takes a value greater than 110;

(e) the probability that a random variable having the normal distribution with $\mu = 5{,}000$ and $\sigma = 1{,}000$ takes a value between 4,000 and 6,000 or the probability that a random variable having the normal distribution with $\mu = 7{,}000$ and $\sigma = 1{,}000$ takes a value between 4,000 and 6,000.

9.19   If a random variable has the normal distribution with $\mu = 80.0$ and $\sigma = 4.8$, find the probabilities that it will take on a value

(a) less than 87.2;   (b) greater than 76.4;

(c) between 81.2 and 86.0;   (d) between 71.6 and 88.4.

9.20   If a random variable has the normal distribution with $\mu = 62.5$ and $\sigma = 12.4$, find the probabilities that it will take on a value

(a) less than 40.1;   (b) greater than 69.3;

(c) between 65.0 and 75.0;   (d) between 57.4 and 67.6.

9.21   A normal distribution has the mean $\mu = 62.4$. Find its standard deviation if 20 percent of the area under the curve lies to the right of 79.2.

9.22   A random variable has a normal distribution with $\sigma = 10$. If the probability that the random variable will take on a value less than 82.5 is 0.8212, what is the probability that it will take on a value greater than 58.3?

⊞ 9.23   Another continuous distribution, called the **exponential distribution,** has many important applications. If a random variable has an exponential distribution with the mean μ, the probability that it will take on a value between 0 and any given nonnegative value of x is $1 - e^{-x/\mu}$ (see Figure 9.15). Here e is the irrational number that also appears in the formula for the normal distribution. Many calculators have keys for computing expressions of the form $e^{-x/\mu}$, and selected values may be obtained from Table XI. Find the prob-

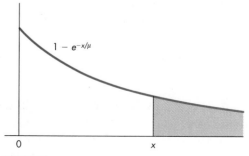

FIGURE 9.15   *Exponential distribution.*

abilities that a random variable having the exponential distribution with the mean $\mu = 10$ will take on a value

(a) less than 4; (b) between 5 and 9; (c) greater than 16.

9.24 The lifetime of a certain electronic component is a random variable that has the exponential distribution with the mean $\mu = 2,000$ hours. Use the formula of Exercise 9.23 to find the probabilities that such a component will last

(a) at most 2,400 hours;

(b) at least 1,600 hours;

(c) between 1,800 and 2,200 hours.

9.25 According to medical research, the time between successive reports of a rare tropical disease is a random variable having the exponential distribution with the mean $\mu = 120$ days. Find the probabilities that the time between successive reports of the disease will

(a) exceed 240 days;

(b) exceed 360 days;

(c) be less than 60 days.

9.26 In the region around a geological fault line, the time between aftershocks that follow a major earthquake is a random variable with the exponential distribution with mean $\mu = 36$ hours. Find the probabilities that the time between successive aftershocks will

(a) be less than 18 hours;

(b) exceed 72 hours;

(c) be between 36 and 108 hours.

9.3 CHECK FOR NORMALITY

There are various ways in which we can test whether an observed distribution has roughly the shape of a normal distribution. The one we present here is crude and largely subjective, but it has the decided advantage that it is very easy to perform.

To illustrate this technique, let us refer again to the sulfur oxides emission data which we used as an example in early chapters of the book. First we convert the cumulative frequencies of the table on page 26 into cumulative percentages by dividing each one by 80, the total frequency, and then multiplying by 100. This yields

Tons of sulfur oxides	Cumulative percentage
Less than 4.95	0.00
Less than 8.95	3.75
Less than 12.95	16.25
Less than 16.95	33.75
Less than 20.95	65.00
Less than 24.95	86.25
Less than 28.95	97.50
Less than 32.95	100.00

where we show the class boundaries instead of the class limits, although this does not really matter unless we continue with the analysis as in Exercise 9.31.

We plot this cumulative percentage distribution on special graph paper, called **normal probability paper** or **arithmetic probability paper.** The resulting graph is called a **normal probability plot.** This graph paper is available at college or university bookstores. The cumulative percent axis is preprinted with a scale suitable for our purposes, and the other scale has equal subdivisions which we label as we use it.

Once the cumulative "less than" percentages have been plotted as in Figure 9.16, we use the following criterion:

> If the points follow pretty much the pattern of a straight line, we consider this as positive evidence that the distribution has roughly the shape of a normal distribution.

Of course "pretty much" and "roughly" are not very precise terms, but we pointed out from the start that this is a crude and largely subjective technique, although it is easy to perform. The most common pattern in which the distribution would be declared "not normal" is one where the rightmost points fall below the straight line determined by the balance of the points. A more rigorous way of checking the "normality" of a distribution of observed data is explained in Exercise 13.97 on page 435.

Returning to Figure 9.16, we find that the points are all close to the dashed line, and we conclude that the distribution of the sulfur oxides emission data has roughly the shape of a normal distribution. Note that in Figure 9.16 we did not plot the cumulative percentages corresponding to 4.95 and 32.95. As we pointed out on page 255, we never quite reach 0 or 100 percent of the area under a normal curve, no matter how far away from the mean we go in either direction.

Normal probability plots can be produced with computer software. Figure 9.17 shows a computer-generated normal probability plot of the sulfur oxides emission data. An advantage of the computer plot is that one need not generate the cumulative frequency distribution. The computer plot also shows more detail.

FIGURE 9.16

Normal probability paper.

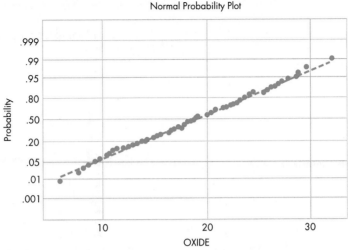

FIGURE 9.17

Normal probability plot
(Minitab 10 for Windows).

Normal Probability Plot

Average: 18.8962
Std Dev: 5.65646
N of data: 80

Anderson-Darling Normality Test
A-Squared: 0.172
p-value: 0.928

◢ EXERCISES

⇦ 9.27 The ages of the 240 persons in a jury pool were classified as follows:

Age group	Number of persons
29 or under	78
30 or over	162

Indicate why the methods of this section cannot be used to determine if this distribution has approximately the shape of a normal distribution.

⇦ 9.28 The following table is a distribution of the amounts of time 200 persons required to complete a certain job application:

Time (minutes)	Number of persons
24 or less	15
25–29	50
30–34	75
35–39	40
40–44	15
45 or over	5
Total	200

Use normal probability paper or computer software to check if this distribution has roughly the shape of a normal distribution.

⇔ 9.29   The following is the distribution of the dollar amounts owed on 180 unpaid electric bills:

Amount (dollars)	Number of bills
49.99 or less	68
50.00– 99.99	26
100.00–149.99	22
150.00–199.99	25
200.00–250.00	39
Total	180

Use normal probability paper or computer software to check whether this distribution has roughly the shape of a normal distribution.

⇔ 9.30   The following is the distribution of the numbers of inquiries a realty firm received about 500 pieces of property:

Number of inquiries	Frequency
3– 6	55
7–10	227
11–14	170
15–18	42
19–22	6
Total	500

Use normal probability paper or computer software to check whether this distribution has roughly the shape of a normal distribution.

⇔ 田 9.31   Normal probability paper can also be used to obtain crude estimates of the mean and the standard deviation of a distribution that has roughly the shape of a normal distribution. To estimate the mean, we observe that 50 percent of the area under any normal curve lies to the left of the mean. Hence, if we check the 50 percent mark on the cumulative percentage scale and go horizontally to the line we fit to the points then the corresponding value on the horizontal scale provides an estimate of the mean of the distribution. To estimate the standard deviation, we observe that the areas under the curve to the left of $z = -1$ and $z = +1$ are roughly 0.16 and 0.84. Hence, if we check 16 percent and 84 percent on the vertical scale, we can judge by the straight line we have fitted to the points what values on the horizontal scale correspond to $z = -1$ and $z = +1$; their difference divided by 2 provides an estimate of the standard deviation of the distribution. Use this method to estimate the mean and the standard deviation of the sulfur oxides emission data from Figure 9.16. Compare with $\bar{x} = 18.85$ and $s = 5.55$ obtained in Chapters 3 and 4.

⇔ 田 9.32   Use the method of Exercise 9.31 to estimate the mean and the standard deviation of the distribution of Exercise 9.28.

⇔ 田 9.33   Normal probability paper can also be used for ungrouped data. Begin by sorting the data values into increasing order. Then one point is plotted for each data value; the point corresponding to the ith largest of n values is given cumulative percentage

$$\frac{i}{n+1} \cdot 100$$

on the vertical scale. For example, the 15th largest of 86 values is given a cumulative percentage of

$$\frac{15}{86+1} \cdot 100 \approx 17.24$$

If n is large, say 30 or more, then the points will be very close together, and thus not all the points need to be plotted. As a reasonable guideline, the points for the 10 smallest and 10 largest values should be plotted, along with every tenth value between those.

Examine the following set of $n = 39$ data values, which have been sorted, and use normal probability paper to assess whether these seem to have roughly the shape of a normal distribution.

51.5	57.9	63.4	63.6	63.9	64.9	66.6	69.8
69.8	70.1	70.2	72.9	73.1	74.0	74.4	75.4
75.6	76.5	77.6	77.9	79.3	79.7	79.8	80.0
82.0	82.0	82.5	83.0	83.9	84.4	85.0	86.4
89.3	91.4	93.6	94.0	94.0	95.3	102.6	

⇧ ⊞ 9.34   The following $n = 49$ values, which have been sorted, were obtained as a random sample.

2.1	2.9	3.6	5.5	6.9	7.4	7.6
9.0	9.5	11.2	11.6	12.9	14.8	15.2
17.6	18.2	19.0	19.2	21.0	21.1	36.1
37.5	42.8	44.6	44.9	47.6	49.5	49.7
54.0	64.4	70.6	79.6	80.0	87.1	89.6
96.8	103.7	104.9	105.3	107.4	107.5	121.6
128.1	132.1	133.4	138.5	167.0	181.0	257.3

Use normal probability paper to assess whether these data seem to have roughly the shape of a normal distribution (see Exercise 9.33).

9.4   APPLICATIONS OF THE NORMAL DISTRIBUTION

Let us now consider some applications where it is assumed in each case that the distribution of the data, or the distribution of the random variable under consideration, can be approximated closely with a normal distribution.

Example

If the amount of cosmic radiation to which a person is exposed while flying by jet across the United States is a random variable having a normal distribution with $\mu = 4.35$ mrem and $\sigma = 0.59$ mrem, find the probabilities that a person on such a flight will be exposed to
(a) more than 5.00 mrem of cosmic radiation;
(b) anywhere from 3.00 to 4.00 mrem of cosmic radiation.

solution

(a) This probability is given by the area of the white region of the lefthand diagram of Figure 9.18, namely, the area under the curve to the right of

$$z = \frac{5.00 - 4.35}{0.59} \approx 1.10$$

Since the entry in Table I corresponding to $z = 1.10$ is 0.3643, we find that the probability is

$$0.5000 - 0.3643 = 0.1357 \quad \text{or approximately } 0.14$$

that a person will be exposed to more than 5.00 mrem of cosmic radiation on such a flight.

FIGURE 9.18

Diagrams for cosmic radiation example.

(b) This probability is given by the area of the white region of the righthand diagram of Figure 9.18, namely, the area under the curve between

$$z = \frac{3.00 - 4.35}{0.59} \approx -2.29 \quad \text{and} \quad z = \frac{4.00 - 4.35}{0.59} \approx -0.59$$

Since the entries in Table I corresponding to $z = 2.29$ and $z = 0.59$ are, respectively, 0.4890 and 0.2224, we find the probability is

$$0.4890 - 0.2224 = 0.2666, \quad \text{or approximately } 0.27$$

that a person will be exposed to anywhere from 3.00 to 4.00 mrem of cosmic radiation on such a flight.   ◪ ◪ ◪

Example

The actual amount of instant coffee that a filling machine deposits into "6-ounce" jars varies from jar to jar, and may be looked upon as a random variable having a normal distribution with a standard deviation of 0.04 ounce. If only 2 percent of the jars are to contain less than 6 ounces of coffee, what must be the mean fill of these jars?

solution

Here we are given $\sigma = 0.04$, $x = 6.00$, a normal-curve area (that of the white region of Figure 9.19), and we are asked to find μ. The value of z for which the entry of Table I is closest to

$$0.5000 - 0.0200 = 0.4800$$

is $z = 2.05$ (for which the table entry is 0.4798). The figure indicates that we seek the corresponding negative value, so we use $z = -2.05$ and establish the relation

$$-2.05 = \frac{6.00 - \mu}{0.04}$$

Then solving for μ, we obtain

$$6.00 - \mu = -2.05(0.04) = -0.082 \quad \text{and} \quad \mu = 6.00 + 0.082 = 6.082 \approx 6.08 \quad ◪ ◪ ◪$$

Although the normal distribution is a continuous distribution that applies to continuous random variables, it is often used to approximate distributions of discrete random variables, which can take on only a finite number of values or as many values as there are positive integers. To do this, we must use the **continuity correction** illustrated in the following example.

FIGURE 9.19

Diagram for instant-coffee filling machine example.

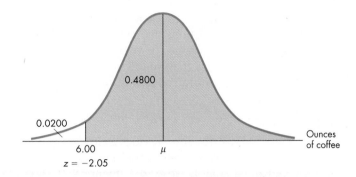

Example

In a study of aggressive behavior, male white mice, returning to their group after four weeks of isolation, average 18.6 fights in the first five minutes, with a standard deviation of 3.3 fights. If we can assume that the distribution of this random variable (the number of fights for each such mouse under the stated conditions) can be approximated closely with a normal distribution, what is the probability that such a mouse will have at least 15 fights in the first five minutes?

solution

The answer is shown by the white area of Figure 9.20; namely, by the area under the curve to the right of 14.5, and not 15 (because the number of fights in which the mouse is involved is a whole number). Hence, if we want to approximate the distribution of this random variable with a normal distribution, we must spread its values over a continuous scale, and we do this by representing each whole number k by the interval from $k - \frac{1}{2}$ to $k + \frac{1}{2}$. For instance, 5 is represented by the interval from 4.5 to 5.5, 10 is represented by the interval from 9.5 to 10.5, 20 is represented by the interval from 19.5 to 20.5, and the probability of 15 or more is shown by the area under the curve to the right of 14.5. Accordingly, we get

$$z = \frac{14.5 - 18.6}{3.3} \approx -1.24$$

and it follows from Table I that the area of the white region of Figure 9.20—the probability that such a mouse will get into at least 15 fights in the first five minutes—is

$$0.5000 + 0.3925 = 0.8925, \quad \text{or approximately } 0.89 \qquad \blacksquare \blacksquare \blacksquare$$

FIGURE 9.20

Diagram for example dealing with aggressive behavior of mice.

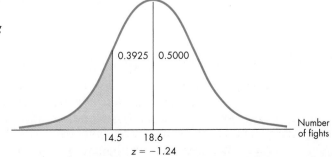

All the examples of this section dealt with random variables having normal distributions, or distributions that can be approximated closely with normal curves. When we observe a value (or values) of a random variable having a normal distribution, we may say that we are sampling a **normal population;** this is consistent with the terminology introduced at the end of Section 8.3.

9.5　　THE NORMAL APPROXIMATION TO THE BINOMIAL DISTRIBUTION

The normal distribution provides a close approximation to the binomial distribution when n, the number of trials, is large and p, the probability of a success on an individual trial, is close to $\frac{1}{2}$. Figure 9.21 shows the histograms of binomial distributions with

$$p = \frac{1}{2} \quad \text{and} \quad n = 2, 5, 10, \text{ and } 25$$

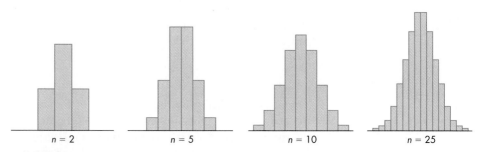

$n = 2$ 　　　 $n = 5$ 　　　 $n = 10$ 　　　 $n = 25$

FIGURE 9.21　　　*Binomial distributions with $p = \frac{1}{2}$.*

and it can be seen that with increasing n these distributions approach the symmetrical bell-shaped pattern of the normal distribution. In fact, normal distributions with the mean $\mu = np$ and the standard deviation $\sigma = \sqrt{np(1 - p)}$ can often be used to approximate binomial probabilities when n is not all that large and p differs quite a bit from $\frac{1}{2}$. Since "not all that large" and "differs quite a bit" are not very precise terms, let us state the following rule of thumb:

It is considered sound practice to use the normal approximation to the binomial distribution only when np and $n(1 - p)$ are both greater than 5; symbolically, when

$$np > 5 \quad \text{and} \quad n(1 - p) > 5$$

Example

Use the normal distribution to approximate the probability of getting 6 heads and 10 tails in 16 flips of a balanced coin, and compare the result with the corresponding value of Table V.

solution

It is reasonable to use the normal approximation since

$$np = 16 \cdot 0.5 = 8 \quad \text{and} \quad n(1 - p) = 16 \cdot (1 - 0.50) = 8$$

are both larger than 5. We will use the continuity correction, as explained on page 271, and represent 6 heads as the interval from 5.5 to 6.5. Hence, we just determine the area of the white region of Figure 9.22. Since

$$\mu = 16 \cdot \frac{1}{2} = 8 \quad \text{and} \quad \sigma = \sqrt{16 \cdot \frac{1}{2} \cdot \frac{1}{2}} = 2$$

we get $\quad z = \dfrac{5.5 - 8}{2} = -1.25 \quad \text{and} \quad z = \dfrac{6.5 - 8}{2} = -0.75$

in standard units for $x = 5.5$ and $x = 6.5$. The entries corresponding to 1.25 and 0.75 in Table I are 0.3944 and 0.2734, and we get

$$0.3944 - 0.2734 = 0.1210$$

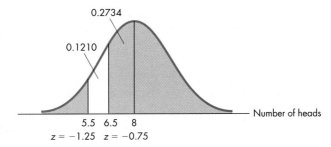

FIGURE 9.22

Normal approximation to a binomial distribution.

for the normal approximation to the probability of getting 6 heads and 10 tails in 16 flips of a balanced coin. Since the corresponding entry in Table V is 0.122, we find that the error of the approximation is 0.001.   ◿ ◿ ◿

Example

A study shows that 40 percent of all self-employed writers in a certain income bracket have Keogh retirement accounts. Use the normal distribution to approximate the probability that among 20 such writers, randomly selected from IRS files, 10 will have Keogh retirement accounts. Also compare the result with the corresponding value in Table V.

solution

It is reasonable to use the normal approximation since

$$np = 20 \cdot 0.4 = 8 \quad \text{and} \quad n(1 - p) = 20 \cdot (1 - 0.4) = 12$$

are both larger than 5. Using the continuity correction, we must find the area of the white region of Figure 9.23, namely, that between 9.5 and 10.5. Since

$$\mu = 20(0.40) = 8 \quad \text{and} \quad \sigma = \sqrt{20(0.40)(0.60)} \approx 2.19$$

we get $\quad z = \dfrac{9.5 - 8}{2.19} \approx 0.685 \quad \text{and} \quad z = \dfrac{10.5 - 8}{2.19} \approx 1.14$

FIGURE 9.23

Normal approximation to a binomial distribution.

in standard units for $x = 9.5$ and $x = 10.5$. The entries corresponding to 0.68 and 0.69 in Table I are 0.2517 and 0.2549, so that by interpolation we find that the area corresponding to 0.685 is

$$\frac{0.2517 + 0.2549}{2} = 0.2533$$

Also the area corresponding to 1.14 is 0.3729. Thus, we get

$$0.3729 - 0.2533 = 0.1196$$

for the normal approximation to the probability that 10 of the 20 self-employed writers will have Keogh retirement accounts. Since the corresponding entry in Table V is 0.117, we find that the error of the approximation is

$$0.1196 - 0.117 = 0.0026 \approx 0.003$$

(We round this error of approximation to three decimals since the exact answer of Table I is given only to three decimals.)   ◪ ◪ ◪

To assess the size of the error of an approximation like this, it usually helps to determine the **percentage error,** namely, the error expressed as a percentage of the quantity we are trying to approximate. For the example above we get

$$\frac{0.003}{0.117} \cdot 100\% \approx 2.6\%.$$

The normal approximation to the binomial distribution comes in very handy when we would otherwise have to use the formula for the binomial distribution repeatedly to calculate the values of many different terms.

Example

Suppose that 5 percent of the adobe bricks shipped by a manufacturer have blemishes. Use the normal distribution to approximate the binomial probability that among 150 adobe bricks shipped by the manufacturer at least eight will have blemishes. Also use the computer printout of Figure 8.4 on page 224 to determine the percentage error of this approximation.

solution

Using the continuity correction, we must find the area of the white region of Figure 9.24, namely, that to the right of 7.5. Since

FIGURE 9.24
Normal approximation to a binomial distribution.

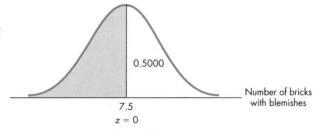

$$\mu = 150(0.05) = 7.5 \quad \text{and} \quad \sigma = \sqrt{150(0.05)(0.95)} \approx 2.67$$

we get

$$z = \frac{7.5 - 7.5}{2.67} = 0$$

in standard units for $x = 7.5$. Thus, the area under the curve to the right of 7.5 is 0.5000, and this is the normal approximation to the binomial probability that at least eight of the 150 adobe bricks will have blemishes. Since the printout of Figure 8.4 shows that the corresponding binomial probability is

$$1 - 0.5228 = 0.4772$$

we find that the error of the approximation is

$$0.5000 - 0.4772 = 0.0228$$

and hence that the percentage error is

$$\frac{0.0228}{0.4772} \cdot 100\% \approx 4.8 \text{ percent}$$ ◪ ◪ ◪

The adequacy of the approximations of the preceding examples depends on how they are to be used. Let us add that in addition to the rule of thumb on page 272, use of the normal approximation to the binomial distribution requires professional judgment. For instance, when p is quite small and we want to approximate the probability of a value that is not too close to the mean, the approximation may be poor even though the rule of thumb on page 272 is satisfied. As the reader will be asked to verify in Exercise 9.55 on page 277 if we had wanted to approximate the probability that there will be only one brick with blemishes among the 150 shipped by the manufacturer, the answer would have been more than twice the correct value. Since we do not expect the reader to become an instant expert at using the normal approximation to the binomial distribution, let us add that we have presented it here mainly because it will be needed in Chapter 13 for large-sample inferences concerning proportions.

 EXERCISES

9.35   If the time to assemble a computer desk from a kit is a random variable having the normal distribution with $\mu = 55$ minutes and $\sigma = 12$ minutes, what are the probabilities that this desk can be assembled in

(a) less than 45 minutes;

(b) anywhere from 45 minutes to 60 minutes;

(c) anywhere from 45 minutes to 75 minutes?

9.36 With reference to Exercise 9.35, for what value of x does it happen that the probability is 0.90 that one can assemble the desk in x minutes or less?

9.37 The reduction of a person's oxygen consumption during periods of transcendental meditation may be looked upon as a random variable having the normal distribution with $\mu = 38.6$ cc per minute and $\sigma = 6.5$ cc per minute. Find the probabilities that during a period of transcendental meditation a person's oxygen consumption will be reduced by

(a) at least 33.4 cc per minute;

(b) at most 34.7 cc per minute.

9.38 The sardines processed by a cannery have a mean length of 4.54 inches with a standard deviation of 0.25 inch. If the distribution of the lengths of the sardines can be approximated closely with a normal distribution, what percentage of the sardines are

(a) shorter than 4.00 inches;

(b) between 4.40 and 4.60 inches long?

9.39 With reference to Exercise 9.38, find x so that only 20 percent of the sardines processed by the cannery are longer than x.

9.40 In a certain photographic process, the developing time of prints may be looked upon as a random variable having the normal distribution with $\mu = 16.20$ seconds and $\sigma = 0.52$ second. Find the probabilities that the time it takes to develop one of the prints will be

(a) at least 17 seconds;

(b) at most 16 seconds;

(c) anywhere from 16 to 17 seconds.

9.41 With reference to the filling-machine example on page 270, show that 97.7 percent of the jars will contain at least 6 ounces of coffee if the machine is adjusted so that $\mu = 6.02$ ounces and $\sigma = 0.01$ ounce.

9.42 In a very large class in European history, the final examination grades have a mean of 71.6 and a standard deviation of 12.6. If it is reasonable to approximate the distribution of these grades with a normal distribution, what percentage of the grades should exceed 79?

9.43 The yearly number of major earthquakes, the world over, is a random variable having approximately the normal distribution with $\mu = 20.8$ and $\sigma = 4.5$. Find the probabilities that in any given year there will be

(a) exactly 19 major earthquakes;

(b) at most 19 major earthquakes;

(c) at least 19 major earthquakes.

9.44 An airline knows that the number of suitcases it loses per week on a certain route is a random variable having approximately the normal distribution with $\mu = 26.2$ and $\sigma = 5.8$. Find the probabilities that in one week on the given route it will lose

(a) exactly 22 suitcases;

(b) at most 22 suitcases;

(c) at least 22 suitcases.

9.45 With reference to the example on page 271, what is the probability that such a mouse will get into exactly 15 fights in the first five minutes?

9.46 Check in each case whether the conditions for the normal approximation to the binomial distribution are satisfied:

(a) $n = 16$ and $p = \frac{1}{4}$;

(b) $n = 65$ and $p = 0.10$;

(c) $n = 120$ and $p = 0.98$.

9.47 Check in each case whether the conditions for the normal approximation to the binomial distribution are satisfied:

(a) $n = 200$ and $p = 0.01$;

(b) $n = 150$ and $p = 0.97$;

(c) $n = 100$ and $p = \frac{1}{8}$;

9.48 Use the normal distribution to approximate the probability of getting 7 heads and 7 tails in 14 flips of a balanced coin. Also refer to Table V to find the error of this approximation.

9.49 Use the normal approximation to the binomial to find the probability of getting exactly 12 heads in 20 flips of a balanced coin. If the exact probability of getting exactly 12 heads in 20 flips is 0.120134, find the error of the approximation.

9.50 Use the normal distribution to approximate the probability that at most 40 of 225 loan applications received by a bank will be refused, if the probability is 0.20 that any such loan application will be refused.

9.51 Use the normal distribution to approximate the probability that at most 20 of 40 clouds seeded with silver iodide will show spectacular growth, if the probability is 0.62 that any cloud seeded with silver iodide will show spectacular growth.

9.52 Use a computer printout of the binomial distribution with $n = 40$ and $p = 0.62$ to find the error of the approximation of Exercise 9.51.

9.53 Use the normal distribution to approximate the probability that at most 12 of 50 patients will get a headache from using a certain kind of medication, if the probability is 0.22 that any one patient will get a headache from using the medication.

9.54 Use a computer printout of the binomial distribution with $n = 50$ and $p = 0.22$ to find the percentage error of the approximation of Exercise 9.53.

9.55 Use the printout of Figure 8.4 on page 224 to show that if we use the normal distribution to approximate the binomial probability with $x = 1$, $n = 150$, and $p = 0.05$, the percentage error is about 117 percent.

9.56 Use the normal distribution to approximate the probability that at least 55 of 90 persons flying across the Atlantic Ocean will feel the effect of the time difference for at least 24 hours, if the probability is 0.70 that any one person flying across the Atlantic Ocean will feel the effect of the time difference for at least 24 hours.

9.57 Use a computer printout of the binomial distribution with $n = 90$ and $p = 0.70$ to find the percentage error of the approximation of Exercise 9.56.

9.58 Use the normal distribution to approximate the probability that at least 150 of 800 subscribers of cable television will pay extra to watch a certain sporting event, if the probability is 0.18 that any one subscriber will pay to watch this sporting event.

9.59 In some situations we can use either the normal approximation or the Poisson approximation to the binomial distribution, in some situations we can use one but not the other, and in some situations we can use neither. Check in each case whether we can use the normal approximation and/or the Poisson approximation to the binomial distribution:

(a) $n = 50$ and $p = \frac{1}{12}$;   (b) $n = 200$ and $p = 0.06$;

(c) $n = 100$ and $p = 0.04$;   (d) $n = 100$ and $p = 0.08$.

9.60 For a certain brand of lawn mower, the probability is 0.07 that it will need in-store servicing before being placed on the sales floor. You wish to find the probability that exactly three of 120 of these lawn mowers will need in-store servicing. Either the normal approximation or the Poisson approximation may be used for this binomial distribution with $n = 120$ and $p = 0.07$.

(a) Find the exact binomial probability that three of 120 of these lawn mowers will need in-store servicing.

(b) Use the normal approximation to obtain a value for this probability.

(c) Use the Poisson approximation to obtain a value for this probability.

⊞ 9.61   In Exercise 9.55 the reader was asked to verify that the normal distribution yields a very poor approximation to the binomial probability with $x = 1$, $n = 150$, and $p = 0.05$. Show that for the Poisson approximation the percentage error is only 15 percent (compared to 117 percent).

9.6   TECHNICAL NOTE (Simulation) ⇧

There are several ways to simulate values of continuous random variables. Tables of **random normal numbers** can be used for this purpose, but it is now more common to utilize computer software. Figure 9.25 shows a computer run that produced 20 values of a random variable having the standard normal distribution.

FIGURE 9.25

Computer simulation of 20 values of a random variable having the standard normal distribution (MINITAB 10 for Windows).

```
MTB  > Random 20 C1;
SUBC >    Normal 0.0 1.0.   – st. D.
MTB  > print C1.                |
                              mean
Data Display


C1
   0.35811       0.89907       0.05196      -0.26583      -0.90180
   1.58087       0.30219      -1.08310       0.53617      -0.17710
  -0.77559      -0.26256       0.08047       0.38734      -1.11132
  -0.66831      -1.07554      -0.76137       1.33531      -0.53266
```

Example

In a certain city, the time it takes the police to respond to emergencies may be regarded as a random variable having the normal distribution with $\mu = 7.3$ minutes and $\sigma = 0.6$ minute. Use computer software to simulate the times that it takes the police in this city to respond to five emergencies.

solution

This is done readily with computer software, and a possible result is shown in Figure 9.26.   ◢ ◢ ◢

FIGURE 9.26

Computer simulation of five values of a random variable having the normal distribution with $\mu = 7.3$ and $\sigma = 0.6$ (MINITAB 10 for Windows).

```
MTB  > Random 5 C1;
SUBC >    Normal 7.3 0.6.
MTB  > print C1.


Data Display


C1
   8.07242       7.05576       7.26181       7.97928       6.85246
```

■ EXERCISES

9.62 The time it takes a person to learn how to operate a certain piece of machinery is a random variable having the normal distribution with $\mu = 5.6$ hours and $\sigma = 1.2$ hours. Simulate the times it takes eight persons to learn how to operate the piece of machinery.

9.63 The scores of college-bound high school seniors on a certain standardized test may be regarded as values of a random variable having the normal distribution with $\mu = 54.3$ and $\sigma = 6.2$. Rounding the results to the nearest whole numbers, simulate the scores of 12 college-bound high school seniors on this test.

9.64 Suppose that the increase in the pulse rate of a person performing a certain strenuous task is a random variable having the normal distribution with $\mu = 28.40$ and $\sigma = 4.17$. Rounding the results to one decimal, simulate the increase in the pulse rate of 20 persons performing the given task.

9.65 The weights of grapefruits shipped by a large orchard are values of a random variable having the normal distribution with $\mu = 19.6$ ounces and $\sigma = 2.2$ ounces. Rounding the results to one decimal, simulate the weights of 24 grapefruits shipped by the orchard.

9.7 CHECKLIST OF KEY TERMS† (*with page references to their definitions*)

⊖ Arithmetic probability paper, 265
Continuity correction, 270
Continuous distribution, 253
⊖ *Exponential distribution,* 264
Normal approximation to binomial
   distribution, 272
Normal distribution, 255
Normal population, 272
⊖ Normal probability paper, 265
⊖ Normal probability plot, 265

Normal-curve areas, 256
Percentage error, 274
Probability density, 253
⊖ Random normal numbers, 278
Standard normal distribution, 256
Standard scores, 257
Standard units, 257
Uniform distribution, 261
z-score, 257

9.8 REVIEW EXERCISES

9.66 The time required for an oil change at the Speedy Oil station is a random variable having the normal distribution with $\mu = 9.2$ minutes and $\sigma = 82$ seconds. Find the probability that an oil change will take

(a) at most 10.6 minutes; (b) anywhere from 9.0 minutes to 11.0 minutes.

9.67 Use the normal distribution to approximate the probability of getting 12 heads in 20 flips of a balanced coin. Refer to Table V to determine the error of this approximation.

9.68 Find the standard-normal-curve area that lies

(a) between $z = 0$ and $z = 1.83$; (b) to the left of $z = 2.50$;

(c) to the right of $z = -0.64$; (d) to the right of $z = 1.24$;

(e) to the left of $z = -0.71$.

9.69 If a random variable has the normal distribution with $\mu = 102.4$ and $\sigma = 3.6$, find the probabilities that it will take on a value

(a) less than 107.8; (b) greater than 99.7;

(c) between 106.9 and 110.5; (d) between 96.1 and 104.2.

†Terms introduced in exercises are shown in *italics*.

9.70   Find the values of

(a) $z_{0.02}$; (b) $z_{0.10}$.

9.71   The following is the distribution of the miles per gallon obtained with 200 cars:

Miles per gallon	Frequency
18.0–19.9	2
20.0–21.9	10
22.0–23.9	19
24.0–25.9	39
26.0–27.9	62
28.0–29.9	37
30.0–31.9	20
32.0–33.9	8
34.0–35.9	3
Total	200

Use normal probability paper or computer software to check whether this distribution has roughly the shape of a normal curve.

9.72   If the probability of a bad reaction to a routine allergy injection is 0.09, use the normal distribution to approximate the probability that at most 20 persons will have a bad reaction, out of 200 receiving routine allergy injections.

9.73   Suppose that the time it takes to complete a certain new tax form is a random variable having the normal distribution with $\mu = 32.6$ minutes and $\sigma = 4.5$ minutes. Simulate the time it takes 12 persons to complete the new tax form.

9.74   Figure 9.27 shows the probability density of a continuous random variable that takes on values on the interval from 0 to $1\frac{1}{2}$.

(a) Verify that the total area under the graph of the density is equal to 1.

(b) Find the probability that the random variable will take a value less than $\frac{3}{4}$.

(c) Find the probability that the random variable will take a value greater than $\frac{1}{2}$.

(d) Find the probability that the random variable will take a value between $\frac{1}{4}$ and $1\frac{1}{4}$.

9.75   The number of complaints received by the complaint department of a department store per day is a random variable that has approximately the normal distribution with $\mu = 48.4$ and $\sigma = 7.5$. Approximately, what are the probabilities that on any one day they will receive

(a) at least 55 complaints;

(b) anywhere from 40 to 50 complaints?

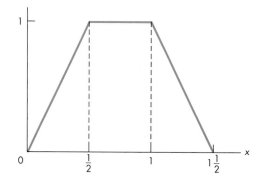

FIGURE 9.27

Diagram for Exercise for 9.74.

9.76   A random variable has a normal distribution with $\sigma = 4.0$. If the probability is 0.9713 that this random variable will take on a value less than 87.6, what is the probability that it will take on a value in excess of 75.0?

9.77   The average time required to perform job A is 90 minutes with a standard deviation of 12 minutes. The average time required to perform job B is 102 minutes with a standard deviation of 18 minutes. If the times have approximately a normal distribution, find

(a) the proportion of time that job A will take longer than the average job B;

(b) the proportion of time that job B will take longer than the average job A.

9.78   Use the normal distribution to approximate the probabilities that a random variable having the binomial distribution with $n = 28$ and $p = 0.31$ will take on a value

(a) less than 9;   (b) anywhere from 7 to 11.

9.79   Find the standard-normal-curve area that lies

(a) between $z = 0$ and $z = -1.11$;

(b) between $z = -0.63$ and $z = 0.63$;

(c) between $z = 0.40$ and $z = 0.55$;

(d) between $z = -1.18$ and $z = -0.68$;

(e) between $z = -1.22$ and $z = 1.82$.

9.80   Check in each case whether the conditions for the normal approximation to the binomial distribution are satisfied:

(a) $n = 40$ and $p = \frac{1}{5}$;   (b) $n = 135$ and $p = \frac{1}{45}$;

(c) $n = 150$ and $p = \frac{1}{25}$; (d) $n = 50$ and $p = 0.95$.

9.81   If the weekly number of muggings reported in a certain precinct is a random variable having the normal distribution with $\mu = 25.3$ and $\sigma = 5.5$, find the probabilities that in any one week

(a) 27 muggings will be reported;

(b) at least 27 muggings will be reported.

9.82   Find z if the standard-normal curve area

(a) between 0 and z is 0.2019;

(b) to the right of z is 0.8810;

(c) to the right of z is 0.1788;

(d) between $-z$ and z is 0.4038.

9.83   To illustrate the Law of Large Numbers that we mentioned in Sections 5.4 and 8.8, use the normal approximation to the binomial distribution to find the probabilities that the proportion of heads will be anywhere from 0.49 to 0.51 when a balanced coin is flipped

(a) 1,000 times;   (b) 10,000 times.

9.9   REFERENCES

More detailed tables of normal-curve areas, as well as tables for some other continuous distributions, may be found in

FISHER, R. A., and YATES, F., *Statistical Tables for Biological, Agricultural and Medical Research.* Cambridge: The University Press, 1954.

PEARSON, E. S., and HARTLEY, H. O., *Biometrika Tables for Statisticians,* Vol. I. New York: John Wiley & Sons, Inc., 1968.

and in other handbooks of statistical tables. Extensive tables of random normal numbers are given in the RAND Corporation tables listed on page 250. Detailed information about various continuous distributions may be found in

HASTINGS, N. A. J., and PEACOCK, J. B., *Statistical Distributions.* London: Butterworth & Company (Publishers) Ltd., 1975.

Further information about the normal approximation to the binomial distribution may be found in

GREEN, J., and ROUND-TURNER, J., "The Error in Approximating Cumulative Binomial and Poisson Probabilities," *Teaching Statistics,* May 1986.

Sampling and Sampling Distributions

A *principal objective of most statistical studies, analyses or investigations is to make sound generalizations, based on samples, about the populations from which the samples originated. Note the word "sound," because the question of when and under what conditions samples permit such generalizations is not easily answered. For instance, if we want to estimate the average amount of money a person spends on a vacation, would we take as our sample the amounts spent by luxury-class passengers on a four-week cruise? If we want to predict the wholesale price of all farm products, would we base this prediction on the price of asparagus alone? Obviously we would not, but just what vacationers and what farm products we should include, and how many of them, is neither obvious nor self-evident.*

In most of the methods we study in the remainder of this book, it will be assumed that we are dealing with random samples. We pay this much attention to random samples, which are defined and discussed in Section 10.1, because they permit valid, or logical, generalizations. As we shall see, however, random sampling is not always feasible, or even desirable, and some alternative sampling procedures are mentioned in the optional Sections 10.2 through 10.5.

In Section 10.6 we introduce the related concept of a sampling distribution, which tells us how quantities determined from samples may vary from sample to sample. Then, in Sections 10.7 through 10.9, we learn how such chance variations can be measured, predicted, and perhaps even controlled. ◪

10.1   RANDOM SAMPLING

In Section 3.1 we distinguished between populations and samples, stating that a population consists of all conceivably possible (or hypothetically possible) observations of a given phenomenon, while a sample is simply part of a population. In what follows, we distinguish further between two kinds of populations: **finite populations** and **infinite populations.**

A population is finite if it consists of a finite, or fixed, number of elements, measurements, or observations. Examples of finite populations are the net weights of the 3,000 cans of paint in a certain production lot, the SAT scores of all the applicants to a given college for the term beginning in the fall of 1995, and the daily high temperatures recorded at a weather station during the years 1985–1995.

In contrast to finite populations, a population is infinite if it contains, hypothetically at least, infinitely many elements. This is the case, for example, when we observe a value of a continuous random variable and there are infinitely many different outcomes. It is also the case when we observe the totals obtained in repeated rolls of a pair of dice, when we repeatedly measure the boiling point of a silicon compound, and when we sample with replacement from a finite population. There is no limit to the number of times that we can roll a pair of dice, no limit to the number of times that we can measure the boiling point of the silicon compound, and no limit to the number of times that we can draw a sample from a finite population and replace it before the next one is drawn.

To present the idea of **random sampling from a finite population,** let us first see how many different samples of size n can be drawn from a finite population of size N. Referring to the rule for the number of combinations of n objects taken r at a time on page 113, we find that, with a change of letters, the answer is $\binom{N}{n}$.

Example

How many different samples of size n can be drawn from a finite population of size N, when
(a) $n = 2$ and $N = 12$;   (b) $n = 3$ and $N = 100$?

solution

(a) There are

$$\binom{12}{2} = \frac{12 \cdot 11}{2!} = 66 \text{ different samples}$$

(b) There are

$$\binom{100}{3} = \frac{100 \cdot 99 \cdot 98}{3!} = 161{,}700 \text{ different samples}$$

Based on the result that there are $\binom{N}{n}$ different samples of size n from a finite population of size N, let us now give the following definition of a **random sample** (sometimes referred to also as a **simple random sample**) from a finite population:

A sample of size n from a finite population of size N is random if it is chosen in such a way that each of the $\binom{N}{n}$ possible samples has the same probability, $\dfrac{1}{\binom{N}{n}}$, of being selected.

For instance, if a population consists of the $N = 5$ elements a, b, c, d, and e (which might be the annual incomes of five persons, the weights of five cows, or the prices of five commodities), there are

$$\binom{5}{3} = 10$$

possible samples of size $n = 3$. They consist of the elements abc, abd, abe, acd, ace, ade, bcd, bce, bde, and cde. If we choose one of these samples in such a way that each sample has the probability $\frac{1}{10}$ of being selected, we call this sample a random sample.

Next comes the question of how random samples are drawn in actual practice. In a simple situation like the one described immediately above, we could write each of the 10 samples on a slip of paper, put them in a hat, shuffle them thoroughly, and then draw one without looking. Obviously, though, this would be impractical in a more realistically complex situation where n and N, or only N, are large. For instance, for $n = 4$ and $N = 200$ we would have to label and draw one of

$$\binom{200}{4} = 64{,}684{,}950$$

slips of paper.

Fortunately, we can draw a random sample from a finite population without listing all possible samples, which we mentioned here only to stress the point that the selection of a random sample must depend entirely on chance. Instead of listing all possible samples, we can write each of the N elements of the finite population on a slip of paper, and draw n of them one at a time without replacement, making sure in each of the successive drawings that all of the remaining elements of the population have the same chance of being selected. As the reader will be asked to verify in Exercise 10.14 on page 289, this procedure also leads to the same probability,

$$\frac{1}{\binom{N}{n}}$$

for each possible sample.

This relatively easy procedure can be simplified further by choosing random numbers instead of drawing slips of paper. We can exploit tables of random numbers for this purpose or, more likely, we can utilize computer software.

Example

Draw a random sample of size $n = 12$ from the population which consists of the amounts of sales tax collected by a city's 247 drugstores in December 1995.

solution

Number the stores from 1 to 247. One possible selection is shown in the computer output of Figure 10.1. As can be seen, the numbers selected are

159	98	63	68	208	85
34	71	241	129	48	216

The drugstores associated with these numbers form the random sample.   ◪ ◪ ◪

Proper random sampling requires that we have a list of all N items in the population, so that we can assign each item one of the numbers from 1 to N. Such a list is called a **sampling frame.** The use of the sampling frame makes it easy to draw random samples with the aid of computers or random number tables. Unfortunately, there are many situations in which it is not possible to construct a sampling frame. For instance, if we want to use a sample to estimate the mean

FIGURE 10.1

Computer-generated random sample (MINITAB 10 for Windows).

```
MTB  > Set C1
DATA >    1( 1 : 247 / 1 )1
DATA >    End.
MTB  > Sample 12 C1 C2.
MTB  > print C2.

Data Display


C2
     159        98       63       68      2Ø8       85
      34        71      241      129       48      216
```

outside diameter of thousands of ball bearings packed in a large crate, or if we want to estimate the mean height of the trees in a forest, it would be impossible to number the ball bearings or the trees, choose random numbers, and then locate and measure the corresponding ball bearings or trees. In these and in many similar situations, all we can do is proceed according to the dictionary definition of the word "random," namely, "haphazard, without aim or purpose." That is, we must not select or reject any element of a population because of its seeming typicalness or lack of it, nor must we favor or ignore any part of a population because of its accessibility or lack of it, and so on. With some reservations, such samples are often treated as if they were random samples.

So far we have discussed random sampling only in connection with finite populations. For infinite populations we say that

> A sample of size n from an infinite population is random if it consists of values of independent random variables having the same distribution.

As we pointed out in connection with the binomial and normal distributions, it is this "same" distribution that we refer to as the population being sampled. Also, by "independent" we mean that the probabilities relating to any one of the random variables are the same regardless of what values may have been observed for the other random variables.

For instance, if we get 2, 5, 1, 3, 6, 4, 4, 5, 2, 4, 1, and 2 in twelve rolls of a die, these numbers constitute a random sample if they are values of independent random variables having the same probability distribution

$$f(x) = \frac{1}{6} \qquad \text{for } x = 1, 2, 3, 4, 5, \text{ or } 6$$

To give another example of a random sample from an infinite population, suppose that eight students obtained the following measurements of the boiling point of a silicon compound: 136, 153, 170, 148, 157, 152, 143, and 150 degrees Celsius. According to the definition, these values constitute a random sample if they are values of independent random variables having the same distribution, say, the normal distribution with $\mu = 152$ and $\sigma = 10$. To judge whether this is actually the case, we would have to ascertain among other things, that the eight students' measuring techniques are equally precise (so that σ is the same for each of the random variables), that there was no collaboration (which might make the random variables dependent), and that there were no impurities in the raw material. In practice, it is not an easy task to judge whether a set of data may be looked upon as a random sample, and we shall go into this further in Section 17.9.

■ EXERCISES

10.1   How many different samples of size $n = 2$ can be selected from a finite population of size
(a) $N = 4$;   (b) $N = 8$;   (c) $N = 20$;   (d) $N = 200$?

10.2   How many different samples of size $n = 3$ can be selected from a finite population of size
(a) $N = 5$;   (b) $N = 12$;   (c) $N = 36$;   (d) $N = 120$?

10.3   What is the probability of each possible sample if
(a) a random sample of size 4 is to be drawn from a finite population of size 12;
(b) a random sample of size 5 is to be drawn from a finite population of size 22?

10.4   With reference to the example on page 285 where we listed all possible samples of size $n = 3$ from the finite population which consists of the elements a, b, c, d, and e, what is the probability that a random sample of size $n = 3$ from this population will contain a specific element, say, the element c?

10.5   List the $\binom{7}{3} = 35$ possible samples of size $n = 3$ that can be drawn from a finite population whose elements are denoted by a, b, c, d, e, f, and g.

10.6   With reference to Exercise 10.5, what is the probability that a random sample of size $n = 3$
(a) will include the element denoted by the letter c;
(b) will include the element denoted by the letter d;
(c) will include the elements denoted by the letters c and d?

10.7   List all possible choices of two of the following six airlines: TWA, American, United, Northwest, Delta, and U.S. Air. If a person randomly selects two of these airlines to study their safety records, find the probability
(a) of each possible sample;
(b) that TWA will be included in the sample.

10.8   A hematologist wants to recheck a sample of $n = 10$ of the 854 blood specimens analyzed by a medical laboratory in a given month. He creates a sampling frame by numbering the specimens as 001, 002, 003, . . . , 853, and 854. Using a computer, he obtains the following sequence of random digits:

> 87823 53256 10686 41497 34560 68314 73474 75120 92638 37130
> 44503 13769 85619 36577 67255 52439 55403 16113 06744 37208
> 04778 24884 43285 56072 02936 33322 46265 60012 35288 53021
> 69328 15666 80382 63848 27829 98564 16683 05034 29066 50739

If he uses the first three digits of each five-digit set (thus starting with 878, 532, 106, . . .), which blood specimens will be selected? (*Note:* In selecting this sample from random digits, the values 000 and all integers from 855 to 899 should be ignored.)

10.9   A county assessor wants to reassess a random sample of 20 of the county's 7,964 one-family homes. She creates a sampling frame by assigning them the numbers

> 0001   0002   . . .   7963   7964

She then obtains the following section of a random number table:

```
23332 57255 99287 46441 91561 67740 45041 13962 44044 92153
53206 35845 30111 72106 85895 06326 43281 46571 30792 29143
39551 80772 94732 65467 01105 92384 28019 88926 69408 12635
95974 75400 34361 41920 87278 92499 58548 78176 98774 75134
```

If she uses the final four digits of each five-digit set (thus starting with 3332, 7255, 9287, ...), which one-family homes will she select? (*Note:* In selecting this sample from random digits, the values 0000 and all integers from 7965 to 9999 should be ignored.)

10.10 A water resources scientist wants to include 12 of the 67 counties of Florida in a ground-water purity survey. He creates a sampling frame by assigning these counties the numbers 01, 02, ..., 67, and then obtains the following sequence of computer-generated random digits;

```
49126 23009 74448 47332 20783 49648 31957 63933 27819 68735
81745 00890 69134 91862 09460 09284 12782 38845 19203 63677
10219 16922 77315 12864 52029 08072 90548 48805 57491 66749
```

If he uses pairs of consecutive digits (and thus starting with 49, 12, 62, 30, ...), which counties will he select? (*Note:* In selecting this sample from random digits, the values 00 and all integers from 68 to 99 should be ignored.)

10.11 Suppose that you have a population of 40 items and you wish to take a sample of size 4. Suppose that you use a random number table to make the selection. What is the probability that the first four numbers you choose will involve no duplicates?

10.12 On page 286 we said that a random sample can be drawn from a finite population by choosing the elements to be included in the sample one at a time, making sure in each of the successive drawings that all remaining elements of the population have the same chance of being selected. Consider the example on page 285, in which samples of size $n = 3$ were to be drawn from the finite population consisting of the elements a, b, c, d, and e. Consider the probability of selecting the sample that consists of the letters b, c, and d.

(a) What is the probability that the first item selected for the sample will be one of the letters b, c, or d?

(b) What is the probability that the first two items selected for the sample will be two of the letters b, c, or d?

(c) What is the probability that the three items selected for the sample will be b, d, and c?

10.13 Use the same kind of argument as in Exercise 10.12 to verify that

(a) each possible random sample of size $n = 3$, drawn one at a time from a finite population of size $N = 100$, has the probability

$$\frac{1}{\binom{100}{3}} = \frac{1}{161{,}700}$$

(b) each possible random sample of size n, drawn one at a time from a finite population of size $N = 200$, has the probability

$$\frac{1}{\binom{200}{3}} = \frac{1}{1{,}313{,}400}$$

10.14 Use the same kind of argument as in Exercise 10.12 to verify that each possible random sample of size n, drawn one at a time from a finite population of size N, has the probability

$$\frac{1}{\binom{N}{n}}$$

10.15   Randy McGill and Susan Martin are both members of a population of 50 students. A researcher is going to select 5 students from this population.
(a) What is the probability that Randy will be in the sample?
(b) What is the probability that Susan will be in the sample?
(c) What is the probability that both Randy and Susan will be in the sample?
(d) Is your solution to part (c) greater than or less than

$$\left(\frac{5}{50}\right)^2 = \frac{1}{100}?$$

10.2   SAMPLE DESIGNS ⇔

The only kind of samples we have discussed so far are random samples, and we did not even consider the possibility that under certain conditions there may be samples that are better (say, easier to obtain, cheaper, or more informative) than random samples, and we did not go into any details about the question of what might be done when random sampling is impossible. Indeed, there are many other ways of selecting a sample from a population, and there is an extensive literature devoted to the subject of designing sampling procedures.

In statistics, a **sample design** is a definite plan, determined completely before any data are actually collected, for obtaining a sample from a given population. Thus, the plan to take a simple random sample of 12 of a city's 247 drugstores by using a table of random numbers in a prescribed way constitutes a sample design. In the next three sections we discuss briefly some of the most widely used kinds of sample designs.

10.3   SYSTEMATIC SAMPLING ⇔

In some instances, the most practical way of sampling is to select, say, every 20th name on a list, every 12th house on one side of a street, every 50th piece coming off an assembly line, and so on. This is called **systematic sampling,** and an element of randomness can be introduced into this kind of sampling by using random numbers to pick the unit with which to start. Although a systematic sample may not be a random sample in accordance with the definition, it is often reasonable to treat systematic samples as if they were random samples; indeed, in some instances, systematic samples actually provide an improvement over simple random samples inasmuch as the samples are spread more evenly over the entire populations.

If the members of the population appear sequentially in time, as with pieces coming off a production line or automobiles approaching a tollbooth, systematic sampling will smoothly spread out the work of sampling over time. This desirable feature of systematic sampling helps reduce the number of clerical errors.

The real danger in systematic sampling lies in the possible presence of hidden periodicities. For instance, if we inspect every 40th piece made by a particular machine, the results would be very misleading if, because of a regularly recurring failure, every 10th piece produced by the machine has blemishes. Also, a systematic sample might yield biased results if we interview the residents of every 12th house along a certain route and it so happens that each 12th house along the route is a corner house on a double lot.

10.4   STRATIFIED SAMPLING ⊖

If we have information about the makeup of a population (that is, its composition) and this is of relevance to our investigation, we may be able to improve on random sampling by **stratification.** This is a procedure that consists of stratifying (or dividing) the population into a number of nonoverlapping subpopulations, or **strata,** and then taking a sample from each stratum. If the items selected from each stratum constitute simple random samples, the entire procedure—first stratification and then random sampling—is called **stratified (simple) random sampling.**

Suppose, for instance, that we want to estimate the mean weight of four persons on the basis of a sample of size 2, and that the (unknown) weights of the four persons are 115, 135, 185, and 205 pounds. Thus, the mean weight we want to estimate is

$$\mu = \frac{115 + 135 + 185 + 205}{4} = 160 \text{ pounds}$$

If we take an ordinary random sample of size 2 from this population, the $\binom{4}{2} = 6$ possible samples are

115 and 135, 115 and 185, 115 and 205, 135 and 185, 135 and 205, 185 and 205

and the corresponding means are 125, 150, 160, 160, 170, and 195. Observe that since each of these samples has the probability $\frac{1}{6}$, the probabilities are $\frac{1}{3}$, $\frac{1}{3}$, and $\frac{1}{3}$ that our error (the difference between the sample mean and $\mu = 160$) will be 0, 10, or 35. Now suppose that we know that two of these persons are men and two are women, and suppose that the (unknown) weights of the men are 185 and 205 pounds, while the (unknown) weights of the women are 115 and 135 pounds. Stratifying our sample (by sex) and randomly choosing one of the two men and one of the two women, we find that there are only the four stratified samples,

115 and 185,   115 and 205,   135 and 185,   135 and 205

The means of these samples are 150, 160, 160, and 170, and now the probabilities are $\frac{1}{2}$ and $\frac{1}{2}$ that our error will be 0 or 10. Clearly, stratification has greatly improved our chances of getting a good (close) estimate of the mean weight of the four persons. See, however, Exercise 10.19 on page 295.

Essentially, the goal of stratification is to form strata in such a way that there is some relationship between being in a particular stratum and the answer sought in the statistical study, and that within the separate strata there is as much homogeneity (uniformity) as possible. In our example there is such a connection between sex and weight and there is much less variability in weight within each of the two groups than there is within the entire population.

In the example above, we used **proportional allocation,** which means that the sizes of the samples from the different strata are proportional to the sizes of the strata. In general, if we divide a population of size N into k strata of size N_1, $N_2, \ldots$, and N_k, and take a sample of size n_1 from the first stratum, a sample of size n_2 from the second stratum, $\ldots$, and a sample of size n_k from the kth stratum, we say that the allocation is proportional if

$$\frac{n_1}{N_1} = \frac{n_2}{N_2} = \cdots = \frac{n_k}{N_k}$$

or if these ratios are as nearly equal as possible. In the example dealing with the weights we had $N_1 = 2$, $N_2 = 2$, $n_1 = 1$, and $n_2 = 1$, so that

$$\frac{n_1}{N_1} = \frac{n_2}{N_2} = \frac{1}{2}$$

and the allocation was, indeed, proportional.

As the reader will be asked to verify in Exercise 10.22 on page 295, allocation is proportional if

Sample Sizes for Proportional Allocation	$n_i = \dfrac{N_i}{N} \cdot n \qquad for\ i = 1, 2, \ldots, and\ k$

where $n = n_1 + n_2 + \cdots + n_k$ is the total size of the sample. When necessary, we use the integers closest to the values given by this formula. See Exercise 10.24 on page 295 and the references at the end of the chapter.

Example

A stratified sample of size $n = 60$ is to be taken from a population of size $N = 4,000$, which consists of three strata of size $N_1 = 2,000$, $N_2 = 1,200$ and $N_3 = 800$. If the allocation is to be proportional, how large a sample must be taken from each stratum?

solution

Substituting into the formula, we obtain

$$n_1 = \frac{2,000}{4,000} \cdot 60 = 30, \quad n_2 = \frac{1,200}{4,000} \cdot 60 = 18, \quad n_3 = \frac{800}{4,000} \cdot 60 = 12 \quad \blacksquare \blacksquare \blacksquare$$

This example illustrates proportional allocation, but we should add that there exist other ways of allocating portions of a sample to the different strata. One of these, called **optimum allocation,** is described in Exercise 10.26 on page 296. It accounts not only for the size of the strata, as in proportional allocation, but also for the variability (of whatever characteristic is of concern) within the strata.

Stratification is not restricted to a single variable of classification, or characteristic, and populations are often stratified according to several characteristics. For instance, in a system-wide survey designed to determine the attitude of its students, say, toward a new tuition plan, a state college system with 17 colleges might stratify its sample not only with respect to the colleges, but also with respect to students' class standing, sex, and major. So, part of the sample would be allocated to junior women in college A majoring in engineering, another part to sophomore men in college L majoring in English, and so on. Up to a point, stratification like this, called **cross stratification,** will increase the precision (reliability) of estimates and other generalizations, and it is widely used, particularly in opinion sampling and market research.

In stratified sampling, the cost of taking random samples from the individual strata is often so high that interviewers are simply given quotas to be filled from the different strata, with few (if any) restrictions on how they are to be filled. For instance, in determining voters' attitudes toward increased medical coverage for elderly persons, an interviewer working a certain area might be told to interview 6 male self-employed homeowners under 30 years of age, 10 female wage earners in the 45–60 age bracket who live in apartments, 3 retired males over 60 who live in trailers, and so on, with the actual selection of the individuals being left to the interviewer's discretion. This is called **quota sampling,** and it is a convenient, relatively inexpensive, and sometimes necessary procedure, but as it is often executed, the resulting samples do not have the essential features of random samples. In the absence of any controls on their choice, interviewers naturally tend to select individuals who are most readily available—persons who work in the same building, shop in the same store, or perhaps reside in the same general area. Quota samples are thus essentially **judgment samples,** and inferences based on such samples generally do not lend themselves to any sort of formal statistical evaluation.

10.5   CLUSTER SAMPLING ⇔

To illustrate another important kind of sampling, suppose that a large foundation wants to study the changing patterns of family expenditures in the San Diego area. In attempting to complete schedules for 1,200 families, the foundation finds that simple random sampling is practically impossible, since suitable lists are not available and the cost of contacting families scattered over a wide area (with possibly two or three callbacks for the not-at-homes) is very high. One way in which a sample can be taken in this situation is to divide the total area of interest into a number of smaller, nonoverlapping areas, say, city blocks. A number of these blocks are then randomly selected, with the ultimate sample consisting of all (or samples of) the families residing in these blocks.

In this kind of sampling, called **cluster sampling,** the total population is divided into a number of relatively small subdivisions, and some of these subdivisions, or clusters, are randomly selected for inclusion in the overall sample. If the clusters are geographic subdivisions, as in the example above, this kind of sampling is also called **area sampling.** To give another example of cluster sampling, suppose that the dean of students of a university wants to know how fraternity men at the school feel about a certain new regulation. He can take a cluster sample by interviewing some or all of the members of several randomly selected fraternities.

Although estimates based on cluster samples are usually not as reliable as estimates based on simple random samples of the same size (see Exercise 10.25 on page 296), they are often more reliable per unit cost. Referring again to the survey of family expenditures in the San Diego area, it is easy to see that it may well be possible to take a cluster sample several times the size of a simple random sample for the same cost. It is much cheaper to visit and interview families living close together in clusters than families selected at random over a wide area.

In practice, several of the methods of sampling we have discussed may well be used in the same study. For instance, if government statisticians want to study the attitude of American elementary school teachers toward certain federal programs, they might first stratify the country by states or some other geographic subdivisions. To take a sample from each stratum, they might then use cluster sampling, subdividing each stratum into a number of smaller geographic subdivisions (say, school districts), and finally, they might use simple random sampling or systematic sampling to select a sample of elementary school teachers within each cluster.

◢ EXERCISES

10.16   The following are average monthly AFDC (Aid to Families with Dependent Children) payments in a recent year by the 50 states, listed in alphabetical order.

```
111  539  216  128  462  283  413  237  193  177
406  257  290  213  325  306  184  168  310  266
279  393  450   92  241  302  319  193  281  313
295  402  183  310  257  257  302  315  353  128
244  116  127  348  418  232  400  166  451  315
```

List the five possible samples of size $n = 10$ that can be taken from this population by starting with one of the first five numbers and then taking each fifth number on the list.

10.17   The following are consecutive monthly figures on the volume of mail (in millions of ton-miles) carried by domestic air operations over a four-year period.

```
67  62  75  67  70  68  64  70  66  73  73   97
76  73  80  78  78  72  75  75  73  83  76  108
84  78  86  85  81  78  78  75  78  86  76  111
79  77  87  84  82  77  79  77  80  84  78  117
```

(a) List the six possible systematic sample of size $n = 8$ that can be taken from the population by starting with one of the first six numbers and then taking each sixth number on the list.

(b) If one of these six samples is randomly chosen to estimate the average volume of mail carried per month, explain why there is a serious risk of getting a very misleading result.

10.18   The rule for systematic sampling needs to be modified if n is not an exact divisor of N. If N/n is not an integer, let k be the next integer; for example, if $N = 73$ and $n = 10$, then $N/n = 7.3$ and we use $k = 8$. Now select one of the N items from the population, using probability $1/N$ for each item. Beginning at the selected item, select each kth item thereafter, continuing until n items have been selected. If you reach the end of the list, continue counting at the beginning of the list.

    (a) Consider a population consisting of 11 items, identified as the letters *a* through *k*. List all possible systematic samples of size $n = 3$ obtained by applying this sampling rule.

    (b) Consider a population consisting of 14 items, identified as the numbers 01 through 14. List all possible systematic samples of size $n = 4$ obtained by applying this sampling rule.

10.19 To generalize the example on page 291, suppose that we want to estimate the mean weight of six persons, whose (unknown) weights are 115, 125, 135, 185, 195, and 205 pounds.

    (a) List all possible random samples of size 2 that can be taken from this population, calculate their means, and determine the probability that the mean of such a sample will differ by more than 5 from 160, the actual mean weight of the six persons.

    (b) Suppose that the first three weights are those of women and the other three are those of men. List all possible stratified samples of size 2 that can be taken by randomly choosing one of the three women and one of the three men, calculate their means, and determine the probability that the mean of such a sample will differ by more than 5 from 160, the actual mean weight of the six persons.

    (c) Suppose that three of the persons, those with weights 125, 135, and 185 pounds, are under 25 years of age, while the remaining are over 25 years of age. List all possible stratified samples of size 2 that can be taken by randomly choosing one of the three younger persons and one of the three older persons, calculate their means, and determine the probability that the mean of such a sample will differ by more than 5 from 160, the actual mean weight of the six persons.

    (d) Compare the results of parts (a), (b), and (c).

10.20 Based on their volumes of sales, 18 of the 24 clothing stores in a city are classified as being small, and the other six are classified as being large. How many different stratified samples of four of these clothing stores can we choose, if

    (a) half of the sample is to be allocated to each of the two strata;

    (b) the allocation is to be proportional?

10.21 Among 240 persons empaneled for jury duty, 120 are white, 80 are black, and 40 are Hispanic. How many different stratified samples of six of the 240 persons can we choose, if

    (a) one-third of the sample is to be allocated to each of the three strata;

    (b) the allocation is to be proportional?

10.22 Verify that if the formula

$$n_i = \frac{N_i}{N} \cdot n \qquad \text{for } i = 1, 2, \ldots, \text{ and } k$$

is used to determine the sample sizes allocated to the *k* strata, then

    (a) the allocation is proportional, that is, the ratios n_i/N_i all equal the same constant;

    (b) the sum of the n_i is equal to *n*.

10.23 A stratified sample of size $n = 80$ is to be taken from a population of size $N = 2{,}000$, which consists of four strata of size $N_1 = 500$, $N_2 = 1{,}200$, $N_3 = 200$, and $N_4 = 100$. If the allocation is to be proportional, how large a sample must be taken from each of the four strata?

10.24 In general, the formula used for the sample sizes in proportional allocation, given on page 292, will not produce integers for the n_i values. Suppose that a population with $k = 3$ strata has sizes

$$N_1 = 62, \qquad N_2 = 20, \qquad N_3 = 18,$$

and that we desire to take a sample of size $n = 12$.

(a) Use the formula for proportional allocation, rounding the n_i values to the nearest integer, and show that the resulting sample sizes sum to 11.

(b) Revise the results of part (a) to make the total sample size equal to 12 by increasing that value of n_i for which the decimal part of $\frac{N_i}{N} \cdot n$ is largest. Then give the values of the ratios N_i/n_i.

(c) Revise the results of part (a) to make the total sample size equal to 12 by increasing that value of n_i for which the ratio N_i/n_i is largest. Then give the values of the ratios N_i/n_i.

The rounding issues presented in this exercise are precisely those of computing the numbers of seats, given to each of the states, in the U.S. House of Representatives. The ratios N_i/n_i correspond to the number of people represented by one congressperson. See the list of references at the end of the chapter.

10.25 With reference to Exercise 10.19, list all possible cluster samples of size 2 that can be taken by randomly choosing either two of the three women or two of the three men, calculate their means, and determine the probability that the mean of such a sample will differ by more than 5 from 160, the actual mean weight of the six persons. If we compare this probability with those obtained in parts (a) and (b) of Exercise 10.19, what does this tell us about the relative merits of simple random sampling, stratified sampling, and cluster sampling in the given situation?

10.26 In stratified sampling with proportional allocation, the importance of differences in stratum size is accounted for by letting the larger strata contribute relatively more items to the sample. However, strata differ not only in size but also in variability, and it would seem reasonable to take larger samples from the more variable strata and smaller samples from the less variable strata. If we let $\sigma_1, \sigma_2, \ldots,$ and σ_k denote the standard deviations of the k strata, we can account for both differences in stratum size and differences in stratum variability, but requiring that

$$\frac{n_1}{N_1\sigma_1} = \frac{n_2}{N_2\sigma_2} = \cdots = \frac{n_k}{N_k\sigma_k}$$

The sample sizes for this kind of allocation, called **optimal allocation** or **Neyman allocation** (in honor of its inventor), are given by the formula

$$n_i = \frac{n \cdot N_i\sigma_i}{N_1\sigma_1 + N_2\sigma_2 + \cdots + N_k\sigma_k}$$

for $i = 1, 2, \ldots,$ and k, where, if necessary, we round to the nearest integer. Verify that

(a) with this formula, the quantities $\dfrac{n_i}{N_i\sigma_i}$ all equal the same constant;

(b) the sum of the n_i is equal to n.

10.27 A sample of size $n = 100$ is to be taken from a population consisting of two strata for which

$$N_1 = 10{,}000, \quad N_2 = 30{,}000, \quad \sigma_1 = 45, \quad \text{and} \quad \sigma_2 = 60$$

To attain optimum allocation, how large a sample must be taken from each of the two strata?

10.28 A sample of size $n = 84$ is to be taken from a population consisting of three strata for which

$$N_1 = 5{,}000, \quad N_2 = 2{,}000, \quad N_3 = 3{,}000, \quad \sigma_1 = 15, \quad \sigma_2 = 18, \quad \sigma_3 = 5$$

To attain optimum allocation, how large a sample must be taken from each of the three strata?

10.29   To estimate the mean of a population on the basis of a stratified sample, we calculate the weighted mean of the means $\bar{x}_1, \bar{x}_2, \ldots,$ and $\bar{x}_k$ obtained for the k strata, using as weights the strata sizes N_i. Verify that for proportional allocation, the weighted mean thus obtained equals the mean of the values obtained for all the strata.

10.30   The records of a casualty insurance company show that among 3,800 claims filed against the company over a period of time 2,600 were minor claims (under \$200), while the other 1,200 were major claims (\$200 or more). To estimate the average size of these claims, the company takes a 1 percent sample, proportionally allocated to the two strata, with the following results (rounded to the nearest dollar):

Minor claims:	42	115	63	78	45	148	195
	66	18	73	55	89	170	41
	92	103	22	138	49	62	88
	113	29	71	58	83		
Major claims:	246	355	872	649	253	338	
	491	860	755	502	488	311	

(a) Find the means of these two samples and then determine their weighted mean, using as weights the two strata sizes $N_1 = 2{,}600$ and $N_2 = 1{,}200$.

(b) Verify that the result of part (a) equals the mean of the combined sample data. This being the case, proportional allocation is said to be **self-weighting.**

10.6   SAMPLING DISTRIBUTIONS

We now introduce the concept of the **sampling distribution** of a statistic, probably the most basic concept of statistical inference. As we shall see, this concept is closely related to the idea of chance variation, or chance fluctuations, mentioned earlier to emphasize the need for measuring the variability of data. In this chapter we concentrate mainly on the sample mean and its sampling distribution, but in some of the exercises on page 312 and in later chapters we also consider the sampling distributions of other statistics.

To illustrate the concept of a sampling distribution, let us construct the one for the mean of a random sample of size $n = 2$ drawn without replacement from the finite population of size $N = 5$, whose elements are the numbers 3, 5, 7, 9, and 11. The mean of this population is

$$\mu = \frac{3 + 5 + 7 + 9 + 11}{5} = 7$$

and its standard deviation is

$$\sigma = \sqrt{\frac{(3-7)^2 + (5-7)^2 + (7-7)^2 + (9-7)^2 + (11-7)^2}{5}} = \sqrt{8}$$

Now, if we take a random sample of size $n = 2$ from this population, there are the $\binom{5}{2} = 10$ possibilities

3 and 5	3 and 7	3 and 9	3 and 11	5 and 7
5 and 9	5 and 11	7 and 9	7 and 11	9 and 11

and their means are 4, 5, 6, 7, 6, 7, 8, 8, 9, and 10. Since each sample has the probability $\frac{1}{10}$, we thus get the following sampling distribution of the mean of a random sample of size $n = 2$ from the given population:

$\bar{x}$	Probability
4	$\frac{1}{10}$
5	$\frac{1}{10}$
6	$\frac{2}{10}$
7	$\frac{2}{10}$
8	$\frac{2}{10}$
9	$\frac{1}{10}$
10	$\frac{1}{10}$

A histogram of this probability distribution is shown in Figure 10.2.

An examination of this sampling distribution reveals some pertinent information relative to the problem of estimating the mean of the given population on the basis of a random sample of size 2. For instance, we see that corresponding to $\bar{x} = 6$, 7, or 8, the probability is $\frac{6}{10}$ that a sample mean will not differ from the population mean $\mu = 7$ by more than 1. Also, corresponding to $\bar{x} = 5$, 6, 7, 8, or 9, the probability is $\frac{8}{10}$ that a sample mean will not differ from the population mean $\mu = 7$ by more than 2. So, if we did not know the mean of the given population and wanted to estimate it with the mean of a random sample of size $n = 2$, the procedure above would give us some idea about the possible size of our error.

Further useful information about this sampling distribution of the mean can be obtained by calculating its mean $\mu_{\bar{x}}$ and its standard deviation $\sigma_{\bar{x}}$, where the subscripts serve to distinguish between these parameters and those of the original population. Using the definitions of the mean and the variance of a probability distribution of pages 232 and 234, we get

$$\mu_{\bar{x}} = 4 \cdot \tfrac{1}{10} + 5 \cdot \tfrac{1}{10} + 6 \cdot \tfrac{2}{10} + 7 \cdot \tfrac{2}{10} + 8 \cdot \tfrac{2}{10} + 9 \cdot \tfrac{1}{10} + 10 \cdot \tfrac{1}{10} = 7$$

and

$$\sigma_{\bar{x}}^2 = (4 - 7)^2 \cdot \tfrac{1}{10} + (5 - 7)^2 \cdot \tfrac{1}{10} + (6 - 7)^2 \cdot \tfrac{2}{10} + (7 - 7)^2 \cdot \tfrac{2}{10}$$
$$+ (8 - 7)^2 \cdot \tfrac{2}{10} + (9 - 7)^2 \cdot \tfrac{1}{10} + (10 - 7)^2 \cdot \tfrac{1}{10} = 3$$

FIGURE 10.2

Sampling distribution of the mean.

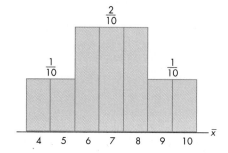

so that $\sigma_{\bar{x}} = \sqrt{3}$. Observe that, at least for this example, $\mu_{\bar{x}}$ equals μ and $\sigma_{\bar{x}}$ is smaller than σ. These relationships are of fundamental importance in statistics, and we shall return to them in Section 10.7.

To give an example of a sampling distribution, we took a very small sample of size $n = 2$ from a very small population of size $N = 5$, but it would be difficult to use the same method to construct the sampling distribution of the mean of a large sample from a large population. We would have to enumerate too many possibilities. For instance, for $n = 10$ and $N = 100$, we would have to list more than 17 trillion samples.

So, to get some idea about the sampling distribution of the mean of a somewhat larger sample from a large finite population, we shall use a **computer simulation.** In other words, we shall leave it to a computer to take repeated random samples from a given population, determine their means, and describe the distribution of these means in various ways. This will give us some idea about the overall shape and some of the key features of the real sampling distribution of the mean for random samples of the given size from the given population.

Figure 10.3 shows the results of a computer simulation where 100 random samples of size $n = 20$ are drawn without replacement from the finite population that consists of the integers from 1 to 1,000. The sample average $\bar{x}$ is calculated for each of the samples, and the distribution of the $\bar{x}$'s is suitably described.†

In Figure 10.3 we first create a population of $N = 1,000$ items, consisting of the integers from 1 to 1,000. The printout indicates that this population has mean $\mu = 500.5$ and standard deviation $\sigma = 288.82$. (See also Exercise 10.56 on page 310.) The 100 samples are not shown, nor are their means shown, but the printout does tell us that the mean of the 100 sample means is 500.24, and the standard deviation of the 100 sample means is 61.77. Further, the printout shows the 100 sample means in a stem-and-leaf display, and we might say that this distribution is fairly symmetrical and bell-shaped. In fact, the overall pattern is quite close to that of a normal curve. This printout applies to the distribution that we obtained by means of the computer simulation involving only 100 random samples of size $n = 20$ drawn without replacement from the finite population that consists of the integers from 1 to 1,000; certainly we expect that it applies to the population of all possible random samples of size $n = 20$.

The results of the simulation support the relationships noted above. The mean of the sampling distribution of the mean is equal to the population mean; although the actual mean of the 100 sample means, 500.24, is not exactly $\mu = 500.5$, it is very close. Also, the standard deviation of the sampling distribution of the mean is less than the population standard deviation; here we note that 61.77 is substantially less than $\sigma = 288.82$.

---

†Each sample of size $n = 20$ is drawn without replacement, but in performing the simulation the population size $N = 1,000$ is restored before the next sample is selected.

FIGURE 10.3

*Computer simulation of a
sampling distribution of
the mean*
(MINITAB 10 for
Windows).

```
MTB  > Set C1
DATA >   1( 1 : 1000 / 1 )1
DATA >   End.
MTB  > Mean C1
Column Mean
   Mean of C1      =        500.50
MTB  > Stdev C1
Column Standard Deviation
   Standard deviation of C1    =        288.82
MTB  > Set C3
DATA > 9999
DATA > end
MTB  > store
Storing in file: MINITAB.MTB
STOR > sample 20 C1 C2
STOR > Let  C4 = Aver(C2)
STOR > stack (C4) (C3) (C3)
STOR > end
MTB  > execute 100 times
Executing from file: MINITAB.MTB
MTB  > lag 1 C3 C5
MTB  > mean C5
Column Mean
   Mean of C5      =        500.24
MTB  > stdev C5
Column Standard Deviation
   Standard deviation of C5    =        61.770
MTB  > Stem-and-Leaf C5;
SUBC >   Increment 50.

Character Stem-and-Leaf Display
Stem-and-leaf of C5   N = 100
Leaf Unit = 10    N*       = 1

    1      3  4
    5      3  7999
   20      4  000222233344444
  (31)     4  5555566666666677777777888999999
   49      5  000000001122222333334444444444
   20      5  55556667777899
    6      6  00123
    1      6  5
```

10.7   THE STANDARD ERROR OF THE MEAN

In most practical situations we cannot proceed as in the two examples of Section 10.6. That is, we cannot enumerate all possible samples or simulate a sampling distribution in order to judge how close a sample mean might be to the mean of the population from which the sample came. Fortunately, though, we can usually get the information we need from two theorems, which express essential facts about sampling distributions of the mean. One of these is discussed below and the other in Section 10.8.

The first of these two theorems expresses formally what we discovered from both of the examples of the preceding section—the mean of the sampling distribution of $\bar{x}$ equals the mean of the population sampled, and the standard deviation of the sampling distribution of $\bar{x}$ is smaller than the standard deviation of the population sampled. It may be phrased as follows: For random samples of size n taken from a population with the mean μ and the standard deviation σ, the sampling distribution of $\bar{x}$ has the mean

Mean of Sampling Distribution of $\bar{x}$

$$\mu_{\bar{x}} = \mu$$

and the standard deviation

Standard Error of the Mean

$$\sigma_{\bar{x}} = \frac{\sigma}{\sqrt{n}} \quad or \quad \sigma_{\bar{x}} = \frac{\sigma}{\sqrt{n}} \cdot \sqrt{\frac{N-n}{N-1}}$$

depending on whether the population is infinite or finite of size N.

It is customary to refer to $\sigma_{\bar{x}}$ as the **standard error of the mean,** where "standard" is used in the sense of an average, as in "standard deviation." Its role in statistics is fundamental, as it measures the extent to which sample means can be expected to fluctuate, or vary, due to chance. If $\sigma_{\bar{x}}$ is small, the chances are good that the mean of a sample will be close to the mean of the population; if $\sigma_{\bar{x}}$ is large, we are more likely to get a sample mean which differs considerably from the mean of the population.

What determines the size of $\sigma_{\bar{x}}$ can be seen from the two formulas above. Both formulas (for infinite and finite populations) show that $\sigma_{\bar{x}}$ increases as the variability of the population increases, and that it decreases as the sample size increases. In fact, it is directly proportional to σ and inversely proportional to the square root of n—for finite populations it decreases even faster due to the n appearing in

$$\sqrt{\frac{N-n}{N-1}}$$

Example

When we take a sample from an infinite population, what happens to the standard error of the mean, and hence to the error we might expect when we use a sample mean to estimate the mean of a population, if the sample size is increased from 50 to 200?

solution

The ratio of the two standard errors is

$$\frac{\frac{\sigma}{\sqrt{200}}}{\frac{\sigma}{\sqrt{50}}} = \frac{\sqrt{50}}{\sqrt{200}} = \sqrt{\frac{50}{200}} = \sqrt{\frac{1}{4}} = \frac{1}{2}$$

and where n is quadrupled, the standard error of the mean is only divided by 2.   ◢ ◢ ◢

The factor $\sqrt{\frac{N-n}{N-1}}$ in the second formula for $\sigma_{\bar{x}}$ is called the **finite population correction factor,** for without it the two formulas for $\sigma_{\bar{x}}$ (for infinite and finite populations) are the same. In practice, it is omitted unless the sample constitutes at least 5 percent of the population, for otherwise it is so close to 1 that it has little effect on the value of $\sigma_{\bar{x}}$. This factor appears also in the standard deviation of the hypergeometric distribution, as in Exercise 8.72 on pages 238–239, using $a + b = N$.

Example

Find the value of the finite population correction factor for $n = 100$ and $N = 10,000$.

solution

Substituting $n = 100$ and $N = 10,000$, we obtain

$$\sqrt{\frac{N-n}{N-1}} = \sqrt{\frac{10,000 - 100}{10,000 - 1}} \approx 0.995^{\dagger}$$

and this is so close to 1 that the correction factor can be omitted for all practical purposes.   ◢ ◢ ◢

Since we stated the two formulas for the standard error of the mean without proof, let us verify the one for finite populations by referring to the results of the two examples of Section 10.6.

Example

With reference to the example on page 297, where we had $n = 2$, $N = 5$, and $\sigma = \sqrt{8}$, verify that the second of the two formulas for $\sigma_{\bar{x}}$ will yield $\sqrt{3}$. This is the value we obtained on pages 298–299.

solution

Substituting $n = 2$, $N = 5$, and $\sigma = \sqrt{8}$ into the second of the two formulas for $\sigma_{\bar{x}}$, we get

$$\sigma_{\bar{x}} = \frac{\sqrt{8}}{\sqrt{2}} \cdot \sqrt{\frac{5-2}{5-1}} = \frac{\sqrt{8}}{\sqrt{2}} \cdot \sqrt{\frac{3}{4}} = \sqrt{\frac{8}{2} \cdot \frac{3}{4}} = \sqrt{3}$$ ◢ ◢ ◢

Example

With reference to the computer simulation of Figure 10.3, where we had $n = 20$, $N = 1,000$, and $\sigma = 288.82$, what value might we have expected for the standard deviation of the 100 sample means?

solution

Substituting $n = 20$, $N = 1,000$, and $\sigma = 288.82$ into the second of the two formulas for $\sigma_{\bar{x}}$ we get

†See the footnote on page 51 regarding the use of the symbol $\approx$.

$$\sigma_{\bar{x}} = \frac{288.82}{\sqrt{20}} \cdot \sqrt{\frac{1{,}000 - 20}{1{,}000 - 1}} \approx 63.97$$

This is reasonably close to 61.77, the value obtained in the computer simulation of Figure 10.3. The discrepancy is due, of course, to chance variation. ◼ ◼ ◼

10.8 THE CENTRAL LIMIT THEOREM

When we use a sample mean to estimate the mean of a population, the uncertainties about our error can be expressed in various ways. When we know the exact sampling distribution of the mean, which we seldom do, we could proceed as in the example on pages 297–298 and calculate the probabilities associated with errors of various size. Also, we always can, but in practice don't, use Chebyshev's theorem and assert with a probability of at least $1 - \frac{1}{k^2}$ that the mean of a random sample will differ from the mean of the population sampled by less than $k \cdot \sigma_{\bar{x}}$.

Example

Based on Chebyshev's theorem with $k = 2$, what can we say about the size of our error, if we are going to use the mean of a random sample of size $n = 64$ to estimate the mean of an infinite population with $\sigma = 20$?

solution

Substituting $n = 64$ and $\sigma = 20$ into the appropriate formula for the standard error of the mean, we get

$$\sigma_{\bar{x}} = \frac{20}{\sqrt{64}} = 2.5$$

and it follows that we can assert with a probability of at least

$$1 - \frac{1}{2^2} = 0.75$$

that the error will be less than $k \cdot \sigma_{\bar{x}} = 2(2.5) = 5$. ◼ ◼ ◼

Here, the trouble is that "at least 0.75" does not tell us enough when in reality the probability may be, say, 0.98 or even 0.999.

Chebyshev's theorem provides the logical connection between errors and the probabilities that they will be committed, but there exists another theorem which, in many instances, enables us to make much stronger probability statements about our potential errors. This theorem, which is the second of the two theorems referred to on page 300, is called the **central limit theorem** and it may be stated as follows:

Central Limit Theorem	*For large samples, the sampling distribution of the mean can be approximated closely with a normal distribution.*

If we combine this theorem with the one of the preceding section, according to which

$$\mu_{\bar{x}} = \mu \quad \text{and} \quad \sigma_{\bar{x}} = \frac{\sigma}{\sqrt{n}}$$

for random samples from infinite populations, we find that if $\bar{x}$ is the mean of a random sample of size n from an infinite population with the mean μ and the standard deviation σ and n is large, then

$$z = \frac{\bar{x} - \mu}{\sigma/\sqrt{n}}$$

is a value of a random variable having approximately the standard normal distribution.

The central limit theorem is of fundamental importance in statistics because it justifies the use of normal-curve methods for a wide range of problems. This theorem applies automatically to sampling from infinite populations. It also applies to sampling from finite populations provided that the sample size n, even though large, is only a small fraction of the population size N. It is difficult to say precisely how large n must be to apply the central limit theorem, but $n = 30$ is usually regarded as sufficient, unless that population distribution has a very unusual shape. When we are actually sampling a normal population, the sampling distribution of the mean $\bar{x}$ is a normal distribution, regardless of the size of n.

Let us now see what probability will take the place of "at least 0.75" if we use the central limit theorem instead of Chebyshev's theorem in the example on page 303.

Example

Based on the central limit theorem, what is the probability that the error will be less than 5, when the mean of a random sample of size $n = 64$ is used to estimate the mean of an infinite population with $\sigma = 20$?

solution

The probability is given by the area of the white region under the curve in Figure 10.4, namely, by the standard-normal-curve area between

$$z = \frac{-5}{20/\sqrt{64}} = -2 \quad \text{and} \quad z = \frac{5}{20/\sqrt{64}} = 2$$

Since the entry in Table I corresponding to $z = 2.00$ is 0.4772, the probability asked for is

$$0.4772 + 0.4772 = 0.9544$$

Thus, the statement that the probability is "at least 0.75" is replaced by the much stronger statement that the probability is about 0.95 (that the mean of a random sample of size $n = 64$ from the given population will differ from the mean of the population by less than 5). ▰ ▰ ▰

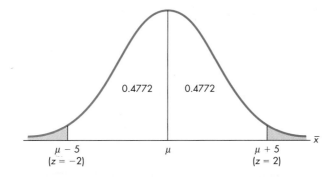

FIGURE 10.4

Sampling distribution of the mean.

The central limit theorem can also be used for finite populations, but a precise description of the situations under which this can be done is rather complicated. The most common proper use is the case in which n is large while $\frac{n}{N}$ is small. This is the case in most political polls.

Since we presented the central limit theorem without proof, let us consider the following example:

Example

In the Figure 10.3 simulation, we created a population with mean $\mu = 500.5$ and standard deviation $\sigma = 288.82$. Based on the central limit theorem, what is the probability that the mean of a sample of size $n = 20$ will differ from $\mu = 500.5$ by 130 or less?

solution

The probability is indicated by the area of the white region under the curve in Figure 10.5. Since

$$\sigma_{\bar{x}} = \frac{288.82}{\sqrt{20}} \cdot \sqrt{\frac{1{,}000 - 20}{1{,}000 - 1}} \approx 63.97$$

this area is the standard-normal curve area between

$$z = \frac{-130}{63.97} \approx -2.03 \quad \text{and} \quad z = \frac{130}{63.97} \approx 2.03$$

FIGURE 10.5

Sampling distribution of the mean.

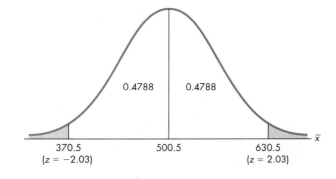

Because the entry in Table I corresponding to $z = 2.03$ is 0.4788, the probability asked for is

$$0.4788 + 0.4788 = 0.9576 \approx 0.96$$

From Figure 10.3 we cannot (because of the grouping) tell exactly how many of the sample means fall between

$$500.5 - 130 = 370.5 \quad \text{and} \quad 500.5 + 130 = 630.5$$

but we can certainly see that only three values lie below 370 or above 630, and this is close to the expected 4 out of 100 on the basis of our calculations. Thus, the simulation provides support for the central limit theorem.   ◢ ◢ ◢

10.9   SOME FURTHER CONSIDERATIONS

In Sections 10.6 through 10.8, our main goal was to introduce the concept of a sampling distribution, and the one that we chose as an illustration was the sampling distribution of the mean. It should be clear, though, that instead of the mean we could have studied the median, the standard deviation, or some other statistic, and investigated its chance fluctuations. So far as the corresponding theory is concerned, this would have required a different formula for the standard error and theory analogous to, yet different from, the central limit theorem.

For instance, for large samples from continuous populations, the **standard error of the median** is approximately

$$\sigma_{\tilde{x}} = 1.25 \cdot \frac{\sigma}{\sqrt{n}}$$

where n is the size of the sample and σ is the population standard deviation. Note that comparison of the two formulas

$$\sigma_{\bar{x}} = \frac{\sigma}{\sqrt{n}} \quad \text{and} \quad \sigma_{\tilde{x}} = 1.25 \cdot \frac{\sigma}{\sqrt{n}}$$

reflects the fact that the mean is generally more reliable than the median (that is, it tends to expose us to smaller errors) when we estimate the mean of a symmetrical population. For symmetrical populations, the means of the sampling distributions of $\bar{x}$ and $\tilde{x}$ are both equal to the population mean μ.

Example

How large a random sample do we need so that its mean is as reliable an estimate of the mean of a symmetrical continuous population as the median of a random sample of size $n = 200$?

solution

Equating the two standard error formulas and substituting $n = 200$ into the one for the standard error of the median, we get

$$\frac{\sigma}{\sqrt{n}} = 1.25 \cdot \frac{\sigma}{\sqrt{200}}$$

which, solved for n, yields $n = 128$. Thus, for the stated purpose, the mean of a random sample of size $n = 128$ is as "good" as the median of a random sample of size $n = 200$. ◩ ◩ ◩

Also, a point worth repeating is that the examples of Section 10.6 were used as teaching aids, designed to convey the idea of a sampling distribution, but they do not reflect what we do in actual practice. In practice, we can seldom list all possible samples, and ordinarily we base an inference on one sample and not on 100 samples. In Chapter 11 and in subsequent chapters we shall go further into the problem of translating theory about sampling distributions into methods of evaluating the merits and shortcomings of statistical procedures.

Another point worth repeating concerns the $\sqrt{n}$ that appears in the denominator of the formula for the standard error of the mean. It makes sense that when n becomes larger and larger, our generalizations will be subject to smaller errors, but the $\sqrt{n}$ in the formula for the standard error of the mean tells us that the gain in reliability is not proportional to the increase in the size of the sample. As we saw, quadrupling the size of the sample will only double the reliability of a sample mean as an estimate of the mean of a population. Indeed, to quadruple the reliability, we would have to multiply the sample size by 16. This relationship between reliability and sample size indicates that there are, to use an economist's expression, diminishing returns to increasing sample size. It seldom pays to take massive large samples.

◩ EXERCISES

10.31   A finite population consists of the $N = 8$ elements

10   10   10   10   10   12   18   40

It can be verified that the mean of this population is $\mu = 15$ and its standard deviation is $\sigma = \sqrt{96} \approx 9.80$.

(a) List the $\binom{8}{2} = 28$ possible samples of size $n = 2$ that can be drawn without replacement from this finite population. *Hint:* In $\binom{5}{2} = 10$ of these samples, both values are equal to 10.

(b) Calculate the mean of each of the 28 samples obtained in part (a).

(c) Assigning probability $\frac{1}{28}$ to each of the samples, construct the sampling distribution of the mean for random samples of size $n = 2$ drawn without replacement from this finite population.

(d) Find the standard deviation of the sampling distribution of the mean for random samples of size $n = 2$ drawn without replacement from this finite population.

10.32   Compare the findings in part (d) of Exercise 10.31 to the formula on page 301 that gives the standard error of the mean.

10.33   A finite population consists of the $N = 6$ numbers 6, 9, 12, 15, 18, and 21. It can easily be verified that the mean of this population is $\mu = 13.5$ and its standard deviation is

$$\sigma = \frac{1}{2}\sqrt{105} \approx 5.12$$

(a) List the 20 possible samples of size $n = 3$ that can be drawn without replacement from this finite population.

(b) Calculate the means of the 20 samples obtained in part (a).

(c) Assigning the probability $\frac{1}{20}$ to each of the samples obtained in part (a), construct the sampling distribution of the mean for random samples of size $n = 3$ drawn without replacement from the given finite population.

(d) What is the probability that the mean of a random sample of size $n = 3$ drawn without replacement from the given population will differ from $\mu = 13.5$ by less than 3?

10.34   With reference to Exercise 10.33, calculate the mean and the standard deviation of the sampling distribution obtained in part (c) and verify the results using the theory of Section 10.7.

10.35   With reference to Exercise 10.33, determine the medians of the 20 samples obtained in part (a). Construct the sampling distribution of the median for random samples of size $n = 3$ drawn without replacement from the given population. Find the probability that the median of such a random sample will differ from $\mu = 13.5$ by less than 3. Compare this probability with the one obtained in part (d) of Exercise 10.33.

10.36   With reference to Exercise 10.33, determine the ranges of the 20 samples obtained in part (a) and construct the sampling distribution of the range for random samples of size $n = 3$ drawn without replacement from the given population.

10.37   When we sample an infinite population, what happens to the standard error of the mean if the sample size is

(a) increased from 60 to 240;   (b) increased from 200 to 450;

(c) increased from 25 to 225;   (d) decreased from 640 to 40?

10.38   In sampling a finite population of size $N = 82$, what happens to the standard error of the mean if the sample size is

(a) increased from 18 to 33;

(b) increased from 33 to 57;

(c) increased from 57 to 81?

10.39   What is the value of the finite population correction factor when

(a) $n = 10$ and $N = 200$;   (b) $n = 10$ and $N = 500$;

(c) $n = 10$ and $N = 2,000$; (d) $n = 20$ and $N = 200$;

(e) $n = 40$ and $N = 400$;   (f) $n = 400$ and $N = 4,000$?

⊞ 10.40   Show that if the mean of a random sample of size n is used to estimate the mean of an infinite population with the standard deviation σ and n is large, there is a fifty–fifty chance that the magnitude of the error will be less than

$$0.6745 \cdot \frac{\sigma}{\sqrt{n}}$$

It has been the custom to refer to this quantity as the **probable error of the mean;** nowadays, it is used mainly in military applications.

(a) If a random sample of size $n = 64$ is drawn from an infinite population with $\sigma = 20.6$, what is the probable error of the mean?

(b) If a random sample of size $n = 100$ is drawn from a very large population (consisting of the fines paid for various traffic violations in a certain county in 1995) with $\sigma = \$18.26$, what is the probable error of the mean? Explain its significance.

10.41 With reference to Exercise 10.16 on page 294, assign each of the systematic samples the probability $\frac{1}{5}$ and calculate the standard deviation of the corresponding sampling distribution of the mean.

10.42 With reference to Exercise 10.17 on page 294, assign each of the systematic samples the probability $\frac{1}{6}$ and calculate the standard deviation of the corresponding sampling distribution of the mean. Compare the result with $\sigma_{\bar{x}} = 3.5$, the standard error of the mean for ordinary random samples of size $n = 8$ from the given finite population.

10.43 In the example on page 291, we compared stratified samples from a population consisting of four weights with ordinary random samples of the same size.

(a) Assigning each of the random samples on page 291, the probability $\frac{1}{6}$, show that the mean and the standard deviation of this sampling distribution of the mean are $\mu_{\bar{x}} = 160$ and $\sigma_{\bar{x}} = 21.0$.

(b) Assigning each of the stratified samples on page 291 the probability $\frac{1}{4}$, show that the mean and the standard deviation of this sampling distribution of the mean are $\mu_{\bar{x}} = 160$ and $\sigma_{\bar{x}} = 7.1$.

Compare the results of parts (a) and (b).

10.44 If $\bar{x}$ is the mean of a stratified random sample of size n obtained by proportional allocation from a finite population of size N, which consists of k strata of size $N_1, N_2, \ldots,$ and N_k, then

$$\sigma_{\bar{x}}^2 = \sum_{i=1}^{k} \frac{(N-n)N_i^2}{nN^2(N_i - 1)} \cdot \sigma_i^2$$

where $\sigma_1^2, \sigma_2^2, \ldots,$ and σ_k^2 are the corresponding variances for the individual strata. Use this formula to verify the result of part (b) of Exercise 10.43.

10.45 In the example on page 291, the two cluster samples, which consist of choosing and weighing either the two women or the two men, have the means 125 and 195. Assigning the probability $\frac{1}{2}$ to each of these means, calculate the standard deviation of this sampling distribution of the mean, and compare it with the corresponding values for ordinary random sampling and stratified sampling obtained in the two parts of Exercise 10.43.

10.46 The mean of a random sample of size $n = 121$ is used to estimate the mean of an infinite population having the standard deviation $\sigma = 33$. What can we assert about the probability that the error will be less than 4.5 if we use

(a) Chebyshev's theorem; (b) the central limit theorem?

10.47 The mean of a random sample of size $n = 25$ is used to estimate the mean of a very large population (consisting of the attention spans of persons over 65), which has a standard deviation of $\sigma = 2.4$ minutes. What can we assert about the probability that the error will be less than 1.2 minutes, if we use

(a) Chebyshev's theorem; (b) the central limit theorem?

10.48 The mean of a random sample of size $n = 100$ is used to estimate the mean daily milk production of a very large population of dairy cows. This population has the standard deviation $\sigma = 3.6$ quarts. Using the central limit theorem, find the probability that the error will be

(a) more than 0.63 quarts; (b) less than 0.45 quarts.

10.49 If measurements of the specific gravity of a metal can be looked upon as a sample from a normal population having the standard deviation $\sigma = 0.025$, what is the probability that the mean of a random sample of size $n = 16$ will be "off" by at most 0.01?

10.50   The population of purchase amounts at a certain all-night convenience store has a mean of $5.20 and a standard deviation of $4.10. What is the probability that the total of 100 purchases, presumably a random sample, will exceed $530?

10.51   If the distribution of the weights of all men traveling by air between Dallas and El Paso has a mean of 163 pounds and a standard deviation of 18 pounds, what is the probability that the combined weight of 36 men traveling on such a flight is more than 6,012 pounds?

10.52   The number of driving miles before a certain kind of tire begins to show wear is, on average, 16,800 miles with a standard deviation of 3,300 miles. A car rental agency buys 36 of these tires for replacement purposes and puts each one on a different car.

(a) Find the probability that the 36 tires will average less than 16,000 miles until they begin to show wear.

(b) Find the probability that the 36 tires will average more than 18,000 miles until they begin to show wear.

(c) Explain why the probabilities in (a) and (b) could not be calculated from the given information if the car rental agency puts four of the 36 tires on each of nine cars.

10.53   Suppose that a population of jelly beans has a mean weight of $\mu = 4.5$ grams and a standard deviation of $\sigma = 0.4$ gram. What is the minimum number of jelly beans to select if you want your sample of jelly beans to have a total weight of at least 200 grams with a probability of 0.90 or more? (*Hint:* Suppose that you took a sample of $n = 60$. Getting a total weight in excess of 200 grams would require that the average weight in the sample exceeds $\frac{200}{60} \approx 3.33$ grams. The probability that the average of a sample of 60 will exceed 3.33 grams is larger than 0.90; therefore 60 jelly beans is too large a sample. Continue this logic to find the minimum sample size.)

10.54   A gourmet chef would like to have 40 pounds of shad roe for a special banquet. Shad roe is sold in "sets" rather than by weight, but the chef knows that the sets come from a population that has the mean weight $\mu = 0.60$ pound and the standard deviation $\sigma = 0.20$ pound. How many sets should the chef order if he wants the probability of reaching the 40 pound objective to be at least 0.90?

10.55   Verify that the mean of a random sample of size $n = 256$ is as reliable an estimate of the mean of a symmetrical continuous population as the median of a random sample of size $n = 400$.

⊞ 10.56   Using the result that the sum of the first n positive integers is

$$\frac{n(n + 1)}{2}$$

and that the sum of their squares is

$$\frac{n(n + 1)(2n + 1)}{6}$$

it can be shown that the mean and the standard deviation of the finite population which consists of the first n positive integers are

$$\mu = \frac{n + 1}{2} \quad \text{and} \quad \sigma = \sqrt{\frac{n^2 - 1}{12}}$$

Verify that these formulas yield the population mean and standard deviation shown in the printout of Figure 10.3 on page 300.

10.10   TECHNICAL NOTE (Simulation) ⇔

Simulation provides an effective way of illustrating, and thus teaching, some of the basic concepts of statistics. In the chapters that follow, the evaluation and interpretation of statistical techniques will often require that we imagine what would happen if experiments are repeated over and over again. Since, most of the time, such repetitions are neither practical nor feasible, we can resort instead to simulations, preferably with the use of computers. Simulation also plays a role in the development of statistical theory, for there are situations where simulation is easier and cheaper than a detailed mathematical analysis.

In earlier chapters we used simulation to generate values of random variables having binomial, Poisson, and normal distributions, and in this chapter we used simulation to generate random samples from specified populations as well as a sampling distribution of the mean. It is hoped that the reader will have the opportunity to generate and study simulations of the sampling distribution of the median, the sampling distribution of s or s^2, or the sampling distributions of some other statistics.

Simulations are most conveniently generated by using computer software. To simplify matters we present in the accompanying table, 40 simulated random samples, each consisting of $n = 5$ values of a random variable having the Poisson distribution with the mean $\lambda = 16$. (The reader may picture these figures as data on the number of emergency calls that an ambulance service receives in an afternoon, the number of cars that arrive at a tollbooth during a five-minute interval, the number of pieces of junk mail that a family receives in a week, and so on.)

Sample						Mean	SD	Median	Sample						Mean	SD	Median
1	22	13	15	18	17	17.0	3.39	17	21	19	10	15	16	18	15.6	3.51	16
2	20	10	15	15	19	15.8	3.96	15	22	16	18	26	14	20	18.8	4.60	18
3	18	12	13	19	9	14.2	4.21	13	23	15	14	21	17	11	15.6	3.71	15
4	12	13	13	14	12	12.8	0.84	13	24	18	8	21	14	15	15.2	4.87	15
5	20	17	16	18	19	18.0	1.58	18	25	19	17	16	13	15	16.0	2.24	16
6	10	11	9	11	11	10.4	0.89	11	26	12	12	20	11	15	14.0	3.67	12
7	16	18	14	9	11	13.6	3.65	14	27	17	9	18	16	9	13.8	4.44	16
8	11	17	19	20	17	16.8	3.49	17	28	10	18	19	13	20	16.0	4.30	18
9	14	19	16	13	21	16.6	3.36	16	29	18	14	23	23	14	18.4	4.51	18
10	17	16	11	17	11	14.4	3.13	16	30	16	13	10	14	20	14.6	3.71	14
11	12	21	10	15	16	14.8	4.21	15	31	15	11	21	8	17	14.4	5.08	15
12	15	26	19	20	15	19.0	4.53	19	32	12	11	19	17	16	15.0	3.39	16
13	13	15	15	13	18	14.8	2.05	15	33	15	16	17	17	16	16.2	0.84	16
14	15	16	16	15	17	15.8	0.84	16	34	20	17	11	19	15	16.4	3.58	17
15	22	15	13	19	11	16.0	4.47	15	35	15	11	14	14	18	14.4	2.51	14
16	18	13	15	11	12	13.8	2.77	13	36	17	22	21	16	20	19.2	2.59	20
17	11	23	12	20	14	16.0	5.24	14	37	22	21	16	15	13	17.4	3.91	16
18	20	8	17	16	13	14.8	4.55	16	38	16	17	20	17	7	15.4	4.93	17
19	16	10	9	19	15	13.8	4.21	15	39	21	18	17	26	25	21.4	4.04	21
20	14	19	16	18	20	17.4	2.41	18	40	12	18	15	14	16	15.0	2.24	15

In the exercises that follow, the reader is asked to use these figures. For convenience, the mean, standard deviation, and median are specified for each of the 40 samples.

EXERCISES

10.57 The column labeled "mean" in the preceding table has a mean of 15.72 and a standard deviation of 1.9958. Compare these results with the corresponding values expected in accordance with the theory of Section 10.7.

10.58 The column labeled "median" in the preceding table has a mean of 15.77 and a standard deviation of 2.0567. Compare this to the standard deviation of the "mean" column.

10.59 Determine the ranges of the 40 samples in the preceding table, and construct a histogram showing how many times each value occurs. Based on these data, what would be reasonable odds that the range of such a sample will be greater than 10?

10.60 For large samples, the formula $\dfrac{\sigma}{\sqrt{2n}}$ may be used to approximate the standard error of s, the standard deviation of the sampling distribution of s. The column labeled "SD" in the preceding table has a mean of 3.41 and a standard deviation of 1.2307. Compare the result with the value obtained by using the formula above with $n = 5$ and $\sigma = \sqrt{16} = 4$.

10.61 Use suitable computer software to simulate 50 random samples of size $n = 3$ from a standard normal population. Calculate the mean of each of the 50 samples; then find the mean and standard deviation of the list of 50 means. Compare these results with values we might expect in accordance with the theory on page 301.

10.11 CHECKLIST OF KEY TERMS[†] (*with page references to their definitions*)

Area sampling, 293
Central limit theorem, 303
Cluster sampling, 293
Computer simulation, 299
Cross stratification, 293
Finite population, 284
Finite population correction factor, 302
Infinite population, 284
Judgment sample, 293
Neyman allocation, 296
Optimum allocation, 296
Probable error of the mean, 308
Proportional allocation, 291

Quota sampling, 293
Random sample, 285
Sample design, 290
Sampling distribution, 297
Sampling frame, 286
Self-weighting, 297
Simple random sample, 285
Standard error of the mean, 301
Standard error of the median, 306
Strata, 291
Stratification, 291
Stratified sampling, 291
Systematic sampling, 290

10.12 REVIEW EXERCISES

10.62 The mean of a random sample of size $n = 81$ is used to estimate the mean of a normal population with $\sigma = 27$. With what probability can we assert that the error of this estimate will be less than 9, if we use

[†]Terms introduced in exercises are shown in *italics*.

(a) Chebyshev's theorem;

(b) the central limit theorem?

10.63 Among 80 persons interviewed for certain jobs by a government agency, 40 are married, 20 are single, 10 are divorced, and 10 are widowed. In how many ways can a 10 percent stratified sample be chosen from among the persons interviewed, if

(a) one-fourth of the sample is to be allocated to each group;

(b) the allocation is proportional?

10.64 A quality control inspector wants to examine 20 of 750 computers that were received as part of a single shipment. He decides to utilize a table of random numbers, obtaining the following values. If he uses the first three digits out of each five-digit block, which ones (by number) will he examine?

18531	52417	31421	91528	94720	12574	28799	34812	20746	14656
38643	14652	56561	23602	10427	88567	66111	49253	73271	63110
76120	79164	66700	30647	56272	80051	72129	99160	67459	34289
80504	13021	08509	05650	24579	84177	43937	28422	41879	37984
88219	19728	34306	92674	44641	43720	86129	76235	70633	80127

10.65 If a random sample of size $n = 3$ is to be chosen from a finite population of size $N = 80$, what is the probability of each possible sample?

10.66 Random samples of size $n = 2$ are drawn from the finite population that consists of the numbers 1, 3, 5, and 7. As can be verified readily, $\mu = 4$ for this population and $\sigma = \sqrt{5}$.

(a) List the six possible samples of size $n = 2$ that can be drawn without replacement from the given population, and calculate their means.

(b) Assigning each of the samples obtained in part (a) the probability $\frac{1}{6}$, construct the sampling distribution of the mean for random samples of size $n = 2$ drawn without replacement from the given population.

(c) Calculate the mean and the standard deviation of the probability distribution obtained in part (b), and compare the results with the values we would expect in accordance with the formulas on page 301.

⇔ 10.67 A finite population consists of four strata of sizes

$$N_1 = 320, \quad N_2 = 200, \quad N_3 = 400, \quad \text{and} \quad N_4 = 80$$

It is believed that the standard deviations within these strata are

$$\sigma_1 = 12, \quad \sigma_2 = 10, \quad \sigma_3 = 18, \quad \text{and} \quad \sigma_4 = 20$$

If a stratified sample of size $n = 50$ is to be taken from this population using optimum allocation, how large should the sample sizes from each of the four strata be?

⇔ 10.68 In Exercise 10.19 on page 295, the reader was asked to compare stratified sampling from a population which consists of the weights of three women and the weights of three men with ordinary random sampling.

(a) Assigning each of the random samples the probability $\frac{1}{15}$, show that $\sigma_{\bar{x}} = 22.7$ for the means of random samples of size $n = 2$ from the given population.

(b) Assigning each of the stratified samples the probability $\frac{1}{9}$, show that $\sigma_{\bar{x}} = 5.8$ for the means of stratified samples of size $n = 2$ from the given population.

Compare the results of parts (a) and (b).

⇔ 10.69 Use the formula of Exercise 10.44 on page 309 to verify the result of part (b) of Exercise 10.68.

⇔ 10.70 With reference to Exercise 10.19 on page 295, how many different cluster samples of size $n = 2$ can we choose from the given population, if we want to choose the weights of two of the women or the weights of two of the men?

10.71   What is the value of the finite population correction factor when

(a) $n = 40$ and $N = 150$;   (b) $n = 25$ and $N = 80$?

10.72   When we sample from an infinite population, what happens to the standard error of the mean if the sample size is

(a) increased from 20 to 500;   (b) decreased from 490 to 40?

10.73   The annual dollar value of homes sold by real estate salespersons in a certain community is 7.5 million dollars, on average, with a standard deviation of 4.4 million dollars. Find the probabilities that in a sample of 36 such salespersons the average annual dollar value of home sales will

(a) be less than 6.5 million dollars;   (b) exceed 9 million dollars.

10.74   The weights of persons who use a certain elevator are normally distributed, at least approximately, with mean $\mu = 130$ pounds and standard deviation $\sigma = 15$ pounds. The elevator contains a sign that says "capacity 3,000 pounds." What is the greatest number of persons that can ride in the elevator while keeping to about 0.05 the probability that the capacity is violated?

10.75   How many different samples of size $n = 4$ can be selected from a finite population of size

(a) $N = 18$;   (b) $N = 30$;   (c) $N = 100$?

10.76   What is the probability of each possible sample if a random sample of size $n = 5$ is to be drawn from a finite population of size $N = 24$?

10.77   The mean of a random sample of size $n = 81$ is used to estimate the mean annual growth of certain plants. Assuming that $\sigma = 3.6$ mm for such data, use the central limit theorem to find the probabilities that this estimate will be off either way by

(a) less than 1.0 mm;   (b) less than 0.5 mm.

⇦ 10.78   With reference to Exercise 10.17 on page 294, list the eight possible systematic samples of size $n = 6$ that can be taken from the given population by starting with one of the first eight numbers and then taking each eighth number on the list.

10.13   REFERENCES

Derivations of the formulas for the standard error of the mean and more general formulations (and proofs) of the central limit theorem may be found in most textbooks on mathematical statistics, for instance, in

FREUND, J. E., *Mathematical Statistics,* 5th ed. Englewood Cliffs, N.J.: Prentice Hall, 1993.

All sorts of information about sampling may be found in

COCHRAN, W. G., *Sampling Techniques,* 3rd ed. New York: John Wiley & Sons, Inc., 1977.

SCHAFFER, R. L., MENDENHALL, W., and OTT, L., *Elementary Survey Sampling,* 2nd ed. Belmont, CA: Duxbury Press, 1979.

SLONIN, M. J., *Sampling in a Nutshell.* New York: Simon and Schuster, 1973.

WILLIAMS, W. H., *A Sampler on Sampling.* New York: John Wiley & Sons, Inc., 1978.

Some books on simulation are referred to among the references at the end of Chapter 8, and the difficulties of drawing a random sample in practice are illustrated by "Was the 1970 Draft Lottery Fair?" in

HOLLANDER, M., and PROSCHAN, F., *The Statistical Exorcist: Dispelling Statistics Anxiety.* New York: Marcel Dekker, Inc., 1984.

The paradoxical problems of proportional allocation to the U.S. House of Representatives are discussed in

BALINSKI, M. L., and YOUNG, H. P., "The Apportionment of Representation," in *Proceedings of Symposia in Applied Mathematics,* American Mathematical Society, Providence, R.I., 1985.

Inferences about means

$\mathcal{P}$*roblems of estimation occur in science, business, athletics, and in everyday life. For example, a psychologist may want to determine adults' reaction time to a particular visual stimulus; a transportation planner may need to know the variation in the distances that people commute to work; and a football coach may want to know what proportion of his team can run 60 yards in less than 8.0 seconds, wearing all their equipment. These are all problems of* **estimation.** *These would be tests of hypotheses if, for instance, the psychologist wishes to decide if the average adult reaction time to the visual stimulus is actually 0.38 second; if the transportation planner wishes to determine if the standard deviation of commuting distance is really 2.5 miles; and if the football coach wants to check whether the actual proportion of his players who can run 60 yards with full equipment in 8.0 seconds is really 75 percent.*

In these examples, the psychologist's problem concerns a population mean; the planner's problem concerns a standard deviation; and the football coach's problem concerns a percentage. These problems are conceptually similar but there are differences in the methods we will use to solve them.

Sections 11.1 through 11.3 concern some general problems of estimation and, in particular, to the estimation of means. Then, after a general introduction to tests of hypotheses in Sections 11.4 and 11.5, Sections 11.6 through 11.10 are devoted to tests of hypotheses about means. Corresponding inferences about the variability of populations and percentages (or proportions) are dealt with in Chapters 12 and 13.

11.1   THE ESTIMATION OF MEANS

To illustrate some of the problems we face when we estimate the mean of a population from sample data, let us refer to a study in which industrial designers want to determine the average (mean) time it takes an adult to assemble an "easy to assemble" toy. Using a random sample, they obtain the following data (in minutes) for 36 persons who assembled the toy:

$$
\begin{array}{cccccccccccc}
17 & 13 & 18 & 19 & 17 & 21 & 29 & 22 & 16 & 28 & 21 & 15 \\
26 & 23 & 24 & 20 & 8 & 17 & 17 & 21 & 32 & 18 & 25 & 22 \\
16 & 10 & 20 & 22 & 19 & 14 & 30 & 22 & 12 & 24 & 28 & 11
\end{array}
$$

The mean of this sample is $\bar{x} = 19.9$ minutes, and in the absence of any other information, this figure can be used as an estimate of μ, the "true" average time it takes an adult to assemble the given toy.

This kind of estimate is called a **point estimate,** since it consists of a single number, or a single point on the real number scale. Although this is the most common way in which estimates are expressed, it leaves room for many questions. For instance, it does not tell us on how much information the estimate is based, and it does not tell us anything about the possible size of the error. And, of course, we must expect an error. This should be clear from our discussion of the sampling distribution of the mean in Chapter 10, where we saw that the chance fluctuations of the mean (and, hence, its reliability as an estimate of μ) depend on two things—the size of the sample and the size of the population standard deviation σ. Thus, we might supplement the estimate, $\bar{x} = 19.9$ minutes, with the information that it is the mean of a random sample of size $n = 36$, whose standard deviation is $s = 5.73$ minutes. Although this does not tell us the actual value of σ, the sample standard deviation can serve as an estimate of this quantity.

Scientific reports often present sample means in this way, together with the values of n and s, but this does not supply readers of the report with a coherent picture unless they have had some formal training in statistics. To take care of this, we refer to the theory of Sections 10.7 and 10.8, and the definition on page 260, according to which $z_{\alpha/2}$ is such that the area to its right under the standard normal curve is $\alpha/2$, and hence the area under the standard normal curve between $-z_{\alpha/2}$ and $z_{\alpha/2}$ is equal to $1 - \alpha$. Making use of the fact that, for large random samples from infinite populations, the sampling distribution of the mean is approximately a normal distribution with

$$\mu_{\bar{x}} = \mu \text{ and } \sigma_{\bar{x}} = \frac{\sigma}{\sqrt{n}}$$

we find from Figure 11.1 that the probability is $1 - \alpha$ that the mean of a large random sample from an infinite population will differ from the mean of the population by at most

$$z_{\alpha/2} \cdot \frac{\sigma}{\sqrt{n}}$$

In other words,

If we are going to use $\bar{x}$ as an estimate of μ, the probability is $1 - \alpha$ that this estimate will be "off" either way by at most:

Maximum Error of Estimate	$E = z_{\alpha/2} \cdot \dfrac{\sigma}{\sqrt{n}}$

FIGURE 11.1

Sampling distribution of the mean.

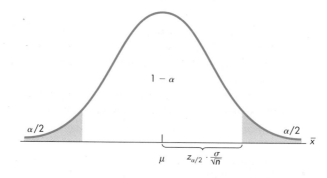

This result applies if n is large, $n \geq 30$, and the population is infinite (or large enough so that the finite population factor need not be used). The two values which are most commonly, though not necessarily, used for $1 - \alpha$ are 0.95 and 0.99, and the corresponding values of $\alpha/2$ are 0.025 and 0.005. As the reader was asked to show in Exercise 9.16 on page 263,

$$z_{0.025} = 1.96 \quad \text{and} \quad z_{0.005} = 2.575$$

Example

A team of efficiency experts intends to use the mean of a random sample of size $n = 150$ to estimate the average mechanical aptitude of assembly-line workers in a large industry (as measured by a certain standardized test). If, based on experience, the efficiency experts can assume that $\sigma = 6.2$ for such data, what can they assert with probability 0.99 about the maximum error of their estimate?

solution

Substituting $n = 150$, $\sigma = 6.2$, and $z_{0.005} = 2.575$ into the formula for E, we have

$$E = 2.575 \cdot \frac{6.2}{\sqrt{150}} \approx 1.30^\dagger$$

Thus, the efficiency experts can assert with probability 0.99 that their error is at most 1.30. ▰ ▰ ▰

Suppose now that the efficiency experts actually collect the necessary data and obtain $\bar{x} = 69.5$. Can they still assert with probability 0.99 that the error of their estimate, $\bar{x} = 69.5$, is at most 130? After all, $\bar{x} = 69.5$ differs from the true (population) mean by at most 1.30, or it does not, and they have no way of knowing whether it is one or the other. Actually, they can make this assertion, but it must be understood that the 0.99 probability applies to the *method* used (getting the sample data and using the formula for E) and not directly to the single problem at hand.

To make this distinction, it has become the custom to use the word "confidence" here instead of "probability."

In general, we make probability statements about future values of random variables (say, the potential error of an estimate) and confidence statements once the data have been obtained.

Accordingly, in our example we can say that the efficiency experts can be 99 percent confident that the error of their estimate, $\bar{x} = 69.5$, is at most 1.30.

Use of the formula for E involves a complication: we need to know the value of the population standard deviation σ. Since σ is not known in most practical situations, we often replace σ with a plausible guess that may cause us to somewhat overstate the error. This approach is conservative, since the statistician is

---

†See the footnote on page 51 regarding the use of the symbol $\approx$.

not promising results better than the data can deliver. Such a situation is explored in Exercises 11.18 and 11.19 on pages 331 and 332.

If the population standard deviation σ is not known, we can also replace σ with an estimate, usually the sample standard deviation s. In general this is considered reasonable provided the sample size is sufficiently large, and by sufficiently large we again mean $n \geq 30$.

Example

With reference to the example on page 317, what can we assert with 95 percent confidence about the maximum error, if we use $\bar{x} = 19.9$ minutes as an estimate of the average time it takes an adult to assemble the given kind of toy?

solution

Substituting $n = 36$, $s = 5.73$ for σ, and $z_{0.025} = 1.96$ into the formula for E, we find that we can assert with 95 percent confidence that the error is at most

$$E = 1.96 \cdot \frac{5.73}{\sqrt{36}} \approx 1.87 \text{ minutes}$$

Of course, the error is at most 1.87 minutes or it is not, and we do not know which is actually the case, but if we had to bet, 95 to 5 (or 19 to 1) would be fair odds that the error is at most 1.87 minutes.   ◪ ◪ ◪

The formula for E can also be used to determine the sample size that is needed to attain a desired degree of precision. Suppose that we want to use the mean of a large random sample to estimate the mean of a population, and we want to be able to assert with probability $1 - \alpha$ that the error of this estimate will be less than some prescribed quantity E. As before, we write

$$E = z_{\alpha/2} \cdot \frac{\sigma}{\sqrt{n}}$$

and upon solving this equation for n we obtain

Sample Size for Estimating μ	$$n = \left(\frac{z_{\alpha/2} \cdot \sigma}{E}\right)^2$$

Example

The dean of a college wants to use the mean of a random sample to estimate the average amount of time students take to get from one class to the next, and she wants to be able to assert with probability 0.95 that her error will be at most 0.25 minute. If she knows from studies of a similar kind that it is reasonable to let $\sigma = 1.50$ minutes, how large a sample will she need?

solution

Substituting $z_{0.025} = 1.96$, $E = 0.25$, and $\sigma = 1.50$ into the formula for n, we have

$$n = \left(\frac{1.96 \cdot 1.50}{0.25}\right)^2 \approx 138.30$$

and we round this up to the next integer, 139. Thus, a random sample of size $n = 139$ is required for the estimate.   ◪ ◪ ◪

Note that the treatment would be the same if we replace "she wants to be able to assert with probability 0.95 that her error *will be* at most 0.25 minute" by "she wants to be able to assert with 95 percent confidence that her error *is* at most 0.25 minute." The difference is in when the assertion is to be made—before or after she collects the data.

This method, as can be seen from the formula and the example, has a shortcoming. It cannot be used unless we know (at least approximately) the value of the population standard deviation σ. When the population standard deviation is not known, we often replace σ with a large but plausible guess. This may cause us to somewhat overstate the needed sample size. Again, this is considered conservative behavior, since the statistician is not promising a sample size too small to deliver the required precision.

In some instances we can begin with a relatively small sample and then use the sample standard deviation as an estimate of σ to determine whether more data are required.

We now introduce a different way of presenting a sample mean together with an assessment of the error we might make if we use it to estimate the mean of the population from which the sample came. As on page 304, we make use of the fact that, for large random samples from infinite populations, the sampling distribution of the mean is approximately a normal distribution with the mean $\mu_{\bar{x}} = \mu$ and the standard deviation $\sigma_{\bar{x}} = \sigma/\sqrt{n}$, so that

$$z = \frac{\bar{x} - \mu}{\sigma/\sqrt{n}}$$

is a value of a random variable having approximately the standard normal distribution. Since the probability is $1 - \alpha$ that a random variable having this distribution will be a value between $-z_{\alpha/2}$ and $z_{\alpha/2}$, namely, that

$$-z_{\alpha/2} < z < z_{\alpha/2}$$

we can substitute into this inequality the foregoing expression for z and get

$$-z_{\alpha/2} < \frac{\bar{x} - \mu}{\sigma/\sqrt{n}} < z_{\alpha/2}$$

If we now apply some fairly simple algebra, we can rewrite this inequality as

Large-sample Confidence Interval for μ	$$\bar{x} - z_{\alpha/2} \cdot \frac{\sigma}{\sqrt{n}} < \mu < \bar{x} + z_{\alpha/2} \cdot \frac{\sigma}{\sqrt{n}}$$

and we can assert with probability $1 - \alpha$ that it will be satisfied for any given sample.[†] In other words, we can assert with $(1 - \alpha)100$ percent confidence that the interval

[†]Since the probability is also $1 - \alpha$ that $-z_{\alpha/2} \leq z \leq z_{\alpha/2}$, some authors substitute $\leq$ for $<$ in this confidence-interval formula. Practically speaking, this does not make any difference.

$$\text{from} \quad \bar{x} - z_{\alpha/2} \cdot \frac{\sigma}{\sqrt{n}} \quad \text{to} \quad \bar{x} + z_{\alpha/2} \cdot \frac{\sigma}{\sqrt{n}},$$

determined on the basis of a large random sample, contains the population mean we are trying to estimate. When σ is unknown and n is at least 30, we replace σ by the sample standard deviation s. If n is at least 30, then the use of s is recommended, even if the value of σ is claimed to be known.

Such an interval is called a **confidence interval,** its endpoints are called **confidence limits,** and $(1 - \alpha)100$ percent is called the **degree of confidence.** As before, the values most often used for the degree of confidence are 95 percent and 99 percent, and the corresponding values of $z_{\alpha/2}$ are 1.96 and 2.575. In contrast to point estimates, the estimates given in the form of a confidence interval are called **interval estimates.** They have the advantage of not requiring further elaboration about their reliability—ensured indirectly by their width and the degree of confidence.

Example

With reference to the example on page 317, where we had $n = 36$, $\bar{x} = 19.9$, and $s = 5.73$, construct a 95 percent confidence interval for the average time it takes an adult to assemble the given kind of toy.

solution

Substituting $n = 36$, $\bar{x} = 19.9$, $s = 5.73$ for σ, and $z_{0.025} = 1.96$ into the confidence interval formula, we get

$$19.9 - 1.96 \cdot \frac{5.73}{\sqrt{36}} < \mu < 19.9 + 1.96 \cdot \frac{5.73}{\sqrt{36}} \quad \text{and} \quad 18.0 < \mu < 21.8$$

The statement that the interval from 18.0 to 21.8 minutes contains the true average assembly time is either true or false. Of course, we do not know whether it is true or false, but we can be 95 percent confident that it is true. We used a method that works 95 percent of the time. Said another way, the interval may contain μ or it may not, but if we had to bet, then 95 to 5 (or 19 to 1) would be fair odds that the interval contains μ.   ◪ ◪ ◪

Had we wanted to construct a 99 percent confidence interval in the preceding example, we would have substituted 2.575 instead of 1.96 for $z_{\alpha/2}$, and we would have obtained $17.4 < \mu < 22.4$. The 99 percent confidence interval is wider than the 95 percent confidence interval—it goes from 17.4 to 22.4 instead of 18.0 to 21.8—illustrating the important fact that

when we increase the degree of confidence, the confidence interval becomes wider and thus tells us less about the quantity we are trying to estimate.

Indeed, as is also illustrated by Exercise 11.8 on page 330, we might say that "the surer we want to be, the less we have to be sure of."

11.2   THE ESTIMATION OF MEANS (Small Samples)

In Section 11.1 we assumed that the samples were large enough, $n \geq 30$, to approximate the sampling distribution of the mean with a normal distribution and, where necessary, to replace σ with s. To develop corresponding methods that apply also to small samples, it is necessary to assume that the populations we are sampling have roughly the shape of normal distributions. We can then base our methods on the statistic

$$t = \frac{\bar{x} - \mu}{s/\sqrt{n}}$$

which is a value of a random variable having the *t* **distribution.** More specifically, this distribution is called the **Student-*t* distribution** or **Student's *t* distribution,** as it was first developed by a statistician, W. S. Gosset, who published his work under the pen name "Student." As is shown in Figure 11.2, the shape of this continuous distribution is very similar to that of the standard normal distribution— like the standard normal distribution, it is bell-shaped and symmetrical with zero mean. The exact shape of the *t* distribution depends on a parameter called the **number of degrees of freedom,** or simply the **degrees of freedom,** which, for the methods of this section, equals $n - 1$, the sample size less one.

FIGURE 11.2

Standard normal distribution and t distribution.

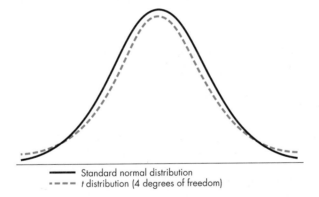

——— Standard normal distribution
- - - - *t* distribution (4 degrees of freedom)

For the standard normal distribution, we defined $z_{\alpha/2}$ in such a way that the area under the curve to its right equals $\alpha/2$, and, hence, the area under the curve between $-z_{\alpha/2}$ and $z_{\alpha/2}$ equals $1 - \alpha$. As is shown in Figure 11.3, the corresponding values for the *t* distribution are $-t_{\alpha/2}$ and $t_{\alpha/2}$. Since these values depend on $n - 1$, the number of degrees of freedom, they must be obtained from a special table, such as Table II at the end of this book, or perhaps a computer. Table II contains among others the values of $t_{0.025}$ and $t_{0.005}$ for 1 through 30 degrees of freedom, and it can be seen that $t_{0.025}$ and $t_{0.005}$ approach the corresponding values for the standard normal distribution as the number of degrees of freedom becomes large.

Now we can proceed as on page 321. Since the probability is $1 - \alpha$ that a random variable having the *t* distribution will take on a value between $-t_{\alpha/2}$ and $t_{\alpha/2}$, namely, that $-t_{\alpha/2} < t < t_{\alpha/2}$, we can substitute into this inequality the expression for *t* above and get

FIGURE 11.3

t distribution.

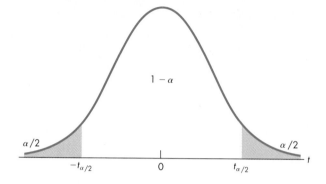

$$-t_{\alpha/2} < \frac{\bar{x} - \mu}{s/\sqrt{n}} < t_{\alpha/2}$$

Applying some relatively simple algebra, we can rewrite this inequality as

Small-sample Confidence Interval for μ	$$\bar{x} - t_{\alpha/2} \cdot \frac{s}{\sqrt{n}} < \mu < \bar{x} + t_{\alpha/2} \cdot \frac{s}{\sqrt{n}}$$

and we can assert with probability $1 - \alpha$ that it will be satisfied for any given sample. The only difference between this confidence interval formula and the large-sample formula (with s substituted for σ) is that $t_{\alpha/2}$ takes the place of $z_{\alpha/2}$.

Example

To test the durability of a new paint for white center lines, a highway department painted test strips across heavily traveled roads in eight different locations, and electronic counters showed that they deteriorated after having been crossed by (to the nearest hundred)

142,600   167,800   136,500   108,300
126,400   133,700   162,000   149,400

cars. Construct a 95 percent confidence interval for the average amount of traffic (car crossings) the new white paint can withstand before it deteriorates.

solution

The mean and the standard deviation of these $n = 8$ values are

$$\bar{x} = 140{,}800 \text{ and } s = 19{,}200$$

to the nearest hundred, and since $t_{0.025}$ for $8 - 1 = 7$ degrees of freedom equals 2.365 (according to Table II), substitution into the formula yields

$$140{,}800 - 2.365 \cdot \frac{19{,}200}{\sqrt{8}} < \mu < 140{,}800 + 2.365 \cdot \frac{19{,}200}{\sqrt{8}}$$

$$124{,}700 < \mu < 156{,}900$$

This result is the desired 95 percent confidence interval for the average amount of traffic (car crossings) that the paint can withstand before it deteriorates. Again, we can't tell for sure whether the interval from 124,700 to 156,900 contains the true average number of car crossings the paint can withstand before it deteriorates, but 95 to 5 would be fair odds that it does. These odds are based on the fact that the method we used—taking a random sample from a normal population and using the formula given above—works 95 percent of the time. ◪ ◪ ◪

Figure 11.4 is a computer printout showing the result we obtained in the preceding example. The differences between

$$124{,}700 \quad \text{and} \quad 124{,}758 \quad \text{and} \quad 156{,}900 \quad \text{and} \quad 156{,}917$$

are due to rounding. Indeed, since the original data were given to the nearest hundred, we rounded the mean, the standard deviation, and the confidence limits to the nearest hundred.

Computer printout for small-sample confidence interval μ (MINITAB 10 for Windows).

```
MTB   > set C1
DATA  > 142600  167800  136500  108300  126400  133700  162000
        149400
DATA  > end
MTB   > TInterval 95.0 C1.


Confidence Intervals


Variable    N      Mean    StDev    SE Mean       95.0 % C.I.
C1          8    140838    19228       6798  (  124751,  156924)
```

The method we used earlier to determine the maximum error we risk with $(1 - \alpha)100$ percent confidence when we use a sample mean to estimate the mean of a population is readily adapted to small samples, provided that the population we are sampling has roughly the shape of a normal distribution. All we have to do is substitute s for σ and $t_{\alpha/2}$ for $z_{\alpha/2}$ in the formula for the maximum error E on page 318.

Example

While performing a certain task under simulated weightlessness, the pulse rate of 12 astronauts increased on the average by 27.33 beats per minute with a standard deviation of 4.28 beats per minute. If we use $\bar{x} = 27.33$ as an estimate of the true average increase of the pulse rate of astronauts performing the given task, what can we assert with 99 percent confidence about the maximum error?

solution

Substituting $s = 4.28$, $n = 12$, and $t_{0.005} = 3.106$ (the entry in Table II for $12 - 1 = 11$ degrees of freedom) into the new formula for E, we obtain

$$E = t_{\alpha/2} \cdot \frac{s}{\sqrt{n}} = 3.106 \cdot \frac{4.28}{\sqrt{12}} \approx 3.84$$

Thus, if we use $\bar{x} = 27.33$ beats per minute as an estimate of the true average increase in the pulse rate of astronauts performing the given task (under the stated conditions), we can assert with 99 percent confidence that our error is at most 3.84 beats per minute.   ◪ ◪ ◪

11.3   THE ESTIMATION OF MEANS (a Bayesian Method) ⬦

In recent years there has been mounting interest in methods of inference where parameters (for example, the population mean μ or the population standard deviation σ) are looked upon as random variables having **prior distributions** that reflect how a person feels about the different values that a parameter can take on. Such prior considerations are then combined with direct sample evidence to obtain **posterior distributions** of the parameters, on which subsequent inferences are based. Since the method used to combine the prior considerations with the direct sample evidence is based on a generalization of Bayes' theorem of Section 6.7, we refer to such inferences as **Bayesian.**

In this section we present a Bayesian method of estimating the mean of a population. As we said, our prior feelings about the possible values of μ are expressed in the form of a prior distribution and, like any distribution, this kind of distribution has a mean and a standard deviation. We shall denote these values by μ_0 and σ_0 and call them the **prior mean** and the **prior standard deviation.**

The method we describe here involves quite a few assumptions, but without them it is nearly impossible to get results that are in an easy-to-use form. So, if we are sampling a population with the mean μ (which we want to estimate) and the standard deviation σ, if the sample is large enough to apply the central limit theorem, and if the prior distribution of μ has roughly the shape of a normal distribution, it can be shown that the posterior distribution of μ is also a normal distribution with the mean

Posterior Mean

$$\mu_1 = \frac{\dfrac{n}{\sigma^2} \cdot \bar{x} + \dfrac{1}{\sigma_0^2} \cdot \mu_0}{\dfrac{n}{\sigma^2} + \dfrac{1}{\sigma_0^2}}$$

and the standard deviation σ_1 given by the formula

Posterior Standard Deviation

$$\frac{1}{\sigma_1^2} = \frac{n}{\sigma^2} + \frac{1}{\sigma_0^2}$$

in which we can solve for σ_1. It can be routinely verified that

$$\sigma_1 = \frac{1}{\sqrt{\dfrac{n}{\sigma^2} + \dfrac{1}{\sigma_0^2}}}$$

Since the posterior mean μ_1 can be used as an estimate of the population mean μ, let us examine some of its most important features. First we note that μ_1 is a weighted mean of $\bar{x}$ and μ_0, and that the weights are $\dfrac{n}{\sigma^2}$ and $\dfrac{1}{\sigma_0^2}$, namely, the reciprocals of the variances of the distribution of $\bar{x}$ and the prior distribution of μ. We see also that when no direct information is available and $n = 0$, the weight assigned $\bar{x}$ is 0, the formula reduces to $\mu_1 = \mu_0$, and the estimate is based entirely on the prior distribution. Without sample data, our estimate will correspond precisely to the prior distribution. When $\sigma_0^2 = \dfrac{\sigma^2}{n}$, our estimate μ_1 is a 50–50 average of μ_0 and $\bar{x}$. As more and more direct evidence becomes available (that is, as n becomes larger and larger), the weight shifts more and more toward the direct sample evidence, the sample mean $\bar{x}$. Finally, we see that when the prior feelings about the possible values of μ are vague (that is, when σ_0 is relatively large), the estimate will be based to a greater extent on $\bar{x}$. However, when there is a great deal of variability in the population which yields the direct sample evidence (that is, when σ is relatively large), the estimate will be based to a greater extent on μ_0.

Once we have determined μ_1 and σ_1, we can actually make probability statements about the population mean μ, which we are trying to estimate. However, with subjective prior feelings and objective data, such probabilities reflect a combination of the corresponding probability concepts and must be interpreted with care.

This procedure requires the specification of μ_0 and σ_0, and it also requires that we know the population standard deviation σ or be willing to estimate it with s. In the case where σ is not known, which is usually the case, some Bayesians will formulate a prior distribution for σ; the resulting estimate for μ is rather complex and has not found wide acceptance.

Example

An investor who is planning to open a new travel agency feels most strongly that he should net on the average $\mu_0 = \$3,600$ per month; also, the subjective prior distribution which he attaches to the various possible values of μ has roughly the shape of a normal distribution with the standard deviation $\sigma_0 = \$130$. If during nine months the operation of the travel agency nets

$$\$3,810 \quad \$3,690 \quad \$3,350 \quad \$3,400 \quad \$3,320$$
$$\$3,250 \quad \$3,430 \quad \$3,600 \quad \$3,670$$

what is the posterior probability that the travel agency will net on the average between $3,500 and $3,600 per month?

solution

The mean and the standard deviation of the sample data are $\bar{x} = 3,502$ and $s = 195$. Using this sample standard deviation to estimate σ, and substituting

$$n = 9, \quad \bar{x} = 3,502, \quad s = 195 \quad \text{for } \sigma, \quad \mu_0 = 3,600, \quad \text{and} \quad \sigma_0 = 130$$

into the formulas for the posterior mean and the posterior standard deviation, we get

$$\mu_1 = \frac{\dfrac{9}{195^2} \cdot 3{,}502 + \dfrac{1}{130^2} \cdot 3{,}600}{\dfrac{9}{195^2} + \dfrac{1}{130^2}} \approx \$3{,}522$$

and

$$\frac{1}{\sigma_1{}^2} = \frac{9}{195^2} + \frac{1}{130^2} \quad \text{and} \quad \sigma_1 \approx 58.1$$

Having found the mean and the standard deviation of the posterior distribution of μ shown in Figure 11.5, we must now determine the area of the white region under the curve, namely, that between

$$z = \frac{3{,}500 - 3{,}522}{58.1} \approx -0.38 \quad \text{and} \quad z = \frac{3{,}600 - 3{,}522}{58.1} \approx 1.34$$

FIGURE 11.5

Posterior distribution of μ.

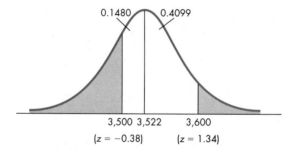

0.1480   0.4099

3,500 3,522   3,600
(z = −0.38)   (z = 1.34)

Since the entries corresponding to $z = 0.38$ and $z = 1.34$ in Table I are 0.1480 and 0.4099, we obtain

$$0.1480 + 0.4099 = 0.5579 \approx 0.56$$

for the (mostly subjective but partly objective) posterior probability that the travel agency will net on the average between \$3,500 and \$3,600 per month.   ◢ ◢ ◢

Example

The investor in the previous example brings his information to a bank as part of his application for a loan. The bank's loan officer, however, has a different prior distribution, and her opinion is that

$$\mu_0 = \$3{,}300 \quad \text{and} \quad \sigma_0 = \$200.$$

If she uses her prior distribution with the same data, what does she calculate as the posterior probability that the travel agency will net on the average between \$3,500 and \$3,600 per month?

solution

The loan officer calculates that

$$\mu_1 = \frac{\dfrac{9}{195^2} \cdot 3{,}502 + \dfrac{1}{200^2} \cdot 3{,}300}{\dfrac{9}{195^2} + \dfrac{1}{200^2}} \approx \$3{,}479$$

and

$$\frac{1}{\sigma_1^2} = \frac{9}{195^2} + \frac{1}{200^2} \approx 0.00026169 \quad \text{and} \quad \sigma_1 \approx 61.8$$

For this analysis she must determine the area under the normal curve between

$$z = \frac{3{,}500 - 3{,}479}{61.8} \approx 0.34 \quad \text{and} \quad z = \frac{3{,}600 - 3{,}479}{61.8} \approx 1.96$$

Since the entries corresponding to $z = 0.34$ and $z = 1.96$ in Table I are 0.1331 and 0.4750, we find

$$0.4750 - 0.1331 = 0.3419 \approx 0.34$$

for her posterior probability that the travel agency will net on the average between \$3,500 and \$3,600 per month. ◪ ◪ ◪

The two preceding examples show that people with different prior opinions will end up with different posterior probabilities. The values claimed by the two people for the interval from \$3,500 to \$3,600, namely 0.56 and 0.34, are not very close.

This brief introduction to **Bayesian inference** serves to bring out the following points: (1) In Bayesian statistics the parameter about which an inference is made is looked upon as a random variable having a distribution of its own, and (2) this kind of inference permits the use of direct as well as collateral information. When we referred to the result of our example as being "mostly subjective but partly objective," we were trying to express the fact that the prior distribution of the investor was probably based on a subjective evaluation of various factors (business conditions in general, for instance, and indirect information about other travel agencies), and that this evaluation was combined with the figures which were actually observed for the nine months. It must also be noted that two persons performing this analysis will likely have different prior distributions and therefore produce different results.

◪ EXERCISES

11.1   To estimate the average serving time at a fast-food restaurant, a consultant noted the time taken by 40 counter servers, a random sample, to complete a standard order (consisting of two burgers, two packages of French fries, and two drinks). The servers averaged 78.4 seconds with a standard deviation of 13.2 seconds to complete the orders.

(a) What can the consultant assert with 95 percent confidence about the maximum error if he uses $\bar{x} = 78.4$ seconds as an estimate of the true average time required to complete this standard order?

(b) Construct a 95% confidence interval for the true average time required to complete the standard order.

11.2   To assess the average weight of a new crop of lemons, a farm manager obtained the weights of 50 new lemons, presumed a random sample. He found an average of 115.2 grams, with a standard deviation of 20.4 grams.

(a) What can the consultant assert with 95 percent confidence about the maximum error if he uses $\bar{x} = 115.2$ grams as an estimate of the true average weight of the lemons?

(b) Construct a 95% confidence interval for the true average weight of the lemons.

11.3   A study of the annual growth of certain cacti showed that 80 of them, selected at random in a certain desert area, grew on the average 3.26 cm with a standard deviation of 1.40 cm.

(a) What can be said with 99 percent confidence about the maximum error if we use $\bar{x} = 3.26$ cm as an estimate of the true average annual growth of the given kind of cactus?

(b) Construct a 99% confidence interval for the true average annual growth of this kind of cactus.

11.4   In a study of work-release plans for jail inmates convicted of nonviolent crimes, it was found that 60 of them, presumed a random sample, were able to keep jobs earning on average $7.22 per hour, with a standard deviation of $2.02 per hour.

(a) What can be said with 95 percent confidence about the maximum error if we use $\bar{x} = \$7.22$ per hour as an estimate of the true hourly earning rate for this population of inmates?

(b) Construct a 95% confidence interval for the true hourly earning rate for this population of inmates.

11.5   A study conducted by an airline showed that a random sample of 120 of its passengers disembarking at Kennedy airport on flights from Europe took on the average 24.15 minutes with a standard deviation of 3.29 minutes to claim their luggage and get through customs. What can they assert with 95 percent confidence about the maximum error, if they use $\bar{x} = 24.15$ minutes as an estimate of the true average time it takes one of their passengers disembarking at Kennedy airport on a flight from Europe to claim his or her luggage and get through customs?

11.6   With reference to the preceding exercise, by how much is the maximum error increased if they want to be 99 percent instead of 95 percent confident?

11.7   With reference to Exercise 11.5, construct a confidence interval for the true average time it takes one of the airline's passengers disembarking at Kennedy airport on a flight from Europe to claim his or her luggage and get through customs, using

(a) 95 percent confidence;   (b) 98 percent confidence;

(c) 99 percent confidence;   (d) 99.5 percent confidence.

11.8   In the example on page 322, the 95 percent confidence interval had a width of

$$21.8 - 18.0 = 3.8 \text{ minutes}$$

and the 99 percent confidence interval had a width of

$$22.4 - 17.4 = 5.0 \text{ minutes.}$$

What would be the width of a corresponding 99.99994 percent confidence interval? Note how greatly the width has increased from the 99 percent confidence interval to the 99.99994 percent confidence interval even though the confidence is increased by less than 1 percentage point.

11.9   A district official intends to use the mean of a random sample of 150 sixth graders from a very large school district to estimate the mean score which all the sixth graders in the district would get if they took a certain arithmetic achievement test. If, based on experience, the official knows that $\sigma = 9.4$ for such data, what can she assert with probability 0.95 about the maximum error? Why did we use the word "probability" here instead of the word "confidence?"

11.10   A sample survey conducted in a rural area in 1994 showed that 250 families spent on the average $252.80 per week on food, with a standard deviation of $28.90. As it is desired to specify the true average weekly food expenditure of families in that area to a fairly narrow interval, construct a 90 percent confidence interval. Explain a possible disadvantage of this procedure.

11.11 A distributor of soft-drink vending machines plans to use the mean number of drinks dispensed during one week by 60 of her machines to estimate the average number dispensed by any one of her machines during one week. If the 60 randomly selected machines had a mean of 255.3 drinks, with a standard deviation of 48.2 drinks, give a 95 percent confidence interval for the true average number dispensed by any one of her machines during one week.

11.12 A random sample of 60 cans of pear halves has a mean weight of 16.1 ounces and a standard deviation of 0.3 ounce. If $\bar{x} = 16.1$ ounces is used as an estimate of the mean weight of all the cans of pear halves in the large lot from which the sample came, with what confidence can we assert that the error of this estimate is at most 0.1 ounce?

田 11.13 If a sample constitutes an appreciable portion of a finite population (say, 5 percent or more), the various formulas of Section 11.1 must be modified by appending the finite population correction factor to the standard error of the mean. For instance, the formula for the maximum error on page 318 becomes

$$ E = z_{\alpha/2} \cdot \frac{\sigma}{\sqrt{n}} \cdot \sqrt{\frac{N - n}{N - 1}} $$

A random sample of 50 scores on a law school's admission test is drawn from the scores of the 420 persons who applied to the law school in 1995. If the sample mean and standard deviation are $\bar{x} = 541$ and $s = 87$, what can we assert with 95 percent confidence about the maximum error, when $\bar{x} = 541$ is used as an estimate of the average score of all 420 applicants?

田 11.14 Use the method of the preceding exercise on the data of Exercise 11.9, given that there are 1,200 sixth graders in the district.

田 11.15 A random sample of 40 drums of a chemical, drawn at random from among 200 such drums whose weights can be assumed to have the standard deviation $\sigma = 10.2$ pounds, has a mean weight of 240.80 pounds. Using the same modification as in Exercise 11.13, construct a 95 percent confidence interval for the mean weight of the 200 drums.

田 11.16 A stratified random sample of size $n = 336$ is allocated proportionally to the four strata of a finite population for which

$$ N_1 = 4,000, \quad N_2 = 6,000, \quad N_3 = 2,000, \quad N_4 = 12,000, $$
$$ \sigma_1 = 20, \quad \sigma_2 = 20, \quad \sigma_3 = 16, \quad \sigma_4 = 30 \text{ cm.} $$

If the mean of this stratified sample is used to estimate the mean of the population,

(a) what can we assert with 95 percent confidence about the maximum error;

(b) what can we assert with 99 percent confidence about the maximum error?

(*Hint:* Use the standard error formula of Exercise 10.44 on page 309.)

田 11.17 Suppose that there are only 3,550 families in the rural area referred to in Exercise 11.10. Use the modification noted in Exercise 11.13 to construct a 90 percent confidence interval for the true average weekly food expenditure. Compare the result with that obtained in Exercise 11.10.

11.18 The manager of a restaurant plans to introduce child-size portions for a number of menu items. As an experiment, she would like to give hamburger patties to a number of six-year-olds in an "all you can eat" situation in order to estimate the average preferred quantity. She believes that the population of children would choose, on the average, somewhere between 2 ounces and 6 ounces, but she has no idea about the standard deviation. She needs to know what to say with 95 percent confidence about the maximum error in using the sample mean to estimate the population mean, if $n = 40$ children are used in the experiment.

(a) Suggest a plausible value for the standard deviation σ and then provide a value for the maximum error, using 95 percent confidence.

(b) Suggest a pessimistic value for the standard deviation σ and then provide a value for the maximum error, using 95 percent confidence.

11.19   A candy distributor wishes to determine the average water content of bottles of maple syrup from a particular New Hampshire producer. The bottles contain 12 ounces of liquid, and she decides to determine the water content of 10 of these bottles, using the sample mean as an estimate of the true population average. What can she say, with probability 0.95, about the maximum error, if the largest possible standard deviation that she is willing to believe is 2.0 ounces?

11.20   It is desired to estimate the mean number of hours of continuous use until a certain kind of computer will first require repairs. If it can be assumed that $\sigma = 48$ hours, how large a sample is needed so that it can be asserted with probability 0.99 that the sample mean will be off by at most 10 hours? Why did we use the word "probability" here, whereas in Exercise 11.12 we used the word "confidence"?

11.21   Suppose that we want to estimate the mean score of junior high school students on a current events test, and to assert with probability 0.90 that the error (meaning the difference between the sample mean and the true mean) will be at most 2.2 points. How large a sample will we need if it can be assumed that $\sigma = 8.0$ points?

11.22   Before bidding on a contract, a contractor wants to be 95 percent confident that he is in error by at most 5 minutes in using the mean of a random sample to estimate the average time it takes a certain kind of adobe brick to harden.

   (a) How large a sample will he need, if he can assume that $\sigma = 24$ minutes for such bricks?

   (b) Why did we use the word "confident" here, whereas in Exercise 11.21 we used the word "probability"?

   (c) Would the solution to (a) be different if we substitute "less than 5 minutes" for "at most 5 minutes"?

11.23   Before purchasing a large shipment of ground meat, a sausage manufacturer wants to be 95 percent confident that he is in error no more than 2.5 grams in estimating the fat content (per 100 grams of meat). If the standard deviation of the fat content (per 100 grams of meat) is assumed to be 8 grams, on how large a sample should he base his estimate?

11.24   The ratio $E^* = E/\sigma$ is the error in standard deviation units. In some situations, lack of knowledge about s makes it difficult to establish realistic values for E. In such cases, specifying E^* is a useful alternative. For example, requiring that E^* be 0.25 or less asks for an error of 0.25σ or less, whatever the value of σ. If a school administrator wants to estimate the average reading achievement score for his whole school by using a sample of children, how large a sample should he take if he wishes to assert, with 95 percent probability, that E^* is at most 0.25?

11.25   Suppose that we wish to estimate μ, the mean time required to learn a specific piece of computer software. How many subjects should we use if we would like the error of estimate to be at most 0.30σ, with a probability of 0.90? As in the previous exercise, the value of σ is not known.

11.26   A computer is programmed to yield values of a random variable having a normal distribution, whose mean and standard deviation are known only to the programmer. Each of 30 students is asked to use the computer to simulate a random sample of size $n = 5$ and then construct a small-sample 90 percent confidence interval for μ. The following are their results:

$$6.30 < \mu < 8.26, \qquad 6.50 < \mu < 7.72, \qquad 6.93 < \mu < 8.01,$$
$$6.60 < \mu < 8.00, \qquad 6.51 < \mu < 7.51, \qquad 6.82 < \mu < 8.66,$$
$$7.02 < \mu < 8.11, \qquad 6.94 < \mu < 7.64, \qquad 6.24 < \mu < 7.26,$$
$$6.87 < \mu < 8.17, \qquad 6.77 < \mu < 8.13, \qquad 6.14 < \mu < 6.82,$$

$$6.83 < \mu < 7.93, \qquad 6.66 < \mu < 8.10, \qquad 6.73 < \mu < 7.49,$$
$$6.41 < \mu < 7.67, \qquad 6.76 < \mu < 7.57, \qquad 6.97 < \mu < 7.47,$$
$$6.01 < \mu < 7.43, \qquad 7.15 < \mu < 7.89, \qquad 6.87 < \mu < 7.81,$$
$$7.35 < \mu < 7.99, \qquad 6.60 < \mu < 8.16, \qquad 6.47 < \mu < 7.81,$$
$$7.01 < \mu < 8.33, \qquad 6.97 < \mu < 7.55, \qquad 6.56 < \mu < 7.48,$$
$$7.13 < \mu < 8.03, \qquad 7.39 < \mu < 8.01, \qquad 5.98 < \mu < 7.68.$$

(a) How many of these 30 confidence intervals would we expect to contain the actual mean of the population sampled? 27

(b) Given that the computer was programmed so that $\mu = 7.30$, how many of the 30 confidence intervals actually contain the mean of the population sampled? Discuss this result. 26

11.27 A major truck-stop owner has kept extensive records on various transactions with his customers. If a random sample of 18 of these records show average sales of 58.22 gallons of diesel fuel with a standard deviation of 4.80 gallons,

(a) construct a 95 percent confidence interval for the mean of the population sampled;

(b) construct a 99 percent confidence interval for the mean of the population sampled;

(c) indicate the maximum error that we can assert with 95 percent confidence if we use $\bar{x} = 58.22$ as an estimate of the truck stop's average sales of diesel fuel;

(d) indicate the maximum error that we can assert with 99 percent confidence if we use $\bar{x} = 58.22$ as an estimate of the truck stop's average sales of diesel fuel.

11.28 There is often some uncertainty about the level of confidence that should be used in constructing intervals. It is claimed that, in general, 99 percent confidence intervals are about 30% longer than the corresponding 95 percent interval. Investigate this claim with the data given in Exercise 11.27, where $n = 18$.

11.29 The excess length of the 99 percent interval over the corresponding 95 percent interval, expressed as a percentage of the length of the 95 percent interval (see Exercise 11.28), is, in fact, determined only by the sample size n.

(a) What is the excess length when $n = 10$?

(b) What is the excess length when $n = 20$?

(c) What is the excess length when $n = 30$?

11.30 Nine bearings manufactured by a certain process have a mean diameter of 0.404 cm and a standard deviation of 0.003 cm. What can be said about the maximum error if $\bar{x} = 0.404$ cm is used as an estimate of the mean diameter of bearings made by the process

(a) with 95 percent confidence;

(b) with 99 percent confidence?

11.31 In an air pollution study a random sample of $n = 12$ specimens collected within a mile downwind from a certain factory contained on the average 2.58 micrograms of suspended benzene-soluble organic matter per cubic foot with a standard deviation of 0.52.

(a) If $\bar{x} = 2.58$ is used as an estimate of the mean of the population sampled, what can be said with 95 percent confidence about the maximum error?

(b) Construct a 95% confidence interval for the mean of the population sampled.

11.32 With reference to the example on page 324, where

$$n = 8, \quad \bar{x} = 140{,}800, \quad \text{and} \quad s = 19{,}200,$$

suppose that 140,800 is used as a point estimate of the average number of car crossings the paint can withstand before it deteriorates. What can we assert with 90 percent confidence about the maximum error?

11.33   With reference to the example on page 325, regarding the increase in pulse rate of astronauts performing a certain task, we had

$$n = 12, \quad \bar{x} = 27.33, \quad \text{and} \quad s = 4.28.$$

Find a confidence interval for the mean of the population sampled, using

(a) 95 percent degree of confidence;

(b) 99 percent degree of confidence.

11.34   On six occasions, presumably a random sample, it took

21   26   24   22   23   22

minutes to clean up a school cafeteria. Using $\bar{x} = 23$ minutes and $s = 1.79$ minutes, construct a 95 percent confidence interval for the average time it takes to clean up this cafeteria.

11.35   In establishing the weight of an ancient coin, its actual weight is of critical importance. Four experts independently weighted a Phoenician tetradrachm and got

14.28   14.34   14.26   and 14.32

grams, yielding

$$\bar{x} = 14.30 \text{ grams} \quad \text{and} \quad s = 0.0365 \text{ gram.}$$

What can we assert with 99 percent confidence about the maximum error when we use 14.30 grams as an estimate of the actual weight of the coin?

11.36   A dentist finds in a routine check that six prison inmates, a random sample, require 2, 3, 6, 0, 4, and 3 fillings. Construct a 90 percent confidence interval for the average number of fillings that are required by the inmates of this (very large) prison.

⊕ 11.37   With reference to the example on page 327, where an investor is planning to open a new travel agency, what prior probability does the investor assign to the agency's netting between \$3,500 and \$3,600 per month? Compare this prior probability with the corresponding posterior probability obtained on page 328.

⊕ 11.38   An actuary feels that the prior distribution of the average annual claims for a certain kind of health insurance coverage is a normal distribution with the mean $\mu_0 = \$352$ and the standard deviation $\sigma_0 = \$12$. She also knows that the claims for this policy vary from one person to another with the standard deviation $\sigma = \$120$. If the claims for ten policies like this average \$440.22, find the posterior mean as a Bayesian estimate of its true average annual claim amount.

⊕ 11.39   With reference to the preceding exercise, what is the posterior probability that the policy's true average annual claim amounts are between \$360 and \$400?

⊕ 11.40   A college professor is making up a final examination in history for a large group of students. His feelings about the average grade they should get is expressed subjectively by a normal distribution which has the mean $\mu_0 = 65.2$ and a standard deviation $\sigma_0 = 1.5$. What prior probability does the professor assign to the event that the average grade of all the students will lie on the interval from 63.0 to 68.0?

⊕ 11.41   With reference to the preceding exercise, suppose that the examination is given to a random sample of 40 of the students and that their grades have a mean $\bar{x} = 72.9$ and a standard deviation $s = 7.4$.

(a) Calculate the posterior mean as a point estimate of the mean grade which all the students will get on the test.

(b) Find the posterior probability which the professor assigns to the event that the average grade of all the students will lie in the interval from 63.0 and 68.0.

⇔ 11.42   In Exercises 11.40 and 11.41, the professor can assess the size of the error by using the prior distribution and using no data.

    (a) Based on the prior distribution, what can he say with 95% confidence if he uses 65.2 as the estimate of the population average?

    (b) Based on the posterior distribution, what can he say with 95% confidence if he uses the posterior mean as the estimate of the population average?

⇔ 11.43   John, the owner of a retail jewelry store, intends to assess his average gross weekly sales for a new product line. Based on information from the vendor of the new line, John believes that the population average of these sales can be expressed subjectively by a normal distribution with a mean of $800 and a standard deviation of $160. For the first 28 weeks during which the new line is sold, John finds that $\bar{x} = \$710$ and $s = \$32$.

    (a) Based on the prior distribution, find the probability that the population average of weekly sales lies in the interval from $560 to $1,040.

    (b) Calculate the posterior mean as a point estimate of the population average weekly sales.

    (c) Find the probability which the posterior distribution assigns to the interval from $560 to $1,040.

11.4   TESTS OF HYPOTHESES

In the introduction to this chapter there are several examples of tests of hypotheses. We mentioned a psychologist who wants to determine whether adults' reaction time to a particular visual stimulus is 0.38 second; a transportation planner who needs to know whether the standard deviation in the distances that people commute to work was 2.5 miles; and a football coach who wants to know whether 75% of his team can run 60 yards in less than 8.0 seconds, wearing all their equipment. Since the psychologist is concerned with a value of μ, the transportation planner about a value of σ, and the football coach about the value of p (the parameter of a binomial population), these are all tests of **statistical hypotheses.**

> A statistical hypothesis is an assertion or conjecture about a parameter, or parameters, of a population; it may also concern the type, or nature, of the population.

With regard to the second part of this definition, we shall see in Section 13.6 how we can test whether it is reasonable to treat a random variable as having a binomial distribution, or perhaps a Poisson distribution, and whether it is reasonable to treat a set of data as coming from a normal population. In this chapter we shall be concerned only with hypotheses about means—the mean of one population or the means of two populations.

    To develop procedures for testing statistical hypotheses, we must always know exactly what to expect when a hypothesis is true, and it is for this reason that we often hypothesize the opposite of what we hope to prove. Suppose, for instance, that we suspect that a dice game is not honest. If we formulate the hypothesis that the dice are crooked, everything would depend on how crooked they are, but if we assume that they are perfectly balanced, we could calculate all the necessary probabilities and take it from there. Also, if we want to show that one method of teaching computer programming is more effective than another, we would hypothesize that the two methods are equally effective; if we want to show that one diet is healthier than another, we hypothesize that they are equally healthy; and if we want to show that a new copper-bearing steel has a higher yield strength than ordinary steel, we hypothesize that the two yield strengths are the same. Since we hypothesize that there is no difference in the effectiveness of the two teaching methods, medically no difference between the two diets, and no difference in the yield strength of the two kinds of steel, we call hypotheses like these **null hypotheses** and denote them by H_0. The term "null hypothesis" is used for any hypothesis set up primarily to see whether it can be rejected.

The idea of setting up a null hypothesis is common even in nonstatistical thinking. It is precisely what we do in criminal proceedings, where an accused is presumed to be innocent until his guilt has been established beyond a reasonable doubt. The presumption of innocence is a null hypothesis.

The hypothesis which we use as an alternative to the null hypothesis, namely, the hypothesis which we accept when the null hypothesis is rejected, is appropriately called an **alternative hypothesis** and is denoted by H_A. It must always be formulated together with the null hypothesis, for otherwise we would not know when to reject H_0. For instance, if the psychologist of the example on page 317 tests the null hypothesis $\mu = 0.38$ second against the alternative hypothesis $\mu > 0.38$ second, he would reject the null hypothesis only if he gets a sample mean which is much greater than 0.38 second. On the other hand, if he uses the alternative hypothesis $\mu \neq 0.38$ second, he would reject the null hypothesis if he gets a sample mean which is much greater than, or much less than, 0.38 second.

As in the preceding illustration, alternative hypotheses usually specify that the population mean (or whatever other parameter may be of concern) is less than, greater than, or not equal to the value assumed under the null hypothesis. For any given problem, the choice of one of these alternatives depends on what we hope to be able to show, or perhaps on where we want to put the burden of proof.

Example

An appliance manufacturer is considering the purchase of a new machine for stamping out sheet metal parts. If μ_0 is the average number of good parts stamped out per hour by his old machine and μ is the corresponding average for the new machine, the manufacturer wants to test the null hypothesis $\mu = \mu_0$ against a suitable alternative. What should the alternative be if:

(a) He does not want to buy the new machine unless it is more productive than the old one;

(b) He wants to buy the new machine (which has some other nice features) unless it is less productive than the old one.

solution

(a) The manufacturer should use the alternative hypothesis $\mu > \mu_0$ and purchase the new machine only if the null hypothesis can be rejected.

(b) The manufacturer should use the alternative hypothesis $\mu < \mu_0$ and purchase the new machine unless the null hypothesis is rejected.

In the preceding example we treat μ_0 as a known number. We wish to make an assertion about μ, the parameter representing the unknown mean for the new machine.

To illustrate in detail the problems we face when testing a statistical hypothesis, suppose that the members of an airport's planning commission are considering the possibility of redesigning the parking facilities. They first want to check the claim that on the average cars remain in the short-term parking area for 42.5 minutes, or whether this figure is too high or too low. Thus, they shall want to test the null hypothesis

$$H_0: \quad \mu = 42.5 \text{ minutes}$$

against the alternative hypothesis

$$H_A: \quad \mu \neq 42.5 \text{ minutes}$$

To perform this test, they instruct a staff member to take a random sample of 50 ticket stubs showing time of arrival and time of departure, with the intention of letting stand the claim if the mean of the sample falls anywhere from 40.5 to 44.5 minutes. Otherwise, they will reject the claim, and in either case they will take whatever action is thus called for in their plans.

This procedure provides a clear-cut criterion for rejecting the claim, but unfortunately it is not infallible. Since the decision is based on a sample, there is the possibility that the sample may not represent the truth. Even in the case in where the true mean is $\mu = 42.5$ minutes, there is the possibility, based on chance alone, that the sample mean may be less than or equal to 40.5 minutes or that it may be greater than or equal to 44.5 minutes. In the case in which, say, the true mean is $\mu = 45.0$ minutes, there is the possibility, based on chance, alone, that the sample mean may fall in the interval between 40.5 to 44.5 minutes. Before adopting any testing criterion, it would seem wise to investigate the chances that it may lead to a wrong decision.

Assuming that it is known from similar studies that $\sigma = 7.6$ minutes for this kind of data, let us first investigate the possibility that the sample mean may be less than or equal to 40.5 minutes or greater than or equal to 44.5 minutes even though the true mean is $\mu = 42.5$ minutes. The probability that this will happen purely due to chance is given by the sum of the areas of the shaded regions of Figure 11.6, and it can easily be determined by approximating the sampling distribution of the mean with a normal distribution. Assuming that the population sampled is large enough to be treated as infinite, we have

$$\sigma_{\bar{x}} = \frac{\sigma}{\sqrt{n}} = \frac{7.6}{\sqrt{50}} \approx 1.07$$

and the dividing lines of the criterion, in standard units, are

$$z = \frac{40.5 - 42.5}{1.07} \approx -1.87 \quad \text{and} \quad z = \frac{44.5 - 42.5}{1.07} \approx 1.87$$

It follows from Table I that the area in each tail of the sampling distribution of Figure 11.6 is

$$0.5000 - 0.4693 = 0.0307$$

FIGURE 11.6

Test criterion and distribution of x̄ if μ = 42.5 minutes.

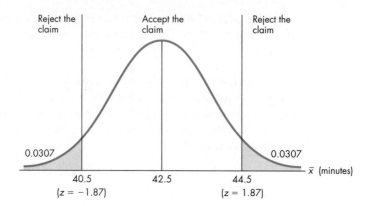

The probability of getting a value in either tail of the sampling distribution and thereby erroneously rejecting the null hypothesis $\mu = 42.5$ minutes, is

$$0.0307 + 0.0307 = 0.0614$$

about 6%. Whether this risk is acceptable is a question for the planning commission. Their decision would depend on the consequences of their making such an error.

Let us now consider the other possibility, where the test fails to detect that μ is not equal to 42.5 minutes. Suppose again, for the sake of argument, that the true mean is $\mu = 45.5$ minutes. Getting a sample mean on the interval from 40.5 minutes to 44.5 minutes would lead to an erroneous acceptance of the claim that $\mu = 42.5$ minutes. The probability that this will occur is given by the shaded area of Figure 11.7. The mean of the sampling distribution is now 45.5, its standard deviation is, as before,

$$\sigma_{\bar{x}} = \frac{7.6}{\sqrt{50}} \approx 1.07$$

and the dividing lines of the criterion, in standard units, are

$$z = \frac{40.5 - 45.5}{1.07} \approx -4.67 \quad \text{and} \quad z = \frac{44.5 - 45.5}{1.07} \approx -0.93$$

FIGURE 11.7

Test criterion and distribution of x̄ if μ = 45.5 minutes

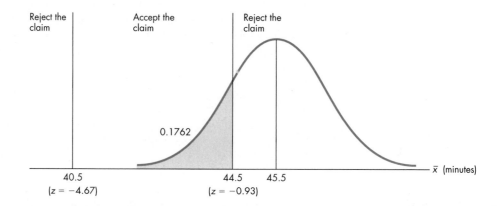

Since the area under the curve to the left of $z = -4.67$ is negligible, it follows from Table I that the shaded region area of Figure 11.7 is

$$0.5000 - 0.3238 = 0.1762$$

or approximately 0.18. This is the probability of erroneously accepting the null hypothesis when actually $\mu = 45.5$ minutes. Again, it is up to the members of the planning commission to decide whether this represents an acceptable risk.

The situation described here is typical of tests of hypothesis, and it may be summarized as in the following table:

	Accept H_0	*Reject H_0*
H_0 is true	Correct decision	Type I error
H_0 is false	Type II error	Correct decision

If the null hypothesis H_0 is true and accepted, or false and rejected, the decision is correct. If H_0 is true and rejected, the decision is incorrect and is a **Type I error.** The probability of committing Type I error is designated by the Greek letter α (alpha). If H_0 is false and accepted, the decision is incorrect and is a **Type II error.** The probability of committing Type II errors is designated by the Greek letter β (beta). In our example, we showed that $\alpha = 0.06$; we also showed that when $\mu = 45.5$ minutes that $\beta = 0.18$.

The scheme outlined above is reminiscent of what we did in Section 7.2. Similar to the decision that the furniture manufacturer had to make in the example on page 193, we now have to decide whether to accept or reject H_0. It is difficult to carry this analogy much further, though, because in actual practice we can seldom associate cash payoffs with the various possibilities, as we did in that example.

Example

Suppose that the planning commission's staff member actually takes the sample and gets $\bar{x} = 41.8$ minutes. What decision will the members of the planning commission make and will it be in error if in reality
  (a) $\mu = 42.5$ minutes;   (b) $\mu = 41.2$ minutes?

solution

Since $\bar{x} = 41.8$ falls in the interval from 40.5 to 44.4, they will accept the null hypothesis that on the average cars remain in the short-term parking area for 42.5 minutes.
  (a) Since the null hypothesis is true and accepted, they will not be making an error.
  (b) Since the null hypothesis is false but accepted, they will be making a Type II error.   ◪ ◪ ◪

In calculating the probability of a Type II error in our example, we arbitrarily chose the alternative value $\mu = 45.5$ minutes. However, in this problem, as in most others, there are infinitely many other alternatives, and for each one of them there is a positive probability β of erroneously accepting H_0. So, in practice we choose some key alternative values and calculate the corresponding probabilities β of committing a Type II error, or we sidestep the issue by proceeding in a way which will be explained in Section 11.5.

FIGURE 11.8

Operating characteristic curve.

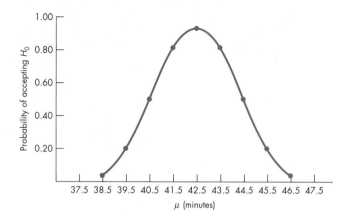

If we do calculate β for various alternative values of μ and plot these probabilities as in Figure 11.8, we obtain a curve which is called the **operating characteristic curve,** or simply the **OC-curve,** of the test criterion. Since the probability of a Type II error is the probability of accepting H_0 when it is false, we "completed the picture" in Figure 11.8 by labeling the vertical scale "Probability of accepting H_0" and plotting at $\mu = 42.5$ minutes the probability of accepting H_0 when it is true, namely,

$$1 - \alpha = 1 - 0.06 = 0.94$$

Examination of the curve of Figure 11.8 shows that the probability of accepting H_0 is greatest when it is true, and that it is still high for small departures from $\mu = 42.5$ minutes. However, for larger and larger departures from $\mu = 42.5$ minutes in either direction, the probabilities of failing to detect them and accepting H_0 become smaller and smaller. In Exercise 11.56 the reader is asked to verify some of the probabilities plotted in Figure 11.8.

If we had plotted the probabilities of rejecting H_0 instead of those of accepting H_0, we would have obtained the graph of the **power function** of the test criterion instead of its operating characteristic curve. The concept of an OC-curve is used more widely in applications, especially in industrial applications, while the concept of a power function is used more widely in matters that are of theoretical interest. A detailed study of operating characteristic curves and power functions is beyond the scope of this text, and the purpose of our example is mainly to show how statistical methods can be used to measure and control the risks one is exposed to when testing hypotheses. Of course, the methods discussed here are not limited to the particular problem concerning the average length of time that cars are parked in a given area—H_0 could be the hypothesis that the average age of divorced women at the time of their divorce is 35.6 years, the hypothesis that an antibiotic is 83 percent effective, the hypothesis that a computer-assisted method of instruction will on the average raise students' scores on a standard achievement test by 8.4 points, and so forth.

◪ EXERCISES

11.44   The average drying time of a manufacturer's paint is 20 minutes. Investigating the effectiveness of a modification in the chemical composition of his paint, the manufacturer wants to test the null hypothesis $\mu = 20$ minutes against a suitable alternative, where μ is the average drying time of the modified paint.

(a) What alternative hypothesis should the manufacturer use if he does not want to make the modification in the chemical composition of the paint unless it decreases the drying time?

(b) What alternative hypothesis should the manufacturer use if the new process is actually cheaper and he wants to make the modification unless it increases the drying time of the paint?

11.45 A city police department is considering replacing the tires on its cars with radial tires. If μ_1 is the average number of miles the old tires last and μ_2 is the average number of miles the new tires will last, the null hypothesis to be tested is $\mu_1 = \mu_2$.

(a) What alternative hypothesis should the department use if it does not want to buy the radial tires unless they are definitely proved to give better mileage? In other words, the burden of proof is put on the radial tires and the old tires are to be kept unless the null hypothesis can be rejected.

(b) What alternative hypothesis should the department use if it is anxious to get the new tires (which have some other good features) unless they actually give poorer mileage than the old tires? Note that now the burden of proof is on the old tires, which will be kept only if the null hypothesis can be rejected.

(c) What alternative hypothesis should the department use so that the rejection of the null hypothesis can lead either to keeping the old tires or to buying the new ones?

11.46 Rework the example on page 339, supposing that $\bar{x} = 45.2$ minutes instead of $\bar{x} = 41.8$ minutes.

11.47 A botanist wishes to test the null hypothesis that the average diameter of the flowers of a particular plant is 9.6 cm. He decides to take a random sample of size $n = 80$ and accept the null hypothesis if the mean of the sample falls between 9.3 cm and 9.9 cm; if the mean of the sample falls outside this interval he will reject the null hypothesis. What decision will he make and will it be in error if

(a) he gets $\bar{x} = 10.2$ cm and $\mu = 9.6$ cm;

(b) he gets $\bar{x} = 10.2$ cm and $\mu = 9.8$ cm;

(c) he gets $\bar{x} = 9.2$ cm and $\mu = 9.6$ cm;

(d) he gets $\bar{x} = 9.2$ cm and $\mu = 9.8$ cm?

11.48 An education specialist is considering the use of instructional material on audiocassettes for a special class of third-grade students with reading difficulties. Students in this class are given a standardized reading test in May of the school year, and μ_1 is the average score obtained after many years of experience. Let μ_2 be the average score for students using the audiocassettes, and assume that high scores are desirable.

(a) What null hypothesis should the education specialist use?

(b) What alternative hypothesis should be used if the specialist does not want to adopt the new cassettes unless they improve the standardized test scores?

(c) What alternative hypothesis should be used if the specialist wants to adopt the new cassettes unless they worsen the standardized test scores?

11.49 Suppose that a psychological testing service is asked to check whether an executive is emotionally fit to assume the presidency of a large corporation. What type of error would it commit if it erroneously rejects the null hypothesis that the executive is fit for the job? What type of error would it commit if it erroneously accepts the null hypothesis that the executive is fit for the job?

11.50 Suppose we want to test the null hypothesis that an antipollution device for cars is effective. Explain under what conditions we would commit a Type I error and under what conditions we would commit a Type II error.

11.51   Whether an error is a Type I error or a Type II error depends on how we formulate the null hypothesis. To illustrate this, rephrase the null hypothesis of the preceding exercise so that the Type I error becomes a Type II error, and vice versa.

11.52   For a given population with $\sigma = 7.2$ cm, we want to test the null hypothesis $\mu = 60$ cm against the alternative hypothesis $\mu < 60$ cm on the basis of a random sample of size $n = 100$. If the null hypothesis is rejected if $\bar{x} \leq 58.5$ cm and is otherwise accepted,

(a) what is the probability of a Type I error?

(b) what is the probability of a Type II error when in reality $\mu = 59$ cm?

11.53   For a certain population of liens against real estate, we feel that $\sigma = \$800$. We want to test the null hypothesis $\mu = \$6{,}000$ against the alternative hypothesis $\mu > \$6{,}000$ on the basis of a random sample of size $n = 150$. If the null hypothesis is rejected if $\bar{x} \geq \$6{,}200$ and is otherwise accepted,

(a) what is the probability of a Type I error?

(b) what is the probability of a Type II error when in reality $\mu = \$6{,}050$?

11.54   For a given population with $\sigma = 21.0$ cm we want to test the null hypothesis $\mu = 255$ cm against the alternative hypothesis $\mu \neq 255$ cm on the basis of a sample of size $n = 36$. If the null hypothesis is rejected when $\bar{x} \leq 248$ cm or $\bar{x} \geq 262$ cm,

(a) find the probability of a Type I error;

(b) find the probability of a Type II error when in reality $\mu = 258.5$ cm.

11.55   For a given population with $\sigma = \$8$ we want to test the null hypothesis $\mu = \$65$ against the alternative hypothesis $\mu > \$65$ on the basis of a sample of size $n = 100$. If the null hypothesis is rejected when $\bar{x} \geq \$66$,

(a) find the probability of a Type I error;

(b) find the probability of a Type II error when in reality $\mu = \$65.50$;

(c) find the probability of a Type II error when in reality $\mu = \$66.50$.

11.56   With reference to the operating characteristic curve of Figure 11.8, verify that the probabilities of Type II errors are

(a) 0.82 when $\mu = 41.5$ minutes or $\mu = 43.5$ minutes;

(b) 0.50 when $\mu = 40.5$ minutes or $\mu = 44.5$ minutes;

(c) 0.18 when $\mu = 39.5$ minutes or $\mu = 45.5$ minutes;

(d) 0.03 when $\mu = 38.5$ minutes or $\mu = 46.5$ minutes.

11.57   Suppose that in the airport parking example on page 337 the criterion is changed so that the null hypothesis $\mu = 42.5$ minutes is rejected if the sample mean is less than 41.0 minutes or greater than 44.0 minutes; otherwise, the null hypothesis is accepted.

(a) What is the probability of a Type I error?

(b) Find the probabilities of Type II errors when

$$\mu = 38.5, \quad 39.5, \quad 40.5, \quad 41.5, \quad 43.5, \quad 44.5, \quad 45.5, \quad \text{or} \quad 46.5 \text{ minutes}$$

and plot the operating characteristic curve.

11.58   In the airport parking example on page 337, we are testing the null hypothesis

$$H_0: \quad \mu = 42.5 \text{ minutes}$$

against the alternative

$$H_A: \quad \mu \neq 42.5 \text{ minutes}$$

and it has been assumed that $\sigma = 7.6$ minutes. Suppose that we decide to use the sample size $n = 60$ (rather than 50), and that we will accept H_0 if the sample mean $\bar{x}$ is anywhere between 40.5 minutes and 44.5 minutes.

(a) What is the probability of a Type I error?

(b) Find the probabilities of Type II errors when

$$\mu = 38.5, \quad 39.5, \quad 40.5, \quad 41.5, \quad 43.5, \quad 44.5, \quad 45.5, \quad 46.5$$

Then plot the operating characteristic curve.

11.5   SIGNIFICANCE TESTS

In the airport parking example of the preceding section, we had less trouble with Type I errors than with Type II errors, because we formulated the null hypothesis as a **simple hypothesis** about the parameter μ; that is, we formulated it so that μ took on a single value and the corresponding probability of a Type I error could be calculated.[†] Had we formulated instead a **composite hypothesis** about the parameter μ, say,

$$\mu \neq 42.5 \text{ minutes}, \quad \mu < 42.5 \text{ minutes}, \quad \text{or} \quad \mu > 42.5 \text{ minutes}$$

where in each case μ can take on more than one possible value, we could not have calculated the probability of a Type I error without specifying how much μ differs from, is less than, or is greater than 42.5 minutes.

In the same example, the alternative hypothesis was the composite hypothesis $\mu \neq 42.5$ minutes, and it took quite some work to calculate the probabilities of Type II errors (for various alternative values of μ) shown in the OC-curve of Figure 11.8. Since this is typical of most practical situations (that is, alternative hypotheses are usually composite), let us illustrate how Type II errors can often be sidestepped altogether.

Studies show that in a certain city licensed drivers average 0.9 traffic ticket per year, with a standard deviation of 0.4. A social scientist suspects that licensed drivers over 65 years of age average more than 0.9 traffic ticket per year, and she checks the 1994 records of 40 randomly selected licensed drivers over 65 in this city. She bases her decision on the following criterion:

> Reject the null hypotheses $\mu = 0.9$ (and accept the alternative $\mu > 0.9$) if the 40 licensed drivers over 65 years of age average 1.0 or more traffic tickets per year; otherwise, reserve judgment, perhaps pending further investigation.

The probability of committing a Type I error with this criterion is given by the area of the shaded region of Figure 11.9, and it equals 0.0571.

If we reserve judgment as in this criterion, there is no possibility of committing a Type II error—no matter what happens, the null hypothesis is never ac-

---

[†]Note that we are applying the term "simple hypothesis" to hypotheses about one specific parameter. Some statisticians use the term "simple hypothesis" only when there are no other unknown parameters and the hypothesis completely specifies the population. The hypothesis H_0: $\mu = 72$ regarding a normally distributed population with unknown standard deviation will be described here as a "simple hypothesis" even though some statisticians would not use this description.

FIGURE 11.9

Test criterion.

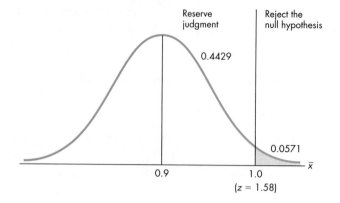

cepted. This would seem to be all right in our example, where the social scientist wants to see primarily whether her suspicion is justified, namely, whether the null hypothesis can be rejected. If it cannot be rejected, this does not mean that she must necessarily accept it; her suspicion may not be completely resolved.

The procedure we have outlined here is called a **significance test,** or a **test of significance.** If the difference between what we expect under the null hypothesis and what we observe in a sample is too large to be reasonably attributed to chance, we reject the null hypothesis. If the difference between what we expect and what we observe is so small that it may well be attributed to chance, we say that the result is **not statistically significant,** or simply that it is **not significant.** We then accept the null hypothesis or reserve judgment, depending on whether a definite decision one way or the other must be reached.

Since "significant" is often used interchangeably with "meaningful" or "important" in everyday language, it must be understood that we are using it here as a technical term. Specifically, the word "significant" is used in situations in which a null hypothesis is rejected. If a result is statistically significant, this does not mean that it is necessarily of any great importance, or that it is of any practical value. Suppose, for instance, that the social scientist of our example takes her sample and gets $\bar{x} = 1.025$. According to the criterion on page 343 this result is statistically significant, meaning that the difference between $\bar{x} = 1.025$ and $\mu = 0.9$ is too big to be attributed to chance. It is possible that no one may care about this result; even an insurance company which ought to be interested might feel that it is simply not worth bothering about.

Returning to the airport parking example, we could convert the criterion on page 337 into that of a significance test by writing

Reject the hypothesis $\mu = 42.5$ minutes (and accept the alternative $\mu \neq 42.5$ minutes) if the mean of the 50 sample values is less than or equal to 40.5 minutes or greater than or equal to 44.5 minutes; reserve judgment if the mean falls anywhere from 40.5 to 44.5 minutes.

So far as the rejection of the null hypothesis is concerned, the criterion has remained unchanged and the probability of a Type I error is still 0.06. However, so far as its acceptance is concerned, the members of the planning commission are now playing it safe by reserving judgment.

Reserving judgment in a significance test is similar to what happens in court proceedings where the prosecution does not have sufficient evidence to get a conviction, but where it would be going too far to say that the defendent definitely did not commit the crime. In general, whether one can afford the luxury of reserving judgment in any given situation depends entirely on the nature of the situation. If a decision must be reached one way or the other, there is no way of avoiding the risk of committing a Type II error.

Since most of the remainder of this book is devoted to significance tests—indeed, most statistical problems which are not problems of estimation or prediction deal with tests of this kind—it will help to perform such tests by proceeding systematically as outlined in the following five steps. The first of these may look simple and straightforward, yet it presents the greatest difficulties to most beginners.

1. We formulate the null hypothesis and an appropriate alternative.

In the airport parking example the null hypothesis is $\mu = 42.5$ minutes, and the alternative hypothesis is $\mu \neq 42.5$ minutes (presumably because the planning commission wanted to protect itself against the possibility that $\mu = 42.5$ minutes may be too high or too low). We refer to this kind of alternative as a **two-sided alternative.** In the traffic ticket example the null hypothesis is $\mu = 0.9$, and the alternative hypothesis is $\mu > 0.9$ (because the social scientist suspected that licensed drivers over 65 average more than 0.9 tickets per year). This is called a **one-sided alternative.** We can also write a one-sided alternative with the inequality going the other way. For instance, if we hope to be able to show that the average time required to do a certain job is less than 15 minutes, we would test the null hypothesis $\mu = 15$ minutes against the alternative hypothesis $\mu < 15$ minutes.

This is not the first time that we concern ourselves with the formulation of hypotheses. In Section 11.4 we mentioned some of the things we must take into account when choosing H_A, but in the example on page 337 as well as in Exercises 11.44 and 11.45 on pages 340 and 341 the null hypothesis is always specified. So, let us see how we go about choosing H_0.

Basically, there are two things we must watch. First, whenever possible we formulate the null hypothesis as a simple hypothesis about the parameter with which we are concerned; second, we formulate the null hypothesis in such a way that its rejection proves the point we hope to make. The reason for choosing H_0 as a simple hypothesis is that it enables us to calculate, or specify, the probability of a Type I error, and we saw how this works in the airport parking example. The reason for choosing the null hypothesis so that its rejection proves the point we hope to make is that in general it is much easier to prove that something is false than to prove that it is true.

Suppose, for instance, that somebody claims that all 6,000 male students attending a certain college weigh at least 145 pounds. To show that this statement is true, we literally have to weigh each of the 6,000 students; however, to show that it is false, we have only to find one student who weighs less than 145 pounds, and that should not be too hard.

Example

A bakery machine fills boxes with crackers, averaging 454 grams (roughly one pound) of crackers per box.

(a) If the management of the bakery is concerned about the possibility that the actual average is different from 454 grams, what null hypothesis and what alternative hypothesis should they use to put this to a test?

(b) If the management of the bakery is concerned about the possibility that the actual average is less than 454 grams, what null hypothesis and what alternative hypothesis should they use to put this to a test?

solution

(a) The words "different from" suggest that the hypothesis $\mu \neq 454$ grams is needed together with the only other possibility, namely, the hypothesis $\mu = 454$ grams. Since the second of these hypotheses is a simple hypothesis, and its rejection (and the acceptance of the other hypothesis) confirms the management's concern, we follow the two rules above by writing

$$H_0: \quad \mu = 454 \text{ grams}$$

$$H_A: \quad \mu \neq 454 \text{ grams}$$

(b) The words "less than" suggest that we need the hypothesis $\mu < 454$ grams, but for the other hypothesis there are many possibilities, including

$$\mu = 454 \text{ grams}, \quad \mu \geq 454 \text{ grams}, \quad \text{and, say,} \quad \mu = 456 \text{ grams}.$$

Two of these (and many others) are simple hypotheses, but since it would be to the bakery's disadvantage to put too many crackers into the boxes, a sensible choice would be

$$H_0: \quad \mu = 454 \text{ grams}$$

$$H_A: \quad \mu < 454 \text{ grams}$$

Note that the null hypothesis is a simple hypothesis and that its rejection (and the acceptance of the alternative) confirms the management's suspicion. ◪ ◪ ◪

Like the first step, the second step looks simple and straightforward, yet it is not without complications.

2. We specify the probability of a Type I error.

When H_0 is a simple hypothesis this can always be done, and we usually set the probability of a Type I error, also called the **level of significance,** at $\alpha = 0.05$ or $\alpha = 0.01$. Testing a simple hypothesis at the 0.05 (or 0.01) level of significance simply means that we are fixing the probability of rejecting H_0 when it is true at 0.05 (or 0.01).

The decision to use 0.05, 0.01, or some other value, depends mostly on the consequences of committing a Type I error. Although it may seem desirable to make the probability of a Type I error small, we cannot make it too small, since this would tend to make the probabilities of serious Type II errors too large, and make it difficult, perhaps exceedingly difficult, to get significant results. The choice of 0.05 or 0.01 and not, say, 0.072 or 0.030, has become a tradition. The use of 0.05 and 0.01 is also related to the availability of statistical tables. While the use of 0.05 or 0.01 has been criticized (see references on page 374), we recommend following statistical tradition. In most of the exercises in this text, the level of significance is noted explicitly.

Let us now see what can be done when the null hypothesis is not a simple hypothesis. Suppose, for instance, that the social scientist of the example on page 343 wants to allow for the possibility that licensed drivers over 65 in the given city might average fewer than 0.9 ticket per year, and hence test the null hypothesis $\mu \leq 0.9$ against the alternative hypothesis $\mu > 0.9$. This means that there is no unique value for the probability of a Type I error, but observe that if μ is less than 0.9, the normal curve of Figure 11.9 is shifted to the left, and the area under the curve to the right of 1.0 becomes less than 0.0571. Thus, if the null hypothesis is $\mu \leq 0.9$, we say that the probability of a Type I error is at most 0.0571, and we write $\alpha \leq 0.0571$. To allow for this possibility, we rewrite the second step as follows:

2. We specify the probability of a Type I error, or the maximum probability of a Type I error.

(This still does not take care of the case where the social scientist wants to test the null hypothesis $\mu < 0.9$ against the alternative hypothesis $\mu \geq 0.9$, but we rarely use null hypotheses given by *strict* inequalities.)

Another difficulty arises in connection with the second step when we cannot, or do not want, to specify the probability of a Type I error, or the maximum probability of a Type I error. This could happen when we do not have enough information about the consequences of Type I errors, or when one person processes the data while another person makes the decisions. What can be done in that case is discussed on pages 351 and 352.

After the null hypothesis, the alternative hypothesis, and the probability (or maximum probability) of a Type I error have been specified, the remaining steps are

3. Based on the sampling distribution of an appropriate statistic, we construct a criterion for testing the null hypothesis against the given alternative hypothesis at the chosen level of significance.

4. We calculate from the data the value of the statistic on which the decision is to be based.

5. We decide whether to reject the null hypothesis, whether to accept it, or whether to reserve judgment.

In the airport parking example we rejected the null hypothesis $\mu = 42.5$ minutes for values of $\bar{x}$ less than 40.5 and also for values of $\bar{x}$ greater than 44.5, and we refer to such a criterion as a **two-sided test** or as a **two-tailed test.** As these names imply, we reject the null hypothesis for values of $\bar{x}$ falling into either tail of its sampling distribution. In the traffic ticket example we rejected the null hypothesis $\mu = 0.9$ for values of $\bar{x}$ greater than 1.0, and we refer to a criterion like this as a **one-sided test** or as a **one-tailed test.** As these names imply, we reject the null hypothesis only for values of $\bar{x}$ falling into one of the two tails of its sampling distribution. In general, a test is said to be two-sided if the null hypothesis is rejected for values of the **test statistic** falling into either tail of its sampling distribution, and it is said to be one-sided if the null hypothesis is rejected only for values of the test statistic falling into one specified tail of its sampling distribution. By "test statistic" we mean the statistic (for instance, the sample mean) on which the test is based. Although there are exceptions, two-sided test criteria are usually used in conjunction with two-sided alternative hypotheses, and one-sided test criteria are usually used in conjunction with one-sided alternative hypotheses.

As part of the third step we must also specify whether the alternative to rejecting the null hypothesis is to accept it or to reserve judgment. This, as we have said, depends on whether we must make a decision one way or the other, or whether the circumstances permit that we delay a decision pending further study. In exercises and examples, the phrase "whether or not" will sometimes be used to indicate that a decision must be reached one way or the other.

In connection with the fifth step, let us point out that we often accept null hypotheses with the tacit hope that we are not exposed to overly high risks of committing serious Type II errors. Of course, if it is necessary we can calculate enough probabilities of Type II errors to get an overall picture from the operating characteristic curve of the test criterion.

Before we consider various special tests for means in the remainder of this chapter, let us point out that the concepts we have introduced here are not limited to tests concerning population means; they apply equally to tests concerning other parameters, or tests concerning the nature, or form, of populations.

◢ EXERCISES

11.59   In a study designed to compare the abilities of eighth-grade boys and girls for a spatial perception test, an educator gets a large difference between their respective sample means. He then concludes that the difference between the corresponding population means is statistically significant. Comment.

11.60   A public opinion poll is conducted on an approaching election to the U.S. Senate. The null hypothesis is that the incumbent candidate will get at least 60 percent of the vote. However, 58 percent of the persons polled favor the incumbent, and this enables the pollster to reject the null hypothesis at the 0.05 level of significance. Since the result is statistically significant, should the candidate be advised to change her campaign strategy?

11.61   The mean age of Mr. and Mrs. Green's three children is 16.3 years while the mean age of Mr. and Mrs. Brown's four children is 12.8 years. Does it make any sense to ask whether the difference between these two means is significant?

11.62 In a study of extrasensory perception, 250 persons were asked to predict patterns on cards drawn at random from a deck, and two of them scored better than could be expected at the 0.01 level of significance. Comment on the conclusion that these two persons must have extraordinary powers.

11.63 During production of spring-loaded postal scales, samples are obtained at regular intervals of time to check at the 0.05 level of significance whether the production process is reliable. The checking is done through use of a known weight of 8.0 ounces, and a scale is deemed acceptable if it indicates any weight between 7.85 ounces and 8.15 ounces. Is there any cause for concern, if in 40 such samples, the null hypothesis that the process is reliable is rejected seven times?

11.64 In a certain experiment, a null hypothesis is rejected at the 0.001 level of significance. Does this mean that the probability is at most 0.001 that the null hypothesis is true?

11.65 It has been claimed that, on the average, the students attending a certain university miss 3.4 lectures per semester per course. One of the deans, concerned that this figure might not be right, plans to put this claim to a test.

(a) What null hypothesis and what alternative should he use?

(b) If the dean plans to base the decision on the mean of a random sample, should he use a one-tailed test or a two-tailed test?

11.66 The manufacturer of a blood-pressure medication claims that, on the average, the medication will lower patients' blood pressure by at least 20 millimeters. A medical research worker suspects this claim and wishes to put it to a test.

(a) What null hypothesis and what alternative should she use?

(b) If she bases her decision on the mean of a random sample, should she use a one-tailed test or a two-tailed test?

11.67 An urban messenger service claims that it can pick up and deliver a package from one downtown location to another within 90 minutes of receiving a telephone request. It is suspected that this 90 minute figure may be too low. What null hypothesis and what alternative hypothesis should be used to test this claim?

11.68 A researcher develops a new topical treatment for acne and wants to show that its performance is not significantly different from that of a popular product currently on the market. Accordingly, he tests the null hypothesis that the population averages for the two products are the same against the two-sided alternative that they are different. He designs an experiment involving six subjects (three using each product) and standard measures of acne severity. The result of the experiment is that the products are not statistically significantly different. Comment.

11.69 A product line inspector is concerned that the average "fill" going into boxes of cornflakes might not be the desired 24 ounces. Letting μ be the relevant population average, she tests the null hypothesis that $\mu = 24$ ounces against the alternative that $\mu \neq 24$ ounces. Based on a random sample of 280 boxes with a sample mean of $\bar{x} = 24.08$ ounces she concludes that the null hypothesis must be rejected and that μ is significantly different from 24 ounces. Comment.

11.70 A lake is repeatedly monitored for concentration levels of a particular pollutant, for which the acceptable level is 0.0082 mg/liter. Letting μ be the average pollution level, a researcher tests the null hypothesis $\mu = 0.0082$ against the alternative $\mu > 0.0082$. Based on a sample of 120 readings with a sample mean of $\bar{x} = 0.0264$ and a sample standard deviation of $s = 0.0022$, he decides that the null hypothesis must be rejected. Comment.

11.6 TESTS CONCERNING MEANS

Having used tests concerning means to illustrate the basic principles of hypothesis testing, we now demonstrate how to proceed in actual practice. In what follows, we depart somewhat from the procedure used in the preceding sections. For example, in the airport parking example as well as in the traffic ticket example we stated the test criterion in terms of $\bar{x}$ (in the first case we rejected the null hypothesis for $\bar{x} \leq 40.5$ or $\bar{x} \geq 44.5$, and in the second case we rejected it for $\bar{x} \geq 1.5$). Now we shall base it on the statistic

Statistic for Test Concerning Mean	$$z = \frac{\bar{x} - \mu_0}{\sigma/\sqrt{n}}$$

where μ_0 is the value of the mean assumed under the null hypothesis. The reason for working with standard units, or z-values, is that it enables us to formulate criteria which are applicable to a great variety of problems, not just one.

The test of this section is essentially a **large-sample test;** that is, we require that the samples are large enough, $n \geq 30$, so that the sampling distribution of the mean can be approximated closely with a normal distribution and z is a value of a random variable having approximately the standard normal distribution. (In the special case where we sample a normal population, z is a value of a random variable having the standard normal distribution regardless of the size of n.)

Thus, we can use the test criteria shown in Figure 11.10 on page 351; depending on the alternative hypothesis, the dividing lines, or **critical values,** of the criteria are $-z_\alpha$ or z_α for the one-sided alternatives, and they are $-z_{\alpha/2}$ and $z_{\alpha/2}$ for the two-sided alternative. As before, z_α and $z_{\alpha/2}$ are such that the area to their right under the standard normal curve is α and $\alpha/2$. Symbolically, we can formulate these criteria as follows:

Alternative hypothesis	Reject the null hypothesis if	Accept the null hypothesis or reserve judgment if
$\mu < \mu_0$	$z \leq -z_\alpha$	$z > -z_\alpha$
$\mu > \mu_0$	$z \geq z_\alpha$	$z < z_\alpha$
$\mu \neq \mu_0$	$z \leq -z_{\alpha/2}$ or $z \geq z_{\alpha/2}$	$-z_{\alpha/2} < z < z_{\alpha/2}$

If the level of significance is 0.05, the dividing lines are -1.645 or 1.645 for the one-sided alternatives, and -1.96 and 1.96 for the two-sided alternative; if the level of significance is 0.01, the dividing lines are -2.33 or 2.33 for the one-sided alternatives, and -2.575 and 2.575 for the two-sided alternative. All these values come directly from Table I.[†]

[†]Some authors exclude the dividing lines from the values for which the null hypothesis is rejected, but this is of no practical consequence since the standard normal distribution is a continuous distribution.

Reject null hypothesis

α

$-z_\alpha$ 0

Alternative hypothesis
$\mu < \mu_0$

Reject null hypothesis

α

0 z_α

Alternative hypothesis
$\mu > \mu_0$

Reject null hypothesis Reject null hypothesis

$\alpha/2$ $\alpha/2$

$-z_{\alpha/2}$ 0 $z_{\alpha/2}$

Alternative hypothesis
$\mu \neq \mu_0$

FIGURE 11.10 *Test criteria for large-sample tests concerning mean.*

Example

Muriel, a surveyor, must determine, based on a random sample of size $n = 35$ readings, whether the height of a certain hill is 724 feet, as recorded. The test is conducted using the 0.05 level of significance and, from a previous survey it is known that the standard deviation is $\sigma = 21$ feet. What will she decide if she gets $\bar{x} = 732$ feet?

solution

1. H_0: $\mu = 724$ feet
   H_A: $\mu \neq 724$ feet
2. $\alpha = 0.05$
3. Reject the null hypothesis if $z \leq -1.96$ or $z \geq 1.96$, where

$$z = \frac{\bar{x} - \mu_0}{\sigma/\sqrt{n}}$$

and otherwise accept the null hypothesis (or reserve judgment).
4. Substituting

$$\mu_0 = 724, \quad \sigma = 21, \quad n = 35, \quad \text{and} \quad \bar{x} = 732$$

into the formula for z, we obtain

$$z = \frac{732 - 724}{21/\sqrt{35}} \approx 2.25$$

5. Since $z = 2.25$ exceeds 1.96, the null hypothesis must be rejected. In other words, the difference between $\bar{x} = 732$ and $\mu_0 = 724$ is significant. ◪ ◪ ◪

If the surveyor had used the 0.01 level of significance in this example, she would not have been able to reject the null hypothesis because $z = 2.25$ falls between -2.575 and 2.575. This illustrates the importance of specifying the level of significance before any calculations are actually made, thus avoiding the temptation of later choosing a level of significance that happens to suit our purpose.

For such problems, some researchers accompany the calculated value of the test statistic with the corresponding **tail probability**, or **p-value**, namely, with the probability of getting a difference between $\bar{x}$ and μ_0 that is numerically greater than or equal to that actually observed. For instance, in the surveyor example, the tail probability is given by the total area under the standard normal curve to the left of $z = -2.25$ and to the right of $z = 2.25$, and that equals

$$2(0.5000 - 0.4878) = 0.0244$$

This practice is not new by any means, but it has been advocated more widely in recent years because of the general availability of computers. For some distributions, computers can provide tail probabilities not directly available from tables.

Quoting tail probabilities is the method referred to on page 347 for problems where we cannot, or do not, want to specify the level of significance. This is feasible, for instance, when we study a set of data without having to reach a decision. It is also feasible when we process a set of data to enable someone else to make a decision. Tail probabilities are provided by most statistical programs, allowing the user to avoid comparing the results with table values and also allowing the user to specify the level of significance.

If it is necessary to make a decision, then we still have the responsibility of specifying the level of significance before we actually perform the test.

In general, *p*-values may be defined as follows: Corresponding to an observed value of a test statistic, the *p*-value is the lowest level of significance at which the null hypothesis could have been rejected. In our example, the *p*-value is 0.0244, and we could have rejected the null hypothesis at the 0.0244 level of significance. We certainly would have rejected the null hypothesis at the actual specified level of significance, $\alpha = 0.05$.

If we wish to base tests of significance on *p*-values, steps 1 and 2 remain the same, but steps 3, 4, and 5 must be modified as follows:

3'. We specify the test statistic.
4'. We calculate the value of the specified test statistic and the corresponding *p*-value from the sample data.
5'. We compare the *p*-value obtained in step 4' with the level of significance α specified in step 2. If the *p*-value is *less than or equal to* α, the null hypothesis must be rejected; otherwise we accept the null hypothesis or reserve judgment.[†]

The test described in this section requires that σ be known. When σ is not known, we substitute for σ the sample standard deviation s. If n is large, say $n \geq 30$, we recommend the use of s even if σ is claimed to be known.

Example

The manager of a trucking firm suspects the claim of a tire salesman that the average lifetime of his tires is at least 28,000 miles. To check the claim, the firm mounts 40 of these tires on its trucks and gets a mean lifetime of 27,563 miles with

---

[†]If test criteria are modified as in the footnote on page 350, *p*-values must be defined in a different way.

a standard deviation of 1,348 miles. What can the manager conclude if the probability of a Type I error is to be at most 0.01?

1. H_0: $\mu \geq 28{,}000$ miles
   H_A: $\mu < 28{,}000$ miles
2. $\alpha \leq 0.01$
3. Since the probability of a Type I error is greatest when $\mu = 28{,}000$ miles, we proceed as if we were testing the null hypothesis $\mu = 28{,}000$ miles against the alternative hypothesis $\mu < 28{,}000$ miles at the 0.01 level of significance. Thus, the null hypothesis must be rejected if $z \leq -2.33$, where

$$z = \frac{\bar{x} - \mu_0}{\sigma/\sqrt{n}}$$

   with σ replaced by s; otherwise, accept the null hypothesis or reserve judgment.
4. Substituting $\mu_0 = 28{,}000$, $\bar{x} = 27{,}563$, $n = 40$, and $s = 1{,}348$ for σ into the formula for z, we get

$$z = \frac{27{,}563 - 28{,}000}{1{,}348/\sqrt{40}} \approx -2.05$$

5. Since $z = -2.05$ is not less than -2.33, the null hypothesis cannot be rejected; in other words, the trucking manager's suspicion that $\mu < 28{,}000$ miles is not confirmed by the data. Whether he goes any further and accepts the null hypothesis is his decision and not a matter of statistics.

It would be acceptable to use H_0: $\mu = 28{,}000$ miles in step 1 and $\alpha = 0.01$ in step 2. Steps 3, 4, and 5 would not be affected by this change.

Let us repeat this procedure using the p-value. In the solution, steps 1 and 2 remain the same, but steps 3, 4, and 5 are replaced by:

3′. The test statistic is

$$z = \frac{\bar{x} - \mu_0}{\sigma/\sqrt{n}}$$

   with σ replaced by s.
4′. Substituting $n = 40$, $\bar{x} = 27{,}563$, $\mu_0 = 28{,}000$, and $s = 1{,}348$ for σ into the formula for z, we get

$$z = \frac{27{,}563 - 28{,}000}{1{,}348/\sqrt{40}} \approx -2.05$$

   and from Table I we find that the p-value, the area under the curve to the left of $z = -2.05$, is 0.0202.
5′. Since 0.0202 is greater than $\alpha = 0.01$, the null hypothesis cannot be rejected. As before, the trucking manager's suspicion is not confirmed. ▪ ▪ ▪

The p-value calculation is sometimes used to avoid the formalism of hypothesis testing, especially in situations where there is no immediate consequence to the accept-or-reject decision. In such cases the *p*-value may be used as a measure of how interesting the data are.

In the truck-tire example, an actual decision is required: the manager must decide what brand of tires to use on his trucks. The end result must be a decision about adopting the specified brand of tires.

Consider next the plight of a social scientist exploring the relationships between family economics and school performance. He could be testing hundreds of hypotheses involving dozens of variables. The work is very complicated, and there are no immediate policy consequences. In this situation, the social scientist can tabulate the hypothesis tests according to their *p*-values. Those tests leading to the lowest *p*-values are the most provocative, and they will certainly be the subject of future discussion. The social scientist need not actually accept or reject the hypotheses, and the use of the *p*-value furnishes a convenient summary.

11.7   TESTS CONCERNING MEANS (Small Samples)

When we do not know the value of the population standard deviation and the sample is small, $n < 30$, we must assume as on page 323 that the population we are sampling has roughly the shape of a normal distribution. We can then base our decision on the statistic

Small-sample Test of Mean

$$t = \frac{\bar{x} - \mu_0}{s/\sqrt{n}}$$

which is a value of a random variable having the *t* distribution (see page 323) with $n - 1$ degrees of freedom. If we cannot fulfill the assumption that the population from which we are sampling has roughly the shape of a normal distribution, then we may have to use one of the alternative tests described in Chapter 17.

The criteria for the **one-sample *t* test,** as this small-sample test is called, are similar to those shown in Figure 11.10 and in the table on page 350. Now the curves represent *t* distributions instead of normal distributions, and z, z_α, and $z_{\alpha/2}$ are replaced by t, t_α, and $t_{\alpha/2}$. As defined on page 323, t_α and $t_{\alpha/2}$ are values for which the area to their right under the *t* distribution are α and $\alpha/2$. All the dividing lines of the criteria may be read from Table II, with the number of degrees of freedom equal to $n - 1$.

Example

The yield of alfalfa from six test plots is

$$1.4 \quad 1.8 \quad 1.1 \quad 1.9 \quad 2.2 \quad 1.2$$

tons per acre. Assuming that these values constitute a sample from a population that has roughly the shape of a normal distribution, test at the 0.05 level of significance whether these values support the contention that the average yield for this type of alfalfa is 1.5 tons per acre.

solution

1. H_0: $\mu = 1.5$
   H_A: $\mu \neq 1.5$
2. $\alpha = 0.05$
3. Reject the null hypothesis if $t \leq -2.571$ or $t \geq 2.571$, where

$$t = \frac{\bar{x} - \mu_0}{s/\sqrt{n}}$$

and 2.571 is the value of $t_{0.025}$ for $6 - 1 = 5$ degrees of freedom; otherwise, state that the data support the contention.

4. First calculating the mean and the standard deviation of the given data, we get $\bar{x} = 1.6$ and $s = 0.434$. Then, substituting these values together with $n = 6$ and $\mu_0 = 1.5$ into the formula for t, we obtain

$$t = \frac{1.6 - 1.5}{0.434/\sqrt{6}} \approx 0.56$$

5. Since $t = 0.56$ falls on the interval from -2.571 to 2.571, the null hypothesis cannot be rejected; in other words, the data support the contention that the average yield of the given kind of alfalfa is 1.5 tons per acre. ◢ ◢ ◢

A computer printout solution of the preceding example is shown in Figure 11.11. It confirms the values we obtained for $\bar{x}$ and t and shows that the tail probability is 0.5965. Since 0.5965 exceeds 0.05, we conclude, as before, that the null hypothesis cannot be rejected.

FIGURE 11.11

Computer printout for one-sample t test (Statistix 4.1).

```
VIEW DATA

  CASE    ALFALFA

     1      1.4
     2      1.8
     3      1.1
     4      1.9
     5      2.2
     6      1.2


ONE-SAMPLE T TEST FOR ALFALFA

NULL HYPOTHESIS:  MU =    1.500
ALTERNATIVE HYP:  MU <>  1.500

MEAN             1.6000
STD ERROR        0.1770
T                  0.56
DF                    5
P                0.5965

  CASES INCLUDED 6       MISSING CASES 0
```

It is still possible, using Table II for the t distribution, to make an interval statement about the p-value. Here we note that $p > 2(0.10) = 0.20$. This is consistent with the 0.5965 value given by the computer program—and with the conclusion that H_0 cannot be rejected.

◢ EXERCISES

11.71   Jeffrey, a law student, wishes to check his professor's contention that convicted forgers spend on the average 8.8 months in jail. He obtains a random sample of 70 such cases from court files and finds that $\bar{x} = 8.2$ months and $s = 2.2$ months.

(a) Test the null hypothesis $\mu = 8.8$ months against the alternative $\mu \neq 8.8$ months, using the 0.01 level of significance.

(b) Find the p-value corresponding to the value of z found in part (a).

(c) Use the p-value to perform the hypothesis test.

11.72   According to the norms established for a reading comprehension test, eighth graders should average 73.2 with a standard deviation of 8.6. If 45 randomly selected eighth graders from a certain school district average 76.7,

(a) test the null hypothesis $\mu = 73.2$ against the alternative hypothesis $\mu > 73.2$ at the 0.01 level of significance;

(b) comment on the district superintendent's claim that her eighth graders are above average;

(c) find the p-value corresponding to the value of z obtained in the test in (a);

(d) use the p-value to perform the hypothesis test.

11.73   The end-of-day shutdown routine at a large factory involves cooling machinery, checking electrical switches, and locking the security fences. Management wants to know if the true average time to perform these tasks is 40 minutes. In a random sample of 34 days, the times to perform the shutdown averages 42 minutes with a standard deviation of 2.1 minutes.

(a) Test the null hypothesis $\mu = 40$ minutes against the alternative $\mu \neq 40$ minutes, using the 0.05 level of significance.

(b) Find the p-value corresponding to the value of z found in part (a).

(c) Use the p-value to perform the hypothesis test.

11.74   A horticulturist wishes to determine whether the honeybees visiting a peach orchard this year differ from the typical weight of 0.85 gram. From previous work in weighing this species of honeybee, the standard deviation of weights is believed to be $\sigma = 0.18$ gram. A sample of 100 honeybees has a mean weight of 0.92 gram with a sample standard deviation of 0.24 gram. At the level of significance 0.05, can we conclude that this year's bees differ from the typical weight?

11.75   A large-sample test concerning a mean yielded a tail probability of 0.005. Can the null hypothesis be rejected at the 0.01 level of significance?

11.76   Tests performed with a random sample of 40 NiCad (nickel-cadmium) computer batteries indicated that they have an average life of 3.60 hours, with a standard deviation of 0.45 hour.

(a) With a probability of Type I error no greater than 0.05, would these data lead you to accept the null hypothesis $\mu \geq 3.75$ hours or the alternative $\mu < 3.75$?

(b) Find the p-value associated with the value of z found in part (a).

(c) Use the p-value to perform the hypothesis test.

11.77   In a study for new sources of food, it is claimed that a pound of a certain kind of fish yields on the average 2.41 ounces of FPC (fish-protein concentrate), which can be used to enrich various food products. A sample of 30 pieces of this fish yielded on the average 2.44 ounces of FPC per pound of fish, with a standard deviation of 0.07 ounce.

(a) Do these data support the claim, using the 0.05 level of significance?

(b) Do these data support the claim, using the 0.01 level of significance?

(c) Find the p-value associated with the value of z.

(d) Using the p-value, determine whether the claim would have been rejected at the 0.02 level of significance.

11.78 If we wish to test the null hypothesis $\mu = \mu_0$ in such a way that the probability of a Type I error is α and the probability of a Type II error is β for the specified alternative value $\mu = \mu_A$, we must take a random sample of size n, where

$$n = \frac{\sigma^2(z_\alpha + z_\beta)^2}{(\mu_A - \mu_0)^2}$$

if the alternative hypothesis is one-sided, and

$$n = \frac{\sigma^2(z_{\alpha/2} + z_\beta)^2}{(\mu_A - \mu_0)^2}$$

if the alternative hypothesis is two-sided.

Suppose, for instance, that for a population with $\sigma = 6$ we want to test the null hypothesis $\mu = 200$ pounds against the alternative hypothesis $\mu < 200$ pounds. How large a sample will we need if the probability of a Type I error is to be 0.05 and the probability of a Type II error is to be 0.05 when $\mu = 198$ pounds? Substituting into the first of the two formulas for n above, we obtain

$$n = \frac{6^2(1.645 + 1.645)^2}{(198 - 200)^2} = 97.4$$

or 98 rounded up to the nearest integer.

(a) Suppose that we want to test the null hypothesis $\mu = 540$ mm against the alternative hypothesis $\mu > 540$ mm for a population whose standard deviation is $\sigma = 88$ mm. How large a sample will we need if the probability of a Type I error is to be 0.05 and the probability of a Type II error is to be 0.10 when $\mu = 560$ mm? Determine also for what values of $\bar{x}$ the null hypothesis will be rejected.

(b) Suppose that we want to test the null hypothesis $\mu = \$650$ against the alternative hypothesis $\mu \neq \$650$ for a population whose standard deviation is $\sigma = \$26$. How large a sample will we need if the probability of a Type I error is to be 0.05 and the probability of a Type II error is to be 0.20 for $\mu = \$670$? Determine also for what values of $\bar{x}$ the null hypothesis will be rejected.

11.79 We wish to test the null hypothesis $\mu = 240$ days against the alternative hypothesis $\mu \neq 240$ days for a population whose standard deviation is at most 14 days. We decide to use the 0.05 level of significance, and we would like the probability of a Type II error to be at most 0.25 when $\mu = 260$ days.

(a) How large a sample will be needed to achieve the objectives?

(b) Does the solution to part (a) suggest that we might need to assume a normally distributed population?

11.80 A random sample of 12 graduates of a secretarial school averages 73.2 words per minute with a standard deviation of 7.9 words per minute on a typing test. Use the 0.05 level of significance to test the null hypothesis that graduates of this secretarial school average 75.0 words per minute on the given test against the alternative that they average less.

11.81 A soft-drink machine is set to dispense 6.0 ounces per cup. If the machine is tested nine times, yielding a mean cup fill of 6.2 ounces with a standard deviation of 0.15 ounce, can we reject the null hypothesis $\mu = 6.0$ ounces against the alternative hypothesis $\mu > 6.0$ ounces at the 0.01 level of significance?

11.82   The manufacturer of a new tranquilizer claims that it will reduce a person's pulse rate by at least 1.5 beats per minute. If the probability of a Type I error is to be at most 0.10, can we reject the manufacturer's claim on the basis of a random sample of 16 persons whose pulse rate was reduced on the average by 1.36 beats per minute with a standard deviation of 0.38 beats per minute?

11.83   The manufacturer of a juice extraction device claims that it can extract at least 42 percent of the weight of an orange in the form of juice. If the probability of a Type I error is to be at most 0.05, can we reject the manufacturer's claim on the basis of a random sample of 20 oranges in which the percentage of extracted juice was 44.5 percent, with a standard deviation of 2.4 percent?

11.84   A company that provides instructions for a certain standardized exam claims that its course will raise scores on the exam by at least 50 points. Can this claim be supported at the 0.05 level of significance if, in a random sample of 40 of its clients, the increases in scores had a mean of 54.6 points, with a standard deviation of 12.0 points?

11.85   A random sample of 5 one-quart cartons of ice cream is drawn from a large production lot. If their mean fat content is 12.6 percent with a standard deviation of 0.51 percent, can we reject the null hypothesis $\mu = 12.0$ percent against the alternative hypothesis $\mu > 12.0$ percent at the 0.01 level of significance?

11.86   A random sample of eight orders from a company's extensive files show that orders for a certain piece of machinery were filled in

$$12 \quad 10 \quad 17 \quad 14 \quad 13 \quad 18 \quad 11 \quad 9$$

days. At the 0.05 level of significance, can we reject the claim that on the average such orders are filled in 10.0 days? It happens that

$$12 + 10 + \cdots + 9 = 104 \text{ and } 12^2 + 10^2 + \cdots + 9^2 = 1{,}424$$

11.87   Peter, an English teacher, wants to determine if Colin's mean reading speed is at least 600 words per minute. What can he conclude if in six 1-minute intervals Colin reads

$$606 \quad 622 \quad 617 \quad 572 \quad 570 \quad 605$$

words? He wants the probability of a Type I error to be at most 0.05. It happens that

$$606 + 622 + \cdots + 605 = 3{,}592$$

and

$$606^2 + 622^2 + \cdots + 605^2 = 2{,}152{,}918$$

11.88   Five measurements of the tar content of in cigarette X yielded

$$14.5 \quad 14.2 \quad 14.4 \quad 14.8 \quad 14.1$$

milligrams per cigarette. This set of five values has $\bar{x} = 14.4$ and $s = 0.274$. You would like to test the null hypothesis H_0: $\mu = 14.1$ (as claimed on the package) using the $\alpha = 0.05$ level of significance.

(a) Would H_0 be accepted against the alternative H_A: $\mu \neq 14.1$?

(b) Would H_0 be accepted against the alternative H_A: $\mu < 14.1$?

(c) Would H_0 be accepted against the alternative H_A: $\mu > 14.1$?

(d) What assumptions are necessary to perform the hypothesis test?

11.89   Five mature dogs of a certain breed weigh 66, 63, 64, 62, and 65 ounces. A kennel club claims that the average for this breed is 60 ounces.

(a) Show that the difference between the mean of this sample and the claim $\mu = 60$ ounces is significant at the 0.05 level of significance.

(b) Suppose that the fifth measurement were recorded as 80 instead of 65. Show that the difference between the mean of this sample and the claimed $\mu = 60$ is no longer significant.

(c) With regard to (b), explain the apparent paradox that while the difference between $\bar{x}$ and 60 has increased, this difference is no longer significant.

11.90   Suppose that an unscrupulous manufacturer wants "scientific proof" that a totally useless chemical additive will improve the mileage yield of their gasoline.

(a) If a research group investigates this additive with one experiment, what is the probability that they will come up with a "significant result" using $\alpha = 0.05$ (to promote the additive with "scientific claims") even though the additive is totally ineffective?

(b) If two independent research groups investigate the additive, what is the probability that at least one of them will come up with a "significant result" even though the additive is totally ineffective?

(c) If 32 independent research groups investigate the additive, what is the probability that at least one of them will come up with a "significant result" even though the additive is totally ineffective?

11.91   Suppose that a pharmaceutical manufacturer would like to find a new ointment to reduce swelling. It produces 20 different medications and tests each one for whether it reduces swelling at the 0.10 level of significance.

(a) What is the probability that at least one of them will "prove" effective even though all of them are totally useless?

(b) What is the probability that more than one will "prove" effective even though all of them are totally useless?

11.92   With reference to Exercise 11.86, use a suitable computer program to determine the tail probability corresponding to the observed value of t. Could we have rejected the claim at the 0.015 level of significance?

11.93   With reference to Exercise 11.87, use a suitable computer program to determine the tail probability corresponding to the observed value of t. What can the teacher conclude, if the probability of a Type I error is to be at most 0.03?

11.94   The standard formulation used by the GreatCoat paint company for its interior wall paint enables a 1 gallon can to cover 250 square feet. The company's research laboratory produces a new formulation, and management is anxious to show that it does not cover significantly less area. Accordingly, they test the hypothesis

$$H_0: \quad \mu = 250 \text{ square feet}$$

against the alternative

$$H_A: \quad \mu < 250 \text{ square feet}$$

The experiment involves 20 cans of the new formulation, and this sample gets mean coverage 237 square feet and a standard deviation of 25 square feet.

(a) Give the value of the test statistic.

(b) What is the p-value associated with this statistic?

(c) After examining the p-value, management decides to use 0.01 as the level of significance. Do the data support the claim, at level of significance 0.01, that the new formulation is not significantly different from the old?

(d) Comment on the appropriateness of selecting the level of significance after observing the p-value.

11.8   DIFFERENCES BETWEEN MEANS

There are many problems where we must decide whether an observed difference between two sample means can be attributed to chance. For instance, we may want to know whether there is really a difference in the average gasoline consumption of two kinds of cars, if sample data show that one kind averages 24.6 miles per gallon while, under the same conditions, the other kind averages 25.7 miles per gallon. Similarly, we may want to decide on the basis of samples whether men can perform a certain task faster than women, whether one kind of ceramic insulator is more brittle than another, whether the average diet in one country is more nutritious than that in another country, and so on.

The method we shall use to test whether an observed difference between two sample means can be attributed to chance, or whether it is statistically significant, is based on the following theory: If $\bar{x}_1$ and $\bar{x}_2$ are the means of two independent random samples, then the mean and the standard deviation of the sampling distribution of the statistic $\bar{x}_1 - \bar{x}_2$ are

$$\mu_{\bar{x}_1 - \bar{x}_2} = \mu_1 - \mu_2 \quad \text{and} \quad \sigma_{\bar{x}_1 - \bar{x}_2} = \sqrt{\frac{\sigma_1^2}{n_1} + \frac{\sigma_2^2}{n_2}}$$

where μ_1, μ_2, σ_1, and σ_2 are the means and the standard deviations of the two populations sampled. It is customary to refer to the standard deviation of this sampling distribution as the **standard error of the difference between two means.**

By "independent" samples we mean that the selection of one sample is in no way affected by the selection of the other. Thus, the theory does not apply to "before and after" kinds of comparisons, nor does it apply, say, if we want to compare the daily caloric consumption of husbands and wives. A special method for comparing the means of dependent samples is explained in Section 11.10.

Then, if we limit ourselves to large samples, $n_1 \geq 30$ and $n_2 \geq 30$, we can base tests of the null hypothesis

$$\mu_1 - \mu_2 = \delta \quad (\textit{delta, the Greek letter for lowercase } d)$$

on the statistic

Statistic for Test of Difference between Two means	$$z = \frac{(\bar{x}_1 - \bar{x}_2) - \delta}{\sqrt{\dfrac{\sigma_1^2}{n_1} + \dfrac{\sigma_2^2}{n_2}}}$$

that is a value of a random variable having approximately the standard normal distribution. Note that we obtained this formula for z by converting to standard units, namely, by subtracting from $\bar{x}_1 - \bar{x}_2$ the mean of its sampling distribution, which under the null hypothesis is $\mu_1 - \mu_2 = \delta$, and then dividing by the standard deviation of its sampling distribution.

Depending on whether the alternative hypothesis is

$$\mu_1 - \mu_2 < \delta, \quad \mu_1 - \mu_2 > \delta, \quad \text{or} \quad \mu_1 - \mu_2 \neq \delta$$

Reject null
hypothesis

Reject null
hypothesis

Reject null
hypothesis

α

$-z_\alpha$ 0

Alternative hypothesis
$\mu_1 - \mu_2 < \delta$

z

α

0   z_α

Alternative hypothesis
$\mu_1 - \mu_2 > \delta$

z

$\alpha/2$ $\alpha/2$

$-z_{\alpha/2}$ 0 $z_{\alpha/2}$

Alternative hypothesis
$\mu_1 - \mu_2 \neq \delta$

z

FIGURE 11.12   *Test criteria for large-sample tests concerning difference between means.*

the criteria we use for the corresponding tests are shown in Figure 11.12. Note that they are like those shown in Figure 11.10 with $\mu_1 - \mu_2$ substituted for μ and δ substituted for μ_0. Analogous to the table on page 350, the criteria for tests of the null hypothesis $\mu_1 - \mu_2 = \delta$ are as follows:

Alternative hypothesis	Reject the null hypothesis if	Accept the null hypothesis or reserve judgment if
$\mu_1 - \mu_2 < \delta$	$z \leq -z_\alpha$	$z > -z_\alpha$
$\mu_1 - \mu_2 > \delta$	$z \geq z_\alpha$	$z < z_\alpha$
$\mu_1 - \mu_2 \neq \delta$	$z \leq -z_{\alpha/2}$ or $z \geq z_{\alpha/2}$	$-z_{\alpha/2} < z < z_{\alpha/2}$

Although δ can be any constant, it is worth noting that in the great majority of problems its value is zero, and we test the null hypothesis of "no difference," namely, the null hypothesis,

$$\mu_1 - \mu_2 = 0 \quad \text{(or simply } \mu_1 = \mu_2\text{)}$$

This procedure is an approximate large-sample test. It is exact only when we know σ_1 and σ_2 and when both of the populations we are sampling are normal.

In most practical situations where σ_1 and σ_2 are unknown, we must make an approximation by substituting for them the sample standard deviations s_1 and s_2. This approximation can be justified by the large sample sizes $n_1 \geq 30$ and $n_2 \geq 30$.

Example

In a study to test whether there is a difference between the average heights of adult females born in two different countries, random samples yielded the following results:

$$n_1 = 120 \qquad \bar{x}_1 = 62.7 \qquad s_1 = 2.50$$
$$n_2 = 150 \qquad \bar{x}_2 = 61.8 \qquad s_2 = 2.62$$

where the measurements are in inches. Use the 0.05 level of significance to test the null hypothesis that the corresponding population means are equal against the alternative hypothesis that they are not equal.

solution

1. H_0: $\delta = 0$
   H_A: $\delta \neq 0$
2. $\alpha = 0.05$
3. Reject the null hypothesis if $z \leq -1.96$ or $z \geq 1.96$, where

$$z = \frac{\bar{x}_1 - \bar{x}_2 - \delta}{\sqrt{\dfrac{\sigma_1^2}{n_1} + \dfrac{\sigma_2^2}{n_2}}}$$

with s_1 and s_2 substituted for σ_1 and σ_2 and using $\delta = 0$; otherwise, accept the null hypothesis or reserve judgment.

4. Substituting

$$n_1 = 120, \ n_2 = 150, \ \bar{x}_1 = 62.7, \ \bar{x}_2 = 61.8,$$

$$s_1 = 2.50 \text{ for } \sigma_1, \ s_2 = 2.62 \text{ for } \sigma_2,$$

and $\delta = 0$ into the formula for z, we obtain

$$z = \frac{62.7 - 61.8}{\sqrt{\dfrac{(2.50)^2}{120} + \dfrac{(2.62)^2}{150}}} \approx 2.88$$

5. Since $z = 2.88$ exceeds 1.96, the null hypothesis must be rejected; in other words, the difference between $\bar{x}_1 = 62.7$ and $\bar{x}_2 = 61.8$ is significant.

Let us now rework this example using the p-value, which requires that we modify steps 3, 4, and 5.

3'.
$$z = \frac{\bar{x}_1 - \bar{x}_2}{\sqrt{\dfrac{\sigma_1^2}{n_1} + \dfrac{\sigma_2^2}{n_2}}}$$

4'.
$$z = \frac{62.7 - 61.8}{\sqrt{\dfrac{(2.50)^2}{120} + \dfrac{(2.62)^2}{150}}} \approx 2.88$$

The area under the normal curve to the right of $z = 2.88$ is 0.0020. This is also the area under the curve to the left of $z = -2.88$, so that the p-value is

$$0.0020 + 0.0020 = 0.0040$$

5'. The p-value is smaller than $\alpha = 0.05$, so that the null hypothesis must be rejected.   ▟ ▟ ▟

It must be noted that there is a certain awkwardness about comparing means when σ_1 and σ_2 have different values (or when the sample values s_1 and s_2 are not close). Consider, for example, two normal populations with means $\mu_1 = 50$ and $\mu_2 = 52$ and standard deviations $\sigma_1 = 5$ and $\sigma_2 = 15$. Though the second population has a larger mean, it is much more likely to produce a value below 40. An investigator faced with situations like this must decide whether the comparison of μ_1 and μ_2 really addresses the relevant problem.

11.9 DIFFERENCES BETWEEN MEANS (Small Samples)

As in Section 11.7, a small-sample test of the significance of the difference between two means may be based on an appropriate t statistic. For this test, which is used when $n_1 < 30$ or $n_2 < 30$, we must assume that our two samples are independent random samples from populations having roughly the shape of normal distributions with the same standard deviation. Then, we can base tests of the null hypothesis $\mu_1 - \mu_2 = \delta$ on the statistic

Statistic for Small Sample Test of Difference between Two Means

$$t = \frac{\bar{x}_1 - \bar{x}_2 - \delta}{\sqrt{\dfrac{(n_1 - 1)s_1^2 + (n_2 - 1)s_2^2}{n_1 + n_2 - 2} \cdot \left(\dfrac{1}{n_1} + \dfrac{1}{n_2}\right)}}$$

which is a value of a random variable having the t distribution with $n_1 + n_2 - 2$ degrees of freedom.

The criteria for the **two-sample t test,** as this small-sample test is called, are similar to those shown in Figure 11.12 and in the table on page 361. Now the curves represent t distributions instead of normal distributions, and z, z_α and $z_{\alpha/2}$ are replaced by t, t_α, and $t_{\alpha/2}$. Like the test of Section 11.8, the two-sample t test is used mainly to test the null hypothesis of "no difference," namely, the null hypothesis

$$\mu_1 - \mu_2 = 0 \qquad \text{(or simply } \mu_1 = \mu_2)$$

The form of this test can be made simpler by noting that it involves an estimate of the standard deviation, which had been assumed the same in the two populations. This estimate is called the **pooled standard deviation** and is defined by

Pooled Standard Deviation

$$s = \sqrt{\frac{(n_1 - 1)s_1^2 + (n_2 \cdot 1)s_2^2}{n_1 + n_2 - 2}}$$

The pooled standard deviation s is always between the values of s_1 and s_2. Using this notation, the test statistic can be written as

Statistic for Small Sample Test of Difference between Two Means

$$t = \frac{\bar{x}_1 - \bar{x}_2 - \delta}{s\sqrt{\dfrac{1}{n_1} + \dfrac{1}{n_2}}}$$

Example

The following random samples are measurements of the heat-producing capacity (in millions of calories per ton) of coal specimens from two mines:

Mine 1: 8,400 8,230 8,380 7,860 7,930
Mine 2: 7,510 7,690 7,720 8,070 7,660

Use the 0.05 level of significance to test whether the difference between the means of these two samples is significant.

solution

We begin by noting the assumption that the two samples are taken from normal populations with equal standard deviations.

1. H_0: $\delta = 0$
   H_A: $\delta \neq 0$
2. $\alpha = 0.05$
3. Reject the null hypothesis if $t \leq -2.306$ or $t \geq 2.306$, where t is given by the formula on page 363 with $\delta = 0$, and 2.306 is the value of $t_{0.025}$ for

$$5 + 5 - 2 = 8$$

degrees of freedom; otherwise, state that the difference between the means of the two samples is not significant.

4. The means and the variances of the two samples are

$$\bar{x}_1 = 8{,}160, \quad \bar{x}_2 = 7{,}730, \quad s_1{}^2 = 63{,}450, \quad \text{and} \quad s_2{}^2 = 42{,}650$$

Substituting these values together with $n_1 = 5$, $n_2 = 5$, and $\delta = 0$ into the formula for t, we have

$$t = \frac{8{,}160 - 7{,}730}{\sqrt{\dfrac{4(63{,}450) + 4(42{,}650)}{5 + 5 - 2} \cdot \left(\dfrac{1}{5} + \dfrac{1}{5}\right)}} \approx 2.95$$

5. Since $t = 2.95$ exceeds 2.306, the null hypothesis must be rejected; in other words, we conclude that the average heat-producing capacity of coal from the two mines is not the same.   ◪ ◪ ◪

Figure 11.13 is a computer printout solution of the preceding example. The line EQUAL VARIANCES, confirms the value we got for t, along with the p-value 0.0184. Since 0.0184 is less than 0.05, we conclude, as before, that the null hypothesis must be rejected. This printout shows other things as well, including the statistic on page 360 of Section 11.8, which it gives under the column for T in the row UNEQUAL VARIANCES.

The procedure of this section is used much more frequently than the procedure of Section 11.8. As noted in the last paragraph of that section, statisticians try to avoid a direct comparison of means when the standard deviations are not equal.

11.10   DIFFERENCES BETWEEN MEANS (Paired Data)

The methods of Sections 11.8 and 11.9 do not apply when the samples are not independent. For instance, they cannot be used when we deal with "before and after" kinds of comparisons, the weights of husbands and wives, and numerous other situations where the data are naturally paired. To handle data of this kind,

FIGURE 11.13

Computer printout for the two-sample t test (Statistix 4.1).

```
VIEW DATA

CASE          CALPERTON      MINE

  1             8400          1
  2             8230          1
  3             8380          1
  4             7860          1
  5             7930          1
  6             7510          2
  7             7690          2
  8             7720          2
  9             8070          2
 10             7660          2


TWO-SAMPLE T TESTS FOR CALPERTON BY MINE

                      SAMPLE
  MINE      MEAN       SIZE      S.D.        S.E.
   1       8160.0       5       251.89      112.65
   2       7730.0       5       206.52      92.358


NULL HYPOTHESIS:  DIFFERENCE =    0.000
ALTERNATIVE HYP:  DIFFERENCE < >  0.000


ASSUMPTION              T        DF        P
EQUAL VARIANCES        2.95      8       0.0184
UNEQUAL VARIANCES      2.95      7.7     0.0192


                        F      NUM DF    DEN DF        P
TESTS FOR EQUALITY
OF VARIANCES           1.49       4         4       0.3549


CASES INCLUDED 10     MISSING CASES 0
```

we work with the (signed) differences of the paired data and test whether these differences may be looked upon as a random sample from a population which has the mean $\mu = \delta$. In most situations we are asking whether $\mu = 0$. If the sample is small, we use the one-sample t test of Section 11.7; otherwise, we use the corresponding large-sample test described in Section 11.6.

Example

The following are the average weekly losses of man-hours due to accidents in 10 industrial plants before and after a certain safety program was put into operation:

45 and 36	73 and 60	46 and 44	124 and 119	33 and 35,
57 and 51	83 and 77	34 and 29	26 and 24	17 and 11

Use the 0.05 level of significance to test whether the safety program is effective.

solution

Since the sample size $n = 10$ is small, we begin by stating the assumptions that the differences constitute a sample from a normal population. The differences are

$$9 \quad 13 \quad 2 \quad 5 \quad -2 \quad 6 \quad 6 \quad 5 \quad 2 \quad 6$$

and for these data we perform the following test:

1. H_0: $\mu = 0$
   H_A: $\mu > 0$ (The alternative is that on the average there were more accidents "before" than "after.")
2. $\alpha = 0.05$
3. Reject the null hypothesis if $t \geq 1.833$, where

$$t = \frac{\bar{x} - \mu_0}{s/\sqrt{n}}$$

and 1.833 is the value of $t_{0.05}$ for $10 - 1 = 9$ degrees of freedom; otherwise, accept the null hypothesis or reserve judgment (as the situation may demand).

4. First calculating the mean and the standard deviation of the ten differences, we get $\bar{x} = 5.2$ and $s = 4.08$. Then, substituting these values together with $n = 10$ and $\mu_0 = 0$ into the formula for t, we have

$$t = \frac{5.2 - 0}{4.08/\sqrt{10}} \approx 4.03$$

5. Since $t = 4.03$ exceeds 1.833, the null hypothesis must be rejected; in other words, we have shown that the industrial safety program is effective. ▰ ▰ ▰

In connection with problems like the preceding one, the one-sample t test is usually referred to as the **paired-sample t test.**

◢ EXERCISES

11.95 A sample study was made of the number of business lunches that executives claim as deductible expenses per month. If 40 executives in the insurance industry averaged 9.4 such deductions with a standard deviation of 3.3 in a given month, while 50 bank executives averaged 7.9 with a standard deviation of 2.9, test at the 0.05 level of significance whether the difference between these two sample means is significant.

11.96 An investigation of repair times for two kinds of photocopying equipment obtained these data values

Equipment Type	Number of Repair Jobs	REPAIR TIMES	
		Mean	Standard Deviation
1	60	84.2	19.4
2	60	91.6	18.8

All times are in minutes.

(a) Test at the 0.01 level of significance whether the difference between these two sample means is significant.

(b) Find the *p*-value (meaning the tail probability) corresponding to the observed value of *z* in part (a).

(c) Use the *p*-value found in part (b) to decide whether the null hypothesis could also have been rejected at the 0.02 level of significance.

(d) Use the *p*-value found in part (b) to decide whether the null hypothesis could also have been rejected at the 0.03 level of significance.

(e) Use the *p*-value found in part (b) to decide whether the null hypothesis could also have been rejected at the 0.04 level of significance.

11.97   Suppose that we want to check whether it is true that on the average men earn in excess of $30 more per week than women in a certain job classification. Sample data indicate the following:

Sex	Number of Workers	WEEKLY SALARY Mean	WEEKLY SALARY Standard Deviation
Male	75	$422.18	$35.20
Female	60	$381.66	$32.65

Test the null hypothesis $\mu_1 - \mu_2 = 30$ against a suitable alternative at the 0.01 level of significance.

11.98   Independent random samples of students from two high schools produced the following scores for a state social-studies exam:

School	Scores										Mean	Standard Deviation
A	78	84	81	78	76	83	79	75	85	81	80	3.3665
B	85	75	83	87	80	79	88	94	87	82	84	5.3955

Use the level of significance $\alpha = 0.05$ to test the claim that students from school A had a lower average than those from school B. Obtain the *p*-value as well.

11.99   To test the claim that the resistance of electric wire can be reduced by at most 0.050 ohm by alloying, 35 values obtained for standard wire yielded

$$\bar{x}_1 = 0.135 \text{ ohm} \quad \text{and} \quad s_1 = 0.004 \text{ ohm}$$

and 35 values obtained for alloyed wire yielded

$$x_2 = 0.082 \text{ ohm} \quad \text{and} \quad s_2 = 0.005 \text{ ohm}$$

What can we conclude about the claim, if the probability of a Type I error is to be at most 0.01?

11.100   Sample surveys conducted in a large county in 1960 and again in 1990 showed that in 1960 the average height of 400 men in the age group from 18 to 24 was 68.4 inches with a standard deviation of 2.6 inches, while in 1990 the average height of 400 men in the same age group was 69.8 inches with a standard deviation of 2.5 inches. Use the 0.05 level of significance to test whether the true average increase in height was 0.6 inch or whether it was greater than that.

11.101   Suppose we want to check whether it is true that on the average men earn more than $30.00 more per week than women in a certain job classification. If sample data show that 80 men earned on the average $353.78 per week with a standard deviation of $18.03, while 80 women earned on the average $315.14 per week with a standard deviation of $21.33, test the null hypothesis $\mu_1 - \mu_2 = 30.00$ against a suitable alternative at the 0.01 level of significance.

11.102   Use the method of the preceding exercise and the data of Exercise 11.99 to construct a 95 percent confidence interval for the true average amount by which the resistance of electric wire can be reduced by alloying.

11.103   Measurements were taken of the hydrogen content (in percent number of atoms) of gases collected from the eruptions of two volcanos. Twelve measurements were taken at each volcano. The data from the first volcano yielded

$$\bar{x}_1 = 41.2 \quad \text{and} \quad s_1 = 5.2$$

while data from the second volcano yielded

$$\bar{x}_2 = 45.8 \quad \text{and} \quad s_2 = 6.7$$

Decide, at the 0.05 level of significance, whether to accept or reject the null hypothesis that there is no difference in hydrogen content in the composition of the gases in the two eruptions.

11.104   Six guinea pigs injected with 0.5 mg of a medication took on the average 15.4 seconds to fall asleep with a standard deviation of 2.2 seconds, while six other guinea pigs injected with 1.5 mg of the medication took on the average 10.6 seconds to fall asleep with a standard deviation of 2.6 seconds. Use the 0.05 level of significance to test whether or not the increase in dosage from 0.5 mg to 1.5 mg reduces the average amount of time it takes a guinea pig to fall asleep by 2.0 seconds.

11.105   In the comparison of two kinds of paint, a consumer-testing service found that four 1-gallon cans of one brand covered on the average 514 square feet with a standard deviation of 32 square feet, while four 1-gallon cans of another brand covered on the average 487 square feet with a standard deviation of 27 square feet. Use the 0.05 level of significance to test whether the difference between the two sample means is significant.

11.106   During one year in two counties, the following number of houses were requested in applications for suburban developments:

County	Number of Houses Requested
G	45 51 66 43 60 68 41 65
R	56 32 61 43 53 22 41

Use the 0.01 level of significance to test whether the difference between the counties is significant. Note any assumptions relevant to the test.

11.107   As part of an industrial training program, some trainees are instructed by method 1 and some by method 2. Both methods involve computer-administered lessons, but method 1 also involves personal attention of an instructor. The assignment of trainees to instructional methods is by random allocation. Random samples of size 10 are taken from large groups of trainees instructed by the two methods. The following values are their scores on a relevant achievement test:

Method	Scores on Achievement Test	Mean	Standard Deviation
1	81 71 79 83 76 75 84 90 83 78	80	5.3955
2	59 65 62 59 57 64 60 56 66 62	61	3.3665

The claim has been made that $\delta \leq 10$, where δ is the average amount by which the personal attention of an instructor will improve a trainee's score. Test this claim at the 0.05 level of significance.

11.108 To compare two kinds of bumper guards, six of each kind were mounted on a compact car. Each car was crashed into a concrete wall at 5 miles per hour, and the following are the costs of the repairs, in dollars:

Bumper Guard	Repair Costs, in Dollars						Mean	Standard Deviation
1	260	310	380	360	290	345	324.17	45.43
2	305	280	265	315	290	310	294.17	43.25

Test at the 0.05 level of significance whether the difference between the means of these two samples is significant. Be sure to note any assumptions that are relevant to the calculations.

11.109 If we substitute the second formula for t on page 363 into $-t_{\alpha/2} < t < t_{\alpha/2}$ and manipulate the inequality algebraically so that the middle term is δ, we obtain a $(1 - \alpha)100$ percent confidence interval for

$$\delta = \mu_1 - \mu_2$$

Use this method and the data of Exercise 11.105 to construct a 95 percent confidence interval for the difference between the true average areas covered with a gallon of the two kinds of paint.

11.110 Following are the weights of 32 patients when they began a weight-reducing diet and two weeks later:

Patient	Before	After	Loss	Patient	Before	After	Loss
1	212	195	17	17	260	249	11
2	193	185	8	18	209	201	8
3	241	225	16	19	198	195	3
4	218	199	19	20	211	196	15
5	205	194	11	21	220	203	17
6	216	193	23	22	245	236	9
7	215	205	10	23	185	169	16
8	198	176	22	24	206	195	11
9	200	188	12	25	189	185	4
10	233	224	9	26	202	195	7
11	258	240	18	27	219	214	5
12	186	174	12	28	263	255	8
13	289	263	26	29	241	228	13
14	250	238	12	30	235	229	6
15	225	213	12	31	200	188	12
16	244	241	3	32	207	193	14
				Mean	221.03	208.88	12.16
				St. Dev.	25.46	24.97	5.70

Use the 0.05 level of significance to test the null hypothesis that the mean weight loss of dieters on this diet for two weeks is 10.0 against the alternative that the loss is greater than that.

⽤ 11.111 The following data were obtained in an experiment designed to check whether there is a systematic difference in the weights obtained with two scales.

Rock Specimen	Scale I	Scale II	Difference
1	12.13	12.17	−0.04
2	17.56	17.61	−0.05
3	9.33	9.35	−0.02
4	11.40	11.42	−0.02
5	28.62	28.61	0.01
6	10.25	10.27	−0.02
7	23.37	23.42	−0.05
8	16.27	16.26	0.01
9	12.40	12.45	−0.05
10	24.78	24.75	0.03
Mean	16.611	16.631	−0.020
St. Dev.	6.7994	6.7873	0.0287

All weights are in grams. Use the 0.01 level of significance to test whether the difference between the means of the weights obtained with the two scales is significant. Be sure to state any assumptions that form the basis for your test.

11.11   CHECKLIST OF KEY TERMS   (*with page references to their definitions*)

11.12 REVIEW EXERCISES

11.112 A random sample of 40 cans of pineapple slices has a mean weight of 15.85 ounces and a standard deviation of 0.23 ounce. If this mean is used as an estimate of the mean weight of all the cans of pineapple slices in the large production lot from which the 40 cans originated, with what confidence can we assert that this estimate is "off" by at most 0.06 ounce?

11.113 A shirt issued for military use has an average useful life of 85 washings, when used in a moderate climate—but will a tropical climate reduce its useful life? A sample of 60 such shirts worn by soldiers in a tropical climate indicates a mean useful life of 76.4 washings, with a standard deviation of 12.8. At the 0.01 level of significance, can we conclude that the use of these shirts in a tropical climate reduces their average useful life?

11.114 Suppose that we want to perform a significance test regarding μ_A and μ_B, which are the average efficiencies of two brands of solar heaters, A and B. Indicate the null and alternative hypotheses which you would use for each of the following situations:

(a) You would like to show that brand A is superior to brand B.

(b) You would like to show that the two brands are not equally efficient.

(c) You would like to show that brand A is not significantly worse than brand B.

(d) You would like to show that brand A is at least as efficient as brand B.

(e) You would like to show that the two brands are equally efficient.

11.115 In a French restaurant, the chef Armand received 26, 21, 14, 22, 18, and 20 orders for coq au vin on six different nights. Construct a 95 percent confidence interval for the number of orders for coq au vin the chef can expect per night.

11.116 A general achievement test is standardized so that eighth graders should average 79.4 with a standard deviation of 4.8. The superintendent of a large school district hopes to show that the eighth graders in her district average better than 79.4. Accordingly, she has the test given to 32 randomly selected eighth graders in her district. By how much must $\bar{x}$, their average, exceed 79.4 to make the difference significant at the 0.01 level of significance?

11.117 Six containers of detergent which were randomly selected from a large display of detergent weighed 15.9, 15.2, 16.2, 15.8, 16.0, and 15.7 ounces. What can we assert with 99 percent confidence about the maximum size of the error if we use the mean of the sample, $\bar{x} = 15.8$ ounces to estimate the mean of the population sampled?

11.118 Lily, a sales manager, believes that the average monthly demand for her product may be described by means of a normal distribution with

$$\mu_0 = 4{,}800 \text{ units} \quad \text{and} \quad \sigma_0 = 260 \text{ units}$$

(a) Thus, what probability does she assign to the true average monthly demand being somewhere between 4,500 to 5,000 units?

(b) If data for 10 months show an average demand of 4,702 units with a standard deviation of 380 units, find the mean and the standard deviation of the posterior distribution.

(c) How would the probability of part (a) be modified in the light of the information given in part (b)?

11.119 Joel, assistant sales manager to Lily in the previous exercise, feels that the average monthly demand may be described by means of a normal distribution with

$$\mu_0 = 4{,}500 \text{ units} \quad \text{and} \quad \sigma_0 = 280 \text{ units}$$

(a) What probability does he assign to the true average monthly demand being some-where on the interval from 4,500 to 5,000 units?

(b) If data for ten months show an average demand of 4,702 units with a standard deviation of 380 units, find the mean and the standard deviation of the posterior distribution.

(c) How would the probability of part (a) be modified with the information given in part (b)?

(d) Why, even though based on the same ten months of data, are the solutions to part (c) of this exercise and part (c) of the previous exercise different?

11.120 An efficiency expert wants to determine the average time it takes a person to buy a week's groceries at a supermarket. If preliminary studies show that it is reasonable to let $\sigma = 4.2$ minutes, how large a sample will be needed to be able to assert with probability 0.95 that the mean of the sample will be "off" by at most 0.4 minute?

11.121 For 15 rounds of golf, played on 15 different courses, two professional golfers had these scores:

Round	Golfer I	Golfer II	Difference
1	71	72	−1
2	69	71	−2
3	70	70	0
4	72	75	−3
5	69	70	−1
6	71	70	1
7	74	72	2
8	68	71	−3
9	70	73	−3
10	71	72	−1
11	69	73	−4
12	70	74	−4
13	73	72	1
14	68	74	−6
15	70	78	−8
Mean	70.333	72.467	−2.133
St. Dev.	1.7182	2.1668	2.7220

If the probability of a Type I error is to be at most 0.05, can we reject the null hypothesis that on the average golfer I is at most 1.5 strokes better than the second?

11.122 In a study of the relationship between family size and intelligence, 40 "only children" had an average IQ of 101.5 with standard deviation of 6.7 and 50 "firstborns" in two-child families had an average IQ of 105.9 with a standard deviation of 5.8. Use the 0.05 level of significance to test whether the difference between these two means is significant.

11.123 Five burlap sacks of potatoes randomly selected from a large lot prepared by a particular distributor in Maine weigh

$$99.7 \quad 99.5 \quad 100.2 \quad 99.2 \quad 99.9$$

pounds. What can we assert with 95 percent confidence about the maximum error, if we use the mean of this sample, $\bar{x} = 99.7$ pounds, to estimate the mean of the population sampled?

11.124 Consider the confidence interval formula on page 321 and the test described on page 350. Suppose that a random sample of size n is taken from a normal population with the mean μ and the standard deviation σ.

(a) Find the set of values covered by the $(1 - \alpha) \cdot 100$ confidence interval for μ.

(b) Consider the test at significance level α of the null hypothesis $\mu = \mu_0$ against the alternative $\mu \neq \mu_0$. Find the set of values for μ_0 for which the null hypothesis cannot be rejected.

(c) Compare the sets obtained in (a) and (b).

11.125 In a statewide election, 1,080,280 votes are cast. Candidate A receives 504,121 votes (about 47%) and candidate B receives 556,158 votes (about 51%). Is it reasonable to ask whether the difference between these two percentages is statistically significant?

11.126 Pauline, a biologist, must determine if the wing span of a certain type of sparrow is anywhere between 14.0 cm and 14.4 cm. She takes a random sample of size $n = 50$ with the intention of accepting the null hypothesis $14.0 \leq \mu \leq 14.4$ if the sample mean $\bar{x}$ is in the interval $13.7 \leq \bar{x} \leq 14.7$, and otherwise rejecting it. If she can assume that $\sigma = 1.0$ cm for the wing spans, find the maximum probability of a Type I error.

11.127 During investigation of an alleged unfair trade practice, the Federal Trade Commission obtains a random sample of 50 "three-ounce" candy bars from a large shipment. If the mean and standard deviation of the sample are 2.96 ounces and 0.11 ounce,

(a) show that the commission (using the 0.01 level of significance) has grounds upon which to proceed against the manufacturer for shortweight selling;

(b) find the p-value associated with the observed value of z and determine whether the null hypothesis could have been rejected at the 0.002 level of significance.

11.128 To compare freshmen's knowledge of history, samples of 50 freshmen from each of two universities were given a special test. If those from the first university have an average score of 67.4 with a standard deviation of 5.0, while those from the second university have an average score of 62.8 with a standard deviation of 4.6, test at the 0.05 level of significance whether the difference between the two sample means is significant.

11.129 Suppose that in the preceding exercise we had wanted to test whether freshmen from the first university score on the average 3.0 points higher on the test than freshman from the second university. Use the data of that exercise to test this conjecture at the 0.05 level of significance.

11.130 The operating rule for a quality control inspection is that "average weights in a sample must be not significantly worse than 90 percent of the standard of 50 pounds." A sample of 180 units shows a mean of 44.6 pounds and a standard deviation of 2.2 pounds. State the null and alternative hypotheses and then perform the test at the 5 percent level of significance.

11.131 In ten trials for gasoline mileage, the following miles per gallon were obtained, using a certain brand of gasoline:

$$28.2 \quad 27.4 \quad 22.9 \quad 26.8 \quad 26.9$$
$$27.4 \quad 28.1 \quad 27.8 \quad 27.4 \quad 28.1$$

The mean of these values is 27.1 miles per gallon, with a standard deviation of 1.5542 miles per gallon. Do these values support or refute the claim that with this brand of gasoline the car averages at least 28 miles per gallon? The probability of a Type I error is to be at most 0.05. Be sure to state any assumptions used in performing the test.

11.132 Carla, the office manager for a law firm, believes that one secretary (Ruth) makes more mistakes than the average of all the others.

(a) If Carla decides that Ruth should be dismissed, and if her belief is confirmed by observations of Ruth's performance, what hypothesis and alternative should Carla set up?

(b) If Carla decides to let Ruth go unless she can prove herself better than the average of all the secretaries, what hypothesis and alternative should the law firm set up?

11.133 A social scientist is studying the ages of executives in top management positions. What null hypothesis and what alternative hypothesis should she use, and under what conditions (accept or reject the null hypothesis) would she prove her point, if she hopes to be able to show that their mean age is

(a) greater than 48;

(b) at least 48?

11.13 REFERENCES

An informal introduction to interval estimation is given under the heading of "How to be precise though vague." in

MORONEY, M. J., *Facts from Figures.* London: Penguin Books, Ltd., 1956.

and some easy reading on estimation and tests of hypotheses may be found in Chapters 12 through 17 of

BROOK, R. J., ARNOLD, G. C., HASSARD, T. H., and PRINGLE, R. M., eds., *The Fascination of Statistics.* New York: Marcel Dekker, Inc., 1986.

A discussion of the theoretical foundation of the t distribution as well as other mathematical details omitted in this book may be found in most textbooks on mathematical statistics. Some of the theory of Bayesian estimation pertaining to Section 11.3 is discussed in Chapter 10 of the book by Freund and Walpole listed on page 314.

A detailed treatment of tests of significance, the choice of the level of significance, tail probabilities, and so forth, may be found in Chapters 26 and 29 of

FREEDMAN, D., PISANI, R., and PURVES, R., *Statistics.* New York: W. W. Norton & Company, Inc., 1978.

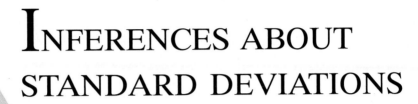

INFERENCES ABOUT STANDARD DEVIATIONS

*I*n Chapter 11 we learned how to judge the size of the error when estimating the mean of a population, how to construct confidence intervals for population means, and how to perform tests of hypotheses about the mean of one population or the means of two populations. All these are very useful statistical techniques, but even more important are the concepts on which they are based: interval estimation, degree of confidence, the Bayesian approach, null and alternative hypotheses, Type I and Type II errors, test of significance, level of significance and tail probability, and above all the concept of statistical significance. Also, we learned about small-sample and large-sample techniques.

As we shall see in this chapter and in subsequent chapters, all these ideas carry over to inferences about population parameters other than the mean, to inferences about the nature of populations, and even to inferences about the randomness of samples. In this chapter we concentrate on population standard deviations, or population variances, which are not only important in their own right, but which must sometimes be estimated or compared before inferences about other parameters can be made. This was the case, for example, in Sections 11.1 and 11.6, where we needed an estimate of the population standard deviation to make inferences about the population mean, and in Section 11.9, where the two-sample t test required that the two populations sampled have equal standard deviations.

In this chapter, Section 12.1 is devoted to the estimation of σ and σ^2, and Sections 12.2 and 12.3 deal with tests of hypotheses about these population parameters.

12.1   THE ESTIMATION OF σ

There are various ways in which we can estimate the standard deviation of a population. We can base such an estimate on special graph paper, as in Exercise 9.31 on page 268, or on the sample range, as in Exercises 4.17 and 4.18 on page 92 and in Exercise 12.15, but usually we base it on the sample standard deviation *s*, introduced in Chapter 4. To illustrate, let us begin with confidence intervals for σ based on *s*, which require that the population we are sampling has roughly the shape of a normal distribution. In that case, the statistic

Chi-square Statistic

$$\chi^2 = \frac{(n-1)s^2}{\sigma^2}$$

called the **chi square statistic** (χ is the lowercase Greek letter *chi*), is a value of a random variable having approximately the **chi-square distribution.** The parameter of this important continuous distribution is called the **number of**

FIGURE 12.1

Chi-square distribution.

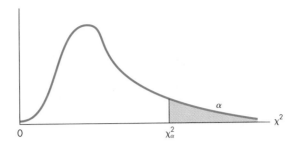

degrees of freedom, just like the parameter of the t distribution. As the chi-square distribution is used here, the number of degrees of freedom is $n - 1$. An example of a chi-square distribution is shown in Figure 12.1. Unlike the normal and t distributions, its domain consists only of the non-negative real numbers.

   Analogous to z_α and t_α, we now define χ^2_α as the value for which the area under the curve to its right (see Figure 12.1) is equal to α; like t_α, this value depends on the number of degrees of freedom and must be obtained from a table, or perhaps a computer. Thus, $\chi^2_{\alpha/2}$ is such that the area under the curve to its right is $\alpha/2$, while $\chi^2_{1-\alpha/2}$ is such that the area under the curve to its left is $\alpha/2$ (see Figure 12.2). For instance, $\chi^2_{0.975}$ is the value for which the area under the curve to its left is 0.025. We made this distinction because the chi-square distribution, unlike the normal and t distributions, is not symmetrical. Values of

$$\chi^2_{0.995}, \quad \chi^2_{0.975}, \quad \chi^2_{0.025}, \quad \text{and} \quad \chi^2_{0.005}$$

among others, are given in Table III at the end of the book for 1, 2, 3, . . ., and 30 degrees of freedom.

   We can now proceed as on pages 321 and 323–324. Since the probability is $1 - \alpha$ that a random variable having a chi-square distribution will take on a value between $\chi^2_{1-\alpha/2}$ and $\chi^2_{\alpha/2}$, namely, that

$$\chi^2_{1-\alpha/2} < \chi^2 < \chi^2_{\alpha/2}$$

we can substitute into this inequality the expression for χ^2 on page 376 and get

$$\chi^2_{1-\alpha/2} < \frac{(n-1)s^2}{\sigma^2} < \chi^2_{\alpha/2}$$

FIGURE 12.2

Chi-square distribution.

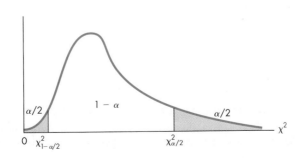

Then applying some relatively simple algebra, we can rewrite this inequality as

Small Sample Confidence Interval for σ^2	$$\frac{(n-1)s^2}{\chi^2_{\alpha/2}} < \sigma^2 < \frac{(n-1)s^2}{\chi^2_{1-\alpha/2}}$$

This is a $100(1 - \alpha)$ percent confidence interval for σ^2, the population variance. By taking square roots, we get a $100(1 - \alpha)$ percent confidence interval for σ, the population standard deviation.[†] It should be emphasized that the use of this interval requires the assumption that the sampled population has roughly the shape of a normal distribution.

Example

A random sample of five hot dogs taken from a large production lot yielded the following data on their fat content: 32.4, 30.9, 33.2, 31.5, and 34.3 percent. Construct a 95 percent confidence interval for σ, which measures the variability of the percentage of fat in the given kind of hot dog.

solution

Since the sample standard deviation is $s = 1.35$ and since the values of $\chi^2_{0.975}$ and $\chi^2_{0.025}$ for $5 - 1 = 4$ degrees of freedom are 0.484 and 11.143 according to Table III, substitution into the confidence interval formula for σ^2 yields

$$\frac{4(1.35)^2}{11.143} < \sigma^2 < \frac{4(1.35)^2}{0.484}$$

$$0.65 < \sigma^2 < 15.06$$

Finally, taking square roots, we get

$$0.81 < \sigma < 3.88$$ ◪ ◪ ◪

The kind of confidence interval we have calculated here is often referred to as a **small-sample confidence interval,** because it is used mainly when n is small, $n < 30$, and, of course, only when it can be assumed that the population sampled has roughly the shape of a normal distribution. For large samples, $n \geq 30$, we make use of the theory that the sampling distribution of s can be approximated with a normal distribution having the mean σ and the standard deviation $\frac{\sigma}{\sqrt{2n}}$ (see Exercise 10.60 on page 312). Converting to standard units, we can thus assert with probability $1 - \alpha$ that

$$-z_{\alpha/2} < \frac{s - \sigma}{\frac{\sigma}{\sqrt{2n}}} < z_{\alpha/2}$$

[†]We could actually present the confidence interval formula for σ by taking the square roots, but this formula would not be computationally helpful. The recommended computation is first to find the interval for σ^2 numerically and then get the interval for σ by taking square roots.

and simple algebra leads to the following **large-sample confidence interval** formula for σ:

Large-sample Confidence Interval for σ	$$\frac{s}{1 + \dfrac{z_{\alpha/2}}{\sqrt{2n}}} < \sigma < \frac{s}{1 - \dfrac{z_{\alpha/2}}{\sqrt{2n}}}$$

Example

The attendance figures at a multiplex movie complex for 80 nonweekend dates (Monday through Thursday) had a sample standard deviation of $s = 102.4$. Construct a 95 percent confidence interval for the standard deviation of the population sampled.

solution

Substituting $n = 80$, $s = 102.4$, and $z_{\alpha/2} = 1.96$ into the confidence interval formula above, we get

$$\frac{102.4}{1 + \dfrac{1.96}{\sqrt{160}}} < \sigma < \frac{102.4}{1 - \dfrac{1.96}{\sqrt{160}}}$$

$$88.66 < \sigma < 121.18$$

This means that we are 95 percent confident that the interval from 88.66 to 121.18 contains σ, the true standard deviation of population generating the nonweekend attendance figures. ◢ ◢ ◢

◪ EXERCISES

12.1   The refractive indices of 18 pieces of glass, randomly selected from a large lot purchased by an optical firm, have a standard deviation of 0.014. Construct a 95 percent confidence interval for σ, the standard deviation of the population sampled.

12.2   A professional bowled 20 games in a tournament and averaged 227.4, with a standard deviation of 16.6. Construct a 95 percent confidence interval for σ, which provides a measure of the bowler's consistency.

12.3   In the example on page 324 we referred to an experiment with a new paint for white center lines, and in the solution we obtained $s = 19,200$ car crossings for the eight locations. Construct a 95 percent confidence interval for σ, which here might measure the consistency of the paint, the consistency with which it is applied, or perhaps the uniformity (say, percentage of heavy trucks) of the traffic.

12.4   With reference to the exercises noted below, construct 95 percent confidence intervals for σ, the standard deviation of the population sampled.

(a) Exercise 11.27, on page 333, in which $n = 18$ and $s = 4.80$ gallons;

(b) Exercise 11.30, on page 333, in which $n = 9$ and $s = 0.003$ cm.

12.5   With reference to the exercises noted below, construct 99 percent confidence intervals for σ, the standard deviation of the population sampled.

(a) Exercise 11.31, on page 333, in which $n = 8$ and $s = 0.56$ microgram;

(b) Exercise 11.81, on page 357, in which $n = 9$ and $s = 0.15$ ounce.

12.6   With reference to the exercises noted below, construct 95 percent confidence intervals for σ^2, the variance of the population sampled.

(a) Exercise 11.86, on page 358, in which $n = 8$ and $s = 3.21$ days;

(b) Exercise 11.87, on page 358, in which $n = 6$ and $s = 22.39$ words.

12.7   With reference to the exercises noted below, construct 95 percent confidence intervals for σ, the standard deviation of the population sampled.

(a) Exercise 11.1, on page 329, in which $n = 40$ and $s = 13.2$ seconds;

(b) Exercise 11.3, on page 330, in which $n = 80$ and $s = 1.40$ cm.

12.8   With reference to the exercises noted below, construct 99 percent confidence intervals for σ, the standard deviation of the population sampled.

(a) Exercise 11.5, on page 330, in which $n = 120$ and $s = 3.29$ minutes;

(b) Exercise 11.10, on page 330, in which $n = 250$ and $s = \$28.90$.

12.9   With reference to Exercise 11.12 on page 331, where we had $n = 60$ and $s = 0.3$ ounce, construct a 95 percent confidence interval for σ^2, the variance of the weight of all the cans of pear halves in the given lot.

⊞ 12.10   Reasonable estimates of the population standard deviation can often be obtained as $\dfrac{Q_3 - Q_1}{1.35}$, where Q_1 and Q_3 are the first and third quartiles. The difference $Q_3 - Q_1$ is often called the **interquartile range.** The list of 32 values below represents the daily numbers of 1-gallon milk cartons sold at a certain supermarket. This list has $\bar{x} = 321.03$ and $s = 25.46$. Compare the value of $\dfrac{Q_3 - Q_1}{1.35}$ with s. For convenience, the list has been sorted into increasing order.

285	302	316	341
286	305	318	344
289	306	319	345
293	307	320	350
298	309	325	358
298	311	333	360
300	312	335	363
300	315	341	389

⊞ 12.11   When we deal with very small samples, good estimates of the population standard deviation can often be obtained on the basis of the sample range (the largest sample value minus the smallest). Such quick estimates of σ are given by the sample range divided by the divisor d, which depends on the size of the sample; for samples from populations having roughly the shape of a normal distribution, its values are shown in the following table for $n = 2, 3, \ldots ,$ and 12:

n	2	3	4	5	6	7	8	9	10	11	12
d	1.13	1.69	2.06	2.33	2.53	2.70	2.85	2.97	3.08	3.17	3.26

For instance, if a psychiatrist saw 11, 9, 14, 8, 7, 11, 15, and 10 patients on eight days, we find that $s = 2.77$, $r = 15 - 7 = 8$, and $d = 2.85$ for $n = 8$. Thus,

$$\frac{8}{2.85} \approx 2.81^{\dagger} \quad \text{and} \quad 2.77$$

are both estimates of the true standard deviation of the number of patients the psychiatrist sees per day. As can be seen, the difference between the two estimates is quite small. In Exercise 11.34 on page 334, a sample of six times to clean up a school cafeteria had

---

†In this book we use the symbol $\approx$ to mean "approximately equal." We use this symbol only at the step where numerical rounding occurs.

values 21, 26, 24, 22, 23, and 22 minutes, resulting in a standard deviation $s = 1.79$ minutes. Use the method based on the range to estimate the true standard deviation, and compare this value with s.

12.12 In Exercise 11.35 on page 334, four weights of an ancient coin were 14.28, 14.34, 14.26, and 14.32 grams, yielding $\bar{x} = 14.30$ grams and $s = 0.0365$ gram. Use the method of Exercise 12.11 to estimate σ, and compare this value with s.

12.13 In Exercise 11.89 on page 358, the weights of five dogs were given as 66, 63, 64, 62, and 65 ounces, with $\bar{x} = 64$ ounces and $s = 1.58$ ounces. Use the method of Exercise 12.11 to estimate σ, and compare this value with s.

12.2 TESTS CONCERNING STANDARD DEVIATIONS

In this section we consider the problem of testing whether a population standard deviation equals a specified constant σ_0, or whether a population variance equals σ_0^2. This kind of test may be required whenever we study the uniformity of a product, process, or operation. For instance, we may want to test whether a certain kind of glass is sufficiently homogeneous for making delicate optical equipment, whether the prior knowledge of a group of students is sufficiently uniform so that they can be taught in one class, whether a lack of uniformity in certain workers' performance may call for stricter supervision, and so forth.

The test of the null hypothesis $\sigma = \sigma_0$, that a population standard deviation equals a specified constant, is based on the same assumptions, the same statistic, and the same sampling theory as the small-sample confidence interval for σ^2 on page 378. Again assuming that our sample is random and comes from a population having roughly the shape of a normal distribution, we use the chi-square statistic:

Small Sample Test Concerning Standard Deviation

$$\chi^2 = \frac{(n-1)s^2}{\sigma_0^2}$$

which is like the one on page 376 with σ replaced by σ_0. As before, the sampling distribution of the statistic is the chi-square distribution with $n - 1$ degrees of freedom.

The test criteria are shown in Figure 12.3; depending on the alternative hypothesis, the dividing lines, or critical values, are $\chi_{1-\alpha}^2$ and χ_α^2 for the one-sided alternatives, and they are $\chi_{1-\alpha/2}^2$ and $\chi_{\alpha/2}^2$ for the two-sided alternative. Symbolically, we can formulate these criteria for testing the null hypothesis $\sigma = \sigma_0$ as follows:

Alternative hypothesis	Reject the null hypothesis if	Accept the null hypothesis or reserve judgment if
$\sigma < \sigma_0$	$\chi^2 \leq \chi_{1-\alpha}^2$	$\chi^2 > \chi_{1-\alpha}^2$
$\sigma > \sigma_0$	$\chi^2 \geq \chi_\alpha^2$	$\chi^2 < \chi_\alpha^2$
$\sigma \neq \sigma_0$	$\chi^2 \leq \chi_{1-\alpha/2}^2$ or $\chi^2 \geq \chi_{\alpha/2}^2$	$\chi_{1-\alpha/2}^2 < \chi^2 < \chi_{\alpha/2}^2$

Alternative hypothesis $\sigma < \sigma_0$ Alternative hypothesis $\sigma > \sigma_0$ Alternative hypothesis $\sigma \neq \sigma_0$

FIGURE 12.3   *Test criteria for tests concerning the equality of two standard deviations.*

The values of $\chi^2_{0.995}$, $\chi^2_{0.99}$, $\chi^2_{0.975}$, $\chi^2_{0.95}$, $\chi^2_{0.05}$, $\chi^2_{0.025}$, $\chi^2_{0.01}$, and $\chi^2_{0.005}$ are given in Table III at the end of the book for 1, 2, 3, ..., and 30 degrees of freedom.

Example

To judge certain safety features of a car, an engineer must know whether the reaction time of drivers to a given emergency situation has a standard deviation of 0.010 second, or whether it is greater than 0.010 second. What can she conclude at the 0.05 level of significance if she gets $s = 0.014$ for a sample of size $n = 15$?

solution

Assuming that the population sampled has roughly the shape of a normal distribution, we can proceed as follows.

1. H_0: $\sigma = 0.010$
   H_A: $\sigma > 0.010$
2. $\alpha = 0.05$
3. Reject the null hypothesis if $\chi^2 \geq 23.685$, where

$$\chi^2 = \frac{(n-1)s^2}{\sigma_0^2}$$

and 23.685 is the value of $\chi^2_{0.05}$ for $15 - 1 = 14$ degrees of freedom.
4. Substituting $n = 15$, $s = 0.014$ and $\sigma_0 = 0.010$ into the formula for χ^2, we get

$$\chi^2 = \frac{14(0.014)^2}{(0.010)^2} \approx 27.44$$

5. Since $\chi^2 = 27.44$ exceeds 23.685, the null hypothesis must be rejected; in other words, the engineer can conclude that the standard deviation of the reaction time of drivers to the given emergency situation is greater than 0.010 second.

The test can also be done through the use of tail probabilities, meaning p-values. Table III gives only selected values for the chi-square distribution, so that we must make an interval statement for the p-value. The value 27.44 falls between $\chi^2_{0.025} = 26.119$ and $\chi^2_{0.01} = 29.141$, and we would state that $0.01 < p < 0.025$.

The test using *p*-values would replace steps 3, 4, and 5 by these:

3′. The test statistic is

$$\chi^2 = \frac{(n-1)s^2}{\sigma_0^2}$$

4′. Substituting $n = 15$, $s = 0.014$, and $\sigma_0 = 0.010$ into the formula for χ^2, we get

$$\chi^2 = \frac{14(0.014)^2}{(0.010)^2} \approx 27.44$$

and from Table III we determine that $0.01 < p < 0.025$.

5′. Since $p < \alpha = 0.05$, the null hypothesis must be rejected. ◪ ◪ ◪

When *n* is large, $n \geq 30$, tests of the null hypothesis $\sigma = \sigma_0$ can be based on the same theory as the large-sample confidence intervals of Section 12.1. That is, we use the statistic

Large-sample Test for Standard Deviation	$z = \dfrac{s - \sigma_0}{\sigma_0/\sqrt{2n}}$

which is a value of a random variable having the standard normal distribution. Thus, the criteria for tests of the null hypothesis $\sigma = \sigma_0$ are like those shown in Figure 11.10 and in the table on page 350, the only difference is that μ and μ_0 are replaced by σ and σ_0.

Example

The specifications for the mass production of certain springs require, among other things, that the standard deviation of their compressed lengths should not exceed 0.040 cm. If a random sample of size $n = 35$ from a certain production lot yields $s = 0.053$ and the probability of a Type I error is not to exceed 0.01, does this constitute evidence for the null hypothesis $\sigma \leq 0.040$ or for the alternative hypothesis $\sigma > 0.040$?

solution

1. H_0: $\sigma \leq 0.040$
   H_A: $\sigma > 0.040$

2. $\alpha \leq 0.01$

3. The null hypothesis must be rejected if $z \geq 2.33$, where

$$z = \frac{s - \sigma_0}{\sigma_0/\sqrt{2n}}$$

and otherwise it must be accepted.

4. Substituting $n = 35$, $s = 0.053$, and $\sigma_0 = 0.040$ into the formula for z, we get

$$z = \frac{0.053 - 0.040}{0.040/\sqrt{70}} \approx 2.72$$

5. Since $z = 2.72$ exceeds 2.33, the null hypothesis must be rejected; in other words, the data show that the production lot does not meet specifications.

The tail probability for this example is 0.0033; since this probability is below 0.01, we would certainly reject the null hypothesis.   ◪ ◪ ◪

12.3   TESTS CONCERNING TWO STANDARD DEVIATIONS

In this section we discuss tests concerning the equality of the standard deviations of two populations. Among other applications, it is sometimes used in connection with the two-sample t test of Section 11.9, where it had to be assumed that the two populations sampled have the same standard deviation. For instance, in the example on page 364 dealing with the heat-producing capacity of coal from two mines, we had $s_1^2 = 63{,}450$ and $s_2^2 = 42{,}650$, and despite what may seem to be a large difference, we assumed that the corresponding population standard deviations were equal. Now we shall put this to a rigorous test.

Given independent random samples for size n_1 and n_2 from populations with the standard deviations σ_1 and σ_2, and assuming that those populations have roughly the shape of normal distributions, we usually base tests of the null hypothesis $\sigma_1 = \sigma_2$ on the **F statistic:**

Test for Equality of Two Standard Deviations	$$F = \frac{s_1^2}{s_2^2} \quad or \quad F = \frac{s_2^2}{s_1^2}, \qquad according\ to\ H_A$$

where s_1 and s_2 are the corresponding sample standard deviations. If the two populations sampled have roughly the shape of normal distributions, it can be shown that such ratios, appropriately called **variance ratios,** are values of random variables having the **F distribution.** This important continuous distribution depends on two parameters called the **numerator** and **denominator degrees of freedom.** These values are $n_1 - 1$ and $n_2 - 1$ if we compute s_1^2/s_2^2. Similarly, these values are $n_2 - 1$ and $n_1 - 1$ if we compute s_2^2/s_1^2.

If we based all the tests on the statistic

$$F = \frac{s_1^2}{s_2^2}$$

we could reject the null hypothesis $\sigma_1 = \sigma_2$ for $F \le F_{1-\alpha}$ when the alternative hypothesis is $\sigma_1 < \sigma_2$ and for $F \ge F_\alpha$ when the alternative hypothesis is $\sigma_1 > \sigma_2$. In this notation, $F_{1-\alpha}$ and F_α are defined in the same way in which we defined the critical values $\chi_{1-\alpha}^2$ and χ_α^2 for the chi-square distribution. Unfortunately, things are not as simple as that. Since there exists a fairly straightforward mathematical relationship between $F_{1-\alpha}$ and F_α (see Exercise 12.28 on page 389), most F tables give only values corresponding to right-hand tails with α less than 0.50; for instance, Table IV at the end of the book contains only values of $F_{0.05}$ and $F_{0.01}$.

FIGURE 12.4

Test criteria for tests concerning the equality of two standard deviations.

One-sided alternative hypothesis   Two-sided alternative hypothesis

For this reason, we use

$$F = \frac{s_2^2}{s_1^2} \quad \text{or} \quad F = \frac{s_1^2}{s_2^2}$$

depending on whether the alternative hypothesis is $\sigma_1 < \sigma_2$ or $\sigma_1 > \sigma_2$, and in either case we reject the null hypothesis for $F \geq F_\alpha$ (see Figure 12.4). When the alternative hypothesis is $\sigma_1 \neq \sigma_2$, we use the greater of the two variance ratios,

$$F = \frac{s_1^2}{s_2^2} \quad \text{or} \quad F = \frac{s_2^2}{s_1^2}$$

and reject the null hypothesis for $F \geq F_{\alpha/2}$ (see Figure 12.4). In all these tests, the degrees of freedom are $n_1 - 1$ and $n_2 - 1$, or $n_2 - 1$ and $n_1 - 1$, depending on which sample variance goes into the numerator and which one goes into the denominator. Symbolically, these criteria for testing the null hypothesis $\sigma_1 = \sigma_2$ are summarized in the following table:

Alternative hypothesis	*Test statistic*	*Reject the null hypothesis if*	*Accept the null hypothesis or reserve judgment if*
$\sigma_1 < \sigma_2$	$F = \dfrac{s_2^2}{s_1^2}$	$F \geq F_\alpha$	$F < F_\alpha$
$\sigma_1 > \sigma_2$	$F = \dfrac{s_1^2}{s_2^2}$	$F \geq F_\alpha$	$F < F_\alpha$
$\sigma_1 \neq \sigma_2$	*The larger of the two ratios*	$F \geq F_{\alpha/2}$	$F < F_{\alpha/2}$

The degrees of freedom are as indicated above.

Example

It is desired to determine whether there is less variability in the gold plating done by company 1 than in the gold plating done by company 2. If independent random samples yielded $s_1 = 0.033$ mil (based on $n_1 = 12$) and $s_2 = 0.061$ mil (based on $n_2 = 10$), test the null hypothesis $\sigma_1 = \sigma_2$ against the alternative hypothesis $\sigma_1 < \sigma_2$ at the 0.05 level of significance.

solution

Assuming that the populations sampled have roughly the shape of normal distributions, we proceed as follows.

1. H_0: $\sigma_1 = \sigma_2$
   H_A: $\sigma_1 < \sigma_2$
2. $\alpha = 0.05$
3. Reject the null hypothesis if $F \geq 2.90$, where

$$F = \frac{s_2^2}{s_1^2}$$

   and 2.90 is the value of $F_{0.05}$ for $10 - 1 = 9$ and $12 - 1 = 11$ degrees of freedom; otherwise, accept the null hypothesis or reserve judgment.
4. Substituting $s_1 = 0.033$ and $s_2 = 0.061$ into the formula for F, we get

$$F = \frac{(0.061)^2}{(0.033)^2} \approx 3.42$$

5. Since $F = 3.42$ exceeds 2.90, the null hypothesis must be rejected; in other words, we conclude that there is less variability in the gold plating done by company 1.

We can also provide the p-value for this example. Since $F_{0.01} = 4.63$ for 9 and 11 degrees of freedom, we note that $0.01 < p < 0.05$. The use of the p-value still allows us to reject the null hypothesis at the 5 percent level of significance. ▱ ▱ ▱

Example

In the example dealing with the coal from two mines on page 363, we had

$$s_1^2 = 63{,}450 \quad \text{and} \quad s_2^2 = 42{,}650$$

for two independent random samples of sizes $n_1 = 5$ and $n_2 = 5$. Use the 0.02 level of significance to test whether there is any evidence that the standard deviations of the two populations sampled are not equal.

solution

Assuming that the populations sampled have roughly the shape of normal distributions, we proceed as follows.

1. H_0: $\sigma_1 = \sigma_2$
   H_A: $\sigma_1 \neq \sigma_2$
2. $\alpha = 0.02$
3. Reject the null hypothesis if $F \geq 15.98$, where

$$F = \frac{s_1^2}{s_2^2} \quad \text{or} \quad F = \frac{s_2^2}{s_1^2}$$

   whichever is larger, and 15.98 is the value of $F_{0.01}$ for $5 - 1 = 4$ and $5 - 1 = 4$ degrees of freedom.

4. Since s_1^2 is greater than s_2^2, we substitute $s_1^2 = 63{,}450$ and $s_2^2 = 42{,}650$ into the first of the two variance ratios and we get

$$F = \frac{63{,}450}{42{,}650} \approx 1.49$$

5. Since $F = 1.49$ does not exceed 15.98, the null hypothesis cannot be rejected; there is no reason why we cannot go ahead with the two-sample t test, which requires that $\sigma_1 = \sigma_2$. ◢ ◢ ◢

In a problem like this where the alternative hypothesis is $\sigma_1 \neq \sigma_2$, Table IV limits us to the 0.02 and 0.10 levels of significance. Had we wanted to use the 0.05 level of significance in the example immediately above, the table referred to on page 391 would have yielded $F_{0.025} = 9.60$ and the conclusion would have been the same.

Since the test described here is very sensitive to departures from the underlying assumptions, it must be used with considerable caution. We say that the test is not **robust.** If the circumstances permit, we replace this test with another more robust procedure.

◢ EXERCISES

12.14 In a random sample the times that 18 women took to complete the written test for their driver's licenses had standard deviation $s = 2.4$ minutes. Use the 0.05 level of significance to test the null hypothesis $\sigma = 2.8$ minutes against the alternative hypothesis $\sigma \neq 2.8$ minutes.

12.15 A random sample of 20 stocks listed on the New York Stock Exchange was obtained, and the one-year rate of return was noted for each. These 20 values had a mean of 8.8 percent with a standard deviation of 1.9 percent. Use the 0.05 level of significance to test the null hypothesis $\sigma = 2.0$ percent against the alternative hypothesis $\sigma < 2.0$ percent.

12.16 With reference to Exercise 11.80 on page 357, where we had $n = 12$ and $s = 7.9$ words per minute, test the null hypothesis $\sigma = 10.0$ words per minute against the alternative $\sigma < 10.0$ words per minute at the 0.01 level of significance.

12.17 With reference to Exercise 11.88 on page 358, in which the tar levels (in milligrams per cigarette) were computed, and in which $n = 5$ and $s = 0.274$ mg per cigarette, test the null hypothesis that σ is at least 0.40 mg per cigarette. The level of significance is to be at most 0.05.

12.18 Veteran inspectors of sheet metal stampings have experienced a standard deviation of measurement of 0.55 square inch. If a new inspector measures 80 stampings with a standard deviation of 0.62 square inch, test at the 0.05 level of significance whether he is making satisfactory measurements or whether his variability is excessive.

12.19 With reference to Exercise 12.18, find the tail probability corresponding to the value obtained for z.

12.20 With reference to Exercise 11.71 on page 356, where we had $n = 70$ and $s = 2.2$ months, test at the 0.01 level of significance whether $\sigma = 2.7$ months for the amount of time that convicted embezzlers spend in jail.

12.21 With reference to Exercise 11.73 on page 356, where we had $n = 34$ and $s = 2.1$ minutes, test at the 0.05 level of significance whether or not $\sigma = 2.5$ minutes for the amount of time it takes the night watchman to walk his round.

12.22   With reference to Exercise 11.76 on page 356, where we had $n = 40$ and $s = 0.45$ hour, test at the 0.05 level of significance whether $\sigma = 0.30$ hour for the battery, or whether it is greater than that.

12.23   Two different lighting techniques are compared by measuring the intensity of light at selected locations in areas lighted by the two methods. If 12 measurements of the first technique have a standard deviation of 2.6 foot-candles and 16 measurements of the second technique have a standard deviation of 4.4 foot-candles, test at the 0.05 level of significance whether the two lighting techniques are equally variable or whether the first technique is less variable than the second.

12.24   The amounts of time required by Dr. L to do routine insurance checkups on 25 patients have a standard deviation of 4.2 minutes, while the amounts of time required by Dr. M to do the same procedure on 21 patients have a standard deviation of 3.0 minutes. Assuming that these data constitute independent random samples, test at the 0.05 level of significance whether the amounts of time for this procedure by these two doctors are equally variable or whether they are more variable for Dr. L.

12.25   In Exercise 11.106 on page 368, the numbers of houses requested by land developers in two counties were compared, with the following results:

County	n	Mean	Standard deviation
G	9	55	10.4403
R	6	36	15.4920

Test at the 0.02 level of significance whether there is any reason to doubt the assumption that $\sigma_G = \sigma_R$, as required for the two-sample t test.

12.26   In Exercise 11.107 on page 368, two industrial training methods were compared, with these results:

Method	n	Mean	Standard deviation
1	10	80	5.3955
2	10	61	3.3665

Test at the 0.10 level of significance whether there is any reason to doubt the assumption that $\sigma_1 = \sigma_2$, as required for the two-sample t test.

12.27   A large commuter railroad records for each train the number of minutes it arrives ahead of schedule. A score of 5 is given to a train that arrives 5 minutes ahead of schedule, and a score of -2 is given to a train that arrives 2 minutes late. A random sample is taken from the records for the previous month for the purpose of comparing rush hour and non-rush hour trains, with these results:

Train type	n	Mean	Standard deviation
Rush hour	21	2.60	5.48
Non-rush hour	16	-3.20	9.42

Test at the 0.10 level of significance the null hypothesis that the two populations sampled have equal standard deviations.

⊞ 12.28   If $F_{1-\alpha}$ is a critical value of F for m and n degrees of freedom and F_α is a critical value of F for n and m degrees of freedom, then

$$F_{1-\alpha} = \frac{1}{F_\alpha}$$

Note that the degrees of freedom are interchanged. In the example on page 385, we had wanted to reject the null hypothesis for

$$F = \frac{s_1^2}{s_2^2} \leq F_{0.95}$$

what would have been the critical value of $F_{0.95}$?

⊞ 12.29   To compare the variability of the lifetimes of two kinds of batteries, we want to test the null hypothesis $\sigma_1 = \sigma_2$ against the alternative hypothesis $\sigma_1 < \sigma_2$. If the sample sizes are $n_1 = 10$ and $n_2 = 8$ and we want to reject the null hypothesis when

$$F = \frac{s_1^2}{s_2^2} \leq F_{1-\alpha}$$

use the method of the preceding exercise to find the value of $F_{1-\alpha}$ for
(a) $\alpha = 0.05$;   (b) $\alpha = 0.01$.

12.4   CHECKLIST OF KEY TERMS[†] (*with page references to their definitions*)

Chi-square distribution, 376	*Interquartile range,* 380
Chi-square statistic, 376	Large-sample confidence interval, 379
Degrees of freedom, 376, 377	Number of degrees of freedom, 376
Denominator degrees of freedom, 384	Numerator degrees of freedom, 384
F distribution, 384	Robust, 387
F statistic, 384	Small-sample confidence interval, 378
	Variance ratio, 384

12.5   REVIEW EXERCISES

12.30   In a random sample of $n = 12$ rounds of golf played on her home course, a golf professional averaged 71.6 with a standard deviation of 2.48. Use the 0.01 level of significance to test the null hypothesis $\sigma = 2.00$ against the alternative hypothesis that her game is actually less consistent.

12.31   Pull strengths in pounds required to break the bond of two kinds of glue are:

Glue	Values				Mean	Standard deviation
1	25.3	19.2	21.1	27.6	22.63	4.6961
	16.9	30.1	17.8	22.9		
	27.2	18.2				
2	26.9	22.5	21.8	23.6	22.14	2.4681
	19.8	21.6	18.7	22.2		

[†]Terms introduced in exercises are shown in *italics*.

Although the two kinds of glue are quite similar on average there is some doubt about whether $\sigma_1 = \sigma_2$. Test at the 0.10 level of significance the null hypothesis that the corresponding population standard deviations are equal.

12.32   In a random sample of 25 servings of a breakfast cereal, the sugar content averaged 10.40 grams with a standard deviation of 1.76 grams. Construct a 95 percent confidence interval for the standard deviation of the population sampled, that is, for the standard deviation of the sugar content in a serving of the given kind of breakfast cereal.

⊞ 12.33   Test runs with 12 models of an experimental engine showed that they operated for the following times (in minutes) using 1 gallon of fuel:

$$25.2 \quad 33.0 \quad 22.4 \quad 30.7 \quad 25.1 \quad 28.3$$
$$26.4 \quad 27.0 \quad 30.2 \quad 29.8 \quad 26.4 \quad 24.5$$

This set of 12 values has a mean of 27.42 and a standard deviation of 3.05. Estimate the population standard deviation using

(a) the sample standard deviation;

(b) the method of Exercise 12.10 on page 380, using the sample quartiles and then
$$\frac{Q_3 - Q_1}{1.35};$$

(c) the method of Exercise 12.11 on page 380, using the sample range with the appropriate divisor.

12.34   In a random sample of 50 income tax returns, the amount due after an audit averaged $880.22 with a standard deviation of $210.71. Construct a 99 percent confidence interval for the true standard deviation of the amount due on an income tax return after such an audit.

12.35   With reference to Exercise 11.103 on page 368, where we had

$$n_1 = 12, \quad n_2 = 12, \quad s_1 = 5.2, \quad \text{and} \quad s_2 = 6.7$$

test at the 0.05 level of significance whether there is more variation in the hydrogen content of gases from the second volcano than there is in the hydrogen content of gases from the first.

12.36   In a random sample, 40 lawyers had an average annual income of $93,520 with a standard deviation of $8,370. If the probability of a Type I error is to be at most 0.05, what can we conclude about the null hypothesis that the standard deviation of the population sampled is at least $10,000?

12.37   With reference to Exercise 11.84 on page 358, where we had $n = 16$ and $s = 0.38$, test the null hypothesis $\sigma = 0.3$ beat against the alternative $\sigma > 0.3$ beat at the 0.05 level of significance.

12.38   In a study of two topical treatments for sunburn, subjects were scored according to the fraction of rash area that was relieved. The relevant data values are these:

Treatment	Number of subjects	FRACTION OF AREA RELIEVED Mean	Standard deviation
G	12	0.68	0.21
R	11	0.62	0.09

Using the 10 percent level of significance, test the null hypothesis that the standard deviations of the populations sampled are equal.

12.6 REFERENCES

Theoretical discussions of the chi-square and F distributions may be found in most textbooks on mathematical statistics; for instance, in

FREUND, J. E., and WALPOLE, R. E., *Mathematical Statistics,* 4th ed. Englewood Cliffs, N.J.: Prentice Hall, 1987.

For more detailed tables of the chi-square and F distributions, see, for example,

PEARSON, E. S., and HARTLEY, H. O., *Biometrika Tables for Statisticians,* Vol. I. New York: John Wiley & Sons, Inc., 1968.

INFERENCES ABOUT PROPORTIONS

*I*n this chapter we deal with count *data, namely, with data obtained by counting rather than measuring. For instance, we concern ourselves with the number of persons who experience some discomfort after they are given a flu vaccine, the number of defectives in a shipment of a manufactured product, the number of television viewers who enjoy a certain situation comedy, the number of tires that last more than 30,000 miles, the number of persons who like their hamburgers with onions, and so forth.*

For the most part, we deal with values of random variables having binomial distributions, so we can use what we learned about this distribution in Chapter 8 and about its approximation by the normal distribution in Section 9.5. In particular, we concern ourselves with the binomial parameter p, *which is the probability of a success on an individual trial. However, when it comes to applications other than games of chance, we usually interpret* p *as the proportion of the time a given kind of event will occur or can be expected to occur.*

Later in the chapter we study methods that apply when each trial has more than two possible outcomes. This is the case, for example, when we count how many persons favor a piece of legislation, are against it, or do not care, or when we count the number of times that a pair of dice comes up 2, 3, 4, ..., 11, or 12. In situations like this we shall assume that we are dealing with multinomial random variables, but we will use approximations rather than the formula of Section 8.6.

In this chapter, Sections 13.1 through 13.4 parallel the work of Chapters 11 and 12, but they deal with inferences about p *instead of* σ *or* μ. *First we concern ourselves with the estimation of* p *(that is, the estimation of proportions, percentages, or probabilities), then we perform tests about the parameter* p *of a binomial population, and finally, we perform tests about the corresponding parameters of two binomial populations. Sections 13.5 and 13.6 deal with tests pertaining to the multinomial case, where each trial permits more than two possible outcomes.* ◼

13.1   THE ESTIMATION OF PROPORTIONS

The information that is usually available for the estimation of a population proportion (percentage, or probability) is a **sample proportion,** $\frac{x}{n}$, where x is the number of times that an event has occurred in n trials. For instance, if a study shows that 54 of 120 cheerleaders, presumably a random sample, suffered what auditory experts called "moderate to severe damage" to their voices, then

$$\frac{x}{n} = \frac{54}{120} = 0.45$$

and we can use this figure as a point estimate of the true proportion of cheer-leaders who are afflicted in this way. Similarly, a supermarket chain might esti-mate the proportion of its shoppers who regularly use discount coupons as 0.68 if a random sample of 300 shoppers included 204 who regularly use discount coupons.

Throughout this section it will be assumed that the situations satisfy, at least approximately, the conditions underlying the binomial distribution:

1. Our information will consist of the number of successes observed in a given number of trials.
2. The trials are independent.
3. The probability of success, the parameter we want to estimate, has the con-stant value p.

Thus, the sampling distribution of the counts on which our methods will be based is the binomial distribution with the mean $\mu = np$ and the standard devi-ation

$$\sigma = \sqrt{np(1-p)}$$

and we know from Section 9.5 that this distribution can be approximated with a normal distribution when np and $n(1-p)$ are both greater than 5. Usually, this requires that n must be large. For $n = 50$, for example, the normal-curve meth-ods discussed here and later in this chapter may be used so long as

$$50p > 5 \text{ and } 50(1-p) > 5;$$

namely, so long as p lies between 0.10 and 0.90. Similarly, for $n = 100$ they may be used so long as p lies between 0.05 and 0.95, and for $n = 200$ they may be used so long as p lies between 0.025 and 0.975. This should give the reader some idea of what we mean here by "n being large."

If we convert to standard units, then for large values of n, the statistic

$$z = \frac{x - np}{\sqrt{np(1-p)}}$$

is a value of a random variable having approximately the standard normal dis-tribution. If we substitute this expression for z into the inequality

$$-z_{\alpha/2} < z < z_{\alpha/2}$$

(as on page 321) and use some relatively simple algebra, we arrive at the in-equality

$$\frac{x}{n} - z_{\alpha/2}\sqrt{\frac{p(1-p)}{n}} < p < \frac{x}{n} + z_{\alpha/2}\sqrt{\frac{p(1-p)}{n}}$$

which looks like a confidence interval formula for p. Indeed, if we use it re-peatedly, the inequality should be satisfied $100(1-\alpha)$ percent of the time, but observe that the unknown parameter p appears not only in the middle, but also in

$$\sqrt{\frac{p(1-p)}{n}}$$

to the left of the first inequality sign and to the right of the other. The quantity $\sqrt{\frac{p(1-p)}{n}}$ is called the **standard error of a proportion,** as it is, in fact, the standard deviation of the sampling distribution of a sample proportion (see Exercise 13.28 on page 403).

To get around this difficulty and, at the same time, simplify the resulting formula, we substitute

$$\hat{p} = \frac{x}{n} \text{ for } p \text{ in } \sqrt{\frac{p(1-p)}{n}}$$

where $\hat{p}$ reads "p-hat." (This kind of notation is widely used in statistics. For instance, when we use the mean of a sample to estimate the mean of a population, we might denote it by $\hat{\mu}$, and when we use the standard deviation of a sample to estimate the standard deviation of a population, we might denote it by $\hat{\sigma}$.) Thus, we get the following **100(1 − α) percent large-sample confidence interval for p:**

Large-sample Confidence Interval for p	$\hat{p} - z_{\alpha/2} \sqrt{\dfrac{\hat{p}(1-\hat{p})}{n}} < p < \hat{p} + z_{\alpha/2} \sqrt{\dfrac{\hat{p}(1-\hat{p})}{n}}$

Example

In a random sample, 136 of 400 persons given a flu vaccine experienced some discomfort. Construct a 95 percent confidence interval for the true proportion of persons who will experience some discomfort from the vaccine.

solution

Substituting $n = 400$, $\hat{p} = \frac{136}{400} = 0.34$, and $z_{0.025} = 1.96$ into the confidence-interval formula, we get

$$0.34 - 1.96 \sqrt{\frac{(0.34)(0.66)}{400}} < p < 0.34 + 1.96 \sqrt{\frac{(0.34)(0.66)}{400}}$$

$$0.294 < p < 0.386$$

As noted previously, an interval like this contains the parameter it is intended to estimate or does not. In any single use of this interval we do not know which is the case, but the 95 percent confidence interval was obtained by a method that works 95 percent of the time. Note also that for $n = 400$ and p on the interval from 0.294 to 0.386, np and $n(1 - p)$ are both much greater than 5, so that n is without question large enough to justify the normal approximation to the binomial distribution. ◪ ◪ ◪

When it comes to small samples, we can construct confidence intervals for p by using a special table, but the resulting intervals are usually so wide that they are not of much value. For example, for $x = 4$ and $n = 10$, the 95 percent confidence interval is $0.12 < p < 0.75$. Clearly, this interval is so wide that it does not tell us very much about the actual value of p.

The large-sample theory presented here can also be used to assess the error we may be making when we use a sample proportion to estimate a population proportion, namely, the binomial parameter p. Proceeding as on page 318, we can assert with probability $1 - \alpha$ that the difference between a sample proportion and p will be at most

$$E = z_{\alpha/2} \sqrt{\frac{p(1-p)}{n}}$$

However, since p is unknown, we substitute for it again the sample proportion $\hat{p}$, and we arrive at the result that

If $\hat{p}$ is used as an estimate of p, we can assert with $100(1 - \alpha)$ percent confidence that the error is at most

Maximum Error of Estimate
$$E = z_{\alpha/2} \sqrt{\frac{\hat{p}(1-\hat{p})}{n}}$$

Like the confidence-interval formula on page 395, this formula requires that n must be large.

Example

In a random sample of 250 persons interviewed while exiting from polling places all over a state, 145 said that they voted for the reelection of the incumbent governor. With 99 percent confidence, what can we say about the maximum error, if we use $\hat{p} = \frac{145}{250} = 0.58$ as an estimate of the actual proportion of the vote which the incumbent governor will get?

solution

Substituting $n = 250$, $\hat{p} = 0.58$, and $z_{0.005} = 2.575$ into the formula for E, we get

$$E = 2.575 \sqrt{\frac{(0.58)(0.42)}{250}} \approx 0.080^{\dagger}$$

Thus, if we use $\hat{p} = 0.58$ as an estimate of the actual proportion of the vote the incumbent governor will get, we can assert with 99 percent confidence that our error is at most 0.080.   ◪ ◪ ◪

As in Section 11.1, we can use the formula for the maximum error to determine how large a sample is needed to attain a desired degree of precision. If we want to use a sample proportion to estimate a population proportion p, and we want to be able to assert with probability $1 - \alpha$ that our error will not exceed some prescribed quantity E, we write as before

$$E = z_{\alpha/2} \sqrt{\frac{p(1-p)}{n}}$$

†See the footnote on page 51 regarding the use of the symbol $\approx$.

Upon solving this equation for *n*, we get

Estimating p (with Some Information About p)	$$n = p(1 - p)\left(\frac{z_{\alpha/2}}{E}\right)^2$$

Since this formula involves *p*, it cannot be used unless we have some information about the possible values that *p* might assume. In that case, we substitute for *p* whichever of its values is closest to $\frac{1}{2}$. Without such information, we make use of the fact that $p(1 - p)$ cannot exceed $\frac{1}{4}$ (which it equals for $p = \frac{1}{2}$) and use the formula

Estimating p (without Information About p)	$$n = \frac{1}{4}\left(\frac{z_{\alpha/2}}{E}\right)^2$$

In either case, since the value we obtain for *n* may well be larger than necessary, we can say that the probability is *at least* $1 - \alpha$ that our error will not exceed *E*.

Example

Suppose that a state highway department wants to estimate what proportion of all trucks operating between two cities carry too heavy a load, and it wants to be able to assert with a probability of at least 0.95 that its error will not exceed 0.04. How large a sample will it need if
(a) it knows that the true proportion lies somewhere on the interval from 0.10 to 0.25;
(b) it has no idea what the true value might be?

solution

(a) Substituting $z_{0.025} = 1.96$, $E = 0.04$, and $p = 0.25$ into the formula for *n*, we get

$$n = (0.25)(0.75)\left(\frac{1.96}{0.04}\right)^2 \approx 450.19$$

and we round this up to the next integer, 451.
(b) Substituting $z_{0.025} = 1.96$, $E = 0.04$, and $p(1 - p) = \frac{1}{4}$ into the formula for *n*, we get

$$n = \frac{1}{4}\left(\frac{1.96}{0.04}\right)^2 = 600.25$$

and we round this up to the next integer, 601. ◢ ◢ ◢

The preceding example illustrates how some knowledge about the values *p* might assume can reduce substantially the sample size needed to attain a desired level of precision. Note also that the solution for *n* is rounded up to the next integer.

13.2   THE ESTIMATION OF PROPORTIONS (a Bayesian Method) ⊖

In Section 13.1 we considered the proportion p (which we tried to estimate) as an unknown constant; in Bayesian estimation this parameter is considered a random variable having a prior distribution which reflects one's belief about the values it can assume. As in the Bayesian estimation of means, we are thus faced with the problem of combining prior information with direct sample evidence.

For example, consider a large company that routinely pays thousands of invoices submitted by its suppliers. Of course, it is of interest to know what proportion of these invoices might contain errors, and interviews of three of the company's executives reveal the following information: Mr. Martin feels that only 0.005 (or a half of 1 percent) of the invoices contain errors; Mr. Green, who is generally regarded to be as reliable in his estimates as Mr. Martin, feels that 0.01 (or 1 percent) of the invoices contain errors; and Mr. Jones, who is generally regarded to be twice as reliable in his estimates as either Mr. Martin or Mr. Green, feels that 0.02 (or 2 percent) of the invoices contain errors. Assuming for the sake of simplicity that $p = 0.005$, $p = 0.01$, and $p = 0.02$ are the only possibilities, we thus have the following **prior probabilities** for the proportion of invoices containing errors:

p	Prior probability
0.005	0.25
0.010	0.25
0.020	0.50

Here the prior probabilities assigned to Mr. Martin's and Mr. Green's estimates are the same, and that assigned to Mr. Jones's estimate is twice as large. The prior probabilities must sum to 1, of course.

Now suppose that a random sample of 200 invoices is carefully checked, and that only one of them contains an error. The probabilities of this happening when $p = 0.005$, $p = 0.010$, or $p = 0.020$ are

$$\binom{200}{1}(0.005)^1(0.995)^{199} \approx 0.37$$

$$\binom{200}{1}(0.010)^1(0.990)^{199} \approx 0.27$$

$$\binom{200}{1}(0.020)^1(0.980)^{199} \approx 0.07$$

where we used the formula for the binomial distribution. Combining these probabilities with the prior probabilities by using the formula for Bayes' theorem (see Section 6.7), we find that the **posterior probability** of $p = 0.005$ is

$$\frac{(0.25)(0.37)}{(0.25)(0.37) + (0.25)(0.27) + (0.50)(0.07)} \approx 0.47$$

while the corresponding posterior probabilities of $p = 0.010$ and $p = 0.020$ are

$$\frac{(0.25)(0.27)}{(0.25)(0.37) + (0.25)(0.27) + (0.50)(0.07)} \approx 0.35$$

$$\frac{(0.50)(0.07)}{(0.25)(0.37) + (0.25)(0.27) + (0.50)(0.07)} \approx 0.18$$

We have thus arrived at the following posterior distribution for the proportion of invoices containing errors:

p	Posterior probability
0.005	0.47
0.010	0.35
0.020	0.18

This distribution reflects the prior judgments as well as the direct sample evidence, and it should not come as a surprise that the highest posterior probability goes to $p = 0.005$—after all, the sample proportion actually equaled

$$\frac{x}{n} = \frac{1}{200} = 0.005$$

To continue, we could use the mean of the posterior distribution, namely,

$$(0.005)(0.47) + (0.010)(0.35) + (0.020)(0.18) = 0.009$$

as a point estimate of the true proportion of invoices containing errors. In contrast to the mean of the prior distribution, which was

$$(0.005)(0.25) + (0.010)(0.25) + (0.020)(0.50) = 0.014$$

the mean of the posterior distribution reflects the prior judgments as well as the direct sample evidence.

In the preceding example it was assumed that p had to be 0.005, 0.010, or 0.020 to simplify the calculations. The method of analysis would have been the same, however, if we had considered 10 different values of p or even 100. In fact, there exist Bayesian techniques, similar to that of Section 11.3, in which p can take on any value on the continuous interval from 0 to 1, and its prior distribution is a continuous curve. The corresponding theory goes considerably beyond the scope of this text, but there is a reference to it on page 442.

EXERCISES

13.1 In using the rule that both np and $n(1 - p)$ must be greater than 5 to use the normal approximation to the binomial distribution,
(a) what values of p are permitted if $n = 250$;
(b) what values of p are permitted if $n = 800$;
(c) what values of n are permitted if $p = 0.04$;
(d) what values of n are permitted if $p = 0.98$?

13.2 In a random sample of 400 persons interviewed in a large city, 288 said that they oppose the construction of any more freeways.

    (a) Construct a 95 percent confidence interval for the corresponding proportion of the population sampled.

    (b) What can we say with 95 percent confidence about the maximum error if we use the sample proportion as an estimate of the population proportion?

13.3   In a random sample of 200 students at a large university, 144 opposed an increase in the humanities requirement and 56 favored an increase in the humanities requirement.

    (a) Give a 95 percent confidence interval for the population proportion opposed to an increase in the humanities requirement.

    (b) Give a 95 percent confidence interval for the population proportion in favor of an increase in the humanities requirement.

    (c) Indicate whether the endpoints of the interval in part (b) can be found from the endpoints of the interval in part (a).

13.4   In a random sample of 500 registered voters in a large city, 214 were registered as Democrats, 208 were registered as Republicans, and 78 were registered Independent.

    (a) Give a 95 percent confidence interval for the proportion of registered voters in the city who are registered as Republicans.

    (b) Give a 95 percent confidence interval for the proportion of registered voters in the city who are registered as Democrats.

    (c) Give a 95 percent confidence interval for the proportion of registered voters in the city who are registered as Independent.

    (d) Indicate whether there are any simple relationships among the endpoints of the intervals found in parts (a), (b), and (c).

13.5   Among 180 fish caught in a certain large lake, 24 were inedible as a result of the chemical pollution of the environment.

    (a) Construct a 99 percent confidence interval for the corresponding true proportion.

    (b) What can we say with 99 percent confidence about the maximum error if we use the sample proportion as an estimate of the population proportion?

13.6   A random sample of 400 shoppers at a supermarket includes 288 who regularly use discount coupons. Construct a 98 percent confidence interval for the true proportion of shoppers at the supermarket who use discount coupons.

13.7   In a random sample of 120 cheerleaders, 54 had suffered moderate to severe damage to their voices. With 90 percent confidence, what can we say about the maximum error if we use the sample proportion $\frac{54}{120} = 0.45$ as an estimate of the true proportion of cheerleaders who are afflicted in this way?

13.8   In a random sample of subway riders in a large city, it was found that 127 out of 305 riders needed to change trains to reach their destinations. Give a 95 percent confidence interval for the corresponding true proportion.

13.9   In a random sample of 400 television viewers interviewed in a certain area, 152 had seen a certain controversial program. With 99 percent confidence what can we say about the maximum error, if we use the sample proportion $\frac{152}{400} = 0.38$, as an estimate of the corresponding true proportion?

13.10   In a random sample of 360 persons eating lunch at a department store cafeteria, only 126 had dessert. If we use $\frac{126}{360} = 0.35$ as an estimate of the corresponding true proportion, with what confidence can we assert that our error is at most 0.10?

13.11   In a random sample of 312 high school seniors in a certain Western state, 176 said that they expected to continue their education at an in-state college or university.

    (a) Construct a 95 percent confidence interval for the corresponding true proportion.

    (b) What can we say with 90 percent confidence about the maximum error if we use $\frac{176}{312} \approx 0.564$ as an estimate of the actual proportion of high school seniors who expect to continue their education at an in-state college or university?

13.12 A random sample of 25 supermarket carts indicates that 11 of them have defective wheels.

(a) Construct a 95 percent confidence interval for the corresponding true proportion.

(b) Does the set of values for p represented by the confidence interval in part (a) permit you to make the normal distribution assumption?

(c) Construct a 99 percent confidence interval for the corresponding true proportion.

(d) Does the set of values for p represented by the confidence interval in part (c) permit you to make the normal distribution assumption?

⊞ 13.13 Instead of the large-sample confidence interval given on page 395, some users prefer the continuity-corrected confidence interval

$$\hat{p} \pm \left(z_{\alpha/2} \sqrt{\frac{\hat{p}(1 - \hat{p})}{n}} + \frac{1}{2n} \right)$$

The justifications for this method are similar to those used in dealing with the normal approximation to the binomial distribution, as on page 271 in Section 9.4.

(a) In terms of n, how much longer than the interval given on page 395 is the continuity-corrected interval?

(b) Give the 95 percent continuity-corrected confidence interval for the situation of Exercise 13.8, in which 127 out of 305 riders needed to change trains to reach their destinations.

(c) Give the 95 percent continuity-corrected confidence interval for the situation of Exercise 13.11, in which 176 of 312 high school seniors in a certain western state said that they expected to continue their education at an in-state college or university.

Use of the continuity correction makes the interval more accurate, in that the actual probability of covering the true value of p is closer to the stated $1 - \alpha$. See the reference list at the end of this chapter.

13.14 In a random sample of 140 supposed UFO sightings, 119 could easily be explained in terms of natural phenomena. Construct a 99 percent confidence interval for the probability that a supposed UFO sighting will easily be explained in terms of natural phenomena.

13.15 In a random sample of 80 persons convicted in U.S. district courts on narcotics charges, 36 received probation. With 95 percent confidence, what can we say about the maximum error. if we use $\frac{36}{80} = 0.45$ as an estimate of the probability that a person convicted in a U.S. district court on narcotics charges will receive probation?

13.16 In a random sample of 240 undergraduate biology students, 84 said that they intend to go on to graduate school. If we use $\frac{84}{240} \cdot 100\% = 35\%$ as an estimate of the true percentage of undergraduate biology students who intend to go on to graduate school, with what confidence can we assert that our error does not exceed 6 percentage points?

⊞ 13.17 When a sample constitutes more than 5 percent of a finite population, and the sample itself is large, we use the same finite population correction factor as in Section 10.7, and hence the following confidence limits for p:

Large-sample Confidence Limits for p (Finite Population)	$\hat{p} \pm z_{\alpha/2} \sqrt{\dfrac{\hat{p}(1 - \hat{p})(N - n)}{n(N - 1)}}$

where N is, as before, the size of the population sampled.

Among the 360 families in an apartment complex a random sample of 100 is interviewed, and it is found that 34 of the families have children of college age. Use the formula above to construct a 95 percent confidence interval for the proportion of all the families living in the apartment complex who have children of college age.

⌗ 13.18   A shoe manufacturer feels that unless its employees agree to a 10 percent wage reduction it cannot stay in business. If in a random sample of 80 of the manufacturer's 400 employees only 24 felt "kindly disposed" to the reduction, use the formula of the preceding exercise to construct a 99 percent confidence interval for the corresponding proportion for all the employees.

13.19   A private opinion pollster is engaged by a politician to estimate what proportion of her constituents favor the decriminalization of certain narcotics violations.

  (a) How large a sample will the pollster have to take to be at least 95 percent sure that the sample proportion is off by at most 0.02?

  (b) How large a sample will the pollster have to take if it is believed that the true proportion in favor of this decriminalization is approximately 0.35?

13.20   Many problems involve the construction of 95 percent confidence intervals, and the value $z_{0.025} \approx 1.96$ is used in the calculations. Some persons make an approximation by replacing 1.96 by 2. Show that the formula for sample size for estimating p (without information about p) on page 397 for 95 percent confidence intervals, replacing 1.96 by 2, reduces to

$$n = \frac{1}{E^2}$$

  (a) Find the sample size needed to have 95 percent confidence that the error is at most 5 percentage points.

  (b) Find the sample size needed to have 95 percent confidence that the error is at most 4 percentage points.

  (c) Find the sample size needed to have 95 percent confidence that the error is at most 2 percentage points.

13.21   A political pollster is engaged by a politician to estimate the proportion of registered voters in his district who plan to vote for him in the next election. Find the sample size needed if he wants, with 95 percent confidence, the poll to be accurate to within

  (a) 8 percentage points;   (b) 4 percentage points;

  (c) 2 percentage points;   (d) 1 percentage point.

13.22   Suppose that we want to estimate what proportion of all drivers exceed the maximum speed limit on a stretch of road between Los Angeles and Bakersfield. How large a sample will we need so that the error of our estimate is at most 0.04 if

  (a) the desired level of confidence is 90 percent;

  (b) the desired level of confidence is 95 percent;

  (c) the desired level of confidence is 99 percent?

13.23   A national manufacturer wants to determine what percentage of purchases of razor blades for use by men is actually made by women. How large a sample of men will the manufacturer need to be at least 98 percent confident that the sample percentage is not off by more than 2.5 percentage points if

  (a) nothing is known about the true proportion;

  (b) there is good reason to believe that the true proportion is at most 0.30?

13.24   In problems involving the estimation of a proportion, there is a trade-off between the level of confidence and the error of estimate. Suppose that we would like to estimate the proportion of wild deer harboring a certain parasite.

  (a) What sample size will be needed if we want the error of estimate to be at most 0.08 and if the desired level of confidence is 90%?

  (b) Using the sample size found in part (a), what is the maximum error if the desired level of confidence is to be 95%?

(c) Using the sample size found in part (a), what is the level of confidence if the maximum error is to be 0.06?

13.25 In planning the operation of a new school, one school board member claims that 4 out of 5 newly hired teachers will stay with the school for more than a year, while another school board member claims that it would be correct to say 7 out of 10. In the past, the two board members have been about equally reliable in their predictions, so that in the absence of direct information we would assign their judgments equal weight. What posterior probabilities would we assign to their claims if it is found that 11 of 12 newly hired teachers stayed with the school for more than a year?

13.26 The landscaping plans for a new hotel call for a row of palm trees along the driveway. The landscape designer tells the owner that if he plants *Washingtonia filifera,* 20 percent of the trees will fail to survive the first heavy frost, the manager of the nursery which supplies the trees tells the owner that 10 percent of the trees will fail to survive the first heavy frost, and the owner's wife tells him that 30 percent of the trees will fail to survive the first heavy frost.

(a) If the owner feels that in this matter the landscape designer is 10 times as reliable as his wife and the manager of the nursery is 9 times as reliable as his wife, what prior probabilities should he assign to these percentages?

(b) If 13 of these palm trees are planted and 2 fail to survive the first heavy frost, what posterior probabilities should the manager assign to the three percentages?

13.27 The method of Section 13.2 can also be used to find the posterior distribution of the number of "successes" in a finite population. Suppose, for instance, that a coin dealer receives a shipment of five ancient coins from abroad, and that, on the basis of past experience, he feels that the probabilities that 0, 1, 2, 3, 4, or all 5 of them are counterfeits are 0.74, 0.11, 0.02, 0.01, 0.02, and 0.10. Since modern methods of counterfeiting have become greatly refined, the cost of authentication has risen sharply and the dealer decides to select one of the coins at random and send it away for authentication. If it turns out that the coin is a forgery, find

(a) the posterior probabilities that 0, 1, 2, 3, or all 4 of the remaining coins are counterfeits;

(b) the mean of the posterior distribution obtained in part (a) and use it to estimate what proportion of the remaining coins are counterfeits.

13.28 Since the proportion of successes is simply the number of successes divided by n, the mean and the standard deviation of the sampling distribution of the proportion of successes may be obtained by dividing by n the mean and the standard deviation of the sampling distribution of the number of successes. Use this argument to verify the standard error formula given on page 395.

13.29 Can it ever happen that the lower end of the large-sample confidence interval for p is less than zero? (*Hint:* Consider what happens if $x = 0$ or $x = 1$ or $x = 2$.)

13.30 The inequality $-z_{\alpha/2} < z < z_{\alpha/2}$ on page 394 is certainly equivalent to the inequality $z^2 < (z_{\alpha/2})^2$.

(a) Show that the substitution of

$$z = \frac{x - np}{\sqrt{np(1 - p)}} \quad \text{into} \quad z^2 < (z_{\alpha/2})^2$$

results in an inequality which can be written as

$$p^2[n^2 + n(z_{\alpha/2})^2] - p[2nx + n(z_{\alpha/2})^2] + x^2 < 0$$

(b) Express the inequality obtained in part (a) using numbers given in Exercise 13.3, namely $n = 200$, $x = 144$, and $z_{\alpha/2} = 1.96$.

(c) Regard the left side of the inequality obtained in part (b) as a quadratic expression in p. Find the values of p for which this quadratic is equal to zero; a 95% confidence interval for p is the interval between these values.

(d) Compare the confidence interval found in part (c) with the interval given in Exercise 13.3, part (a). (*Note*: The confidence intervals should be very similar because the sample size n is large. With smaller values of n the two methods will differ noticeably.)

13.3   TESTS CONCERNING PROPORTIONS

Now we concern ourselves with tests of hypotheses that enable us to decide, on the basis of sample data, whether the true value of a proportion (percentage, or probability) equals, is greater than, or is less than a given constant. These tests make it possible, for example, to determine whether the actual proportion of fifth graders who can name the governor of their state is 0.35, whether it is true that 10 percent of IRS employees' answers to taxpayers' telephone inquiries are in error, or whether the probability is really 0.25 that the downtime of a new computer will exceed two hours in any given week.

Questions of this kind are usually decided on the basis of the observed number of successes in n trials, or the observed proportion of successes. We will make the same assumptions as we did in Section 13.1, enabling us to use the binomial distribution. These assumptions are that the information will consist of the number of successes observed in a given number of trials, that the trials are independent, and that the probability of success has the constant value p. We will be testing hypotheses about the parameter p.

When n is small, tests concerning proportions can be based directly on tables of binomial probability, as illustrated by the following example:

Example

It has been claimed that more than 70 percent of the students attending a large university are opposed to a plan to increase student fees in order to build new parking facilities. If 15 of 18 students selected at random at that university are opposed to the plan, test the claim at the 0.05 level of significance.

solution

The structure of binomial probabilities in Table V makes it easiest to organize this test through the use of p-values, as described on pages 351–352.

1. H_0: $p = 0.70$
   H_A: $p > 0.70$

2. $\alpha = 0.05$

3′. The test statistic is the number of students in the sample opposed to the plan, namely $x = 15$.

4′. Table V shows that for $n = 18$ and $p = 0.70$ the probability of 15 or more successes is

$$0.105 + 0.046 + 0.013 + 0.002 = 0.166$$

Thus, $p = 0.166$.

5'. Since 0.166 is greater than 0.05, the null hypothesis cannot be rejected; in other words, the data do not support the claim that more than 70 percent of the students at the given university are opposed to the plan. We accept the null hypothesis or defer judgment. ▰ ▰ ▰

We used the procedure based on p-values because, for tests based on a binomial table, this alternative procedure can save a good deal of work. As the reader will be asked to verify in Exercise 13.39, this is true, particularly, when a test is two-tailed, as in the example that follows.

Example

It has been claimed that 40 percent of all shoppers can identify a highly advertised trade mark. If, in a random sample, 13 of 20 shoppers were able to identify the trade mark, test at the 0.05 level of significance whether to accept the null hypothesis $p = 0.40$ or the alternative hypothesis $p \neq 0.40$.

solution

1. H_0: $p = 0.40$
   H_A: $p \neq 0.40$

2. $\alpha = 0.05$

3'. The test statistic is x, the number of shoppers who can identify the trade mark; here $x = 13$.

4'. Table V shows that for $n = 20$ and $p = 0.40$ the probability of 13 or fewer successes is

$$1 - (0.005 + 0.001) = 0.994$$

and that the probability of 13 or more successes is

$$0.015 + 0.005 + 0.001 = 0.021$$

In a two-tailed test, the p-value is twice the smaller of these two numbers. Here,

$$p = 2(0.021) = 0.042$$

5'. Since 0.042 is less than 0.05, the null hypothesis must be rejected; in other, words, the data show that the true percentage of shoppers who can identify the trade mark is not 40 percent. ▰ ▰ ▰

When n is large, tests concerning proportions (percentages, or probabilities) may be based on the normal-curve approximation to the binomial distribution. Using the same z-statistic which led to the large-sample confidence interval formula for p on page 394, we base tests of the null hypothesis $p = p_0$ on the statistic[†]

[†]Some statisticians make a continuity correction here by substituting $x - \frac{1}{2}$ or $x + \frac{1}{2}$ for x in the formula for z, whichever makes z closer to zero. However, when n is large the effect of this correction is usually negligible.

| *Large-sample Test Concerning Proportion* | $$z = \frac{x - np_0}{\sqrt{np_0(1 - p_0)}}$$ |

which is a value of a random variable having approximately the standard normal distribution. The test criteria are like those shown in Figure 11.10 with p and p_0 substituted for μ and μ_0; analogous to the table on page 350, the criteria for tests of the null hypothesis $p = p_0$ are as follows:

Alternative hypothesis	*Reject the null hypothesis if*	*Accept the null hypothesis or reserve judgment if*
$p < p_0$	$z \leq -z_\alpha$	$z > -z_\alpha$
$p > p_0$	$z \geq z_\alpha$	$z < z_\alpha$
$p \neq p_0$	$z \leq -z_{\alpha/2}$ or $z \geq z_{\alpha/2}$	$-z_{\alpha/2} < z < z_{\alpha/2}$

Example

A television critic claims that 80 percent of all viewers find the noise level of a certain commercial objectionable. If a random sample of 320 television viewers includes 245 who find the noise level of the commercial objectionable, test at the 0.05 level of significance whether the difference between the sample proportion,

$$\frac{245}{320} \approx 0.766, \quad \text{and} \quad p_0 = 0.80$$

is significant.

solution

1. H_0: $p = 0.80$
   H_A: $p \neq 0.80$
2. $\alpha = 0.05$
3. Reject the null hypothesis if $z \leq -1.96$ or $z \geq 1.96$, where

$$z = \frac{x - np_0}{\sqrt{np_0(1 - p_0)}}$$

Otherwise, state that the difference between the sample proportion and $p = 0.80$ is not significant.
4. Substituting $n = 320$, $x = 245$, and $p_0 = 0.80$ into the formula for z, we get

$$z = \frac{245 - 320(0.80)}{\sqrt{320(0.80)(0.20)}} \approx -1.54$$

5. Since $z = -1.54$ falls on the interval from -1.96 to 1.96, the null hypothesis cannot be rejected; in other words, we conclude that the difference between $\frac{245}{320} \approx 0.766$ and $p = 0.80$ is not significant. ◪ ◪ ◪

■ ◪ EXERCISES

13.31   A doctor claims that only 10 percent of all persons exposed to a certain amount of radiation will feel any ill effects. If, in a random sample, 5 of 18 persons exposed to such radiation feel some ill effects, test the null hypothesis $p = 0.10$ against the alternative hypothesis $p > 0.10$ at the 0.05 level of significance.

13.32   The manufacturer of a spot remover claims that his product removes 90 percent of all spots. If, in a random sample, the spot remover removes 11 of 16 spots, test the null hypothesis $p = 0.90$ against the alternative hypothesis $p < 0.90$ at the 0.05 level of significance.

13.33   It has been claimed that 20 percent of all undergraduate business students will take advanced work in accounting. In a random sample of 12 undergraduate business students, 5 say that they will take advanced work in accounting. Test the claimed value of 20 percent, using the alternative hypothesis $p > 0.20$ and the 0.05 level of significance.

13.34   It has been claimed that at least 60 percent of all purchasers of a certain computer program will call the manufacturer's hotline within one month of purchase. If 3 of 14 software purchasers selected at random called the hotline within one month of purchase, test the claim at the 0.05 level of significance (one-tailed criterion).

13.35   In a random sample, 12 of 14 industrial accidents were due to unsafe working conditions. Use the 0.05 level of significance to test the hypothesis that 50 percent of all industrial accidents are due to unsafe working conditions against the alternative hypothesis $p \neq 50$ percent.

13.36   A food processor wants to know whether the probability is really 0.60 that a customer will prefer a new kind of packaging to the old. If, in a random sample, 7 of 18 customers prefer the new kind of packaging to the old kind, test the null hypothesis $p = 0.60$ against the alternative hypothesis $p \neq 0.60$ at the 0.05 level of significance.

13.37   In a random sample, 5 of 12 medical students said that they will go into private practice soon after they finish their internships. If the probability of a Type I error is to be at most 0.05, does this support or refute the claim that at least 70 percent of all medical students plan to go into private practice soon after they finish their internships?

13.38   A random sample of size $n = 15$ is to be used to test the null hypothesis $p = 0.70$ against the alternative $p < 0.70$. For what values of x, the observed number of successes, will the null hypothesis be rejected if

     (a) the level of significance is 0.10;

     (b) the level of significance is 0.05;

     (c) the level of significance is 0.01?

13.39   In the example on page 405, we tested the null hypothesis $p = 0.40$ against the alternative hypothesis $p \neq 0.40$. For what values of x, the number of shoppers in the sample of size $n = 20$ who can identify the trademark, would the null hypothesis be rejected if

     (a) the level of significance is 0.10;

     (b) the level of significance is 0.05;

     (c) the level of significance is 0.01?

13.40   In a random sample of 200 automobile accidents, it was found that 64 were due at least in part to driver fatigue. Use the 0.05 level of significance to test whether or not this supports the claim that 35 percent of all automobile accidents are due at least in part to driver fatigue.

13.41   In a study of aviophobia, a psychologist claims that 30 percent of all women are afraid of flying. If, in a random sample, 41 of 150 women are afraid of flying, test the null hypothesis $p = 0.30$ against the alternative hypothesis $p \neq 0.30$ at the 0.05 level of significance.

13.42 In a random sample of 600 cars making right turns at a certain intersection, 157 pulled into the wrong lane. Test the claim that 30 percent of all drivers make this mistake at the given intersection, using the level of significance

(a) $\alpha = 0.05$;   (b) $\alpha = 0.01$.

13.43 An airline claims that at most 6 percent of all its lost luggage is never found. Test this claim, if, in a random sample, 17 of 200 pieces of the airline's lost luggage are not found and the probability of a Type I error is not to exceed 0.01.

13.44 To check an ambulance service's claim that at least 40 percent of its calls are life-threatening emergencies, a random sample was taken from its files, and it was found that 49 of 150 calls were life-threatening emergencies. If the probability of a Type I error is not to exceed 0.05, what can we conclude about the ambulance service's claim?

13.45 A food chemist notes that 90 percent of the bricks of a certain cheddar cheese will remain mold-free for three months under standard refrigeration. A variation is made in the salt content of this cheese, and a sample of 15 bricks of the modified cheese are kept under standard refrigeration for three months.

(a) Suppose that only 11 of the bricks remain mold-free. At the 5 percent level of significance, test the null hypothesis $p = 0.90$ against the alternative hypothesis $p \neq 0.90$.

(b) Suppose that all 15 of the bricks remain mold-free. At the 5 percent level of significance, test the null hypothesis $p = 0.90$ against the alternative hypothesis $p \neq 0.90$. What can you say about this experiment's ability to detect p larger than 0.90?

13.46 For each of 400 simulated random samples, a statistics class determined a 90 percent confidence interval for μ, and it found that 368 of them contained the mean of the population sampled, the other 32 did not. At the 0.05 level of significance, is there evidence to doubt whether the method employed actually yields 90 percent confidence intervals?

13.47 A slightly bent coin was flipped 400 times, coming up heads 166 times. At the 0.05 level of significance, can you reject the null hypothesis $p = 0.5$ against the alternative $p \neq 0.5$?

13.4 DIFFERENCES BETWEEN PROPORTIONS

There are many problems where we must decide whether an observed difference between two sample proportions can be attributed to chance, or whether it is indicative of the fact that the corresponding population proportions are not equal. For instance, we may want to decide on the basis of sample data whether there is a difference between the actual proportions of persons with and without flu shots who catch the disease, or we may want to test on the basis of samples whether two manufacturers of electronic equipment ship equal proportions of defectives.

The method we shall use here to test whether an observed difference between two sample proportions is significant, or whether it can be attributed to chance, is based on the following theory: If x_1 and x_2 are the numbers of successes obtained in n_1 trials of one kind and n_2 of another, the trials are all independent, and the corresponding probabilities of a success are, respectively, p_1 and p_2, then the sampling distribution of

$$\frac{x_1}{n_1} - \frac{x_2}{n_2}$$

has the mean $p_1 - p_2$ and the standard deviation

$$\sqrt{\frac{p_1(1-p_1)}{n_1} + \frac{p_2(1-p_2)}{n_2}}$$

It is customary to refer to this standard deviation as the **standard error of the difference between two proportions.**

When we test the null hypothesis $p_1 = p_2 (= p)$ against an appropriate alternative hypothesis, the mean of the sampling distribution of the difference between two sample proportions is $p_1 - p_2 = 0$, and the standard error formula can be written

$$\sqrt{p(1-p)\left(\frac{1}{n_1} + \frac{1}{n_2}\right)}$$

where p is usually estimated by **pooling** the data and substituting for p the combined sample proportion

$$\hat{p} = \frac{x_1 + x_2}{n_1 + n_2}$$

which, as before, reads "p-hat." Then, converting to standard units, we obtain the statistic

Test Concerning Difference between Two Proportions	$z = \dfrac{\dfrac{x_1}{n_1} - \dfrac{x_2}{n_2}}{\sqrt{\hat{p}(1-\hat{p})\left(\dfrac{1}{n_1} + \dfrac{1}{n_2}\right)}}$ with $\hat{p} = \dfrac{x_1 + x_2}{n_1 + n_2}$

which, for large samples, is a value of a random variable having approximately the standard normal distribution. To make this formula appear more compact, we can substitute in the numerator $\hat{p}_1$ for $\frac{x_1}{n_1}$ and $\hat{p}_2$ for $\frac{x_2}{n_2}$.

The test criteria are again like those shown in Figure 11.10 with p_1 and p_2 substituted for μ and μ_0; analogous to the table on page 350 the criteria for tests of the null hypothesis $p_1 = p_2$ are as follows:

Alternative hypothesis	Reject the null hypothesis if	Accept the null hypothesis or reserve judgment if
$p_1 < p_2$	$z \le -z_\alpha$	$z > -z_\alpha$
$p_1 > p_2$	$z \ge z_\alpha$	$z < z_\alpha$
$p_1 \ne p_2$	$z \le -z_{\alpha/2}$ or $z \ge z_{\alpha/2}$	$-z_{\alpha/2} < z < z_{\alpha/2}$

Example

To test the effectiveness of a new pain-relieving drug, 80 patients at a clinic were given a pill containing the drug and 80 others were given a placebo containing only powdered sugar. If 56 of the patients in the first group and 38 of those in the

second group felt a beneficial effect, what can we conclude at the 0.01 level of significance about the effectiveness of the new drug?

solution

1. H_0: $p_1 = p_2$
   H_A: $p_1 > p_2$
2. $\alpha = 0.01$
3. Reject the null hypothesis if $z \geq 2.33$, where z is given by the formula on
   page 409; otherwise, accept it or reserve judgment.
4. Substituting

$$x_1 = 56, \quad x_2 = 38, \quad n_1 = 80, \quad n_2 = 80, \quad \text{and} \quad \hat{p} = \frac{56 + 38}{80 + 80} = 0.5875$$

into the formula for z we get

$$z = \frac{\frac{56}{80} - \frac{38}{80}}{\sqrt{(0.5875)(0.4125)\left(\frac{1}{80} + \frac{1}{80}\right)}} \approx 2.89$$

5. Since $z = 2.89$ exceeds 2.33, the null hypothesis must be rejected; in other
   words, we conclude that the new drug is effective. ▰ ▰ ▰

The method we have described here applies to tests of the null hypothesis $p_1 =
p_2$, but it can easily be modified (see Exercise 13.55 on page 414) so that it ap-
plies also to tests of the null hypothesis $p_1 - p_2 = \delta$ (*delta,* the Greek letter for
lowercase *d*). Also, when the alternative hypothesis is $p_1 \neq p_2$, but not when it is
$p_1 < p_2$ or $p_1 > p_2$, we can base the test on a different statistic, which is somewhat
easier to calculate. This method is described in Exercise 13.83 on page 428.

There are also many problems in which we must decide whether differences
among more than two sample proportions are significant, or whether they can
be attributed to chance. For instance, if 24 of 200 brand *A* tires, 21 of 200 brand
B tires, 18 of 200 brand *C* tires, and 33 of 200 brand *D* tires failed to last 20,000
miles we may want to decide whether the differences among

$$\frac{24}{200} = 0.120, \quad \frac{21}{200} = 0.105, \quad \frac{18}{200} = 0.090, \quad \text{and} \quad \frac{33}{200} = 0.165$$

are significant, or whether they may be due to chance. Problems of this type can
be treated separately, but we will consider them as a special case of the problem
treated in Section 13.5.

In problems involving proportions, there is often the need to go beyond testing the null hypothesis that the two proportions are equal. Indeed, when the null
hypothesis is rejected we need to make some statement summarizing the way in
which the proportions are unequal.

A simple description consists of the difference $\hat{p}_1 - \hat{p}_2$, which can be regarded
as an estimate of the population difference $p_1 - p_2$. A technique for giving a confidence interval for $p_1 - p_2$ is discussed in Exercise 13.57. The statistic $\hat{p}_1 - \hat{p}_2$ is
sometimes called the **rate difference.** The null hypothesis H_0: $p_1 = p_2$ can of

course be written as H_0: $p_1 - p_2 = 0$, which is a statement about the population rate difference.

Other descriptions have come into common use. It is helpful to display the data in the form of a 2-by-2 table:

	Success	*Failure*	*Total*
Group 1	x_1	$n_1 - x_1$	n_1
Group 2	x_2	$n_2 - x_2$	n_2

For simplicity of notation, it helps to shorten this to

	Success	*Failure*	*Total*
Group 1	A	B	$A + B$
Group 2	C	D	$C + D$

so that $A = x_1$, $B = n_1 - x_1$, and so on.

We have already noted the rate difference $\hat{p}_1 - \hat{p}_2$, which equals

$$\frac{A}{A + B} - \frac{C}{C + D}$$

It can now be noted that $\frac{A}{B}$ is the observed odds in group 1, since

$$\frac{A}{B} = \frac{\dfrac{A}{A + B}}{\dfrac{B}{A + B}} = \frac{\hat{p}_1}{1 - \hat{p}_1}$$

In a similar fashion, $\frac{C}{D}$ is the observed odds in group 2. The statistic

$$\frac{A/B}{C/D}, \quad \text{which equals} \quad \frac{AD}{BC}$$

is called the **odds ratio.** The null hypothesis H_0: $p_1 = p_2$ can of course be written as

$$H_0: \quad \frac{p_1/(1 - p_1)}{p_2/(1 - p_2)} = 1$$

which is a statement about the population odds ratio.

The odds ratio is used heavily in medical investigations, since it tends to be relatively stable over changing definitions of experimental conditions. For instance, a study to compare an active headache treatment to a placebo (a sugar pill) in terms of ability to relieve headache symptoms within 15 minutes produced these values:

	Relief?		
	Yes	*No*	*Total*
Active	10	90	100
Placebo	5	95	100

The rate difference $\hat{p}_1 - \hat{p}_2$ is equal to

$$\frac{10}{100} - \frac{5}{100} = 0.05$$

while the odds ratio is

$$\frac{10 \cdot 95}{90 \cdot 5} \approx 2.11$$

A rerun of the experiment on different subjects, noting relief within one hour, produced the following:

	Relief?		
	Yes	*No*	*Total*
Active	34	16	50
Placebo	24	26	50

For this second study, the rate difference is

$$\frac{34}{50} - \frac{24}{50} = 0.20$$

and the odds ratio is

$$\frac{34 \cdot 26}{16 \cdot 24} \approx 2.30$$

It can be seen that changing the duration of the experiment from 15 minutes to one hour caused a substantial change in the rate difference but only a minor change in the odds ratio. The references at the end of this chapter suggest reasons why the odds ratio tends to remain stable as the terms of the experiment are changed.

In some medical studies, the two groups consist of persons who have or who have not been exposed to some potentially toxic substance, which the columns denote as the presence or absence of some disease. For such studies, the data look like this:

		Disease?		
		Yes	*No*	*Total*
Exposed to potentially toxic substance?	*Yes*	A	B	A + B
	No	C	D	C + D

For the $A + B$ persons exposed to the substance, the estimated risk of getting the disease is

$$\hat{p}_1 = \frac{A}{A + B}, \quad \text{whereas} \quad \hat{p}_2 = \frac{C}{C + D}$$

is the estimated risk for those not exposed to the substance. In this context, we could employ the rate difference or the odds ratio, as noted above, but we can also give the **risk ratio**

$$\frac{\hat{p}_1}{\hat{p}_2} = \frac{A/(A + B)}{C/(C + D)}$$

If the risk ratio is equal to 2, the interpretation is that someone exposed to the toxic substance is twice as likely to get the disease as someone who has not been exposed.

The risk ratio is also called the **rate ratio.** The risk ratio and the rate difference are not appropriate measures to use when the exposure status is determined after the fact. For example, one cannot use these measures if the investigation works from groups of diseased and nondiseased persons and then inquires about past exposure to possibly toxic substances.

There are hypothesis tests and confidence intervals for these statistics, but such tests go beyond the level of this text. The field of **epidemiology** concerns the use of such statistical information in determining health risk. The reference list contains sources for this fascinating field.

EXERCISES

13.48 One method of seeding clouds was successful in 57 of 150 attempts, while another method was successful in 33 of 100 attempts. At the 0.05 level of significance, can we conclude that the first method is better than the second?

13.49 One mail solicitation for a charity brought 412 responses to 5,000 letters and another, more expensive, mail solicitation brought 311 responses to 3,000 letters. Use the 0.01 level of significance to test the null hypothesis that the two solicitations are equally effective against the alternative that the more expensive one is more effective.

13.50 In a random sample of 250 full-time students at a large university, 146 reported that they had made nontextbook purchases at the university bookstore. In a separate random sample of 200 part-time students at the same university 102 reported that they had made nontextbook purchases at the university bookstore. At the 0.05 level of significance, test the null hypothesis that the corresponding population proportions are equal against the alternative that the full-time students are more likely to make nontextbook purchases at the university bookstore.

13.51 A study showed that 74 of 200 persons who saw a deodorant advertised during the telecast of a baseball game and 86 of 200 other persons who saw it advertised on a variety show remembered two hours later the name of the deodorant. Use the 0.05 level of significance to test whether or not the difference between the two sample proportions, $\frac{74}{200} = 0.37$ and $\frac{86}{200} = 0.43$, is significant.

13.52 A random sample of 100 high school students were asked whether they would turn to their parents for help with a homework assignment in mathematics, and another random sample of 100 high school students were asked the same question with regard to a homework assignment in English. If 62 students in the first sample and 44 students in the second sample would turn to their parents for help, test at the 0.05 level of significance whether the difference between the two sample proportions, $\frac{62}{100}$ and $\frac{44}{100}$, may be attributed to chance.

13.53   The owner of an automobile repair shop offers a fresh donut to each customer in his waiting room. When he used 144 donuts from Tasty-Yum Bakery, he noted that 98 were eaten completely while the remaining 46 were partially eaten and discarded. When he used 144 donuts from Topps Bakery, he noted that 121 were eaten completely. At the 0.05 level of significance test whether the difference between the sample proportions is significant.

13.54   Among 500 marriage license applications, chosen at random twelve years ago, 48 of the women were at least one year older than the men, and among 500 marriage license applications, chosen at random eight years later, 85 of the women were at least one year older than the men. Use the 0.05 level of significance to test whether or not there was an actual increase in the proportion of women on marriage license applications who were at least one year older than the men.

13.55   To test the null hypothesis that the difference between two population proportions equals some constant δ (*delta,* the Greek letter for lowercase *d*), we can use the statistic

Test Concerning Difference between Two Proportions

$$z = \frac{\hat{p}_1 - \hat{p}_2 - \delta}{\sqrt{\dfrac{\hat{p}_1(1 - \hat{p}_1)}{n_1} + \dfrac{\hat{p}_2(1 - \hat{p}_2)}{n_2}}}$$

which, for large samples, is a value of a random variable having approximately the standard normal distribution. In this formula, $\hat{p}_1$ and $\hat{p}_2$ denote the two sample proportions,

$$\frac{x_1}{n_1} \quad \text{and} \quad \frac{x_2}{n_2}$$

The test criteria are like those of Figure 11.12 on page 361 and the table on page 361 with p_1 and p_2 substituted for μ_1 and μ_2.

(a) In a true-false test, a test item is considered to be good if it discriminates between well-prepared and poorly prepared students. If 205 of 250 well-prepared students and 137 of 250 poorly prepared students answer a certain test item correctly, test at the 0.05 level of significance whether to accept the null hypothesis $p_1 - p_2 = 0.20$ or the alternative hypothesis $p_1 - p_2 > 0.20$.

(b) To check on regional preferences, a chain of donut houses interviews random samples of shoppers in North Carolina and in Vermont. Asked whether they prefer the chain's donuts to those of all its competitors, 177 of 500 persons interviewed in North Carolina and 110 of 400 persons interviewed in Vermont answered "Yes." Test at the 0.05 level of significance whether the corresponding true proportion for North Carolina exceeds that for Vermont by more than 0.06.

13.56   A medical research worker wants to compare two flavor bases for use in children's medicines. She used two groups consisting of 200 children each, finding that 136 of 200 children liked the cherry base and that 107 of 200 liked the orange base. At the 0.05 level of significance, test the claim that the true percentage for the cherry base exceeds the true percentage for the orange base by 0.15. As the alternative, use the statement that the difference between the rates is not 0.15.

13.57   If we substitute the formula for z of Exercise 13.55 into $-z_{\alpha/2} < z < z_{\alpha/2}$, and manipulate the inequality algebraically so that the middle term is δ, we obtain a $100(1 - \alpha)$ percent confidence interval for

$$\delta = p_1 - p_2$$

Use this method and the data of part (b) of Exercise 13.55 to construct a 99 percent confidence interval for the difference between the true proportions of shoppers in North Carolina and in Vermont who prefer the donut chain's donuts to those of all its competitors.

13.58 Use the method of Exercise 13.57 and the data of Exercise 13.56 to construct a 98 percent confidence interval for the difference between the true percentages of children who
like the cherry and orange flavor bases.

13.59 Show that if $p_1 = p_2$, then the corresponding odds ratio is equal to 1.

13.60 The odds ratio that compares population 1 to population 2 is given as

$$\frac{p_1/(1 - p_1)}{p_2/(1 - p_2)}$$

(a) Show that the odds ratio which compares population 2 to population 1 is the recip-
rocal of the above.

(b) If the odds ratio that compares population 1 to population 2 is 0.80, what is the odds
ratio that compares population 2 to population 1?

(c) If $p_R = 0.60$ and $p_J = 0.75$, what odds ratios could you use to compare populations
R and J?

13.61 In a survey about on-campus parking, 36 of 80 freshmen expressed a desire for more
parking spaces, while 53 of 70 juniors expressed a desire for more parking spaces.

(a) At the 0.05 level of significance, is the difference between the freshmen and juniors
statistically significant?

(b) Provide the rate difference and the odds ratio that compare the two groups.

13.62 An epidemiologist concerned with the possibility that caffeine consumption reduces the
probability of conception for women attempting to become pregnant followed two groups
of women for 15 months. All women who enrolled in the study were attempting to become pregnant. The women in one group consumed no caffeine at all, and the women in
the other group ingested more than 300 milligrams per day. She noted then the number
of women who did not become pregnant within 12 months:

		Conception delayed past 12 months?		
		Yes	*No*	
Caffeine consumption	*None*	21	179	200
	>300	35	125	160

(a) Formulate and test at the 0.05 level of significance the null hypothesis which asks
whether there is any significant difference between the rates of delayed pregnancies
for the two groups of women.

(b) Summarize the difference between the two groups of women in terms of the rate difference.

(c) Summarize the difference between the two groups of women in terms of the rate
ratio.

(d) Summarize the difference between the two groups of women in terms of the odds
ratio.

This exercise was motivated by the article by Cynthia Stanton and Ronald Gray in the
American Journal of Epidemiology, December 15, 1995.

13.63 It has been noted that the risk ratio and odds ratio are nearly equal when the disease is
uncommon. The table below shows the number of cases of stroke in a six-year period
among younger (under 65 years at start of study) and older (over 65 years) men who were
not taking medication to reduce blood pressure:

Stroke?

	Yes	No
Older	70	1,020
Younger	65	3,400

(a) Formulate and test at the 0.05 level of significance the null hypothesis that asks whether there is any significant difference between the rates of stroke for the two groups of men.

(b) Summarize the difference between the two groups of men in terms of the rate difference.

(c) Summarize the difference between the two groups of men in terms of the rate ratio.

(d) Summarize the difference between the two groups of men in terms of the odds ratio.

(e) Which of the measures given in parts (b), (c), and (d) are most nearly equal?

This exercise was motivated by the article by Lindenstrom et al. in the *American Journal of Epidemiology*, December 15, 1995.

13.64   Two experiments were conducted to compare new products H and Q for relief from itching due to insect bites to a currently marketed product identified as CMP. Unfortunately, the two experiments used different definitions of "relief" and also followed the subjects for different lengths of time. The results were the following:

Experiment 1:

Relief?

	Yes	No	Total
New product H	16	24	40
CMP	12	28	40

Experiment 2:

Relief?

	Yes	No	Total
New product Q	45	5	50
CMP	36	14	50

Each of the new products performed better than the currently marketed product in its separate experiment. Which of products H and Q seems to be superior? Why?

13.5   ANALYSIS OF AN $r \times c$ TABLE

The method we describe in this section applies to two kinds of problems. These two kinds differ conceptually, but they are analyzed in the same way. In the first kind of problem we deal with trials or experiments in which we will have control over the sample sizes for separate experimental groups. In the second kind of problem we will have control only over the total sample size.

In both kinds of problems we will deal with situations in which there are two or more possible outcomes. This includes the binomial case, where there are always two possible outcomes, but it may include situations in which we note whether an undergraduate is a freshman, sophomore, junior, or senior.

As an example of the first kind of problem, consider a survey in which independent random samples of 80 single persons, 120 married persons, and 100 persons who are widowed or divorced were asked whether "friends and social life," "job or primary activity," or "health and physical condition" contribute most to their general happiness. The results are shown in the following table, called a 3 × 3 table (where 3 × 3 reads "3 by 3"), as it contains three rows and three columns:

	Single	*Married*	*Widowed or divorced*
Friends and social life	41	49	42
Job or primary activity	27	50	33
Health and physical condition	12	21	25
	80	120	100

There are three separate samples, the column totals are the fixed sample sizes, and each trial (each person interviewed) permits three different outcomes. Note that the row totals,

$$41 + 49 + 42 = 132, \qquad 27 + 50 + 33 = 110$$

and

$$12 + 21 + 25 = 58,$$

depend on the responses of the persons interviewed, and hence on chance. In general, a table like this, with r rows and c columns, is called an **$r \times c$** ("r by c") **table.**

In the second kind of problem where the method of this section applies, the column totals as well as the row totals are left to chance. Suppose, for instance, that we want to investigate whether there is a relationship between the qualification test scores of persons who have gone through a certain job-training program and their subsequent performance on the job. Suppose, furthermore, that a random sample of 400 cases taken from very extensive files yielded the following results:

		Performance			
		Poor	*Fair*	*Good*	
	Below average	67	64	25	156
Qualification test scores	Average	42	76	56	174
	Above average	10	23	37	70
		119	163	118	400

Here there is only one sample, the **grand total** of 400 is its fixed size, and each trial (each case chosen from the files) permits nine different outcomes. It is mainly in connection with problems like this that $r \times c$ tables are referred to as **contingency tables.**

Before we demonstrate how $r \times c$ tables are analyzed, let us examine what null hypotheses we shall want to test. In the problem dealing with the different factors which contribute most to one's happiness, we want to test the null hypothesis that the probabilities of the three choices ("friends and social life," "job or primary activity," or "health and physical condition") are the same for each group. Symbolically, if p_{ij} is the probability of obtaining a response belonging to the ith row and the jth column, the null hypothesis is

$$H_0: \quad p_{11} = p_{12} = p_{13}$$

$$p_{21} = p_{22} = p_{23}$$

$$p_{31} = p_{32} = p_{33}$$

where the p's must add up to 1 for each column.[†] The alternative hypothesis is that the p's are not all equal for at least one row, namely,

$$H_A: \quad p_{i1}, p_{i2} \text{ and } p_{i3} \text{ are not all equal for at least one value of } i.$$

In the other kind of problem, the one immediately above, we are concerned with the null hypothesis that on the job performance of persons who have gone through the training program is independent of their qualification test scores. In general, the alternative hypotheses are

H_0:   The two variables under consideration are independent.

H_A: The two variables are not independent.

Despite the differences we have described, the analysis of an $r \times c$ table is the same for both kinds of situations, and we shall illustrate it here by analyzing the second example. If the null hypothesis of independence is true, the probability of randomly choosing a person whose qualification test score is below average and whose on the job performance is poor is given by the product of the probability of choosing a person whose qualification test score is below average and the probability of choosing a person whose on the job performance is poor. Using the total of the first row, the total of the first column, and the grand total for the entire table to estimate these probabilities, we get

$$\frac{67 + 64 + 25}{400} = \frac{156}{400}$$

for the probability of choosing a person whose qualification test score is below average. Similarly, we find

[†]We could also say that we are testing the null hypothesis that we are sampling three **multinomial populations** (as in Section 8.6) with identical probabilities for the three groups of people.

$$\frac{67 + 42 + 10}{400} = \frac{119}{400}$$

for the probability of choosing a person whose on the job performance is poor. Hence, we estimate the probability of choosing a person whose qualification test score is below average and whose on the job performance is poor as $\frac{156}{400} \cdot \frac{119}{400}$, and in a sample of size 400 we would expect to find

$$400 \cdot \frac{156}{400} \cdot \frac{119}{400} = \frac{156 \cdot 119}{400} \approx 46.4$$

persons who fit this description.

In the final step of the preceding paragraph, $\frac{156 \cdot 119}{400}$ is just the product of the total of the first row and the total of the first column divided by the grand total for the entire table. Indeed, the argument which led to this result can be used to show that in general

The expected frequency for any cell of an $r \times c$ table may be obtained by multiplying the total of the row to which it belongs by the total of the column to which it belongs and then dividing by the grand total for the entire table.

With this rule we get an expected frequency of

$$\frac{156 \cdot 163}{400} \approx 63.6$$

for the second cell of the first row, and

$$\frac{174 \cdot 119}{400} \approx 51.8 \quad \text{and} \quad \frac{174 \cdot 163}{400} \approx 70.9$$

for the first two cells of the second row.

It is not necessary to calculate all the expected frequencies in this way, as it can be shown that the sum of the expected frequencies for any row or column must equal the sum of the corresponding observed frequencies (see Exercises 13.87 and 13.88). Therefore, we can get some of the expected frequencies by subtraction from row or column totals. For instance, for our example we get

$$156 - 46.4 - 63.6 = 46.0$$

for the third cell of the first row,

$$174 - 51.8 - 70.9 = 51.3$$

for the third cell of the second row, and

$$119 - 46.4 - 51.8 = 20.8$$

$$163 - 63.6 - 70.9 = 28.5$$

$$118 - 46.0 - 51.3 = 20.7$$

for the three cells of the third row. These results are summarized in the following table, where the expected frequencies are shown in parentheses below the corresponding observed frequencies:

| | | Performance | | |
		Poor	Fair	Good
	Below average	67 (46.4)	64 (63.6)	25 (46.0)
Qualification test score	Average	42 (51.8)	76 (70.9)	56 (51.3)
	Above average	10 (20.8)	23 (28.5)	37 (20.7)

To test the null hypothesis under which the **expected cell frequencies** were calculated, we compare them with the **observed cell frequencies.** It stands to reason that the null hypothesis should be rejected if the discrepancies between the observed and expected frequencies are large, and that it should be accepted (or at least that we reserve judgment) if the discrepancies between the observed and expected frequencies are small.

Denoting the observed frequencies by the letter o and the expected frequencies by the letter e, we base this comparison on the following **chi-square statistic:**

Statistic for Analysis of r × c Table	$$\chi^2 = \sum \frac{(o - e)^2}{e}$$

If the null hypothesis is true, χ^2 is a value of a random variable having approximately the chi-square distribution (see page 376) with $(r - 1)(c - 1)$ degrees of freedom. When $r = 3$ and $c = 3$ as in our example, the number of degrees of freedom is

$$(3 - 1)(3 - 1) - 4$$

It should be observed that, after we had calculated four of the expected frequencies with the rule on page 419, all the remaining expected frequencies were automatically determined by subtraction from row or column totals. Some statisticians prefer the alternative formula

Alternative Formula for Chi-square Statistic	$$\chi^2 = \sum \frac{o^2}{e} - n$$

where n is the grand total of the frequencies for the entire table. This alternative formula does simplify the calculations, but the original formula shows more clearly how χ^2 is actually affected by the discrepancies between the o's and the e's.

Since we shall want to reject the null hypothesis when the discrepancies between the o's and e's are large, we use the test criterion shown in Figure 13.1;
symbolically, we reject the null hypothesis at the α level of significance if $\chi^2 \geq$
χ^2_α. Remember, though, that this test is only an approximate large-sample test,
and it is recommended that it not be used when one (or more) of the expected
frequencies is less than 5. The values of χ^2_α may be read from Table III at the
end of the book, where, for the most part, they are given to three decimals. In
practice, there is seldom any need to carry more than two decimals in calculating the value of the χ^2 statistic.

Example

With reference to the illustration on page 420, test at the 0.01 level of significance
whether the on the job performance of persons who have gone through the training program is independent of their qualification test score.

solution

1. H_0: On the job performance and qualification test score are independent.
   H_A: On the job performance and qualification test score are not independent.

2. $\alpha = 0.01$

3. Reject the null hypothesis if $\chi^2 \geq 13.277$, where

$$\chi^2 = \Sigma \frac{(o - e)^2}{e}$$

and 13.277 is the value of $\chi^2_{0.01}$ for $(3 - 1)(3 - 1) = 4$ degrees of freedom;
otherwise, accept the null hypothesis or reserve judgment.

4. Substituting the observed and expected frequencies from the table on page
420 into the formula for χ^2, we get

$$\chi^2 = \frac{(67 - 46.4)^2}{46.4} + \frac{(64 - 63.6)^2}{63.6} + \frac{(25 - 46.0)^2}{46.0}$$

$$+ \frac{(42 - 51.8)^2}{51.8} + \frac{(76 - 70.9)^2}{70.9} + \frac{(56 - 51.3)^2}{51.3}$$

$$+ \frac{(10 - 20.8)^2}{20.8} + \frac{(23 - 28.5)^2}{28.5} + \frac{(37 - 20.7)^2}{20.7}$$

$$\approx 40.89$$

FIGURE 13.1

Test criterion.

5. Since $\chi^2 = 40.89$ exceeds 13.277, the null hypothesis must be rejected; that is, we conclude that there is a relationship between qualification test score and on the job performance.   ▰ ▰ ▰

A computer printout of the preceding chi-square analysis is shown in Figure 13.2. The difference between the values of χ^2 obtained above and in Figure 13.2 is due to rounding. Since the calculations involved in χ^2 can be exhausting, we strongly recommend that χ^2 be calculated by computer. Some computer programs also give the tail probability corresponding to the observed value of χ^2 when the null hypothesis is true. For our example it is about 0.00000003; this exquisitely precise figure cannot be taken too literally since the distribution of χ^2 is only an approximation.

The method which we used here to analyze the $r \times c$ table applies also when the column totals are fixed sample sizes, as in the "greatest contribution to happiness" example on page 417. In that case, the rule by which we multiply the row total by the column total and then divide by the grand total has to be justified in a different way (see Exercise 13.86 on page 429), but this is of no conse-

---

FIGURE 13.2

Computer printout for analysis of $r \times c$ table, obtained after entering data in program spreadsheet. (MINITAB 10 for Windows).

```
MTB > print C1 C2 C3

Data Display

Row     C1      C2      C3

  1     67      64      25
  2     42      76      56
  3     10      23      37

MTB > ChiSquare C1 C2 C3

Chi-Square Test

Expected counts are printed below observed counts

             C1        C2        C3      Total
    1        67        64        25        156
           46.41     63.57     46.02

    2        42        76        56        174
           51.76     70.90     51.33

    3        10        23        37         70
           20.83     28.52     20.65

Total       119       163       118        400

ChiSq =   9.135  +   0.003  +   9.601 +
          1.842  +   0.366  +   0.425 +
          5.627  +   1.070  +  12.945 = 41.014
df = 4,  p = 0.000
```

quence—the expected frequencies are determined in exactly the same way. Actually, there exists an alternative way of analyzing $r \times c$ tables, which is preferable when we are dealing with ordinal data. Clearly, the three performance ratings in our example (poor, fair, and good) were ordered, and so were the three levels of test score (below average, average, and above average). The alternate method is discussed in Section 16.4, beginning on page 541. Other relevant references are given on page 442.

In the analysis of $r \times c$ tables, the special case where $r = 2$ and the column totals are fixed sample sizes has many important applications. Here we are testing, in fact, for significant differences among c sample proportions, and we can simplify our notation by letting $p_1, p_2, \ldots,$ and p_c denote the corresponding true proportions.

Example

The following table shows the results of a study in which independent random samples of workers in three parts of the country were asked whether they feel that unemployment or inflation is a more serious problem:

	Northeast	Midwest	Southwest
Unemployment	87	73	66
Inflation	113	77	84
	200	150	150

Test at the 0.05 level of significance whether the differences among the sample proportions of workers who chose unemployment,

$$\frac{87}{200} = 0.435, \qquad \frac{73}{150} \approx 0.487, \qquad \text{and} \qquad \frac{66}{150} = 0.440$$

are significant.

solution

1. H_0: $p_1 = p_2 = p_3$
   H_A: $p_1, p_2,$ and p_3 are not all equal.
2. $\alpha = 0.05$
3. Reject the null hypothesis if $\chi^2 \geq 5.991$, where

$$\chi^2 = \Sigma \frac{(o - e)^2}{e}$$

and 5.991 is the value of $\chi^2_{0.05}$ for $(2 - 1)(3 - 1) = 2$ degrees of freedom; otherwise, state that the differences among the three sample proportions are not significant.

4. Since the total for the first row is $87 + 73 + 66 = 226$, we get expected frequencies of

$$\frac{226 \cdot 200}{500} = 90.4 \qquad \text{and} \qquad \frac{226 \cdot 150}{500} = 67.8$$

for the first two cells of the first row of the table. Then, by subtraction, we get

$$226 - 90.4 - 67.8 = 67.8$$

for the third cell of the first row, and

$$200 - 90.4 = 109.6$$
$$150 - 67.8 = 82.2$$
$$150 - 67.8 = 82.2$$

for the three cells of the second row. Finally, substituting all these values together with the observed frequencies into the formula for x^2, we get

$$x^2 = \frac{(87 - 90.4)^2}{90.4} + \frac{(73 - 67.8)^2}{67.8} + \frac{(66 - 67.8)^2}{67.8}$$
$$+ \frac{(113 - 109.6)^2}{109.6} + \frac{(77 - 82.2)^2}{82.2} + \frac{(84 - 82.2)^2}{82.2}$$
$$\approx 1.048$$

5. Since $x^2 = 1.048$ does not exceed 5.991, the null hypothesis cannot be rejected; in other words, the differences among the three sample proportions are not significant.   ◩ ◩ ◩

Note that in an application like this the number of degrees of freedom is simply $c - 1$. Also, for $c = 2$ we have here an alternative method for testing the significance of the difference between two sample proportions (as in Section 13.4), but it can be used only when the alternative hypothesis is $p_1 \neq p_2$.

Let us also remind the reader that all these tests are approximate large-sample tests, which should not be used when one (or more) of the expected frequencies is less than 5. However, we can often combine some rows or combine some columns in such a way that none of the expected frequencies is less than 5.

◩ EXERCISES

13.65   Use the alternative formula on page 420 to recalculate the value of x^2 obtained on page 421 for the 3 × 3 contingency table.

13.66   Use the alternative formula on page 420 to recalculate the value of x^2 obtained on pages 423–424 for the comparison of the three sample proportions.

13.67   Suppose that we ask 200 automotive dealers selling American cars, 150 automotive dealers selling European cars, and 200 automotive dealers selling Japanese cars whether they expect sales to go down, remain the same, go up, or whether they can't tell. What hypotheses shall we want to test, if we are going to perform a chi-square analysis of the resulting 4 × 3 table?

13.68   Suppose that we take a random sample of 400 persons living in federal housing projects and classify each one according to whether he or she has part-time employment, full-time employment, or no employment, and also according to whether he or she has 0, 1, 2, 3, or 4 or more children. What hypotheses shall we want to test, if we are going to perform a chi-square analysis of the resulting 3 × 5 table?

13.69 Suppose that we take random samples of voters in Memphis, Nashville, Knoxville, and Chattanooga, and ask them whether they favor an increase in the state tax on cigarettes. What hypotheses shall we want to test, if we are going to perform a chi-square analysis of the resulting 2 × 4 table?

13.70 In a study to determine whether there is a relationship between bank employees' standard of dress and their professional advancement, a random sample of size $n = 300$ yielded the results shown in the following table:

	Speed of advancement		
	Slow	Average	Fast
Very well dressed	32	56	32
Well dressed	28	69	22
Poorly dressed	15	33	13
	75	158	67

Test at the 0.05 level of significance, preferably with the help of a computer, whether there is a real relationship between standard of dress and speed of professional advancement.

13.71 A sample survey, designed to show how students attending a large university get to their classes, yielded the following results:

	Freshman	Sophomore	Junior	Senior
Walk	104	87	89	72
Automobile	22	29	35	43
Bicycle	46	34	37	32
Other	28	50	39	53
	200	200	200	200

Test at the 0.05 level of significance, preferably with the help of a computer, the null hypothesis that the same proportions of freshmen, sophomores, juniors, and seniors use these means of transportation.

13.72 The following sample data pertain to shipments received by a large firm from three different vendors:

	Vendor A	Vendor B	Vendor C
Rejected	12	8	20
Not perfect but acceptable	23	12	30
Perfect	85	60	110

Use the 0.01 level to test, preferably with the help of a computer, whether the three vendors ship products of equal quality.

13.73   A market research organization wants to determine, on the basis of the following information, whether there is a relationship between the size of a tube of toothpaste which a shopper buys and the number of persons in the shopper's household:

		Number of persons			
		1–2	*3–4*	*5–6*	*7 or more*
	Giant	23	116	78	43
Size of tube bought	Large	54	25	16	11
	Small	31	68	39	8

With the help of a computer, decide at the 0.01 level of significance, whether there is a relationship between the two variables.

13.74   Of a group of 200 persons suffering anxiety disorders, 100 received psychotherapy and 100 received psychological counseling. A panel of psychiatrists determined after six months whether their condition had deteriorated, remained unchanged, or improved. The results are shown in the following table. Use the 0.05 level of significance, preferably with the help of a computer, to test whether the two treatment methods are equally effective.

	Psychotherapy	*Psychological counseling*
Deteriorated	8	11
Unchanged	58	62
Improved	34	27

13.75   In a study of students' parents' feelings about a required course in sex education, a random sample of 360 parents are classified according to whether they have one, two, or three or more children in the school system, and also whether they feel that the course is poor, adequate, or good. The results are as shown in the following table. Test at the 0.05 level of significance, preferably with the help of a computer, whether there is a relationship between parents' reaction to the course and the number of children they have in school.

	Number of children		
	1	*2*	*3 or more*
Poor	48	40	12
Adequate	55	53	29
Good	57	46	20

13.76 If the analysis of a contingency table shows that there is a relationship between the two variables under consideration, the strength of the relationship may be measured by the **contingency coefficient**

Contingency Coefficient

$$C = \sqrt{\frac{\chi^2}{\chi^2 + n}}$$

where χ^2 is the value of the chi-square statistic obtained for the table and n is the grand total of all the frequencies. This coefficient takes on values between 0 (corresponding to independence) and a maximum value less than 1 depending on the size of the table; for instance, it can be shown that for a 3 × 3 table the maximum value of C is $\sqrt{2/3} = 0.82$.

(a) Calculate the value of C for the second example on page 417, concerning the relationship between qualification test score and on-the-job performance. The value of χ^2 was computed on page 421.

(b) Find C for the contingency table of Exercise 13.73.

13.77 A market research study shows that among 100 men, 100 women, and 200 children interviewed, there were 44, 53, and 133 who did not like the flavor of a new toothpaste. Use the 0.05 level of significance to decide whether or not the differences among the three sample proportions, $\frac{44}{100} = 0.44$, $\frac{53}{100} = 0.53$, and $\frac{133}{200} = 0.665$, are significant.

13.78 On page 410 we referred to a study in which 24 of 200 brand A tires, 21 of 200 brand B tires, 18 of 200 brand C tires, and 33 of 200 brand D tires failed to last 20,000 miles. Based on these figures and at the 0.05 level of significance, is there a difference in the durability of the four kinds of tires?

13.79 The following table shows the results of a survey in which random samples of the parents of 12th graders in three school districts were asked whether they are for or against the removal of certain controversial books from a required reading list:

	District 1	*District 2*	*District 3*
For the removal of the books	8	13	12
Against the removal of the books	52	67	48

At the 0.05 level of significance, and preferably with the assistance of a computer, are the differences among the sample proportions

$$\frac{8}{60} \approx 0.133, \qquad \frac{13}{80} \approx 0.162, \qquad \text{and} \qquad \frac{12}{60} = 0.200$$

significant?

13.80 Tests are made on the ability of three materials to withstand extreme temperature changes, with these results:

Material	Number tested	Number crumbled
A	120	43
B	80	28
C	100	23

Test at the 0.05 level of significance, preferably with the help of a computer, whether the probability of crumbling is the same for all three materials.

13.81   The following table shows the results of a study in which random samples of the members of five large unions were asked whether they are for or against a certain political candidate:

	Union 1	Union 2	Union 3	Union 4	Union 5
For the candidate	74	81	69	75	91
Against the candidate	26	19	31	25	9

At the 0.01 level of significance, and preferably with the assistance of a computer, can we conclude that the differences among the five sample proportions are significant?

13.82   The z test for comparing two proportions, introduced on page 409, considers x_1 out of n_1 successes in one group and x_2 out of n_2 successes in a second group. The information can be displayed in this table:

	Success	Failure
Group 1	x_1	$n_1 - x_1$
Group 2	x_2	$n_2 - x_2$

Suppose that we relabel the entries so that $x_1 = A$, $n_1 - x_1 = B$, $x_2 = C$, and $n_2 - x_2 = D$. Then the table is:

	Success	Failure
Group 1	A	B
Group 2	C	D

Let $N = A + B + C + D = n_1 + n_2$ be the total number of items. Show that the z test for comparing two proportions can be expressed as

$$z = \frac{\sqrt{N}(AD - BC)}{\sqrt{A + B)(C + D)(A + C)(B + D)}}$$

13.83   For the data in a 2×2 table relabeled as in Exercise 13.82, show that

$$x^2 = \frac{N(AD - BC)^2}{(A + B)(C + D)(A + C)(B + D)}$$

and hence that x^2 is the square of the value of z.

13.84   Consider Exercise 13.52 on page 413 in which $A = 62$, $B = 38$, $C = 44$, and $D = 56$. Analyze these values as a 2×2 table, and verify that the value obtained here for x^2 equals the square of the value originally obtained for z.

13.85   Suppose that all the values in an $r \times c$ table are doubled. Show that this will double the value of x^2.

13.86 Use an argument similar to that on page 419 to show that the rule for calculating the expected frequencies for an $r \times c$ table (multiplying the row total by the column total and then dividing by the grand total) applies also when the column totals are fixed sample sizes.

13.87 Verify that if the expected frequencies for an $r \times c$ table are calculated with the rule on page 419, the sum of the expected frequencies for any row equals the sum of the corresponding observed frequencies.

13.88 Verify that if the expected frequencies for an $r \times c$ table are calculated with the rule on page 419, the sum of the expected frequencies for any column equals the sum of the corresponding observed frequencies.

13.6 GOODNESS OF FIT

In this section we consider another application of the chi-square criterion, comparing an observed frequency distribution with a distribution we might expect according to theory or assumptions. We refer to such a comparison as a test of **goodness of fit.**

To illustrate, suppose that we consider a table of random digits, supposedly constructed in such a way that each digit is a value of a random variable with takes on the values 0, 1, 2, 3, 4, 5, 6, 7, 8, and 9 with equal probabilities of 0.10. The table below shows a tabulation based on 250 digits from such a table, which can be generated by computer. The actual counts of the digits are shown in the "observed frequency" column.

Digit	Probability	Observed frequency o	Expected frequency e
0	0.10	21	25
1	0.10	28	25
2	0.10	24	25
3	0.10	33	25
4	0.10	23	25
5	0.10	21	25
6	0.10	23	25
7	0.10	23	25
8	0.10	21	25
9	0.10	33	25
		250	250

The expected frequencies in the right-hand column were obtained by multiplying each of the probabilities of 0.10 by 250, the total number of digits counted.

To test whether the discrepancies between the observed and expected frequencies can be attributed to chance, we use the same chi-square statistic as in Section 13.5:

Statistic for Test of Goodness of Fit

$$x^2 = \sum \frac{(o - e)^2}{e}$$

In using this formula, we calculate $\dfrac{(o-e)^2}{e}$ separately for each class of the distribution. Then, if the value we get for x^2 exceeds x_α^2, we reject the null hypothesis on which the expected frequencies are based at the level of significance α. The number of degrees of freedom is $k-m-1$, where k is the number of terms $\dfrac{(o-e)^2}{e}$ added in the formula for x^2, and m is the number of parameters of the probability distribution which have to be estimated from the sample data. The role of m will be made clear in the examples that follow.

Example

Based on the observed frequencies in the table given above, test at the 0.05 level of significance whether there is any indication that the digits in the table may not be regarded as random.

solution

1. H_0: The probability of each digit is 0.10.
   H_A: The probabilities are not all 0.10.
2. $\alpha = 0.05$
3. Reject the null hypothesis if $x^2 \geq 16.919$, where

$$x^2 = \Sigma \frac{(o-e)^2}{e}$$

and 16.919 is the value of $x_{0.05}^2$ for

$$k - m - 1 = 10 - 0 - 1 = 9$$

degrees of freedom; otherwise, state that there is no indication that the digits in the random number table may not be regarded as random. (Here $m = 0$ since none of the parameters of the probability distribution had to be estimated from the sample data.)

4. Substituting the observed and expected frequencies from the table on page 429 into the formula for x^2, we get

$$x^2 = \frac{(21-25)^2}{25} + \frac{(28-25)^2}{25} + \cdots + \frac{(33-25)^2}{25} = 7.92$$

5. Since $x^2 = 7.92$ does not exceed 16.919, the null hypothesis cannot be rejected. In other words, there is no indication that the digits may not be regarded as random. ◢ ◢ ◢

To give an example where we must estimate a parameter of the probability distribution from the observed data, suppose that a person takes a bus to and from work, and the following table shows how many times, Monday through Friday, the buses were late arriving at the respective stops in 100 weeks:

Number of times buses were late	Number of weeks
0	0
1	2
2	8
3	19
4	29
5	26
6	13
7	3
8	0
9	0
10	0

Based on this information, we want to test, using $\alpha = 0.05$, whether the data may be regarded as values of a random variable having a binomial distribution.

We know that $n = 10$, but since p is unknown, it will have to be estimated from the given data. We do this by calculating the mean of the observed data, putting it equal to np (the expression for the mean of the binomial distribution), and solving for p. Thus, we get

$$\bar{x} = \frac{0 \cdot 0 + 1 \cdot 2 + 2 \cdot 8 + \cdots + 10 \cdot 0}{100} = 4.2$$

Therefore, we solve $np = 10p = 4.2$, obtaining $p = 0.42$. Since the binomial probabilities for $n = 10$ and $p = 0.42$ cannot be obtained from Table V at the end of this book, we shall use a computer program, as in the example on page 213. The results of this computer run are shown in Figure 13.3. Then copying the probabilities in the column $P(X = x)$ from Figure 13.3, we get

FIGURE 13.3

Computer printout of the binomial distribution with n = 10 and p = 0.42 (MINITAB 10 for Windows).

```
MTB > Set C1
DATA>   1(0 : 10 / 1)1
DATA>   End
MTB > PDF C1;
SUBC>   Binomial 10 0.42.

Probability Density Function

Binomial with n = 10 and p = 0.420000

         x        P(X = x)
     0.00         0.0043
     1.00         0.0312
     2.00         0.1017
     3.00         0.1963
     4.00         0.2488
     5.00         0.2162
     6.00         0.1304
     7.00         0.0540
     8.00         0.0147
     9.00         0.0024
    10.00         0.0002
```

Number of times buses were late	Binomial probability	Observed frequency o	Expected frequency e
0	0.0043	0	0.4
1	0.0312	2	3.1
2	0.1017	8	10.2
3	0.1963	19	19.6
4	0.2488	29	24.9
5	0.2162	26	21.6
6	0.1304	13	13.0
7	0.0540	3	5.4
8	0.0147	0	1.5
9	0.0024	0	0.2
10	0.0002	0	0.0

where the expected frequencies in the right-hand column were obtained by multiplying each of the binomial probabilities by 100 and then rounding to one decimal.

The sampling distribution of the χ^2 statistic which we use to compare the o's and the e's is only approximately a chi-square distribution. Therefore, we must be sure that none of the expected frequencies is less than 5, as we did on page 421. We can accomplish this by combining the first three classes and the final four classes. This leaves us with

Number of times buses were late	Observed frequency o	Expected frequency e
2 or less	10	13.7
3	19	19.6
4	29	24.9
5	26	21.6
6	13	13.0
7 or more	3	7.1

where we added the frequencies of the respective classes. Now we proceed as before.

Example

Test at the 0.05 level of significance whether the data on page 431 may be regarded as values of a random variable having a binomial distribution.

solution

1. H_0: Random variable has a binomial distribution.
   H_A: Random variable does not have a binomial distribution.
2. $\alpha = 0.05$
3. Reject the null hypothesis if $\chi^2 \geq 9.488$, where

$$\chi^2 = \Sigma \, \frac{(o - e)^2}{e}$$

and 9.488 is the value of $\chi^2_{0.05}$ for $6 - 1 - 1 = 4$ degrees of freedom; otherwise, accept the null hypothesis or reserve judgment. Here $k = 6$ since six terms were used to obtain χ^2, after combining classes. Also, $m = 1$ since p had to be estimated from the data observed.

4. Substituting the observed and expected frequencies from the table given above into the formula for χ^2, we get

$$\chi^2 = \frac{(10 - 13.7)^2}{13.7} + \frac{(19 - 19.6)^2}{19.6} + \frac{(29 - 24.9)^2}{24.9}$$

$$+ \frac{(26 - 21.6)^2}{21.6} + \frac{(13 - 13.0)^2}{13.0} + \frac{(3 - 7.1)^2}{7.1}$$

$$\approx 5.0$$

5. Since $\chi^2 = 5.0$ does not exceed 9.488, the null hypothesis cannot be rejected; in other words, there is no real evidence that the random variable (the number of buses that are late per week) does not have a binomial distribution. ◪ ◪ ◪

The method illustrated here is used generally to test how well distributions, expected on the basis of theory or assumptions, fit, or describe, observed data. Thus, in the exercises that follow we shall test also whether observed distributions have (at least approximately) the shape of Poisson and normal distributions.

◪ EXERCISES

13.89   To see whether a die is balanced, it is rolled 720 times, and the following results are obtained:

Number	Frequency
1	129
2	107
3	98
4	132
5	136
6	118
Total	720

At the 0.05 level of significance, do these results support the hypothesis that the die is balanced?

13.90   Ten years' data show that in a given city there were no bank robberies in 57 months, one bank robbery in 36 months, two bank robberies in 15 months, and three or more bank robberies in 12 months. At the 0.05 level of significance, does this substantiate the claim that the probabilities of 0, 1, 2, or 3 or more bank robberies in any one month are 0.40, 0.30, 0.20, and 0.10?

13.91   Four coins are tossed 320 times and 0, 1, 2, 3, and 4 heads showed 14, 68, 108, 104, and 26 times. Using the probabilities from Exercise 5.53 on page 127, namely, $\frac{1}{16}, \frac{4}{16}, \frac{6}{16}, \frac{4}{16}$, and $\frac{1}{16}$, test at the 0.05 level of significance whether it is reasonable to suppose that the coins are balanced and randomly tossed.

13.92   A quality control specialist takes daily samples of four lawn mowers coming off an assembly line. On 200 consecutive working days, she obtains the following:

Number of lawn mowers requiring adjustments	Number of days
0	105
1	76
2	17
3	2
4	0
Total	200

Use the 0.05 level of significance to test the null hypothesis that the data may be looked upon as random samples from a binomial population with $n = 4$ and $p = 0.10$.

13.93   In 400 five-minute intervals the air-traffic control of an airport received 0, 1, 2, 3, 4, 5, 6, 7, and 8 or more radio messages with respective frequencies of 2, 12, 54, 76, 68, 76, 45, 41, and 26. Use the 0.05 level of significance to test whether the number of radio messages which they receive during a five-minute interval is a random variable having the Poisson distribution with $\lambda = 4.6$, namely, that the probabilities for 0, 1, 2, 3, 4, 5, 6, 7, and 8 or more calls are 0.010, 0.046, 0.107, 0.163, 0.187, 0.173, 0.132, 0.087, and 0.095.

13.94   For 300 consecutive working days, a baker prepares three large chocolate cakes, and those not sold on the same day are donated to a charitable food bank. Given the data shown in the following table, test at the 0.05 level of significance whether they may be looked upon as values of a random variable having a binomial distribution:

Number of cakes sold	Number of days
0	2
1	14
2	46
3	238

Use the formula for the binomial distribution to calculate the required probabilities.

13.95   Consider the information presented in Exercise 13.92. Test at the 0.05 level of significance whether the data may be looked upon as random samples from a binomial population with $n = 4$.

13.96   The following is the distribution of the hourly number of car drivers requesting gasoline at a rural gas station:

Car drivers requesting gasoline per hour	Frequency
0	33
1	68
2	96
3	98
4	106
5	65
6	25
7	8
8	1
Total	500

Find the mean of this distribution, and using it as an estimate of the parameter λ, fit a Poisson distribution. That is, determine the corresponding Poisson probabilities by using the formula for the Poisson distribution, possibly using a calculator or suitable statistical software. Multiply each of the probabilities by the total frequency 500 to determine expected frequencies. Test at the 0.01 level of significance whether the hourly number of drivers requesting gasoline may be looked upon as a random variable having a Poisson distribution.

13.97   The following is the distribution of the number of minutes it took 80 persons to complete a certain tax form:

Time to complete form (minutes)	Frequency
10–14	8
15–19	28
20–24	27
25–29	12
30–34	4
35–39	1
Total	80

As can easily be verified, the mean of this distribution is $\bar{x} = 20.7$ and its standard deviation is $s = 5.4$. To test the null hypothesis that these data constitute a random sample from a normal population, proceed with the following steps:

(a) Find the probabilities that a random variable having a normal distribution with $\mu = 20.7$ and $\sigma = 5.4$ will take on a value less than 14.5, between 14.5 and 19.5, between 19.5 and 24.5, between 24.5 and 29.5, between 29.5 and 34.5, and greater than 34.5.

(b) Changing the first and last classes of the distribution to "14 or less" and "35 or more," find the expected normal curve frequencies corresponding to the six classes of the distribution by multiplying the probabilities obtained in part (a) by the total frequency of 80.

(c) Test at the 0.05 level of significance whether the given data may be looked upon as a random sample from a normal population.

13.98   The following are the scores of 200 persons on a screening test required of applicants by a firm specializing in executive placement:

Score	Number of persons
20–24	3
25–29	12
30–34	50
35–39	75
40–44	40
45–49	15
50–54	4
55–59	1
Total	200

As can easily be verified, the mean of this distribution is $\bar{x} = 37.10$ and its standard deviation is $s = 5.85$. To test the null hypothesis that these data constitute a random sample from a normal population, proceed with the following steps:

(a) Find the probabilities that a random variable having a normal distribution with $\mu = 37.10$ and $\sigma = 5.85$ will take on a value less than 24.5, between 24.5 and 29.5, between 29.5 and 34.5, between 34.5 and 39.5, between 39.5 and 44.5, between 44.5 and 49.5, between 49.5 and 54.5, and greater than 54.5.

(b) Changing the first and last classes of the distribution to "24 or less" and "55 or more," find the expected normal curve frequencies corresponding to the eight classes of the distribution by multiplying the probabilities obtained in part (a) by the total frequency of 200.

(c) Test at the 0.05 level of significance whether the given data may be looked upon as a random sample from a normal population.

13.7   CHECKLIST OF KEY TERMS† *(with page references to their definitions)*

$100(1 - \alpha)$ percent large-sample confidence interval for p, 395

Cell, 419

Chi-square statistic, 420

Contingency coefficient, 427

Contingency table, 418

Count data, 393

Expected cell frequencies, 420

Goodness of fit, 429

Grand total, 418

Multinomial population, 418

Observed cell frequencies, 420

Odds ratio, 411

Pooling, 409

⇔ Posterior probability, 398

⇔ Prior probability, 398

$r \times c$ table, 417

Rate difference, 410

Rate ratio, 413

Risk ratio, 413

Sample proportion, 393

Standard error of a proportion, 395

Standard error of the difference between two proportions, 409

13.8   REVIEW EXERCISES

13.99   An airline has four daily flights between two cities. A monitoring of arrival times on 250 days gave this information:

Number of late flights	Frequency
0	106
1	98
2	35
3	9
4	2
Total	250

Using the 0.05 level of significance, test whether these data may be looked upon as a random sample of size $n = 250$ from a binomial population.

†Terms in italics are introduced in exercises.

13.100   In a random sample of 90 persons shopping at a department store, 63 made at least one purchase. Construct a 95 percent confidence interval for the probability that any one person shopping at the department store will make at least one purchase.

13.101   The following table shows how samples of the residents of three federally financed housing projects replied to the question whether they would continue to live there if they had the choice:

	Project 1	Project 2	Project 3
Yes	63	84	69
No	37	16	31

Test at the 0.01 level of significance whether the differences among the three sample proportions (of "yes" answers) may be attributed to chance.

13.102   Based on the result of $n = 15$ trials, we want to test the null hypothesis $p = 0.40$ against the alternative hypothesis $p > 0.40$. If we reject the null hypothesis when the number of successes is 8 or more (and accept the null hypothesis otherwise), find:

(a) the probability of a Type I error;

(b) the probability of a Type II error when $p = 0.50$;

(c) the probability of a Type II error when $p = 0.60$.

13.103   In a study conducted at a large airport, 86 of 300 persons who had just gotten off a plane and 42 of 200 persons who were about to board a plane admitted that they were afraid of flying.

(a) Use the z statistic to test at the 0.01 level of significance whether the difference between the corresponding sample proportions is significant.

(b) Use the χ^2 statistic to perform the test in part (a).

(c) Indicate whether there is any relationship between z and χ^2 for this problem.

13.104   In a random sample of 200 retired persons, 137 stated that they prefer living in an apartment to living in a one-family home. At the 0.05 level of significance, does this refute the claim that 60 percent of all retired persons prefer living in an apartment to living in a one-family home?

13.105   In accordance with the rule that np and $n(1 - p)$ must both be greater than 5, for what values of p can we use the normal approximation to the binomial distribution when $n = 400$?

13.106   A sample check reveals that 186 of 200 of a professional football team's season-ticket holders intend to renew their tickets for the next season. Construct a 95 percent confidence interval for the true proportion of the team's season-ticket holders who intend to renew their tickets for the next season.

13.107   An undercover police officer wishes to determine what percentage of vendors at flea markets collect state sales tax. How large a sample will he need if he wants to assert with 95 percent confidence that the error of his estimate is at most 0.06 if:

(a) he has no idea about the true value;

(b) he is certain that the true value is in the range of 10 percent to 30 percent?

13.108   Among 120 trucks stopped at a road block, 42 were overloaded. If we use the sample proportion, $\frac{42}{120} = 0.35$, to estimate the corresponding true proportion, what can we say with 98 percent confidence about the maximum error?

13.109   A geneticist found that in independent random samples of 100 men and 100 women there were 31 men and 24 women with a certain minor blood disorder. Can he conclude at the 0.01 level of significance that the corresponding true proportion for men is significantly greater than that for women?

(a) Comment on the formulation of this question.

(b) Restate the question as it should have been asked, and answer it by performing the appropriate test.

13.110 In $n = 13$ trials, a certain garden fungicide was effective 11 times.

(a) Find the tail probability, meaning p-value, if we wish to test the null hypothesis that the fungicide is effective 50 percent of the time against the alternative hypothesis that it is effective more than 50 percent of the time.

(b) Can the null hypothesis be rejected at the 0.01 level of significance?

13.111 Interviews of samples of 250 men and 250 women with minor personal problems yielded these results:

	Men	*Women*
Never been in therapy	146	123
Therapy for six months or less	28	31
Therapy for more than six months	76	96
	250	250

(a) If we perform a chi-square analysis of this 3×2 table, what hypothesis will we be testing?

(b) At the 0.05 level of significance, and preferably with the assistance of a computer, perform the hypothesis test of part (a).

13.112 In an experiment, an interviewer of job applicants is asked to write down his first impression (favorable or unfavorable) after 2 minutes and his final impression at the end of the interview. Use the following data and the 0.01 level of significance to test the interviewer's claim that his first and final impressions are the same 90 percent of the time:

		First impression	
		Favorable	*Unfavorable*
Final impression	*Favorable*	186	33
	Unfavorable	54	127

13.113 To see whether a newly discovered manuscript can be attributed to a famous nineteenth-century historian, his literary style was analyzed statistically, and it was found, among other things, that in many samples of 1,000 words of text material he used the word "from" 0 to 4 times 43 percent of the time, 5 to 7 times 32 percent of the time, and 8 or more times 25 percent of the time. Now, if in 20 samples of 1,000 words of text material from the newly discovered manuscript, the word "from" is used 0 to 4 times, 5 to 7 times, and 8 or more times in 15, 3, and 2 of the samples, is this evidence at the 0.05 level of significance that the manuscript is not the work of this historian?

13.114 Fifty chronic headache sufferers participated in an experiment in which they used products A and B on two separate headaches. The data from these subjects is summarized in this table:

	Relief with product B?	
	Yes	*No*
Yes	22	8
No	6	14

Relief with Product A? — Yes / No rows

What hypothesis will we test if we are going to perform a chi-square analysis of this 2 × 2 table?

13.115 The following is the distribution of the sulfur oxides emission data obtained on pages 22–23.

Tons of sulfur oxides	Frequency
5.0– 8.9	3
9.0–12.9	10
13.0–16.9	14
17.0–20.9	25
21.0–24.9	17
25.0–28.9	9
29.0–32.9	2
Total	80

We showed on page 68 that $\bar{x} = 18.85$, and it can be verified that $s = 5.55$. Test at the 0.05 level of significance whether the data may be looked upon as a random sample from a normal population.

13.116 The purchasing agent of a firm feels that the probability is 0.80 that any one of several shipments of steel recently received will meet specifications. The head of the firm's quality control department feels that this probability is 0.90, and the chief engineer feels (somewhat more pessimistically) that it is 0.60.

(a) If the managing director of the firm feels that in this matter the purchasing agent is 10 times as reliable as the chief engineer while the head of the quality control department is 14 times as reliable as the chief engineer, what prior probabilities would he assign to their claims?

(b) If five of the shipments are inspected and only two meet specifications, what posterior probabilities should the managing director of the firm assign to the respective claims?

13.117 Among the 500 children at a summer camp, a random sample of 120 are interviewed and only 27 of them prefer being at camp to vacationing with their parents. Use the formula of Exercise 13.17 on page 401 to construct a 95 percent confidence interval for the actual proportion of all the children at that camp who prefer being there to traveling with their parents.

13.118 Tests of the fidelity and the selectivity of 190 radios produced the results shown in the following table:

		Fidelity		
		Low	*Average*	*High*
	Low	7	12	31
Selectivity	*Average*	35	59	18
	High	15	13	0

Use the 0.01 level of significance to test the null hypothesis that fidelity is independent of selectivity.

13.119 With reference to the preceding exercise, calculate the value of the contingency coefficient defined in Exercise 13.76 on page 427.

13.120 Tests are made on the proportion of defective castings produced by two molds. If in a random sample of 100 castings from mold A there were 12 defectives and in a random sample of 200 castings from mold B there were 39 defectives, test at the 0.05 level of significance whether the corresponding true proportion for mold B exceeds that for mold A by more than 0.04.

13.121 In a random sample of 500 voters in a large city, 285 favor a new issue of municipal bonds. If we use $\frac{285}{500} = 0.57$ as an estimate of the true proportion of voters in this city who favor the bonds, what can we say with 99 percent confidence about the maximum error of this estimate?

13.122 A political leader hires a private poll to estimate what percentage of residents of his precinct believe a rumor about him spread by his opponent. How large a sample will the poll have to take to be able to assert with a probability of at least 0.90 that the sample percentage will be within 5 percent of the true value?

13.123 Suppose that we want to test the null hypothesis $p = 0.30$ on the basis of the number of successes, x, in 14 trials. For what values of x would we reject the null hypothesis if the level of significance and the alternative hypothesis are, respectively,

(a) $\alpha = 0.05$ and $p \neq 0.30$;

(b) $\alpha = 0.05$ and $p > 0.30$;

(c) $\alpha = 0.05$ and $p < 0.30$;

(d) $\alpha = 0.10$ and $p \neq 0.30$? Hint: Refer to Table V, Binomial Probabilities.

13.124 Among 210 persons with alcohol problems admitted to the psychiatric emergency room of a hospital, the day of the week of admission was as follows:

Day of admission	Mon.	Tues.	Wed.	Thurs.	Fri.	Sat.	Sun.	Total
Frequency:	26	23	19	25	33	44	40	210

Use the 0.05 level of significance to test the null hypothesis that the psychiatric emergency room can expect equally many persons with alcohol problems on each day of the week.

13.125 When asked to identify Jean-Jacques Rousseau, 28 of 120 persons said that he is a deep-sea diver. If the probability of a Type I error is to be at most 0.05, does this substantiate the claim that at least 30 percent of all persons make this mistake?

13.126 A large manufacturer hires many handicapped workers. To see whether their handicaps affect their performance, the personnel manager obtained the following sample data:

		Deaf	Blind	Other handicap	No handicap
	Above average	11	3	14	36
Performance	Average	24	11	39	134
	Below average	5	6	7	30
		40	20	60	200

Explain why a "standard" chi-square analysis with $(3 - 1)(4 - 1) = 6$ degrees of freedom cannot be performed.

13.127   There are various ways in which the data of Exercise 13.126 can be salvaged. Use one of them and perform a suitable chi-square analysis at the 0.05 level of significance.

13.128   The method of Section 13.2 can also be used to find the posterior distribution of the parameter λ of a Poisson distribution. Suppose, for instance, that several brokers are discussing the sale of a large estate, and that one of them feels that a newspaper ad should produce three serious inquiries, a second feels that it should produce five serious inquiries, and a third feels that it should produce six.

(a) If in the past the second broker has been twice as reliable as the first and the first has been three times as reliable as the third, what prior probabilities should we assign to their claims?

(b) How would these probabilities be affected if the ad actually produced only one serious inquiry and it can be assumed that the number of serious inquiries is a random variable having the Poisson distribution with either $\lambda = 3$, $\lambda = 5$, or $\lambda = 6$ corresponding to the three claims?

13.129   Four coins are tossed 240 times and 0, 1, 2, 3, or 4 heads showed 32, 96, 62, 42, and 8 times. Use the 0.01 level of significance to test whether it is reasonable to suppose that the coins are balanced and randomly tossed.

13.130   It costs more to test a certain type of ammunition than to manufacture it, and, hence, only two rounds are tested from each large lot. If lots are accepted without further inspection when both rounds function according to specifications, find the actual proportion of defectives for which this test procedure will cause a lot to be subjected to further inspection with a probability of 0.19.

13.131   The pigs at a certain animal research farm can contract swine flu during the winter. As part of an experiment, some of the pigs (randomly selected) were given an anti-flu vaccine while others were left unvaccinated. It was then noted which of them contracted swine flu during the winter:

| | | Contracted swine flu? | | |
		Yes	No	Total
Vaccinated	No	46	56	102
	Yes	28	77	105

(a) Give the risk ratio related to a pig's being unvaccinated.

(b) Use the χ^2 test to determine if the vaccination has a significant effect. Use the 0.05 level of significance.

13.9   REFERENCES

Tables for confidence limits for proportions, including those for small samples, were first published in Vol. 26 (1934) of *Biometrika*, a statistical journal. They have been reproduced in many textbooks, including the first five editions of this book, and among current texts they may be found, for example, in

MAXWELL, E. A., *Introduction to Statistical Thinking.* Englewood Cliffs, N.J.: Prentice Hall, 1983.

The theory which underlies the various tests of this chapter is discussed in most textbooks on mathematical statistics; for instance, in Chapters 8 and 12 of the book by Freund and Walpole listed below. Details about contingency tables may be found in

Everitt, B. S., *The Analysis of Contingency Tables.* New York: John Wiley & Sons, Inc., 1977.

In recent years, research has been done on the analysis of $r \times c$ tables with ordinal categorical variables. A readable introduction to this topic can be found in

Freund, J. E., and Simon, G. A., *Statistics: A First Course,* 5th ed. Englewood Cliffs, N.J.: Prentice Hall, 1991.

More advanced material may be found in

Agresti, A., *Analysis of Ordinal Categorical Data.* New York: John Wiley & Sons, Inc., 1984.

Goodman, L. A., *The Analysis of Cross-Classified Data Having Ordered Categories.* Cambridge, Mass.: Harvard University Press, 1984.

An extension of the Bayesian method of Section 13.2 to the case where p can take on any value on the continuous interval from 0 to 1, and its prior distribution is a continuous curve, is discussed in Chapter 10 of

Freund, J. E., and Walpole, E. R., *Mathematical Statistics,* 4th ed. Englewood Cliffs, N.J.: Prentice Hall, 1987.

A very useful summary of the measures that can be computed in a 2-by-2 table, along with the statistical applications, is found in

Fleiss, J. L., *Statistical Methods for Rates and Proportions,* 2nd ed. New York: John Wiley & Sons, Inc., 1981.

The stability of the odds ratio is discussed in Chapter 2 of

Agresti, A., *Categorical Data Analysis.* New York: John Wiley & Sons, Inc., 1990.

Controversy about the proper construction of the binomial confidence interval can be found in

Simon, G., "Should we use the t point for binomial confidence intervals?" *Teaching Statistics,* 1996.

The use of categorical data in epidemiology is explained in an easy-to-read form in

MacMahon, B., and Pugh, T., *Epidemiology: Principles and Methods.* Boston: Little, Brown and Company, 1970.

A clean presentation of epidemiological methods is

Campbell, M. J., and Machin, D., *Medical Statistics: A Commonsense Approach,* 2nd ed. Chichester, West Sussex, England: John Wiley & Sons, Inc., 1993.

ANALYSIS OF VARIANCE

*T*his chapter extends Sections 11.8 and 11.9 by considering whether the observed differences of more than two sample means can be attributed to chance. For instance, we may want to decide on the basis of sample data whether there really is a difference in the effectiveness of three methods of foreign language instruction. We might also wish to judge whether there is a real difference in the average mileage obtained with five kinds of gasoline, or whether there is a real difference in the durability of six kinds of exterior house paint. The method to be used for these situations is the analysis of variance, or ANOVA.

The analysis of variance can be used to sort out several questions at once. Regarding foreign language instruction, for instance, we can also ask whether the results we observe are due to the differences in the instructional methods and not due to the teachers or textbooks. Our ability to deal with these questions will lead us the subject of **experimental design**, the planning of experiments so that meaningful questions can be asked and put to a test.

Following the introductory example in Section 14.1, and the discussion of **randomization** in Section 14.2, we present the analysis of variance in Section 14.3. Section 14.4 introduces the **multiple comparisons** question, the technique for sorting out the interpretations in cases of statistical significance. The notion of blocking in Section 14.5 leads to the general consideration of the two-way experiment in Section 14.6. Various useful extensions are introduced in the remaining sections of this chapter. ◪

14.1   DIFFERENCES AMONG *k* MEANS: AN EXAMPLE

We introduce the kind of problem we face by means of an example. Suppose that we want to compare the cleansing action of three detergents on the basis of the following whiteness readings made on 15 swatches of white cotton cloth, first soiled with motor oil and then washed in an agitator-type washing machine:

						Mean	Variance	Standard deviation
Detergent A:	77	81	71	76	80	77	15.50	3.937
Detergent B:	72	58	74	66	70	68	40.00	6.325
Detergent C:	76	85	82	80	77	80	13.50	3.674

The means of these three samples are certainly unequal, and we would like to know whether the differences among them are significant or whether they can be attributed to chance.

In problems like this, we will use μ_1, μ_2, ..., μ_k to represent the averages of the k populations sampled. We want to test the null hypothesis

$$\mu_1 = \mu_2 = \cdots = \mu_k$$

Differences Among k Means: An Example SECTION 14.1   445

against the alternative that these μ's are not all equal.[†] The null hypothesis would be supported if the differences among the sample means are small, while the alternative would be supported if at least some of the differences among the sample means are large. We need a measure of the discrepancies among the $\bar{x}$'s, the sample means, along with a rule which tells us when the null hypothesis should be rejected.

Let us make two assumptions that are critical to the method by which we shall analyze our problem:

1. The populations we are sampling can be approximated closely with normal distributions.
2. These populations all have the same standard deviation.

For our example, we observe values sampled from three populations, one for each detergent. We will assume that each of the three populations has approximately the shape of a normal distribution and further that all three populations have the same standard deviation σ. It should be noted that we do not know the value of σ. The three populations may or may not have equal means; indeed, our precise task is to reach a decision about this issue.

The analysis of variance method is based on two different estimates of σ^2. The first estimate will tend to be larger than σ^2 if the alternative hypothesis is correct. The second estimate will tend to be around σ^2 whether the null hypothesis is correct or the alternative hypothesis is correct. Our decision will be based upon the ratio of these two estimates.

For the first estimate of σ^2, we will examine the variance of the $\bar{x}$'s as a measure of the differences among them. We first determine the mean of the whiteness values, getting

$$\frac{77 + 68 + 80}{3} = 75$$

Using the formula on page 83, which defines the sample variance we obtain

$$s_{\bar{x}}^2 = \frac{(77 - 75)^2 + (68 - 75)^2 + (80 - 75)^2}{3 - 1} = 39$$

The subscript $\bar{x}$ is used to show that this is the variance of the sample means.

If it is really true that $\mu_1 = \mu_2 = \mu_3$, then the $\bar{x}$ values form a sample of size three from a population with standard deviation

[†]In connection with work later in this chapter, we write these means as

$$\mu_1 = \mu + \alpha_1, \quad \mu_2 = \mu + \alpha_2, \quad \ldots, \quad \text{and} \quad \mu_k = \mu + \alpha_k$$

The symbol μ, where

$$\mu = \frac{\mu_1 + \mu_2 + \cdots + \mu_k}{k}$$

is called the **grand mean,** and the α's, whose sum is zero (see Exercise 14.20 on page 462), are called the **treatment effects.** In this notation, we test the null hypothesis $\alpha_1 = \alpha_2 = \cdots = \alpha_k = 0$ against the alternative that the α's are not all zero.

$$\sigma_{\bar{x}} = \frac{\sigma}{\sqrt{n}}$$

where n is the size of each sample. In our example, each of the three samples consists of five values, so that $n = 5$. Thus, we can look on $s_{\bar{x}}^2$ as an estimate of

$$\sigma_{\bar{x}}^2 = \left(\frac{\sigma}{\sqrt{n}}\right)^2 = \frac{\sigma^2}{n}$$

and therefore $n \cdot s_{\bar{x}}^2$ as an estimate of σ^2. For our example, we have

$$n \cdot s_{\bar{x}}^2 = 5 \cdot 39 = 195$$

as our estimate of σ^2, the common variance of the three populations.

Let us consider the second estimate of σ^2. Under our assumptions that each population has the same standard deviation, we could use any of s_1^2, s_2^2, or s_3^2 as a second estimate. It will be somewhat more effective to use their average. By averaging, or **pooling,** these three values are

$$\frac{s_1^2 + s_2^2 + s_3^2}{3} = \frac{15.50 + 40.00 + 13.50}{3} = 23$$

We now have two estimates of σ^2,

$$n \cdot s_{\bar{x}}^2 = 195 \quad \text{and} \quad \frac{s_1^2 + s_2^2 + s_3^2}{3} = 23$$

The first estimate, based on the variation among the $\bar{x}$'s, is much larger than the second, which is based on the variation within samples and, hence, measures variation due to chance. This suggests that the population means are probably not all equal and that the null hypothesis ought to be rejected. We put this comparison on a rigorous basis through use of the statistic referred to as an **F statistic** or as a **variance ratio:**

Test Concerning Differences Among Means	$F = \dfrac{\textit{estimate of } \sigma^2 \textit{ based on the variation among the } \bar{x}\textit{'s}}{\rule{6cm}{0pt}}$

If the null hypothesis is true and the assumptions we made are valid, the sampling distribution of this statistic is the F distribution, which we introduced in Chapter 12. Since the null hypothesis will be rejected only when F is large (that is, when the variation among the $\bar{x}$'s is too great to be attributed to chance), we base our decision on the criterion of Figure 14 1. For $\alpha = 0.05$ or 0.01, the values of F_α may be looked up in Table IV at the end of the book, and if we compare the means of k random samples of size n, we have $k - 1$ degrees of freedom for the numerator and $k(n - 1)$ degrees of freedom for the denominator.

Returning to our numerical example, we find that $F = \frac{195}{23} \approx 8.48$, and since this exceeds 6.93, which is the value of $F_{0.01}$ for

$$k - 1 = 3 - 1 = 2 \quad \text{and} \quad k(n - 1) = 3(5 - 1) = 12$$

FIGURE 14.1

Test criterion.

degrees of freedom, the null hypothesis must be rejected at the 0.01 level of significance. In other words, the differences among the three sample means are too large to be attributed entirely to chance.

The technique described in this section is the simplest form of an **analysis of variance.** This technique is quite rewarding, and we explore further aspects of it in Section 14.3.

EXERCISES

14.1   Samples of dried oats in 3-pound containers were assessed for the weight (in grams) of grain-dust residue at the bottoms of the containers. The containers were produced by three different manufacturers, and the results were these:

Manufacturer						Mean	Variance
1	17	12	13	11	12	13	5.5
2	22	15	17	11	20	17	18.5
3	11	13	17	15	19	15	10.0

(a) For these data, calculate $n \cdot s_{\bar{x}}^2$, the mean of the variances of the three samples, and the value of F.

(b) Test at the 0.05 level of significance whether the differences among the means of the three samples can be attributed to chance.

14.2   Margaret, a horticulturist, is experimenting with methods to keep garden slugs away from marigolds. She has 20 small plots of marigolds, and she randomly allocates five plots to each of four different methods of slug control. The controls are put in place at 6 P.M., and the slugs counted at 10 P.M. The results are as follows:

Method						Mean	Variance
A	13	14	17	19	22	17	13.5
B	4	5	10	3	3	5	8.5
C	24	28	31	30	22	27	15.0
D	12	11	6	13	8	10	8.5

Method A uses saucers of stale beer, method B uses diatomaceous earth around the plant stems, method C uses nothing at all, and method D is a commercial anti-slug spray.

(a) For these data, calculate $n \cdot s_{\bar{x}}^2$, the mean of the variances of the four samples, and the value of F.

(b) Test at the 0.05 level of significance whether the differences among the means of the four samples can be attributed to chance.

14.3   The following are the mileages obtained by a test driver, using 3 gallons of five brands of gasoline:

Brand				Mean	Variance
A	25.3	26.3	26.4	26.0	0.37
B	23.6	24.9	25.6	24.7	1.03
C	24.6	24.9	26.1	25.2	0.63
D	22.2	22.8	23.1	22.7	0.21
E	26.7	25.8	26.1	26.2	0.21

(a) For these data, calculate $n \cdot s_{\bar{x}}^2$, the mean of the variances of the five samples, and the value of F.

(b) Test at the 0.05 level of significance whether the differences among the means of the five samples can be attributed to chance.

14.4   Following are the caloric values of the fat contents of meals served at three elementary schools. Eight meals were sampled from each school.

School									Mean	Variance
1	145	140	119	138	148	139	150	125	138	118.29
2	135	131	129	143	148	139	151	128	138	76.29
3	146	141	138	154	135	129	133	144	140	64.00.

(a) For these data, calculate $n \cdot s_{\bar{x}}^2$, the mean of the variances of the three samples, and the value of F.

(b) Test at the 0.05 level of significance whether the differences among the means of the three samples can be attributed to chance.

14.5   The following are the fourth-grade reading comprehension scores on a standardized test for random samples of students from three large schools.

School 1:	81	83	77	72	86	92	83	78	80	75
School 2:	73	112	66	104	95	81	62	76	129	90
School 3:	84	89	81	76	79	83	85	74	80	78

Explain why the method described in Section 14.1 should probably not be used to test for significant differences among the three sample means.

14.6   The following are the weights (in pounds) of a random sample of basketball players in three different leagues:

Conference X:	186	195	212	169	188	195	175	201
Conference Y:	205	114	127	186	179	117	191	124
Conference Z:	173	195	203	212	195	189	190	169

Explain why the method described in Section 14.1 should probably not be used to test for significant differences among the three sample means.

14.2 THE DESIGN OF EXPERIMENTS: RANDOMIZATION

In the example of the preceding section it may have seemed perfectly natural to conclude that the three detergents are not equally effective; and yet, a moment's reflection will show that this conclusion is not so "natural" at all. For all we know, the swatches cleaned with detergent B may have been more soiled than the others, the washing times may have been longer for detergent C, there may have been differences in water hardness or water temperature, and even the instruments used to make the whiteness readings may have gone out of adjustment after the readings for detergents A and C were made.

It is entirely possible, of course, that the differences among the three sample means, 77, 68, and 80, are due largely to differences in the quality of the three detergents, but we have just listed several other factors that could be responsible. It is important to remember that a significance test may show that differences among sample means are too large to be attributed to chance, but it cannot say why the differences occur.

In general, if we want to show that one factor (among others) can be considered the cause of an observed phenomenon, we must somehow make sure that none of the other factors can reasonably be held responsible. There are various ways in which this can be done; for instance, we can conduct a rigorously **controlled experiment** where all variables except the one of concern are held fixed. To do this in the example dealing with the three detergents, we might soil the swatches with exactly equal amounts of motor oil, always use exactly the same washing time, water of exactly the same temperature and hardness, and inspect the measuring instruments after each use. Under these rigid conditions, significant differences among the sample means cannot be due to differently soiled swatches, or differences in washing time, water temperature, water hardness, or measuring instruments. On the positive side, the differences show that the detergents are not all equally effective if they are used in this narrowly restricted way. Of course, we cannot say whether the same differences would exist if the washing time is longer or shorter, if the water has a different temperature or hardness, and so on.

Such carefully controlled experiments are difficult to achieve in practice. For example, it would have been difficult in our illustration to be sure that the instruments really were measuring identically on repeated washings, or that the wash cycles were performed identically. Even with careful control, it might also happen that some factor, not considered or not carefully controlled, was responsible for the differences in whiteness. We protect ourselves against these extraneous factors through **randomization**. We design our experiment so that the variations caused by extraneous factors can all be combined under the general heading of "chance."

In our example dealing with the three detergents, we could accomplish this by numbering the swatches (which generally will not be exactly equally soiled) from 1 to 15, specifying the random order in which they are to be washed and measured, and randomly selecting the five swatches which are to be washed with each of the three detergents. When all the variations due to uncontrolled extraneous factors can thus be included under the heading of chance variation, we refer to the design of the experiment as a **completely randomized design.**

As should be apparent, randomization protects against the effects of the extraneous factors only in a probabilistic sort of way. For instance, in our example it is possible, though very unlikely, that detergent A will be assigned randomly to the five swatches which happen to be the least soiled, or that the water happens to be coldest when we wash the five swatches with detergent B. For this reason, we often try to control some of the factors and randomize the others, and thus use designs that are somewhere between the two extremes described.

Randomization protects against the effects of factors that cannot be controlled perfectly. The experimenter is not relieved of the responsibility of designing the experiment carefully simply because randomization will be used. In our example, an honest effort should be made to prepare the swatches as equally soiled as possible.

Finally, we must make this very important point: *Randomization should be used even if the experimenter believes that all effects are carefully controlled.* In our example, an experimenter who has taken steps to control the quantity of motor oil on the swatches, the wash temperature, the water hardness, and so on, must still use randomization to assign the swatches to the detergents.

The use of randomization is a cornerstone of experimental science. An experiment where randomization was possible, but not used, can never be taken completely seriously.

14.3   ONE-WAY ANALYSIS OF VARIANCE

The analysis of variance expresses a measure of the total variation in a set of data as a sum of terms, each attributed to a specific source or cause. In this section, we show the use of the analysis of variance for experiments planned as completely randomized designs. In the detergent example of Section 14.1, two sources of variation are

1. actual differences in the cleansing action of the three detergents;

2. chance, usually called **experimental error.**

Experiments involving chance and just one experimental factor, such as the detergents lead to a **one-way analysis of variance.** Other versions of the analysis of variance are our concern later in this chapter.

As a measure of the total variation of kn observations consisting of k samples of size n, we use the **total sum of squares**[†]

$$SST = \sum_{i=1}^{k} \sum_{j=1}^{n} (x_{ij} - \bar{x}_{..})^2$$

where x_{ij} is the jth observation of the ith sample ($i = 1, 2, \ldots, k$ and $j = 1, 2, \ldots, n$), and $\bar{x}_{..}$ is the **grand mean,** the mean of all the kn measurements or

---

[†]The use of double subscripts and double summations is treated briefly in Section 3.8.

observations. Note that if we divide the total sum of squares *SST* by $kn - 1$, we get the variance of the combined data.

If we let $\bar{x}_{i\cdot}$ denote the mean of the *i*th sample (for $i = 1, 2, \ldots, k$), we can now write the following identity, which forms the basis of a **one-way analysis of variance:**[†]

One-way Analysis of Variance, n Observations in each of k groups.	$$SST = n \cdot \sum_{i=1}^{k} (\bar{x}_{i\cdot} - \bar{x}_{\cdot\cdot})^2 + \sum_{i=1}^{k} \sum_{j=1}^{n} (x_{ij} - \bar{x}_{i\cdot})^2$$

It is customary to refer to the first term on the right, the quantity that measures the variation among the sample means, as the **treatment sum of squares,** *SS(Tr)*, and to the second term, which measures the variation within the individual samples, as the **error sum of squares,** *SSE*. The choice of the word "treatment" is explained by the origin of many analysis-of-variance techniques in agricultural experiments where different fertilizers, for example, are regarded as different **treatments** applied to the soil. So, we shall refer to the three detergents in our example as three different treatments, and in other problems we may refer to four nationalities as four different treatments, five different advertising campaigns as five different treatments, and so on. The word "error" in "error sum of squares" pertains to the experimental error, or chance.

Using such notation, the identity for a one-way analysis of variance reads

$$SST = SS(Tr) + SSE$$

and since its proof requires quite a bit of algebraic manipulation, let us merely verify it numerically for the three-detergents example of Section 14.1. Substituting the original whiteness readings, the three sample means, and the grand mean (see pages 444 and 445) into the formulas for the three sums of squares, we get

$$
\begin{aligned}
SST = \quad & (77 - 75)^2 + (81 - 75)^2 + (71 - 75)^2 + (76 - 75)^2 + (80 - 75)^2 \\
+ \; & (72 - 75)^2 + (58 - 75)^2 + (74 - 75)^2 + (66 - 75)^2 + (70 - 75)^2 \\
+ \; & (76 - 75)^2 + (85 - 75)^2 + (82 - 75)^2 + (80 - 75)^2 + (77 - 75)^2 \\
= \quad & 666
\end{aligned}
$$

$$SS(Tr) = 5[(77 - 75)^2 + (68 - 75)^2 + (80 - 75)^2] = 390$$

[†]This identity may be derived by writing the total sum of squares as

$$SST = \sum_{i=1}^{k} \sum_{j=1}^{n} (x_{ij} - \bar{x}_{\cdot\cdot})^2 = \sum_{i=1}^{k} \sum_{j=1}^{n} [(\bar{x}_{i\cdot} - \bar{x}_{\cdot\cdot}) + (x_{ij} - \bar{x}_{i\cdot})]^2$$

and then expanding the squares $[(\bar{x}_{i\cdot} - \bar{x}_{\cdot\cdot}) + (x_{ij} - \bar{x}_{i\cdot})]^2$ by means of the binomial theorem and simplifying algebraically.

$$SSE = (77-77)^2 + (81-77)^2 + (71-77)^2 + (76-77)^2 + (80-77)^2$$
$$+ (72-68)^2 + (58-68)^2 + (74-68)^2 + (66-68)^2 + (70-68)^2$$
$$+ (76-80)^2 + (85-80)^2 + (82-80)^2 + (80-80)^2 + (77-80)^2$$
$$= 276$$

and it can be seen that

$$SS(Tr) + SSE = 390 + 276 = 666 = SST$$

Although this may not be apparent immediately, what we have done here is very similar to what we did in Section 14.1. Indeed, $SS(Tr)$ divided by $k-1$ equals the quantity which we denoted by $n \cdot s_{\bar{x}}^2$ and put into the numerator of the F statistic on page 446. Called the **treatment mean square,** it measures the variation among the sample means and it is denoted by $MS(Tr)$. Thus,

$$MS(Tr) = \frac{SS(Tr)}{k-1}$$

and for the three-detergent example we get $MS(Tr) = \frac{390}{2} = 195$. This equals the value we got for $n \cdot s_{\bar{x}}^2$ on page 446 (see also Exercise 14.23 on page 462).

Similarly, SSE divided by $k(n-1)$ equals the mean of the k sample variances, $\frac{1}{3}(s_1^2 + s_2^2 + s_3^2)$ in our example, which we put into the denominator of the F statistic on page 446. Called the **error mean square,** it measures the variation within the samples and it is denoted by MSE. Thus,

$$MSE = \frac{SSE}{k(n-1)}$$

and for the three-detergent example we get

$$MSE = \frac{276}{3(5-1)} = \frac{276}{12} = 23$$

This equals the value we got for $\frac{1}{3}(s_1^2 + s_2^2 + s_3^2)$ on page 446 (see also Exercise 14.23 on page 462).

Since F is defined on page 446 as the ratio of these two measures of the variation among the sample means and within the samples, we can now write

Test Concerning Differences Among Means

$$F = \frac{MS(Tr)}{MSE}$$

In practice, we display the work required for the determination of F in the following kind of table, called an **analysis of variance table:**

Source of variation	Degrees of freedom	Sum of squares	Mean square	F
Treatments	$k - 1$	$SS(Tr)$	$MS(Tr)$	$\dfrac{MS(Tr)}{MSE}$
Error	$k(n - 1)$	SSE	MSE	
Total	$kn - 1$	SST		

The degrees of freedom for treatments and error are the numerator and denominator degrees of freedom referred to on page 446. Note that they equal the quantities we divide into the sums of squares to obtain the corresponding mean squares.

After we have calculated F, we proceed as in Section 14.1. Assuming again that the populations sampled can be approximated closely with normal distributions and that they have equal standard deviations, we reject the null hypothesis

$$\mu_1 = \mu_2 = \cdots = \mu_k$$

against the alternative hypotheses that these μ's are not all equal (or, in the notation introduced in the footnote to page 445, the null hypothesis

$$\alpha_1 = \alpha_2 = \cdots = \alpha_k = 0$$

against the alternative hypothesis that these treatment effects are not all zero), if the value obtained for F is greater than or equal to F_α for $k - 1$ and $k(n - 1)$ degrees of freedom.

Example

Use the sums of squares on page 452 to construct an analysis of variance table for the three-detergent example, and test at the 0.01 level of significance whether or not the three detergents are equally effective.

solution

Since $k = 3$, $n = 5$, $SST = 666$, $SS(Tr) = 390$, and $SSE = 276$, we get $k - 1 = 2$, $k(n - 1) = 12$, $MS(Tr) = \frac{390}{2} = 195$, $MSE = \frac{276}{12} = 23$, and $F = \frac{195}{23} \approx 8.48$. All these results are summarized in the following table:

Source of variation	Degrees of freedom	Sum of squares	Mean square	F
Treatments	2	390	195	8.48
Error	12	276	23	
Total	14	666		

Note that the total degrees of freedom is simply the sum of the degrees of freedom for treatments and error (see also Exercise 14.23 on page 462).

Finally, since $F =$ exceeds 6.93, the value of $F_{0.01}$ for 2 and 12 degrees of freedom, the null hypothesis that the three detergents are equally effective must be rejected.   ▰ ▰ ▰

The calculations for our detergent example are aided by the fact that the three means, as well as the overall mean, are integers. In most situations, the calculations can be quite tedious, and we must exploit the following computing formulas. In these formulas, $T_{i.}$ denotes the sum of the values for the ith sample, and $T_{..}$ denotes the **grand total** of all the data.

Computing Formulas for Sums of Squares, n Observations, k Groups	

$$SST = \sum_{i=1}^{k} \sum_{j=1}^{n} x_{ij}^2 - \frac{1}{kn} \cdot T_{..}^2 , \qquad SS(Tr) = \frac{1}{n} \cdot \sum_{i=1}^{k} T_{i.}^2 - \frac{1}{kn} \cdot T_{..}^2$$

and by subtraction

$$SSE = SST - SS(Tr)$$

Example

Use these computing formulas to verify the sums of squares on page 452 for the three-detergent example.

solution

Substituting $k = 3$, $n = 5$, $T_{1.} = 385$, $T_{2.} = 340$, $T_{3.} = 400$, $T_{..} = 1{,}125$ and $\Sigma\Sigma\, x^2 = 85{,}041$ into the formulas, we now have

$$SST = 85{,}041 - \tfrac{1}{15}(1{,}125)^2 = 85{,}041 - 84{,}375 = 666$$

$$SS(Tr) = \tfrac{1}{5}[385^2 + 340^2 + 400^2] - 84{,}375 = 390$$

$$SSE = 666 - 390 = 276$$

As can be seen, these results are identical with the ones obtained before.   ▰ ▰ ▰

A computer printout of the analysis of variance of this section is shown in Figure 14.2. Besides the degrees of freedom, the sums of squares, the mean squares, and the value of F, it provides information which permits further comparisons among the population means. We shall not go into this here. Some statistical software also gives the tail probability, namely, the probability of getting a value greater than or equal to the observed value of F when the null hypothesis is true. For our example it is given as 0.005.

The method discussed here applies only when the sample sizes are all equal, but minor modifications make it applicable also when the sample sizes are not all equal. If the ith sample is of size n_i, the computing formulas for the sums of squares become

FIGURE 14.2

Computer printout for one-way analysis of variance (MINITAB 10 for Windows).

```
MTB > print c1 c2

Data Display

Row     C1    C2

  1      1    77
  2      1    81
  3      1    71
  4      1    76
  5      1    80
  6      2    72
  7      2    58
  8      2    74
  9      2    66
 10      2    70
 11      3    76
 12      3    85
 13      3    82
 14      3    80
 15      3    77


MTB > Oneway c2 c1.

One-Way Analysis of Variance

Analysis of Variance on C2
Source    DF        SS        MS        F         p
C1         2      390.0     195.0     8.48     0.005
Error     12      276.0      23.0
Total     14      666.0
                                    Individual 95% CIs For Mean
                                    Based on Pooled StDev
Level      N      Mean      StDev   ----+-------+-------+-------+-
    1      5    77.000      3.937                   (-----*-----)
    2      5    68.000      6.325    (------*------)
    3      5    80.000      3.674                       (------*------)
                                    ----+-------+-------+-------+-
Pooled StDev =    4.796             66.0    72.0    78.0    84.0
```

Computing Formulas for Sums of Squares (Unequal Sample Sizes)	

$$SST = \sum_{i=1}^{k} \sum_{j=1}^{n_i} x_{ij}^2 - \frac{1}{N} \cdot T_{..}^2, \qquad SS(Tr) = \sum_{i=1}^{k} \frac{T_i^2}{n_i} - \frac{1}{N} \cdot T_{..}^2$$

and by subtraction

$$SSE = SST - SS(Tr)$$

where $N = n_1 + n_2 + \cdots + n_k$. The only other change is that the degrees of freedom numbers are $k - 1$ for treatments, $N - k$ for error, and $N - 1$ total.

Example

A laboratory technician wants to compare the breaking strength of three kinds of thread. Originally he had planned to repeat each determination six times. Not having enough time, however, he has to base his analysis on the following results (in ounces):

Thread 1:	18.0	16.4	15.7	19.6	16.5	18.2
Thread 2:	21.1	17.8	18.6	20.8	17.9	19.0
Thread 3:	16.5	17.8	16.1			

Perform an analysis of variance to test at the 0.05 level of significance whether the differences among the sample means are significant.

solution

1. H_0: $\mu_1 = \mu_2 = \mu_3$
   H_A: The μ's are not all equal.

2. $\alpha = 0.05$

3. Reject the null hypothesis if $F \geq 3.89$, where F is to be determined by an analysis of variance and 3.89 is the value of $F_{0.05}$ for $k - 1 = 3 - 1 = 2$ and $N - k = 15 - 3 = 12$ degrees of freedom; otherwise, accept the null hypothesis or reserve judgment.

4. Substituting $n_1 = 6$, $n_2 = 6$, $n_3 = 3$, $N = 15$, $T_{1.} = 104.4$, $T_{2.} = 115.2$, $T_{3.} = 50.4$, $T_{..} = 270.0$, and $\Sigma\Sigma\, x^2 = 4{,}897.46$ into the computing formulas for the sums of squares, we get

$$SST = 4{,}897.46 - \frac{1}{15}\,(270.0)^2 = 37.46$$

$$SS(Tr) = \frac{104.4^2}{6} + \frac{115.2^2}{6} + \frac{50.4^2}{3} - \frac{1}{15}\,(270.0)^2 = 15.12$$

$$SSE = 37.46 - 15.12 = 22.34$$

Since the degrees of freedom are $k - 1 = 3 - 1 = 2$, $N - k = 15 - 3 = 12$, and $N - 1 = 14$, we then obtain

$$MS(Tr) = \frac{15.12}{2} = 7.56, \quad MSE = \frac{22.34}{12} \approx 1.86, \quad F = \frac{7.56}{1.86} \approx 4.06$$

and all these results are summarized in the following analysis of variance table:

Source of variation	Degrees of freedom	Sum of squares	Mean square	F
Treatments	2	15.12	7.56	4.06
Error	12	22.34	1.86	
Total	14	37.46		

5. Since $F = 4.06$ exceeds 3.89, the null hypothesis must be rejected; in other words, we conclude that there is a difference in the strength of the three kinds of thread.

This example could also utilize the *p*-value. The final three steps would be these:

3'. The statistic is

$$F = \frac{MS(Tr)}{MSE}$$

4'. Find

$$F = \frac{7.56}{1.86} = 4.06$$

Since $F = 4.06$ falls between 3.89 and 6.93, the values of $F_{0.05}$ and $F_{0.01}$ for 2 and 12 degrees of freedom, we find that $0.01 < p < 0.05$.

5'. Since the level of significance was specified as $\alpha = 0.05$, we conclude, as before, that the null hypothesis must be rejected. Had the level of significance not been specified, we might simply have stated that $0.01 < p < 0.05$. ▰ ▰ ▰

14.4   MULTIPLE COMPARISONS

When the F test of an analysis of variance indicates statistical significance, the null hypothesis of equal treatments is rejected. However, the F test provides no specific guidance to the consumer as to which of the treatments should be preferred. For example, suppose that 30 subjects tested six different toothpaste preparations for 1 week, five subjects using each toothpaste, with the following scores in mean reduction of dental plaque:

Toothpaste						Average
1	1.32	1.71	2.52	2.55	1.78	1.976
2	2.59	2.27	2.75	1.39	1.78	2.156
3	2.72	2.31	1.25	1.28	1.43	1.798
4	0.92	2.61	1.79	2.92	1.97	2.042
5	3.24	2.77	3.02	3.65	2.49	3.034
6	1.92	2.65	2.00	2.93	1.91	2.282

High values suggest greater plaque-fighting effectiveness. The analysis of variance produces an F statistic that is significant at the 0.05 level. While the toothpaste with the highest mean plaque-reduction score, number 5, certainly appears to be superior to toothpaste 3, we are not sure whether we can declare toothpaste number 5 to be significantly better than toothpaste number 6. We could of course perform an ordinary t test to compare these two products, but there are altogether

$$\binom{6}{2} = \frac{6 \cdot 5}{2 \cdot 1} = 15$$

tests that compare the respective pairs of products. If we perform so many tests, then we will likely reject one or more of the null hypotheses by chance alone, even if all are true.

The area of study called **multiple comparisons** has been developed to help devise procedures for properly controlling the Type I error probabilities in conducting these comparisons. This is a complicated topic. There are misunderstandings of this topic by non-experts, and a number of issues have not been clarified even by the experts. Here we present one method, suitable for use in making decisions among many acceptable consumer product brands: the **studentized range.**[†] This method is designed for comparing pairs of means. The form that we present here applies only in the case where all of the sample sizes are equal.

You are invited to refer to the references at the end of the chapter to learn about methods for handling the case of unequal sample sizes. The references also deal with other methods of multiple comparisons, such as the Bonferroni, Duncan, Dunnett, Neuman–Keuls, least significant difference, and Scheffe methods. There are additional techniques devoted to forming groups of means that are deemed not significantly different from each other; these are also indicated in the references.

For our toothpaste example, the analysis of variance table is:

Source of variation	Degrees of freedom	Sum of squares	Mean square	F
Treatments	5	4.69835	0.93967	2.69
Error	24	8.37660	0.34902	
Total	29	13.0749		

We are testing the null hypothesis

$$H_0: \quad \mu_1 = \mu_2 = \cdots = \mu_6$$

This is to be rejected if $F \geq 2.62$, where 2.62 is $F_{0.05}$, obtained from Table IV using

$$k - 1 = 6 - 1 = 5 \quad \text{and} \quad k(n - 1) = 6(5 - 1) = 24$$

degrees of freedom. Since $F = 2.69 > 2.62$, we reject the null hypothesis. It is helpful now to compare the toothpaste products to determine which pairs are significantly different.

The studentized range procedure has been devised to control the overall probability of making at least one Type I error in comparing the different pairs

[†]**Studentizing** is the process of dividing a statistic by a statistically independent estimate of scale. The expression is derived from the *nom de plume* of W. S. Gosset, who first introduced the process in 1907 by discussing the distribution of the mean divided by the sample standard deviation.

of means. It asserts that two treatments (say treatment i and treatment j) are significantly different if their means ($\bar{x}_i$ and $\bar{x}_j$) are such that

$$|\bar{x}_i - \bar{x}_j| \geq \frac{q_\alpha}{\sqrt{n}} s$$

where s is the square root of the error mean square and q_α is taken from Table XII. The α in this notation refers to the level of significance, and Table XII covers the usual cases $\alpha = 0.05$ and $\alpha = 0.01$. Table XII covers many different sizes of experiments, and in this table k is the number of treatments and $k(n-1)$ the number of degrees of freedom. Of course, $k(n-1)$ is the number of degrees of freedom in the Error line of the analysis of variance table.

In applying the studentized range method to the toothpaste data, it helps to sort the products according to their mean plaque-reduction score:

3	1	4	2	6	5
1.798	1.976	2.042	2.156	2.282	3.034

The cutoff point required by the studentized range method is $\dfrac{q_\alpha}{\sqrt{n}} s$. We note that

$$s = \sqrt{0.34902} \approx 0.5908, \quad n = 5, \quad \text{and} \quad q_{0.05} = 4.37$$

using Table XII with

$$k = 6 \quad \text{and} \quad k(n-1) = 6(5-1) = 24$$

It follows that any two means can be declared significantly different if their difference, in absolute value, exceeds

$$\frac{q_\alpha}{\sqrt{n}} s = \frac{4.37}{\sqrt{5}} \, 0.5908 \approx 1.155$$

The outermost difference in this experiment, namely that between toothpastes 5 and 3, is 1.236. This exceeds 1.155, a significant difference.

But what of our question regarding the comparison of toothpaste number 5 versus toothpaste number 6? Their difference in means is 0.712, less than 1.115. Therefore, these two products cannot be declared significantly different. The consumer can conclude that toothpaste number 5 performed best in this experiment, but that it cannot be deemed statistically significantly different from products numbered 1, 4, 2, or 6. Indeed, the only significantly pairwise comparison is that involving toothpaste number 5 and toothpaste number 3. This statement is insightful and helpful to the consumer. It can be concisely written out by underlining the six treatments as follows:

$$\underline{3 \quad 1 \quad 4 \quad 2 \quad 6} \quad \underline{ 5}$$

where two treatment differences are deemed satistically significant only if they are not underlined by the same line.

■ EXERCISES

14.7   An experiment is performed to determine which of three golf ball brands, *A, B,* or *C,* will attain the greatest distance when driven from a tee. Criticize the experiment if:

(a) one golf pro hits all the brand *A* balls, another hits all the brand *B* balls, and a third hits all the brand *C* balls;

(b) all brand *A* balls are hit first, brand *B* balls next, and brand *C* balls last.

14.8   Flora, a botanist wants to compare three kinds of tulips having, respectively, red, white, and yellow flowers. She has four bulbs of each kind and plants them in a flower bed in the following pattern, where *R, W,* and *Y* denote the three colors:

```
R   R   R   R
W   W   W   W
Y   Y   Y   Y
```

When the plants reach maturity, Flora measures their height and performs an analysis of variance. Criticize this experiment and indicate how it might be improved.

⊞ 14.9   To compare three weight-reducing diets, five of 15 persons are assigned randomly to each of the diets. After they have been on these diets for two weeks, a one-way analysis of variance is performed on their weight losses to test the null hypothesis that the three diets are equally effective. It has been claimed that this procedure cannot yield a valid conclusion because the five persons who originally weighed the most might be assigned to the same diet. Verify that the probability of this happening by chance is about 0.001.

⊞ 14.10   With reference to the preceding exercise, suppose that five of the 15 persons are assigned randomly to each of the three diets, but it is discovered subsequently that the five persons who orginally weighed the most are all assigned to the same diet. Should the one-way analysis of variance still be performed?

14.11   Rework part (b) of Exercise 14.1 on page 447 by performing an analysis of variance. Use the computational formulas on page 454. You will find the following numbers helpful:

$$T_{1.} = 65, \quad T_{2.} = 85, \quad T_{3.} = 75$$

$$T_{..} = 225, \quad \sum_{i=1}^{3} \sum_{j=1}^{5} x_{ij}^2 = 3{,}551$$

14.12   Rework part (b) of Exercise 14.2 on page 447 by performing an analysis of variance. Use the computational formulas on page 454. You will find the following numbers helpful:

$$T_{1.} = 85, \quad T_{2.} = 25, \quad T_{3.} = 135, \quad T_4 = 50$$

$$T_{..} = 295, \quad \sum_{i=1}^{4} \sum_{j=1}^{5} x_{ij}^2 = 5{,}897$$

14.13   Rework part (b) of Exercise 14.3 on page 448 by performing an analysis of variance. Use the computational formulas on page 454; You will find the following numbers helpful:

$$T_{1.} = 78.0, \quad T_{2.} = 74.1, \quad T_{3.} = 75.6, \quad T_4 = 68.1$$

$$T_5 = 78.6, \quad T_{..} = 374.4, \quad \sum_{i=1}^{5} \sum_{j=1}^{3} x_{ij}^2 = 9{,}373.48$$

14.14 Rework part (b) of Exercise 14.4 on page 448 by performing an analysis of variance. Use the computational formulas on page 454. You will find the following numbers helpful:

$$T_{1.} = 1{,}104, \quad T_{2.} = 1{,}104, \quad T_{3.} = 1{,}120$$

$$T_{..} = 3{,}328, \quad \sum_{i=1}^{3} \sum_{j=1}^{8} x_{ij}^2 = 463{,}314$$

14.15 The following are the numbers of mistakes made on five occasions by four wordprocessor operators, setting a technical report:

Operator 1:	10	13	9	11	12
Operator 2:	11	13	8	16	12
Operator 3:	10	15	13	11	15
Operator 4:	15	7	11	12	9

At the 0.05 level of significance, can we conclude that there is a real difference in the numbers of mistakes made in general by the four operators?

14.16 The following data show the yields of soybeans (in bushels per acre) planted 2 inches apart on essentially similar plots with the rows 20, 24, 28, and 32 inches apart:

20 in.	24 in.	28 in.	32 in.
23.1	21.7	21.9	19.8
22.8	23.0	21.3	20.4
23.2	22.4	21.6	19.3
23.4	21.1	20.2	18.5
23.6	21.9	21.6	19.1
21.7	23.4	23.8	21.9

Test at the 0.05 level of significance whether the differences among the four sample means can be attributed to chance.

14.17 A large marketing firm uses many photocopy machines, several of each of four different models. During the last six months, the office manager has tabulated for each machine the average number of minutes per week that it is out of service due to repairs, resulting in the following data:

Model G:	56	61	68	42	82	70
Model H:	74	77	92	63	54	
Model K:	25	36	29	56	44	48 38
Model M:	78	105	89	112	61	

Test at the 0.01 level of significance whether the differences among the four sample means can be attributed to chance.

The following facts may be helpful: The group totals are $T_G = 379$, $T_H = 360$, $T_J = 276$, and $T_M = 445$. The grand total is 1,460. Also,

$$\sum_{i=1}^{4} \sum_{j=1}^{n_i} x_{ij}^2 = 104{,}500$$

14.18 When used with three different lubricants, a specific group of machine parts show the following weight losses (in milligrams) due to friction:

Lubricant X:	10	13	12	10	14	8	12	13			
Lubricant Y:	9	8	12	9	8	11	7	6	8	11	9
Lubricant Z:	6	7	7	5	9	8	4	10			

Test at the 0.01 level of significance whether the differences among the three sample means are significant. The treatment totals are 92, 98, and 56, with a grand total of 246. The sum of squares is 2,412.

14.19 To study its performance, a newly designed motorboat was timed over a marked course under various wind and water conditions. Use the following data (in minutes) to test, at the 0.05 level of significance, whether the differences among the three sample means are significant:

Calm conditions:	26	19	16	22		
Moderate conditions:	25	27	25	20	18	23
Choppy conditions:	23	25	28	31	26	

The totals for the three conditions are 83, 138, and 133, with a grand total of 354. The sum of squares is 8,584.

14.20 With reference to the footnote to page 445, verify that the sum of the treatment effects, the α's, is equal to zero.

14.21 Verify that $kn - 1$, the expression given for the total degrees of freedom in the table on page 453, equals the sum of $k - 1$ and $k(n - 1)$, namely, the sum of the degrees of freedom for treatments and error.

14.22 Verify that the quantity referred to as the Pooled StDev (the pooled standard deviation) in Figure 14.2 is the square root of the value obtained for $\frac{1}{3}(s_1^2 + s_2^2 + s_3^2)$ on page 446.

⊞ 14.23 Verify symbolically that for a one-way analysis of variance

(a) $\dfrac{SS(Tr)}{k - 1} = n \cdot s_{\bar{x}}^2$; (b) $\dfrac{SSE}{k(n - 1)} = \dfrac{1}{k} \cdot \sum_{i=1}^{k} s_i^2$

where s_i^2 is the variance of the ith sample.

14.24 If $k = 2$ and we are testing the null hypothesis $\mu_1 = \mu_2$ against the alternative hypothesis $\mu_1 \neq \mu_2$, the one-way analysis of variance is equivalent to the two-sample t test of Section 11.9. Indeed, it can be shown that F must equal t^2, where F and t are the statistics on which the respective tests are based. Perform an analysis of variance for the data of Exercise 11.106 on page 368 and show that the value obtained for F equals the square of the value obtained for t in Exercise 11.106.

14.25 The values below are the percentages of the previous year's fruit yield for apple trees managed under eight different spraying schedules, with six trees used for each spraying schedule. The value 130, for example, indicates that the tree's yield was 130% of the previous year. Large values are thus to be interpreted as favorable.

Schedule							Mean
A	130	98	128	106	139	121	120.33
B	142	133	122	131	132	141	133.50
C	114	141	95	123	118	140	121.83
D	77	99	84	76	70	75	80.17
E	109	86	113	101	103	112	104.00
F	148	143	111	142	131	100	129.17
G	149	129	134	108	119	126	127.50
H	92	129	111	103	107	125	111.17

(a) Give the analysis of variance F statistic and, at the 0.05 level, note whether this is significant. For these data, it happens that

$$SS(Tr) = 12,696.2 \quad \text{and} \quad SSE = 7,818.7$$

(b) Analyze these values using the studentized range method at the 0.05 level of significance and advise an arborist who would like to employ one of these methods.

14.26 The following data are the weights of five football linemen, randomly selected from the rosters of four different high school teams.

Team						Mean
1	196	237	215	211	228	217.4
2	214	216	220	235	215	220.0
3	201	223	240	241	224	225.8
4	194	197	193	225	207	203.2

The analysis of variance for these data produced $F = 2.39$ on 3 and 16 degrees of freedom. The error mean square was $MSE = 192.4250$.

(a) Show that this F statistic is not significant at the 5% level.

(b) Using the 0.05 level of significance, find the cutoff for which the studentized range method will declare significance for a difference between two means. Show that, by this method, that there are no significant pairwise differences.

14.5 THE DESIGN OF EXPERIMENTS: BLOCKING

To introduce another important concept in the design of experiments, suppose that a reading comprehension test is given to random samples of eighth graders from each of four schools, and that the results are

School A:	87	70	92
School B:	43	75	56
School C:	70	66	50
School D:	67	85	79

The means of these four samples are 83, 58, 62, and 77, and since the differences among them are very large, it would seem reasonable to conclude that there are some real differences in the average reading comprehension of eighth graders in the four schools. This does not follow, however, from a one-way analysis of variance. We get

Source of variation	Degrees of freedom	Sum of squares	Mean square	F
Treatments	3	1,278	426	2.90
Error	8	1,176	147	
Total	11	2,454		

and since $F = 2.90$ is less than 4.07, the value of $F_{0.05}$ for 3 and 8 degrees of freedom, the null hypothesis (that the population means are all equal) cannot be rejected at the 0.05 level of significance.

The reason for this is that there are not only considerable differences among the four means, but also very large differences among the values within the samples. In the first sample they range from 70 to 92, in the second sample from 43 to 75, in the third sample from 50 to 70, and in the fourth sample from 67 to 85. Giving this some thought, it would seem reasonable to conclude that these differences within the samples may well be due to differences in ability, an extraneous factor (we might call it a "nuisance" factor) which was randomized by taking a random sample of eighth graders from each school. Thus, variations due to differences in ability were included in the experimental error; this "inflated" the error sum of squares which went into the denominator of the F statistic, and the results were not significant.

To avoid this kind of situation, we could hold the extraneous factor fixed, but this will seldom give us the information we want. In our example, we could limit the study to eighth graders with a scholastic grade-point average (GPA) of 90 or above, but then the results would apply only to eighth graders with a GPA of 90 or above. Another possibility is to vary the known source of variability (the extraneous factor) deliberately over as wide a range as necessary, and to do it in such a way that the variability it causes can be measured and, hence, eliminated from the experimental error. This means that we should plan the experiment in such a way that we can perform a **two-way analysis of variance,** in which the total variability of the data is partitioned into three components attributed, respectively, to treatments (in our example, the four schools), the extraneous factor, and experimental error.

As we shall see later, this can be accomplished in our example by randomly selecting from each school one eighth grader with a low GPA, one eighth grader with a typical GPA, and one eighth grader with a high GPA, where "low," "typical," and "high" are presumably defined in a rigorous way. Suppose, then, that we proceed in this way and get the results shown in the following table:

	Low GPA	*Typical GPA*	*High GPA*
School A	71	92	89
School B	44	51	85
School C	50	64	72
School D	67	81	86

What we have done here is called **blocking,** and the three levels of GPA are called **blocks.** In general, blocks are the levels at which we hold an extraneous factor fixed, so that we can measure its contribution to the total variability of the data by means of a two-way analysis of variance. In the scheme we chose for our example, we are dealing with **complete blocks**—they are complete in the sense that each treatment appears the same number of times in each block. There is one eighth grader from each school in each block.

Suppose, furthermore, that the order in which the students are tested may have some effect on the results. If the order is randomized within each block (that is, for each level of GPA), we refer to the design of the experiment as a **randomized block design.**

14.6 TWO-WAY ANALYSIS OF VARIANCE

In this section we present the theory of a **two-way analysis of variance** in connection with experiments where blocking is used to reduce the error sum of squares, and, hence, we refer to the two variables under consideration as "treatments" and "blocks." As we shall indicate later, the same kind of analysis applies also to **two-factor experiments,** where both variables are of material concern.

Before we go into any details, let us point out that there are essentially two ways of analyzing such two-variable experiments, and they depend on whether the two variables are independent, or whether there is an **interaction.** Suppose, for instance, that a tire manufacturer is experimenting with different kinds of treads, and finds that one kind is especially good for use on dirt roads while another kind is especially good for use on hard pavement. If this is the case, we say that there is an interaction between road conditions and tread design. On the other hand, if each of the treads is affected equally by the different road conditions, we would say that there is no interaction and that the two variables (road conditions and tread design) are independent. In this book we shall study only the case where there is no interaction.[†]

To formulate the hypotheses to be tested in the two-variable case, let us write μ_{ij} for the population mean that corresponds to the ith treatment and the jth block. In our example, μ_{ij} is the average reading comprehension score in the ith school for eighth graders with grade point average level j. We express this as

$$\mu_{ij} = \mu + \alpha_i + \beta_j$$

As in the footnote to page 445, μ is the grand mean (the average of all the population means μ_{ij}), and the α_i are the treatment effects (whose sum is zero). Correspondingly, we refer to the β_j as the **block effects** (whose sum is also zero), and write the two null hypotheses we want to test as

$$\alpha_1 = \alpha_2 = \cdots = \alpha_k = 0 \quad \text{and} \quad \beta_1 = \beta_2 = \cdots = \beta_n = 0$$

The alternative to the first null hypothesis (which in our illustration amounts to the hypothesis that the average reading comprehension of eighth graders is the same in all four schools) is that the treatment effects α_i are not all zero; the alternative to the second null hypothesis (which in our illustration amounts to the hypothesis that the average reading comprehension of eighth graders is the same for all three levels of GPA) is that the block effects β_j are not all zero.

[†]From a technical point of view, it can happen that the no-interaction model $\mu_{ij} = \mu + \alpha_i + \beta_j$ introduced on this page is inadequate and needs to be replaced by the interaction model $\mu_{ij} = \mu + \alpha_i + \beta_j + \gamma_{ij}$.

To test the second of the null hypotheses, we need a quantity, similar to the treatment sum of squares, which measures the variation among the block means (58, 72, and 83 for the data on page 464. So, if we let $T_{.j}$ denote the total of all the values in the jth block, substitute it for $T_{i.}$ in the computing formula for $SS(Tr)$ on page 454, sum on j instead of i, and interchange n and k, we obtain, analogous to $SS(Tr)$ the **block sum of squares:**

Block Sum of Squares

$$SSB = \frac{1}{k} \cdot \sum_{j=1}^{n} T_{.j}^2 - \frac{1}{kn} \cdot T_{..}^2$$

In a two-way analysis of variance (with no interaction) we compute SST and $SS(Tr)$ according to the formulas on page 454, SSB according to the formula immediately above, and then we get SSE by subtraction. Since

$$SST = SS(Tr) + SSB + SSE$$

we have

Error Sum of Squares (Two-way Analysis)

$$SSE = SST - [SS(Tr) + SSB]$$

Observe that the error sum of squares for a two-way analysis of variance does not equal the error sum of squares for a one-way analysis of variance performed on the same data, even though we denote both with the symbol SSE. In fact, we are now partitioning the error sum of squares for the one-way analysis of variance into two terms: the block sum of squares, SSB, and the remainder which is the new error sum of squares, SSE.

We can now construct the following analysis-of-variance table for a two-way analysis of variance (with no interaction):

Source of variation	Degrees of freedom	Sum of squares	Mean square	F
Treatments	$k - 1$	$SS(Tr)$	$MS(Tr) = \dfrac{SS(Tr)}{k - 1}$	$\dfrac{MS(Tr)}{MSE}$
Block	$n - 1$	SSB	$MSB = \dfrac{SSB}{n - 1}$	$\dfrac{MSB}{MSE}$
Error	$(k - 1)(n - 1)$	SSE	$MSE = \dfrac{SSE}{(k - 1)(n - 1)}$	
Total	$kn - 1$	SST		

The mean squares are again the sums of squares divided by their respective degrees of freedom, and the two F values are the mean squares for treatments and blocks divided by the mean square for error. Also, the degrees of freedom for blocks are $n - 1$ (like those for treatments with n substituted for k), and the degrees of freedom for error are found by subtracting the degrees of freedom for treatments and blocks from $kn - 1$, the total number of degrees of freedom:

$$(kn - 1) - (k - 1) - (n - 1) = kn - k - n + 1 = (k - 1)(n - 1)$$

Thus, in the significance test for treatments the numerator and denominator degrees of freedom for F are $k - 1$ and $(k - 1)(n - 1)$, and in the significance test for blocks the numerator and denominator degrees of freedom for F are $n - 1$ and $(k - 1)(n - 1)$.

Example

With reference to the data on page 464, namely,

	Low GPA	Typical GPA	High GPA
School A	71	92	89
School B	44	51	85
School C	50	64	72
School D	67	81	86

test at the 0.05 level of significance whether the differences among the means obtained for the four schools (treatments) are significant, and also whether the differences among the means obtained for the three levels of GPA (blocks) are significant.

solution

1. H_0's: $\alpha_1 = \alpha_2 = \alpha_3 = \alpha_4 = 0$
   $\beta_1 = \beta_2 = \beta_3 = 0$
   H_A's: The treatment effects are not all equal to zero; the block effects are not all equal to zero.

2. $\alpha = 0.05$ for both tests.

3. For treatments, reject the null hypothesis if $F \geq 4.76$, where F is to be determined by a two-way analysis of variance and 4.76 is the value of $F_{0.05}$ for

   $$k - 1 = 4 - 1 = 3 \quad \text{and} \quad (k - 1)(n - 1) = (4 - 1)(3 - 1) = 6$$

   degrees of freedom. For blocks, reject the null hypothesis if $F \geq 5.14$, where F is to be determined by a two-way analysis of variance and 5.14 is the value of $F_{0.05}$ for

   $$n - 1 = 3 - 1 = 2 \quad \text{and} \quad (k - 1)(n - 1) = (4 - 1)(3 - 1) = 6$$

   degrees of freedom. If either null hypothesis cannot be rejected, accept it or reserve judgment.

4. Substituting $k = 4$, $n = 3$, $T_{1.} = 252$, $T_{2.} = 180$, $T_{3.} = 186$, $T_{4.} = 234$, $T_{.1} = 232$, $T_{.2} = 288$, $T_{.3} = 332$, $T_{..} = 852$, and $\Sigma\Sigma x^2 = 63,414$ into the computing formulas for the sums of squares, we get

$$SST = 63,414 - \tfrac{1}{12}(852)^2 = 63,414 - 60,492 = 2,922$$

$$SS(Tr) = \tfrac{1}{3}[252^2 + 180^2 + 186^2 + 234^2] - 60,492 \approx 1,260$$

$$SSB = \tfrac{1}{4}[232^2 + 288^2 + 332^2] - 60,492 = 1,256$$

$$SSE = 2.922 - [1,260 + 1,256] = 406$$

Since the degrees of freedom are $k - 1 = 4 - 1 = 3$, $n - 1 = 3 - 1 = 2$,

$$(k - 1)(n - 1) = (4 - 1)(3 - 1) = 6, \quad \text{and} \quad kn - 1 = 4 \cdot 3 - 1 = 11$$

we then get

$$MS(Tr) = \frac{1,260}{3} = 420, \quad MSB = \frac{1,256}{2} = 628, \quad MSE = \frac{406}{6} \approx 67.67,$$

$$F = \frac{420}{67.67} \approx 6.21 \text{ for treatments,} \quad \text{and} \quad F = \frac{628}{67.67} \approx 9.28 \text{ for blocks}$$

and all these results are summarized in the following analysis-of-variance table:

Source of variation	Degrees of freedom	Sum of squares	Mean square	F
Treatments	3	1,260	420	6.21
Blocks	2	1,256	628	9.28
Error	6	406	67.67	
Total	11	2,922		

5. For treatments, since $F = 6.21$ exceeds 4.76, the null hypothesis must be rejected; for blocks, since $F = 9.28$ exceeds 5.14, the null hypothesis must be rejected. In other words, we conclude that the average reading comprehension of eighth graders is not the same for the four schools, and also that it is not the same for the three levels of GPA.   ▰ ▰ ▰

Observe that by blocking we were able to show that the differences among the means obtained for the four schools are significant, whereas without blocking, in the experiment described on page 463, the differences among the means obtained for the four schools were not significant.

Needless to say, perhaps, there exists extensive software for a two-way analysis of variance. Many of the programs, including the one used for the printout shown in Fig. 14.3, provide a considerable amount of additional information. Because the calculations of this section are complicated and error-prone, all serious use of the analysis of variance is performed by computer.

```
MTB > print C1 C2 C3

Data Display

Row    C1    C2    C3

  1     1     1    71
  2     1     2    44
  3     1     3    50
  4     1     4    67
  5     2     1    92
  6     2     2    51
  7     2     3    64
  8     2     4    81
  9     3     1    89
 10     3     2    85
 11     3     3    72
 12     3     4    86

MTB  > Twoway c3 c1 c2;
SUBC >    Means c1 c2.

Two-way Analysis of Variance

Analysis of Variance for C3
Source         DF         SS          MS
C1              2      1256.0       628.0
C2              3      1260.0       420.0
Error           6       406.0        67.7
Total          11      2922.0

                         Individual 95% CI
        C1    Mean    -+--------+--------+--------+--------+
         1    58.0     (------*------)
         2    72.0               (------*------)
         3    83.0                       (------*------)
                      -+--------+--------+--------+--------+
                     48.0     60.0     72.0     84.0     96.0

                         Individual 95% CI
        C2    Mean    --------+--------+--------+--------+-
         1    84.0                      (------*------)
         2    60.0     (------*------)
         3    62.0      (------*------)
         4    78.0                (------*------)
                      --------+--------+--------+--------+-
                             60.0     72.0     84.0     96.0
```

As we pointed out on page 465, a two-way analysis of variance can also be used in connection with **two-factor experiments,** where both variables (factors) are of material concern. It could be used, for example, in the analysis of the following data collected in an experiment designed to test whether the range of a missile flight (in miles) is affected by differences among launchers and also by differences among fuels (see Exercise 14.33 on page 471):

	Fuel 1	Fuel 2	Fuel 3	Fuel 4
Launcher X	45.9	57.6	52.2	41.7
Launcher Y	46.0	51.0	50.1	38.8
Launcher Z	45.7	56.9	55.3	48.1

Note that we used a different format for this table to distinguish between two-factor experiments (where uncontrolled extraneous factors are usually randomized over the entire experiment) and experiments where we deal with treatments and blocks.

Also, when a two-way analysis of variance is used in this way, we usually call the two variables **factor A** and **factor B** (instead of treatments and blocks) and write SSA instead of $SS(Tr)$; we still write SSB, but now B stands for the factor B instead of blocks.

Throughout this section we have assumed exactly one observation in each treatment-by-block combination, so that the experiment consists of exactly kn data values. Experiments with more than one observation in each treatment-by-block combination are done frequently, but we shall not discuss them in this book.

◢ EXERCISES

14.27 To compare the amounts of time that three television stations allot to commercials, Laura, a researcher, measures the time devoted to commercials in random samples of 15 shows on each station. To her dismay, she discovers that there is so much variation within the samples—for one station the figures vary from 6 to 35 minutes—that it is virtually impossible to get significant results. Is there a way in which she might overcome this obstacle?

14.28 To compare five word processors, A, B, C, D, and E, four persons, 1, 2, 3, and 4, were timed in preparing a certain kind of report on each of the machines. The results (in minutes) are shown in the following table:

	1	2	3	4
A	49.1	48.2	52.3	57.0
B	47.5	40.9	44.6	49.5
C	76.2	46.8	50.1	55.3
D	50.7	43.4	47.0	52.6
E	55.8	48.3	82.6	57.8

Explain why these data should not be analyzed by the method of Section 14.5.

14.29 The following are the cholesterol contents (in milligrams per package) which four laboratories obtained for 6-ounce packages of three very similar diet foods:

	Laboratory 1	Laboratory 2	Laboratory 3	Laboratory 4
Diet food A	3.7	2.8	3.1	3.4
Diet food B	3.1	2.6	2.7	3.0
Diet food C	3.5	3.4	3.0	3.3

Perform a two-way analysis of variance, using the 0.01 level of significance for both tests.

14.30 The calorie content of six different brands of orange juice were determined by three different machines. The numbers below are the determination in calories per 6 fluid ounces:

Orange juice brand

	A	B	C	D	E	F
Machine 1	89	97	92	105	100	91
Machine 2	92	101	94	110	100	95
Machine 3	90	98	94	109	99	94

Perform a two-way analysis of variance, using the 0.01 level of significance for both tests.

14.31 A laboratory technician measured the breaking strength of each of five kinds of linen threads by using four different measuring instruments. I_1, I_2, I_3, and I_4 and obtained the following results (in ounces):

	I_1	I_2	I_3	I_4
Thread 1	20.9	20.4	19.9	21.9
Thread 2	25.0	26.2	27.0	24.8
Thread 3	25.5	23.1	21.5	24.4
Thread 4	24.8	21.2	23.5	25.7
Thread 5	19.6	21.2	22.1	21.1

Perform a two-way analysis of variance, using the 0.05 level of significance for both tests.

14.32 The following are eight consecutive weeks' earnings (in dollars) of three salespersons who sell cosmetics door-to-door:

	\multicolumn{8}{c}{Week Number}
	1	2	3	4	5	6	7	8
Salesperson 1	186	222	198	216	210	194	203	219
Salesperson 2	197	203	194	208	220	209	190	205
Salesperson 3	174	213	190	197	233	206	199	221

(a) Use a one-way analysis of variance and the 0.05 level of significance to test the null hypothesis that on the average the three salespersons' weekly earnings are the same.

(b) Retest the null hypothesis of part (a), regarding the successive weeks as blocks.

14.33 With reference to the missile-range data on page 470, perform a two-way analysis of variance, using the 0.05 level of significance for both tests.

14.34 The following are the numbers of defectives produced by four workmen operating, in turn, three different machines:

Workman

		B_1	B_2	B_3	B_4
	A_1	35	38	41	32
Machine	A_2	31	40	38	31
	A_3	36	35	43	25

Perform a two-way analysis of variance, using the 0.05 level of significance for both tests.

14.7   THE DESIGN OF EXPERIMENTS: REPLICATION

In Section 14.5 we showed how we can increase the amount of information to be gained from an experiment by blocking, that is, by eliminating the effect of an extraneous factor. Another way to increase the amount of information to be gained from an experiment is to increase the volume of the data. For instance, in the example on page 463, we might increase the size of the samples and give the reading comprehension test to twenty eighth graders from each school instead of three. For more complicated designs, the same thing can be accomplished by executing the entire experiment more than once. and this is called **replication.** With reference to the example on page 463, we might conduct the experiment (select and test twelve eighth graders) in one week, and then replicate (repeat) the entire experiment in the next week.

Conceptually, replication does not present any difficulties, but computationally it does, and that is why we shall not go into this any further. Indeed, if an experiment requiring a two-way analysis of variance is replicated, it will then require a three-way analysis of variance, since replication, itself, may be a source of variation in the data. For instance, this might be the case in our example if it got very hot and humid during the second week, making it difficult for the students to concentrate.

14.8   LATIN SQUARES ⇔

In Section 14.5 we saw how blocking can be used to eliminate the variability due to one extraneous factor from the experimental error, and, in principle, two or more extraneous sources of variation can be handled in the same way. The only real problem is that this may inflate the size of an experiment beyond practical bounds. Suppose, for instance, that in the example dealing with the reading comprehension of eighth graders we would also like to eliminate whatever variability there may be due to differences in age (12, 13, or 14) and in sex. Allowing for all possible combinations of GPA, age, and sex, we will have to use $3 \cdot 3 \cdot 2 = 18$ different blocks, and if there is to be one eighth grader from each school in each block, we will have to select and test $18 \cdot 4 = 72$ eighth graders in all. If we also wanted to eliminate whatever variability there may be due to ethnic background, for which we might consider five categories, this would raise the required number of eighth graders to $72 \cdot 5 = 360$.

In this section we will show how problems like this can sometimes be resolved, at least in part, by planning experiments as **Latin squares.** At the same time, we also hope to impress upon the reader that it is through proper design that experiments can be made to yield a wealth of information. To give an example, suppose that a market research organization wants to compare four ways of packaging a breakfast food, but it is concerned about possible regional differences in the popularity of the breakfast food, and also about the effects of promoting the breakfast food in different ways. So, it decides to test market the different kinds of packaging in the northeastern, southeastern, northwestern, and southwestern parts of the United States and to promote them with discounts, lotteries, coupons, and two-for-one sales. Thus, there are $4 \cdot 4 = 16$ blocks (combinations of regions and methods of promotion) and it would take $16 \cdot 4 = 64$

market areas (cities) to promote each kind of packaging once within each block within each region of the country. Such a marketing project would be incredibly expensive. Moreover, the test markets must be separated from each other so that the promotion methods do not interfere with each other, and the United States simply does not have 64 sufficiently widely separated test markets. It is of interest to note, however, that with proper planning 16 market areas (cities) will suffice. To illustrate, let us consider the following arrangement, called a **Latin square,** in which the letters *A, B, C,* and *D* represent the four kinds of packaging:

	Discounts	*Lotteries*	*Coupons*	*2-for-1 sales*
Northeast	*A*	*B*	*C*	*D*
Southeast	*B*	*C*	*D*	*A*
Northwest	*C*	*D*	*A*	*B*
Southwest	*D*	*A*	*B*	*C*

In general, a Latin square is a square array of the letters *A, B, C, D,* . . . , of the English (Latin) alphabet, which is such that each letter occurs once and only once in each row and in each column.

The Latin square above, looked upon as an experimental design, requires that discounts be used with packaging *A* in a city in the Northeast, with packaging *B* in a city in the Southeast, with packaging *C* in a city in the Northwest, and with packaging *D* in a city in the Southwest; that lotteries be used with packaging *B* in a city in the Northeast, with packaging *C* in a city in the Southeast, with packaging *D* in a city in the Northwest, and with packaging *A* in a city in the Southwest; and so on. Note that each kind of promotion is used once in each region and once with each kind of packaging; each kind of packaging is used once in each region and once with each kind of promotion; and each region is used once with each kind of packaging and once with each kind of promotion. As we shall see, this will enable us to perform an analysis of variance leading to significance tests for all three variables.

The analysis of an $r \times r$ Latin square is very similar to a two-way analysis of variance. The total sum of squares and the sums of squares for rows and columns are calculated in the same way in which we previously calculated *SST*, *SS(Tr)*, and *SSB*, but we must find an extra sum of squares which measures the variability due to the variable represented by the letters *A, B, C, D,* . . . , namely, a new treatment sum of squares. The formula for this sum of squares is

Treatment Sum of Squares for Latin Square

$$SS(Tr) = \frac{1}{r} \cdot (T_A^2 + T_B^2 + T_C^2 + \cdots) - \frac{1}{r^2} \cdot T_{..}^2$$

where T_A is the total of the observations corresponding to treatment *A*, T_B is the total of the observations corresponding to treatment *B*, and so forth. Finally, the error sum of squares is again obtained by subtraction:

Error Sum of Squares for Latin Square	$SSE = SST - [SSR + SSC + SS(Tr)]$

where SSR and SSC are the sums of squares for rows and columns.

We can now construct the following analysis-of-variance table for the analysis of an $r \times r$ Latin square:

Source of variation	Degrees of freedom	Sum of squares	Mean square	F
Rows	$r - 1$	SSR	$MSR = \dfrac{SSR}{r-1}$	$\dfrac{MSR}{MSE}$
Columns	$r - 1$	SSC	$MSC = \dfrac{SSC}{r-1}$	$\dfrac{MSC}{MSE}$
Treatments	$r - 1$	SS(Tr)	$MS(Tr) = \dfrac{SS(Tr)}{r-1}$	$\dfrac{MS(Tr)}{MSE}$
Error	$(r-1)(r-2)$	SSE	$MSE = \dfrac{SSE}{(r-1)(r-2)}$	
Total	$r^2 - 1$	SST		

The mean squares are again the sums of squares divided by their respective degrees of freedom, and the three *F*-values are the mean squares for rows, columns, and treatments divided by the mean square for error. The degrees of freedom for rows, columns, and treatments are all $r - 1$, and, by subtraction, the degree of freedom for error is

$$(r^2 - 1) - (r - 1) - (r - 1) - (r - 1) = r^2 - 3r + 2 = (r - 1)(r - 2)$$

Thus, for each of the three significance tests the numerator and denominator degrees of freedom for F are $r - 1$ and $(r - 1)(r - 2)$.

Example

Suppose that in the breakfast-food study referred to on page 472, the market research organization actually gets the data shown in the following table, where the figures are a week's sales in $10 thousand:

	Discounts	Lotteries	Coupons	2-for-1 sales
Northeast	A 48	B 38	C 42	D 53
Southeast	B 39	C 43	D 50	A 54
Northwest	C 42	D 50	A 47	B 44
Southwest	D 46	A 48	B 46	C 52

Analyze this Latin square, using the 0.05 level of significance for each test.

<u>solution</u>

1. H_0's: The row, column, and treatment effects (defined as in the footnote to page 445 and on page 465) are all equal to zero.

   H_A's: The respective effects are not all equal to zero.

2. $\alpha = 0.05$ for each test.

3. For rows, columns, or treatments, reject the null hypothesis if $F \geq 4.76$, where the Fs are obtained by means of an analysis of variance, and 4.76 is the value of $F_{0.05}$ for $r - 1 = 4 - 1 = 3$ and $(r - 1)(r - 2) = (4 - 1)(4 - 2) = 6$ degrees of freedom.

4. Substituting $r = 4$, $T_{1.} = 181$, $T_{2.} = 186$, $T_{3.} = 183$, $T_{4.} = 192$, $T_{.1} = 175$, $T_{.2} = 179$, $T_{.3} = 185$, $T_{.4} = 203$, $T_A = 197$, $T_B = 167$, $T_C = 179$, $T_D = 199$, $T_{..} = 742$, and $\Sigma\Sigma\, x^2 = 34{,}756$ into the computing formulas for the sums of squares, we get

$$SST = 34{,}756 - \tfrac{1}{16}(742)^2 = 34{,}756 - 34{,}410.25 = 345.75$$

$$SSR = \tfrac{1}{4}[181^2 + 186^2 + 183^2 + 192^2] - 34{,}410.25 = 17.25$$

$$SSC = \tfrac{1}{4}[175^2 + 179^2 + 185^2 + 203^2] - 34{,}410.25 = 114.75$$

$$SS(Tr) = \tfrac{1}{4}[197^2 + 167^2 + 179^2 + 199^2] - 34{,}410.25 = 174.75$$

$$SSE = 345.75 - [17.25 + 114.75 + 174.75] = 39.00$$

The remainder of the work is shown in the following analysis-of-variance table:

Source of variation	Degrees of freedom	Sum of squares	Mean square	F
Rows (regions)	3	17.25	$\dfrac{17.25}{3} = 5.75$	$\dfrac{5.75}{6.5} \approx 0.88$
Columns (promotion methods)	3	114.75	$\dfrac{114.75}{3} = 38.25$	$\dfrac{38.25}{6.5} \approx 5.88$
Treatments (packaging)	3	174.75	$\dfrac{174.75}{3} = 58.25$	$\dfrac{58.25}{6.5} \approx 8.96$
Error	6	39.00	$\dfrac{39.00}{6} = 6.5$	
Total	15	345.75		

5. For rows, since $F = 0.88$ is less than 4.76, the null hypothesis cannot be rejected; for columns, since $F = 5.88$ exceeds 4.76, the null hypothesis must be rejected; for treatments, since $F = 8.96$ exceeds 4.76, the null hypothesis must be rejected. In other words, we conclude that differences in promotion and packaging, but not the different regions, affect the breakfast food's sales. ◢ ◢ ◢

The calculations for the analysis of variance for the Latin square can of course be done by computer, and the work for this example is shown in Figure 14.4. Since there is considerable arithmetic involved in a Latin square experiment, we recommend that computers always be used for their analysis.

FIGURE 14.4

Computer printout for Latin square analysis of variance, using GLM (general linear model) command (MINITAB 10 for Windows).

```
MTB > print C1 C2 C3 C4

Data Display

Row    C1    C2    C3    C4

 1     1     1     1     48
 2     1     2     2     38
 3     1     3     3     42
 4     1     4     4     53
 5     2     1     2     39
 6     2     2     3     43
 7     2     3     4     50
 8     2     4     1     54
 9     3     1     3     42
10     3     2     4     50
11     3     3     1     47
12     3     4     2     44
13     4     1     4     46
14     4     2     1     48
15     4     3     2     46
16     4     4     3     52

MTB > GLM c4 = c1 c2 c3.

General Linear Model

Factor    Levels    Values
C1           4        1    2    3    4
C2           4        1    2    3    4
C3           4        1    2    3    4

Analysis of Variance for C4

Source    DF     Seq SS      Adj SS     Adj MS      F        P
C1         3     17.250      17.250      5.750    0.88    0.500
C2         3    114.750     114.750     38.250    5.88    0.032
C3         3    174.750     174.750     58.250    8.96    0.012
Error      6     39.000      39.000      6.500
Total     15    345.750
```

14.9 THE DESIGN OF EXPERIMENTS: SOME FURTHER CONSIDERATIONS ◇

There are many other experimental designs besides the ones we have discussed, and they serve a great variety of special purposes. Widely used, for example, are the **incomplete block designs,** which apply when it is impossible to have each treatment in each block.

The need for such a design arises, for instance, when we want to compare 13 kinds of tires but cannot put them all on a test car at the same time. Numbering the tires from 1 to 13, we might use the following experimental design:

Test run	Kinds of tires				Test run	Kinds of tires			
1	1	2	4	10	8	8	9	11	4
2	2	3	5	11	9	9	10	12	5
3	3	4	6	12	10	10	11	13	6
4	4	5	7	13	11	11	12	1	7
5	5	6	8	1	12	12	13	2	8
6	6	7	9	2	13	13	1	3	9
7	7	8	10	3					

Here there are 13 test runs, or blocks, and since each kind of tire appears together with each other kind of tire once within the same block, the design is referred to as a **balanced incomplete block design.** The fact that each kind of tire appears together with each other kind of tire once within the same block is important; it facilitates the statistical analysis because it assures that we have the same amount of information for comparing each pair of tires. In general, the analysis of incomplete block designs is fairly complicated, and we shall not go into it here, as it has been our purpose only to demonstrate what can be accomplished by the careful design of an experiment.

EXERCISES

14.35 Suppose that we want to compare the number of defective pieces produced by four machine operators working on five different machine parts (1, 2, 3, 4, and 5) in three different shifts (I, II, and III).

(a) If the machine operators are to be regarded as the "treatments," list the blocks (combinations of machine parts and shifts) that would be required if each part is to be produced in each shift.

(b) How many observations would be required if each machine operator is to work once on each machine part during each shift?

14.36 An agronomist wants to compare the yield of 16 varieties of corn, and at the same time study the effect of five different fertilizers and two methods of irrigation. How many test plots must he plant if each variety of corn is to be grown once with each possible combination of fertilizers and methods of irrigation?

14.37 A pharmaceutical manufacturer wants to market a new cold remedy that is actually a combination of four medications, and wants to experiment first with two dosages for each medication. If A_L and A_H denote the low and high dosage of medication A, B_L and B_H the low and high dosage of medication B, C_L and C_H the low and high dosage of medication C, and D_L and D_H the low and high dosage of medication D, list the 16 preparations that must be tested if each dosage of each medication is to be used once in combination with each dosage of each of the other medications.

14.38 Making use of the fact that each of the letters must occur once and only once in each row and each column, complete the following Latin squares:

(a)

	A	
B		

(b)

	A		
		B	
A	C		
	C		

(c)

	A	E		
		B		E
C			A	
D				
				D

14.39 The sample data in the following 3×3 Latin square are the scores in an American history test obtained by nine college students of various ethnic backgrounds and of various professional interests, who were taught by instructors A, B, and C:

	Ethnic background		
	Mexican	German	Polish
Law	A 75	B 86	C 69
Medicine	B 95	C 79	A 86
Engineering	C 70	A 83	B 93

Analyze this Latin square, using the 0.05 level of significance for each test.

14.40 To compare four different brands of golf-balls, A, B, C, and D, each kind was driven by each of four golf pros, P_1, P_2, P_3, and P_4, using once each four different drivers, D_1, D_2, D_3, and D_4. The distances from the tee to the points where the balls came to rest (in yards) were as shown in the following table:

	D_1	D_2	D_3	D_4
P_1	D 231	B 215	A 261	C 199
P_2	C 234	A 300	B 280	D 266
P_3	A 301	C 208	D 247	B 255
P_4	B 253	D 258	C 210	A 290

Analyze this Latin square, using the 0.05 level of significance for each test.

⇕ 14.41   Among nine persons interviewed in a poll, three are Easterners, three are Southerners, and three are Westerners. By profession, three of them are teachers, three are lawyers, and three are doctors, and no two of the same profession come from the same part of the United States. Also, three are Democrats, three are Republicans, and three are Independents, and no two of the same political affiliation are of the same profession or come from the same part of the United States. If one of the teachers is an Easterner and an Independent, another teacher is a Southerner and a Republican, and one of the lawyers is a Southerner and a Democrat, what is the political affiliation of the doctor who is a Westerner? (*Hint:* Construct a 3 × 3 Latin square. This exercise is a simplified version of a famous problem posed by R. A. Fisher in his classical work *The Design of Experiments.*)

⇕ 14.42   To test their ability to make decisions under pressure, the nine senior executives of a company are to be interviewed by each of four psychologists. As it takes a psychologist a full day to interview three of the executives, the schedule for the interviews is arranged as follows, where the nine executives are denoted by *A, B, C, D, E, F, G, H,* and *I:*

Day	Psychologist	Executives		
March 2	I	B	C	?
March 3	I	E	F	G
March 4	I	H	I	A
March 5	II	C	?	H
March 6	II	B	F	A
March 9	II	D	E	?
March 10	III	D	G	A
March 11	III	C	F	?
March 12	III	B	E	H
March 13	IV	B	?	I
March 16	IV	C	?	A
March 17	IV	D	F	H

Replace the six question marks with the appropriate letters, given that each of the nine executives is to be interviewed together with each of the other executives once and only once on the same day. Note that this will make the arrangement a balanced incomplete block design, which may be important because each executive is tested together with each other executive once under identical conditions.

⇕ 14.43   A newspaper regularly prints the columns of seven writers but has room for only three in each edition. Complete the following schedule, in which the writers are numbered 1–7, so that each writer's column appears three times per week, and a column of each writer appears together with a column of each other writer once per week.

Day	Writers		
Monday	1	2	3
Tuesday	4		
Wednesday	1	4	5
Thursday	2		
Friday	1	6	7
Saturday	5		
Sunday	2	4	6

14.10 CHECKLIST OF KEY TERMS (*with page references to their definitions*)

Analysis of variance, 447
Analysis-of-variance table, 452
⇔ Balanced incomplete block design, 477
Block effects, 465
Block sum of squares, 466
Blocking, 464
Blocks, 464
Complete blocks, 464
Completely randomized design, 449
Controlled experiment, 449
Error mean square, 452
Error sum of squares, 451
Experimental design, 444
Experimental error, 450
F statistic, 446
Factors, 470
Grand mean, 445, 450
Grand total, 454

⇔ Incomplete block design, 476
Interaction, 465
⇔ Latin square, 472
Multiple comparison, 458
One-way analysis of variance, 450
Pooling, 446
Randomization, 449
Randomized block design, 465
Replication, 472
Studentized range, 458
Total sum of squares, 450
Treatment effects, 445
Treatment mean square, 452
Treatment sum of squares, 451
Treatments, 451
Two-factor experiment, 465
Two-way analysis of variance, 464, 465
Variance ratio, 446

14.11 REVIEW EXERCISES

14.44   With reference to the golf-ball experiment of Exercise 14.7 on page 460, criticize the experiment if all the A balls are hit from the No. 1 tee, all the B balls are hit from the No. 2 tee, and all the C balls are hit from the No. 3 tee.

14.45   To find the best arrangement of instruments on a control panel of an airplane, three different arrangements were tested by simulating emergency conditions and observing the reaction time required to correct the condition. The reaction times (in tenths of a second) of 12 pilots (randomly assigned to the different arrangements) were as follows:

Arrangement 1:	8	15	10	11
Arrangement 2:	16	11	14	19
Arrangement 3:	12	7	13	8

(a) Calculate $n \cdot s_{\bar{x}}^2$ for these data, and also the mean of the variances of the three samples and the value of F.

(b) Test at the 0.01 level of significance whether the differences among the three sample means can be attributed to chance.

14.46   Rework part (b) of the preceding exercise, using the computing formulas to obtain the necessary sums of squares. Compare the values of F obtained here and in part (a) of the preceding exercise.

⇔ 14.47   A school has seven department heads who are assigned to seven different committees as shown in the following table:

Committee	Department heads			
Textbooks	Dodge,	Fleming,	Griffith,	Anderson
Athletics	Bowman,	Evans,	Griffith,	Anderson
Band	Bowman,	Carlson,	Fleming,	Anderson
Dramatics	Bowman,	Carlson,	Dodge,	Griffith
Tenure	Carlson,	Evans,	Fleming,	Griffith
Salaries	Bowman,	Dodge,	Evans,	Fleming
Discipline	Carlson,	Dodge,	Evans,	Anderson

(a) Verify that this arrangement is a balanced incomplete block design.

(b) If Dodge, Bowman, and Carlson are (in that order) appointed chairpersons of the first three committees, how will the chairpersons of the other four committees have to be chosen so that each of the department heads is chairperson of one of the committees?

14.48 Give the degrees of freedom for treatments, blocks, and errors in a two-way analysis of variance with:

(a) $k = 6$ and $n = 7$; (b) $k = 6$ and $n = 10$;
(c) $k = 5$ and $n = 4$; (d) $k = 8$ and $n = 7$.

14.49 The sample data in the following table are the grades in a statistics test obtained by nine college students from three majors who were taught by three different instructors:

	Instructor A	Instructor B	Instructor C
Marketing	77	88	71
Finance	88	97	81
Insurance	85	95	72

Analyze this two-factor experiment, using the 0.05 level of significance.

14.50 The figures in the following 5×5 Latin square are the numbers of minutes engines E_1, E_2, E_3, E_4, and E_5, tuned up by mechanics M_1, M_2, M_3, M_4, and M_5, ran with a gallon of fuel A, B, C, D, or E:

	E_1	E_2	E_3	E_4	E_5
M_1	A 31	B 24	C 20	D 20	E 18
M_2	B 21	C 27	D 23	E 25	A 31
M_3	C 21	D 27	E 25	A 29	B 21
M_4	D 21	E 25	A 33	B 25	C 22
M_5	E 21	A 37	B 24	C 24	D 20

Analyze this Latin square, using the 0.01 level of significance for each of the tests of significance.

14.51   The manager of a restaurant wants to determine whether the sales of chicken dinners depend on how this entree is described on the menu. He has three kinds of menus printed, listing chicken dinners among the other entrees or featuring them as "Chef's Special," or as "Gourmet's Delight," and he intends to use each kind of menu on six different Sundays. Actually, the manager collects only the following data, showing the number of chicken dinners sold on twelve Sundays:

Listed among other entrees:	76	94	85	77
Featured as Chef's Special:	109	117	102	92	115
Featured as Gourmet's Delight:	100	83	102		

Perform a one-way analysis of variance at the 0.05 level of significance.

14.52   A food chemist is considering the use of four spices in a recipe for chili with beans. Let *A, B, C,* and *D* denote that the four spices are used, while *a, b, c,* and *d* denote that they are not used. Then *AbcD,* for example, denotes that the first and fourth spices are used and the second and third are not used.

(a) List the 16 possible ways in which the food chemist can use or not use these four spices.

(b) In how many of the 16 ways are the first two spices both used?

14.53   To study the earnings of faculty members in certain areas from speeches, writing, and consulting, a research worker interviews six groups of faculty members:

(1) four male assistant professors of economics;

(2) four male professors of economics;

(3) four female professors of statistics;

(4) four male associate professors of economics;

(5) four female assistant professors of statistics;

(6) four female associate professors of statistics.

If he combines groups 1 and 5, groups 2 and 3, and groups 4 and 6, and then performs an analysis of variance with $k = 3$ and $n = 8$, and gets a significant value of F, to what sources of variation (sex, rank, or subject) can this be attributed?

14.54   With reference to the preceding exercise, explain why there is no way in which the research worker can use the data to test whether there is a significant difference that can be attributed to sex.

14.55   The following data are the amounts of time (in minutes) that it took a person to drive to work, Monday through Friday, along four different routes:

	Monday	*Tuesday*	*Wednesday*	*Thursday*	*Friday*
Route 1	27	26	26	32	23
Route 2	28	29	27	30	26
Route 3	30	34	31	34	27
Route 4	29	28	31	31	27

Perform a two-way analysis of variance, using the 0.05 level of significance for both tests.

14.56 The following values are the numbers of computer modem cards produced by each of four assembly lines over 12 workdays.

Line													Mean
1	904	852	861	770	877	929	955	836	870	843	847	864	867.33
2	835	857	822	796	808	832	777	830	808	862	843	802	822.67
3	873	803	855	851	856	857	873	830	921	886	834	939	864.83
4	839	849	913	840	843	892	841	807	875	898	976	822	866.25

(a) Give the analysis of variance F statistic and, at the 0.05 level, note whether this is significant. For these data, it happens that

$$SS(Tr) = 17{,}047.2 \quad \text{and} \quad SSE = 71{,}773.2.$$

(b) Analyze these values using the studentized range method at the 0.05 level of significance and comment on the performance of the four assembly lines.

14.12 ☑ REFERENCES

The following are some of the many books that have been written on the subject of analysis of variance:

GUENTHER, W. C., *Analysis of Variance,* Englewood Cliffs, N.J.: Prentice-Hall, Inc., 1964.

SNEDECOR, G. W., and COCHRAN, W. G., *Statistical Methods, 6th ed.* Ames, Iowa: Iowa State University Press, 1973.

Problems relating to the design of experiments are also treated in the above books and in

ANDERSON, V. L., and McLEAN, R. A., *Design of Experiments: A Realistic Approach,* New York: Marcel Dekker. Inc., 1974.

BOX, G. E. P., HUNTER, W. G., and HUNTER, J. S., *Statistics for Experimenters,* New York: John Wiley & Sons, Inc., 1978.

COCHRAN, W. G., and COX, G. M., *Experimental Design, 2nd ed.* New York: John Wiley & Sons, Inc., 1957.

FINNEY, D. J., *An Introduction to the Theory of Experimental Design.* Chicago: The University of Chicago Press, 1960.

FLEISS, J., *The Design and Analysis of Clinical Experiments,* New York. John Wiley & Sons, Inc., 1986.

HICKS, C. R., *Fundamental Concepts in the Design of Experiments, 2nd ed.* New York: Holt, Rinehart and Winston, 1973.

ROMANO, A., *Applied Statistics for Science and Industry.* Boston: Allyn and Bacon, Inc., 1977.

A table of Latin squares for $r = 3, 4, 5, \ldots,$ and 12 may be found in the above-mentioned book by W. G. Cochran and G. M. Cox.

Informally, some questions of experimental design are discussed in Chapters 18 and 19 of

BROOK, R. J., ARNOLD, G. C., HASSARD, T. H., and PRINGLE, R. M., eds., *The Fascination of Statistics.* New York: Marcel Dekker, Inc., 1986.

The topic of multiple comparisons is covered authoritatively in

HOCHBERG, Y., and TAMHANE, A. *Multiple Comparison Procedures.* New York: John Wiley & Sons, Inc., 1987.

REGRESSION

I n many statistical investigations, the main goal is to establish relationships which make it possible to predict one or more variables in terms of others. For instance, studies are made to predict the future sales of a product in terms of its price, a person's weight loss in terms of the number of weeks he or she has been on an 800-calories-per-day diet, family expenditures on medical care in terms of family income, the per capita consumption of certain food items in terms of their nutritional value and the amount of money spent advertising them on television, and so forth.

Of course, it would be ideal if we could predict one quantity exactly in terms of another, but this is seldom possible. In most instances we must be satisfied with predicting averages or expected values. For instance, we cannot predict exactly how much money a specific college graduate will earn ten years after graduation, but given suitable data we can predict the average earnings of all college graduates ten years after graduation. Similarly, we can predict the average yield of a variety of wheat in terms of the total rainfall in July, and we can predict the expected grade-point average of a student starting law school in terms of his or her IQ. This problem of predicting the average value of one variable in terms of the known value of another variable (or the known values of other variables) is called the problem of **regression.** *This term dates back to Francis Galton (1822–1911), who used it first in connection with a study of the relationship between the heights of fathers and sons.*

After a general introduction to curve fitting and the method of least squares in Sections 15.1 and 15.2, questions concerning inferences based on least-squares lines are discussed in Section 15.3, and problems where predictions are based on more than one variable and problems where the relationship is not linear are treated in the two optional sections, Sections 15.4 and 15.5. ◪

15.1   CURVE FITTING

Whenever possible, we try to express, or approximate, relationships between known quantities and quantities that are to be predicted in terms of mathematical equations. This has been very successful in the natural sciences, where it is known, for instance, that at a constant temperature the relationship between the volume, y, and the pressure, x, of a gas is given by the formula

$$y = \frac{k}{x}$$

where k is a numerical constant. Also, it has been shown that the relationship between the size of a culture of bacteria, y, and the length of time, x, it has been exposed to certain environmental conditions is given by the formula

$$y = a \cdot b^x$$

where a and b are numerical constants. More recently, equations like these have also been used to describe relationships in the behavioral sciences, the social sciences, and other fields. For instance, the first of the equations above is often used in economics to describe the relationship between price and quantity demanded, and the second has been used to describe the growth of one's vocabulary or the accumulation of wealth.

Whenever we use observed data to arrive at a mathematical equation that describes the relationship between two variables—a procedure known as **curve fitting**—we must face three kinds of problems:

1. We must decide what kind of curve, and hence what kind of predicting equation we want to use.
2. We must find the particular equation which is best in some sense.
3. We must investigate certain questions regarding the merits of the particular equation, and of predictions made from it.

The second of these problems is discussed in some detail in Section 15.2, and the third in Section 15.3.

The first kind of problem is usually decided by direct inspection of the data. We plot the data on ordinary (arithmetic) graph paper, sometimes on special graph paper with special scales (see Section 15.5), and we decide by visual inspection upon the kind of curve (a straight line, a parabola, ...) that best describes the overall pattern of the data. There are methods by which this can be done more objectively, but they are fairly advanced and they will not be discussed in this book.

Insofar as our work here is concerned, we shall concentrate mainly on **linear equations** in two unknowns. They are of the form

$$y = a + bx$$

where a is the **y-intercept** (the value of y for $x = 0$) and b is the **slope** of the line (namely, the change in y which accompanies an increase of one unit in x)[†]. Linear equations are useful and important not only because many relationships are actually of this form, but also because they often provide close approximations to relationships that would otherwise be difficult to describe in mathematical terms.

The term "linear equation" arises from the fact that the graph of $y = a + bx$ is a straight line. That is, all pairs of values of x and y which satisfy an equation of the form $y = a + bx$ constitute points which fall on a straight line. In practice,

---

[†]In other branches of mathematics, linear equations in two unknowns are often written as $y = mx + b$. Of course, such choices of notation are arbitrary, but the one used widely in statistics, $y = a + bx$, has the advantage that it lends itself readily to generalizations. For instance, the equation of a parabola can be written as $y = a + bx + cx^2$.

FIGURE 15.1

Graph of linear equation.

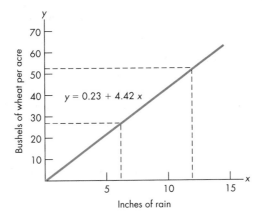

the values of a and b are usually estimated from observed data, and once they have been determined, we can substitute values of x into the equation and calculate the corresponding predicted values of y.

To illustrate, suppose that we are given data on a midwestern county's yield of wheat y (in bushels per acre), and its annual rainfall x (in inches measured from September through August) and that by the method discussed in Section 15.2 we obtain the predicting equation

$$y = 0.23 + 4.42x$$

(see Exercise 15.7). The corresponding graph is shown in Figure 15.1, and it should be observed that for any pair of values of x and y which are such that $y = 0.23 + 4.42x$, we get a point (x, y) which falls on the line. Substituting $x = 6$, for instance, we find that when there is an annual rainfall of 6 inches, we can expect a yield of

$$y = 0.23 + 4.42 \cdot 6 = 26.75$$

bushels per acre; similarly, substituting $x = 12$, we find that when there is an annual rainfall of 12 inches, we can expect a yield of

$$y = 0.23 + 4.42 \cdot 12 = 53.27$$

bushels per acre. The points $(6, 26.75)$ and $(12, 53.27)$ lie on the straight line of Figure 15.1, and this is true for any other points obtained in the same way.

15.2 THE METHOD OF LEAST SQUARES

Once we have decided to fit a straight line to a given set of data, we face the second kind of problem, namely, that of finding the equation of the particular line which in some sense provides the best possible fit. To show what is involved, let us consider the following sample data obtained in a study of the relationship between the number of years that applicants for certain foreign service jobs studied German in high school or college and the scores that they received in a proficiency test in that language:

Number of years x	Score in test y
3	57
4	78
4	72
2	58
5	89
3	63
4	73
5	84
3	75
2	48

If we plot the points that correspond to these ten pairs of values as in Figure 15.2, we observe that, even though the points do not all fall on a straight line, the overall pattern of the relationship is reasonably well described by the straight line. There is no noticeable departure from linearity in the scatter of the points, so we feel justified in deciding that a straight line is a suitable description of the underlying relationship.

We now face the problem of finding the equation of the line that in some sense provides the best fit to the data and which, it is hoped, will later yield the best possible predictions of *y* from *x*. Logically speaking, there is no limit to the number of straight lines that can be drawn on a piece of graph paper. Some of these lines would fit the data so poorly that we could not consider them seriously, but many others would seem to provide more or less good fits, and the problem is to find the one line which fits the data best in some well-defined sense. If all the points actually fall on a straight line there is no problem, but this is an extreme case rarely encountered in practice. In general, we have to be satisfied with a line having certain desirable properties, short of perfection.

The criterion which, today, is used almost exclusively for defining a best fit dates back to the early part of the nineteenth century and the work of the

FIGURE 15.2

Data on number of years German studied and score on test.

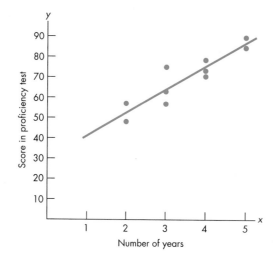

French mathematician Adrien Legendre; it is known as the **method of least squares.** As will be used here, this method requires that the line that we fit to our data be such that the sum of the squares of the vertical distances from the points to the line is a minimum.

To explain why this is done, let us refer to the following data which might represent the numbers of correct answers, x and y, that four students got on two parts of a multiple-choice test:

x	y
4	6
9	10
1	2
6	2

In Figure 15.3 we plotted the corresponding data points, and through them we drew two lines to describe the overall pattern.

If we use the horizontal line in the diagram on the left to predict y for the given values of x, we would get $y = 5$ in each case, and the errors of these predictions are

$$6 - 5 = 1, \quad 10 - 5 = 5, \quad 2 - 5 = -3 \quad \text{and } 2 - 5 = -3$$

In Figure 15.3, they are the vertical distances from the points to the line.

The sum of these errors is

$$1 + 5 + (-3) + (-3) = 0$$

but this is no indication of their size and we find ourselves in a position similar to that on page 83, which led to the definition of the standard deviation. Squaring the errors as we squared the deviations from the mean on page 83, we find that the sum of the squares of the errors is

$$1^2 + 5^2 + (-3)^2 + (-3)^2 = 44.$$

Now let us consider the line in the diagram on the right, which was drawn so that it passes through the points (1, 2) and (9, 10); as can easily be verified, its equation is $y = 1 + x$. Judging by eye, this line seems to provide a much better

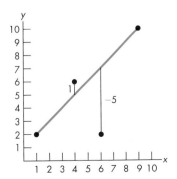

fit than the horizontal line in the diagram on the left, and if we use it to predict *y* for the given values of *x*, we would get

$$1 + 4 = 5, \quad 1 + 9 = 10, \quad 1 + 1 = 2, \quad \text{and} \quad 1 + 6 = 7$$

The errors of these predictions, which in the figure on the right are the vertical distances from the points to the line, are

$$6 - 5 = 1, \quad 10 - 10 = 0, \quad 2 - 2 = 0, \quad \text{and} \quad 2 - 7 = -5$$

The sum of these errors is

$$1 + 0 + 0 + (-5) = -4,$$

which is numerically greater than the sum we obtained for the errors made with the other line of Figure 15.3, but this is of no consequence. The sum of the squares of the errors is now

$$1^2 + 0^2 + 0^2 + (-5)^2 = 26,$$

and this is much less than the 44 which we obtained before. In this sense, the line on the right provides a much better fit to the data than the horizontal line on the left.

We can go even one step further, and ask for the equation of the line for which the sum of the squares of the errors is least, and in Exercise 15.12 on page 498 the reader is asked to verify that its equation is $y = \frac{15}{17} + \frac{14}{17}x$ for our example. We refer to this line as a **least-squares line.**

To show how a least-squares line is actually fitted to a set of **data points,** that is, to a set of paired data, let us consider *n* pairs of numbers $(x_1, y_1), (x_2, y_2), \ldots,$ and (x_n, y_n), which might represent such things as the thrust and the speed of *n* rockets, the height and weight of *n* persons, the reading rate and reading comprehension of *n* students, or the number of persons unemployed in two cities in *n* years. If we write the equation of the line as

$$\hat{y} = a + bx$$

where the symbol $\hat{y}$ (*y*-hat) is used to distinguish between an observed value of *y* and the corresponding value $\hat{y}$ on the line, the least-squares criterion requires that we minimize the sum of the squares of the differences between the *y*'s and the $\hat{y}$'s (see Figure 15.4). This means that we must find the numerical values of the constants *a* and *b* appearing in the equation $\hat{y} = a + bx$ for which

$$\Sigma(y - \hat{y})^2 = \Sigma[y - (a + bx)]^2$$

is as small as possible. As it takes calculus or fairly tedious algebra to find the expressions for *a* and *b* that minimize $\Sigma (y - \hat{y})^2$, let us merely state the result that they are given by the solutions for *a* and *b* of the following system of two linear equations:

Normal Equations	
	$\Sigma y = na + b(\Sigma x)$
	$\Sigma xy = a(\Sigma x) + b(\Sigma x^2)$

FIGURE 15.4

Least-squares line.

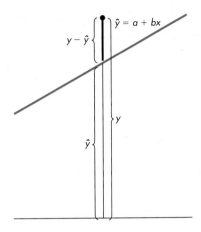

In these equations, called the **normal equations,** n is the number of pairs of observations, $\Sigma\, x$ and $\Sigma\, y$ are the sums of the observed x's and y's, $\Sigma\, x^2$ is the sum of the squares of the x's, and $\Sigma\, xy$ is the sum of the products obtained by multiplying each x by the corresponding y.

Example

Fit a least-squares line to the data on page 488, which pertain to the numbers of years that certain applicants for foreign service jobs have studied German in high school or college and the scores they received in a proficiency test in that language.

solution

The sums needed for substitution into the normal equations are obtained by performing the calculations shown in the following table:

Number of years x	Test score y	x^2	xy
3	57	9	171
4	78	16	312
4	72	16	288
2	58	4	116
5	89	25	445
3	63	9	189
4	73	16	292
5	84	25	420
3	75	9	225
2	48	4	96
35	697	133	2,554

(There are many desk calculators, or hand-held calculators, on which the various sums can be accumulated directly, so that there is no need to fill in all the details.

Indeed, on some calculators the values of a and b can be obtained directly by recording the data and then pressing the appropriate buttons.) Substituting

$$\Sigma\, x = 35, \quad \Sigma\, y = 697, \quad \Sigma\, x^2 = 133, \quad \Sigma\, xy = 2{,}554, \quad \text{and} \quad n = 10$$

into the normal equations, we get

$$697 = 10a + 35b$$
$$2{,}554 = 35a + 133b$$

and we must now solve these two simultaneous linear equations for a and b. There are many ways in which this can be done. Using the so-called method of elimination, we get $a = 31.55$ and $b = 10.90$. ◪ ◪ ◪

As an alternative to this procedure we now develop a number of formulas that will be extremely useful in later calculations that we will make in connection with least-squares problems.

Useful Formulas for Least-squares Calculations

$$\bar{x} = \frac{\Sigma\, x}{n}, \qquad \bar{y} = \frac{\Sigma\, y}{n}$$

$$S_{xx} = \Sigma\, x^2 - \frac{(\Sigma\, x)^2}{n}, \qquad S_{yy} = \Sigma\, y^2 - \frac{(\Sigma\, y)^2}{n}, \qquad S_{xy} = \Sigma\, xy - \frac{(\Sigma\, x)\cdot(\Sigma\, y)}{n}$$

The formulas for $\bar{x}$ and $\bar{y}$ are familiar. The new formulas S_{xx}, S_{xy}, and S_{yy} will appear in many of the formulas that follow. They provide an easy numerical technique for solving the normal equations.

Solutions of Normal Equations

$$b = \frac{S_{xy}}{S_{xx}}, \qquad a = \bar{y} - b\bar{x}$$

The computational process for finding the least-squares estimates (the solutions of the normal equations) involves several steps. First find the values of the five sums

$$\Sigma\, x, \quad \Sigma\, y, \quad \Sigma\, x^2, \quad \Sigma\, y^2, \quad \text{and} \quad \Sigma\, xy$$

Then find the five quantities

$$\bar{x}, \quad \bar{y}, \quad S_{xx}, \quad S_{xy}, \quad S_{yy}$$

Finally, use the formulas above to find b and a. Note that you must find b first since a is calculated in terms of b. The quantity S_{yy} has not been used yet, but will appear in Section 15.3.

Example

Use these formulas to rework the preceding example.

solution

First substituting $n = 10$ and the various sums obtained in the table on page 491 into the formulas for S_{xx} and S_{xy}, we get

$$S_{xx} = 133 - \frac{1}{10}(35)^2 = 10.5$$

$$S_{xy} = 2{,}554 - \frac{1}{10}(35)(697) = 114.5$$

Thus,

$$b = \frac{114.5}{10.5} \approx 10.90 \quad \text{and} \quad a = \frac{697}{10} - 10.90\,\frac{35}{10} = 31.55 \qquad \blacksquare\ \blacksquare\ \blacksquare$$

As you may well suspect, there exists computer software for fitting least-squares lines. A printout obtained by means of such a program is shown in Figure 15.5. The values of a and b are shown to be 31.533 and 10.905 in the col-

FIGURE 15.5

Computer printout for the last squares line.

(MINITAB 10 for Windows)

```
MTB > print C1 C2

Data Display

Row   C1   C2

 1    3    57
 2    4    78
 3    4    72
 4    2    58
 5    5    89
 6    3    63
 7    4    73
 8    5    84
 9    3    75
10    2    48

MTB  >  Regress c2 1 c1;
SUBC >      Constant.

Regression Analysis

The regression equation is
C2 = 31.5 + 10.9 C1

Predictor      Coef     Stdev    t-ratio        p
Constant     31.533     6.360       4.96    0.000
C1           10.905     1.744       6.25    0.000

s = 5.651    R-sq = 83.0%    R-sq(adj) = 80.9%

Analysis of Variance

SOURCE          DF        SS        MS       F        p
Regression       1    1248.6    1248.6   39.09    0.000
Error            8     255.5      31.9
Total            9    1504.1

Unusual Observations
Obs.       C1       C2      Fit    Stdev.Fit    Residual    St.Resid
  9      3.00    75.00    64.25         1.99       10.75       2.03R

R denotes an obs. with a large st. resid.
```

umn headed "Coef," and the differences between these values and those obtained above the figure are due to rounding. The bottom part of the printout is not needed here, but we shall refer to it in Chapter 16.

Once we have determined the equation of a least-squares line, we can use it to make predictions.

Example

Use the least-squares line $\hat{y} = 31.55 + 10.90x$ to predict the proficiency score of an applicant who has studied German in high school or college for two years.

solution

Substituting $x = 2$ into the equation, we get

$$\hat{y} = 31.55 + 10.90(2) = 53.35$$

and this is the best prediction we can make in the least-squares sense.   ◤ ◤ ◤

When we make a prediction like this, we cannot really expect that we will always hit the answer right on the nose; in fact, we cannot possibly be right when the answer has to be a whole number, as in our illustration, and our prediction is 53.35. With reference to this example, it would be unreasonable to expect that every applicant who has studied German for a given number of years will get the same score in the proficiency test; indeed, the data on page 488 show that this is not the case. Thus, to make meaningful predictions based on least-squares lines, we must look upon the values of $\hat{y}$ obtained by substituting given values of x as averages, or expected values. Interpreted in this way, we refer to least-squares lines as **regression lines,** or better as **estimated regression lines,** since the values of a and b are estimated on the basis of sample data. Questions relating to the goodness of these estimates are discussed in Section 15.3.

In this section we have considered only the problem of fitting a straight line to paired data. More generally, the method of least squares can also be used to fit other kinds of curves and to derive predicting equations in more than two unknowns. The problem of fitting some curves other than straight lines by the method of least squares is discussed briefly in Section 15.5, and a simple example of a predicting equation in more than two unknowns is given in Section 15.4.

◢ EXERCISES

15.1   A dog which had six hours of obedience training made five mistakes at a dog show, a dog which had twelve hours of obedience training made six mistakes, and a dog which had eighteen hours of obedience training made only one mistake. If we let x denote the number of hours of obedience training and y the number of mistakes, which of the two lines

$$y = 10 - \frac{1}{2}x \quad \text{or} \quad y = 8 - \frac{1}{3}x$$

provides a better fit to the three data points in the sense of least squares?

15.2   With reference to the preceding exercise, is the line which provides the better fit a least-squares line?

15.3 The following table shows how many weeks six persons worked at an automobile inspection station and the number of cars each one inspected between noon and 2 p.m. on a given day:

Number of weeks employed x	Number of cars inspected y
2	13
7	21
9	23
1	14
5	15
12	21

For these data,

$$\Sigma\, x = 36, \quad \Sigma\, x^2 = 304, \quad \Sigma\, y = 107, \quad \Sigma\, y^2 = 2{,}001, \quad \text{and} \quad \Sigma\, xy = 721$$

(a) Find the equation of the least-squares line which will enable us to predict y in terms of x.

(b) Use part (a) to estimate how many cars someone who has been working at the inspection station for eight weeks can be expected to inspect during the given two-hour period.

(c) Explain why you would not use the results of part (a) to predict the number of cars that would be inspected during the given two-hour period by someone who has been working at the inspection station for 120 weeks.

15.4 The following table shows the number of hours a runner has run during each of eight consecutive weeks and the corresponding times in which she ran a mile at the end of the week:

Number of hours run	Times of mile (minutes)
13	5.2
15	5.1
18	4.9
20	4.6
19	4.7
17	4.8
21	4.6
16	4.9

For these data,

$$\Sigma\, x = 139, \quad \Sigma\, x^2 = 2{,}465, \quad \Sigma\, y = 38.8, \quad \Sigma\, y^2 = 188.52, \quad \text{and} \quad \Sigma\, xy = 670.2$$

(a) Find the equation of the least-squares line which will allow us to predict the runner's time for the mile from the number of hours she ran that week.

(b) Predict how fast the runner would run a mile at the end of a week in which she ran for 18 hours.

(c) Explain why your solution to part (b) is different from the 4.9 minutes which she actually achieved at the end of the third week (during which she ran for 18 hours).

15.5 Market research shows that if a new toy is priced at $1.50 it will yield a profit of $72,000, if it is priced at $2.00 it will yield a profit of $40,000, and if it is priced at $2.40 it will yield a profit of $28,800. Discerning a fairly linear pattern, the toy manufacturer fits a least-squares line and gets

$$\hat{y} = 142{,}623 - 48{,}656x$$

where x is the price in dollars and y is the profit in dollars. Can the toy manufacturer conclude that if he literally gives the toys away at ten cents apiece, he can expect a profit of

$$\hat{y} = 142{,}623 - 48{,}656(0.10) = \$137{,}757?$$

15.6   The following data pertain to the chlorine residue in a swimming pool at various times after it has been treated with chemicals:

Number of hours	Chlorine residue (parts per million)
0	2.2
2	1.8
4	1.5
6	1.4
8	1.1
10	1.1
12	0.9

For these data,

$$\Sigma\, x = 42, \quad \Sigma\, x^2 = 364, \quad \Sigma\, y = 10, \quad \Sigma\, y^2 = 15.52, \quad \text{and} \quad \Sigma\, xy = 48.6$$

The reading at 0 hour was taken immediately after the chemical treatment was completed.

(a) Fit a least-squares line from which we can predict the chlorine residue in terms of the number of hours since the pool has been treated with chemicals.

(b) Use the equation of the least-squares line to estimate the chlorine residue in the pool 5 hours after it has been treated with chemicals.

(c) Use the equation of the least-squares line to estimate the chlorine residue in the pool 8 hours after it has been treated with chemicals. Why is your answer somewhat different from the 1.1 parts per million actually observed at 8 hours?

(d) Suppose that you learned that the data values given above were all taken over a 12-hour period on the same day. Why might the results parts (a), (b), and (c) be misleading?

15.7   Verify that the equation of the example on page 487 can be obtained by fitting a least-squares line to the following data:

Rainfall (inches)	Yield of wheat (bushels per acre)
12.9	62.5
7.2	28.7
11.3	52.2
18.6	80.6
8.8	41.6
10.3	44.5
15.9	71.3
13.1	54.4

For these data,

$$\Sigma\, x = 98.1, \quad \Sigma\, x^2 = 1{,}299.85, \quad \Sigma\, y = 435.8, \quad \Sigma\, y^2 = 25{,}705, \quad \text{and} \quad \Sigma\, xy = 5{,}772.6504$$

15.8 The following are the midterm and final examination grades of eight students in a course in European history:

Midterm	Final examination
75	81
66	57
92	95
86	77
65	71
44	62
60	63
79	84

For these data,

$$\Sigma\, x = 567, \quad \Sigma\, x^2 = 41{,}843, \quad \Sigma\, y = 590, \quad \Sigma\, y^2 = 44{,}674, \quad \text{and} \quad \Sigma\, xy = 42{,}958$$

(a) Find the equation of the least-squares line which will enable us to predict final examination grades in this course from midterm grades.

(b) Use the least-squares equation obtained in part (a) to predict the final examination grade of a student who got a 68 on the midterm test.

15.9 1983 government statistics show that for couples with 0, 1, 2, or 3 children, the relationship between the number of children, x, and family income in dollars, y, is fairly well described by the least-squares line

$$\hat{y} = 22{,}000 + 2{,}500x$$

If a childless couple has twins, will this increase their income by

$$2{,}500(2) = \$5{,}000?$$

15.10 The following show the improvement (gain in reading speed) of eight students in a speed-reading program, and the number of weeks they have been in the program:

Number of weeks x	Speed gain (words per minute) y
3	86
5	118
2	49
8	193
6	164
9	232
3	73
4	109

For these data,

$$\Sigma\, x = 40, \quad \Sigma\, x^2 = 244, \quad \Sigma\, y = 1{,}024, \quad \Sigma\, y^2 = 158{,}900, \quad \text{and} \quad \Sigma\, xy = 6{,}217$$

(a) Plot the eight data points to verify that it is reasonable to assume that the relationship between average speed gain and time is linear.

(b) Find the equation of the least-squares line which will enable us to predict speed gain from the number of weeks that a student has been in the program.

(c) Use the results of part (b) to predict the speed gain of a student after he or she has been in the program for seven weeks.

15.11   A sociologist exploring the relationship between family size and food bills selected at random six female customers at a supermarket. Each selected customer was asked how many children under the age of 18 lived with her, and she was also asked the number of quarts of milk consumed weekly by her household, on average. The data resulting from this inquiry are these:

Number of children under 18	Weekly milk consumption (quarts)
2	14
2	20
2	9
2	25
2	16
2	14

The sociologist wanted to find the least-squares line which would enable her to predict the milk consumption from the number of children. What computational problems will be encountered?

15.12   Verify for the example on page 489 that the equation of the least-squares line is $y = \frac{15}{17} + \frac{14}{17}x$, and calculate the corresponding sum of the squares of the vertical deviations from the points to the line. How does this sum of squares compare with those obtained for the other two lines on pages 489 and 490?

15.13   A study of the relationship between the IQ's of husbands and wives yielded the least-squares equation $\hat{y} = 48 + 0.5x$, where x is the IQ of the husband and y is the IQ of the wife. Given that this equation is based on the following data:

x	y
90	90
114	102
102	

where one of the y-values has been misplaced, find the missing value of y.

15.14   Raw material used in the production of a synthetic fiber is stored in a place which has no humidity control. Measurements of the relative humidity in the storage place and the moisture content of a sample of the raw material (both in percentages) on 12 days yielded the following results:

Humidity	Moisture content
46	12
53	14
37	11
42	13
34	10
29	8
60	17
44	12
41	10
48	15
33	9
40	13

For these data,

$$\Sigma\, x = 507, \quad \Sigma\, x^2 = 22{,}265, \quad \Sigma\, y = 144, \quad \Sigma\, y^2 = 1{,}802 \quad \text{and} \quad \Sigma\, xy = 6{,}314$$

(a) Fit a least-squares line from which we can predict the moisture content in terms of the humidity.

(b) Use the result of part (a) to estimate the moisture content when the relative humidity is 38 percent.

15.15 Suppose that in the preceding exercise we had wanted to estimate what humidity will yield a moisture content of 10 percent. We could substitute $\hat{y} = 10$ into the equation obtained in part (a) of the preceding exercise and solve for x, but this would not provide an estimate in the least-squares sense. To make the best possible least-squares predictions, or estimates, of humidity in terms of moisture content, we denote the moisture contents by x, the humidity readings by y, and then fit a least-squares line to these data. Find the equation of this line and use it to estimate the humidity which will yield a moisture content of 10 percent.

15.16 When the x's are equally spaced (that is, when the differences between successive values of x are all equal), the calculation of a and b can be simplified by coding the x's by assigning them the values

$$..., \quad -3, \quad -2, \quad -1, \quad 0, \quad 1, \quad 2, \quad 3, \quad ...$$

when n is odd, and the values

$$..., \quad -5, \quad -3, \quad -1, \quad 1, \quad 3, \quad 5, \quad ...$$

when n is even. With this coding, the sum of the x's is zero, and the formulas for a and b on page 492 become

$$a = \frac{\Sigma\, y}{n} \quad \text{and} \quad b = \frac{\Sigma\, xy}{\Sigma\, x^2}$$

Of course, the equation of the resulting least-squares line expresses y in terms of the coded x's, and we have to account for this when we use the equation to make predictions.

(a) During its first five years of operation, a company's gross income from sales was 1.4, 2.1, 2.6, 3.5, and 3.7 million dollars. Fit a least-squares line and, assuming that the trend continues, predict the company's gross income from sales during its sixth year of operation.

(b) At the end of eight successive years, a manufacturing company had 1.0, 1.7, 2.3, 3.1, 3.5, 3.4, 3.9, and 4.7 million dollars invested in plants and equipment. Fit a least-squares line and, assuming that the trend continues, predict the company's investment in plants and equipment at the end of the tenth year.

15.17 Ten bright students from a certain high school were ranked among themselves according to their performance on the PSAT test and then again according to their performance on the SAT test, for which they had extensive tutoring. The results were as follows:

Rank on PSAT test x	Rank on SAT test	Change in rank y
1	4	−3
2	7	−5
3	5	−2
4	3	1
5	8	−3
6	10	−4
7	1	6
8	2	6
9	9	0
10	6	4

For these data,

$$\Sigma\, x = 55, \quad \Sigma\, x^2 = 385, \quad \Sigma\, y = 0, \quad \Sigma\, y^2 = 152, \quad \Sigma\, xy = 76$$

(a) Verify that the equation of the least-squares line fit to these data is

$$\hat{y} = -5.07 + 0.92x$$

(b) Substitute $x = 1$ and $x = 10$ into the equation obtained in part (a), and thus determine the expected change in rank of the students who ranked first and tenth on the PSAT test.

(c) Can we conclude that the extensive tutoring had a positive effect on the lower-scoring students and an adverse effect on the higher-scoring students?

⊞ 15.18   The following are alternative formulas for the symbolic solution of the two normal equations:

$$a = \frac{(\Sigma\, y)(\Sigma\, x^2) - (\Sigma\, x)(\Sigma\, xy)}{n(\Sigma\, x^2) - (\Sigma\, x)^2}, \qquad b = \frac{n(\Sigma\, xy) - (\Sigma\, x)(\Sigma\, y)}{n(\Sigma\, x^2) - (\Sigma\, x)^2}$$

(a) Use these formulas to recalculate the values of a and b obtained for the example on pages 491–492.

(b) Use these formulas to rework Exercise 15.8.

15.3   REGRESSION ANALYSIS

In the preceding section we use a least-squares line to predict that someone who has studied German in high school or college for two years will score 53.35 in the proficiency test, but even if we interpret the line correctly as a regression line (that is, treat predictions made from it as averages or expected values), there are questions that remain to be answered. For instance,

> How good are the values we obtained for a and b in the least-squares equation $\hat{y} = 31.55 + 10.90x$?

> How good an estimate is $\hat{y} = 53.35$ of the average score of persons who have had two years of German in high school or college?

After all, $a = 31.55$, $b = 10.90$, and $\hat{y} = 53.35$ for $x = 2$ are only estimates based on sample data, and if we base our work on ten other applicants for such foreign service jobs, the method of least squares would probably yield different values for a and b, and a different value for $\hat{y}$ for $x = 2$. Also, for making predictions, we might ask

> Can we give an interval for which we can assert with some degree of confidence that it will contain the score of a person who has studied German in high school or college for two years?

With regard to the first of these questions, we said that $a = 31.55$ and $b = 10.90$ are "only estimates based on sample data," and this implies the existence of corresponding true values, usually denoted by α and β and referred to as the **regression coefficients.** Accordingly, there is also a true regression line

$$\mu_{y|x} = \alpha + \beta x$$

where $\mu_{y|x}$ is the true mean of y for a given value of x. To distinguish between the Roman letters (a, b) and the Greek letters (α, β), we refer to a and b as the **estimated regression coefficients.**

To clarify the idea of a true regression line, let us consider Figure 15.6, where we have drawn the distributions of y for several values of x. With reference to our numerical example, these curves are the distributions of the proficiency scores of persons who have had one, two, or three years of German in high school or college, and to complete the picture we can visualize similar curves for all other values of x within the range of values under consideration. Note that the means of all the distributions of Figure 15.6 lie on the true regression line $\mu_{y|x} = \alpha + \beta x$.

In **linear regression analysis** we assume that the x's are constants, not values of random variables, and that for each value of x the variable to be predicted, y, has a certain distribution (as pictured in Figure 15.6) whose mean is $\alpha + \beta x$. In **normal regression analysis** we assume, furthermore, that these distributions are all normal distributions with the same standard deviations σ.

Based on these assumptions, it can be shown that the estimated regression coefficients a and b, obtained by the method of least squares, are values of random variables having normal distributions with the means α and β and the standard deviations

$$\sigma\sqrt{\frac{1}{n} + \frac{\bar{x}^2}{S_{xx}}} \quad \text{and} \quad \frac{\sigma}{\sqrt{S_{xx}}}$$

The estimated regression coefficients a and b are, however, not statistically independent. Note that both of these standard error formulas require that we estimate σ, the common standard deviation of the normal distributions pictured in Figure 15.6. Otherwise, the x's are assumed to be constants, so there is no problem in determining $\bar{x}$ and S_{xx}. The estimate of σ we shall use is called the **standard error of estimate** and it is denoted by s_e. Its formula is

FIGURE 15.6

Distributions of y for

given values of x.

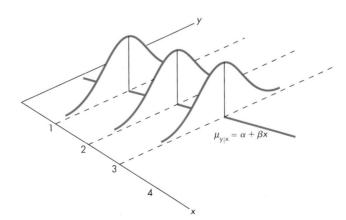

$$s_e = \sqrt{\frac{\Sigma\,(y - \hat{y})^2}{n - 2}}$$

where, again, the y's are the observed values of y and the $\hat{y}$'s are the corresponding values on the least-squares line. Observe that s_e^2 is the sum of the squares of the vertical deviations from the points to the line (namely, the quantity which we minimized by the method of least squares) divided by $n - 2$.

The formula above defines s_e, but in practice we calculate its value by means of the computing formula

Standard Error of Estimate
(Computing Formula)

$$s_e = \sqrt{\frac{S_{yy} - \dfrac{(S_{xy})^2}{S_{xx}}}{n - 2}}$$

The symbol S_{yy} was defined on page 492.

Example

Find s_e for the least-squares line which we fit to the data pertaining to the numbers of years that certain applicants for foreign service jobs have studied German in high school or college and the scores which they received in a proficiency test in that language.

solution

Since $n = 10$ and we indicated on page 493 that $S_{xx} = 10.5$ and $S_{xy} = 114.5$, the only other quantity needed is S_{yy}. Calculating

$$\Sigma\,y^2 = 57^2 + 78^2 + \cdots + 48^2 = 50{,}085$$

and copying $\Sigma\,y = 697$ from the table on page 491, we get

$$S_{yy} = 50{,}085 - \tfrac{1}{10}(697)^2 = 1{,}504.1$$

and hence

$$s_e = \sqrt{\frac{1{,}504.1 - (114.5)^2/10.5}{10 - 2}} \approx 5.651$$

The result we obtained here can also be read from the printout of Figure 15.5.

If we make all the assumptions of normal regression analysis (see page 501), inferences about the regression coefficients α and β can be based on the statistics

Inferences About
Regression Coefficients

$$t = \frac{a - \alpha}{s_e\sqrt{\dfrac{1}{n} + \dfrac{\bar{x}^2}{S_{xx}}}}, \qquad t = \frac{b - \beta}{\dfrac{s_e}{\sqrt{S_{xx}}}}$$

whose sampling distributions are t distributions with $n - 2$ degrees of freedom. Note that the quantities in the denominators are estimates of the corresponding standard errors with s_e substituted for σ.

The following example illustrates how we test hypotheses about either of the regression coefficients α and β.

Example

Suppose that it has been claimed that $\beta = 12.5$ in the example dealing with the applicants for the foreign service jobs and their proficiency in German, and that the whole study was actually made to test this claim at the 0.05 level of significance.

solution

1. H_0: $\beta = 12.5$
   H_A: $\beta \neq 12.5$

2. $\alpha = 0.05$

3. Reject the null hypothesis if $t \leq -2.306$ or $t \geq 2.306$, where

$$t = \frac{b - \beta}{s_e/\sqrt{S_{xx}}}$$

and 2.306 is the value of $t_{0.025}$ for $10 - 2 = 8$ degrees of freedom; otherwise, accept the null hypothesis or reserved judgment.

4. Since we know from page 493 and the above that $b = 10.90$, $S_{xx} = 10.5$, and $s_e = 5.651$, substitution of these values together with $\beta = 12.5$ yields

$$t = \frac{10.90 - 12.5}{5.651/\sqrt{10.5}} \approx -0.92$$

5. Since $t = -0.92$ falls on the interval from -2.306 and 2.306, the null hypothesis cannot be rejected; that is, there is no real evidence that the slope is not $\beta = 12.5$.   ◰ ◰ ◰

We could have saved ourselves some work in the preceding example by referring to the printout of Figure 15.5 on page 493. In the column that is headed "Stdev" it shows that the estimated standard error, the quantity which goes into the denominator of the t statistic, is 1.744, so we can write directly

$$t = \frac{10.90 - 12.5}{1.744} \approx -0.92$$

Tests concerning the regression coefficient α are performed in the same way, except that we use the first of the two t statistics on page 502. In most practical applications, however, the regression coefficient α is not of much interest—it is just the y-intercept, namely, the value of y which corresponds to $x = 0$. In many cases it has no real meaning.

To construct confidence intervals for the regression coefficients α and β, we substitute for the middle term of $-t_{\alpha/2} < t < t_{\alpha/2}$ the appropriate t statistic from page 502. Then, simple algebra leads to the formulas

Confidence Limits for Regression Coefficients

$$a \pm t_{\alpha/2} \cdot s_e \sqrt{\frac{1}{n} + \frac{\bar{x}^2}{S_{xx}}} \quad \text{and} \quad b \pm t_{\alpha/2} \cdot \frac{s_e}{\sqrt{S_{xx}}}$$

where the degree of confidence is $(1 - \alpha)100$ percent and $t_{\alpha/2}$ is the entry in Table II for $n - 2$ degrees of freedom.

Example

The following data show the average numbers of hours that six students spent on homework per week and their grade-point indexes for the courses they took in a given semester:

Hours spent on homework x	Grade-point index y
15	2.0
28	2.7
13	1.3
20	1.9
4	0.9
10	1.7

Construct a 95 percent confidence interval for β, the amount by which a student in the population sampled can expect to raise his or her grade-point index by studying an extra hour per week.

solution

First calculating the necessary sums we get

$$\Sigma x = 90, \quad \Sigma y = 10.5, \quad \Sigma x^2 = 1,694, \quad \Sigma xy = 181.1, \quad \text{and} \quad \Sigma y^2 = 20.29$$

so that

$$S_{xx} = 1,694 - \tfrac{1}{6}(90)^2 = 344$$

$$S_{yy} = 20.29 - \tfrac{1}{6}(10.5)^2 = 1.915$$

$$S_{xy} = 181.1 - \tfrac{1}{6}(90)(10.5) = 23.6$$

Then we get

$$b = \frac{23.6}{344} \approx 0.0686, \quad s_e = \sqrt{\frac{1.915 - \frac{(23.6)^2}{344}}{6 - 2}} \approx 0.272$$

and since $t_{0.025} = 2.776$ for $6 - 2 = 4$ degrees of freedom, we arrive at the confidence limits

$$0.0686 \pm 2.776 \cdot \frac{0.272}{\sqrt{344}}$$

or 0.0686 ± 0.0407. Rounding to three decimals, we can write the 95 percent confidence interval for β as

$$0.028 < \beta < 0.109$$

This confidence interval is rather wide, and this is due to two things—the very small size of the sample and the variation measured by s_e, namely, the variation among the grade-point indexes of students doing the same amount of homework. ◪ ◪ ◪

The work we have done here can be simplified greatly by using a printout like that of Figure 15.5 on page 493. For our new example we get the printout shown in Figure 15.7, and we find that $b = 0.0686$ and that the estimate of the standard error, by which we have to multiply $t_{\alpha/2}$, is 0.01467. Using again $t_{0.025} = 2.776$, we thus get the confidence limits

$$0.0686 \pm 2.776(0.01467) \quad \text{or} \quad 0.0686 \pm 0.0407$$

This is precisely the value we had before.

To answer the second question asked on page 500, the one concerning the estimation, or prediction, of the average value of y for a given value of x, we use

```
MTB > print c1 c2

Data Display

Row      C1      C2

  1      15      2.0
  2      28      2.7
  3      13      1.3
  4      20      1.9
  5       4      0.9
  6      10      1.7

MTB  >  Regress c2 1 c1;
SUBC >       Constant.

Regression Analysis

The regression equation is
C2 = 0.721 + 0.0686 C1

Predictor         Coef        Stdev       t-ratio          p
Constant        0.7209       0.2464          2.93      0.043
C1              0.06860      0.01467         4.68      0.009

s = 0.2720      R-sq = 84.5%        R-sq(adj) = 80.7%

Analysis of Variance

SOURCE           DF          SS           MS          F          p
Regression        1      1.6191       1.6191      21.88      0.009
Error             4      0.2959       0.0740
Total             5      1.9150
```

a method that is very similar to the one just discussed. Basing our argument on another t statistic, we arrive at the following $(1 - \alpha)100$ percent confidence limits for $\mu_{y|x_0}$, the mean of y when $x = x_0$:

Confidence Limits for Mean of y When x = x₀	$(a + bx_0) \pm t_{\alpha/2} \cdot s_e \sqrt{\dfrac{1}{n} + \dfrac{(x_0 - \bar{x})^2}{S_{xx}}}$

As before, the number of degrees of freedom is $n - 2$ and the corresponding value of $t_{\alpha/2}$ may be read from Table II.

Example

Referring again to the data on page 488, suppose that we want to estimate the mean proficiency score of applicants who have had two years of German in high school or college. Construct a 99 percent confidence interval for this mean.

solution

Copying

$$\Sigma x = 35, \quad S_{xx} = 10.5, \quad a + bx_0 = 31.55 + 10.90(2) = 53.35, \quad s_e = 5.651$$

from pages 493 and 502, and substituting these values together with

$$n = 10, \quad \bar{x} = \frac{35}{10} = 3.5, \quad \text{and} \quad t_{0.005} = 3.355$$

(for $10 - 2 = 8$ degrees of freedom) into the confidence interval formula, we get

$$53.35 \pm (3.355)(5.651) \cdot \sqrt{\frac{1}{10} + \frac{(2 - 3.5)^2}{10.5}}$$

or 53.35 ± 10.63. Hence, we can write the 99 percent confidence interval for the mean proficiency scores of applicants with two years of German in high school or college as

$$42.72 < \mu_{y|x} < 63.98$$

The third question asked on page 500 differs from the other two in that it does not concern the estimation of a population parameter, but the prediction of a single future observation. The endpoints of an interval for which we can assert with a given degree of confidence that it will contain such an observation are called **limits of prediction,** and the calculation of such limits will answer the third kind of question. Basing our argument on yet another t statistic, we arrive at the following $(1 - \alpha)100$ percent limits of prediction for a value of y when $x = x_0$:

Limits of Prediction	$(a + bx_0) \pm t_{\alpha/2} \cdot s_e \sqrt{1 + \dfrac{1}{n} + \dfrac{(x_0 - \bar{x})^2}{S_{xx}}}$

Again, the number of degrees of freedom is $n - 2$, and the corresponding value of $t_{\alpha/2}$ may be read from Table II.

Example

Referring again to the example on page 488, find 99 percent limits of prediction for the proficiency score of an applicant who has studied German in high school or college for two years.

solution

Noting that the only difference between the limits above and the confidence limits for $\mu_{y|x_0}$ is that we add 1 to the quantity under the square-root sign, we can immediately write the limits of prediction as

$$53.35 \pm (3.355)(5.51) \cdot \sqrt{1 + \frac{1}{10} + \frac{(2 - 3.5)^2}{10.5}} \quad \text{or} \quad 53.35 \pm 21.74$$

Thus, the 99 percent limits of prediction are 31.61 and 75.09.

The interval for $\mu_{y|x}$, the mean score of all students who have had two years of German, is considerably shorter than the interval of the previous example, which applies to a prediction for one person.

Let us remind the reader that all these methods are based on the very stringent assumptions of normal regression analysis. Furthermore, if we base more than one inference on the same data, we will run into problems with regard to the levels of significance and/or degrees of confidence. The random variables on which the various procedures are based are clearly not independent.

EXERCISES

15.19 With reference to Exercise 15.3 on page 495, test the null hypothesis $\beta = 1.2$ (namely, the hypothesis that each additional week on the job adds 1.2 to the number of cars a person can be expected to inspect in the given period of time) against the alternative hypothesis $\beta < 1.2$ at the 0.05 level of significance.

15.20 With reference to Exercise 15.6 on page 496, test the null hypothesis $\beta = -0.12$ against the alternative hypothesis $\beta > -0.12$ at the 0.05 level of significance. Also, state in words what hypothesis is being tested.

15.21 The following table shows the assessed values and the selling prices of eight houses, constituting a random sample of all the houses sold recently in a suburban area:

Assessed value (thousands of dollars)	Selling price (thousands of dollars)
140.3	163.4
172.0	218.3
132.5	155.2
144.8	174.0
127.9	148.8
151.6	181.1
180.4	223.2
158.0	192.5

For these data,

$$\Sigma\, x = 1207.5, \quad \Sigma\, x^2 = 184{,}640.51, \quad \Sigma\, y = 1{,}456.5, \quad \Sigma\, y^2 = 270{,}530.63, \quad \text{and}$$

$$\Sigma\, xy = 223{,}398.38$$

Assessed values are used for local tax purposes and do not necessarily represent actual value.

(a) Fit a least-squares line which will enable us to predict the selling price of a house in that area in terms of its assessed value.

(b) Test the null hypothesis $\beta = 1.1$ against the alternative hypothesis $\beta > 1.1$ at the 0.05 level of significance.

15.22   The following data show the advertising expenses (expressed as a percentage of total expenses) and the net operating profits (expressed as a percentage of total sales) in a random sample of six drugstores:

Advertising expenses	Net operating profit
1.5	3.6
1.0	2.8
2.8	5.4
0.4	1.9
1.3	2.9
2.0	4.3

For these data,

$$\Sigma\, x = 9.0, \quad \Sigma\, x^2 = 16.94, \quad \Sigma\, y = 20.9, \quad \Sigma\, y^2 = 80.47, \quad \text{and} \quad \Sigma\, xy = 36.45$$

(a) Fit a least-squares line which will enable us to predict net operating profits in terms of advertising expenses.

(b) Test the null hypothesis $\beta = 1.60$ against the alternative hypothesis $\beta \neq 1.60$ at the 0.01 level of significance.

15.23   With reference to the Exercise 15.6 on page 496, test the null hypothesis $\alpha = 2.1$ against the alternative hypothesis $\alpha < 2.1$ at the 0.05 level of significance. Also state in words what hypothesis is being tested.

冊 15.24   With reference to the example on page 504, test the null hypothesis $\alpha = 0.85$ against the alternative hypothesis $\alpha < 0.85$ at the 0.05 level of significance, getting the value of a and the estimate of the standard error directly from Figure 15.7.

15.25   The following sample data show the demand for a product (in thousands of units) and its price (in cents) charged in six different market areas:

Price x	18	10	14	11	16	13
Demand y	9	125	57	90	22	79

For these data,

$$\Sigma\, x = 82, \quad \Sigma\, x^2 = 1{,}166, \quad \Sigma\, y = 382, \quad \Sigma\, y^2 = 33{,}780, \quad \text{and} \quad \Sigma\, xy = 4{,}579$$

(a) Fit a least-squares line from which we can predict the demand for the product in terms of its price.

(b) Construct a 95 percent confidence interval for β and explain in words what quantity is thus being estimated.

15.26　With reference to Exercise 15.14 on page 498 construct a 99 percent confidence interval for β.

15.27　With reference to Exercise 15.22, construct a 98 percent confidence interval for β and state in words what quantity is thus being estimated.

15.28　With reference to Exercise 15.6 on page 496, construct a 95 percent confidence interval for α.

15.29　With reference to Exercise 15.22, construct a 99 percent confidence interval for α.

⊞ 15.30　With reference to the example on page 488, the one dealing with the language proficiency of applicants to certain foreign service jobs, construct a 99 percent confidence interval for α, getting the value of a and the estimate of the standard error directly from Figure 15.5.

15.31　With reference to Exercise 15.3 on page 495, construct a 95 percent confidence interval for the average number of cars a person will inspect in the given time period if he or she has been working at the inspection station for eight weeks. (See also Exercise 15.34.)

15.32　With reference to Exercise 15.21, construct a 95 percent confidence interval for the average selling price of a house in the given suburban area which has an assessed value of $145,000. (See also Exercise 15.35.)

15.33　With reference to Exercise 15.22, construct a 95 percent confidence interval for the mean net operating profits (expressed as a percentage of total sales) when the advertising expenses are 2.0 percent of total expenses.

15.34　With reference to Exercise 15.3 on page 495, find 95 percent limits of prediction for the number of cars a person will inspect in the given time period if he or she has been working at the inspection station for eight weeks.

15.35　With reference to Exercise 15.21, find 95 percent limits of prediction for the selling price of a house in the given suburban area which has an assessed value of $145,000.

15.36　True or false?

(a) A confidence interval for the mean of y for a given value of x can be made as narrow as we want by making n sufficiently large.

(b) The difference between upper and lower limits of prediction can be made as small as we want by making n sufficiently large.

15.37　Verify that the following formula for s_e is equivalent to the one given on page 502.

$$s_e = \sqrt{\frac{S_{xx} \cdot S_{yy} - (S_{xy})^2}{(n-2)S_{xx}}}$$

Also use this alternative formula to recalculate the value of s_e given on page 504.

15.4　MULTIPLE REGRESSION ⇔†

Although there are many problems where one variable can be predicted quite accurately in terms of another, it stands to reason that predictions should improve if one considers additional relevant information. For instance, we should be able to make better predictions of the performance of newly hired teachers if we consider not only their education, but also their years of experience and their personality. Also, we should be able to make better predictions of a new textbook's success if we consider not only the quality of the work, but also the potential demand and the competition.

†This section is marked optional because the calculations, while possible by calculator for very small problems, generally require computer software.

Many mathematical formulas can serve to express relationships among more than two variables, but most commonly used in statistics (partly for reasons of convenience) are linear equations of the form

$$y = b_0 + b_1 x_1 + b_2 x_2 + \cdots + b_k x_k$$

Here y is the variable which is to be predicted, $x_1, x_2, \dots$, and x_k are the k known variables on which predictions are to be based, and $b_0, b_1, b_2, \dots$, and b_k are numerical constants which must be determined from observed data.

To illustrate, consider the following equation which was obtained in a study of the demand for different meats:

$$\hat{y} = 3.489 - 0.090 x_1 + 0.064 x_2 + 0.019 x_3$$

Here y denotes the total consumption of federally inspected beef and veal in millions of pounds, x_1 denotes a composite retail price of beef in cents per pound, x_2 denotes a composite retail price of veal in cents per pound, and x_3 denotes income as measured by a certain payroll index. With this equation, we can predict the total consumption of federally inspected beef and veal on the basis of specified values of x_1, x_2, and x_3.

The problem of determining a linear equation in more than two variables which best describes a given set of data is that of finding numerical values for $b_0, b_1, b_2, \dots$, and b_k. This is usually done by the method of least squares; that is, we minimize the sum of squares $\Sigma (y - \hat{y})^2$, where as before the y's are the observed values and the $\hat{y}$'s are the values calculated by means of the linear equation. In principle, the problem of determining the values of $b_0, b_1, b_2, \dots$, and b_k is the same as it is in the two-variable case, but manual solutions may be very tedious because the method of least squares requires that we solve as many normal equations as there are unknown constants $b_0, b_1, b_2, \dots$, and b_k. For instance, when there are two independent variables x_1 and x_2, and we want to fit the equation

$$y = b_0 + b_1 x_1 + b_2 x_2$$

we must solve the three normal equations

Normal Equations (Two Independent Variables)	
	$\Sigma y = n \cdot b_0 + b_1 (\Sigma x_1) + b_2 (\Sigma x_2)$
	$\Sigma x_1 y = b_0 (\Sigma x_1) + b_1 (\Sigma x_1^2) + b_2 (\Sigma x_1 x_2)$
	$\Sigma x_2 y = b_0 (\Sigma x_2) + b_1 (\Sigma x_1 x_2) + b_2 (\Sigma x_2^2)$

Here $\Sigma x_1 y$ is the sum of the products obtained by multiplying each given value of x_1 by the corresponding value of y, $\Sigma x_1 x_2$ is the sum of the products obtained by multiplying each given value of x_1 by the corresponding value of x_2, and so on.

Example

The following data show the number of bedrooms, the number of baths, and the prices at which eight one-family houses sold recently in a certain community:

Number of bedrooms x_1	Number of baths x_2	Price (dollars) y
3	2	78,800
2	1	74,300
4	3	83,800
2	1	74,200
3	2	79,700
2	2	74,900
5	3	88,400
4	2	82,900

Find a linear equation which will enable us to predict the average sales price of a one-family house in the given community in terms of the number of bedrooms and the number of baths.

solution

The quantities needed for substitution into the three normal equations are $n = 8$,

$$\Sigma x_1 = 25, \quad \Sigma x_2 = 16, \quad \Sigma y = 637,000, \quad \Sigma x_1^2 = 87,$$

$$\Sigma x_1 x_2 = 55, \quad \Sigma x_2^2 = 36, \quad \Sigma x_1 y = 2,031,100, \quad \text{and} \quad \Sigma x_2 y = 1,297,700$$

and we get

$$637,000 = 8b_0 + 25b_1 + 16b_2$$

$$2,031,100 = 25b_0 + 87b_1 + 55b_2$$

$$1,297,700 = 16b_0 + 55b_1 + 36b_2$$

We could solve these equations by the method of elimination or by using determinants, but in view of the rather tedious calculations, such work is left to computers. So, let us refer to the printout of Figure 15.8. Here we find in the column headed "Coef" that

$$b_0 = 65,191.7, \quad b_1 = 4,133.3, \quad \text{and} \quad b_2 = 758.3$$

and in the line immediately above the coefficients that, after rounding, the least-squares equation becomes

$$\hat{y} = 65,192 + 4,133x_1 + 758x_2$$

This equation tells us that (in the given community and at the time the study was made) each extra bedroom adds on the average $4,133, and each bath $758 to the sales price of a house. ◪ ◪ ◪

Example

Based on the result of the preceding example, predict the sales price of a three-bedroom house with two baths.

solution

Substituting $x_1 = 3$ and $x_2 = 2$ into the equation obtained above, we get

$$\hat{y} = 65,192 + 4,133(3) + 758(2) = \$79,107$$

or approximately $79,100.

    Although we shall not go into the subject here, let us point out that most printouts like that of Figure 15.8 also provide information which makes it easy to test hypotheses about the true regression coefficients (the quantities estimated by $b_0, b_1, b_2, \ldots$) or to construct confidence intervals.

FIGURE 15.8

Computer printout for multiple regression.
(MINITAB 10 for Windows).

```
MTB > print c1 c2 c3

Data Display

Row    C1     C2        C3
 1      3      2      78800
 2      2      1      74300
 3      4      3      83800
 4      2      1      74200
 5      3      2      79700
 6      2      2      74900
 7      5      3      88400
 8      4      2      82900


MTB  >  Regress c3 2 c1 c2;
SUBC >        Constant.


Regression Analysis


The regression equation is
C3 = 65192 + 4133 C1 + 758 C2


Predictor        Coef       Stdev     t-ratio         p
Constant      65191.7       418.0      155.96     0.000
C1             4133.3       228.6       18.08     0.000
C2              758.3       340.5        2.23     0.076


s = 370.4    R-sq = 99.6%    R-sq(adj) = 99.5%

Analysis of Variance

SOURCE         DF           SS          MS        F        p
Regression      2    185269168    92634584   675.34    0.000
Error           5       685833      137167
Total           7    185955008


SOURCE         DF       SEQ SS
    C1          1    184588800
    C2          1       680364
```

15.38 The following are data on the ages and incomes of a random sample of five executives working for a large multinational company, and the number of years each went to college:

Age x_1	Years college x_2	Income (dollars) y
38	4	81,700
46	0	73,300
39	5	89,500
43	2	79,800
32	4	69,900

(a) Fit an equation of the form $y = b_0 + b_1x_1 + b_2x_2$ to the given data.

(b) Use the equation obtained in part (a) to estimate the average income of 39-year-old executives with four years of college who work for this company.

15.39 The following are sample data provided by a moving company on the weights of six shipments, the distances they were moved, and the damage that was incurred:

Weight (thousands of pounds) x_1	Distance (thousands of miles) x_2	Damage (dollars) y
4.0	1.5	160
3.0	2.2	112
1.6	1.0	69
1.2	2.0	90
3.4	0.8	123
4.8	1.6	186

(a) Fit an equation of the form $y = b_0 + b_1x_1 + b_2x_2$ to the given data.

(b) Use the equation obtained in part (a) to predict the damage when a shipment weighing 2,400 pounds is moved 1,200 miles.

(c) Repeat part (b) for a shipment weighing 2,400 pounds and moving 1,500 miles.

(d) Repeat part (b) for a shipment weighing 3,600 pounds and moving 1,200 miles.

(e) Repeat part (b) for a shipment weighing 3,600 pounds and moving 1,500 miles.

15.40 The following data were collected to determine the relationship between two processing variables and the hardness of a certain kind of steel:

Hardness (Rockwell 30-T) y	Copper content (percent) x_1	Annealing temperature (degrees F) x_2
78.9	0.02	1,000
55.2	0.02	1,200
80.9	0.10	1,000
57.4	0.10	1,200
85.3	0.18	1,000
60.7	0.18	1,200

(a) Fit an equation of the form $y = b_0 + b_1x_1 + b_2x_2$ to the given data.

(b) Use the equation obtained in part (a) to predict the hardness of the steel when its copper content is 0.14 percent and the annealing temperature is 1,100 degrees F.

⇔ 15.41   When the x_1's and/or the x_2's are equally spaced, the calculation of b_0, b_1, b_2, ..., can usually be simplified by using coding like that of Exercise 15.16 on page 499. Rework the preceding exercise after coding the three x_1-values -1, 0, and 1, and the two x_2-values -1 and 1.

15.5   NONLINEAR REGRESSION ⇔

When data depart more or less widely from linearity, we must consider fitting some curve other than a straight line. In this section we first give two cases where the relationship is not linear but the method of Section 15.2 can nevertheless be employed; then we give an example of **polynomial curve fitting** by fitting a **parabola** whose equation is

$$y = a + bx + cx^2$$

It is common practice to plot paired data on various kinds of graph paper, to see whether there are scales for which the points fall close to a straight line. Of course, when this is the case for ordinary graph paper, we proceed as in Section 15.2. If it is the case when we use **semilog paper** (with equal subdivisions for x and a logarithmic scale for y, as shown in Figure 15.10), this indicates that an **exponential curve** will provide a good fit. The equation of such a curve is

$$y = a \cdot b^x$$

or in logarithmic form

$$\log y = \log a + x(\log b)$$

which is a linear equation in x and $\log y$, where "log" stands for logarithm to the base 10.[†] Observe that if we write A for $\log a$, B for $\log b$, and Y for $\log y$, the equation becomes $Y = A + Bx$, which is the usual equation of a straight line.

For finding an exponential curve, we can simply apply the procedure on page 492 to the problem expressed as $Y = A + Bx$.

Example

The following are data on a company's net profits during the first six years that it has been in business:

Year	Net profit (thousands of dollars)
1	112
2	149
3	238
4	354
5	580
6	867

[†]The work is equally valid for any logarithm base. This section uses base 10 logarithms, but certainly base e can be used as well.

FIGURE 15.9

Net profits plotted

FIGURE 15.10

Net profits plotted

Figure 15.9, where these data are plotted on ordinary graph paper, shows that the relationship is not linear, but Figure 15.10, where a logarithmic scale is used for the *y*'s, shows that the overall pattern is remarkably "straightened out." Thus, fit an exponential curve to the given data.

solution

Obtaining the logarithms of the *y*'s with a calculator, or perhaps with a logarithm table, we find that

x	y	$Y = \log y$
1	112	2.0492
2	149	2.1732
3	238	2.3766
4	354	2.5490
5	580	2.7634
6	867	2.9380

Then we note that $n = 6$, and we find

$$\Sigma\, x = 21, \quad \Sigma\, x^2 = 91, \quad \Sigma\, Y = 14.8494, \quad \text{and} \quad \Sigma\, xY = 55.1664$$

These calculations are found using $Y = \log y$. This enables us to find

$$\bar{x} = 3.5, \qquad \bar{Y} = 2.4749,$$

$$S_{xx} = 91 - \frac{(21)^2}{6} = 17.5, \quad \text{and} \quad S_{xY} = 55.1664 - \frac{(21)(14.8494)}{6} = 3.1935$$

Then

$$B = \frac{S_{xY}}{S_{xx}} \approx 0.1825 \quad \text{and} \quad A = \bar{Y} - B\bar{x} = 2.4749 - (0.1825)(3.5) \approx 1.8362$$

516   C H A P T E R 15   *Regression*

The equation which describes the relationship is then

$$\hat{Y} = \log \hat{y} = 1.8362 + 0.1825x$$

Since 1.8362 and 0.1825 are the estimates corresponding to $\log a$ and $\log b$, we find by taking antilogarithms that $a = 68.58$ and $b = 1.52$. Thus, the equation of the exponential curve which best describes the relationship between the company's net profit and the number of years it has been in business is given by

$$\hat{y} = 68.58(1.52)^x$$

where $\hat{y}$ is in thousands of dollars.

Once we have fit an exponential curve to a set of paired data, we can predict a future value of y by substituting into its equation the corresponding value of x, but it is usually more convenient to substitute x into the logarithmic form of the equation, namely,

$$\log \hat{y} = \log a + x(\log b)$$

Example

With reference to the preceding example, predict the company's net profit for the eighth year that it will have been in business.

solution

Substituting $x = 8$ into the logarithmic form of the exponential curve, we get

$$\log \hat{y} = 1.8362 + 8(0.1825) = 3.2962$$

and hence $\hat{y} = 1,980$ or $1,980,000.

If points representing paired data fall close to a straight line when plotted on **log-log paper** (with logarithmic scales for both x and y), this indicates that an equation of the form

$$y = a \cdot x^b$$

will provide a good fit. In the logarithmic form, the equation of such a **power function** is

$$\log y = \log a + b(\log x)$$

which is a linear equation in $\log x$ and $\log y$. (Writing A, X, and Y for $\log a$, $\log x$, and $\log y$, the equation becomes

$$Y = A + bX$$

which is the usual equation of a straight line.) For finding a power curve, we can simply apply the procedure on page 492 to the problem expressed as $Y = A + bX$. The work in fitting a power function is similar to that required to fit an exponential curve, and we shall not illustrate it here. In Exercises 15.45 and 15.46 on page 520 you will find data to which the method can be applied.

When the values of y first increase and then decrease, or first decrease and then increase, a **parabola** having the equation

$$y = a + bx + cx^2$$

will often provide a good fit. This equation can also be written as

$$y = b_0 + b_1x + b_2x^2$$

to conform with the notation of Section 15.4, and we can therefore look upon parabolas as linear equations in the two unknowns $x_1 = x$ and $x_2 = x^2$. Thus, fitting a parabola to a set of paired data is nothing new—we simply use the method of Section 15.4.

Example

The following are data on the drying time of a varnish and the amount of a certain chemical additive:

Amount of additive (grams) x	Drying time (hours) y
1	7.2
2	6.7
3	4.7
4	3.7
5	4.7
6	4.2
7	5.2
8	5.7

(a) Fit a parabola which, as would appear from Figure 15.11, should be the right kind of curve to fit to the given data.
(b) Use the result of part (a) to predict the drying time of the varnish when 6.5 grams of the chemical are added.

Parabola fitted to

varnish-drying-time data.

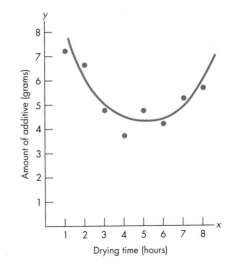

solution

(a) Using a computer to fit a linear equation of the form

$$\hat{y} = b_0 + b_1x_1 + b_2x_2$$

to the following data

$x_1 = x$	$x_2 = x^2$	y
1	1	7.2
2	4	6.7
3	9	4.7
4	16	3.7
5	25	4.7
6	36	4.2
7	49	5.2
8	64	5.7

we get the printout shown in Figure 15.12 on the opposite page. Here, the co-efficients are $b_0 = 9.2446$, $b_1 = -2.0149$, and $b_2 = 0.19940$, and if we round to two decimals we can write the equation of the parabola as

$$\hat{y} = 9.24 - 2.01x + 0.20x^2$$

(b) Substituting $x = 6.5$ into the equation, we get

$$\hat{y} = 9.24 - 2.01(6.5) + 0.20(6.5)^2 \approx 4.62 \text{ hours}$$ ◪ ◪ ◪

On pages 516–517 we introduced parabolas as curves which bend once—that is, their values first increase and then decrease, or first decrease and then increase. For patterns which bend more than once, **polynomial equations** of higher degree, such as

$$y = a + bx + cx^2 + dx^3 \quad \text{or} \quad y = a + bx + cx^2 + dx^3 + ex^4$$

can be fitted by the same technique. In practice, we often use sections of such curves, especially parts of parabolas, when there is only a slight curvature in the pattern we want to describe (see Exercise 15.50 on page 521).

◪ EXERCISES

15.42 Fit an exponential curve to the following data on the percentage of the radial tires made by a certain manufacturer that are still usable after having been driven the given number of miles:

Miles driven (thousands) x	Percentage usable y
1	97.2
2	91.8
5	82.5
10	64.4
20	41.0
30	29.9
40	17.6
50	11.3

Also estimate the percentage of the tires we can expect to be usable after they have been driven for 25,000 miles.

```
MTB > print c1 c2 c3

Data Display

Row     C1      C2      C3

  1      1       1      7.2
  2      2       4      6.7
  3      3       9      4.7
  4      4      16      3.7
  5      5      25      4.7
  6      6      36      4.2
  7      7      49      5.2
  8      8      64      5.7

MTB  >  Regress  c3  2  c1  c2;
SUBC >       Constant.

Regression Analysis

The regression equation is
C3 = 9.24 - 2.01 C1 + 0.199 C2

Predictor        Coef      Stdev     t-ratio       p
Constant       9.2446     0.7645      12.09     0.000
C1            -2.0149     0.3898      -5.17     0.004
C2            0.19940    0.04228       4.72     0.005

s = 0.5480      R-sq = 85.3%      R-sq(adj) = 79.4%

Analysis of Variance

SOURCE        SF         SS         MS         F          p
Regression     2     8.7173     4.3586     14.51     0.008
Error          5     1.5015     0.3003
Total          7    10.2187

SOURCE        DF     SEQ SS
C1             1     2.0372
C2             1     6.6801
```

15.43 The following data pertain to the growth of a colony of bacteria in a culture medium:

Days since inoculation x	Bacteria count (thousands) y
2	112
4	148
6	241
8	363
10	585

Fit an exponential curve and use it to estimate the bacteria count at the end of the fifth day.

15.44 When the *x*'s are equally spaced, the calculations needed to fit an exponential curve can be simplified appreciably by using coding like that of Exercise 15.16 on page 499.

(a) Coding the years −5, −3, −1, 1, 3, and 5, rework the illustration on page 515.

(b) What coded value of *x* do we have to substitute into the least-squares equation obtained in part (a), if we want to predict the company's profit for the eighth year?

15.45 The following data pertain to the demand for a product (in thousands of units) and its price (in cents) charged in five different market areas:

Price	20	16	10	11	14
Demand	22	41	120	89	56

Fit a power function and use it to estimate the demand when the price of the product is 12 cents.

15.46 The following data pertain to the volume of a gas (in cubic inches) and its pressure (in pounds per square inch), when the gas is compressed at a constant temperature:

Volume *x*	Pressure *y*
50	16.0
30	40.1
20	78.0
10	190.5
5	532.2

Fit a power function and use it to estimate the pressure of this gas when it is compressed to a volume of 15 cubic inches.

15.47 The following are data on the amount of fertilizer applied to the soil, *x* in pounds per square foot, and the yield of a certain food crop, *y* in pounds per square yard:

x	*y*
0.5	32.0
1.1	34.3
2.2	15.7
0.2	20.8
1.6	33.5
2.0	21.5

(a) Plot these data to verify that it is reasonable to fit a parabola.

(b) Fit a parabola by the method of least squares.

(c) Use the equation obtained in part (a) to predict the yield when 1.5 pounds of the fertilizer are applied per square foot.

15.48 In the years 1978–1983 the production of uranium in the United States was 18,490, 18,730, 21,850, 19,240, 13,430, and 10,600 short tons (according to the 1985 *Statistical Abstract of the United States*). Code the years −5, −3, −1, 1, 3, and 5, and fit a parabola by the method of least squares.

15.49 In the years 1977–1983 there were 3.1, 3.2, 3.2, 3.0, 3.2, 3.8, and 4.1 million new passports issued in the United States (according to the 1985 *Statistical Abstract of the United States*). Code the years −3, −2, −1, 0, 1, 2, and 3, and fit a parabola by the method of least squares.

15.50 Fit a parabola to the data of Exercise 15.45 and use it to estimate the demand when the price of the product is 12 cents.

15.51 Market research shows that weekly sales of a new candy bar will be related to its price as follows:

Price (cents)	Weekly sales (number of bars)
50	232,000
55	194,000
60	169,000
65	157,000

Finding that the parabola

$$\hat{y} = 1,130,000 - 28,000x + 200x^2$$

provides an excellent fit, the person conducting the study substitutes $x = 85$, gets $y = 195,000$, and then predicts that weekly sales will total 195,000 if the candy is priced at 85 cents. Comment on this argument.

15.6 ☑ CHECKLIST OF KEY TERMS (*with page references to their definitions*)

Curve fitting, 486
Data points, 490
Estimated regression coefficients, 501
Estimated regression line, 494
⊖ Exponential curve, 514
Least-squares line, 490
Limits of prediction, 506
Linear equation, 486
Linear regression analysis, 501
⊖ Log-log paper, 516
Method of least squares, 489
⊖ Multiple regression, 509

Normal equations, 491
Normal regression analysis, 501
⊖ Parabola, 514
⊖ Polynomial equation, 514, 518
⊖ Power function, 516
Regression, 485
Regression coefficients, 501
Regression line, 494
⊖ Semilog paper, 514
Slope, 486
Standard error of estimate, 501
y-intercept, 486

15.7 ☑ REVIEW EXERCISES

15.52 The following are the numbers of hours which ten persons (interviewed as part of a sample survey) spent watching television, x, and reading books or magazines, y, per week:

x	y
18	7
25	5
19	1
12	5
12	10
27	2
15	3
9	9
12	8
18	4

For these data,

$$\Sigma x = 167, \quad \Sigma x^2 = 3{,}101, \quad \Sigma y = 54, \quad \Sigma y^2 = 374, \quad \text{and} \quad \Sigma xy = 798$$

(a) Fit a least-squares line which will enable us to predict y in terms of x.

(b) If a person spends 20 hours watching television per week, predict how many hours he or she will spend reading books or magazines.

15.53 With reference to the preceding exercise, construct a 95 percent confidence interval for the regression coefficient β.

15.54 With reference to Exercise 15.52, construct a 99 percent confidence interval for the number of hours a person who watches 20 hours of television per week can be expected to read books or magazines per week.

15.55 For the last five months, the ice cream sales, in thousands of gallons, for a certain chain of supermarkets were 46, 55, 57, 52, and 44. Use coding like that of Exercise 15.16 on page 499 to fit a parabola for these data.

15.56 The following are data on the average weekly profit (in $1,000) of five restaurants, their seating capacities, and the average daily traffic (in thousands of cars) which passes their locations:

Seating capacity x_1	Traffic count x_2	Weekly net profit y
120	19	23.8
200	8	24.2
150	12	22.0
180	15	26.2
240	16	33.5

(a) Use the method of least squares to fit an equation of the form

$$y = b_0 + b_1 x_1 + b_2 x_2$$

to these data.

(b) Use the equation obtained in part (a) to predict the average weekly net profit of a restaurant with a seating capacity of 210 at a location where the daily traffic count averages 14,000 cars.

15.57 The following data pertain to the cosmic-ray doses measured at various altitudes:

Altitude (hundreds of feet) x	Dose rate (mrem/year) y
0.5	28
4.5	30
7.8	32
12.0	36
48.0	58
53.0	69

Fit an exponential curve and use it to estimate the cosmic radiation at 6,000 feet.

15.58 The following are the high school averages, x, and first-year college grade-point indexes, y, of ten students:

x	y
3.0	2.6
2.7	2.4
3.8	3.9
2.6	2.1
3.2	2.6
3.4	3.3
2.8	2.2
3.1	3.2
3.5	2.8
3.3	2.5

For these data,

$$\Sigma\, x = 31.4, \quad \Sigma\, x^2 = 99.88, \quad \Sigma\, y = 27.6, \quad \Sigma\, y^2 = 78.96, \quad \text{and} \quad \Sigma\, xy = 88.23$$

(a) Fit a least-squares line which will enable us to predict first-year college grade-point indexes in terms of high school averages.

(b) Use the equation obtained in part (a) to predict the first-year college grade-point index of a student with a high school average of 2.5.

15.59 With reference to the preceding exercise, test the null hypothesis $\beta = 0.50$ against the alternative hypothesis $\beta > 0.50$ at the 0.05 level of significance.

15.60 The following are the processing times (minutes), x, and hardness readings, y, of certain machine parts:

x	y
20	282
34	275
19	171
10	142
24	145
31	340
25	282
13	105
29	233

For these data

$$\Sigma\, x = 205, \quad \Sigma\, x^2 = 5{,}189, \quad \Sigma\, y = 1{,}975, \quad \Sigma\, y^2 = 486{,}017, \quad \text{and} \quad \Sigma\, xy = 48{,}851$$

(a) Fit a least-squares line which will enable us to predict hardness from processing time.

(b) Use the equation obtained in part (a) to predict the hardness reading of a machine part which was processed for 25 minutes.

15.61 With reference to the preceding exercise, test the null hypothesis $\alpha = 55.0$ against the alternative hypothesis $\alpha \neq 55.0$ at the 0.01 level of significance.

15.62 With reference to Exercise 15.60, find 95 percent limits of prediction for the hardness reading of a machine part which has been processed for 25 minutes.

15.63 The following data show the scores which ten students got in an examination, their total SAT (Scholastic Aptitude Test) scores, and the number of hours that they studied for the examination:

Number of hours studied x_1	SAT score x_2	Score in examination y
9	1,160	70
3	1,013	38
16	1,022	90
19	995	99
6	1,180	59
11	1,117	75
14	1,062	77
12	1,207	84
6	1,014	49
9	1,008	61

(a) Use the method of least squares to fit an equation of the form $y = b_0 + b_1 x_1 + b_2 x_2$.

(b) Use the equation obtained in part (a) to predict the scores of students with these combinations of SAT scores and study times:

Number of hours studied	SAT score
12	1,000
18	1,000
12	1,200
18	1,200

15.8   REFERENCES

Methods of deciding which kind of curve to fit to a given set of paired data may be found in books on numerical analysis and in more advanced texts in statistics. Further information about the material of this chapter may be found in

CHATTERJEE, S., and PRICE, B., *Regression Analysis by Example,* 2nd ed. New York: John Wiley & Sons, Inc., 1991.

DANIEL, C., and WOOD, F., *Fitting Equations to Data, 2nd ed.* New York: John Wiley & Sons, Inc., 1980.

DRAPER, N. R., and SMITH, H., *Applied Regression Analysis, 2nd ed.* New York: John Wiley & Sons, Inc., 1981.

EZEKIEL, M., and FOX, K. A., *Methods of Correlation and Regression Analysis, 3rd ed.* New York: John Wiley & Sons, Inc., 1959.

GUNST, R. F., and MASON, R. L., *Regression Analysis and Its Applications. A Data-Oriented Approach.* New York: Marcel Dekker, Inc., 1980.

HARRIS, R. J., *A Primer of Multivariate Statistics.* New York: Academic Press, Inc., 1971.

MOSTELLER, F., and TUKEY, J. W., *Data Analysis and Regression.* Reading, Mass: Addison-Wesley Publishing Company, Inc., 1977.

WEISBERG, S., *Applied Linear Regression, 2nd ed.* New York: John Wiley & Sons, Inc., 1985

WONNACOTT, T. H., and WONNACOTT, R. J., *Regression: A Second Course in Statistics.* New York: John Wiley & Sons, Inc., 1981.

CORRELATION

*H*aving *learned how to fit a least-squares line to paired data, we turn now to the problem of determining how well such a line actually fits the data. Of course, we can get some idea of this by inspecting a diagram which shows the line together with the data, but to demonstrate how we can be more objective, let us refer back to the original data of the example dealing with the foreign service job applicants' proficiency in German, namely:*

Years studied German x	Score in test y
3	57
4	78
4	72
2	58
5	89
3	63
4	73
5	84
3	75
2	48

As can be seen from this table, there are substantial differences among the scores, the smallest being 48 and the largest being 89. However, we also see that the 48 was obtained by a person who had studied German for two years, while the 89 was obtained by a person who had studied German for five years, and this suggests that the differences among the scores may well be due, at least in part, to differences in the length of time that the applicants had studied German. This observation raises the following question, which we shall answer in this chapter: Of the total variation among the y's, how much can be attributed to the relationship between the two variables x and y (that is, to the fact that the observed y's correspond to different values of x), and how much can be attributed to chance?.

In Section 16.1 we introduce the coefficient of correlation as a measure of the strength of the linear relationship between two variables, in Section 16.2 we study how to interpret it, and in Section 16.3 we study related problems of inference; the problems of multiple and partial correlation will be touched upon lightly in Section 16.5. ◪

16.1   THE COEFFICIENT OF CORRELATION

Regarding the question raised in the chapter opening above, we are faced here with an analysis of variance. Figure 16.1 shows what we mean. As can be seen from the diagram, the deviation of an observed value of y from the mean of all the y's, $y - \bar{y}$, can be written as a sum of two parts. The first part is the deviation of $\hat{y}$ (the value on the line corresponding to an observed value of x) from the mean of all the y's, $\hat{y} - \bar{y}$; the second part is the deviation of the observed

FIGURE 16.1

Illustration to show that
$y - \bar{y} = (y - \hat{y}) + (\hat{y} - \bar{y}).$

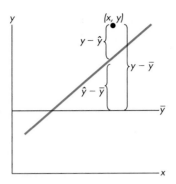

value of y from the corresponding value on the line, $y - \hat{y}$. Symbolically, we write

$$y - \bar{y} = (\hat{y} - \bar{y}) + (y - \hat{y})$$

for any observed value y, and if we square the expressions on both sides of this identity and sum over all n values of y, we find that algebraic simplifications lead to

$$\Sigma\,(y - \bar{y})^2 = \Sigma\,(\hat{y} - \bar{y})^2 + \Sigma\,(y - \hat{y})^2$$

The quantity on the left above measures the total variation of the y's and we call it the **total sum of squares;** note that $\Sigma\,(y - \bar{y})^2$ is just the variance of the y's multiplied by $n - 1$. The first of the two sums on the right, $\Sigma\,(\hat{y} - \bar{y})^2$, is called the **regression sum of squares** and it measures that part of the total variation of the y's which can be ascribed to the relationship between the two variables x and y; indeed, if all the points lie on the least-squares line, then $y = \hat{y}$ and the regression sum of squares equals the total sum of squares. In practice, this is hardly, if ever, the case, and the fact that all the points do not lie on a least-squares line is an indication that there are other factors than differences among the x's which affect the values of y. It is customary to combine all these other factors under the general heading of "chance." Chance variation is thus measured by the amounts by which the points deviate from the line; specifically, it is measured by $\Sigma\,(y - \hat{y})^2$, called the **residual sum of squares,** which is the second of the two components into which we partitioned the total sum of squares.

To determine these sums of squares for the example dealing with the language proficiency of certain foreign service job applicants, we could substitute the values of y given on page 526, $\bar{y}$, and the values of $\hat{y}$ obtained by substituting the x's into

$$\hat{y} = 31.55 + 10.90x$$

(see page 494), but there are simplifications. First, for $\Sigma\,(y - \bar{y})^2$ we have the computing formula

$$S_{yy} = \Sigma\,y^2 - \frac{1}{n}(\Sigma\,y)^2$$

and on page 502 we show that it equals 1,504.1 for our example. Second, $\Sigma\,(y - \hat{y})^2$ is the quantity which we minimized by the method of least squares, and which appears in the numerator of the formula for s_e. Copying the numerator from its computing formula on page 502, we get

$$\Sigma \, (y - \hat{y})^2 = S_{yy} - \frac{(S_{xy})^2}{S_{xx}}$$

and

$$1{,}504.1 - \frac{(114.5)^2}{10.5} \approx 255.50$$

for our example. (The values of S_{xx} and S_{xy} are determined on page 493.) Finally, by subtraction, the regression sum of squares is given by

$$\Sigma \, (\hat{y} - \overline{y})^2 = \Sigma \, (y - \overline{y})^2 - \Sigma \, (y - \hat{y})^2 = S_{yy} - \left(S_{yy} - \frac{(S_{xy})^2}{S_{xx}} \right) = \frac{(S_{xy})^2}{S_{xx}}$$

and for our example we get

$$\frac{(114.5)^2}{10.5} \approx 1{,}248.6$$

It is of interest to note that all the quantities we have calculated here could have been obtained directly from the computer printout of Figure 15.5 on page 493. Under Analysis of Variance, in the column headed *SS*, we find that the total sum of squares is 1,504.1, the residual (or error) sum of squares is 255.5, and the regression sum of squares is 1,248.6.

We are now ready to examine the sums of squares, and comparing the regression sum of squares with the total sum of squares, we find that

$$\frac{\Sigma \, (\hat{y} - \overline{y})^2}{} = \frac{1{,}248.6}{1{,}504.1} \approx 0.83$$

is the proportion of the total variation of the scores which can be attributed to the relationship with x, namely, to the differences in the number of years which the applicants had studied German in high school or college. This quantity is referred to as the **coefficient of determination** and is denoted by r^2. Note that the coefficient of determination is also given in the printout of Figure 15.5 on page 493; near the middle it says "R-sq = 83.0%."

If we take the square root of the coefficient of determination, we get the **coefficient of correlation,** denoted by the letter r. Its sign is chosen so that it is like that of the estimated regression coefficient b, and for our example, where b is positive, we get

$$r = \sqrt{0.83} \approx 0.91$$

It follows that the correlation coefficient is positive when the least-squares line has an upward slope, namely, when the relationship between x and y is such that small values of y tend to go with small values of x and large values of y tend to go with large values of x. Also, the correlation coefficient is negative when the least-squares line has a downward slope, namely, when large values of y tend to go with small values of x and small values of y tend to go with large values of x. Examples of **positive** and **negative correlations** are shown in the first two diagrams of Figure 16.2 on the following page.

FIGURE 16.2

Types of correlation.

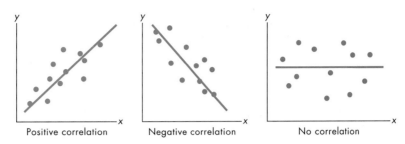

Positive correlation   Negative correlation   No correlation

Since part of the variation of the y's cannot exceed their total variation, $\Sigma (y - \hat{y})^2$ cannot exceed $\Sigma (y - \bar{y})^2$, and it follows from the formula defining r that correlation coefficients must lie on the interval from -1 to $+1$. If all the points actually fall on a straight line, the residual sum of squares, $\Sigma (y - \hat{y})^2$, is zero,

$$\Sigma (\hat{y} - \bar{y})^2 = \Sigma (y - \bar{y})^2$$

and the resulting value of r, -1 or $+1$, is indicative of a perfect fit. If, however, the scatter of the points is such that the least-squares line is a horizontal line coincident with $\bar{y}$ (that is, a line with slope 0 which intersects the y-axis at $a = \bar{y}$), then

$$\Sigma (y - \hat{y})^2 = \Sigma (y - \bar{y})^2 \quad \text{and} \quad r = 0$$

In that case none of the variation of the y's can be attributed to their relationship with x, and the fit is so poor that knowledge of x is of no help in predicting y. The predicted value of y is $\bar{y}$ regardless of x. An example of this is shown in the third diagram of Figure 16.2.

The formula that defines r shows clearly the nature, or essence, of the coefficient of correlation, but in actual practice it is seldom used to determine its value. To derive a computing formula for r, we first substitute

$$\Sigma (y - \bar{y})^2 = S_{yy} \quad \text{and} \quad \Sigma (\hat{y} - \bar{y})^2 = \frac{(S_{xy})^2}{S_{xx}}$$

from page 528 into the formula for r^2, getting

$$r^2 = \frac{(S_{xy})^2}{S_{xx} \cdot S_{yy}}$$

and hence that

Formula for Coefficient of Correlation	$r = \dfrac{S_{xy}}{\sqrt{S_{xx} \cdot S_{yy}}}$

For convenient reference, we remind you that

$$S_{xx} = \Sigma x^2 - \frac{1}{n} (\Sigma x)^2$$

$$S_{yy} = \Sigma y^2 - \frac{1}{n} (\Sigma y)^2$$

$$S_{xy} = \Sigma xy - \frac{1}{n} (\Sigma x)(\Sigma y)$$

Example

The following are the scores which 12 students received in final examinations in economics and anthropology:

Economics	Anthropology
51	74
68	70
72	88
97	93
55	67
73	73
95	99
74	73
20	33
91	91
74	80
80	86

Calculate r.

solution

First calculating the necessary sums, we get

$$\Sigma x = 850, \quad \Sigma x^2 = 65,230, \quad \Sigma y = 927, \quad \Sigma y^2 = 74,883, \quad \text{and} \quad \Sigma xy = 69,453$$

Then, substituting these values together with $n = 12$ into the formulas for S_{xx}, S_{yy}, S_{xy}, and finally r, we find that

$$S_{xx} = 65,230 - \tfrac{1}{12}(850)^2 \approx 5,021.67$$
$$S_{yy} = 74,883 - \tfrac{1}{12}(927)^2 = 3,272.25$$
$$S_{xy} = 69,453 - \tfrac{1}{12}(850)(927) = 3,790.5$$

and

$$r = \frac{3,790.5}{\sqrt{(5,026.7)(3,272.25)}} \approx 0.935$$

Observe that if S_{xy} is positive, then both b and r will be positive; negative S_{xy} leads to negative b and r.

The quantity S_{xy} in the numerator of the formula for r is actually a computing formula for

$$\Sigma(x - \bar{x})(y - \bar{y})$$

which, divided by n, is called the first **product moment.** For this reason, r is also referred to at times as the **product-moment coefficient of correlation.** Note that in $\Sigma (x - \bar{x})(y - \bar{y})$ we add the products obtained by multiplying the deviation of each x from $\bar{x}$ by the deviation of the corresponding y from $\bar{y}$. In this way we literally measure how the x's and y's vary together. If their relationship is such that large values of x tend to go with large values of y, and small values of x with small values of y, the deviations $x - \bar{x}$ and $y - \bar{y}$ tend to be both positive or both negative, and most of the products $(x - \bar{x})(y - \bar{y})$ will be positive. On the other hand, if the relationship is such that large values of x tend to go with small values of y, and small values of x with large values of y, the deviations $x - \bar{x}$ and $y - \bar{y}$ tend to be of opposite sign, and most of the products $(x - \bar{x})(y - \bar{y})$ will be negative. For this reason, $\Sigma (x - \bar{x})(y - \bar{y})$, divided by $n - 1$, is called the **sample covariance.**

16.2 THE INTERPRETATION OF r

When r equals $+1$, -1, or 0, there is no problem about the interpretation of the coefficient of correlation. As we have already indicated, it is $+1$ or -1, when all the points actually fall on a straight line, and it is zero when the fit of the least-squares line is so poor that knowledge of x does not help in the prediction of y. In general, the definition of r tells us that $100r^2$ is the percentage of the total variation of the y's which is explained by, or is due to, their relationship with x. This itself is an important measure of the relationship between two variables; beyond this, it permits valid comparisons of the strength of several relationships. For instance, if $r = 0.80$ in one study and $r = 0.40$ in another study, it would be very misleading to report that the 0.80 correlation is twice as good or twice as strong as the 0.40 correlation. When $r = 0.80$, then

$$100\%(0.80)^2 = 64\%$$

of the variation of the y's is accounted for by the relationship with x, and when $r = 0.40$, only

$$100\%(0.40)^2 = 16\%$$

of the variation of the y's is accounted for by the relationship with x. Thus, in the sense of "percentage of variation accounted for" we can say that the 0.80 correlation is four times as strong as the 0.40 correlation. In the same way, we say that a relationship for which $r = 0.60$ is nine times as strong as a relationship for which $r = 0.20$.

There are several pitfalls in the interpretation of the coefficient of correlation. First, it is often overlooked that r measures only the strength of linear relationships; second, it should be remembered that a strong correlation (a value of r close to $+1$ or -1, does not necessarily imply a cause–effect relationship.

If r is calculated indiscriminately, for instance, for the three sets of data of Figure 16.3, we get $r = 0.75$ in each case, but it is a meaningful measure of the strength of the relationship only in the first case. In the second case there is a very strong curvilinear relationship between the two variables, and in the third case six of the seven points actually fall on a straight line, but the seventh point is so far off that it suggests the possibility of a gross error of measurement or an error in recording the data. Thus, before we calculate r, we should always plot the data to see whether there is reason to believe that the relationship is, in fact, linear.

The fallacy of interpreting a high value of r (that is, a value close to $+1$ or -1), as an indication of a cause–effect relationship, is best explained with a few examples. Frequently used as an illustration, is the high positive correlation be-

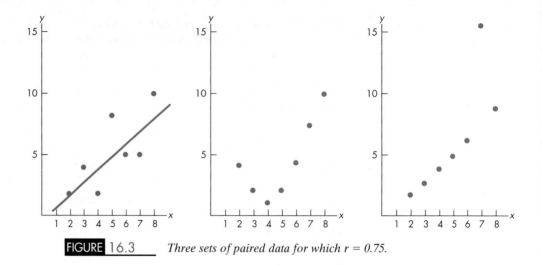

FIGURE 16.3   *Three sets of paired data for which r = 0.75.*

tween the annual sales of chewing gum and the incidence of crime in the United States. Obviously, one cannot conclude that crime might be reduced by prohibiting the sale of chewing gum; both variables depend upon the size of the population, and it is this mutual relationship with a third variable (population size) which produces the positive correlation. Another example is the strong positive correlation which was observed between the number of storks seen nesting in English villages and the number of children born in the same villages. We leave it to the reader's ingenuity to explain why there might be a strong correlation in this case in the absence of any cause–effect relationship.

■ EXERCISES

16.1   Use the values of S_{xx}, S_{yy}, and S_{xy} obtained on page 504 to calculate r for the data dealing with the gradepoint indexes of six students and the average amount of time they spent on homework per week.

16.2   The following are the numbers of minutes it took 12 mechanics to assemble a piece of machinery in the morning, x, and in the late afternoon, y:

x	y
12	14
11	11
9	14
13	11
10	12
11	15
12	12
14	13
10	16
9	10
11	10
12	14

For these data,

$$S_{xx} = 25.6667, \quad S_{xy} = -0.3333, \quad S_{yy} = 42.6667$$

Find the value of r.

16.3   With reference to the preceding exercise, what percentage of the variation of the y's is due to differences among the x's?

16.4   After a student calculated r for a large set of paired data, she discovered to her dismay that the variable which should have been labeled x was labeled y and the variable which should have been labeled y was labeled x. Is there any reason for being dismayed?

16.5   The following table shows the percentages of the vote predicted by a poll for eight candidates for the U.S. Senate in different states, x, and the percentages of the vote which they actually received, y:

x	y
43	50
46	42
51	57
59	55
41	46
53	48
52	53
62	56

For these data,

$$S_{xx} = 378.875, \quad S_{xy} = 185.875, \quad \text{and} \quad S_{yy} = 196.875$$

Find the value of r.

16.6   After a student computed the correlation between height and weight for a large number of people, he realized that the weights were given in kilograms and the heights were given in centimeters. He wanted to obtain the correlation between height in inches and weight in pounds. If there are 0.3937 inch per centimeter and 2.2 pounds per kilogram, how should he correct his calculations?

16.7   If we calculate r for each of the following sets of data, should we be surprised if we get $r = 1$ and $r = -1$? Explain your answers.

(a)

x	y
6	9
14	11

(b)

x	y
12	5
8	15

16.8   The following data were obtained in a study of the relationship between the resistance (ohms) and the failure time (minutes) of certain overloaded resistors:

Resistance	Failure time
48	45
28	25
33	39
40	45
36	36
39	35
46	36
40	45
30	34
42	39
44	51
48	41
39	38
34	32
47	45

For these data,

$$S_{xx} = 577.60, \quad S_{xy} = 413.40, \quad S_{yy} = 596.93$$

Calculate r and determine what percentage of the variation in failure time is due to differences in resistance.

16.9   A student computed the correlation between height and weight for a large group of third grade school children and obtained a value of $r = 0.32$. She was unable to decide whether she should conclude that being tall causes a child to put on more weight or that having excess weight enables a child to grow taller. Help her solve this dilemma.

16.10   State in each case whether you would expect a positive correlation, a negative correlation, or no correlation:

(a) the ages of husbands and wives;

(b) the amount of rubber on tires and the number of miles they have been driven;

(c) the number of hours that golfers practice and their scores;

(d) shoe size and IQ;

(e) the weight of the load of trucks and their gasoline consumption.

16.11   State in each case whether you would expect a positive correlation, a negative correlation, or no correlation:

(a) pollen count and the sale of anti-allergy drugs;

(b) income and education;

(c) the number of sunny days in August in Detroit and the attendance at the Detroit Zoo;

(d) shirt size and sense of humor;

(e) number of persons getting flu shots and number of persons catching the flu.

16.12   With reference to Exercise 15.40 on page 513, calculate r for the copper content and the hardness of the given specimens of steel. For these data,

$$S_{x_1 x_1} = 0.0256, \, S_{x_1 y} = 42.792, \quad \text{and} \quad S_{yy} = 895.9733$$

16.13   With reference to Exercise 15.38 on page 513, calculate r for each of the following pairs of variables:

(a) age and income;

(b) age and years college;

(c) years college and income.

For these data

$$S_{x_1x_1} = 113.20, \quad S_{x_1x_2} = -33, \quad S_{x_2x_2} = 16, \quad S_{x_1y} = 24{,}780, \quad S_{x_2y} = 30{,}900,$$
$$\text{and} \quad S_{yy} = 233{,}352{,}000$$

16.14 If $r = 0.41$ for one set of paired data and $r = 0.29$ for another set of paired data, compare the strengths of the two relationships.

16.15 In a medical study it was found that $r = 0.70$ for the weight of babies six months old and their weight at birth, and that $r = 0.60$ for the weight of babies six months old and their average daily intake of food. Give a counterexample to show that it is not valid to conclude that weight at birth and food intake together account for

$$100\%(0.70)^2 + 100\%(0.60)^2 = 85\%$$

of the variation of babies' weight when they are six months old. Can you explain why the conclusion is not valid?

16.16 Working with various socioeconomic data for the years 1975–1982, a researcher got $r = 0.9225$ for the number of foreign language degrees offered by U.S. colleges and universities and the mileage of railroad track owned by U.S. railroads. Can we conclude that

$$100\%(0.9225)^2 \approx 85.1\%$$

of the variation in the foreign language degrees is accounted for by differences in the ownership of railroad track?

开 16.17 Correlation methods can be used to study internal relationships within a series of data collected at regular intervals. Such data are called **time series** and are commonly encountered in economics, where data are reported annually, monthly, weekly, and so on. The following numbers are total gross sales (in thousands of dollars) for 15 consecutive weeks at a wholesale beverage store:

$$\begin{array}{ccccc} 60 & 58 & 62 & 56 & 47 \\ 44 & 48 & 49 & 47 & 42 \\ 41 & 42 & 46 & 44 & 50 \end{array}$$

We can see how the sales may be related to sales in previous weeks by computing the **autocorrelation coefficients** corresponding to various time lags. For example, the autocorrelation coefficient of lag 1 compares y_t, the sales in week t, with y_{t-1}, the sales in week $t-1$. This requires the computation of the correlation coefficient for these pairs of values:

$$\begin{array}{l} y_t: \quad 60 \ \ 58 \ \ 62 \ \ 56 \ \ 47 \ \ 44 \ \ 48 \ \ 49 \ \ 47 \ \ 42 \ \ 41 \ \ 42 \ \ 46 \ \ 44 \\ y_{t-1}: \ 58 \ \ 62 \ \ 56 \ \ 47 \ \ 44 \ \ 48 \ \ 49 \ \ 47 \ \ 42 \ \ 41 \ \ 42 \ \ 46 \ \ 44 \ \ 50 \end{array}$$

Observe that there are only 14 pairs in this list.

Similarly, the autocorrelation coefficient of lag 2 requires the computation of the correlation coefficient for these 13 pairs of values:

$$\begin{array}{l} y_t: \quad 60 \ \ 58 \ \ 62 \ \ 56 \ \ 47 \ \ 44 \ \ 48 \ \ 49 \ \ 47 \ \ 42 \ \ 41 \ \ 42 \ \ 46 \\ y_{t-2}: \ 62 \ \ 56 \ \ 47 \ \ 44 \ \ 48 \ \ 49 \ \ 47 \ \ 42 \ \ 41 \ \ 42 \ \ 46 \ \ 44 \ \ 50 \end{array}$$

(a) Find the value of the autocorrelation coefficient of lag 1. The relevant sums of squares are

$$S_{y_t y_t} = 650, \quad S_{y_t y_{t-1}} = 465, \quad \text{and} \quad S_{y_{t-1} y_{t-1}} = 522.8571$$

(b) Find the value of the autocorrelation coefficient of lag 2. The relevant sums of squares are

$$S_{y_t y_t} = 623.0769, \quad S_{y_t y_{t-2}} = 277.3077, \quad \text{and} \quad S_{y_{t-2} y_{t-2}} = 421.2308$$

⊞ 16.18   Correlation methods are sometimes used to study the relationship between two time series of data. For the years 1983–1996 (14 years in all) a large textile manufacturer notes
it spending on research and development (R&D) and its share of the market, as follows:

Year	R&D (millions of dollars)	Market share (%)
1983	0.8	20.4
1984	0.5	18.6
1985	0.8	19.1
1986	1.0	18.0
1987	1.0	18.2
1988	0.9	19.6
1989	0.8	20.0
1990	1.2	20.4
1991	1.0	19.2
1992	0.9	20.5
1993	0.8	20.8
1994	1.0	18.9
1995	1.0	19.0
1996	0.8	19.8

To see whether and how the market share may be related to expenditure on R&D in
prior years, let x_t denote the company's R&D expenditures in year t and let y_t denote the
market share in year t.

(a) Calculate the correlation coefficient for y_t and x_{t-1}.

(b) Calculate the correlation coefficient for y_t and x_{t-2}.

(c) Calculate the correlation coefficient for y_t and x_{t-3}.

(d) Calculate the correlation coefficient for y_t and x_{t-4}.

(e) Discuss the apparent duration of the effect of expenditure on research and development on the company's share of the market.

For instance, part (a) asks for the correlation for the data organized as:

Year	Previous year R&D (millions of dollars)	Market share (%)
1984	0.8	18.6
1985	0.5	19.1
1986	0.8	18.0
1987	1.0	18.2
1988	1.0	19.6
1989	0.9	20.0
1990	0.8	20.4
1991	1.2	19.2
1992	1.0	20.5
1993	0.9	20.8
1994	0.8	18.9
1995	1.0	19.0
1996	1.0	19.8

There are only 13 years in this display. Note that the market share for 1984 is paired with
the R&D expenditures for 1983.

Part (b) involves only 12 years. The market share for 1985 is paired with the R&D expenditures for 1983.

Part (c) involves 11 years, and part (d) involves 10 years.

These time-lag correlations are called **cross correlations.**

For part (a), the relevant sums of squares are

$$S_{x_{t-1}x_{t-1}} = 0.34, \quad S_{x_{t-1}y_t} = 0.24, \quad \text{and} \quad S_{y_t y_t} = 9.3092$$

For part (b), the relevant sums of squares are

$$S_{x_{t-2}x_{t-2}} = 0.3292, \quad S_{x_{t-2}y_t} = 1.3658, \quad \text{and} \quad S_{y_t y_t} = 8.6292$$

For part (c), the relevant sums of squares are

$$S_{x_{t-3}x_{t-3}} = 0.3164, \quad S_{x_{t-3}y_t} = 0.9982, \quad \text{and} \quad S_{y_t y_t} = 8.4891$$

For part (d), the relevant sums of squares are

$$S_{x_{t-4}x_{t-4}} = 0.3090, \quad S_{x_{t-4}y_t} = -0.2460, \quad \text{and} \quad S_{y_t y_t} = 6.0440.$$

16.3 CORRELATION ANALYSIS

When r is calculated on the basis of sample data, we may get a strong positive or negative correlation purely by chance, even though there is actually no relationship whatever between the two variables under consideration.

Suppose, for instance, that we take a pair of dice, one red and one green, roll

Red die x	Green die y
4	5
2	2
4	6
2	1
6	4

them five times, and get the following results:

Presumably, there is no relationship between x and y, the numbers of points showing on the two dice. It is hard to see why large values of x should go with large values of y and small values of x with small values of y, but calculating r, we get the surprisingly high value $r = 0.66$. This raises the question of whether something is wrong with the assumption that there is no relationship between x and y, and to answer it we shall have to see whether the high value of r may be attributed to chance.

When a correlation coefficient is calculated from sample data, as in the above example, the value we get for r is only an estimate of a corresponding parameter, the **population correlation coefficient,** which we denote by ρ (the Greek letter *rho*). What r measures for a sample, ρ measures for a population.

To make inferences about ρ on the basis of r, we shall have to make several assumptions about the distributions of the random variables whose values we observe. In **normal correlation analysis** we make the same assumptions as in normal regression analysis (see page 501), except that the x's are not constants, but values of a random variable having a normal distribution.

Since the sampling distribution of r is rather complicated under these assumptions, it is common practice to base inferences about ρ on the **Fisher Z transformation**, a change of scale from r to Z, which is given by

$$Z = \frac{1}{2} \cdot \ln \frac{1 + r}{1 - r}$$

Here the abbreviation ln denotes "natural logarithm," that is, logarithm to the base e, where $e = 2.71828 \ldots$.[†] This transformation is named after R. A. Fisher, a prominent statistician, who showed that under the assumptions of normal correlation analysis and for any value of ρ, the distribution of Z is approximately normal with

$$\mu_Z = \frac{1}{2} \cdot \ln \frac{1 + \rho}{1 - \rho} \quad \text{and} \quad \sigma_Z = \frac{1}{\sqrt{n - 3}}$$

Hence,

Statistic for Inferences About ρ	$z = \dfrac{Z - \mu_Z}{\sigma_Z} = (Z - \mu_Z)\sqrt{n - 3}$

has approximately the standard normal distribution. The application of this theory is greatly facilitated by the use of Table IX at the end of the book, which gives the values of Z corresponding to

$$r = 0.00, \quad 0.01, \quad 0.02, \quad 0.03, \quad \ldots, \quad \text{and} \quad 0.99$$

Observe that only positive values are given in this table; if r is negative, we simply look up $-r$ and take the negative of the corresponding Z. Note also that the formula for μ_Z is like that for Z with r replaced by ρ; therefore, Table IX can be used to look up values of μ_Z corresponding to given values of ρ.

Example

Use the 0.05 level of significance to test the null hypothesis of no correlation (that is, the null hypothesis $\rho = 0$) for the example where we rolled a pair of dice five times and got $r = 0.66$.

solution

1. H_0: $\rho = 0$
   H_A: $\rho \neq 0$
2. $\alpha = 0.05$
3. Since $\mu_Z = 0$ for $\rho = 0$, reject the null hypothesis if $z \leq -1.96$ or $z \geq 1.96$, where

$$z = Z \cdot \sqrt{n - 3}$$

[†]Fisher's Z requires that base e logarithms be used.

Otherwise, state that the value of r is not significant.

4. Substituting $n = 5$ and $Z = 0.793$, the value of Z corresponding to $r = 0.66$ according to Table IX, we get

$$z = 0.793 \sqrt{5 - 3} \approx 1.12$$

5. Since $z = 1.12$ falls on the interval from -1.96 to 1.96, the null hypothesis cannot be rejected; in other words, the value obtained for r is not significant, as should have been expected. ◾◾◾

An alternative way of handling this kind of problem (namely, testing the null hypothesis $\rho = 0$) is given in Exercise 16.23 on page 541.

Example

With reference to the example dealing with the proficiency scores of certain applicants for foreign service jobs, where we had $n = 10$ and $r = 0.91$, test the null hypothesis $\rho = 0.70$ against the alternative hypothesis $\rho > 0.70$ at the 0.05 level of significance.

solution

1. H_0: $\rho = 0.70$
   H_A: $\rho > 0.70$
2. $\alpha = 0.05$
3. Reject the null hypothesis if $z \geq 1.645$, where $z = (Z - \mu_Z)\sqrt{n - 3}$ and otherwise, accept the null hypothesis or reserve judgment.
4. Substituting $n = 10$, $Z = 1.528$ corresponding to $r = 0.91$, and $\mu_Z = 0.867$ corresponding to $\rho = 0.70$ according to Table IX, we get

$$z = (1.528 - 0.867)\sqrt{10 - 3} \approx 1.75$$

5. Since $z = 1.75$ exceeds 1.645, the null hypothesis must be rejected; we conclude that $\rho > 0.70$ for the proficiency scores of applicants to the foreign service jobs and the number of years that they have studied German in high school or college. ◾◾◾

To construct confidence intervals for ρ, we first construct confidence intervals for μ_Z, and then convert to r and ρ by means of Table IX. A confidence interval formula for μ_Z may be obtained by substituting

$$z = (Z - \mu_Z)\sqrt{n - 3}$$

for the middle term of the double inequality $-z_{\alpha/2} < z < z_{\alpha/2}$, and then manipulating the terms algebraically so that the middle term is μ_Z. This leads to the following $100(1 - \alpha)$ percent confidence interval for μ_Z:

Confidence interval for μ_Z

$$Z - \frac{z_{\alpha/2}}{\sqrt{n - 3}} < \mu_Z < Z + \frac{z_{\alpha/2}}{\sqrt{n - 3}}$$

Example

If $r = 0.62$ for the cost estimates of two mechanics for a random sample of 30 repair jobs, construct a 95 percent confidence interval for the population correlation coefficient.

solution

Getting $Z = 0.725$, corresponding to $r = 0.62$, from Table IX, and substituting it together with $n = 30$ and $z_{0.025} = 1.96$ into the above confidence interval formula for μ_Z, we find that

$$0.725 - \frac{1.96}{\sqrt{27}} < \mu_Z < 0.725 + \frac{1.96}{\sqrt{27}} \quad \text{or} \quad 0.348 < \mu_Z < 1.102$$

Finally, looking up the values of r which come closest to $Z = 0.348$ and $Z = 1.102$ in Table IX, we get the 95 percent confidence interval

$$0.33 < \rho < 0.80$$

for the true strength of the linear relationship between cost estimates made by the two mechanics.   ◣ ◣ ◣

Example

If $r = 0.20$ for a random sample of $n = 40$ paired data, construct a 95 percent confidence interval for ρ.

solution

Getting $Z = 0.203$, corresponding to $r = 0.20$, from Table IX, and substituting it together with $n = 40$ and $z_{0.025} = 1.96$ into the above confidence interval formula for μ_Z, we find that

$$0.203 - \frac{1.96}{\sqrt{37}} < \mu_Z < 0.203 + \frac{1.96}{\sqrt{37}} \quad \text{or} \quad -0.119 < \mu_Z < 0.525$$

Then, looking up in Table IX the values of r which come closest to $Z = 0.119$ and $Z = 0.525$, we get the 95 percent confidence interval

$$-0.12 < \rho < 0.48$$

for the population correlation coefficient.   ◣ ◣ ◣

◪ EXERCISES

16.19   With reference to Exercise 16.2 on page 532, test the null hypothesis of no correlation at the 0.05 level of significance.

16.20   With reference to Exercise 16.8 on page 533, test the null hypothesis $\rho = 0$ against the alternative hypothesis $\rho \neq 0$ at the 0.05 level of significance.

16.21   With reference to Exercise 15.14 on page 498,

(a) calculate r for the given data;

(b) test at the 0.05 level of significance whether the value of r obtained in part (a) is significant.

16.22   With reference to Exercise 15.7 on page 496,

(a) determine what percentage of the variation in the yield can be attributed to differ-ence in the rainfall;

(b) test the null hypothesis of no correlation (between rainfall and yield) at the 0.01 level of significance.

16.23   Under the assumptions of normal correlation analysis, the test of the null hypothesis $\rho = 0$ may also be based on the statistic

$$t = \frac{r \sqrt{n-2}}{}$$

which has the t distribution with $n - 2$ degrees of freedom. Use this statistic to test in each case whether the value of r is significant at the 0.05 level of significance:

(a) $n = 12$ and $r = 0.50$;   (b) $n = 20$ and $r = 0.62$.

16.24   Use the t statistic of the preceding exercise to test in each case whether the value of r is significant at the 0.01 level of significance:

(a) $n = 14$ and $r = 0.78$;   (b) $n = 16$ and $r = 0.51$.

16.25   Use the t statistic of Exercise 16.24 to rework Exercise 16.19.

16.26   Wit h reference to Exercise 15.7 on page 496,

(a) use the t statistic of Exercise 16.24 to test the null hypothesis of no correlation;

(b) find the t statistic which tests the null hypothesis $\beta = 0$;

(c) compare the results of (a) and (b).

16.27   The t statistic given in Exercise 16.24 is numerically identical to the t statistic which tests $\beta = 0$ in the regression of Y on X. Show that this is so by expressing both t statistics in terms of S_{xx}, S_{xy}, S_{yy}, and n.

16.28   In a study of the relationship between the death rate from lung cancer and the per capita consumption of cigarettes twenty years earlier, data for $n = 9$ countries yielded $r = 0.73$. At the 0.05 level of significance, test the null hypothesis $\rho = 0.50$ against the alternative hypothesis $\rho > 0.50$.

16.29   In a study of the relationship between the available heat (per cord) of green wood and air-dried wood, data for $n = 13$ kinds of wood yielded $r = 0.94$. Use the 0.01 level of sig-nificance to test the null hypothesis $\rho = 0.75$ against the alternative hypothesis $\rho \neq 0.75$.

16.30   If $n = 18$ and $r = -0.64$ for certain paired data, test the null hypothesis $\rho = -0.30$ against the alternative hypothesis $\rho < -0.30$ at the 0.05 level of significance.

16.31   Assuming that the conditions underlying normal correlation analysis are met, use the Fisher Z transformation to construct approximate 95 percent confidence intervals for ρ when

(a) $r = 0.80$ and $n = 15$;   (b) $r = -0.22$ and $n = 30$;   (c) $r = 0.64$ and $n = 100$.

16.32   Assuming that the conditions underlying normal correlation analysis are met, use the Fisher Z transformation to construct approximate 99 percent confidence intervals for ρ when

(a) $r = -0.87$ and $n = 19$;   (b) $r = 0.39$ and $n = 24$;   (c) $r = 0.16$ and $n = 40$.

16.4   CORRELATIONS FOR COUNT DATA ⇔

Correlations can also be computed for cross-classified count data, provided that both categories of classifications are ordered. This is the analysis suggested in Section 13.5 when we first encountered such data, and the details will be com-pleted here. The data in the table below indicate the numbers of broken eggs in each of 600 cartons received at a particular supermarket loading dock. The data have been displayed in this fashion to find out if there is any relationship between egg size and the tendency to break.

	0	1	2	3	4	Total
Medium	52	26	12	7	3	100
Large	98	35	10	6	1	150
X-Large	188	40	16	4	2	250
Jumbo	80	16	3	1	0	100

Number of broken eggs

This table must be read carefully. The shipment involved 100 cartons of medium eggs; of these 100 cartons, 52 cartons had no broken eggs, 26 cartons had one broken egg, and so on.

A great many analyses are possible for such data. We could, for example, compute the χ^2 statistic to test whether the probabilities of the various numbers of broken eggs are the same for each size category. We could also utilize the fact that there are four different types of cartons, and we could do an analysis of variance. These methods are both described in Chapters 13 and 14, and they are both valid. The χ^2 statistic ignores the orderings on the sizes of the eggs and on the numbers of broken eggs. The analysis of variance utilizes the numbers of broken eggs as data values, but ignores ordering on the sizes of the eggs. These analyses are valid tests of the null hypothesis of no relation between size of egg and likelihood of breakage, but they are less likely to produce significant test statistics than the test based on the correlation coefficient.

We can calculate the correlation coefficient most easily by assigning integer scores to the numbers of broken eggs and to the egg sizes. The numbers of broken eggs are already given as integers 0, 1, 2, 3, and 4, and we should not alter these scores. The egg sizes can be encoded in many ways, but it is simplest to assign the values as 1, 2, 3, and 4. The choice of scores is of course subjective. The row totals will be needed in the calculations, and these are already provided in the table. The column totals can be found to be 418, 117, 41, 18, and 6. We had 418 cartons with no broken eggs, 117 cartons with one broken egg, 41 with two broken eggs, 18 with three broken, and 6 with four broken. There were 600 cartons in this problem, and indeed

$$418 + 117 + 41 + 18 + 6 = 600$$

Let x correspond to the egg size. The possible values for x are 1, 2, 3, and 4, so that

$$\Sigma\, x = 100 \cdot 1 + 150 \cdot 2 + 250 \cdot 3 + 100 \cdot 4 = 1{,}550$$

In similar fashion we can find

$$\Sigma\, x^2 = 100 \cdot 1^2 + 150 \cdot 2^2 + 250 \cdot 3^2 + 100 \cdot 4^2 = 4{,}550$$

Let y correspond to the number of broken eggs. The possible values for y are 0, 1, 2, 3, and 4. Then

$$\Sigma\, y = 418 \cdot 0 + 117 \cdot 1 + 41 \cdot 2 + 18 \cdot 3 + 6 \cdot 4 = 277$$

We will then find

$$y^2 = 418 \cdot 0^2 + 117 \cdot 1^2 + 41 \cdot 2^2 + 18 \cdot 3^2 + 6 \cdot 4^2 = 539$$

The sum Σxy is also needed. This will use the individual entries of the table, and it is calculated as

$$
\begin{aligned}
\Sigma xy = \ & 52 \cdot 0 + 26 \cdot 1 + 12 \cdot 2 + 7 \cdot\ 3 + 3 \cdot\ 4 \\
+ \ & 98 \cdot 0 + 35 \cdot 2 + 10 \cdot 4 + 6 \cdot\ 6 + 1 \cdot\ 8 \\
+ \ & 188 \cdot 0 + 40 \cdot 3 + 16 \cdot 6 + 4 \cdot\ 9 + 2 \cdot 12 \\
+ \ & 80 \cdot 0 + 16 \cdot 4 + \ 3 \cdot 8 + 1 \cdot 12 + 0 \cdot 16 \\
= \ & 613
\end{aligned}
$$

We can now find

$$S_{xx} = 4{,}550 - \frac{1550^2}{600} \approx 545.8333$$

$$S_{yy} = 539 - \frac{277^2}{600} \approx 411.1183$$

$$S_{xy} = 613 - \frac{1{,}550 \cdot 277}{600} \approx -102.5833$$

We substitute these into the formula for r to obtain

$$r = \frac{-102.5833}{\sqrt{(545.8333)(411.1183)}} \approx -0.2166$$

The numeric value of r conveys much more information about the data than would the chi-squared test or the analysis of variance. There are many steps in the calculations for r, and use of a computer is recommended.

16.5 MULTIPLE AND PARTIAL CORRELATION ☺

In Section 16.1 we introduced the coefficient of correlation as a measure of goodness of the fit of a least-squares line to a set of paired data. If predictions are to be made with an equation of the form

$$\hat{y} = b_0 + b_1 x_1 + b_2 x_2 + \cdots + b_k x_k$$

obtained by the method of least squares as in Section 15.4, we define the **multiple correlation coefficient** in the same way in which we originally defined r. We take the square root of the quantity

$$\frac{\Sigma(\hat{y} - \bar{y})^2}{}$$

which is the proportion of the total variation of the y's that can be attributed to the relationship with the x's. The only difference is that we now calculate $\hat{y}$ by means of the multiple regression equation instead of the equation $\hat{y} = a + bx$.

Example

In the example on page 510, where we derived the multiple regression equation

$$\hat{y} = 65{,}192 + 4{,}133x_1 + 758x_2$$

it can be shown that

$$\Sigma(\hat{y} - \bar{y})^2 = 185{,}269{,}168 \quad \text{and} \quad \Sigma(y - \bar{y})^2 = 185{,}955{,}008$$

What is the value of the multiple correlation coefficient? (Actually, these values were obtained with a continuation of the computer program which yielded the printout shown in Figure 15.8 on page 512. The square of the multiple correlation coefficient is identified as R–sq in Figure 15.8.)

solution

Since

$$\frac{185{,}269{,}168}{185{,}955{,}008} \approx 0.9963$$

it follows that the multiple correlation coefficient is $\sqrt{0.9963} \approx 0.998$. ◤ ◤ ◤

This example also serves to illustrate that adding more independent variables in a correlation study may not be sufficiently productive to justify the extra work. As it can be shown that $r = 0.996$ for y and x_1 alone, it is apparent that very little is gained by considering also x_2. In other words, predictions based on the number of bedrooms alone are virtually as good as predictions which account also for the number of baths. The situation is quite different, though, in Exercise 16.37, where two independent variables together account for a much higher proportion of the total variation in y than does either x_1 or x_2 alone.

When we discussed the problem of correlation and causation, we showed that a strong correlation between two variables may be due entirely to their dependence on a third variable. We illustrated this with the examples of chewing gum sales and the crime rate, and child births and the number of storks. To give another example, let us consider the two variables x_1, the weekly amount of hot chocolate sold by a refreshment stand at a summer resort, and x_2, the weekly number of visitors to the resort. If, on the basis of suitable data, we get $r = -0.30$ for these variables, this should come as a surprise—after all, we would expect more sales of hot chocolate when there are more visitors, and vice versa, and hence a positive correlation.

However, if we think for a moment, we may surmise that the negative correlation of -0.30 may well be due to the fact that the variables x_1 and x_2 are both related to a third variable x_3, the average weekly temperature at the resort. If the temperature is high, there will be more visitors, but they will prefer cold drinks to hot chocolate; if the temperature is low, there will be fewer visitors, but they will prefer hot chocolate to cold drinks. So, let us suppose that further data yield $r = -0.70$ for x_1 and x_3, and $r = 0.80$ for x_2 and x_3. These values seem reasonable since low sales of hot chocolate should go with high temperatures and vice versa, while the number of visitors should be high when the temperature is high, and low when the temperature is low.

In the preceding example, we should really have investigated the relationship between x_1 and x_2 (hot chocolate sales and the number of visitors to the resort) when all other factors, primarily temperature, are held fixed. As it is seldom possible to control matters to such an extent, it has been found that a statistic called the **partial correlation coefficient** does a fair job of eliminating the effects of other variables. If we write the ordinary correlation coefficients for x_1 and x_2, x_1 and x_3, and x_2 and x_3, as r_{12}, r_{13}, and r_{23}, the partial correlation coefficient for x_1 and x_2 with x_3 fixed is given by

Partial Correlation Coefficient	$$r_{12.3} = \dfrac{r_{12} - r_{13} \cdot r_{23}}{\sqrt{1 - r_{13}^2}\sqrt{1 - r_{23}^2}}$$

Example

Calculate $r_{12.3}$ for the example above.

solution

Substituting $r_{12} = -0.30$, $r_{13} = -0.70$, and $r_{23} = 0.80$ into the formula for $r_{12.3}$, we get

$$r_{12.3} = \frac{(-0.30) - (-0.70)(0.80)}{\sqrt{1 - (-0.70)^2}\sqrt{1 - (0.80)^2}} \approx 0.607$$

This result shows that, as we expected, there is a positive relationship between the sales of hot chocolate and the number of visitors to the resort when the effect of differences in temperature is eliminated.   ◪ ◪ ◪

We have given this example mainly to illustrate what we mean by partial correlation, but it also serves as a reminder that correlation coefficients can be very misleading unless they are interpreted with care. Partial correlation coefficients do not solve the problem of interpreting ordinary correlation coefficients, so they should also be used with considerable caution.

◪ EXERCISES

⇧ 16.33   The data in the table shown at the end of this Exercise summarize the results of a survey question given to 122 students at a particular college. The question, "Do you favor the retention of the college's current humanities requirements?" had seven response categories. These categories ranged from "strongly disagree" to "strongly agree." Compute the correlation coefficient to assess the relationship between opinion and year in college. Assign the scores 1, 2, 3, and 4 to the rows of the table. To the columns of the table assign scores −3, −2, −1, 0, 1, 2, and 3.

Responses of 122 college students to a question on the humanities requirement

	Very strongly disagree	Strongly disagree	Disagree	Neutral	Agree	Strongly agree	Very strongly agree	Total
Freshman	2	1	2	14	8	3	1	31
Sophomore	0	2	2	9	8	4	2	27
Junior	1	0	0	10	13	2	2	28
Senior	1	0	1	8	17	5	4	36
Total	4	3	5	41	46	14	9	122

16.34 Exercise 13.70 on page 425 examined the relationship between bank employees' standard of dress and their professional advancement. Compute a correlation coefficient between these two variables, using evenly spaced scores. (*Hint:* The arithmetic will be relatively simple with scores −1, 0, and 1 for each of the variables.)

16.35 Residents of a long-term health-care facility were asked to rate the quality of a new chicken salad recipe, choosing responses from the list *poor, acceptable, good,* and *delicious*. In fact, the residents were given, at random, one of three different versions of the chicken salad recipe, differing only in the amount of salt. Here is a summary of their responses:

	Poor	*Acceptable*	*Good*	*Delicious*
100 mg salt	6	4	1	0
200 mg salt	0	2	7	3
400 mg salt	0	1	4	5

The salt amounts are specified in milligrams of sodium per 4 ounces of chicken salad.

(a) Compute the correlation coefficient between the amount of salt and the ratings, using evenly spaced scores.

(b) Compute the correlation coefficient between these variables, using evenly spaced scores for the ratings and scores 1, 2, and 4 for the salt amounts.

(c) If you repeated part (b), using scores -1, 0, and 2 for the salt amounts, would you get the same value for the correlation coefficient?

⟘ 16.36 In a multiple regression problem, the regression sum of squares is

$$\Sigma (\hat{y} - \bar{y})^2 = 45{,}225$$

and the total sum of squares is

$$\Sigma (y - \bar{y})^2 = 136{,}210$$

Find the value of the multiple correlation coefficient.

⟘ 16.37 Use the least-squares equation obtained in Exercise 15.38 on page 513 to calculate $\hat{y}$ for each of the five executives. Then determine the values of

$$\Sigma (\hat{y} - \bar{y})^2 \quad \text{and} \quad \Sigma (y - \bar{y})^2$$

and calculate the multiple correlation coefficient. Also compare the result with the values obtained for r in parts (a) and (c) of Exercise 16.13 on page 534.

16.38 Use the least-squares equation obtained in Exercise 15.39 on page 513 to calculate $\hat{y}$ for each of the six shipments. Then calculate the regression sum of squares, the total sum of squares, and the multiple correlation coefficient.

16.39 An experiment was conducted to determine if the height of certain rose bushes can be predicted on the basis of the amount of rose fertilizer and the amount of irrigation that is applied to the soil. For predicting the height on the basis of both variables, they obtained a multiple correlation coefficient of 0.58; for predicting the height on the basis of the amount of rose fertilizer alone they got $r = 0.66$. Comment on these results.

16.40 Using the illustration on pages 544 and 545, find the partial correlation coefficient for x_1 (sales of hot chocolate) and x_3 (temperature) when x_2 (number of visitors) remains fixed.

16.41 Use the results of Exercise 16.13 on page 534 to find:

(a) the partial correlation coefficient for age and income when years of college remains fixed;

(b) the partial correlation coefficient for years of college and income when age remains fixed.

16.42 An experiment yielded the following results:

$$r_{12} = 0.80, \quad r_{13} = -0.70, \quad \text{and} \quad r_{23} = 0.90$$

Explain why these figures cannot all be correct.

16.6 ◪ CHECKLIST OF KEY TERMS[†] (*with page references to their definitions*)

[†]Terms shown in italics are introduced in the exercises.

16.7 ☑ REVIEW EXERCISES

16.43   If $r = 0.45$ for one set of paired data and $r = 0.90$ for another, is the 0.90 correlation twice as strong as the 0.45 correlation?

⊖ 16.44   Use the least-squares equation obtained in Exercise 15.56 on page 522 to calculate $\hat{y}$ for each of the five restaurants. Then calculate the regression and total sums of squares, and the multiple correlation coefficient.

16.45   If $r = 0.56$ for one set of paired data and $r = -0.97$ for another, compare the strengths of the two relationships.

16.46   Working a homework assignment, Sue obtained

$$S_{xx} = 145.22, \quad S_{xy} = -210.58, \quad \text{and} \quad S_{yy} = 287.45$$

for a given set of paired data. Explain why there must be an error in her calculations.

16.47   A set of $n = 22$ paired observations yielded $r = 0.36$. Test the null hypothesis of no correlation at the 0.05 level of significance:

(a) using the test based on the Fisher Z transformation;

(b) using the t statistic of Exercise 16.23 on page 541.

16.48   The following data pertain to a study of the effects of environmental pollution on wildlife; in particular, the relationship between DDT and the thickness of the eggshells of certain birds:

DDT residue in yolk lipids (parts per million)	Thickness of eggshells (millimeters)
117	0.49
65	0.52
303	0.37
98	0.53
122	0.49
150	0.42

If x is used for the DDT residue and y for the shell thickness, then

$$S_{xx} = 34{,}873.50, \quad S_{xy} = -23.89, \quad \text{and} \quad S_{yy} = 0.0194$$

Calculate r for these data.

16.49   With reference to the preceding exercise, test at the 0.05 level of significance whether the value obtained for r is significant.

16.50   If $r = 0.25$ for the ages of a group of college students and their knowledge of foreign affairs, what percentage of the variation of their knowledge of foreign affairs can be attributed to differences in age?

16.51   Assuming that the conditions underlying normal correlation analysis are met, use the Fisher Z transformation to construct approximate 95 percent confidence intervals for ρ when:

(a) $r = 0.44$ and $n = 20$;   (b) $r = -0.32$ and $n = 38$

16.52   State in each case whether you would expect a positive correlation, a negative correlation, or no correlation:

(a) the number of hours that sprinters practice and the time in which they run 100 yards;

(b) family expenditures on food and family expenditures on clothing;

(c) daily high humidity and the Dow Jones index;

(d) malpractice insurance claims and malpractice insurance rates.

16.53 In a multiple regression problem, the residual sum of squares is

$$\Sigma\,(y - \hat{y})^2 = 926$$

and the total sum of squares is

$$\Sigma\,(y - \bar{y})^2 = 1{,}702$$

Find the value of the multiple correlation coefficient.

16.54 Calculate r for the data of Exercise 15.52 on pages 521 and 522 and test the null hypothesis of no correlation at the 0.01 level of significance.

16.55 The following are the numbers of inquiries which a real estate agency received in eight weeks about houses for rent, x, and houses for sale, y:

x	y
60	82
72	85
47	62
38	53
17	29
45	50
33	69
57	88

For these data,

$$S_{xx} = 2{,}068.8750, \quad S_{xy} = 2{,}111.25, \quad S_{yy} = 2{,}907.50$$

Calculate r.

16.56 With reference to the preceding exercise, test the null hypothesis $\rho = 0.70$ against the alternative hypothesis $\rho > 0.70$ at the 0.05 level of significance.

16.57 In connection with the study referred to in Exercise 16.16 on page 000, the researcher coded the years -3, -2, -1, 0, 1, 2, 3, and 4, and got $r = -0.9725$ for the coded years and the number of foreign language degrees conferred, and $r = -0.9821$ for the coded years and the ownership of railroad track. Find the partial correlation coefficient for the number of foreign language degrees conferred and the ownership of railroad track when time is held fixed.

16.8 ◢ REFERENCES

More detailed information about multiple and partial correlation may be found in

EZEKIEL, M., and FOX, K. A., *Methods of Correlation and Regression Analysis, 3rd ed.* New York: John Wiley & Sons, Inc., 1959.

HARRIS, R. J., *A Primer of Multivariate Statistics.* New York: Academic Press, Inc., 1975.

and an advanced theoretical treatment is given in Volume 2 of

KENDALL, M. G., and STUART, A., *The Advanced Theory of Statistics, 3rd ed.* New York: Hafner Press, 1973.

Volume 1 of this book provides the theoretical foundation of significance tests for r.

CHAPTER

17

NONPARAMETRIC TESTS

$\mathcal{M}$*ost of the tests cited in Chapters 11 through 16 require specific assumptions about the population, or populations, sampled. In many cases we must assume that the populations have roughly the shape of normal distributions, that their variances are known or are known to be equal, or that the samples are independent. Since there are many situations where it is doubtful whether all the necessary assumptions can be met, statisticians have developed alternative procedures based on less stringent assumptions, known as* **nonparametric tests.**

Aside from the fact that nonparametric tests can be used under more general conditions than the standard tests they replace, they are often easier to explain and understand; moreover, in many nonparametric tests the computational burden is so light that they come under the heading of "quick and easy" or "shortcut" techniques. For all these reasons, nonparametric tests are quite popular, and extensive literature is devoted to their theory and application.

In Sections 17.1 and 17.2 we present the sign test as a nonparametric alternative to tests concerning means and tests concerning differences between means based on paired data. Another nonparametric test that serves the same purpose but is more concise, is given in Sections 17.3 and 17.4. In Sections 17.5 through 17.7 we present a nonparametric alternative to tests concerning differences between means based on independent samples and a somewhat similar nonparametric alternative to the one-way analysis of variance. In Sections 17.8 through 17.10 we learn how to test the randomness of a sample after the data have actually been obtained; and in Section 17.11 we present a nonparametric test of the significance of a relationship between paired data. In Section 17.12 we mention some of the weaknesses of nonparametric methods, and in Section 17.13 we present a list of the various nonparametric tests and the "standard" tests that they replace. ∎

17.1   THE SIGN TEST

Except for the large-sample tests, the tests concerning means in Chapter 11 are based on the assumption that the populations sampled have roughly the shape of normal distributions. When this assumption is untenable in practice, these standard tests can be replaced by any one of several nonparametric alternatives, and these are the subject matter of Sections 17.1 through 17.7.

Our first, and simplest, alternative is the **sign test,** which we study in this section and in Section 17.2.

The **one-sample sign test** applies when we sample a continuous population, so that the probability of getting a sample value less than the median and the probability of getting a sample value greater than the median are both $\frac{1}{2}$. It is helpful to note that the sign test involves the population median. Of course, if the population is symmetrical, the mean μ and median $\tilde{\mu}$ are the same.

To test the null hypothesis $\tilde{\mu} = \tilde{\mu}_0$ against an appropriate alternative on the basis of a random sample of size n, we replace each sample value greater than $\tilde{\mu}_0$ with a plus sign and each sample value less than $\tilde{\mu}_0$ with a minus sign. Then we test the null hypothesis that the number of plus signs are the values of a random variable having the binomial distribution with $p = \frac{1}{2}$. If any sample value equals $\tilde{\mu}_0$ exactly, which may certainly happen with rounded data, we simply discard it.

To perform a one-sample sign test when the sample is small, we refer directly to a table of binomial probabilities, such as Table V at the end of this book. When the sample is large, we use the normal approximation to the binomial distribution, as illustrated in Section 17.2.

Example

The following data constitute a random sample of 15 measurements of the octane rating of a specific brand of gasoline:

$$97.5 \quad 95.2 \quad 97.3 \quad 96.0 \quad 96.8 \quad 100.3 \quad 97.4 \quad 95.3$$
$$93.2 \quad 99.1 \quad 96.1 \quad 97.6 \quad 98.2 \quad 98.5 \quad 94.9$$

Use the one-sample sign test to test the null hypothesis $\tilde{\mu} = 98.5$ against the alternative hypothesis $\tilde{\mu} < 98.5$ at the 0.01 level of significance.

solution

Since one of the sample values equals 98.5, it must be discarded and the sample size for the one-sample sign test is only $n = 14$.

1. H_0: $\tilde{\mu} = 98.5$
   H_A: $\tilde{\mu} < 98.5$
2. $\alpha = 0.01$
3'. The test statistic is x itself, the number of plus signs.
4'. Replacing each value greater than 98.5 with a plus sign and each value less than 98.5 with a minus sign, the 14 sample values not equal to 98.5 yield

$$- \; - \; - \; - \; - \; + \; - \; - \; - \; + \; - \; - \; - \; -$$

Thus, $x = 2$ and Table V show that for $n = 14$ and $p = 0.50$, the probability that $x \leq 2$ is

$$0.001 + 0.006 = 0.007$$

The p-value is, then, 0.007.
5'. Since 0.007 is less than 0.01, the null hypothesis must be rejected. We conclude that the median octane rating of the specific brand of gasoline is less than 98.5.   ◢ ◢ ◢

In this example, we used the alternative method for testing the hypothesis, as mentioned on pages 351–352. The alternate method, using the p-value, will be easier for many of the nonparametric procedures.

The sign test can also be used when we deal with paired data as in Section 11.10. For such problems, each pair of sample values is replaced with a plus sign if the first value minus the second is positive, and with a minus sign if the first value minus the second is negative. Obviously, we can determine the sign of the difference by simply noting which value is larger. For paired data, the sign test asks whether the median of the population of these differences is zero.[†]

Example

It is possible that the appraisals of one real estate appraiser are higher than those of a competitor's. To put this assumption to a test, both are asked to appraise a sample of nine real estate properties, and the following are their estimates (in dollars):

Property	Appraiser 1	Appraiser 2
1	79,250	77,380
2	110,230	106,450
3	93,750	95,100
4	88,360	86,000
5	121,300	118,960
6	124,820	122,630
7	105,220	101,710
8	106,660	109,850
9	83,500	80,760

Use the sign test at the 0.05 level of significance to test the null hypothesis $\tilde{\mu}_D = 0$, where $\tilde{\mu}_D$ is the median of the population of differences, first appraiser minus second appraiser. Use the alternative $\tilde{\mu}_D > 0$, which suggests that the first appraiser quotes higher values.

solution

1. H_0: $\tilde{\mu}_D = 0$
    H_A: $\tilde{\mu}_D > 0$
2. $\alpha = 0.05$
3′. The test statistic is x, the number of plus signs.
4′. Replacing each pair of values with a plus sign if the first value is greater than the second, and with a minus sign if the first value is smaller than the second, we get

$$+ \quad + \quad - \quad + \quad + \quad + \quad + \quad - \quad +$$

Thus $x = 7$ and Table V shows that for $n = 9$ and $p = 0.50$, the probability of $x \geq 7$ is

$$0.070 + 0.018 + 0.002 = 0.090$$

The p-value is 0.090.

[†]If the two populations have roughly the same shape, whether symmetric or not, and if the two values are independent, then the sign test can be regarded as a test of whether the two populations have the same mean (or median).

5'. Since 0.090 exceeds 0.05, the null hypothesis cannot be rejected. The data do not confirm the notion that the first appraiser's estimates are on the average higher than those of the second appraiser.   ◿ ◿ ◿

When the sign test is used in this way, it is referred to as the **paired-sample sign test.** As in the one-sample sign test, we have to discard sample pairs when the two values are the same.

17.2   THE SIGN TEST (Large Samples)

When np and $n(1 - p)$ are both greater than 5, so that we can use the normal approximation to the binomial distribution, we can base the sign test on the large-sample test of Section 13.3, namely on the statistic

$$z = \frac{x - np_0}{\sqrt{np_0(1 - p_0)}}$$

with $p_0 = 0.50$, which has approximately the standard normal distribution.

Example

The following are two supervisors' ratings of the performance of a random sample of a large company's employees, on a scale of 0 to 100:

Supervisor 1	Supervisor 2	Supervisor 1	Supervisor 2
88	73	79	79
69	67	65	77
97	81	95	82
60	73	88	84
82	78	91	93
90	82	68	66
65	62	77	76
77	80	74	74
86	81	85	78

Use the paired-sample sign test at the 0.02 level of significance to check whether the difference between the means of the two sets of ratings, 79.8 and 77.0, can be attributed to chance.

solution

Since two pairs of equal ratings have to be discarded, the sample size for the sign test is only $n = 16$.

1. H_0: $\tilde{\mu}_D = 0$
   H_A: $\tilde{\mu}_D \neq 0$
2. $\alpha = 0.02$

3. If x is the number of plus signs (positive differences between the ratings of supervisors 1 and 2), reject the null hypothesis if $z \leq -2.33$ or $z \geq 2.33$, where

$$z = \frac{x - np_0}{\sqrt{np_0(1 - p_0)}}$$

with $p_0 = 0.50$; otherwise, accept it or reserve judgment.

4. Replacing each positive difference with a plus sign and each negative difference with a minus sign, we get

$$+ \; + \; + \; - \; + \; + \; + \; - \; + \; - \; + \; + \; - \; + \; + \; +$$

for the sixteen unequal pairs. Thus, $x = 12$ and

$$z = \frac{12 - 16(0.50)}{\sqrt{16(0.50)(0.50)}} = 2.00$$

5. Since $z = 2.00$ falls between -2.33 and 2.33, the null hypothesis cannot be rejected; in other words, the difference between the mean ratings of the two supervisors is not significant. ◢ ◢ ◢

EXERCISES

17.1 On 14 occasions, a random sample, Mike, a city employee, had to wait

4.5 8.6 7.3 7.0 2.5 6.1 8.9 6.5 6.3 1.6 5.8 6.3 5.9 9.0

minutes for the bus he takes to work. Use the sign test based on Table V and the 0.05 level of significance to test the null hypothesis $\tilde{\mu} = 6.0$ (that the median wait is 6.0 minutes) against the alternative hypothesis $\tilde{\mu} \neq 6.0$.

17.2 A random sample of nine women interviewed at a shopping mall indicated that they had been living in the area for

62 48 55 37 25 87 60 41 18

months. Use the sign test based on Table V and the 0.05 level of significance to test the null hypothesis $\tilde{\mu} = 30$ (that the median time living in the area is 30 months for the population of women using the shopping mall). Use the alternative hypothesis $\tilde{\mu} > 30$.

17.3 The following random-sample data are the weights (in grams) of 14 packages of a specific granola bar:

100.8 100.0 102.6 100.3 98.2 101.0 100.5
102.5 100.0   97.1 103.6 100.9   99.8 101.0

Use the sign test based on Table V and the 0.01 level of significance to test the null hypothesis $\tilde{\mu} = 100.0$ (that the median weight of that population of granola bars is 100 grams) against the alternative $\tilde{\mu} \neq 100.0$.

17.4 After playing four rounds of golf at a country club, a random sample of 10 professionals had total scores of

280 282 279 278 283 280 279 280 287 283

Use the sign test at the 0.05 level of significance to test the null hypothesis $\tilde{\mu} = 284$ (that the median score is 284 for the population of golfers from which these are sampled) against the alternative $\tilde{\mu} < 284$.

17.5   Following are the number of passengers carried on flights No. 136, Chicago to Phoenix, and No. 137, Phoenix to Chicago, on 7 days:

Day	Flight 136	Flight 137
1	232	189
2	255	249
3	249	251
4	265	230
5	236	218
6	240	233
7	249	236

Use the sign test based on Table V and the 0.01 level of significance to test the null hypothesis $\tilde{\mu}_D = 0$, where $\tilde{\mu}_D$ is the median of the Flight 136 minus Flight 137 differences. Use the alternative $\tilde{\mu}_D > 0$.

17.6   Use the paired-sample sign test to rework the example on page 365, which deals with the losses of man-hours before and after a certain safety program was put into operation.

17.7   Use the paired-sample sign test to rework Exercise 11.111 on pages 369–370.

17.8   Following are the miles per gallon obtained with 40 tankfuls of a certain kind of gasoline:

$$
\begin{array}{llllllll}
24.1 & 25.0 & 24.8 & 24.3 & 24.2 & 25.3 & 24.2 & 23.6 \\
24.5 & 24.4 & 24.5 & 23.2 & 24.0 & 23.8 & 23.8 & 25.3 \\
24.5 & 24.6 & 24.0 & 25.2 & 25.2 & 24.4 & 24.7 & 24.1 \\
24.6 & 24.9 & 24.1 & 25.8 & 24.2 & 24.2 & 24.8 & 24.1 \\
25.6 & 24.5 & 25.1 & 24.6 & 24.3 & 25.2 & 24.7 & 23.3
\end{array}
$$

Use the sign test at the 0.01 level of significance to test the null hypothesis $\tilde{\mu} = 24.2$ (that the median of the population of mileages is 24.2 miles per gallon) against the alternative hypothesis $\tilde{\mu} > 24.2$.

17.9   Use the normal approximation to the binomial distribution to rework Exercise 17.3.

17.10   In a study of the braking efficiency of standard passenger cars on dry, clean, level pavement, 21 drivers traveling 30 miles per hour were able to stop in these distances (measured in feet):

$$
\begin{array}{lllllll}
79 & 68 & 80 & 90 & 67 & 71 & 75 \\
84 & 85 & 65 & 77 & 66 & 80 & 82 \\
71 & 76 & 68 & 78 & 80 & 78 & 68
\end{array}
$$

Use the sign test at the 0.05 level of significance to test the null hypothesis $\tilde{\mu} = 79$ against the alternative $\tilde{\mu} < 79$, where $\tilde{\mu}$ is the median stopping distance, at 30 miles per hour for the population of drivers from which the sample was obtained.

17.11   The following values are the numbers of hamburgers and frankfurters sold by a seaside refreshment stand on 25 consecutive business days:

Day	Hamburgers	Frankfurters	Day	Hamburgers	Frankfurters
1	142	171	14	166	171
2	166	190	15	168	192
3	105	88	16	156	158
4	179	184	17	220	241
5	205	244	18	208	206
6	117	119	19	147	160
7	182	186	20	155	165
8	155	166	21	163	171
9	172	168	22	102	90
10	199	231	23	124	124
11	211	221	24	182	193
12	168	155	25	211	224
13	143	170			

Use the sign test at the 0.05 level of significance to test the null hypothesis $\tilde{\mu}_D = 0$, where $\tilde{\mu}_D$ is the median of the population of hamburger minus frankfurter differences. Use the alternative $\tilde{\mu}_D < 0$.

17.12 The following are the number of employees absent from two government agencies on 25 days:

	Agency			Agency	
Day	A	B	Day	A	B
1	24	29	14	32	40
2	32	45	15	30	33
3	36	36	16	46	42
4	33	39	17	38	50
5	41	48	18	34	37
6	45	36	19	45	39
7	33	41	20	32	37
8	38	39	21	44	32
9	46	40	22	25	33
10	32	39	23	45	48
11	37	30	24	35	33
12	34	45	25	30	35
13	41	42			

Use the sign test at the 0.05 level of significance to test the null hypothesis $\tilde{\mu}_D = 0$, where $\tilde{\mu}_D$ is the median of the population of daily agency A minus agency B absences. Use the alternative hypothesis $\tilde{\mu}_D < 0$.

17.13 Use the normal approximation to the binomial distribution to rework Exercise 17.5.

17.3 RANK SUMS: THE SIGNED-RANK TEST

The sign test is not difficult to perform and has intuitive appeal, but it is wasteful of information because it utilizes only the signs of the differences between the observations and $\tilde{\mu}_0$ in the one-sample case, or the signs of the differences between the pairs of observations in the paired-sample case. For this reason an alternative nonparametric test, the **signed-rank test**, also called the **Wilcoxon signed-rank test**, is often preferred.

In this test, we rank the differences without regard to their signs, assigning rank 1 to the smallest numerical difference (that is, to the smallest difference in absolute value), rank 2 to the second smallest numerical difference, ..., and rank n to the largest numerical difference. Zero differences are, again, discarded, and if two or more differences are numerically equal, we assign each one the mean of the ranks which they jointly occupy. Then we base the test on T^+, the sum of the ranks of the positive differences, T^-, the sum of the ranks of the negative differences, or T, the smaller of the two.

We will discuss the signed-rank test as it pertains to the median of the population.[†] The signed-rank test, like the sign test, can be applied to a single sample of values. The signed-rank test, again like the sign test, can be applied to paired samples, as in the example on page 553.[‡]

To illustrate this procedure, we refer to the first example of Section 17.1, where we are given 15 measurements of the octane rating of a certain kind of gasoline and use the one-sample sign test to test the null hypothesis $\tilde{\mu} = 98.5$ against the alternative hypothesis $\tilde{\mu} < 98.5$ at the 0.01 level of significance. These measurements are shown in the first column of the following table:

Measurements	Differences	Ranks
97.5	−1.0	4
95.2	−3.3	12
97.3	−1.2	6
96.0	−2.5	10
96.8	−1.7	7
100.3	1.8	8
97.4	−1.1	5
95.3	−3.2	11
93.2	−5.3	14
99.1	0.6	2
96.1	−2.4	9
97.6	−0.9	3
98.2	−0.3	1
98.5	0.0	
94.9	−3.6	13

The differences between the measurements and $\mu = 98.5$ are given in the second column. In ranking the differences in column 3 we ignore the signs of the differences, so the smallest numerical difference is 0.3 (after we discarded the zero difference), the next smallest is 0.6, ..., and the largest is 5.3, the ranks are as shown in the third column. It follows that

$$T^+ = 8 + 2 = 10$$

$$T^- = 4 + 12 + 6 + 10 + 7 + 5 + 11 + 14 + 9 + 3 + 1 + 13 = 95$$

[†]In fact, however, this test is really about a different quantity, a "pseudomedian," which is the median of the population obtained by taking the mean of two independent values. If the population is symmetrical, there is no need for concern, since the mean, median, and pseudomedian will all be the same.

[‡]The assumption of symmetrical populations is much more credible for differences based on paired samples.

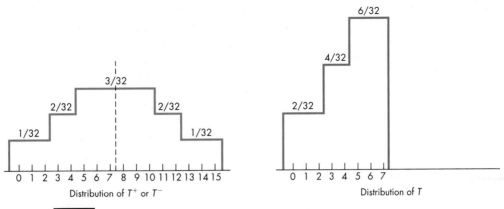

FIGURE 17.1   *Distributions of T^+, T^-, and T for $n = 5$.*

and hence $T = 10$. Since $T^+ + T^-$ is always the sum of the integers from 1 to n, namely, $\dfrac{n(n + 1)}{2}$, we could have obtained T^- more readily by subtracting

$$T^+ = 10 \quad \text{from} \quad \frac{14 \cdot 15}{2} = 105$$

There were no ties in this example, but where there are ties, we assign to each of the tied differences the mean of the ranks that they occupy jointly. More details about this may be found on page 565.

The close relationship between T^+, T^-, and T, is reflected also by their sampling distributions, which are pictured in Figure 17.1, for the special case where $n = 5$. To simplify the construction of tables of critical values, we shall base all tests of the null hypothesis $\tilde{\mu} = \tilde{\mu}_0$ on the distribution of T and reject it for values falling into the left-hand tail. We have to be careful, though, to use the right statistic and the right critical value. When $\tilde{\mu} < \tilde{\mu}_0$ then T^+ tends to be small, so when the alternative hypothesis is $\tilde{\mu} < \tilde{\mu}_0$ we base the test on T^+; when $\tilde{\mu} > \tilde{\mu}_0$ then T^- tends to be small, so when the alternative hypothesis is $\tilde{\mu} > \tilde{\mu}_0$ we base the test on T^-; and when $\tilde{\mu} \neq \tilde{\mu}_0$ then either T^+ or T^- tends to be small, so when the alternative hypothesis is $\tilde{\mu} \neq \tilde{\mu}_0$ we base the test on T. These relationships are summarized in the following table:

Alternative hypothesis	Reject the null hypothesis if	Accept the null hypothesis or reserve judgment if
$\tilde{\mu} < \tilde{\mu}_0$	$T^+ \leq T_{2\alpha}$	$T^+ > T_{2\alpha}$
$\tilde{\mu} > \tilde{\mu}_0$	$T^- \leq T_{2\alpha}$	$T^- > T_{2\alpha}$
$\tilde{\mu} \neq \tilde{\mu}_0$	$T \leq T_\alpha$	$T > T_\alpha$

The necessary values of T_α, (the largest values of T for which the probability of $T \leq T_\alpha$ does not exceed α) may be found in Table VI at the end of the book.

The blank spaces in the table indicate that the null hypothesis cannot be rejected regardless of the value we obtain for the test statistic. Note that the same critical values serve for tests at different levels of significance, depending on whether the alternative hypothesis is one-sided or two-sided.

Example

With reference to the octane ratings on page 552, use the signed-rank test at the 0.01 level of significance to test the null hypothesis $\tilde{\mu} = 98.5$ against the alternative hypothesis $\tilde{\mu} < 98.5$.

solution

1. H_0: $\tilde{\mu} = 98.5$
   H_A: $\tilde{\mu} < 98.5$
2. $\alpha = 0.01$
3. Reject the null hypothesis if $T^+ \leq 16$, where 16 is the value of $T_{0.02}$ for $n = 14$; otherwise, accept it or reserve judgment.
4. As shown on page 558, $T^+ = 10$.
5. Since $T^+ = 10$ is less than 16, the null hypothesis must be rejected; as on page 552, we conclude that the median octane rating of the given kind of gasoline is less than 98.5.   ◪ ◪ ◪

The signed-rank test can also be used in place of the paired-sample sign test. The procedure is exactly the same, but we describe the null hypothesis as $\tilde{\mu}_D = 0$, where $\tilde{\mu}_D$ is the median of the population of differences.[†] The alternative hypotheses are either $\tilde{\mu}_D < 0$, $\tilde{\mu}_D > 0$, or $\tilde{\mu}_D \neq 0$; in using the one-sided alternatives, we must be careful regarding the order in which the differences are taken.

17.4   RANK SUMS: THE SIGNED-RANK TEST (Large Samples)

When n is 15 or more, it is considered reasonable to assume that the distributions of T^+ and T^- can be approximated closely with normal curves. In that case we can base all tests on either T^+ or T^-, and as it does not matter which one we choose, we shall use here the statistic T^+.

Based on the assumption that each difference is as likely to be positive as negative, it can be shown that the mean and the standard deviation of the sampling distribution of T^+ are

Mean and Standard Deviation of T^+ Statistic

$$\mu_{T^+} = \frac{n(n+1)}{4} \quad and \quad \sigma_{T^+} = \sqrt{\frac{n(n+1)(2n+1)}{24}}$$

[†]As noted in the footnote on page 558, the actual quantity being tested is a "pseudomedian," but for paired samples it is quite reasonable to use the median.

Thus, for large samples, in this case, $n \geq 15$, we can base the signed-rank test on the statistic

Large-sample Signed-rank Test	$$z = \frac{T^+ - \mu_{T^+}}{\sigma_{T^+}}$$

which is a value of a random variable having approximately the standard normal distribution. When the alternative hypothesis is $\tilde{\mu} \neq \tilde{\mu}_0$ (or $\tilde{\mu}_1 \neq \tilde{\mu}_2$), we reject the null hypothesis if $z \leq -z_{\alpha/2}$ or $z \geq z_{\alpha/2}$; when the alternative hypothesis is $\tilde{\mu} > \tilde{\mu}_0$ (or $\tilde{\mu}_1 > \tilde{\mu}_2$), we reject the null hypothesis if $z \geq z_\alpha$; and when the alternative hypothesis is $\tilde{\mu} < \tilde{\mu}_0$ (or $\tilde{\mu}_1 < \tilde{\mu}_2$), we reject the null hypothesis if $z \leq -z_\alpha$.

Example

Following are the weights (in pounds) before and after, of 16 persons who stayed on a certain weight-reducing diet for 2 weeks:

Before	After	Before	After
169.0	159.9	143.8	145.1
188.6	181.3	198.2	185.5
222.1	209.0	166.9	158:6
160.1	162.3	142.9	145.4
187.5	183.5	160.5	159.5
202.5	197.6	198.7	190.6
167.8	171.4	149.7	149.0
214.3	202.1	181.6	183.1

Use the large-sample signed-rank test at the 0.05 level of significance to test whether the weight-reducing diet is effective.

solution

1. H_0: $\tilde{\mu}_1 = \tilde{\mu}_2$
   H_A: $\tilde{\mu}_1 > \tilde{\mu}_2$
2. $\alpha = 0.05$
3. Reject the null hypothesis if $z \geq 1.645$, where

$$z = \frac{T^+ - \mu_{T^+}}{\sigma_{T^+}}$$

and otherwise reserve judgment.

4. The differences and the ranks of their absolute values are shown in the following table:

Before	After	Difference	Rank
169.0	159.9	9.1	13
188.6	181.3	7.3	10
222.1	209.0	13.1	16
160.1	162.3	−2.2	5
187.5	183.5	4.0	8
202.5	197.6	4.9	9
167.8	171.4	−3.6	7
214.3	202.1	12.2	14
143.8	145.1	−1.3	3
198.2	185.5	12.7	15
166.9	158.6	8.3	12
142.9	145.4	−2.5	6
160.5	159.5	1.0	2
198.7	190.6	8.1	11
149.7	149.0	0.7	1
181.6	183.1	−1.5	4

It follows that

$$T^+ = 13 + 10 + 16 + 8 + 9 + 14 + 15 + 12 + 2 + 11 + 1 = 111$$

and since

$$\mu_{T+} = \frac{16 \cdot 17}{4} = 68 \quad \text{and} \quad \sigma_{T+} = \sqrt{\frac{16 \cdot 17 \cdot 33}{24}} \approx 19.34$$

we finally obtain

$$z = \frac{111 - 68}{19.34} \approx 2.22$$

5. Since $z = 2.22$ exceeds 1.645, the null hypothesis must be rejected; we conclude that the weight-reducing diet is effective. ◢ ◢ ◢

▨ EXERCISES

17.14   In 10 consecutive games, a high school basketball player scored

12   19   11   25   18   8   16   17   14   20

points. Using the signed-rank procedure, test at the 0.05 level of significance the null hypothesis $\tilde{\mu} = 15$ points against the alternative $\tilde{\mu} > 15$. Assume that the population is approximately symmetric, so that $\tilde{\mu}$ represents the median, and also the mean, of this population.

17.15   On what statistic do we base our decision and for what values of the statistic do we reject the null hypothesis, if we have a random sample of size $n = 10$ and are using the signed-rank test at the 0.05 level of significance to test the null hypothesis $\tilde{\mu} = \tilde{\mu}_0$ against the alternative hypothesis

(a) $\tilde{\mu} \neq \tilde{\mu}_0$;   (b) $\tilde{\mu} > \tilde{\mu}_0$;   (c) $\tilde{\mu} < \tilde{\mu}_0$?

17.16   Rework the preceding exercise with the level of significance changed to 0.01.

17.17   On what statistic do we base our decision and for what values of the statistic do we reject the null hypothesis, if we have a random sample of $n = 12$ pairs of values and we are using the signed-rank test at the 0.01 level of significance to test the null hypothesis $\tilde{\mu}_D = 0$ against the alternative

(a) $\tilde{\mu}_D > 0$;　　(b) $\tilde{\mu}_D \neq 0$;　　(c) $\tilde{\mu}_D < 0$?

17.18　Rework the preceding exercise with the level of significance changed to 0.05.

17.19　In a random sample of 13 issues, the Jersey Journal listed

$$32 \quad 27 \quad 41 \quad 29 \quad 36 \quad 34 \quad 52 \quad 31 \quad 30 \quad 22 \quad 38 \quad 47 \quad 35$$

apartments for rent. Use the signed-rank test at the 0.05 level of significance to test the null hypothesis $\tilde{\mu} = 40$ against the alternative hypothesis

(a) $\tilde{\mu} < 40$;　　(b) $\tilde{\mu} \neq 40$.

Assume that the data values are sampled from a symmetrical population.

17.20　Use the signed-rank test to rework Exercise 17.1 on page 555.

17.21　Use the signed-rank test to rework Exercise 17.3 on page 555.

17.22　In a random sample taken at a public playground, it took

$$38 \quad 43 \quad 36 \quad 29 \quad 44 \quad 28 \quad 40 \quad 50 \quad 39 \quad 47 \quad 33$$

minutes to play a set of tennis. Use the signed-rank test at the 0.05 level of significance to test whether or not it takes on the average 35 minutes to play a set of tennis at that public playground.

17.23　Jan, a psychologist, observed children riding a playground swing, for the purpose of noting how long each child remained on the swing. She clocked for 11 children, these values (in minutes):

$$3.0 \quad 5.5 \quad 3.4 \quad 6.2 \quad 2.9 \quad 9.0 \quad 5.2 \quad 3.8 \quad 4.4 \quad 12.5 \quad 8.0$$

Assuming that these values are sampled from a symmetrical population, use the signed-rank test at the 0.05 level of significance to test whether the median time on the swing is 3.5 minutes.

17.24　In a random sample of nine summer days, two cities in Arizona reported the following high temperatures:

Day	City 1	City 2
1	108	105
2	101	103
3	101	105
4	116	109
5	111	106
6	113	112
7	114	108
8	112	102
9	112	103

Use the sign test at the 0.05 level of significance to test whether the two cities' mean daily high summer temperature is the same.

17.25　Following are the number of 3-month and 6-month certificates of deposit (CD's) that a bank sold on a sample of 16 business days:

3-month CD's	6-month CD's	3-month CD's	6-month CD's
35	30	51	31
27	17	33	43
24	26	42	34
44	30	41	25
29	28	18	33
30	23	29	26
29	22	33	22
36	24	37	32

Test at the 0.05 level of significance whether the bank sells equally many of the two varieties against the alternative that it sells more of the three-month CD's using

(a) the signed-rank test based on Table VI;

(b) the large-sample signed-rank test.

17.26   Use the signed-rank test to rework Exercise 17.5 on page 556.

17.27   A sample of 24 pieces of luggage carried by an airline on transoceanic flights had the following weights (in pounds):

```
32.0  49.9  63.3  46.4  36.1  42.5
48.1  50.0  52.4  27.7  44.7  40.9
35.5  48.2  38.6  52.6  36.9  43.2
66.0  40.8  41.7  41.3  35.1  35.6
```

Test at the 0.05 level of significance whether the median weight of the luggage pieces carried on such flights is 37.0 pounds. Assume that the population sampled is approximately symmetrical and use

(a) the signed-rank test based on Table VI;

(b) the large-sample signed-rank test.

17.28   Following is a random sample of the scores obtained by husbands and wives on a spatial abilities test:

Husband	Wife	Husband	Wife
108	103	125	120
104	116	96	98
103	106	107	117
112	104	115	130
99	99	101	100
105	94	110	101
102	110	103	96
112	128	105	99
119	106	124	120
106	103	113	116

Use the large-sample signed-rank test at the 0.05 level of significance to test whether husbands and wives do equally well on this particular test.

17.5   RANK SUMS: THE *U* TEST

We now consider a nonparametric alternative to the two-sample *t* test, concerning the difference between two means. It is called the **U test** or, sometimes, the **rank-sum test** and is also known as the **Wilcoxon test** or the **Mann–Whitney test,** named after statisticians who contributed to its development. The various names reflect the manner in which the calculations are organized, and are all logically equivalent.

With this test we are able to test whether two independent samples come from identical populations. In particular, we can test the null hypothesis $\mu_1 = \mu_2$ without having to assume that the populations sampled have roughly the shape of normal distributions.[†] In fact, the test requires only that the populations be continuous (to avoid ties), and even that requirement is not critical so long as the number of ties is small.

To illustrate how the U test is performed, suppose that we want to compare the grain size of sand obtained from two different locations on the moon on the basis of the following diameters (in millimeters):

Location 1: 0.37 0.70 0.75 0.30 0.45 0.16 0.62 0.73 0.33
Location 2: 0.86 0.55 0.80 0.42 0.97 0.84 0.24 0.51 0.92 0.69

The means of these two samples are 0.49 and 0.68, and their difference seems large, but it remains to be seen whether that is significant.

To perform the U test we first arrange the data jointly, as if they comprise one sample, in an increasing order of magnitude. For our data we get

0.16 0.24 0.30 0.33 0.37 0.42 0.45 0.51 0.55 0.62
 1   2   1   1   1   2   1   2   2   1

0.69 0.70 0.73 0.75 0.80 0.84 0.86 0.92 0.97
 2   1   1   1   2   2   2   2   2

where we indicate for each value whether it came from location 1 or location 2. Assigning the data, in this order, the ranks 1, 2, 3, . . . , and 19, we find that the values of the first sample (location 1) occupy ranks 1, 3, 4, 5, 7, 10, 12, 13, and 14, while those of the second sample (location 2) occupy ranks, 2, 6, 8, 9, 11, 15, 16, 17, 18, and 19. There are no ties here between values in different samples, but if there are, we assign each of the tied observations the mean of the ranks which they jointly occupy. For instance, if the third and fourth values are the same, we assign each the rank

$$\frac{3 + 4}{2} = 3.5$$

and if the ninth, tenth, and eleventh values are the same, we assign each the rank

$$\frac{9 + 10 + 11}{3} = 10$$

When there are ties among values belonging to the same sample, it does not matter how they are ranked. For instance, if the third and fourth values are the

[†]Technically, this procedure tests the null hypothesis that zero is the median of the distribution of $X_1 - X_2$, where X_1 and X_2 are randomly selected observations from the two populations. If we can assume that the two populations have the same shape, then the test may properly be described in terms of the means μ_1 and μ_2. One can construct examples in which $\mu_1 = \mu_2$ but the median of the distribution of $X_1 - X_2$ is not zero.

same but belong to the same sample, it does not matter which one is ranked 3 and which one is ranked 4.

Now, if there is an appreciable difference between the means of the two populations, most of the lower ranks are likely to go to the values of one sample while most of the higher ranks are likely to go to the values of the other sample. The test of the null hypothesis that the two samples come from identical populations may thus be based on W_1, the sum of the ranks of the values of the first sample, or on W_2, the sum of the ranks of the values of the second sample. In practice, it does not matter which sample we refer to as sample 1 and which sample we refer to as sample 2, and whether we base the test on W_1 or W_2. (When the sample sizes are unequal, we usually let the smaller of the two samples be sample 1; however, this is not required for the work in this book.)

If the sample sizes are n_1 and n_2, the sum of W_1 and W_2 is simply the sum of the first $n_1 + n_2$ positive integers, which is known to be

$$\frac{(n_1 + n_2)(n_1 + n_2 + 1)}{2}$$

This formula enables us to find W_2 if we know W_1, and vice versa. For our illustration we get

$$W_1 = 1 + 3 + 4 + 5 + 7 + 10 + 12 + 13 + 14 = 69$$

and since the sum of the first 19 positive integers is $\frac{19 \cdot 20}{2} = 190$, it follows that

$$W_2 = 190 - 69 = 121$$

(This value is the sum of the ranks 2, 6, 8, 9, 11, 15, 16, 17, 18, and 19.)

The hypothesis testing decision could be based on W_1 or W_2, but it is somewhat easier to use the statistics

U_1 and U_2 Statistics

$$U_1 = W_1 - \frac{n_1(n_1 + 1)}{2} \quad \text{or} \quad U_2 = W_2 - \frac{n_2(n_2 + 1)}{2}$$

or on the statistic U, which is always equal to the smaller of the two. The resulting tests have the advantage that they lend themselves readily to the construction of tables of critical values. Not only do U_1 and U_2 take on values on the same interval from 0 to $n_1 n_2$—indeed, their sum is always equal to $n_1 n_2$—but they have identical distributions symmetrical about $\frac{n_1 n_2}{2}$. The relationship between the sampling distributions of U_1, U_2, and U is shown in Figure 17.2 for the special case where $n_1 = 3$ and $n_2 = 3$.

The null hypothesis is $\mu_1 = \mu_2$ and, as in Section 17.3, we shall base all tests on the sampling distribution of one and the same statistic, here the statistic U, and reject it for values falling into the left-hand tail. Again, we have to be careful, though, to use the right statistic and the right critical value. When $\mu_1 < \mu_2$ then U_1 will tend to be small, so when the alternative hypothesis is $\mu_1 < \mu_2$ we base the test on U_1; when $\mu_1 > \mu_2$ then U_2 will tend to be small, so when the al-

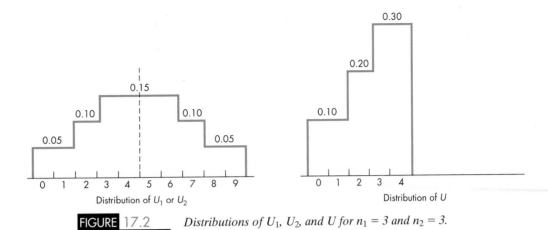

FIGURE 17.2   *Distributions of U_1, U_2, and U for $n_1 = 3$ and $n_2 = 3$.*

ternative hypothesis is $\mu_1 > \mu_2$ we base the test on U_2; and when $\mu_1 \neq \mu_2$ then either U_1 or U_2 will tend to be small, so when the alternative hypothesis is $\mu_1 \neq \mu_2$ we base the test on U. All this is summarized in the following table:

Alternative hypothesis	Reject the null hypothesis if	Accept the null hypothesis or reserve judgment if
$\mu_1 < \mu_2$	$U_1 \leq U_{2\alpha}$	$U_1 > U_{2\alpha}$
$\mu_1 > \mu_2$	$U_2 \leq U_{2\alpha}$	$U_2 > U_{2\alpha}$
$\mu_1 \neq \mu_2$	$U \leq U_\alpha$	$U > U_\alpha$

The necessary values of U_α, which are the largest values of U for which the probability of $U \leq U_\alpha$ does not exceed α, may be found in Table VII at the end of the book; the blank spaces in the table indicate that the null hypothesis cannot be rejected regardless of the value we obtain for the test statistic. Note that the same critical values serve for tests at different levels of significance depending on whether the alternative hypothesis is one-sided or two-sided.

Example

With reference to the grain-size data on page 565, use the U test at the 0.05 level of significance to test whether or not the two samples come from populations with equal means.

solution

1. H_0: $\mu_1 = \mu_2$
   H_A: $\mu_1 \neq \mu_2$
2. $\alpha = 0.05$
3. Reject the null hypothesis if $U \leq 20$, where 20 is the value of $U_{0.05}$ for $n_1 = 9$ and $n_2 = 10$; otherwise, reserve judgment.
4. Having already shown on page 566 that $W_1 = 69$ and $W_2 = 121$, we get

$$U_1 = 69 - \frac{9 \cdot 10}{2} = 24, \qquad U_2 = 121 - \frac{10 \cdot 11}{2} = 66$$

and, hence, $U = 24$. Note that $U_1 + U_2 = 24 + 66 = 90$, which equals $n_1 n_2 = 9 \cdot 10$.

5. Since $U = 24$ is greater than 20, the null hypothesis cannot be rejected; in other words, we cannot conclude that there is a difference in the mean grain size of sand from the two locations on the moon.   ◪ ◪ ◪

Example

The following are the burning times (rounded to the nearest tenth of a minute) of random samples of two kinds of emergency flares:

Brand 1:	17.2	18.1	19.3	21.1	14.4	13.7	18.8	15.2	20.3	17.5
Brand 2:	13.6	19.1	11.8	14.6	14.3	22.5	12.3	13.5	10.9	14.8

Use the U test at the 0.05 level of significance to test whether it is reasonable to say that on the average brand 1 flares are better (last longer) than brand 2 flares.

solution

1. H_0: $\mu_1 = \mu_2$
   H_A: $\mu_1 > \mu_2$
2. $\alpha = 0.05$
3. Reject the null hypothesis if $U_2 \leq 27$, where 27 is the value of $U_{0.10}$ for $n_1 = 10$ and $n_2 = 10$; otherwise, accept it or reserve judgment.
4. Ranking the data jointly according to size, we find that the values of the second sample occupy ranks 5, 16, 2, 9, 7, 20, 3, 4, 1, and 10, so that

$$W_2 = 5 + 16 + 2 + 9 + 7 + 20 + 3 + 4 + 1 + 10 = 77$$

and

$$U_2 = 77 - \frac{10 \cdot 11}{2} = 22$$

5. Since $U_2 = 22$ is less than 27, the null hypothesis must be rejected; we conclude that brand 1 flares are, indeed, better than brand 2 flares.   ◪ ◪ ◪

17.6   RANK SUMS: THE *U* TEST (Large Samples)

The large-sample U test may be based on either U_1 or U_2 as defined on page 566, but since the resulting tests are equivalent and it does not matter which sample we denote sample 1 and which sample we denote sample 2, we shall use here the statistic U_1.

Based on the assumption that the two samples come from identical continuous populations, it can be shown that the mean and the standard deviation of the sampling distribution of U_1 are[†]

[†]When there are ties in rank the formula for the standard deviation provides only an approximation, but if the number of ties is small, there is usually no need to make any correction.

Mean and Standard Deviation of U_1 Statistic	$\mu_{U_1} = \dfrac{n_1 n_2}{2}$ and $\sigma_{U_1} = \sqrt{\dfrac{n_1 n_2 (n_1 + n_2 + 1)}{12}}$

Observe that these formulas remain the same when we interchange the subscripts 1 and 2, but this should not come as a surprise—as we pointed out on page 566, the distributions of U_1 and U_2 are the same.

Furthermore, if n_1 and n_2 are both greater than 8, the sampling distribution of U_1 can be approximated closely by a normal distribution. Thus, we base the test of the null hypothesis $\mu_1 = \mu_2$ on the statistic

Statistic for Large-sample U Test	$z = \dfrac{U_1 - \mu_{U_1}}{\sigma_{U_1}}$

which has approximately the standard normal distribution. When the alternative hypothesis is $\mu_1 \neq \mu_2$, we reject the null hypothesis if $z \leq -z_{\alpha/2}$ or $z \geq z_{\alpha/2}$; when the alternative hypothesis is $\mu_1 > \mu_2$, we reject the null hypothesis if $z \geq z_\alpha$; and when the alternative hypothesis is $\mu_1 < \mu_2$, we reject the null hypothesis if $z \leq -z_\alpha$.

Example

The following are the weight gains (in pounds) of two random samples of young turkeys fed two different diets but otherwise kept under identical conditions:

Diet 1: 16.3 10.1 10.7 13.5 14.9 11.8 14.3 10.2
12.0 14.7 23.6 15.1 14.5 18.4 13.2 14.0

Diet 2: 21.3 23.8 15.4 19.6 12.0 13.9 18.8 19.2
15.3 20.1 14.8 18.9 20.7 21.1 15.8 16.2

Use the large-sample U test at the 0.01 level of significance to test the null hypothesis that the two populations sampled are identical against the alternative hypothesis that on the average the second diet produces a greater gain in weight.

solution

1. H_0: $\mu_1 = \mu_2$
   H_A: $\mu_1 < \mu_2$
2. $\alpha = 0.01$
3. Reject the null hypothesis if $z \leq -2.33$, where

$$z = \frac{U_1 - \mu_{U_1}}{\sigma_{U_1}}$$

and otherwise accept the null hypothesis or reserve judgment.

4. Ranking the data jointly according to size, we find that the values of the first sample occupy ranks

21 1 3 8 15 4 11 2 5.5 13 31 16 12 22 7 10

(The 5th and 6th values are both equal to 12.0, so we assign each the rank 5.5.) Thus

$$W_1 = 1 + 2 + 3 + 4 + 5.5 + 7 + 8 + 10 + 11 + 12 + 13$$
$$+ 15 + 16 + 21 + 22 + 31$$
$$= 181.5$$

and

$$U_1 = 181.5 - \frac{16 \cdot 17}{2} = 45.5$$

Since

$$\mu_{U_1} = \frac{16 \cdot 16}{2} = 128 \quad \text{and} \quad \sigma_{U_1} = \sqrt{\frac{16 \cdot 16 \cdot 33}{12}} \approx 26.53$$

it follows that

$$z = \frac{45.5 - 128}{26.53} \approx -3.11$$

5. Since $z = -3.11$ is less than -2.33, the null hypothesis must be rejected; we conclude that on the average the second diet produces a greater gain in weight. ◪ ◪ ◪

17.7   RANK SUMS: THE *H* TEST

The ***H* test,** or **Kruskal–Wallis test,** is a rank-sum test that serves to test the assumption that k independent random samples come from identical populations, and in particular that the null hypothesis $\mu_1 = \mu_2 = \cdots = \mu_k$, against the alternative that these means are not all equal.[†] Unlike the standard test which it replaces (the one-way analysis of variance of Section 14.3) it does not require the assumption that the populations sampled have, at least approximately, normal distributions.

As in the U test, the data are ranked jointly from low to high as though they constitute a single sample. Then, if R_i is the sum of the ranks assigned to the n_i values of the ith sample and $n = n_1 + n_2 + \cdots + n_k$, the H test is based on the statistic

Statistic for H Test

$$H = \frac{12}{n(n+1)} \sum_{i=1}^{k} \frac{R_i^2}{n_i} - 3(n+1)$$

[†]The null hypothesis is, technically, that zero is the median of each of the

$$\binom{k}{2} = \frac{k(k-1)}{2}$$

differences $X_i - X_j$, where X_i and X_j are randomly selected values from two of the populations. If we can assume that all populations have the same shape, then it is proper to describe the test in terms of the means $\mu_1, \mu_2, \ldots, \mu_k$.

If the null hypothesis is true and each sample has at least five observations, it is generally considered reasonable to approximate the sampling distribution of H with a chi-squared distribution having $k - 1$ degrees of freedom.[†] Consequently, we reject the null hypothesis $\mu_1 = \mu_2 = \cdots = \mu_k$ and accept the alternative hypothesis that these means are not all equal, when the value we get for H equals or exceeds χ_α^2 for $k - 1$ degrees of freedom.

Example

Students are randomly assigned to groups which are taught Spanish by three different methods: (1) classroom instruction and language laboratory, (2) only classroom instruction, and (3) only self-study in language laboratory. Following are the final examination scores of samples of students from the three groups:

Method 1:   94 88 91 74 86 97
Method 2:   85 82 79 84 61 72 80
Method 3:   89 67 72 76 69

Use the H test at the 0.05 level of significance to test the null hypothesis that the populations sampled are identical against the alternative hypothesis that their means are not all equal.

solution

1. H_0: $\mu_1 = \mu_2 = \mu_3$
   H_A: μ_1, μ_2 and μ_3 are not all equal.
2. $\alpha = 0.05$
3. Reject the null hypothesis if $H \geq 5.991$, which is the value of $\chi^2_{0.05}$ for $3 - 1 = 2$ degrees of freedom; otherwise, accept it or reserve judgment.
4. Arranging the data jointly according to size, we get

   61 67 69 72 72 74 76 79 80 82 84 85 86 88 89 91 94 97

   Assigning the data, in this order, the ranks 1, 2, 3, ..., and 18, we find that

   $$R_1 = 6 + 13 + 14 + 16 + 17 + 18 = 84$$

   $$R_2 = 1 + 4.5 + 8 + 9 + 10 + 11 + 12 = 55.5$$

   $$R_3 = 2 + 3 + 4.5 + 7 + 15 = 31.5$$

   and it follows that

   $$H = \frac{12}{18 \cdot 19}\left(\frac{84^2}{6} + \frac{55.5^2}{7} + \frac{31.5^2}{5}\right) - 3 \cdot 19 \approx 6.67$$

5. Since $H = 6.67$ exceeds 5.991, the null hypothesis must be rejected; we conclude that the three methods of instruction are not all equally effective.   ◪ ◪ ◪

[†]When the sample sizes are small, one can use special tables for this test. These are cited in some of the references at the end of this chapter.

EXERCISES

17.29   On what statistic do we base our decision and for what values of the statistic do we reject the null hypothesis $\mu_1 = \mu_2$ if we have random samples of sizes $n_1 = 9$ and $n_2 = 9$ and are using the U test based on Table VII to test the null hypothesis against the alternative hypothesis

(a) $\mu_1 > \mu_2$ with significance level 0.05;

(b) $\mu_1 \neq \mu_2$ with significance level 0.05;

(c) $\mu_1 < \mu_2$ with significance level 0.05;

(d) $\mu_1 > \mu_2$ with significance level 0.01;

(e) $\mu_1 \neq \mu_2$ with significance level 0.01;

(f) $\mu_1 < \mu_2$ with significance level 0.01?

17.30   On what statistic do we base our decision and for what values of the statistic do we reject the null hypothesis $\mu_1 = \mu_2$ if we have random samples of sizes $n_1 = 10$ and $n_2 = 14$ and are using the U test based on Table VII to test the null hypothesis against the alternative hypothesis

(a) $\mu_1 > \mu_2$ with significance level 0.05;

(b) $\mu_1 \neq \mu_2$ with significance level 0.05;

(c) $\mu_1 < \mu_2$ with significance level 0.05;

(d) $\mu_1 > \mu_2$ with significance level 0.01;

(e) $\mu_1 \neq \mu_2$ with significance level 0.01;

(f) $\mu_1 < \mu_2$ with significance level 0.01?

17.31   On what statistic do we base our decision and for what values of the statistic do we reject the null hypothesis $\mu_1 = \mu_2$, if we are using the U test based on Table VII at the 0.05 level of significance to test the null hypothesis against the alternative hypothesis $\mu_1 \neq \mu_2$, and we have

(a) $n_1 = 4$ and $n_2 = 6$;   (b) $n_1 = 9$ and $n_2 = 8$;

(c) $n_1 = 5$ and $n_2 = 12$ (d) $n_1 = 7$ and $n_2 = 3$?

17.32   Rework the preceding exercise with the alternative hypothesis changed to $\mu_1 > \mu_2$.

17.33   Explain why there is no value in Table VII for $U_{0.05}$ corresponding to $n_1 = 3$ and $n_2 = 3$. (*Hint*: Refer to Figure 17.2 on page 567.)

17.34   Following are the scores which random samples of students from two minority groups obtained on a current events test:

Minority group 1:	73	82	39	68	91	75
	89	67	50	86	57	65
Minority group 2:	51	42	36	53	88	59
	49	66	25	64	18	76

Use the U test based on Table VII to test at the 0.05 level of significance whether or not students from the two minority groups can be expected to score equally well on this test.

17.35   The following are the number of minutes taken by random samples of 15 men and 12 women to complete a written test given for the renewal of their driver's licenses:

Men:	9.9	7.4	8.9	9.1	7.7	9.7	11.8	7.5
	9.2	10.0	10.2	9.5	10.8	8.0	11.0	
Women:	8.6	10.9	9.8	10.7	9.4	10.3		
	7.3	11.5	7.6	9.3	8.8	9.6		

Use the U test based on Table VII to test at the 0.05 level of significance whether or not $\mu_1 = \mu_2$, where μ_1 and μ_2 are the average amounts of time it takes men and women to complete the test.

17.36   The following are figures on the numbers of burglaries committed in a city in random samples of six days in the spring and six days in the fall:

Spring: 36   25   32   38   28   35
Fall: 27   20   15   29   18   22

Use the *U* test based on Table VII to test at the 0.05 level of significance whether there are on the average equally many burglaries per day in the spring and in the fall, or whether there are on the average fewer in the fall.

17.37   The following are the Rockwell hardness numbers obtained for six aluminum die castings randomly selected from production lot *A* and eight from production lot *B*

Production lot A: 75   56   63   70   58   74
Production lot B: 63   85   77   80   86   76   72   82

Use the *U* test based on Table VII to test at the 0.05 level of significance whether the castings of production lot *B* are on the average harder than those of production lot *A*.

17.38   Following are the weekly food expenditures of two-child families chosen at random from two suburbs of a large city:

Suburb F: 176.19   184.00   179.89   182.78
                198.45   187.38   182.50   190.60

Suburb G: 175.76   178.51   187.91   175.12
                190.19   167.36   187.16

Use the *U* test based on Table VII to test at the 0.01 level of significance whether such weekly food expenditures are on the average higher in suburb *F* than in suburb *G*.

17.39   Use the large-sample *U* test to rework the example on page 565, which deals with the grain size of sand from two locations on the moon.

17.40   Use the large-sample *U* test to rework the example on page 568, which deals with the burning times for two kinds of emergency flares.

17.41   An examination, designed to assess their knowledge of American history, was given to random samples of 20 freshmen at each of two major universities; their grades were

University A: 58   62   69   70   72   73   76   77   78   80
                    84   87   90   90   91   92   93   96   97   98

University B: 34   37   45   56   62   63   63   66   68   71
                    74   74   75   75   78   88   88   88   89   94

For convenience, the scores have been arranged in increasing order. Use the *U* test at the 0.05 level of significance to decide whether there is a difference in the average knowledge of American history between freshmen entering the two universities.

17.42   Following are data for the breaking strength (in pounds) of random samples of two kinds of 2-inch cotton ribbons:

Type I ribbon: 133   144   165   169   171   176   180   181
                      182   183   186   187   194   197   198   200

Type II ribbon: 134   154   159   161   164   164   164   169
                      170   172   175   176   185   189   194   198

For convenience, the values have been arranged in increasing order. Use the *U* test at the 0.05 level of significance to test the claim that type I ribbon is, on the average, stronger than type II ribbon.

17.43   Use the large-sample *U* test to rework Exercise 17.34.

17.44   Use the large-sample *U* test to rework Exercise 17.35.

17.45   Following are the miles per gallon a test driver obtained from random samples of six tankfuls of each of three brands of gasoline:

Gasoline 1:   15   24   27   29   30   32
Gasoline 2:   17   20   22   28   32   33
Gasoline 3:   18   19   22   23   25   32

For convenience, the values have been sorted by increasing order. Use the H test at the 0.05 level of significance to test the claim that there is no difference in the true average mileage yield of the three kinds of gasoline.

17.46   Use the H test to rework part (b) of Exercise 14.1 on page 447.

17.47   Use the H test to rework Exercise 14.15 on page 461.

17.48   Use the H test to rework Exercise 14.16 on page 461.

17.49   To compare four bowling balls, a professional bowler bowls five games with each ball and gets the following scores:

Bowling ball D: 221   232   207   198   212
Bowling ball E: 202   225   252   218   226
Bowling ball F: 210   205   189   196   216
Bowling ball G: 229   192   247   220   208

Use the H test at the 0.05 level of significance to test the null hypothesis that on the average the bowler performs equally well with the four bowling balls.

17.50   Three groups of guinea pigs, injected with 0.5, 1.0, and 1.5 mg respectively, of a tranquilizer, fell asleep in the following number of seconds:

0.5 mg dose: 7.8   8.2   10.0   10.2
              10.9   12.7   13.7   14.0
1.0 mg dose: 7.5   7.9   8.8   9.7   10.5
              11.0   12.5   12.9   13.1   13.3
1.5 mg dose: 7.2   8.0   8.5   9.0
               9.4   11.3   11.5   12.0

For convenience, the values have been arranged in increasing order. Use the H test at the 0.01 level of significance to test the null hypothesis that the differences in dosage have no effect on the length of time it takes guinea pigs to fall asleep.

17.8   TESTS OF RANDOMNESS: RUNS

All the methods of inference studied in this book are based on the assumption that our samples are random; yet, there are many applications where it is difficult to determine whether this assumption is justifiable. This is true, particularly, when we have little or no control over the selection of the data, as is the case, for example, when we rely on whatever records are available to make long-range predictions of the weather, when we use whatever data are available to estimate the mortality rate of a disease, or when we use sales records for past months to make predictions of a department store's future sales. None of this information constitutes a random sample in the strict sense.

There are several methods of judging the randomness of a sample on the basis of the order in which the observations are obtained; they enable us to decide, after the data have been collected, whether patterns that look suspiciously nonrandom may be attributed to chance. The technique we describe here and in the next two sections, the **u test,** is based on the **theory of runs.**

A **run** is a succession of identical letters (or other kinds of symbols) which is followed and preceded by different letters or no letters at all. To illustrate, consider the following arrangement of healthy, H, and diseased, D, elm trees that were planted many years ago along a country road:

$$H\,H\,H\,H\,\underline{D\,D\,D}\,\underline{H\,H\,H\,H\,H\,H\,H}\,\underline{D\,D}\,\underline{H\,H}\,\underline{D\,D\,D\,D}$$

Using underscore rules to combine the letters which constitute the runs, we find that there are runs of four H's, three D's, seven H's, two D's, two H's, and four D's. This set of values represents six runs.

The **total number of runs** appearing in an arrangement of this kind is often a good indication of a possible lack of randomness. If there are too few runs, we might suspect a definite grouping or clustering, or perhaps a trend; if there are too many runs, we might suspect some sort of repeated alternating, or cyclical, pattern. In the example above there seems to be a definite clustering—the diseased trees seem to come in groups—but it remains to be seen whether this is significant or whether it can be attributed to chance.

If there are n_1 letters of one kind, n_2 letters of another kind, and u runs, we base this kind of decision on the following criterion:

Reject the null hypothesis of randomness if

$$u \le u'_{\alpha/2} \qquad \text{or} \qquad u \ge u_{\alpha/2}$$

where $u'_{\alpha/2}$ and $u_{\alpha/2}$ are given in Table VIII for values of n_1 and n_2 through 15, and $\alpha = 0.05$ and $\alpha = 0.01$.

In the construction of Table VIII, $u'_{\alpha/2}$ is the largest value for which the probability of $u \le u'_{\alpha/2}$ does not exceed $\alpha/2$, and $u_{\alpha/2}$ is the smallest value for which the probability of $u \ge u_{\alpha/2}$ does not exceed $\alpha/2$. The blank spaces in the table indicate that the null hypothesis cannot be rejected for values in that tail of the sampling distribution, regardless of the value we obtain for u.

Example

With reference to the arrangement of healthy and diseased trees cited above, use the u test at the 0.05 level of significance to test the null hypothesis of randomness against the alternative hypothesis that the arrangement is not random.

solution

1. H_0:   Arrangement is random.
   H_A: Arrangement is not random.
2. $\alpha = 0.05$.
3. Reject the null hypothesis if $u \le 6$ or $u \ge 17$, where 6 and 17 are the values of $u'_{0.025}$ and $u_{0.025}$ for $n_1 = 13$ and $n_2 = 9$; otherwise, accept it or reserve judgment.
4. $u = 6$ by inspection of the data.
5. Since $u = 6$ equals the value of $u'_{0.025}$, the null hypothesis must be rejected; we conclude that the arrangement of healthy and diseased elm trees is not

random. (There are too few runs and it appears that the diseased trees come in clusters.)   ◪ ◪ ◪

17.9   TESTS OF RANDOMNESS: RUNS (Large Samples)

Under the null hypothesis that n_1 letters of one kind and n_2 letters of another kind are arranged at random, it can be shown that the mean and the standard deviation of u, the total number of runs, are

Mean and Standard Deviation of u	$$\mu_u = \frac{2n_1 n_2}{n_1 + n_2} + 1 \quad and \quad \sigma_u = \sqrt{\frac{2n_1 n_2(2n_1 n_2 - n_1 - n_2)}{(n_1 + n_2)^2(n_1 + n_2 - 1)}}$$

Furthermore, if neither n_1 nor n_2 is less than 10, the sampling distribution of u can be approximated closely by a normal distribution. Thus, we base the test of the null hypothesis of randomness on the statistic

Statistics for Large-sample u Test	$$z = \frac{u - \mu_u}{\sigma_u}$$

which has approximately the standard normal distribution. If the alternative hypothesis is that the arrangement is not random, we reject the null hypothesis for $z \leq -z_{\alpha/2}$ or $z \geq z_{\alpha/2}$; if the alternative hypothesis is that there is a clustering or a trend, we reject the null hypothesis for $z \leq -z_\alpha$; and if the alternative hypothesis is that there is an alternating, or cyclical, pattern, we reject the null hypothesis for $z \geq z_\alpha$.

Example

The following is an arrangement of men, M, and women, F, lined up to purchase tickets for a rock concert:

M F M F M M M F M F M M M F F M M M M F F M F M
(cont.) M M F M M M F F F M F M M M F M F M M M M F F M

Test for randomness at the 0.05 level of significance.

solution

1. H_0:   Arrangement is random.
   H_A: Arrangement is not random.
2. $\alpha = 0.05$
3. Reject the null hypothesis if $z \leq -1.96$ or $z \geq 1.96$, where

$$z = \frac{u - \mu_u}{\sigma_u}$$

and otherwise accept the null hypothesis or reserve judgment.
4. Since $n_1 = 30$, $n_2 = 18$, and $u = 27$, we get

$$\mu_u = \frac{2 \cdot 30 \cdot 18}{30 + 18} + 1 = 23.5$$

$$\sigma_u = \sqrt{\frac{2 \cdot 30 \cdot 18(2 \cdot 30 \cdot 18 - 30 - 18)}{(30 + 18)^2(30 + 18 - 1)}} \approx 3.21$$

and, hence,

$$z = \frac{27 - 23.5}{3.21} \approx 1.09$$

5. Since $z = 1.09$ falls on the interval from -1.96 to 1.96, the null hypothesis cannot be rejected; in other words, there is no real evidence to indicate that the arrangement is not random.   ◪ ◪ ◪

17.10   TESTS OF RANDOMNESS: RUNS ABOVE AND BELOW THE MEDIAN

The u test is not limited to testing the randomness of sequences of attributes, such as the H's and D's, or M's and W's, of our examples. Any sample consisting of numerical measurements or observations can be treated similarly by using the letters a and b to denote values falling above and below the median of the sample. Numbers equal to the median are omitted. The resulting sequence of a's and b's (representing the data in their original order) can then be tested for randomness on the basis of the total number of runs of a's and b's, namely, the total number of **runs above and below the median.** Depending on the size of n_1 and n_2, we use Table VIII or the large-sample test of Section 17.9.

Example

On 24 successive runs between two cities, a bus carried

| 24 | 19 | 32 | 28 | 21 | 23 | 26 | 17 | 20 | 28 | 30 | 24 |
| 13 | 35 | 26 | 21 | 19 | 29 | 27 | 18 | 26 | 14 | 21 | 23 |

passengers. Use the total number of runs above and below the median to test at the 0.01 level of significance whether it is reasonable to treat these data as if they constitute a random sample.

solution

Since the median of the data is 23.5, we get the following arrangement of values above and below the median:

a b a a b b a b b a a a b a a b b a a b a b b b

1. H_0:   Arrangement is random.
    H_A: Arrangement is not random.

2. $\alpha = 0.01$

3. Reject the null hypothesis if $u \leq 6$ or $u \geq 20$, where 6 and 20 are the values of $u'_{0.005}$ and $u_{0.005}$ for $n_1 = 12$ and $n_2 = 12$; otherwise, accept the null hypothesis or reserve judgment.

4. $u = 14$ by inspection of the above arrangement of a's and b's.

5. Since $u = 14$ falls between 6 and 20, the null hypothesis cannot be rejected; in other words, there is no real evidence to indicate that the data do not constitute a random sample.   ◪ ◪ ◪

EXERCISES

17.51 Following is the order in which a broker received buy, *B*, and sell, *S*, orders for a certain stock:

$$B\ B\ B\ B\ B\ B\ B\ B\ S\ S\ B\ S\ S\ S\ S\ S\ B\ B\ B\ B\ B$$

Test for randomness at the 0.05 level of significance.

17.52 Betsy buys gasoline either at a Texaco station, *T*, or at a Mobil station, *M*, and the following arrangement shows the order of the stations from which she bought gasoline over a certain period of time:

$$T\ T\ T\ M\ T\ M\ T\ M\ M\ T\ T\ M\ T\ M\ T\ M\ T\ M\ M\ T\ M\ T$$

Test for randomness at the 0.05 level of significance.

17.53 Test at the 0.01 level of significance whether the following arrangement of defective, *D*, and nondefective, *N*, pieces coming off an assembly line may be regarded as random:

$$N\ N\ N\ N\ N\ N\ N\ N\ D\ D\ D\ D\ N\ N\ N\ D\ D\ N\ N\ N$$

17.54 The following arrangement indicates whether 50 consecutive persons interviewed by a pollster are for, *F*, or against, *A*, an increase in the state gasoline tax to build more roads:

$$A\ A\ A\ F\ A\ F\ A\ A\ A\ A\ F\ F\ A\ A\ F\ A\ A\ A\ A\ A\ F\ A\ A\ F\ F$$
$$(\text{cont.})\ A\ A\ F\ A\ A\ A\ A\ F\ A\ F\ F\ A\ A\ A\ A\ A\ F\ A\ A\ F\ A\ A\ A\ A\ F$$

Test for randomness at the 0.05 level of significance.

17.55 A user of a random number table extracted this sequence of 50 digits:

18469 76565 25695 21164 04836 80483 64661 28031 57163 77464

Representing each 0, 2, 4, 6, and 8 by the letter *e* (for even) and each 1, 3, 5, 7, and 9 by the letter *o* (for odd), test at the 0.05 level of significance whether the arrangement of the 50 digits may be regarded as random.

17.56 To test whether a radio signal contains a message or constitutes random noise, an interval of time is subdivided into a number of very short intervals and for each of these it is determined whether the signal strength exceeds, *E*, or does not exceed, *N*, a certain level of background noise. Test at the 0.05 level of significance whether the following arrangement, thus obtained, may be regarded as random, and hence that the signal contains no message and may be regarded as random noise:

$$E\ N\ N\ N\ N\ E\ N\ E\ N\ N\ N\ E\ E\ N\ N\ N\ E\ E\ N\ E\ N\ N\ N\ E\ N\ N\ N\ E\ E\ N\ N\ N$$
$$(\text{cont.})\ N\ N\ E\ E\ N\ E\ N\ N\ E\ N\ N\ N\ E\ E\ E\ N\ N\ N\ E\ N\ E\ N\ N\ N\ N\ E\ N$$

17.57 Flip a coin 60 times and test at the 0.05 level of significance whether the resulting sequence of *H*'s and *T*'s (heads and tails) may be regarded as random.

17.58 Use the large-sample runs test to rework Exercise 17.52.

17.59 The following sequence of *C*'s and *A*'s shows the order in which 50 cars with Arizona license plates, *A*, or California license plates, *C*, crossed the Colorado river entering Arizona from Blythe, California:

C A A C A C C A C C C A A C A A A A C C C A C C C
(cont.) A A C C C A C A A C C C C A C A A A C C A C A A A

Test for randomness at the 0.05 level of significance.

17.60 The following are the numbers of students absent from a large school on 24 consecutive days:

29 25 31 28 30 28 33 31 35 29 31 33
35 28 36 30 33 26 30 28 32 31 38 27

Use the 0.01 level of significance to test whether there is any indication that the data should not be treated as if they were a random sample.

17.61 The following are the numbers of lunches that an insurance agent claimed as business deductions in 30 consecutive months:

6 7 5 6 8 6 8 6 6 4 3 2 4 4 3
4 7 5 6 8 6 6 3 4 2 5 4 4 3 7

Test for randomness at the 0.01 level of significance.

17.62 The total number of retail stores opening for business and also quitting business within the calendar years 1948–1980 in a large city were

108 103 109 107 125 142 147 122 116 153 144
162 143 126 145 129 134 137 143 150 148 152
125 106 112 139 132 122 138 148 155 146 158

Making use of the fact that the median is 138, test at the 0.05 level of significance whether there is a real trend.

17.63 The following are the examination grades of 40 students in the order in which they finished an examination:

75 95 77 93 89 83 69 77 92 88
62 64 91 72 76 83 50 65 84 67
63 54 58 76 70 62 65 41 63 55
32 58 61 68 54 28 35 49 82 60

Making use of the fact that the median is 66, test at the 0.05 level of significance whether there is a real trend.

17.64 The following are six year's quarterly sales (in millions of dollars) of a manufacturer of heavy machinery:

83.8 102.5 121.0 90.5 106.6 104.8 114.7 93.6
98.9 96.9 122.6 85.6 103.2 96.9 118.0 92.1
100.5 92.9 125.6 79.2 110.8 95.1 125.6 86.7

Making use of the fact that the median is 99.7, test at the 0.05 level of significance whether there is a real cyclical pattern.

17.11 RANK CORRELATION

Since the significance test for r of Section 16.3 is based on very stringent assumptions, we sometimes use a nonparametric alternative that can be applied under much more general conditions. This test of the null hypothesis of no correlation is based on the **rank-correlation coefficient,** often called **Spearman's rank-correlation coefficient** and denoted by r_S.

To calculate the rank-correlation coefficient for a given set of paired data, we first rank the *x*'s among themselves from low to high or high to low; then we rank the *y*'s in the same way, find the sum of the squares of the differences, *d*, between the ranks of the *x*'s and the *y*'s, and substitute into the formula

Rank-correlation Coefficient	$$r_S = 1 - \frac{6(\Sigma\, d^2)}{n(n^2 - 1)}$$

where *n* is the number of pairs of *x*'s and *y*'s. When there are ties in rank, we proceed as before and assign to each of the tied observations the mean of the ranks which they jointly occupy.

Example

Following are the numbers of hours that 10 students studied for an examination and the grades which they received:

Number of hours studied x	Grade in examination y
9	56
5	44
11	79
13	72
10	70
5	54
18	94
15	85
2	33
8	65

Calculate r_S.

solution

Ranking the *x*'s among themselves from low to high and also the *y*'s, we get the ranks shown in the first two columns of the following table:

Rank of x	Rank of y	d	d²
5	4	1.0	1.00
2.5	2	0.5	0.25
7	8	−1.0	1.00
8	7	1.0	1.00
6	6	0.0	0.00
2.5	3	−0.5	0.25
10	10	0.0	0.00
9	9	0.0	0.00
1	1	0.0	0.00
4	5	−1.0	1.00
			4.50

Then, determining the d's and their squares, and substituting $n = 10$ and $\Sigma\, d^2 = 4.50$ into the formula for r_S, we obtain

$$r_S = 1 - \frac{66(4.50)}{10(10^2 - 1)} \approx 0.97 \qquad \blacksquare\ \blacksquare\ \blacksquare$$

As can be seen from this example, r_S is not difficult to compute manually, and this is why it is sometimes used instead of r when no calculator is available. When there are no ties, r_S actually equals the correlation coefficient r calculated for the two sets of ranks; when ties exist there may be a small (but usually negligible) difference. Of course, by using ranks instead of the original data we lose some information, but this is usually offset by the computational ease of the rank-correlation coefficient. It is worthwhile to note that r and r_S estimate different population quantities, so that it frequently happens that r and r_S are not numerically close, although they are close for this example, since the value of r is 0.96.

The main advantage in using r_S is that we can test the null hypothesis of no correlation without having to make any assumptions about the populations sampled. Under the null hypothesis of no correlation—indeed, the null hypothesis that the x's and the y's are randomly matched—the sampling distribution of r_S has the mean 0 and the standard deviation

$$\sigma_{r_S} = \frac{1}{\sqrt{n - 1}}$$

Since this sampling distribution can be approximated with a normal distribution even for relatively small values of n, we base the test of the null hypothesis on the statistic which has approximately the standard normal distribution.

Statistic for Testing Significance of r_S	$z = \dfrac{r_S - 0}{1/\sqrt{n - 1}} = r_S\sqrt{n - 1}$

Example

With reference to the preceding example where we had $n = 10$ and $r_S = 0.97$, test the null hypothesis of no correlation at the 0.01 level of significance.

solution

1. H_0: $\rho = 0$ (no correlation)
   H_A: $\rho \neq 0$
2. $\alpha = 0.01$
3. Reject the null hypothesis if $z \leq -2.575$ or $z \geq 2.575$, where $z = r_S\sqrt{n - 1}$ and otherwise, accept it or reserve judgment.
4. For $n = 10$ and $r_S = 0.97$ we get

$$z = 0.97\ \sqrt{10 - 1} = 2.91$$

5. Since $z = 2.91$ exceeds 2.575, the null hypothesis must be rejected; we conclude that there is a relationship between study time and grades in the population sampled.   ◪ ◪ ◪

EXERCISES

17.65   Twelve weeks' sales (where the units are $10,000) of a downtown department store, x, and its suburban branch, y, are

x	y
71	49
64	31
67	45
58	24
80	68
63	30
69	40
59	37
76	62
60	22
66	35
55	19

Calculate r_S.

17.66   Calculate r_S for the following sample data representing the number of minutes it took 12 mechanics to assemble a piece of machinery in the morning, x, and in the late afternoon, y:

x	y
10.8	15.1
16.6	16.8
11.1	10.9
10.3	14.2
12.0	13.8
15.1	21.5
13.7	13.2
18.5	21.1
17.3	16.4
14.2	19.3
14.8	17.4
15.3	19.0

17.67   Test at the 0.05 level of significance whether the value obtained for r_S in the preceding exercise is significant.

17.68   With reference to Exercise 15.21 on page 507, calculate r_S and test whether it is significant at the 0.05 level of significance.

17.69   With reference to Exercise 15.60 on page 523, calculate r_S and test whether it is significant at the 0.01 level of significance.

17.70   If a sample of $n = 18$ pairs of data yielded $r_S = 0.39$, is this rank-correlation coefficient significant at the 0.05 level of significance?

17.71 If a sample of $n = 40$ pairs of data yielded $r_S = 0.48$, is this rank-correlation coefficient significant at the 0.01 level of significance?

17.72 The following table shows how a panel of nutrition experts and a panel of heads of household ranked 15 breakfast foods on their palatability:

Breakfast food	Nutrition experts	Heads of household
I	7	5
II	3	4
III	11	8
IV	9	14
V	1	2
VI	4	6
VII	10	12
VIII	8	7
IX	5	1
X	13	9
XI	12	15
XII	2	3
XIII	15	10
XIV	6	11
XV	14	13

Calculate r_S as a measure of the consistency of the two rankings.

17.73 The following are the rankings which three judges gave to the work of ten artists:

Judge A:	5	8	4	2	3	1	10	7	9	6
Judge B:	3	10	1	4	2	5	6	7	8	9
Judge C:	8	5	6	4	10	2	3	1	7	9

Calculate r_S for each pair of rankings and decide
(a) which two judges are most alike in their opinions about these artists;
(b) which two judges differ the most in their opinions about these artists.

17.12 SOME FURTHER CONSIDERATIONS

Although nonparametric tests have a great deal of intuitive appeal and are widely applicable, it should not be overlooked that they are usually **less efficient** than the standard tests which they replace. To illustrate what we mean here by "less efficient," let us refer to the example on pages 306–307, where we show that the mean of a random sample of size $n = 128$ is as reliable an estimate of the mean of a symmetrical population as the median of a random sample of size $n = 200$. Thus, the median requires a larger sample, and this is what we mean when we say that it is "less efficient."

Put another way, nonparametric tests tend to be wasteful of information. The sign test and paired-sample sign tests are especially wasteful, whereas the other procedures introduced in this chapter are only slightly wasteful. Nonparametric tests should not be used indiscriminately when the assumptions underlying the corresponding standard tests are satisfied.

In actual practice, nonparametric procedures are used frequently to confirm conclusions of standard tests if there is some uncertainty about the validity of the assumptions underlying the standard tests. It is fortunate that the nonparametric tests and standard tests generally reach similar conclusions. Nonparametric tests are indispensable for situations in which the sample sizes are very small, since there will not be enough data to form an opinion one way or the other about the validity of assumptions.

17.13   SUMMARY

The table which follows summarizes the various nonparametric tests we have discussed (except for the tests of randomness based on runs) and the corresponding standard tests which they replace. In each case we cite the section or sections of the book where they are discussed.

Null hypothesis	Standard tests	Nonparametric tests
$\mu = \mu_0$	One-sample t test: (Section 11.7) or corresponding large-sample test (Section 11.6)	One-sample sign test (Sections 17.1 and 17.2) or signed-rank test (Sections 17.3 and 17.4)
$\mu_1 = \mu_2$ (independent samples)	Two-sample t test: (Section 11.9) or corresponding large-sample test (Section 11.8)	U test (Sections 17.5 and 17.6)
$\mu_1 = \mu_2$ (paired data)	Paired-sample t test: (Section 11.10) or corresponding large-sample test (Section 11.10)	Paired-sample sign test: (Sections 17.1 and 17.2) or signed-rank test (Sections 17.3 and 17.4)
$\mu_1 = \mu_2 = \cdots = \mu_k$	One-way analysis of variance (Section 14.3)	H test: (Section 17.7)
$\rho = 0$	Test based on Fisher Z transformation (Section 16.3)	Test based on rank-correlation coefficient: (Section 17.11)

Note also that tests of randomness are discussed in sections 17.8, 17.9, and 17.10; there are no corresponding standard tests.

17.14   CHECKLIST OF KEY TERMS   (*with page references to their definitions*)

H test, 570
Kruskal–Wallis test, 570
Mann–Whitney test, 564
Nonparametric tests, 551
One-sample sign test, 551
Paired-sample sign test, 554

Rank sum test, 564
Rank-correlation coefficient, 579
Runs, 575
Runs above and below the median, 577
Sign test, 551
Signed-rank test, 557

Spearman's rank-correlation coefficient, 579
Theory of runs, 574
Total number of runs, 575
u test, 574

U test, 564
Wilcoxon signed-rank test, 557
Wilcoxon test, 564

17.15 REVIEW EXERCISES

17.74 Following are the prices (in dollars) charged for a certain camera in a random sample of 15 discount stores:

57.25 58.14 54.19 56.17 57.21 55.38 54.75 57.29
57.80 54.50 55.00 56.35 54.26 60.23 53.99

Use the sign test based on Table V to test at the 0.05 level of significance whether or not the median price charged for the camera in the population sampled is $55.00.

17.75 Use the signed-rank test based on Table VI to rework the preceding exercise.

17.76 Use the large-sample sign test to rework Exercise 17.74.

17.77 The following sequence shows whether a certain member was present, *P*, or absent, *A*, at twenty consecutive meetings of a fraternal organization:

P P P P P P P P A P P P P P P P A A A A

At the 0.05 level of significance, is there any real indication of a lack of randomness?

17.78 Following are the numbers of minutes that patients had to wait for their appointments with four doctors:

Doctor A: 18 26 29 22 16
Doctor B: 9 11 28 26 15
Doctor C: 20 13 22 25 10
Doctor D: 21 26 39 32 24

Use the *H* test at the 0.05 level of significance to test the null hypothesis that the means of the populations sampled are equal against the alternative hypothesis that these means are not all equal.

17.79 Following are data on the percentage kill of two kinds of insecticides used against mosquitos:

Insecticide X: 41.9 46.9 44.6 43.9 42.0 44.0
41.0 43.1 39.0 45.2 44.6 42.0
Insecticide Y: 45.7 39.8 42.8 41.2 45.0 40.2
40.2 41.7 37.4 38.8 41.7 38.7

Use the *U* test based on Table VII to test at the 0.05 level of significance whether or not the two insecticides are on the average equally effective.

17.80 Use the large-sample *U* test to rework the preceding exercise.

17.81 Following are the batting averages, *x*, and home runs hit, *y*, by a random sample of 15 major league baseball players during the first half of the season:

x	y
0.252	12
0.305	6
0.299	4
0.303	15
0.285	2
0.191	2
0.283	16
0.272	6
0.310	8
0.266	10
0.215	0
0.211	3
0.272	14
0.244	6
0.320	7

Calculate the rank-correlation coefficient and test whether it is significant at the 0.01 level of significance.

17.82 Following are the numbers of persons who attended a "singles only" dance on twelve Saturdays:

172 208 169 232 123 165 197 178 221 195 209 182

Use the sign test based on Table V to test at the 0.05 level of significance whether or not the true median of the population sampled is $\tilde{\mu} = 169$.

17.83 Use the signed-rank test based on Table VI to rework the preceding exercise.

17.84 Use the large-sample sign test to rework Exercise 17.82.

17.85 Following are the numbers of burglaries committed in two cities on twenty days:

City A	City B	City A	City B
83	80	105	104
98	87	117	102
115	86	86	100
112	122	150	108
77	102	119	124
103	94	111	91
116	81	137	103
136	96	160	153
156	158	121	140
83	127	143	105

Use the large-sample sign test at the 0.05 level of significance to test whether or not on the average there are as many burglaries per day in the two cities.

17.86 Use the large-sample signed-rank test to rework the preceding exercise.

17.87 On what statistic do we base our decision and for what values of the statistic do we reject the null hypothesis $\mu_1 = \mu_2$, if we have random samples of size $n_1 = 8$ and $n_2 = 11$ and are using the U test based on Table VII at the 0.05 level of significance to test the null hypothesis against the alternative hypothesis

(a) $\mu_1 < \mu_2$; (b) $\mu_1 > \mu_2$; (c) $\mu_1 \neq \mu_2$?

17.88 The following sequence shows whether a television news program had at least 25 percent of a city's viewing audience, A, or less than 25 percent, L, on 36 consecutive weekday evenings:

$$L\ L\ L\ L\ A\ A\ L\ L\ L\ A\ L\ L\ L\ A\ A\ A\ A\ L$$
$$\text{(cont.)}\ A\ L\ L\ L\ A\ A\ L\ L\ L\ L\ L\ A\ L\ L\ L\ L\ L\ A$$

Test for randomness at the 0.05 level of significance.

17.89 If $r_S = 0.27$ for $n = 25$ paired data, is this rank-correlation coefficient significant at the 0.05 level of significance?

17.90 Following are the scores of 16 golfers for the first two rounds of a tournament:

Day 1	Day 2	Day 1	Day 2
68	71	71	72
73	76	73	74
70	73	68	69
74	71	70	72
69	72	73	70
72	74	71	75
67	70	67	69
72	68	73	71

Use the sign test at the 0.05 level of significance to test whether on the average the hundreds of golfers (from which these 16 may be regarded as a sample) participating in the tournament scored equally well on the first two days or whether they tended to score lower on the first day.

17.91 Following are the closing prices of a commodity (in dollars) on twenty consecutive trading days:

$$378\ \ 379\ \ 379\ \ 378\ \ 377\ \ 376\ \ 374\ \ 374\ \ 373\ \ 373$$
$$374\ \ 375\ \ 376\ \ 376\ \ 376\ \ 375\ \ 374\ \ 374\ \ 373\ \ 374$$

Test for randomness at the 0.01 level of significance.

17.92 Use the large-sample sign test to rework Exercise 17.27 on page 564.

17.93 Following are the numbers of minutes it took two ambulance services to reach the scenes of accidents:

Ambulance service 1:	9.3	5.5	13.1	10.0	7.6
	9.2	11.2	6.4	14.0	10.3

Ambulance service 2:   12.7   6.6   9.1   4.5   7.2 6.4 7.5

Assuming that the data constitute random samples, use the U test at the 0.05 level of significance to test the null hypothesis that on the average the two ambulance services respond with equal speed against the alternative hypothesis that on the average the first ambulance service is slower.

17.94 On what statistic do we base our decision and for what values of the statistic do we reject the null hypothesis $\mu_1 = \mu_2$, if we have a random sample of $n = 11$ pairs of values and are using the signed-rank test at the 0.01 level of significance to test the null hypothesis against the alternative hypothesis

(a) $\mu_1 < \mu_2$;   (b) $\mu_1 > \mu_2$;   (c) $\mu_1 \neq \mu_2$?

17.95 Rework the preceding exercise with the level of significance changed to 0.05.

17.16   REFERENCES

Further information about the nonparametric tests discussed in this chapter and many others may be found in

CONOVER, W. J., *Practical Nonparametric Statistics.* New York: John Wiley & Sons, Inc., 1971.

DANIEL, W. W., *Applied Nonparametric Statistics.* Boston: Houghton Mifflin Company, 1978.

GIBBONS, J. D., *Nonparametric Statistical Inference.* New York: McGraw-Hill Book Company, 1971.

LEHMANN, E. L., *Nonparametrics: Statistical Methods Based on Ranks.* San Francisco: Holden-Day, Inc., 1975.

MOSTELLER, F., and ROURKE, R. E. K., *Sturdy Statistics, Nonparametrics and Order Statistics.* Reading, Mass.: Addison-Wesley Publishing Company, Inc., 1973.

NOETHER, G. E., *Elements of Nonparametric Statistics, 2nd ed.* New York: John Wiley & Sons, Inc., 1976.

RANDLES, R., and WOLFE, D., *Introduction to the Theory of Nonparametric Statistics.* New York: John Wiley & Sons, Inc., 1979.

SIEGEL, S., *Nonparametric Statistics for the Behavioral Sciences.* New York: McGraw-Hill Book Company, 1956.

STATISTICAL TABLES

<table>
<tr><td colspan="11" align="center">TABLE I   Normal-Curve Areas</td></tr>
<tr><td colspan="11">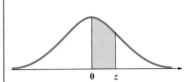 Table I entries are the probabilities that a random variable having the standard normal distribution will take on a value between 0 and z; they are given by the shaded area between 0 and z under the curve in the adjacent figure.</td></tr>
</table>

z	0.00	0.01	0.02	0.03	0.04	0.05	0.06	0.07	0.08	0.09
0.0	0.0000	0.0040	0.0080	0.0120	0.0160	0.0199	0.0239	0.0279	0.0319	0.0359
0.1	0.0398	0.0438	0.0478	0.0517	0.0557	0.0596	0.0636	0.0675	0.0714	0.0753
0.2	0.0793	0.0832	0.0871	0.0910	0.0948	0.0987	0.1026	0.1064	0.1103	0.1141
0.3	0.1179	0.1217	0.1255	0.1293	0.1331	0.1368	0.1406	0.1443	0.1480	0.1517
0.4	0.1554	0.1591	0.1628	0.1664	0.1700	0.1736	0.1772	0.1808	0.1844	0.1879
0.5	0.1915	0.1950	0.1985	0.2019	0.2054	0.2088	0.2123	0.2157	0.2190	0.2224
0.6	0.2257	0.2291	0.2324	0.2357	0.2389	0.2422	0.2454	0.2486	0.2517	0.2549
0.7	0.2580	0.2611	0.2642	0.2673	0.2704	0.2734	0.2764	0.2794	0.2823	0.2852
0.8	0.2881	0.2910	0.2939	0.2967	0.2995	0.3023	0.3051	0.3078	0.3106	0.3133
0.9	0.3159	0.3186	0.3212	0.3238	0.3264	0.3289	0.3315	0.3340	0.3365	0.3389
1.0	0.3413	0.3438	0.3461	0.3485	0.3508	0.3531	0.3554	0.3577	0.3599	0.3621
1.1	0.3643	0.3665	0.3686	0.3708	0.3729	0.3749	0.3770	0.3790	0.3810	0.3830
1.2	0.3849	0.3869	0.3888	0.3907	0.3925	0.3944	0.3962	0.3980	0.3997	0.4015
1.3	0.4032	0.4049	0.4066	0.4082	0.4099	0.4115	0.4131	0.4147	0.4162	0.4177
1.4	0.4192	0.4207	0.4222	0.4236	0.4251	0.4265	0.4279	0.4292	0.4306	0.4319
1.5	0.4332	0.4345	0.4357	0.4370	0.4382	0.4394	0.4406	0.4418	0.4429	0.4441
1.6	0.4452	0.4463	0.4474	0.4484	0.4495	0.4505	0.4515	0.4525	0.4535	0.4545
1.7	0.4554	0.4564	0.4573	0.4582	0.4591	0.4599	0.4608	0.4616	0.4625	0.4633
1.8	0.4641	0.4649	0.4656	0.4664	0.4671	0.4678	0.4686	0.4693	0.4699	0.4706
1.9	0.4713	0.4719	0.4726	0.4732	0.4738	0.4744	0.4750	0.4756	0.4761	0.4767
2.0	0.4772	0.4778	0.4783	0.4788	0.4793	0.4798	0.4803	0.4808	0.4812	0.4817
2.1	0.4821	0.4826	0.4830	0.4834	0.4838	0.4842	0.4846	0.4850	0.4854	0.4857
2.2	0.4861	0.4864	0.4868	0.4871	0.4875	0.4878	0.4881	0.4884	0.4887	0.4890
2.3	0.4893	0.4896	0.4898	0.4901	0.4904	0.4906	0.4909	0.4911	0.4913	0.4916
2.4	0.4918	0.4920	0.4922	0.4925	0.4927	0.4929	0.4931	0.4932	0.4934	0.4936
2.5	0.4938	0.4940	0.4941	0.4943	0.4945	0.4946	0.4948	0.4949	0.4951	0.4952
2.6	0.4953	0.4955	0.4956	0.4957	0.4959	0.4960	0.4961	0.4962	0.4963	0.4964
2.7	0.4965	0.4966	0.4967	0.4968	0.4969	0.4970	0.4971	0.4972	0.4973	0.4974
2.8	0.4974	0.4975	0.4976	0.4977	0.4977	0.4978	0.4979	0.4979	0.4980	0.4981
2.9	0.4981	0.4982	0.4982	0.4983	0.4984	0.4984	0.4985	0.4985	0.4986	0.4986
3.0	0.4987	0.4987	0.4987	0.4988	0.4988	0.4989	0.4989	0.4989	0.4990	0.4990

SOURCE: Abridged from Table I of A. Hald, *Statistical Tables and Formulas* (New York: Wiley), 1952. Reproduced by permission of A. Hald and the publisher, John Wiley & Sons, Inc.
Also, for $z = 4.0$, 5.0, and 6.0, the areas are 0.49997, 0.4999997, and 0.499999999.

TABLE II   Critical Values of *t*

Table II entries are values for which the area to their right under the *t* distribution with given degrees of freedom (the shaded area to the right of t_α) is equal to α.

df	$t_{0.100}$	$t_{0.050}$	$t_{0.025}$	$t_{0.010}$	$t_{0.005}$
1	3.078	6.314	12.706	31.821	63.657
2	1.886	2.920	4.303	6.965	9.925
3	1.638	2.353	3.182	4.541	5.841
4	1.533	2.132	2.776	3.747	4.604
5	1.476	2.015	2.571	3.365	4.032
6	1.440	1.943	2.447	3.143	3.707
7	1.415	1.895	2.365	2.998	3.499
8	1.397	1.860	2.306	2.896	3.355
9	1.383	1.833	2.262	2.821	3.250
10	1.372	1.812	2.228	2.764	3.169
11	1.363	1.796	2.201	2.718	3.106
12	1.356	1.782	2.179	2.681	3.055
13	1.350	1.771	2.160	2.650	3.012
14	1.345	1.761	2.145	2.624	2.977
15	1.341	1.753	2.131	2.602	2.947
16	1.337	1.746	2.120	2.583	2.921
17	1.333	1.740	2.110	2.567	2.898
18	1.330	1.734	2.101	2.552	2.878
19	1.328	1.729	2.093	2.539	2.861
20	1.325	1.725	2.086	2.528	2.845
21	1.323	1.721	2.080	2.518	2.831
22	1.321	1.717	2.074	2.508	2.819
23	1.319	1.714	2.069	2.500	2.807
24	1.318	1.711	2.064	2.492	2.797
25	1.316	1.708	2.060	2.485	2.787
26	1.315	1.706	2.056	2.479	2.779
27	1.314	1.703	2.052	2.473	2.771
28	1.313	1.701	2.048	2.467	2.763
29	1.311	1.699	2.045	2.462	2.756
30	1.310	1.697	2.042	2.457	2.750
40	1.303	1.684	2.021	2.423	2.704
60	1.296	1.671	2.000	2.390	2.660
120	1.289	1.658	1.980	2.358	2.617
∞	1.282	1.645	1.960	2.326	2.576

TABLE III Critical Values of χ^2

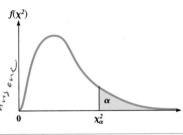

Table III entries are values for which the area to their right under the chi-square distribution with given degrees of freedom (the area to the right of χ_α^2) is equal to α.

D.F.	$\chi_{0.995}^2$	$\chi_{0.99}^2$	$\chi_{0.975}^2$	$\chi_{0.95}^2$	$\chi_{0.05}^2$	$\chi_{0.025}^2$	$\chi_{0.01}^2$	$\chi_{0.005}^2$
1	0.0000393	0.000157	0.000982	0.00393	3.841	5.024	6.635	7.879
2	0.0100	0.0201	0.0506	0.103	5.991	7.378	9.210	10.597
3	0.0717	0.115	0.216	0.352	7.815	9.348	11.345	12.838
4	0.207	0.297	0.484	0.711	9.488	11.143	13.277	14.860
5	0.412	0.554	0.831	1.145	11.070	12.832	15.086	16.750
6	0.676	0.872	1.237	1.635	12.592	14.449	16.812	18.548
7	0.989	1.239	1.690	2.167	14.067	16.013	18.475	20.278
8	1.344	1.646	2.180	2.733	15.507	17.535	20.090	21.955
9	1.735	2.088	2.700	3.325	16.919	19.023	21.666	23.589
10	2.156	2.558	3.247	3.940	18.307	20.483	23.209	25.188
11	2.603	3.053	3.816	4.575	19.675	21.920	24.725	26.757
12	3.074	3.571	4.404	5.226	21.026	23.337	26.217	28.300
13	3.565	4.107	5.009	5.892	22.362	24.736	27.688	29.819
14	4.075	4.660	5.629	6.571	23.685	26.119	29.141	31.319
15	4.601	5.229	6.262	7.261	24.996	27.488	30.578	32.801
16	5.142	5.812	6.908	7.962	26.296	28.845	32.000	34.267
17	5.697	6.408	7.564	8.672	27.587	30.191	33.409	35.718
18	6.265	7.015	8.231	9.390	28.869	31.526	34.805	37.156
19	6.844	7.633	8.907	10.117	30.144	32.852	36.191	38.582
20	7.434	8.260	9.591	10.851	31.410	34.170	37.566	39.997
21	8.034	8.897	10.283	11.591	32.671	35.479	38.932	41.401
22	8.643	9.542	10.982	12.338	33.924	36.781	40.289	42.796
23	9.260	10.196	11.689	13.091	35.172	38.076	41.638	44.181
24	9.886	10.856	12.401	13.848	36.415	39.364	42.980	45.558
25	10.520	11.524	13.120	14.611	37.652	40.646	44.314	46.928
26	11.160	12.198	13.844	15.379	38.885	41.923	45.642	48.290
27	11.808	12.879	14.573	16.151	40.113	43.194	46.963	49.645
28	12.461	13.565	15.308	16.928	41.337	44.461	48.278	50.993
29	13.121	14.256	16.047	17.708	42.557	45.722	49.588	52.336
30	13.787	14.953	16.791	18.493	43.773	46.979	50.892	53.672

SOURCE: Based on Table 8 of *Biometrika Tables for Statisticians*, Volume I (Cambridge University Press, 1954), by permission of the *Biometrika* trustees.

TABLE IV   Critical Values of F: Values of $F_{0.05}$

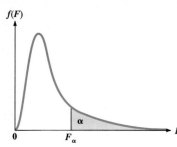

Table IV entries are values for which the area to their right under the F distribution with given degrees of freedom (the shaded area to the right of F_α) is equal to α.

ν_2	Numerator Degrees of Freedom								
	1	2	3	4	5	6	7	8	9
1	161.4	199.5	215.7	224.6	230.2	234.0	236.8	238.9	240.5
2	18.51	19.00	19.16	19.25	19.30	19.33	19.35	19.37	19.38
3	10.13	9.55	9.28	9.12	9.01	8.94	8.89	8.85	8.81
4	7.71	6.94	6.59	6.39	6.26	6.16	6.09	6.04	6.00
5	6.61	5.79	5.41	5.19	5.05	4.95	4.88	4.82	4.77
6	5.99	5.14	4.76	4.53	4.39	4.28	4.21	4.15	4.10
7	5.59	4.74	4.35	4.12	3.97	3.87	3.79	3.73	3.68
8	5.32	4.46	4.07	3.84	3.69	3.58	3.50	3.44	3.39
9	5.12	4.26	3.86	3.63	3.48	3.37	3.29	3.23	3.18
10	4.96	4.10	3.71	3.48	3.33	3.22	3.14	3.07	3.02
11	4.84	3.98	3.59	3.36	3.20	3.09	3.01	2.95	2.90
12	4.75	3.89	3.49	3.26	3.11	3.00	2.91	2.85	2.80
13	4.67	3.81	3.41	3.18	3.03	2.92	2.83	2.77	2.71
14	4.60	3.74	3.34	3.11	2.96	2.85	2.76	2.70	2.65
15	4.54	3.68	3.29	3.06	2.90	2.79	2.71	2.64	2.59
16	4.49	3.63	3.24	3.01	2.85	2.74	2.66	2.59	2.54
17	4.45	3.59	3.20	2.96	2.81	2.70	2.61	2.55	2.49
18	4.41	3.55	3.16	2.93	2.77	2.66	2.58	2.51	2.46
19	4.38	3.52	3.13	2.90	2.74	2.63	2.54	2.48	2.42
20	4.35	3.49	3.10	2.87	2.71	2.60	2.51	2.45	2.39
21	4.32	3.47	3.07	2.84	2.68	2.57	2.49	2.42	2.37
22	4.30	3.44	3.05	2.82	2.66	2.55	2.46	2.40	2.34
23	4.28	3.42	3.03	2.80	2.64	2.53	2.44	2.37	2.32
24	4.26	3.40	3.01	2.78	2.62	2.51	2.42	2.36	2.30
25	4.24	3.39	2.99	2.76	2.60	2.49	2.40	2.34	2.28
26	4.23	3.37	2.98	2.74	2.59	2.47	2.39	2.32	2.27
27	4.21	3.35	2.96	2.73	2.57	2.46	2.37	2.31	2.25
28	4.20	3.34	2.95	2.71	2.56	2.45	2.36	2.29	2.24
29	4.18	3.33	2.93	2.70	2.55	2.43	2.35	2.28	2.22
30	4.17	3.32	2.92	2.69	2.53	2.42	2.33	2.27	2.21
40	4.08	3.23	2.84	2.61	2.45	2.34	2.25	2.18	2.12
60	4.00	3.15	2.76	2.53	2.37	2.25	2.17	2.10	2.04
120	3.92	3.07	2.68	2.45	2.29	2.17	2.09	2.02	1.96
∞	3.84	3.00	2.60	2.37	2.21	2.10	2.01	1.94	1.88

Denominator Degrees of Freedom

SOURCE: From M. Merrington and C. M. Thompson, "Tables of Percentage Points of the Inverted Beta (F)-Distribution." *Biometrika*, 1943, 33, 73–88. Reproduced by permission of the *Biometrika* Trustees.

TABLE IV   Critical Values of F: Values of $F_{0.05}$ (concluded)

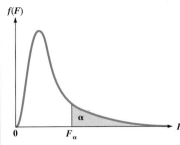

$f(F)$

α

F_α

F

0

Table IV entries are values for which the area to their right under the F distribution with given degrees of freedom (the shaded area to the right of F_α) is equal to α.

ν_2 \\ ν_1	\multicolumn{10}{c}{**Numerator Degrees of Freedom**}										
	10	**12**	**15**	**20**	**24**	**30**	**40**	**60**	**120**	**∞**
1	241.9	243.9	245.9	248.0	249.1	250.1	251.1	252.2	253.3	254.3
2	19.40	19.41	19.43	19.45	19.45	19.46	19.47	19.48	19.49	19.50
3	8.79	8.74	8.70	8.66	8.64	8.62	8.59	8.57	8.55	8.53
4	5.96	5.91	5.86	5.80	5.77	5.75	5.72	5.69	5.66	5.63
5	4.74	4.68	4.62	4.56	4.53	4.50	4.46	4.43	4.40	4.36
6	4.06	4.00	3.94	3.87	3.84	3.81	3.77	3.74	3.70	3.67
7	3.64	3.57	3.51	3.44	3.41	3.38	3.34	3.30	3.27	3.23
8	3.35	3.28	3.22	3.15	3.12	3.08	3.04	3.01	2.97	2.93
9	3.14	3.07	3.01	2.94	2.90	2.86	2.83	2.79	2.75	2.71
10	2.98	2.91	2.85	2.77	2.74	2.70	2.66	2.62	2.58	2.54
11	2.85	2.79	2.72	2.65	2.61	2.57	2.53	2.49	2.45	2.40
12	2.75	2.69	2.62	2.54	2.51	2.47	2.43	2.38	2.34	2.30
13	2.67	2.60	2.53	2.46	2.42	2.38	2.34	2.30	2.25	2.21
14	2.60	2.53	2.46	2.39	2.35	2.31	2.27	2.22	2.18	2.13
15	2.54	2.48	2.40	2.33	2.29	2.25	2.20	2.16	2.11	2.07
16	2.49	2.42	2.35	2.28	2.24	2.19	2.15	2.11	2.06	2.01
17	2.45	2.38	2.31	2.23	2.19	2.15	2.10	2.06	2.01	1.96
18	2.41	2.34	2.27	2.19	2.15	2.11	2.06	2.02	1.97	1.92
19	2.38	2.31	2.23	2.16	2.11	2.07	2.03	1.98	1.93	1.88
20	2.35	2.28	2.20	2.12	2.08	2.04	1.99	1.95	1.90	1.84
21	2.32	2.25	2.18	2.10	2.05	2.01	1.96	1.92	1.87	1.81
22	2.30	2.23	2.15	2.07	2.03	1.98	1.94	1.89	1.84	1.78
23	2.27	2.20	2.13	2.05	2.01	1.96	1.91	1.86	1.81	1.76
24	2.25	2.18	2.11	2.03	1.98	1.94	1.89	1.84	1.79	1.73
25	2.24	2.16	2.09	2.01	1.96	1.92	1.87	1.82	1.77	1.71
26	2.22	2.15	2.07	1.99	1.95	1.90	1.85	1.80	1.75	1.69
27	2.20	2.13	2.06	1.97	1.93	1.88	1.84	1.79	1.73	1.67
28	2.19	2.12	2.04	1.96	1.91	1.87	1.82	1.77	1.71	1.65
29	2.18	2.10	2.03	1.94	1.90	1.85	1.81	1.75	1.70	1.64
30	2.16	2.09	2.01	1.93	1.89	1.84	1.79	1.74	1.68	1.62
40	2.08	2.00	1.92	1.84	1.79	1.74	1.69	1.64	1.58	1.51
60	1.99	1.92	1.84	1.75	1.70	1.65	1.59	1.53	1.47	1.39
120	1.91	1.83	1.75	1.66	1.61	1.55	1.50	1.43	1.35	1.25
∞	1.83	1.75	1.67	1.57	1.52	1.46	1.39	1.32	1.22	1.00

Denominator Degrees of Freedom

TABLE IV   Critical Values of F: Values of $F_{0.01}$

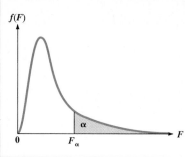

Table IV entries are values for which the area to their right under the F distribution with given degrees of freedom (the shaded area to the right of F_α) is equal to α.

ν_1 \ ν_2	Numerator Degrees of Freedom								
	1	2	3	4	5	6	7	8	9
1	4,052	4,999.5	5,403	5,625	5,764	5,859	5,928	5,982	6,022
2	98.50	99.00	99.17	99.25	99.30	99.33	99.36	99.37	99.39
3	34.12	30.82	29.46	28.71	28.24	27.91	27.67	27.49	27.35
4	21.20	18.00	16.69	15.98	15.52	15.21	14.98	14.80	14.66
5	16.26	13.27	12.06	11.39	10.97	10.67	10.46	10.29	10.16
6	13.75	10.92	9.78	9.15	8.75	8.47	8.26	8.10	7.98
7	12.25	9.55	8.45	7.85	7.46	7.19	6.99	6.84	6.72
8	11.26	8.65	7.59	7.01	6.63	6.37	6.18	6.03	5.91
9	10.56	8.02	6.99	6.42	6.06	5.80	5.61	5.47	5.35
10	10.04	7.56	6.55	5.99	5.64	5.39	5.20	5.06	4.94
11	9.65	7.21	6.22	5.67	5.32	5.07	4.89	4.74	4.63
12	9.33	6.93	5.95	5.41	5.06	4.82	4.64	4.50	4.39
13	9.07	6.70	5.74	5.21	4.86	4.62	4.44	4.30	4.19
14	8.86	6.51	5.56	5.04	4.69	4.46	4.28	4.14	4.03
15	8.68	6.36	5.42	4.89	4.56	4.32	4.14	4.00	3.89
16	8.53	6.23	5.29	4.77	4.44	4.20	4.03	3.89	3.78
17	8.40	6.11	5.18	4.67	4.34	4.10	3.93	3.79	3.68
18	8.29	6.01	5.09	4.58	4.25	4.01	3.84	3.71	3.60
19	8.18	5.93	5.01	4.50	4.17	3.94	3.77	3.63	3.52
20	8.10	5.85	4.94	4.43	4.10	3.87	3.70	3.56	3.46
21	8.02	5.78	4.87	4.37	4.04	3.81	3.64	3.51	3.40
22	7.95	5.72	4.82	4.31	3.99	3.76	3.59	3.45	3.35
23	7.88	5.66	4.76	4.26	3.94	3.71	3.54	3.41	3.30
24	7.82	5.61	4.72	4.22	3.90	3.67	3.50	3.36	3.26
25	7.77	5.57	4.68	4.18	3.85	3.63	3.46	3.32	3.22
26	7.72	5.53	4.64	4.14	3.82	3.59	3.42	3.29	3.18
27	7.68	5.49	4.60	4.11	3.78	3.56	3.39	3.26	3.15
28	7.64	5.45	4.57	4.07	3.75	3.53	3.36	3.23	3.12
29	7.60	5.42	4.54	4.04	3.73	3.50	3.33	3.20	3.09
30	7.56	5.39	4.51	4.02	3.70	3.47	3.30	3.17	3.07
40	7.31	5.18	4.31	3.83	3.51	3.29	3.12	2.99	2.89
60	7.08	4.98	4.13	3.65	3.34	3.12	2.95	2.82	2.72
120	6.85	4.79	3.95	3.48	3.17	2.96	2.79	2.66	2.56
∞	6.63	4.61	3.78	3.32	3.02	2.80	2.64	2.51	2.41

SOURCE: From M. Merrington and C. M. Thompson, "Tables of Percentage Points of the Inverted Beta (F)-Distribution," *Biometrika*, 1943, 33, 73–88. Reproduced by permission of the *Biometrika* Trustees.

TABLE IV Critical Values of F: Values of $F_{0.01}$ (concluded)

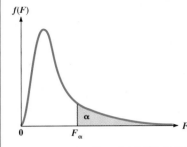

Table IV entries are values for which the area to their right under the F distribution with given degrees of freedom (the shaded area to the right of F_α) is equal to α.

ν_1	Numerator Degrees of Freedom ν_2									
	10	12	15	20	24	30	40	60	120	∞
1	6,056	6,106	6,157	6,209	6,235	6,261	6,287	6,313	6,339	6,366
2	99.40	99.42	99.43	99.45	99.46	99.47	99.47	99.48	99.49	99.50
3	27.23	27.05	26.87	26.69	26.60	26.50	26.41	26.32	26.22	26.13
4	14.55	14.37	14.20	14.02	13.93	13.84	13.75	13.65	13.56	13.46
5	10.05	9.89	9.72	9.55	9.47	9.38	9.29	9.20	9.11	9.02
6	7.87	7.72	7.56	7.40	7.31	7.23	7.14	7.06	6.97	6.88
7	6.62	6.47	6.31	6.16	6.07	5.99	5.91	5.82	5.74	5.65
8	5.81	5.67	5.52	5.36	5.28	5.20	5.12	5.03	4.95	4.86
9	5.26	5.11	4.96	4.81	4.73	4.65	4.57	4.48	4.40	4.31
10	4.85	4.71	4.56	4.41	4.33	4.25	4.17	4.08	4.00	3.91
11	4.54	4.40	4.25	4.10	4.02	3.94	3.86	3.78	3.69	3.60
12	4.30	4.16	4.01	3.86	3.78	3.70	3.62	3.54	3.45	3.36
13	4.10	3.96	3.82	3.66	3.59	3.51	3.43	3.34	3.25	3.17
14	3.94	3.80	3.66	3.51	3.43	3.35	3.27	3.18	3.09	3.00
15	3.80	3.67	3.52	3.37	3.29	3.21	3.13	3.05	2.96	2.87
16	3.69	3.55	3.41	3.26	3.18	3.10	3.02	2.93	2.84	2.75
17	3.59	3.46	3.31	3.16	3.08	3.00	2.92	2.83	2.75	2.65
18	3.51	3.37	3.23	3.08	3.00	2.92	2.84	2.75	2.66	2.57
19	3.43	3.30	3.15	3.00	2.92	2.84	2.76	2.67	2.58	2.49
20	3.37	3.23	3.09	2.94	2.86	2.78	2.69	2.61	2.52	2.42
21	3.31	3.17	3.03	2.88	2.80	2.72	2.64	2.55	2.46	2.36
22	3.26	3.12	2.98	2.83	2.75	2.67	2.58	2.50	2.40	2.31
23	3.21	3.07	2.93	2.78	2.70	2.62	2.54	2.45	2.35	2.26
24	3.17	3.03	2.89	2.74	2.66	2.58	2.49	2.40	2.31	2.21
25	3.13	2.99	2.85	2.70	2.62	2.54	2.45	2.36	2.27	2.17
26	3.09	2.96	2.81	2.66	2.58	2.50	2.42	2.33	2.23	2.13
27	3.06	2.93	2.78	2.63	2.55	2.47	2.38	2.29	2.20	2.10
28	3.03	2.90	2.75	2.60	2.52	2.44	2.35	2.26	2.17	2.06
29	3.00	2.87	2.73	2.57	2.49	2.41	2.33	2.23	2.14	2.03
30	2.98	2.84	2.70	2.55	2.47	2.39	2.30	2.21	2.11	2.01
40	2.80	2.66	2.52	2.37	2.29	2.20	2.11	2.02	1.92	1.80
60	2.63	2.50	2.35	2.20	2.12	2.03	1.94	1.84	1.73	1.60
120	2.47	2.34	2.19	2.03	1.95	1.86	1.76	1.66	1.53	1.38
∞	2.32	2.18	2.04	1.88	1.79	1.70	1.59	1.47	1.32	1.00

Denominator Degrees of Freedom

TABLE V   Binomial Probabilities

*All values omitted in this table are **0.0005** or less.*

n	x	0.05	0.1	0.2	0.3	0.4	0.5	0.6	0.7	0.8	0.9	0.95
2	0	0.902	0.810	0.640	0.490	0.360	0.250	0.160	0.090	0.040	0.010	0.002
	1	0.095	0.180	0.320	0.420	0.480	0.500	0.480	0.420	0.320	0.180	0.095
	2	0.002	0.010	0.040	0.090	0.160	0.250	0.360	0.490	0.640	0.810	0.902
3	0	0.857	0.729	0.512	0.343	0.216	0.125	0.064	0.027	0.008	0.001	
	1	0.135	0.243	0.384	0.441	0.432	0.375	0.288	0.189	0.096	0.027	0.007
	2	0.007	0.027	0.096	0.189	0.288	0.375	0.432	0.441	0.384	0.243	0.135
	3		0.001	0.008	0.027	0.064	0.125	0.216	0.343	0.512	0.729	0.857
4	0	0.815	0.656	0.410	0.240	0.130	0.062	0.026	0.008	0.002		
	1	0.171	0.292	0.410	0.412	0.346	0.250	0.154	0.076	0.026	0.004	
	2	0.014	0.049	0.154	0.265	0.346	0.375	0.346	0.265	0.154	0.049	0.014
	3		0.004	0.026	0.076	0.154	0.250	0.346	0.412	0.410	0.292	0.171
	4			0.002	0.008	0.026	0.062	0.130	0.240	0.410	0.656	0.815
5	0	0.774	0.590	0.328	0.168	0.078	0.031	0.010	0.002			
	1	0.204	0.328	0.410	0.360	0.259	0.156	0.077	0.028	0.006		
	2	0.021	0.073	0.205	0.309	0.346	0.312	0.230	0.132	0.051	0.008	0.001
	3	0.001	0.008	0.051	0.132	0.230	0.312	0.346	0.309	0.205	0.073	0.021
	4			0.006	0.028	0.077	0.156	0.259	0.360	0.410	0.328	0.204
	5				0.002	0.010	0.031	0.078	0.168	0.328	0.590	0.774
6	0	0.735	0.531	0.262	0.118	0.047	0.016	0.004	0.001			
	1	0.232	0.354	0.393	0.303	0.187	0.094	0.037	0.010	0.002		
	2	0.031	0.098	0.246	0.324	0.311	0.234	0.138	0.060	0.015	0.001	
	3	0.002	0.015	0.082	0.185	0.276	0.312	0.276	0.185	0.082	0.015	0.002
	4		0.001	0.015	0.060	0.138	0.234	0.311	0.324	0.246	0.098	0.031
	5			0.002	0.010	0.037	0.094	0.187	0.303	0.393	0.354	0.232
	6				0.001	0.004	0.016	0.047	0.118	0.262	0.531	0.735
7	0	0.698	0.478	0.210	0.082	0.028	0.008	0.002				
	1	0.257	0.372	0.367	0.247	0.131	0.055	0.017	0.004			
	2	0.041	0.124	0.275	0.318	0.261	0.164	0.077	0.025	0.004		
	3	0.004	0.023	0.115	0.227	0.290	0.273	0.194	0.097	0.029	0.003	
	4		0.003	0.029	0.097	0.194	0.273	0.290	0.227	0.115	0.023	0.004
	5			0.004	0.025	0.077	0.164	0.261	0.318	0.275	0.124	0.041
	6				0.004	0.017	0.055	0.131	0.247	0.367	0.372	0.257
	7					0.002	0.008	0.028	0.082	0.210	0.478	0.698
8	0	0.663	0.430	0.168	0.058	0.017	0.004	0.001				
	1	0.279	0.383	0.336	0.198	0.090	0.031	0.008	0.001			
	2	0.051	0.149	0.294	0.296	0.209	0.109	0.041	0.010	0.001		
	3	0.005	0.033	0.147	0.254	0.279	0.219	0.124	0.047	0.009		
	4		0.005	0.046	0.136	0.232	0.273	0.232	0.136	0.046	0.005	
	5			0.009	0.047	0.124	0.219	0.279	0.254	0.147	0.033	0.005
	6			0.001	0.010	0.041	0.109	0.209	0.296	0.294	0.149	0.051
	7				0.001	0.008	0.031	0.090	0.198	0.336	0.383	0.279
	8					0.001	0.004	0.017	0.058	0.168	0.430	0.663

TABLE V   Binomial Probabilities   (continued)

*All values omitted in this table are **0.0005** or less.*

n	x	0.05	0.1	0.2	0.3	0.4	0.5	0.6	0.7	0.8	0.9	0.95
9	0	0.630	0.387	0.134	0.040	0.010	0.002					
	1	0.299	0.387	0.302	0.156	0.060	0.018	0.004				
	2	0.063	0.172	0.302	0.267	0.161	0.070	0.021	0.004			
	3	0.008	0.045	0.176	0.267	0.251	0.164	0.074	0.021	0.003		
	4	0.001	0.007	0.066	0.172	0.251	0.246	0.167	0.074	0.017	0.001	
	5		0.001	0.017	0.074	0.167	0.246	0.251	0.172	0.066	0.007	0.001
	6			0.003	0.021	0.074	0.164	0.251	0.267	0.176	0.045	0.008
	7				0.004	0.021	0.070	0.161	0.267	0.302	0.172	0.063
	8					0.004	0.018	0.060	0.156	0.302	0.387	0.299
	9						0.002	0.010	0.040	0.134	0.387	0.630
10	0	0.599	0.349	0.107	0.028	0.006	0.001					
	1	0.315	0.387	0.268	0.121	0.040	0.010	0.002				
	2	0.075	0.194	0.302	0.233	0.121	0.044	0.011	0.001			
	3	0.010	0.057	0.201	0.267	0.215	0.117	0.042	0.009	0.001		
	4	0.001	0.011	0.088	0.200	0.251	0.205	0.111	0.037	0.006		
	5		0.001	0.026	0.103	0.201	0.246	0.201	0.103	0.026	0.001	
	6			0.006	0.037	0.111	0.205	0.251	0.200	0.088	0.011	0.001
	7			0.001	0.009	0.042	0.117	0.215	0.267	0.201	0.057	0.010
	8				0.001	0.011	0.044	0.121	0.233	0.302	0.194	0.075
	9					0.002	0.010	0.040	0.121	0.268	0.387	0.315
	10						0.001	0.006	0.028	0.107	0.349	0.599
11	0	0.569	0.314	0.086	0.020	0.004						
	1	0.329	0.384	0.236	0.093	0.027	0.005	0.001				
	2	0.087	0.213	0.295	0.200	0.089	0.027	0.005	0.001			
	3	0.014	0.071	0.221	0.257	0.177	0.081	0.023	0.004			
	4	0.001	0.016	0.111	0.220	0.236	0.161	0.070	0.017	0.002		
	5		0.002	0.039	0.132	0.221	0.226	0.147	0.057	0.010		
	6			0.010	0.057	0.147	0.226	0.221	0.132	0.039	0.002	
	7			0.002	0.017	0.070	0.161	0.236	0.220	0.111	0.016	0.001
	8				0.004	0.023	0.081	0.177	0.257	0.221	0.071	0.014
	9				0.001	0.005	0.027	0.089	0.200	0.295	0.213	0.087
	10					0.001	0.005	0.027	0.093	0.236	0.384	0.329
	11							0.004	0.020	0.086	0.314	0.569
12	0	0.540	0.282	0.069	0.014	0.002						
	1	0.341	0.377	0.206	0.071	0.017	0.003					
	2	0.099	0.230	0.283	0.168	0.064	0.016	0.002				
	3	0.017	0.085	0.236	0.240	0.142	0.054	0.012	0.001			
	4	0.002	0.021	0.133	0.231	0.213	0.121	0.042	0.008	0.001		
	5		0.004	0.053	0.158	0.227	0.193	0.101	0.029	0.003		
	6			0.016	0.079	0.177	0.226	0.177	0.079	0.016		
	7			0.003	0.029	0.101	0.193	0.227	0.158	0.053	0.004	
	8			0.001	0.008	0.042	0.121	0.213	0.231	0.133	0.021	0.002
	9				0.001	0.012	0.054	0.142	0.240	0.236	0.085	0.017
	10					0.002	0.016	0.064	0.168	0.283	0.230	0.099
	11						0.003	0.017	0.071	0.206	0.377	0.341
	12							0.002	0.014	0.069	0.282	0.540

TABLE V   Binomial Probabilities   (continued)

*All values omitted in this table are **0.0005** or less.*

n	x	p 0.05	0.1	0.2	0.3	0.4	0.5	0.6	0.7	0.8	0.9	0.95
13	0	0.513	0.254	0.055	0.010	0.001						
	1	0.351	0.367	0.179	0.054	0.011	0.002					
	2	0.111	0.245	0.268	0.139	0.045	0.010	0.001				
	3	0.021	0.100	0.246	0.218	0.111	0.035	0.006	0.001			
	4	0.003	0.028	0.154	0.234	0.184	0.087	0.024	0.003			
	5		0.006	0.069	0.180	0.221	0.157	0.066	0.014	0.001		
	6		0.001	0.023	0.103	0.197	0.209	0.131	0.044	0.006		
	7			0.006	0.044	0.131	0.209	0.197	0.103	0.023	0.001	
	8			0.001	0.014	0.066	0.157	0.221	0.180	0.069	0.006	
	9				0.003	0.024	0.087	0.184	0.234	0.154	0.028	0.003
	10				0.001	0.006	0.035	0.111	0.218	0.246	0.100	0.021
	11					0.001	0.010	0.045	0.139	0.268	0.245	0.111
	12						0.002	0.011	0.054	0.179	0.367	0.351
	13							0.001	0.010	0.055	0.254	0.513
14	0	0.488	0.229	0.044	0.007	0.001						
	1	0.359	0.356	0.154	0.041	0.007	0.001					
	2	0.123	0.257	0.250	0.113	0.032	0.006	0.001				
	3	0.026	0.114	0.250	0.194	0.085	0.022	0.003				
	4	0.004	0.035	0.172	0.229	0.155	0.061	0.014	0.001			
	5		0.008	0.086	0.196	0.207	0.122	0.041	0.007			
	6		0.001	0.032	0.126	0.207	0.183	0.092	0.023	0.002		
	7			0.009	0.062	0.157	0.209	0.157	0.062	0.009		
	8			0.002	0.023	0.092	0.183	0.207	0.126	0.032	0.001	
	9				0.007	0.041	0.122	0.207	0.196	0.086	0.008	
	10				0.001	0.014	0.061	0.155	0.229	0.172	0.035	0.004
	11					0.003	0.022	0.085	0.194	0.250	0.114	0.026
	12					0.001	0.006	0.032	0.113	0.250	0.257	0.123
	13						0.001	0.007	0.041	0.154	0.356	0.359
	14							0.001	0.007	0.044	0.229	0.488
15	0	0.463	0.206	0.035	0.005							
	1	0.366	0.343	0.132	0.031	0.005						
	2	0.135	0.267	0.231	0.092	0.022	0.003					
	3	0.031	0.129	0.250	0.170	0.063	0.014	0.002				
	4	0.005	0.043	0.188	0.219	0.127	0.042	0.007	0.001			
	5	0.001	0.010	0.103	0.206	0.186	0.092	0.024	0.003			
	6		0.002	0.043	0.147	0.207	0.153	0.061	0.012	0.001		
	7			0.014	0.081	0.177	0.196	0.118	0.035	0.003		
	8			0.003	0.035	0.118	0.196	0.177	0.081	0.014		
	9			0.001	0.012	0.061	0.153	0.207	0.147	0.043	0.002	
	10				0.003	0.024	0.092	0.186	0.206	0.103	0.010	0.001
	11				0.001	0.007	0.042	0.127	0.219	0.188	0.043	0.005
	12					0.002	0.014	0.063	0.170	0.250	0.129	0.031
	13						0.003	0.022	0.092	0.231	0.267	0.135
	14							0.005	0.031	0.132	0.343	0.366
	15								0.005	0.035	0.206	0.463

TABLE V Binomial Probabilities (continued)

*All values omitted in this table are **0.0005** or less.*

n	x	p=0.05	0.1	0.2	0.3	0.4	0.5	0.6	0.7	0.8	0.9	0.95
16	0	0.440	0.185	0.028	0.003							
	1	0.371	0.329	0.113	0.023	0.003						
	2	0.146	0.275	0.211	0.073	0.015	0.002					
	3	0.036	0.142	0.246	0.146	0.047	0.009	0.001				
	4	0.006	0.051	0.200	0.204	0.101	0.028	0.004				
	5	0.001	0.014	0.120	0.210	0.162	0.067	0.014	0.001			
	6		0.003	0.055	0.165	0.198	0.122	0.039	0.006			
	7			0.020	0.101	0.189	0.175	0.084	0.019	0.001		
	8			0.006	0.049	0.142	0.196	0.142	0.049	0.006		
	9			0.001	0.019	0.084	0.175	0.189	0.101	0.020		
	10				0.006	0.039	0.122	0.198	0.165	0.055	0.003	
	11				0.001	0.014	0.067	0.162	0.210	0.120	0.014	0.001
	12					0.004	0.028	0.101	0.204	0.200	0.051	0.006
	13					0.001	0.009	0.047	0.146	0.246	0.142	0.036
	14						0.002	0.015	0.073	0.211	0.275	0.146
	15							0.003	0.023	0.113	0.329	0.371
	16								0.003	0.028	0.185	0.440
17	0	0.418	0.167	0.023	0.002							
	1	0.374	0.315	0.096	0.017	0.002						
	2	0.158	0.280	0.191	0.058	0.010	0.001					
	3	0.041	0.156	0.239	0.125	0.034	0.005					
	4	0.008	0.060	0.209	0.187	0.080	0.018	0.002				
	5	0.001	0.017	0.136	0.208	0.138	0.047	0.008	0.001			
	6		0.004	0.068	0.178	0.184	0.094	0.024	0.003			
	7		0.001	0.027	0.120	0.193	0.148	0.057	0.009			
	8			0.008	0.064	0.161	0.185	0.107	0.028	0.002		
	9			0.002	0.028	0.107	0.185	0.161	0.064	0.008		
	10				0.009	0.057	0.148	0.193	0.120	0.027	0.001	
	11				0.003	0.024	0.094	0.184	0.178	0.068	0.004	
	12				0.001	0.008	0.047	0.138	0.208	0.136	0.017	0.001
	13					0.002	0.018	0.080	0.187	0.209	0.060	0.008
	14						0.005	0.034	0.125	0.239	0.156	0.041
	15						0.001	0.010	0.058	0.191	0.280	0.158
	16							0.002	0.017	0.096	0.315	0.374
	17								0.002	0.023	0.167	0.418
18	0	0.397	0.150	0.018	0.002							
	1	0.376	0.300	0.081	0.013	0.001						
	2	0.168	0.284	0.172	0.046	0.007	0.001					
	3	0.047	0.168	0.230	0.105	0.025	0.003					
	4	0.009	0.070	0.215	0.168	0.061	0.012	0.001				
	5	0.001	0.022	0.151	0.202	0.115	0.033	0.004				
	6		0.005	0.082	0.187	0.166	0.071	0.015	0.001			
	7		0.001	0.035	0.138	0.189	0.121	0.037	0.005			
	8			0.012	0.081	0.173	0.167	0.077	0.015	0.001		
	9			0.003	0.039	0.128	0.185	0.128	0.039	0.003		
	10			0.001	0.015	0.077	0.167	0.173	0.081	0.012		
	11				0.005	0.037	0.121	0.189	0.138	0.035	0.001	

TABLE V   Binomial Probabilities   (concluded)

*All values omitted in this table are **0.0005** or less.*

n	x	p=0.05	0.1	0.2	0.3	0.4	0.5	0.6	0.7	0.8	0.9	0.95
	12				0.001	0.015	0.071	0.166	0.187	0.082	0.005	
	13					0.004	0.033	0.115	0.202	0.151	0.022	0.001
	14					0.001	0.012	0.061	0.168	0.215	0.070	0.009
	15						0.003	0.025	0.105	0.230	0.168	0.047
	16						0.001	0.007	0.046	0.172	0.284	0.168
	17							0.001	0.013	0.081	0.300	0.376
	18								0.002	0.018	0.150	0.397
19	0	0.377	0.135	0.014	0.001							
	1	0.377	0.285	0.068	0.009	0.001						
	2	0.179	0.285	0.154	0.036	0.005						
	3	0.053	0.180	0.218	0.087	0.017	0.002					
	4	0.011	0.080	0.218	0.149	0.047	0.007	0.001				
	5	0.002	0.027	0.164	0.192	0.093	0.022	0.002				
	6		0.007	0.095	0.192	0.145	0.052	0.008	0.001			
	7		0.001	0.044	0.153	0.180	0.096	0.024	0.002			
	8			0.017	0.098	0.180	0.144	0.053	0.008			
	9			0.005	0.051	0.146	0.176	0.098	0.022	0.001		
	10			0.001	0.022	0.098	0.176	0.146	0.051	0.005		
	11				0.008	0.053	0.144	0.180	0.098	0.017		
	12				0.002	0.024	0.096	0.180	0.153	0.044	0.001	
	13				0.001	0.008	0.052	0.145	0.192	0.095	0.007	
	14					0.002	0.022	0.093	0.192	0.164	0.027	0.002
	15					0.001	0.007	0.047	0.149	0.218	0.080	0.011
	16						0.002	0.017	0.087	0.218	0.180	0.053
	17							0.005	0.036	0.154	0.285	0.179
	18							0.001	0.009	0.068	0.285	0.377
	19								0.001	0.014	0.135	0.377
20	0	0.358	0.122	0.012	0.001							
	1	0.377	0.270	0.058	0.007							
	2	0.189	0.285	0.137	0.028	0.003						
	3	0.060	0.190	0.205	0.072	0.012	0.001					
	4	0.013	0.090	0.218	0.130	0.035	0.005					
	5	0.002	0.032	0.175	0.179	0.075	0.015	0.001				
	6		0.009	0.109	0.192	0.124	0.037	0.005				
	7		0.002	0.055	0.164	0.166	0.074	0.015	0.001			
	8			0.022	0.114	0.180	0.120	0.035	0.004			
	9			0.007	0.065	0.160	0.160	0.071	0.012			
	10			0.002	0.031	0.117	0.176	0.117	0.031	0.002		
	11				0.012	0.071	0.160	0.160	0.065	0.007		
	12				0.004	0.035	0.120	0.180	0.114	0.022		
	13				0.001	0.015	0.074	0.166	0.164	0.055	0.002	
	14					0.005	0.037	0.124	0.192	0.109	0.009	
	15					0.001	0.015	0.075	0.179	0.175	0.032	0.002
	16						0.005	0.035	0.130	0.218	0.090	0.013
	17						0.001	0.012	0.072	0.205	0.190	0.060
	18							0.003	0.028	0.137	0.235	0.189
	19								0.007	0.058	0.270	0.377
	20								0.001	0.012	0.122	0.358

n	$T_{0.10}$	$T_{0.05}$	$T_{0.02}$	$T_{0.01}$
4				
5	1			
6	2	1		
7	4	2	0	
8	6	4	2	0
9	8	6	3	2
10	11	8	5	3
11	14	11	7	5
12	17	14	10	7
13	21	17	13	10
14	26	21	16	13
15	30	25	20	16
16	36	30	24	19
17	41	35	28	23
18	47	40	33	28
19	54	46	38	32
20	60	52	43	37
21	68	59	49	43
22	75	66	56	49
23	83	73	62	55
24	92	81	69	61
25	101	90	77	68

TABLE VI Critical Values of T

SOURCE: From F. Wilcoxon and R. A. Wilcox, *Some Rapid Approximate Statistical Procedures*, American Cyanamid Company, Pearl River, N.Y., 1964. Reproduced with permission of American Cyanamid Company.

TABLE VII Critical Values of $U_{0.10}$

n_1 \ n_2	2	3	4	5	6	7	8	9	10	11	12	13	14	15
2				0	0	0	1	1	1	1	2	2	3	3
3		0	0	1	2	2	3	4	4	5	5	6	7	7
4		0	1	2	3	4	5	6	7	8	9	10	11	12
5	0	1	2	4	5	6	8	9	11	12	13	15	16	18
6	0	2	3	5	7	8	10	12	14	16	17	19	21	23
7	0	2	4	6	8	11	13	15	17	19	21	24	26	28
8	1	3	5	8	10	13	15	18	20	23	26	28	31	33
9	1	4	6	9	12	15	18	21	24	27	30	33	36	39
10	1	4	7	11	14	17	20	24	27	31	34	37	41	44
11	1	5	8	12	16	19	23	27	31	34	38	42	46	50
12	2	5	9	13	17	21	26	30	34	38	42	47	51	55
13	2	6	10	15	19	24	28	33	37	42	47	51	56	61
14	3	7	11	16	21	26	31	36	41	46	51	56	61	66
15	3	7	12	18	23	28	33	39	44	50	55	61	66	72

TABLE VII Critical Values of $U_{0.05}$

n_1 \ n_2	2	3	4	5	6	7	8	9	10	11	12	13	14	15
2							0	0	0	0	1	1	1	1
3				0	1	1	2	2	3	3	4	4	5	5
4			0	1	2	3	4	4	5	6	7	8	9	10
5		0	1	2	3	5	6	7	8	9	11	12	13	14
6		1	2	3	5	6	8	10	11	13	14	16	17	19
7		1	3	5	6	8	10	12	14	16	18	20	22	24
8	0	2	4	6	8	10	13	15	17	19	22	24	26	29
9	0	2	4	7	10	12	15	17	20	23	26	28	31	34
10	0	3	5	8	11	14	17	20	23	26	29	33	36	39
11	0	3	6	9	13	16	19	23	26	30	33	37	40	44
12	1	4	7	11	14	18	22	26	29	33	37	41	45	49
13	1	4	8	12	16	20	24	28	33	37	41	45	50	54
14	1	5	9	13	17	22	26	31	36	40	45	50	55	59
15	1	5	10	14	19	24	29	34	39	44	49	54	59	64

SOURCE: Table VII is based on Table 11.4 of D. B. Owen, *Handbook of Statistical Tables*, © 1962. U.S. Department of Energy. Published by Addison-Wesley Publishing Company, Inc., Reading, Mass. Reprinted with permission of the publisher.

TABLE VII Critical Values of $U_{0.02}$

n_1 \ n_2	2	3	4	5	6	7	8	9	10	11	12	13	14	15
2												0	0	0
3						0	0	1	1	1	2	2	2	3
4				0	1	1	2	3	3	4	5	5	6	7
5			0	1	2	3	4	5	6	7	8	9	10	11
6			1	2	3	4	6	7	8	9	11	12	13	15
7		0	1	3	4	6	7	9	11	12	14	16	17	19
8		0	2	4	6	7	9	11	13	15	17	20	22	24
9		1	3	5	7	9	11	14	16	18	21	23	26	28
10		1	3	6	8	11	13	16	19	22	24	27	30	33
11		1	4	7	9	12	15	18	22	25	28	31	34	37
12		2	5	8	11	14	17	21	24	28	31	35	38	42
13	0	2	5	9	12	16	20	23	27	31	35	39	43	47
14	0	2	6	10	13	17	22	26	30	34	38	43	47	51
15	0	3	7	11	15	19	24	28	33	37	42	47	51	56

TABLE VII Critical Values of $U_{0.01}$

n_1 \ n_2	3	4	5	6	7	8	9	10	11	12	13	14	15
3							0	0	0	1	1	1	2
4				0	0	1	1	2	2	3	3	4	5
5			0	1	1	2	3	4	5	6	7	7	8
6		0	1	2	3	4	5	6	7	9	10	11	12
7		0	1	3	4	6	7	9	10	12	13	15	16
8		1	2	4	6	7	9	11	13	15	17	18	20
9	0	1	3	5	7	9	11	13	16	18	20	22	24
10	0	2	4	6	9	11	13	16	18	21	24	26	29
11	0	2	5	7	10	13	16	18	21	24	27	30	33
12	1	3	6	9	12	15	18	21	24	27	31	34	37
13	1	3	7	10	13	17	20	24	27	31	34	38	42
14	1	4	7	11	15	18	22	26	30	34	38	42	46
15	2	5	8	12	16	20	24	29	33	37	42	46	51

n_1 \ n_2	4	5	6	7	8	9	10	11	12	13	14	15
TABLE VIII Critical Values of $u_{0.025}$												
4		9	9									
5	9	10	10	11	11							
6	9	10	11	12	12	13	13	13	13			
7		11	12	13	13	14	14	14	14	15	15	15
8		11	12	13	14	14	15	15	16	16	16	16
9			13	14	14	15	16	16	16	17	17	18
10			13	14	15	16	16	17	17	18	18	18
11			13	14	15	16	17	17	18	19	19	19
12			13	14	16	16	17	18	19	19	20	20
13				15	16	17	18	19	19	20	20	21
14				15	16	17	18	19	20	20	21	22
15				15	16	18	18	19	20	21	22	22

n_1 \ n_2	2	3	4	5	6	7	8	9	10	11	12	13	14	15
TABLE VIII Critical Values of $u'_{0.025}$														
2											2	2	2	2
3					2	2	2	2	2	2	2	2	2	3
4				2	2	2	3	3	3	3	3	3	3	3
5			2	2	3	3	3	3	3	4	4	4	4	4
6		2	2	3	3	3	3	4	4	4	4	5	5	5
7		2	2	3	3	3	4	4	5	5	5	5	5	6
8		2	3	3	3	4	4	5	5	5	6	6	6	6
9		2	3	3	4	4	5	5	5	6	6	6	7	7
10		2	3	3	4	5	5	5	6	6	7	7	7	7
11		2	3	4	4	5	5	6	6	7	7	7	8	8
12	2	2	3	4	4	5	6	6	7	7	7	8	8	8
13	2	2	3	4	5	5	6	6	7	7	8	8	9	9
14	2	2	3	4	5	5	6	7	7	8	8	9	9	9
15	2	3	3	4	5	6	6	7	7	8	8	9	9	10

SOURCE: Table VIII is adapted, by permission, from F. S. Swed and C. Eisenhart, "Tables for testing randomness of grouping in a sequence of alternatives," *Annals of Mathematical Statistics*, Vol. 14.

TABLE VIII Critical Values of $u_{0.005}$

n_1 \ n_2	5	6	7	8	9	10	11	12	13	14	15
5		11									
6	11	12	13	13							
7		13	13	14	15	15	15				
8		13	14	15	15	16	16	17	17	17	
9			15	15	16	17	17	18	18	18	19
10			15	16	17	17	18	19	19	19	20
11			15	16	17	18	19	19	20	20	21
12				17	18	19	19	20	21	21	22
13				17	18	19	20	21	21	22	22
14				17	18	19	20	21	22	23	23
15					19	20	21	22	22	23	24

TABLE VIII Critical Values of $u'_{0.005}$

n_1 \ n_2	3	4	5	6	7	8	9	10	11	12	13	14	15
3										2	2	2	2
4						2	2	2	2	2	2	2	3
5				2	2	2	2	3	3	3	3	3	3
6			2	2	2	3	3	3	3	3	3	4	4
7			2	2	3	3	3	3	4	4	4	4	4
8		2	2	3	3	3	3	4	4	4	5	5	5
9		2	2	3	3	3	4	4	5	5	5	5	6
10		2	3	3	3	4	4	5	5	5	5	6	6
11		2	3	3	4	4	5	5	5	6	6	6	7
12	2	2	3	3	4	4	5	5	6	6	6	7	7
13	2	2	3	3	4	5	5	5	6	6	7	7	7
14	2	2	3	4	4	5	5	6	6	7	7	7	8
15	2	3	3	4	4	5	6	6	7	7	7	8	8

TABLE IX Values of $Z = \frac{1}{2} \cdot \ln \frac{1 + r}{1 - r}$									
r	0.00	0.01	0.02	0.03	0.04	0.05	0.06	0.07	0.08	0.09
0.0	0.000	0.010	0.020	0.030	0.040	0.050	0.060	0.070	0.080	0.090
0.1	0.100	0.110	0.121	0.131	0.141	0.151	0.161	0.172	0.182	0.192
0.2	0.203	0.213	0.224	0.234	0.245	0.255	0.266	0.277	0.288	0.299
0.3	0.310	0.321	0.332	0.343	0.354	0.365	0.377	0.388	0.400	0.412
0.4	0.424	0.436	0.448	0.460	0.472	0.485	0.497	0.510	0.523	0.536
0.5	0.549	0.563	0.576	0.590	0.604	0.618	0.633	0.648	0.662	0.678
0.6	0.693	0.709	0.725	0.741	0.758	0.775	0.793	0.811	0.829	0.848
0.7	0.867	0.887	0.908	0.929	0.950	0.973	0.996	1.020	1.045	1.071
0.8	1.099	1.127	1.157	1.188	1.221	1.256	1.293	1.333	1.376	1.422
0.9	1.472	1.528	1.589	1.658	1.738	1.832	1.946	2.092	2.298	2.647

For negative values of r, insert a minus sign in front of the corresponding Z's, and vice versa.

TABLE X Binomial Coefficients

For $r > 10$, it may be necessary to make use of the identity $\binom{n}{r} = \binom{n}{n-r}$

n	$\binom{n}{0}$	$\binom{n}{1}$	$\binom{n}{2}$	$\binom{n}{3}$	$\binom{n}{4}$	$\binom{n}{5}$	$\binom{n}{6}$	$\binom{n}{7}$	$\binom{n}{8}$	$\binom{n}{9}$	$\binom{n}{10}$
0	1										
1	1	1									
2	1	2	1								
3	1	3	3	1							
4	1	4	6	4	1						
5	1	5	10	10	5	1					
6	1	6	15	20	15	6	1				
7	1	7	21	35	35	21	7	1			
8	1	8	28	56	70	56	28	8	1		
9	1	9	36	84	126	126	84	36	9	1	
10	1	10	45	120	210	252	210	120	45	10	1
11	1	11	55	165	330	462	462	330	165	55	11
12	1	12	66	220	495	792	924	792	495	220	66
13	1	13	78	286	715	1287	1716	1716	1287	715	286
14	1	14	91	364	1001	2002	3003	3432	3003	2002	1001
15	1	15	105	455	1365	3003	5005	6435	6435	5005	3003
16	1	16	120	560	1820	4368	8008	11440	12870	11440	8008
17	1	17	136	680	2380	6188	12376	19448	24310	24310	19448
18	1	18	153	816	3060	8568	18564	31824	43758	48620	43758
19	1	19	171	969	3876	11628	27132	50388	75582	92378	92378
20	1	20	190	1140	4845	15504	38760	77520	125970	167960	184756

TABLE XI	Values of e^{-x}						
x	e^{-x}	x	e^{-x}	x	e^{-x}	x	e^{-x}
0.0	1.0000	2.5	0.082085	5.0	0.006738	7.5	0.00055308
0.1	0.9048	2.6	0.074274	5.1	0.006097	7.6	0.00050045
0.2	0.8187	2.7	0.067206	5.2	0.005517	7.7	0.00045283
0.3	0.7408	2.8	0.060810	5.3	0.004992	7.8	0.00040973
0.4	0.6703	2.9	0.055023	5.4	0.004517	7.9	0.00037074
0.5	0.6065	3.0	0.049787	5.5	0.004087	8.0	0.00033546
0.6	0.5488	3.1	0.045049	5.6	0.003698	8.1	0.00030354
0.7	0.4966	3.2	0.040762	5.7	0.003346	8.2	0.00027465
0.8	0.4493	3.3	0.036883	5.8	0.003028	8.3	0.00024852
0.9	0.4066	3.4	0.033373	5.9	0.002739	8.4	0.00022487
1.0	0.3679	3.5	0.030197	6.0	0.002479	8.5	0.00020347
1.1	0.3329	3.6	0.027324	6.1	0.002243	8.6	0.00018411
1.2	0.3012	3.7	0.024724	6.2	0.002029	8.7	0.00016659
1.3	0.2725	3.8	0.022371	6.3	0.001836	8.8	0.00015073
1.4	0.2466	3.9	0.020242	6.4	0.001662	8.9	0.00013639
1.5	0.2231	4.0	0.018316	6.5	0.001503	9.0	0.00012341
1.6	0.2019	4.1	0.016573	6.6	0.001360	9.1	0.00011167
1.7	0.1827	4.2	0.014996	6.7	0.001231	9.2	0.00010104
1.8	0.1653	4.3	0.013569	6.8	0.001114	9.3	0.00009142
1.9	0.1496	4.4	0.012277	6.9	0.001008	9.4	0.00008272
2.0	0.1353	4.5	0.011109	7.0	0.000912	9.5	0.00007485
2.1	0.1225	4.6	0.010052	7.1	0.000825	9.6	0.00006773
2.2	0.1108	4.7	0.009095	7.2	0.000747	9.7	0.00006128
2.3	0.1003	4.8	0.008230	7.3	0.000676	9.8	0.00005545
2.4	0.0907	4.9	0.007447	7.4	0.000611	9.9	0.00005017

TABLE XII Critical Values of $q_{0.05}$

Studentized Range Percentage Points

D.F. \ k	3	4	5	6	7	8	9	10	11
1	27.0	32.8	37.1	40.4	43.1	45.4	47.4	49.1	50.6
2	8.33	9.80	10.9	11.7	12.4	13.0	13.5	14.0	14.4
3	5.91	6.83	7.50	8.04	8.48	8.85	9.18	9.46	9.72
4	5.04	5.76	6.29	6.71	7.05	7.35	7.60	7.83	8.03
5	4.60	5.22	5.67	6.03	6.33	6.58	6.80	7.00	7.17
6	4.34	4.90	5.31	5.63	5.90	6.12	6.32	6.49	6.65
7	4.17	4.68	5.06	5.36	5.61	5.82	6.00	6.16	6.30
8	4.04	4.53	4.89	5.17	5.40	5.60	5.77	5.92	6.05
9	3.95	4.42	4.76	5.02	5.24	5.43	5.60	5.74	5.87
10	3.88	4.33	4.65	4.91	5.12	5.31	5.46	5.60	5.72
11	3.82	4.26	4.57	4.82	5.03	5.20	5.35	5.49	5.61
12	3.77	4.20	4.51	4.75	4.95	5.12	5.27	5.40	5.51
13	3.74	4.15	4.45	4.69	4.89	5.05	5.19	5.32	5.43
14	3.70	4.11	4.41	4.64	4.83	4.99	5.13	5.25	5.36
15	3.67	4.08	4.37	4.60	4.78	4.94	5.08	5.20	5.31
16	3.65	4.05	4.33	4.56	4.74	4.90	5.03	5.15	5.26
17	3.63	4.02	4.30	4.52	4.71	4.86	4.99	5.11	5.21
18	3.61	4.00	4.28	4.50	4.67	4.82	4.96	5.07	5.17
19	3.59	3.98	4.25	4.47	4.65	4.79	4.92	5.04	5.14
20	3.58	3.96	4.23	4.45	4.62	4.77	4.90	5.01	5.11
24	3.53	3.90	4.17	4.37	4.54	4.68	4.81	4.92	5.01
30	3.49	3.85	4.10	4.30	4.46	4.60	4.72	4.82	4.92
40	3.44	3.79	4.04	4.23	4.39	4.52	4.64	4.74	4.82
60	3.40	3.74	3.98	4.16	4.31	4.44	4.55	4.65	4.73
120	3.36	3.69	3.92	4.10	4.24	4.36	4.47	4.56	4.64
∞	3.31	3.63	3.86	4.03	4.17	4.29	4.39	4.47	4.55

TABLE XII Critical Values of $q_{0.05}$ (concluded)

Studentized Range Percentage Points

D.F. \ k	12	13	14	15	16	20	24	28	32	36	40
1	52.0	53.2	54.3	55.4	56.3	59.6	62.1	64.2	66.0	67.6	68.9
2	14.8	15.1	15.4	15.7	15.9	16.8	17.5	18.0	18.5	18.9	19.3
3	9.95	10.2	10.4	10.5	10.7	11.2	11.7	12.1	12.4	12.6	12.9
4	8.21	8.37	8.53	8.66	8.79	9.23	9.58	9.88	10.1	10.3	10.5
5	7.32	7.47	7.60	7.72	7.83	8.21	8.51	8.76	8.98	9.17	9.33
6	6.79	6.92	7.03	7.14	7.24	7.59	7.86	8.09	8.28	8.45	8.60
7	6.43	6.55	6.66	6.76	6.85	7.17	7.42	7.63	7.81	7.97	8.11
8	6.18	6.29	6.39	6.48	6.57	6.87	7.11	7.31	7.48	7.63	7.76
9	5.98	6.09	6.19	6.28	6.36	6.64	6.87	7.06	7.22	7.36	7.49
10	5.83	5.94	6.03	6.11	6.19	6.47	6.69	6.87	7.02	7.16	7.28
11	5.71	5.81	5.90	5.98	6.06	6.33	6.54	6.71	6.86	6.99	7.11
12	5.62	5.71	5.80	5.88	5.95	6.21	6.41	6.59	6.73	6.86	6.97
13	5.53	5.63	5.71	5.79	5.86	6.11	6.31	6.48	6.62	6.74	6.85
14	5.46	5.55	5.64	5.71	5.79	6.03	6.22	6.39	6.53	6.65	6.75
15	5.40	5.49	5.57	5.65	5.72	5.96	6.15	6.31	6.45	6.56	6.67
16	5.35	5.44	5.52	5.59	5.66	5.90	6.08	6.24	6.37	6.49	6.59
17	5.31	5.39	5.47	5.54	5.61	5.84	6.03	6.18	6.31	6.43	6.53
18	5.27	5.35	5.43	5.50	5.57	5.79	5.98	6.13	6.26	6.37	6.47
19	5.23	5.32	5.39	5.46	5.53	5.75	5.93	6.08	6.21	6.32	6.42
20	5.20	5.28	5.36	5.43	5.49	5.71	5.89	6.04	6.17	6.28	6.37
24	5.10	5.18	5.25	5.32	5.38	5.59	5.76	5.91	6.03	6.13	6.23
30	5.00	5.08	5.15	5.21	5.27	5.48	5.64	5.77	5.89	5.99	6.08
40	4.90	4.98	5.04	5.11	5.16	5.36	5.51	5.64	5.75	5.85	5.93
60	4.81	4.88	4.94	5.00	5.06	5.24	5.39	5.51	5.62	5.71	5.79
120	4.71	4.78	4.84	4.90	4.95	5.13	5.27	5.38	5.48	5.57	5.64
∞	4.62	4.69	4.74	4.80	4.85	5.01	5.14	5.25	5.35	5.43	5.50

TABLE XII Critical Values of $q_{0.01}$

Studentized Range Percentage Points

D.F. \ k	3	4	5	6	7	8	9	10	11	12
1	135	164	186	202	216	227	237	246	253	260
2	19.0	22.3	24.7	26.6	28.2	29.5	30.7	31.7	32.6	33.4
3	10.6	12.2	13.3	14.2	15.0	15.6	16.2	16.7	17.1	17.5
4	8.12	9.17	9.96	10.6	11.1	11.6	11.9	12.3	12.6	12.8
5	6.98	7.80	8.42	8.91	9.32	9.67	9.97	10.2	10.5	10.7
6	6.33	7.03	7.56	7.97	8.32	8.61	8.87	9.10	9.30	9.49
7	5.92	6.54	7.01	7.37	7.68	7.94	8.17	8.37	8.55	8.71
8	5.64	6.20	6.63	6.96	7.24	7.47	7.68	7.86	8.03	8.18
9	5.43	5.96	6.35	6.66	6.92	7.13	7.33	7.50	7.65	7.78
10	5.27	5.77	6.14	6.43	6.67	6.88	7.06	7.21	7.36	7.49
11	5.15	5.62	5.97	6.25	6.48	6.67	6.84	6.99	7.13	7.25
12	5.05	5.50	5.84	6.10	6.32	6.51	6.67	6.81	6.94	7.06
13	4.96	5.40	5.73	5.98	6.19	6.37	6.53	6.67	6.79	6.90
14	4.90	5.32	5.63	5.88	6.09	6.26	6.41	6.54	6.66	6.77
15	4.84	5.25	5.56	5.80	5.99	6.16	6.31	6.44	6.56	6.66
16	4.79	5.19	5.49	5.72	5.92	6.08	6.22	6.35	6.46	6.56
17	4.74	5.14	5.43	5.66	5.85	6.01	6.15	6.27	6.38	6.48
18	4.70	5.09	5.38	5.60	5.79	5.94	6.08	6.20	6.31	6.41
19	4.67	5.05	5.33	5.55	5.74	5.89	6.02	6.14	6.25	6.34
20	4.64	5.02	5.29	5.51	5.69	5.84	5.97	6.09	6.19	6.29
24	4.55	4.91	5.17	5.37	5.54	5.69	5.81	5.92	6.02	6.11
30	4.46	4.80	5.05	5.24	5.40	5.54	5.65	5.76	5.85	5.93
40	4.37	4.70	4.93	5.11	5.27	5.39	5.50	5.60	5.69	5.76
60	4.28	4.60	4.82	4.99	5.13	5.25	5.36	5.45	5.53	5.60
120	4.20	4.50	4.71	4.87	5.01	5.12	5.21	5.30	5.38	5.44
∞	4.12	4.40	4.60	4.76	4.88	4.99	5.08	5.16	5.23	5.29

SOURCE: Adapted from H. L. Harter (1969), *Order Statistics and Their Use in Testing and Estimation. Vol. 1: Tests Based on Range and Studentized Range of Samples From a Normal Population*, Aerospace Research Laboratories, U.S. Air Force.

TABLE XII   Critical Values of $q_{0.01}$ (concluded)

Studentized Range Percentage Points

k D.F.	13	14	15	16	20	24	28	32	36	40
1	266	272	277	282	298	311	321	330	338	345
2	34.1	34.9	35.4	36.0	38.0	39.5	40.8	41.8	42.8	43.6
3	17.9	18.3	18.5	18.8	19.8	20.6	21.2	21.7	22.2	22.6
4	13.1	13.4	13.5	13.7	14.4	15.0	15.4	15.8	16.1	16.4
5	10.9	11.1	11.2	11.4	11.9	12.4	12.7	13.0	13.3	13.5
6	9.65	9.81	9.95	10.1	10.5	11.0	11.2	11.5	11.7	11.9
7	8.86	9.00	9.12	9.24	9.65	9.97	10.2	10.5	10.7	10.9
8	8.31	8.44	8.55	8.66	9.03	9.33	9.57	9.78	9.96	10.1
9	7.91	8.03	8.13	8.23	8.57	8.85	9.08	9.27	9.44	9.59
10	7.60	7.72	7.81	7.91	8.23	8.49	8.70	8.88	9.04	9.19
11	7.36	7.47	7.56	7.65	7.95	8.20	8.40	8.58	8.73	8.86
12	7.17	7.27	7.36	7.44	7.73	7.97	8.16	8.33	8.47	8.60
13	7.01	7.11	7.19	7.27	7.55	7.78	7.96	8.12	8.26	8.39
14	6.87	6.97	7.05	7.13	7.40	7.62	7.79	7.95	8.08	8.20
15	6.76	6.85	6.93	7.00	7.26	7.48	7.65	7.80	7.93	8.05
16	6.66	6.75	6.82	6.90	7.15	7.36	7.53	7.67	7.80	7.92
17	6.57	6.66	6.73	6.81	7.05	7.26	7.42	7.56	7.69	7.80
18	6.50	6.58	6.66	6.73	6.97	7.17	7.33	7.47	7.59	7.70
19	6.43	6.51	6.59	6.65	6.89	7.09	7.24	7.38	7.50	7.61
20	6.37	6.45	6.52	6.59	6.82	7.02	7.17	7.30	7.42	7.52
24	6.19	6.27	6.33	6.39	6.61	6.79	6.94	7.06	7.17	7.27
30	6.01	6.08	6.14	6.20	6.41	6.58	6.71	6.83	6.93	7.02
40	5.84	5.90	5.96	6.02	6.21	6.37	6.49	6.60	6.70	6.78
60	5.67	5.73	5.79	5.84	6.02	6.16	6.28	6.38	6.47	6.55
120	5.51	5.57	5.61	5.66	5.83	5.96	6.07	6.16	6.24	6.32
∞	5.35	5.40	5.45	5.49	5.65	5.77	5.87	5.95	6.03	6.09

ANSWERS TO ODD-NUMBERED EXERCISES

CHAPTER 1

1.3 (a) Persons coming out of the building housing the national headquarters of a political party are more likely to support that party.
(b) December (pre-Christmas) spending is not typical of spending throughout the year.

1.7 (a) The conclusion follows from the data.
(b) The conclusion follows from the data.
(c) The conclusion goes beyond the data.
(d) The conclusion follows from the data.

1.9 (a) and (b) are numeric descriptions of the data, while (c) and (d) make generalizations which go beyond the data.

1.11 (a) Ordinal; (b) nominal; (c) ordinal; (d) nominal. In (d), removal of the "no opinion" category would leave ordinal data.

1.13 Since IQ scores are rescaled z-scores (see Section 4.3), it is unrealistic to interpret the above as three times a "smartness" difference.

1.15 (a) It requires a generalization.
(b) The conclusion is purely descriptive.
(c) The conclusion is purely descriptive.
(d) The conclusion entails a generalization.

1.17 (a) Persons walking near a government office may have some relationship to the government and thus have non-typical opinions.
(b) The use of the word "denied" introduces a bias.

1.19 (a) "Indian art" may be interpreted as art from India or as art of American Indians.
(b) Many persons will not respond honestly to questions about their personal habits.

1.21 The data are only ordinal data and should not have been added.

1.23 (a) The conclusion follows from the data.
(b) The conclusion follows directly from the data.
(c) Generalization.
(d) Generalization.

CHAPTER 2

2.1

15	8
16	13667
17	0122478
18	2
19	1
20	1

NOTE: 15 | 8 means 158

2.3

3	29
4	2456888
5	0126
6	12

NOTE: 3 | 2 means $320

2.5

16	4
16	
17	02
17	68
18	0123
18	668
19	334
19	8
20	
20	58
21	0
21	
22	
22	5

NOTE: 16 | 4 means 164

2.7

4	027
5	135889
6	0123679
7	123
8	0

NOTE: 4 | 0 means 40

2.9 160–169, 170–179, 180–189, 190–199, 200–209, 210–219, 220–229, 230–239, 240–249, 250–259, and 260–269.

2.11 148.0–149.9, 150.0–151.9, 152.0–153.9, 154.0–155.9, 156.0–157.9, 158.0–159.9, 160.0–161.9.

The class width is 2, and the intervals begin at 148, 150, 152, and so on.

2.13 (a) Yes; (b) no; (c) yes; (d) no; (e) no.

2.15 (a) 89; (b) 36; (c) through (f) cannot be determined.

2.17 (a) $0.00–49.99, $50.00–99.99, $100.00–149.99, $150.00–199.99, $200.00–249.99, $250.00–299.99, $300.00 and no upper limit.

 (b) −$0.005, $49.995, $99.995, $149.995, $199.995, $249.995, $299.995.

The final class has no upper boundary.

 (c) $24.995, $74.995, $124.995, $174.995, $224.995, $274.995.

The final class does not have a class mark.

 (d) Does not exist.

2.19 (a) −0.5, 12.5, 25.5, 38.5, 51.5.

 (b) 0–12, 13–25, 26–38, and 39–51.

2.21 The second and third classes overlap. Also, there is no provision for values from $49.91 to $49.99.

2.23

Grades	Percentage
30–39	7.5
40–49	5.0
50–59	5.0
60–69	25.0
70–79	30.0
80–89	17.5
90–99	10.0
Total	100.0

2.25

Weights	Frequency
80– 89	2
90– 99	3
100–109	9
110–119	13
120–129	13
130–139	7
140–149	3
Total	50

2.27

Weights	Frequency
80 or more	50
90 or more	48
100 or more	45
110 or more	36
120 or more	23
130 or more	10
140 or more	3
150 or more	0

2.29 (a)

Number of Customers	Percentage
40–44	3.33
45–49	7.50
50–54	15.00
55–59	27.50
60–64	31.67
65–69	10.83
70–74	2.50
75–79	1.67
Total	100.00

(b)

Number of Customers	Percentage
Less than 40	0.00
Less than 45	3.33
Less than 50	10.83
Less than 55	25.83
Less than 60	53.33
Less than 65	85.00
Less than 70	95.83
Less than 75	98.33
Less than 80	100.00

2.31 (a)

mpg	Frequency
More than 22.4	40
More than 22.9	38
More than 23.4	35
More than 23.9	28
More than 24.4	20
More than 24.9	6
More than 25.4	1
More than 25.9	0
Total	168

(b)

mpg	Percentage
More than 22.4	100.0
More than 22.9	95.0
More than 23.4	87.5
More than 23.9	70.0
More than 24.4	50.0
More than 24.9	15.0
More than 25.4	2.5
More than 25.9	0.0

2.33

Number of mistakes	Frequency
0	17
1	21
2	8
3	7
4	5
5	2
Total	60

2.35

Means of transportation	Frequency
Bus	8
Car	18
Plane	10
Train	4
Total	40

2.37 Defective merchandise could include merchandise of incorrect color or size, or be damaged during delivery.

2.39

Amount in Dollars	Frequency
Less than 20.00	22
Less than 40.00	69
Less than 60.00	135
Less than 80.00	170
Less than 100.00	191
Less than 120.00	200

2.45 Misleading because we tend to compare areas rather than the heights.

2.47 209°, 52°, 35°, 10°, 46°, and 8°.

2.51 15–21, 22–28, 29–35, 36–42, 43–49, and 50–56.

2.53 7, 10, 20, 22, 10, 2, and 1.

2.55 7, 17, 37, 59, 69, 71, and 72.

2.57 (a) No; (b) yes; (c) yes; (d) no.

2.59 100, 73.33, 31.67, 10, 3.33, and 0.

2.61 18,000–20,499, 20,500–22,999, 23,000–25,499, 25,500–27,999, 28,000–30,499, 30,500–32,999.

2.63 6.0–7.9, 8.0–9.9, 10.0–11.9, 12.0–13.9, 14.0–15.9.

2.65 (a) 1,253, 1,250, 1,254, 1,258, 1,257, 1,256, and 1,255;

(b) 3,467, 3,405, 3,419, and 3,448;

(c) 11, 10, 18, 16, 17, 17, 22, 24, 20, 21, 21, 23, 29, 26, 27, 27, 33, 31, 32, 38, 35, and 42.

2.69 Some may not have finished high school.

CHAPTER 3

3.1 (a) This would be regarded as a population if we are interested only in this single company.
(b) This would be regarded as a sample if we are interested generally in the expenses of computer support groups of many companies.

3.3 (a) These would be regarded as a population if the set of 23 department stores constitutes a single chain of stores run under one central management.
(b) These would be regarded as a sample if these were 23 stores out of a larger chain or if the 23 stores were completely unrelated.

3.5 41.8.

3.7 (a) 11.9; (b) $67.

3.9 58.1.

3.11 The bridge is safe.

3.13 $6.90.

3.15 (a) 4.01 ounces; (b) 0.075 ounce.

3.17 (a) $\frac{7}{8}$; (b) $\frac{2}{3}$.

3.19 (a) 1.6; (b) 4; (c) 96 on the fourth day and 192 cases on the fifth day.

3.21 (a) The harmonic mean of 60 and 30 is indeed 40.
(b) The harmonic mean of $45 and $36 is indeed $40.
(c) 72.

3.23 $41,192.63.

3.25 0.865 hour.

3.27 (a) The median is the 13th value.
(b) The median is the mean of the 16th and 17th values.

3.29 The median is 52.

3.31 The median is 55.

3.33 (a) $\bar{x} = 0.8$. (b) The median is 0.
(c) 9 values are above the mean, 11 values are below the mean.
(d) 9 values are above the median, no value is below the median.

3.35 (a) The median is 140 minutes.

3.37 $\bar{x} = 110.5\%$. The median is 92%.

3.41 The manufacturers of car C can use the midrange.

3.43 (a) The median is 67.
(b) Q_1 is 58; Q_3 is 70.

3.45

	n	Median	Lower quartile	Upper quartile
(a)	40	20.5	10.5	30.5
(b)	41	21	10.5	31.5
(c)	42	21.5	11	32
(d)	43	22	11	33

Half-integers refer to the means of the values in the surrounding positions.

3.47 Q_1 is 32; Q_3 is 84.5.

3.49 59.5.

3.53 7.

3.55 (a) 146. (b) 149. (c) There is no mode.

3.57 (a) The mean is 581.2, the median is 591.5, and the mode is 514.
(b) The mean is 580, the median is 590, and the mode is 480.
(c) The mean is 585, the median is 600, and the mode is 600.
(d) The mean and median are altered only modestly by rounding. The mode can change radically when data are rounded.

3.59 $\bar{x} = 56.45$.

3.61 (a) $\tilde{x} = \$10.61$.
(b) $P_{20} = -\$35.48$; $P_{80} = \$37.88$.

3.63 $\bar{x} = 7.8$.

3.65 (a) 3.7 and 10.6;
(b) $P_5 = 0.2$ and $P_{98} = 19.5$.

3.67 (a) $\tilde{x} = 37.49$;
(b) $P_{20} = 29.75$;
$P_{40} = 35.47$;
$P_{60} = 39.52$;
$P_{80} = 46.61$.

3.69 We find the mean of the distribution to be 117.5. The original data values have mean 117.88, so that the grouping error is only $117.5 - 117.88 = -0.38$.

3.71 For Exercise 3.69, the class interval is 10, and the grouping error is -0.38. For Exercise 3.70, the class interval is 5, while the grouping error is -0.0075.

3.73 (a) $x_1 + x_2 + x_3 + x_4 + x_5 + 5$;
(b) $3(y_1 + y_2 + y_3 + y_4)$;
(c) $3(x_1 + x_2 + x_3 + x_4)$.

3.75 (a) 25; (b) 14; (c) 70; (d) 430.

3.77 (a) For $j = 1$, the sum is 7;
For $j = 2$, the sum is 4;
For $j = 3$, the sum is -2;
For $j = 4$, the sum is 10.

(b) For $i = 1$, the sum is 4;
For $i = 2$, the sum is 8;
For $i = 3$, the sum is 7.

3.81 (a) $39 < 121$.
(b) $42 < 100$.
(c) take $n = 2$, $a_1 = 1$, $a_2 = -1$.
$\Sigma a_i^2 = 1 + 1 = 2 > (\Sigma a_i)^2 = (1 - 1)^2 = 0$.

3.83 (a) $2{,}300 < (2 + 3 + 5)(100 + 200 + 300) = 6{,}000$.
(b) $240 < (0 + 2 + 0 + 4)(0 + 20 + 0 + 50) = 420$.

3.85 The median is 1.575; Q_1 is 1.375; Q_3 is 1.74.

3.87 13.7.

3.89 15.17.

3.91 (a) Position 16;
(b) the mean of the values in positions 40 and 41.

3.93 The median is 27.75; Q_1 is 25.8; Q_3 is 30.5.

3.95 The total number of store visits by the 12 persons is $12 \cdot 5.75 = 69$. Therefore, it is not possible that 7 or more of these persons shopped in 10 or more stores.

3.97 The median is in the 12th position. The lower quartile is in the 6th position. The upper quartile is in the 18th position.

3.99 From the stem-and-leaf display the median is 41.5. If you go back to the original list to locate the median, you could give its value as 41.95.

3.101 (a) $Q_1 = 19.6$; (b) $Q_3 = 29.5$;
(c) $P_{40} = 23.0$; (d) $P_{80} = 30.4$.

3.103 It is possible that the mean salary is higher at company B. Here is a very simple situation in which this can happen:

Company	Male Employees		Female Employees	
	Number	Mean Salary	Number	Mean Salary
A	1	$30,000	2	$24,000
B	2	$28,000	1	$23,000

The mean salary at company A is $26,000; the mean salary at company B is $26,333.

CHAPTER 4

4.1 8 seconds.

4.3 The range is $1\frac{1}{8}$ for stock A and $\frac{3}{8}$ for stock B.

4.5 The interquartile range is then 2.5.

4.7 The interquartile range is 12 feet.

4.9 12.5.

4.11 (a) $s = 0.18$.

4.13 (a) $s = 3.77$.

4.15 (a) 2.31; (b) 54.77; (c) 10.69.

4.17 The range is 4, and the standard deviation is 2.06. The claim is certainly reasonable.

4.19 (b) 1.89.

4.21 (a) $\frac{35}{36}$; (b) $\frac{143}{144}$.

4.23 Since $k = 0.5 < 1$, Chebyshev's theorem won't work.

4.25 (a) 96%; (b) 98.4%; (c) 99%; (d) 99.75%.

4.27 (a) Between 0.230 and 0.290;
(b) between 0.215 and 0.305.

4.31 The z-score for the first man is 2.2, and the z-score for the second man is 1.95. The first man is more seriously overweight.

4.33 The coefficient of variation for the first patient is 7.55%. The coefficient of variation for the second patient is 6.32%.

4.35 9.4%.

4.37 (a) $\bar{x} = 24.5$ and $\tilde{x} = 24.21$;
(b) $s = 9.90$.

4.39 $s\kappa = 0.30$.

4.41 $s\kappa = -0.37$. Distribution is fairly symmetrical.

4.43 The data are highly skewed with the tail on the right.

4.45 Distribution is fairly symmetrical.

4.47 The frequencies corresponding to 0, 1, 2, and 3 are 28, 17, 4, and 1; data are highly skewed with the tail on the righthand side.

4.49 Data are highly skewed with the tail on the righthand side.

4.51 There are no "whiskers" on either side; the data are U-shaped.

4.53 $\frac{5}{9}$.

4.55 The values show a very slight positive skewness.

4.57 $\sigma^2 = 2$, which equals $\frac{5^2 - 1}{12}$.

4.59 $z = 1.14$.

4.61 (a) 17.75; (b) 5.66.

4.63 796.88 and 111.56.

4.65 (a) 22; (b) 12 and 29.

4.67 (a) 55.6%; (b) 75%; (c) 84%.

4.69 103.74.   **4.71** $V = 3.77\%$.

CHAPTER 5

5.3 (a) There are exactly three ways in which the student can study for a total of 5 hours over the three nights.
(b) There are four ways.

5.5 There are 12 ways.

5.7 30 ways.

5.9 There are 8 ways.

5.11 There are 96 ways.

5.13 240.

5.15 There are 1,024 pizzas.

5.17 (a) False; (b) false; (c) true; (d) true.

5.19 1,862,784.

5.21 6,609,600.

5.23 40,320.

5.25 (a) 384; (b) 1,152; (c) 2,880; (d) 1,152; (e) 2,880.

5.27 (a) 180; (b) 60; (c) 20; (e) 34,650.

5.29 (b) 120; (c) 5,040; (d) 144.

5.31 1,365.   **5.33** 210.   **5.35** 3,003.

5.37 (a) 56; (b) 56; (c) 8.

5.39 18,900.

5.45 (a) Row 7 is 1 7 21 35 35 21 7 1; (b) 35.

5.47 (a) 35; (b) 20; (c) 15; (d) easily verified, $20 + 15 = 35$.

5.49 (a) $\frac{1}{221}$; (b) $\frac{11}{221}$; (c) $\frac{25}{102}$; (d) $\frac{1}{17}$.

5.51 (a) $\frac{1}{6}$; (b) $\frac{1}{2}$.

5.53 $\frac{1}{16}, \frac{4}{16}, \frac{6}{16}, \frac{4}{16}$, and $\frac{1}{16}$.

5.55 (a) $\frac{25}{54}$; (b) $\frac{29}{54}$; (c) $\frac{11}{54}$; (d) $\frac{1}{3}$.

5.57 $1/n$.

5.59 (a) 0.837; (b) 0.159; (c) 0.004.

5.61 (a) $\frac{2}{7}$; (b) $\frac{1}{21}$.

5.63 0.753.   **5.65** 0.170.   **5.67** 0.191.

5.73 (a) 108; (b) 110.

5.75 0.1632.   **5.77** $\frac{4}{36}$.

5.79 1,048,576.

5.81 (a) 2; (b) 3; (c) 0; (d) 1.

5.83 (a) 336; (b) 336; (c) 2,016.

5.85 1.58×10^{10}.

5.87 $\frac{1}{32}, \frac{5}{32}, \frac{10}{32}, \frac{10}{32}, \frac{5}{32}, \frac{1}{32}$.

5.89 0.81.

5.91 (a) 0.511; (b) 0.279; (c) 0.139; (d) 0.002.

5.93 768.

5.95 If the identities of the individuals matter, the number of ways is 93,024. The number of ways without regard to the identities is 3,876.

CHAPTER 6

6.1 (a) {a, c, d, f, g}; (b) {a, b, c, e, f, g}; (c) {e}.

6.3 (a) {6, 7, 8, 9, 10}; (b) {4, 5}; (c) {8, 9, 10};

(d) $\{1, 2, 3, 4, 5\}$.

6.5 (a) $\{8\}$ is the event that a person chooses a color other than red, yellow, blue, green, brown, white, or purple.
(b) This is an empty set.
(c) $\{1, 2, 3, 4, 5\}$ is the event that a person chooses red, yellow, blue, green, or brown.
(d) $\{3, 4, 8\}$ is the event that a person chooses blue, green, and another color not red, yellow, brown, white, or purple.

6.7 (a) The first salesman sells one car.
(b) The second salesman sells more cars than the first salesman, or the first salesman sells no cars.
(c) The salesmen sell the same number of cars.
(d) The first salesman sells more cars than the second salesman.

6.9 (a) $(0, 2), (1, 1), (2, 0)$;
(b) $(2, 0), (1, 0)$;
(c) $(0, 0), (2, 0), (1, 0), (1, 1)$.

6.11 T and U are not mutually exclusive; T and V are not mutually exclusive; T and W are mutually exclusive; U and V are mutually exclusive; U and W are mutually exclusive, and V and W are not mutually exclusive.

6.13 (b) $K = \{(0, 2), (0, 3), (1, 2)\}$,
$L = \{(1, 0), (2, 0), (2, 1), (3, 0)\}$; and
$M = \{(0, 3), (1, 2), (2, 1), (3, 0)\}$.
(c) K and L are mutually exclusive; K and M are not mutually exclusive, and L and M are not mutually exclusive.

6.15 (a) $\{A, D\}$; (b) $\{C, E\}$; (c) $\{B\}$; (d) $\{A, C, E\}$.

6.17 Region 1 represents the event that a driver has both kinds of insurance; region 2 represents the event that a driver has liability insurance but no collision insurance; region 3 represents the event that a driver has collision insurance but no liability insurance; region 4 represents the event that a driver has neither kind of insurance.

6.19 Region 1 represents the event that the flight leaves Denver on time and arrives in Houston on time; region 2 represents the event that the flight leaves Denver on time but does not arrive in Houston on time; region 3 represents the event that the flight does not leave Denver on time but arrives in Houston on time; region 4 represents the event that the flight does not leave Denver on time and does not arrive in Houston on time.

6.21 60 of the players are men who do not use a two-handed backhand.

6.23 (a) 3, 5, 6 and 8; (b) 2 and 7; (c) 1 and 3; (d) 7 and 8.

6.25 (a) Region 5; (b) regions 1 and 2 together; (c) regions 3, 5, and 6 together; (d) regions 1, 3, 4, and 6 together.

6.29 (a) $P(C' \cap T)$; (b) $P(C' \cap T')$.

6.31 (a) $P(R')$; (b) $P(D' \cap R)$; (c) $P(V' \cup D')$.

6.33 (a) The third rule; (b) the first rule; (c) the second rule; (d) the first rule.

6.35 (a) The third rule;
(b) second probability cannot exceed the first;
(c) the two events are not mutually exclusive;
(d) the first postulate.

6.37 Postulate 3 and postulate 2.

6.39 Postulate 1.

6.41 Q and R are not mutually exclusive.

6.43 (a) 0.38; (b) 0.10; (c) 0.90.

6.45 (a) 0.998; (b) 0.007; (c) 0.993.

6.47 (a) 3 to 2; (b) 11 to 5; (c) 7 to 2.

6.49 9 to 4.

6.51 (a) $\frac{34}{55}$; (b) $\frac{11}{13}$; (c) $\frac{5}{6}$.

6.53 (a) $p = \frac{1}{4}$; (b) $p < \frac{1}{4}$.

6.55 Since running for the House and running for the Senate are mutually exclusive, we ask if $\frac{1}{3} + \frac{1}{5}$ is equal to $\frac{7}{12}$. Since it is not equal, his probabilities are inconsistent.

6.57 He should assign odds of 19 to 11 against either of them winning.

6.59 (a) Yes; (b) no; (c) yes; (d) no.

6.61 Bets (a) and (b) are attractive.

6.63 (a) 0.52; (b) 0.71; (c) 0.48.

6.65 (a) 0.64; (b) 0.98; (c) 0.82; (d) 0.12.

6.67 (a) $\frac{2}{3}$; (b) $\frac{2}{9}$; (c) $\frac{2}{15}$; (d) $\frac{2}{15}$.

6.69 (a) 0.55; (b) 0.53; (c) 0.23; (d) 0.80.

6.71 0.95.

6.73 (a) 0.35; (b) 0.65.

6.75 (a) 0.27; (b) 0.40; (c) 0.60.

6.77 (a) There must be a mistake.
(b) There must be a mistake.

6.79 (a) $P(Q \mid W)$; (b) $P(W' \mid Q)$; (c) $P(Q' \mid W')$.

6.81 (a) The probability that a worker who meets the production quota is well trained.
(b) The probability that a worker who is well trained will not meet the production quota.
(c) The probability that a worker who does not meet the production quota is not well trained.

6.83 (a) $P(E \mid G)$; (b) $P(G' \mid A')$; (c) $P(A \mid E \cap G)$.

6.85 The probability that
(a) an applicant who is employed will have the application approved;
(b) an applicant who is not employed will not have the application approved;
(c) an applicant who has the application approved will not be employed or not have a good credit rating.

6.87 (a) $\frac{36}{80}$; (b) $\frac{20}{80}$; (c) $\frac{24}{80}$; (d) $\frac{8}{80}$; (e) $\frac{24}{36}$; (f) $\frac{8}{20}$; (g) $\frac{8}{44}$; (h) $\frac{72}{80}$.

6.91 (a) $\frac{2}{5}$; (b) $\frac{1}{2}$.

6.93 (a) 0.90; (b) 0.15.   **6.95** 0.30.

6.97 (a) $\frac{1}{16}$; (b) $\frac{1}{17}$.   **6.99** (a) $\frac{22}{145}$; (b) $\frac{4}{25}$.

6.103 A and C are independent.

6.105 Events M and N are not independent.

6.107 $\frac{1}{256}$.

6.109 (a) $P(X\mid \text{red, deck } A) = \frac{5}{10}$
$> P(X\mid \text{green, deck } A) = \frac{14}{30}$.
(b) $P(X\mid \text{red, deck } B) = \frac{5}{25}$
$> P(X\mid \text{green, deck } B) = \frac{2}{15}$.
(d) For the combined deck
$P(X\mid \text{red, combined deck}) = \frac{10}{35}$
$< P(X\mid \text{green, combined deck}) = \frac{16}{45}$.

6.111 $\frac{1}{12}$.   **6.113** 0.0288.

6.115 (a) 0.0616; (b) 0.5325.

6.117 (a) 0.242; (b) 0.5372.

6.119 0.8051.

6.121 (a) $P(D\mid T) \approx 0.246$.
(b) $P(D'\mid T') \approx 0.999$.

6.123 (a) 0.601; (b) 0.81.

6.125 The most likely cause of the explosion is C_4, purposeful action.

6.127 The probability that the other coin is also a penny, is $\frac{2}{3}$.

6.131 (a) 0.076; (b) ≈ 0.421.

6.133 0.0046.

6.135 The two events are independent.

6.137 (a) $\frac{5}{24}$; (b) $\frac{13}{16}$; (c) $\frac{40}{77}$.

6.139 0.68.

6.141 (a) 0.38; (b) 0.42; (c) 0.50.

6.143 Any bet is plausible for which the odds favoring the 49ers translates to a probability between 0.636 and 0.714.

6.145 $n = 91$.

6.147 (a) $\frac{94}{125}$; (b) $\frac{4}{5}$; (c) $\frac{4}{5}$;
(d) $\frac{40}{47}$; (e) $\frac{11}{25}$; (f) $\frac{20}{31}$.

6.149 0.224.

6.151 The probabilities are consistent.

6.153 (a) $P(R\mid F) \approx 0.187$; (b) $P(R'\mid F') \approx 0.998$.

6.155 (a) $\frac{1}{4,096}$; (b) $\frac{1}{4,096}$.

6.157 (a) The person will visit Portugal, but neither Belgium nor England.
(b) The person will visit Belgium and England.
(c) The person will visit Belgium, but not England.
(d) The person will visit Belgium and/or Portugal, but not England.
(e) The person will visit neither Belgium nor England.

6.159 (a) 0.0435; (b) 0.632.

6.161 (c) A much higher percentage of the patients in Hospital B are high risk cases than in Hospital A.

CHAPTER 7

7.1 $0.20.   **7.3** $0.23.

7.5 (a) $5,000 for each player.
(b) $6,500 and $3,500.
(c) $8,500 and $1,500.

7.7 Draw from box 2.

7.9 $5\frac{13}{16}$.   **7.11** $1.16.   **7.13** 1.81.

7.15 (a) $p < \frac{1}{4}$; (b) $p > 0.15$.

7.17 $p < 0.571$.   **7.19** $89.

7.21 It is not rational to pay $4.

7.23 It is not worth her time.

7.25 (a) The expected distances are $45\frac{1}{3}$ miles (shopping center first) and 44 miles (barn first), so his preferred strategy is to go to the barn first.
(b) Both expected distances are 45 miles, so the two choices are equivalent.

7.27 It does not matter whether they continue the operation.

7.29 The expected profits are $59,200 and $73,600. Delaying the expansion maximizes the expected profit.

7.31 (a) Expand now.
(b) Stock 4 pies.

7.33 (a) The expected value of perfect information is 2 miles.
(b) The expected value of perfect information is $1,575,000. It would be worthwhile to spend the $500,000.

7.35 (a) $132; (b) $192.

7.37 The midrange, which is $2,000.

7.39 63.   **7.41** $p < 0.60$.

7.43 $1,900.   **7.45** $26.00.

7.47 At least $\frac{2}{3}$, but less than $\frac{3}{4}$.

7.49 (a) $p > 0.10$; (b) $p < 0.10$; (c) $p = 0.10$.

7.51 The expected value of perfect information is $3.60; it is worthwhile to spend $2.40 for the call.

7.53 Hotel B.

7.55 The midrange, which is 31.5 miles per gallon.

CHAPTER 8

8.1 (a) No; (b) no; (c) yes.

8.3 (a) Yes; (b) no; (c) yes; (d) no.

8.5 0.311.   **8.7** 0.278.

8.9 0.201.

8.11 (a) 0.251; (b) 0.251.

8.13 (a) 0.301; (b) 0.957; (c) 0.250; (d) 0.791.

8.15 (a) 0.397; (b) 0.941; (c) 0.010.

8.17 (a) 0.203; (b) 0.316; (c) 0.050.

8.19 The probabilities are 0.010, 0.060, 0.161, 0.251, 0.251, 0.167, 0.074, 0.021, 0.004, and 0.000.

8.21 (a) 0.311; (b) 0.230; (c) 0.654.

8.23 (b) $f(0) = \frac{729}{4,096}$, $f(1) = \frac{1,458}{4,096}$,

$f(2) = \frac{1,215}{4,096}$, $f(3) = \frac{540}{4,096}$,

$f(4) = \frac{135}{4,096}$, $f(5) = \frac{18}{4,096}$,

$f(6) = \frac{1}{4,096}$.

8.25 (a) 0.0864; (b) 0.0791; (c) 0.0630.

8.27 (a) 15 is not enough.
(b) 20 is not enough.
(c) 30 is more than what is needed.
(d) 21 is the smallest number.

8.29 0.018.

8.31 (a) 0.044; (b) 0.2967; (c) 0.4747; (d) 0.1846.

8.33 (a) 0.833; (b) 0.455; (c) 0.773.

8.35 (a) Not satisfied; (b) satisfied; (c) satisfied; (d) not satisfied.

8.37 (a) 0.206218. (b) 0.204800. (c) The error is -0.001418. In percentage terms, this is -0.69%.

8.39 0.038.

8.41 0.0459.

8.43 (a) Satisfied; (b) not satisfied; (c) not satisfied.

8.45 0.1680.

8.47 (a) 0.159; (b) 0.803; (c) 0.765.

8.49 (a) 0.163; (b) 0.936.

8.51 (a) 0.116; (b) 0.170; (c) 0.351.

8.53 0.0988; (b) 0.0034.

8.55 (a) 0.049; (b) 0.056.

8.57 0.029.

8.59 (a) 0.0179; (b) 0.0716.

8.61 (a) 1.3; (b) 0.81; (c) 0.81.

8.63 $\mu = 0.98$, therefore $\sigma = 1.21$.

8.65 (a) $\mu = 4.805$ and $\sigma^2 = 1.909$;
(b) $\mu = 4.8$ and $\sigma^2 = 1.92$.

8.67 $\mu = 16$ and $\sigma = 1.79$.

8.69 (a) $\mu = 230$, $\sigma = 10.72$;
(b) $\mu = 200$, $\sigma = 12.91$;
(c) $\mu = 72$, $\sigma = 6.79$;
(d) $\mu = 36$, $\sigma = 5.75$;
(e) $\mu = 442$, $\sigma = 11.89$.

8.71 (a) $\mu = 0.937$; (b) $\mu = 0.9375$.

8.73 (a) $\sigma = 0.7856$; (b) $\sigma = 0.7474$.

8.75 $\mu = 0.799$.

8.77 $\sigma = 0.8905$.

8.79 The probability is at least 0.75.

8.81 $k = 5$.
(a) The probability is at least 0.96 that the number of heads will be between 4,750 and 5,250, and hence that the proportion of heads will be between 0.475 and 0.525.
(b) The probability is at least 0.96 that the number of heads will be between 497,500 and 502,500, and hence that the proportion of heads will be between 0.4975 and 0.5025.

8.83 (a) 00–24, 25–74, and 75–99.

8.87 (a) 0000–2465, 2466–5917, 5918–8334, 8335–9462, 9463–9857, 9858–9968, 9969–9994, and 9995–9999.

8.91 (a) 1.39; (b) 3.33.

8.93 (a) Their total is 0.98.
(b) $f(4)$ is negative.
(c) Their total is 1.25.

8.95 0.082.

8.97 00–45, 46–72, 73–87, 88–95, and 96–99.

8.99 (a) Satisfied; (b) not satisfied; (c) not satisfied.

8.101 (a) 0.1985; (b) 0.8109; (c) 0.8693.

8.103 (a) At least $\frac{48}{49}$; (b) at least 0.84.

8.105 (a) The hypergeometric probability is $\dfrac{\binom{1393}{48}\binom{35}{2}}{\binom{1428}{50}}$.
(b) The binomial probability is 0.223551.
(c) The Poisson probability is 0.220480.

8.107 $\mu = 2.092$ and $\sigma^2 = 1.836$.

8.109 (a) 0.382; (b) 0.930; (c) 0.079.

8.111 (a) 0.146; (b) 0.957; (c) 0.189.

8.113 (a) $\mu = 2.5$, $\sigma = 1.06$;
(b) $\mu = 0.15$, $\sigma = 0.372$;
(c) $\mu = 0.15$, $\sigma = 0.385$;
(d) $\mu = 21$, $\sigma = 1.27$.

CHAPTER 9

9.1 (a) The total area under the curve is $(4 - 1)\frac{1}{4} = \frac{3}{4} < 1$.
(b) $f(x) < 0$ for $1 < x < \frac{7}{4}$.

9.3 (a) 0.625; (b) 0.8.

9.5 $\frac{7}{16}$.

9.7 (a) The first area is bigger;
(b) the first area is bigger;
(c) the first area is bigger;
(d) the two areas are equal;
(e) the first area is bigger;
(f) the second area is bigger;
(g) the two areas are equal;
(h) the first area is bigger.

9.9 (a) 0.3078; (b) 0.4515; (c) 0.3156; (d) 0.6064;
(e) 0.9032; (f) 0.2148.

9.11 (a) 0.5792; (b) 0.1251; (c) 0.5871; (d) 0.3708;
(e) 0.1271; (f) 0.7764; (g) 0.1804.

9.13 (a) $z = \pm 1.48$; (b) $z = -0.74$; (c) $z = 1.12$;
(d) $z = \pm 2.17$.

9.15 (a) $z = \pm 0.53$; (b) $z = \pm 1.56$;
(c) $z = \pm 0.44$; (d) $z = \pm 2.03$.

9.17 (a) The first probability is bigger;
(b) the second probability is bigger;
(c) the first probability is bigger;
(d) the first probability is bigger.

9.19 (a) 0.9332; (b) 0.7734; (c) 0.2957; (d) 0.9198.

9.21 20.

9.23 (a) 0.330; (b) 0.200; (c) 0.202.

9.25 (a) 0.135; (b) 0.050; (c) 0.393.

9.27 We only have two points, which will always fit a line.

9.31 Roughly, $\mu = 18.6$ and $\sigma = 5.4$.

9.33 The data were obtained from a normally distributed population.

9.35 (a) 0.203; (b) 0.459; (c) 0.749.

9.37 (a) 0.7881; (b) 0.2743.

9.39 4.75.

9.41 97.72%.

9.43 (a) 0.0809; (b) 0.3859; (c) 0.6950.

9.45 0.0661.

9.47 (a) Not satisfied; (b) not satisfied; (c) satisfied.

9.49 $\mu = 10$, $\sigma = 2.236$. The probability is 0.120, and the error is

$$0.120 - 0.120134 = -0.000134.$$

9.51 $\mu = 24.8$ and $\sigma = 3.07$. The probability is 0.0808.

9.53 $\mu = 11$ and $\sigma = 2.93$. The probability is 0.6950.

9.55 From the printout of Figure 8.4, the probability is 0.0036. $\mu = 7.5$ and $\sigma = 2.67$. The probability is 0.0078. The error is 0.0042, and the percentage error is 117%.

9.57 The probability is 0.97256. The error is -0.00244, and the percentage error is -0.25%.

9.59 (a) We cannot use the normal approximation; we cannot use the Poisson approximation.
(b) We can use the normal approximation; we cannot use the Poisson approximation.
(c) We cannot use the normal approximation; we can use the Poisson approximation.
(d) We can use the normal approximation; we can use the Poisson approximation.

9.61 The error is 0.000525, and the percentage error is 15%.

9.67 $\mu = 10$ and $\sigma = 2.236$. The probability is 0.1200 and the error is 0.000.

9.69 (a) 0.9332; (b) 0.7734; (c) 0.0934; (d) 0.6514.

9.75 (a) 0.2090; (b) 0.4933.

9.77 0.1587 longer for job A; 0.7486 longer for job B.

9.79 (a) 0.3665; (b) 0.4714; (c) 0.0534; (d) 0.1293;
(e) 0.8544.

9.81 (a) 0.0683; (b) 0.4129.

9.83 (a) $\mu = 500$ and $\sigma = 15.81$. The probability is 0.4908.
(b) $\mu = 5,000$ and $\sigma = 50$. The probability is 0.9556.

CHAPTER 10

10.1 (a) 6; (b) 28; (c) 190; (d) 19,900.

10.3 (a) $\frac{1}{495}$; (b) $\frac{1}{26,334}$.

10.7 (a) $\frac{1}{15}$; (b) $\frac{1}{3}$.

10.9

3332	7255	6441	1561	7740
5041	3962	4044	2153	3206
5845	0111	2106	5895	6326
3281	6571	0792	0772	4732

10.11 0.8568.

10.15 (a) $\frac{1}{10}$; (b) $\frac{1}{10}$; (c) 0.0082; (d) less than 0.01.

10.17 (a) Combine the data for January and July, those for February and August, those for March and September, those for April and October, those for May and November, and those for June and December.
(b) The sixth sample contains all the high figures for December.

10.19 (a) Here are the sample means:

120	165
125	160
150	165
155	170
160	190
130	195
155	200
160	

The probability that the sample mean will differ from the population mean 160 by more than 5 is $\frac{8}{15}$.
(b) Here are the means of the stratified samples:

150	165
155	160
160	165
155	170
160	

The probability that the sample mean will differ from the population mean 160 by more than 5 is $\frac{2}{9}$.
(c) Here are the stratified sample means:

120	170
160	150
165	190
125	195
165	

The probability that the sample mean will differ from the population mean 160 by more than 5 is $\frac{2}{3}$.
(d) The results of the relevant stratification in (b) improved greatly on the simple random sampling of (a). The stratification proposed in (d) was actually destructive for the task of estimating the mean weight.

10.21 (a) 17,598,672,000; (b) 35,498,176,000.

10.23 $n_1 = 20$, $n_2 = 48$, $n_3 = 8$, $n_4 = 4$.

10.25 The means are 120, 125, 130, 190, 195, and 200. The probability is 1. Stratified sampling is better than simple random sampling, which in turn is better than cluster sampling.

10.27 $n_1 = 20$, $n_2 = 80$.

10.31 (c)

Mean	Probability
10	10/28
11	5/28
14	5/28
15	1/28
25	5/28
26	1/28
29	1/28

(d) 6.414.

10.33 (c)

x	9	10	11	12	13	14	15	16	17	18
$f(x)$	$\frac{1}{20}$	$\frac{1}{20}$	$\frac{2}{20}$	$\frac{3}{20}$	$\frac{3}{20}$	$\frac{3}{20}$	$\frac{3}{20}$	$\frac{2}{20}$	$\frac{1}{20}$	$\frac{1}{20}$

(d) 0.80.

10.35

x	9	10	11	12	13	14	15	16	17	18
$f(x)$	$\frac{4}{20}$	$\frac{0}{20}$	$\frac{0}{20}$	$\frac{6}{20}$	$\frac{0}{20}$	$\frac{0}{20}$	$\frac{6}{20}$	$\frac{0}{20}$	$\frac{0}{20}$	$\frac{4}{20}$

The median is much less likely to be close to 13.5.

10.37 (a) Divided by 2; (b) divided by 1.5; (c) divided by 3; (d) multiplied by 4.

10.39 (a) 0.9771; (b) 0.9909; (c) 0.9977; (d) 0.9511; (e) 0.9499; (f) 0.9488.

10.41 $\sigma_{\bar{x}} = 32.08$.

10.43 (a) $\mu_{\bar{x}} = 160$ and $\sigma_{\bar{x}} = 21.0$.
(b) $\mu_{\bar{x}} = 160$ and $\sigma_{\bar{x}} = 7.1$.

10.45 $\mu_{\bar{x}} = 160$ and $\sigma_{\bar{x}} = 35$.

10.47 $\sigma_{\bar{x}} = 0.48$. (a) At least 0.84; (b) 0.9876.

10.49 $\sigma_{\bar{x}} = 0.00625$. The probability is 0.8904.

10.51 0.0918.

10.53 The smallest sample size is $n = 46$.

10.57 The mean 15.72 is compared to $\mu = 16$. The standard deviation 1.9958 is compared to $\sigma_{\bar{x}}$ 1.79.

10.59 The odds are 31 to 9 against it.

10.63 (a) 300,105,000; (b) 1,736,410,000.

10.65 $\frac{1}{82,160}$.

10.67 $n_1 = 16$, $n_2 = 8$, $n_3 = 29$, $n_4 = 7$.

10.69 $\sigma_{\bar{x}} = 5.8$.

10.71 (a) 0.859; (b) 0.834.

10.73 (a) 0.0869; (b) 0.0202.

10.75 (a) 3,060; (b) 27,405; (c) 3,921,225.

10.77 $\sigma_{\bar{x}} = 0.4$. (a) 0.9876; (b) 0.7888.

CHAPTER 11

11.1 (a) 4.09 seconds; (b) (74.31 seconds, 82.49 seconds).

11.3 (a) 0.403 cm; (b) (2.857 cm, 3.663 cm).

11.5 0.59.

11.7 (a) 24.15 ± 0.589; (b) 24.15 ± 0.700;
(c) 24.15 ± 0.773; (d) 24.15 ± 0.844.

11.9 1.50. The sample has not yet been taken.

11.11 $243.1 < \mu < 267.5$.

11.13 22.7.

11.15 $237.96 < \mu < 243.64$ pounds.

11.17 $249.90 < \mu < 255.70$.

11.19 The maximum error, using $\sigma = 2.0$ and 95% confidence, will be at most 1.24 ounces.

11.21 $n = 36$.

11.23 $n \geq 40$.

11.25 $n \geq 31$.

11.27 (a) (55.83, 60.61); (b) (54.94, 61.50);
(c) 2.39; (d) 3.28.

11.29 (a) 44%; (b) 37%; (c) 35%.

11.31 (a) 0.33; (b) 2.58 ± 0.33.

11.33 (a) $24.61 < \mu < 30.05$; (b) $23.49 < \mu < 31.17$.

11.35 0.11 gram.

11.37 0.2794.

11.39 Posterior standard deviation is 11.44. The probability in this distribution between $360 and $400 is 0.4990.

11.41 (a) $\mu_1 = 70.0$; (b) $\sigma_1 = 0.92$. The probability is 0.0150.

11.43 (a) 0.8664. (b) $\mu_1 = \$710.19$.
(c) $\sigma_1 \approx 6.04$; thus the probability is 100%.

11.45 (a) Use the alternative $\mu_2 > \mu_1$, and switch to the radial tires only if the null hypothesis can be rejected.
(b) Use the alternative $\mu_2 < \mu_1$, and switch to the radial tires unless the null hypothesis can be rejected.
(c) Use the alternative $\mu_2 \neq \mu_1$.

11.47 (a) (error); (b) (correct); (c) (error); (d) (correct).

11.49 If it erroneously rejects, the testing service commits a Type I error. If it erroneously accepts, the testing service commits a Type II error.

11.51 Use the null hypothesis that the device is not effective.

11.53 (a) 0.0011; (b) 0.989.

11.55 (a) 0.1056; (b) 0.7340; (c) 0.2660.

11.57 (a) 0.1616.
(b) 0.0096 for $\mu = 38.5$ and $\mu = 46.5$,
0.0808 for $\mu = 39.5$ and $\mu = 45.5$,
0.3192 for $\mu = 40.5$ and $\mu = 44.5$,
0.6712 for $\mu = 41.5$ and $\mu = 43.2$.

11.59 For population means, there is either a difference or no difference.

11.61 It does not make sense since we are not dealing with sample data.

11.63 Purely by chance, 2 times can be expected. So 7 times is worrisome.

11.65 (a) $H_0: \mu = 3.4$, and $H_A: \mu \neq 3.4$.
(b) Two-tailed test.

11.67 $H_0: \mu = 90$, and $H_A: \mu > 90$.

11.69 $\bar{x} = 24.08$ is so close that we are unconcerned.

11.71 (a) $z = -2.28$. The null hypothesis cannot be rejected.
(b) $p = 0.0226$.
(c) $p > \alpha$. The null hypothesis cannot be rejected.

11.73 (a) $z = 5.55$. The null hypothesis must be rejected.
(b) $p < 0.0000001$.
(c) Since $p < \alpha$, the null hypothesis is rejected.

11.75 Since 0.005 is less than 0.01, the null hypothesis must be rejected.

11.77 $z = 2.35$.
(a) The null hypothesis must be rejected.
(b) The null hypothesis cannot be rejected.
(c) 0.0188. (d) The null hypothesis would have been rejected at 0.02 level.

11.79 (a) $n = 4$; (b) yes.

11.81 $t = 4.00$. The null hypothesis must be rejected.

11.83 $t = 4.66$. The null cannot be rejected.

11.85 $t = 2.63$. The null hypothesis cannot be rejected.

11.87 $t = -0.14$. The null hypothesis cannot be rejected.

11.89 (a) $t = 5.66$. The null hypothesis must be rejected.
(b) $t = 2.11$. The null hypothesis cannot be rejected.
(c) Though the distance between $\bar{x}$ and 60 has increased, so has the value of s.

11.91 (a) 0.8784; (b) 0.6082.

11.93 The tail probability is 0.3668.

11.95 $z = 2.26$. The null hypothesis must be rejected.

11.97 $z = 0.31$. The null hypothesis cannot be rejected.

11.99 $z = 2.78$. The null hypothesis must be rejected.

11.101 $z \approx 2.77$. The null hypothesis must be rejected.

11.103 $t = -1.88$. The null hypothesis cannot be rejected.

11.105 $t = 1.29$. The null hypothesis cannot be rejected.

11.107 $t = 4.98$. The null hypothesis must be rejected.

11.109 $-24.2 < \delta < 78.2$.

11.111 $t = -2.204$. The null hypothesis cannot be rejected.

11.113 $z = -5.2$. The null hypothesis must be rejected.

11.115 $15.95 < \mu < 24.39$.

11.117 0.56 ounce.

11.119 (a) 0.4633. (b) $\sigma_1 = 110.60$. (c) 0.9434. (d) The two analyses used different prior distributions and come up with different answers.

11.121 $t = -0.90$. The null hypothesis cannot be rejected.

11.123 0.473 pound.

11.125 No, we are dealing with actual votes.

11.127 (a) $z = -2.57$. The null hypothesis must be rejected. (b) $p = 0.0051$. The null hypothesis could not have been rejected at the 0.002 level.

11.129 $z = 1.67$. The null hypothesis cannot be rejected.

11.131 $t = -1.831$. The null hypothesis cannot be rejected.

11.133 (a) Use alternative hypothesis $\mu > 48$; she would prove her point if the null hypothesis can be rejected. (b) Use alternative hypothesis $\mu < 48$; she would prove her point if the null hypothesis cannot be rejected.

CHAPTER 12

12.1 $0.0105 < \sigma < 0.0210$.

12.3 $12,700 < \sigma < 39,100$.

12.5 (a) $0.329 < \sigma < 1.490$; (b) $0.091 < \sigma < 0.366$.

12.7 (a) $10.83 < \sigma < 16.90$; (b) $1.21 < \sigma < 1.66$.

12.9 $0.065 < \sigma^2 < 0.133$.

12.11 The estimate of σ based on the range is 1.98, compared to $s = 1.79$.

12.13 The estimate of σ based on the range is 1.72, compared to $s = 1.58$.

12.15 $\chi^2 = 17.15$. The null hypothesis cannot be rejected.

12.17 $\chi^2 = 1.88$. The null hypothesis cannot be rejected.

12.19 0.0537.

12.21 $z = -1.32$. The null hypothesis cannot be rejected.

12.23 $F = 2.86$. The null hypothesis must be rejected.

12.25 $F = 2.202$. The null hypothesis cannot be rejected.

12.27 $F = 2.95$. The null hypothesis must be rejected.

12.29 (a) $F_{0.95} = 0.304$; (b) $F_{0.99} = 0.178$.

12.31 $F = 3.62$ The null hypothesis cannot be rejected.

12.33 (a) 3.05; (b) 3.59; (c) 3.25.

12.35 $F = 1.66$. The null hypothesis cannot be rejected.

12.37 $\chi^2 = 24.07$. The null hypothesis cannot be rejected.

CHAPTER 13

13.1 (a) $0.02 < p < 0.98$; (b) $0.00625 < p < 0.99375$; (c) $n > 125$; (d) $n > 250$.

13.3 (a) 0.72 ± 0.062; (b) 0.28 ± 0.062; (c) $0.218 = 1 - 0.782$ and $0.342 = 1 - 0.658$.

13.5 (a) 0.1333 ± 0.0654; (b) at most 0.0654.

13.7 0.075.

13.9 0.0625.

13.11 (a) 0.564 ± 0.055. (b) 0.046.

13.13 (b) 0.416 ± 0.057; (c) 0.564 ± 0.0567.

13.15 0.109.

13.17 0.34 ± 0.079.

13.19 (a) 2,401; (b) 2,185.

13.21 (a) 156; (b) 625; (c) 2,500; (d) 10,000.

13.23 (a) 2,172; (b) 1,825.

13.25 0.256.

13.27 (a) 0.145, 0.053, 0.039, 0.105, and 0.658. (b) $\mu_1 = 3.08$.

13.31 $p = 0.028$. The null hypothesis must be rejected.

13.33 $p = 0.073$. The null hypothesis cannot be rejected.

13.35 $p = 0.007$. The null hypothesis must be rejected.

13.37 $p = 0.038$. The null hypothesis must be rejected.

13.39 (a) $x \leq 4$ or $x \geq 13$; (b) $x \leq 3$ or $x \geq 13$; (c) $x \leq 2$ or $x \geq 15$.

13.41 $z = -0.71$. The null hypothesis cannot be rejected.

13.43 $z = 1.49$. The null hypothesis cannot be rejected.

13.45 (a) $p = 0.11$. The null hypothesis cannot be rejected. (b) $p = 0.412$. The null hypothesis cannot be rejected. This experiment simply does not have the ability to detect a p bigger than 0.90.

13.47 $z = -3.4$. The null hypothesis must be rejected.

13.49 $z = -3.21$. The null hypothesis must be rejected.

13.51 $z = -1.22$. The null hypothesis cannot be rejected.

13.53 $z = -3.19$. The null hypothesis must be rejected.

13.55 (a) $z = 1.81$. The null hypothesis must be rejected. (b) $z = 0.61$. The null hypothesis cannot be rejected.

13.57 0.079 ± 0.080; $-0.001 < p_1 - p_2 < 0.159$.

13.61 (a) $z = -3.88$. The null hypothesis must be rejected. (b) Rate difference is -0.31; odds ratio of freshman to junior is 0.258.

13.63 (a) $z = 8.25$. The null hypothesis must be rejected. (b) 0.0495. (c) 3.59. (d) 3.78. (e) (c) and (d).

13.65 40.9.

13.67 The null hypothesis is that the probabilities of the four response categories are the same for each of the three types of dealers.

13.69 The null hypothesis is that the probability of favoring the tax increase is the same for each of the four cities.

13.71 $\chi^2 = 25.5$. The null hypothesis must be rejected.

13.73 $\chi^2 = 88.9$. The null hypothesis must be rejected.

13.75 $\chi^2 = 4.01$. The null hypothesis cannot be rejected.

13.77 $\chi^2 = 14.92$. The null hypothesis must be rejected.

13.79 $\chi^2 = 0.97$. The null hypothesis cannot be rejected.

13.81 $\chi^2 = 16.55$. The null hypothesis must be rejected.

13.89 $\chi^2 = 9.48$. The null hypothesis cannot be rejected.

13.91 $\chi^2 = 13.8$. The null hypothesis must be rejected.

13.93 $\chi^2 = 15.4$. The null hypothesis must be rejected.

13.95 $\chi^2 = 0.3$ with one degree of freedom. The null hypothesis cannot be rejected.

13.97 (a) The probabilities are 0.1251, 0.2878, 0.3451, 0.1904, 0.0464, and 0.0052.
(b) The expected frequencies are 10.0, 23.0, 27.6, 15.2, 3.7, and 0.4. The fourth, fifth, and sixth classes are combined.
(c) $\chi^2 = 1.77$. The null hypothesis cannot be rejected.

13.99 $p \approx 0.20$. The expected frequencies are 102.5, 102.5, 38.5, 6.5, and 0.5. Combining the last two classes, $\chi^2 = 2.92$. The null hypothesis cannot be rejected.

13.101 $\hat{p} = 0.72$, $\chi^2 = 11.6$. The null hypothesis must be rejected.

13.103 (a) $z = 1.92$. The null hypothesis cannot be rejected.
(b) $\chi^2 = 3.7$. The null hypothesis cannot be rejected. (c) $z^2 \approx \chi^2$.

13.105 $0.0125 < p < 0.9875$.

13.107 (a) 267; (b) 225.

13.109 (a) We talk about significant differences between sample data, or significant differences between sample data and population parameters, but not about significant differences between population parameters.
(b) Either delete the word "significantly" or substitute the word "sample" for the word "true." $z = 1.11$. The null hypothesis cannot be rejected.

13.111 $\chi^2 = 4.445$. The null hypothesis cannot be rejected.

13.113 $\chi^2 = 8.37$. The null hypothesis must be rejected.

13.115 $\chi^2 = 1.3$. The null hypothesis cannot be rejected.

13.117 0.225 ± 0.065 and $0.160 < p < 0.290$.

13.119 0.47.   13.121 0.057.

13.123 (a) $x = 0$ or $x \geq 9$; (b) $x \geq 8$; (c) $x \leq 1$; (d) $x \leq 1$ or $x \geq 8$.

13.125 $z = -1.59$. The null hypothesis cannot be rejected.

13.127 $\chi^2 = 2.49$. The null hypothesis cannot be rejected.

13.129 $\chi^2 = 58.24$. We decide that either the coins are not balanced or that they were not flipped properly (or both).

13.131 (a) 1.69. (b) $\chi^2 = 7.59$. The null hypothesis should be rejected.

CHAPTER 14

14.1 (a) $n \cdot s_{\bar{x}}^2 = 20$. The mean of the variances is 11.33. Thus $F = 1.77$.
(b) Cannot reject the null hypothesis.

14.3 (a) $n \cdot s_{\bar{x}}^2 = 5.889$. The mean of the variances is 0.49. Thus $F = 12.02$.
(b) Reject the null hypothesis.

14.5 The standard deviations within the groups are very unequal.

14.7 (a) It will be impossible to distinguish the effects of the balls from the effects of the golf pros.
(b) It will be impossible to distinguish the effects of the balls from the effects of time sequence.

14.9 $\frac{1}{1,001}$.

14.11 $F = 1.77$. The null hypothesis cannot be rejected.

14.13 $F = 12.02$. The null hypothesis must be rejected.

14.15 $F = 0.68$. The null hypothesis cannot be rejected.

14.17 $F = 11.70$. The null hypothesis must be rejected.

14.19 $F = 3.19$. The null hypothesis cannot be rejected.

14.25 (a) $F = 9.28$.
(b) The standard for comparing two treatments is 25.80. We can find the following pairs significantly different:

D	vs.	H
D	vs.	A
D	vs.	C
D	vs.	G
D	vs.	F
D	vs.	B

E vs. B

14.27 She might consider only programs of the same length, or she might use the program lengths as blocks and perform a two-way analysis of variance.

14.29 $F = 6.62$ for treatments and $F = 4.86$ for blocks. Both null hypotheses must be rejected.

14.31 $F = 8.31$ for treatments and $F = 0.58$ for blocks. The null hypothesis for treatments must be rejected; the null hypothesis for blocks cannot be rejected.

14.33 $F = 4.43$ for factor A and $F = 17.06$ for factor B. The null hypothesis for factor A cannot be rejected; the null hypothesis for factor B must be rejected.

14.35 (a) 1 and I, 2 and I, 3 and I, 4 and I, 5 and I, 1 and II, 2 and II, 3 and II, 4 and II, 5 and II, 1 and III, 2 and III, 3 and III, 4 and III, and 5 and III. (b) 60.

14.37 $A_L B_L C_L D_L$, $A_L B_L C_L D_H$, $A_L B_L C_H D_L$, $A_L B_L C_H D_H$, $A_L B_H C_L D_L$, $A_L B_H C_L D_H$, $A_L B_H C_H D_L$, $A_L B_H C_H D_H$, $A_H B_L C_L D_L$, $A_H B_L C_L D_H$, $A_H B_L C_H D_L$, $A_H B_L C_H D_H$, $A_H B_H C_L D_L$, $A_H B_H C_L D_H$, $A_H B_H C_H D_L$, $A_H B_H C_H D_H$.

14.39 $F = 27.12$ for rows, $F = 2.57$ for columns, and $F = 94.51$ for treatments. The null hypothesis for rows (professional interest) must be rejected; the null hypotheses for columns (ethnic background) cannot be rejected; the null hypothesis for treatments (instructors) must be rejected.

14.41 The doctor who is a Westerner is a Republican.

14.43 2 must appear together with 5 and 7 on Thursday.
4 must appear together with 3 and 7 on Tuesday.
5 must appear together with 3 and 6 Saturday.

14.45 (a) $n \cdot s_{\bar{x}}^2 = 28$. The mean of the variances is 9.56, and $F = 2.93$.
(b) $F = 2.93$. The null hypothesis cannot be rejected.

14.47 (a) It is a balanced incomplete block design because the seven department heads are not all serving together on a committee, but each department head serves together with each other department head on two committees.
(b) There are two solutions:
Griffith—Dramatics
Anderson—Discipline
Evans—Tenure or salaries
Fleming—Salaries or tenure

14.49 $F = 15.21$ for factor A and $F = 52.99$ for factor B. Both null hypotheses must be rejected.

14.51 $F = 6.83$. The null hypothesis must be rejected.

14.53 Attributed to rank.

14.55 $F = 7.75$ for treatments and $F = 8.06$ for blocks. The null hypothesis for treatments (routes) must be rejected; the null hypothesis for blocks (days of the week) must be rejected.

CHAPTER 15

15.1 For the first line the sum of the squares of the errors is 8. For the second line the sum of the squares of the

errors is 6. The second line provides a better fit.

15.3 (a) $b = 0.898$ and $a = 12.445$. (b) 19.6. (c) 131.1.

15.5 The conclusion does not follow; we cannot extrapolate for $0.10.

15.7 $\hat{y} = 0.23 + 4.42x$.

15.9 No.

15.11 $S_{xx} = 0$. This makes it impossible to determine the regression slope.

15.13 105.

15.15 $\hat{x} = 4.954 + 3.108y$. For $y = 10$, the predicted value is $\hat{x} = 36.03$.

15.17 (a) $\hat{y} = -5.07 + 0.92x$.
(b) For $x = 1$, $\hat{y} = -4.15$; for $x = 10$, $\hat{y} = 4.13$.

15.19 $t = -1.21$. The null hypothesis cannot be rejected.

15.21 (a) $\hat{y} = 43.242 + 1.493x$;
(b) $t = 6.962$. The null hypothesis must be rejected.

15.23 $t = -2.76$. The null hypothesis must be rejected.

15.25 (a) $\hat{y} = 257.19 - 14.16x$. (b) $-18.14 < \beta < -10.18$.

15.27 $1.160 < \beta < 1.806$.

15.29 $0.592 < \alpha < 1.926$.

15.31 (16.6, 22.6).

15.33 $4.01 < \mu_{y|2} < 4.44$.

15.35 ($166,044, $180,442).

15.39 (a) $\hat{y} = 14.56 + 30.11x_1 + 12.16x_2$.
(b) $101.42. (c) $105.06.
(d) $137.55. (e) $141.20.

15.41 (a) $\hat{y} = 69.73 + 2.975x_1 - 11.97x_2$. (b) 71.2.

15.43 $\hat{y} = 68.9(1.23)^x$; for $x = 5$, $y = 197$ thousand.

15.45 $\hat{y} = 27,200 \cdot x^{-2.36}$; for $x = 12$, $\hat{y} = 77.2$.

15.47 $\hat{y} = 14.789 + 38.892x - 17.559x^2$;
for $x = 1.5$, $\hat{y} = 33.6$.

15.49 $\hat{y} = 3.143 + 0.15x + 0.057x^2$.

15.51 The parabola cannot be used for values of x beyond the range of values of x investigated, because it turns up again for larger values of x.

15.53 $-0.652 < \beta < -0.013$.

15.55 $\hat{y} = 56.66 - 5.1x_1 - 2.93x_2$.

15.57 $\hat{y} = 28.3(1.02)^x$; for $x = 60$, $\hat{y} = 74.2$.

15.59 $t = 2.47$. The null hypothesis must be rejected.

15.61 $t = -0.09$. The null hypothesis cannot be rejected.

15.63 (a) $\hat{y} = -32.702 + 3.819x_1 + 0.058x_2$.

(b) 71.13; 94.04; 82.73; 105.64.

CHAPTER 16

16.1 0.92.   **16.3** 0.01%.   **16.5** 0.68.

16.7 The line that passes through the two points of part (a) has a positive slope and $r = +1$; the line which passes through the two points of part (b) has a negative slope and $r = -1$.

16.9 A correlation shows only association.

16.11 There is (a) a positive correlation; (b) a positive correlation; (c) a positive correlation; (d) no correlation; (e) a negative correlation.

16.13 (a) 0.15; (b) -0.78; (c) 0.51.

16.15 The conclusion is not valid.

16.17 (a) 0.7976; (b) 0.5413.

16.19 $z = -0.030$. The null hypothesis cannot be rejected.

16.21 (a) $r = 0.92$. (b) $z = 4.767$. The null hypothesis must be rejected.

16.23 (a) $t = 1.83$. The null hypothesis cannot be rejected. (b) $t = 3.35$. The null hypothesis must be rejected.

16.25 $t = -0.03$. The null hypothesis cannot be rejected.

16.29 $z = 2.42$. The null hypothesis cannot be rejected.

16.31 (a) $0.49 < \rho < 0.93$; (b) $-0.54 < \rho < 0.15$; (c) $0.51 < \rho < 0.74$.

16.33 $r = 0.223$.

16.35 (a) $r = 0.733$. (b) $r = 0.652$. (c) The value of r will not be altered.

16.37 $r = 0.9998$.

16.39 The multiple correlation coefficient cannot be less.

16.41 (a) $r_{13.2} = 1.00$; (b) $r_{23.1} = 1.00$.

16.43 The second relation is four times as strong.

16.47 $z = 1.64$. We cannot reject the null hypothesis. (b) $t = 1.73$. We cannot reject the null hypothesis.

16.49 $z = -2.75$. The null hypothesis must be rejected.

16.51 (a) $0 < \rho < 0.74$; (b) $-0.58 < \rho < 0$.

16.53 0.68.   **16.55** 0.86.   **16.57** r is 0.86.

CHAPTER 17

17.1 The probability of $x \geq 9$ is 0.212. The null hypothesis cannot be rejected.

17.3 The probability of $x \leq 9$ is 0.981, and the probability of $x \geq 9$ is 0.073. The null hypothesis cannot be rejected.

17.5 The probability of $x \geq 6$ is 0.63. The null hypothesis cannot be rejected.

17.7 The probability of $x \geq 3$ is 0.945. The probability of $x \leq 3$ is 0.172. The null hypothesis cannot be rejected.

17.9 $z = 1.73$. The null hypothesis cannot be rejected.

17.11 $z = -2.86$. Reject H_0.

17.13 $z = 1.82$. The null hypothesis cannot be rejected.

17.15 (a) Use T and reject the null hypothesis if $T \leq 8$. (b) Use T^- and reject the null hypothesis if $T^- \leq 11$. (c) Use T^+ and reject the null hypothesis if $T^+ \leq 11$.

17.17 (a) Use T^- and reject the null hypothesis if $T^- \leq 10$. (b) Use T and reject the null hypothesis if $T \leq 7$. (c) Use T^+ and reject the null hypothesis if $T^+ < 10$.

17.19 (a) $T^+ = 18$. The null hypothesis must be rejected. (b) $T^+ = 18$, $T^- = (13)(14)/2 - 18 = 73$, so that $T = 18$. The null hypothesis cannot be rejected.

17.21 $T^- = 8 + 11 + 1 = 20$, $T^+ = (12)(13)/2 - 20 = 58$, and $T = 20$. The null hypothesis cannot be rejected.

17.23 $T = 13$. The null hypothesis cannot be rejected.

17.25 (a) $T^- = 25.5$. The null hypothesis must be rejected. (b) $z = 2.20$. The null hypothesis must be rejected.

17.27 (a) $T^- = 42$, $T^+ = (24)(25)/2 - 42 = 258$ and $T = 42$. The null hypothesis must be rejected. (b) $z = (258 - 150)/35 \approx 3.09$. The null hypothesis must be rejected.

17.29 (a) We use the statistic U_2 and reject the null hypothesis if $U_2 \leq 21$. (b) We use the statistic U and reject the null hypothesis if $U \leq 17$. (c) We use the statistic U_1 and reject the null hypothesis if $U_1 \leq 21$. (d) We use the statistic U_2 and reject the null hypothesis if $U_2 \leq 14$. (e) We use the statistic U and reject the null hypothesis if $U \leq 11$. (f) We use the statistic U_1 and reject the null hypothesis if $U_1 \leq 14$.

17.31 (a) $U \leq 2$ (b) $U \leq 15$ (c) $U \leq 11$ (d) $U \leq 1$

17.33 For $n_1 = 3$ and $n_2 = 3$, the probability of $U \leq 0$ is 0.10, which already exceeds 0.05.

17.35 $U_1 = 88$, $U_2 = 92$, and $U = 88$. The null hypothesis must be rejected.

17.37 $W_1 = 26.5$ so that $U_1 = 5.5$. The null hypothesis must be rejected.

17.39 $z = (24 - 45)/12.25 \approx -1.71$. The null hypothesis cannot be rejected.

17.41 $z = (289 - 200)/36.97 \approx 2.41$. The null hypothesis must be rejected.

17.43 $z = (110 - 72)/17.32 \approx 2.19$. The null hypothesis must be rejected.

17.45 $H \approx 0.85$. The null hypothesis cannot be rejected.

17.47 $H = 1.91$. The null hypothesis must be rejected.

17.49 $H \approx 4.51$. The null hypothesis cannot be rejected.

17.51 $n_1 = 14$, $n_2 = 8$, and $u = 5$. The null hypothesis must be rejected.

17.53 $n_1 = 14$, $n_2 = 6$, and $u = 5$. The null hypothesis cannot be rejected.

17.55 $z = (23 - 25.64)/3.45 \approx -0.77$.

17.59 $z = (26 - 25.95)/3.49 \approx 0.01$. The null hypothesis cannot be rejected.

17.61 $n_1 = 14$, $n_2 = 13$, and $u = 5$. The null hypothesis must be rejected.

17.63 $z = (12 - 21)/3.12 \approx -2.88$.

17.65 $r_S = 1 - (6.26)/(12)(143) \approx 0.91$.

17.67 $z \approx 2.16$. The null hypothesis must be rejected.

17.69 $r_S = 1 - 6 (35.5)/9.80 \approx 0.70$ and $Z = 0.70 \sqrt{8} = 1.98$. The null hypothesis cannot be rejected.

17.71 $z = 3.00$. The null hypothesis must be rejected.

17.73 $r_S \approx 0.61$ for judges A and B, $r_S \approx -0.05$ for judges A and C, and $r_S \approx -0.18$ for judges B and C.

(a) the rankings of judges A and B are most alike.

(b) the rankings of judges B and C differ the most.

17.75 $T^+ = 86$, $T^- = 19$, and we get $T = 19$. The null hypothesis must be rejected.

17.77 $n_1 = 15$, $n_2 = 5$, and $u = 4$. The null hypothesis must be rejected.

17.79 $U_1 = 109$, $U_2 = 35$, and $U = 35$. The null hypothesis must be rejected.

17.81 $r_S = 0.39$, $z \approx 1.46$. The null hypothesis cannot be rejected.

17.83 $T^+ = 55$, $T^- = 11$, and we get $T = 11$. The null hypothesis must be rejected.

17.85 $z = 1.34$. The null hypothesis cannot be rejected.

17.87 (a) We use the statistic U_1 and reject the null hypothesis if $U_1 \leq 23$.

(b) We use the statistic U_2 and reject the null hypothesis if $U_2 \leq 23$.

(c) We use the statistic U and reject the null hypothesis if $U \leq 19$.

17.89 $z = 1.32$. The null hypothesis cannot be rejected.

17.91 $n_1 = 9$, $n_2 = 9$, and $u = 4$. The null hypothesis must be rejected.

17.93 $U_2 = 18.5$. The null hypothesis cannot be rejected.

17.95 (a) We use the statistic T^+ and reject the null hypothesis if $T^+ \leq 14$.

(b) We use the statistic T^- and reject the null hypothesis if $T^- \leq 14$.

(c) We use the statistic T and reject the null hypothesis if $T \leq 11$.

INDEX